The Scottish Islands

The Scottish

A Comprehensive Guide t

Eilean an Tigh and Garbh Eilean from Eilean Mhuire

Islands
HAMISH HASWELL-SMITH

Every Scottish Island

CANONGATE

First published in Great Britain

in 1996 by Canongate Books Ltd

14 High Street, Edinburgh EH1 1TE

0 86241 579 9

The publishers acknowledge subsidy

from the Scottish Arts Council

towards the publication of this volume.

British Library Cataloguing-in-Publication Data

A Catalogue record for this book is available on

request from the British Library

Typeset and designed by Sarah Merrill Mowat

Printed and Bound in Great Britain

by Butler & Tanner Ltd, Frome, Somerset

To Jean

Author's Note

MY ORIGINAL INTENTION was merely to compile, for my personal satisfaction, a list of the Scottish islands equivalent to 'Munro's Tables of the 3000ft Mountains of Scotland ' (published by the Scottish Mountaineering Trust). This factually-interesting little book satisfies the aspirations of 'Munro-baggers' and I considered that, as someone who enjoyed landing on islands, to grade islands by size instead of mountains by height, would be an interesting exercise and serve me well.

It was during the long labour of calculation that I realised that, like most island-collectors, the pleasure of landing on 'new' territory becomes secondary to the desire to explore and appreciate the island for itself alone. The research became more and more absorbing as the years rolled by. My original simple statistical database of island names and areas grew into an amorphous mass of information from many sources. In the end I had to call a halt and try to return to the logical structure with which I began the quest.

I am only too aware that the information contained here will always be incomplete. Sometimes it has been abbreviated for reasons of space; more often the scarce facts have had to be wrested with difficulty from diverse sources. I have endeavoured to check them assiduously and where possible referred back to original records but, even so, I know there will be errors and omissions. If you are an island resident or owner, I apologise if I have omitted something of particular interest, and if you are a specialist (and in Scotland we are particularly fortunate in having experts in every conceivable field) your comments and corrections would be appreciated for a future edition.

It is quite astonishing how many of our islands were still populated a few decades ago and whose inhabitants are no longer easily traced. All their unrecorded wisdom will vanish with them and so, with every passing year, more and more of our common heritage is being forgotten or lost by neglect.

Contents

Acknowledgements

THIS BOOK would not have been possible without *Jandara* – a 41' Moody sloop – who, like every woman, has few faults and many virtues. She possesses four of us – a farmer, a baker, a quantity-surveyor, and me. Three of our wives are called Jean and one is called Ann so, by convoluted reasoning in kitchen Gaelic, her name derives from 'Jean-Ann-andara' – the second wife.

Our partnership has survived for more than a decade and its success is probably due to our diverse personalities. The farmer, Craig Hutcheson, has a boyish sense of humour, a healthy appetite, and a considerable practical aptitude when he cares to apply it. He plays the 'daft laddie' to perfection but is nobody's fool. The baker, Ian Terris, is a business man and world traveller who wakens everyone at five in the morning and doesn't know the meaning of *sotto voce*. But he is a competent seaman, a genuine friend, and always steady and reliable in a crisis. Peter Crabb, the quantity-surveyor, is a meticulous handyman who has a steady and considered approach to every problem and a love of the great outdoors. Being 6'-5" tall he is also our spare mast. Peter shares my star-sign – if one accepts such nonsense – and coughs discreetly at our occasional minor divergences of opinion. My only comment on my own personality is to thank my partners for their indulgence.

I am fortunate that my partners share my enthusiasm for 'collecting' and exploring islands and that my other sailing friends also accept the challenge wholeheartedly. Among the latter I must particularly mention Harry Holmes, a cocky Yorkshireman and erstwhile Commodore of the Royal Forth Yacht Club, and his wife Brenda, a marvellous cook among her many other attributes; George Steedman, a fellow architect, and steadfast crew on some memorable voyages; and my cousin, Dr Ronald Howie, who has recently taught me a thing or two.

We try to explore every island 'in depth' but conditions are sometimes difficult. A heavy swell and seaweed on the rocks can be a considerable hazard but a conquest doesn't 'count' unless one has truly landed, even if detailed exploration in such cases has to await the next favourable opportunity.

I would like to thank the many kind people who have been so generous with their help. In particular, I wish to record my appreciation for the invaluable information given to me by:

Kenneth John Smith of Earshader, Mrs Anna Mackinnon of Ardroil, Angus McLean of Brenish, Norman Buchanan and his son of Valtos, Uig, and D. Murdie of Bernera, all of the Isle of Lewis.

Donald Macdonald of Lingerbay, Isle of Harris.

Donald MacKillop of Berneray, Sound of Harris.

D J Campbell of Lochmaddy, Isle of North Uist.

Dorota Rychlik of Vaila.

Margaret Wilkes, Head of the Map Library of the National Library of Scotland, and members of staff.

Dr David H Caldwell, National Museums of Scotland.

Mrs I Dickson of the Census Division of the General Register Office of Scotland.

My sincere thanks also to:

Betty Kirkpatrick, Albert Morris, and Norman G Masson, for their encouragement and friendly advice.

Kenneth Mackenzie for his information on Scottish birdlife.

The late Bobby Tulloch of Yell for his vast knowledge of Shetland which he divulged so generously.

The late Norman MacCaig for his ready support and permission to include some lines from his poems.

CLAMSHELL CAVE, STAFFA (3-AP)

Preface

THERE ARE few parts of the world which possess such magic and mystery as the seas around Scotland. Some six thousand miles of contorted coastline (69% of the total United Kingdom coastline) create a wonderland of islands and mountains and rocks and stacks and secret inlets and remote, uninhabited places. This is an area of breathtaking beauty with a character formed not only by the proximity of mountains and sea but also by the complexity of the geography and the geology, of the climate and the social history. It is a serene yet chaotic landscape in which every isle has a distinct personality. Each is an individual entity with differences so remarkable that the mere crossing of a short stretch of water can be like visiting another continent.

What is the fascination of an island?

Why do we experience such a thrill at being surrounded by water, cut off from the rest of mankind, imprisoned on a miniature world? Is it because an island is of human scale, easy to comprehend, safe and defensible when the world beyond is big and terrifying? Who hasn't dreamed of being marooned on the proverbial desert island? For generations islands have been a theme of literature and poetry and, more recently, of radio and film. Utopia, Atlantis, *Robinson Crusoe, Treasure Island, 'Desert Island Discs'* – to name a few. It is a long list.

I have found Scottish islands so intriguing that the lack of a ready source of information on them has been a great frustration. The sheer excitement of landing on – and exploring – another island can be tempered by having little fore-knowledge of what to look for and where to go. Is there an archaeological ruin worth seeing? – a cave worth visiting? – uncommon birdlife? It is the ' – you mean to say you were in Venice and you didn't even see St Marks?!' syndrome. This is particularly true as the available time ashore is usually severely limited.

Reach for a book on Scottish islands – there are any number of excellent ones – and time after time the same subjects turn up: Mull, Arran, Lewis, Islay, mainland Orkney or Shetland (because they are large), Staffa (because of Fingal's cave), Iona (for its history and

mystery) . . . and so on: possibly thirty or forty islands in all.

But what about the rest?

What about Hellisay or Killegray? Fuday or Fuiay? Uyea or Wiay? Hascosay or Mingulay?

Scotland has 165 islands of forty hectares and over (i.e. approximately one hundred acres or one-sixth of a square mile) and that figure is based on my very restrictive rules of classification which will be explained later. It doesn't include 'bridged' islands like Skye, or Seil, or the Black Isle; it counts the whole of the Uists and Benbecula as only one island; it excludes the hundreds of islands which are less than forty hectares (islets like the Bass Rock and Staffa); and, yet, there are still *165 islands* to be described and, hopefully, visited?

'Collecting' islands isn't easy anywhere but Scottish islands present a particularly difficult, but exciting, challenge – much harder than the collection of mere mountains. Most of the large islands are well-served with transport and accommodation but it's a different matter for the smaller, or more remote, islands. Is there an anchorage or even a place to land? Will the weather or tides permit a landing? And once having achieved a landing, what is the opportunity for exploration? How long dare one stay ashore?

No one, to the best of my knowledge, has ever yet landed on every one of the 165 islands listed here. And it may be a long time before anyone does if for no other reason than that a few islands, such as Boreray in the St Kilda group, demand a very rare combination of ideal tidal and weather conditions, youthful confidence, and the agility of a mountain goat. Even so, this is no reason not to take each challenge one at a time – or section by section – and still build up a handsome score. A few general statistics may highlight how easy it is to start. Of the 165 listed islands: sixty-one were still populated at the time of the 1991 census; forty-nine have scheduled ferry services (and at least thirteen more provide informal services on request or by agreement); twenty-two have airstrips or airfields; eighteen have scheduled air services; twenty-seven provide hotel accommodation, and most of the

A TYPICAL 'CLEIT' ABOVE VILLAGE BAY , ST KILDA (9-1)

populated islands also provide B&B, hostel accommodation, or campsites.

The problem with writing about remote and uninhabited places is that doing so can destroy just what we find so attractive. I remember meeting a couple on an island visit who were from the south coast of England. 'We sail and explore these waters every year,' they said, 'but we don't tell anyone about it. These are secret places, far away from people. Why attract the crowds?'

I understand this viewpoint, yet I am taking a calculated risk that newcomers will visit these secret places, not just to chalk up another conquest, but because they have poetry in their souls and a true love of islands; that they will appreciate that it takes only one castaway beer can or cigarette packet to destroy the next visitor's pleasure; and that they will understand that it is common courtesy to respect the privacy of island-owners, avoid causing damage, and when possible ask permission to land and explore.

* * *

Before I could start collating information about islands I was faced with a difficult problem of definition.

What, exactly, is an island?

The dictionary says it is 'a mass of land, but not a continent, surrounded with water'. That defines maximum size, but do remember that size changes with every ebb and flow of the tide. The 1861 Census defined an island as 'any piece of solid land surrounded by water which affords sufficient vegetation to support one or two sheep, or is inhabited by man'. That is not a very scientific definition for minimum size – if one is needed – but it again confirms that an island must be surrounded by water. But does this mean permanently surrounded by water? What if there is a linking sandbank when the tide is out? The definition also seems to allow a bridge or tunnel connection whilst definitely precluding a causeway because that would interrupt the surrounding ring of water.

In the end I had to arrive at my own definition:

An island is a piece of land or group of pieces of land which is entirely surrounded by seawater at Lowest Astronomical Tide and to which there is no permanent means of dry access.

This satisfies my belief that the quality of insularity requires isolation.

In other words, if you can walk across to a piece of land without wading through sea-water, even if it is only at the time of the lowest of tides, then that piece of land is not an island. And, similarly, land accessible by bridge, causeway or tunnel is not an island.

Likewise, if a number of 'islands' are accessible to each other at low water, or by bridge, tunnel or causeway, they should be considered one, single island.

By this definition the Uists, Benbecula and their many adjoining satellites ('drying' or 'tidal' islands) count as one large island. And Skye, with a bridge to the mainland, no longer counts as an island. Although some, I know, will disagree with this definition because it may seem unduly restrictive; loosening the parameters leads to so many unresolvable situations that the exercise becomes pointless. Take a close look at the coast of Benbecula to see what I mean.

One requirement in my definition, however, is quite arbitrary: 'seawater'. I have restricted myself to ocean islands. There are plenty of Scottish islands which meet the above definition in every other respect but happen to be surrounded by fresh loch or river water. Maybe, some-one someday will want to list them. My only excuse for not doing so is that there is already more than a lifetime's interest in the seaward islands.

Format and Overview

The Scottish islands have been divided into twelve geographical areas or sections.

Every island of forty or more hectares in area (i.e. approximately 100 acres or more) has been separately classified and tabulated.

On each island map:

The sea area is overlaid with a grid of 5-cable squares (i.e. half a nautical mile or nearly one kilometre) to allow instant comparison of scale and distance.

Pale blue colour indicates approximate sea areas of less than 2m depth or areas of potential risk.

Grey-blue colour indicates tidal areas of rock, sand, or foreshore which cover at high water.

The scale shows kilometres and statute miles (not nautical miles).

Every piece of land which is less than the minimum area for classification but which could still justifiably be called an island or an islet is at least mentioned together with any information of interest. If there is a lot of interesting information then this is either given in the introduction to the section or put in a separate appendix. Occasionally, some of the 'drying' or 'tidal' islands have also merited this treatment.

Information for each of the one hundred and sixty-five classified islands has been presented in the following manner:

NAME

There were four main language groups from which Scottish place-names have evolved:

Brythonic (or P-Celtic). This was probably an older Celtic language than Gaelic. It was spoken by the ancient Britons of the Clyde valley and the Picts may also have spoken it, or a language closely allied to it. It is represented today by the Welsh, Cornish and Breton languages.

Gaelic (or Q-Celtic). This is the Celtic language still spoken today in Scotland and Ireland, although in many different forms. It originated in Ireland, came over with the Scottish settlers and Christian missionaries, and by the 9th century was spoken in much of Scotland.

Norse. Many Viking invaders settled in the Western Isles bringing their language with them and these islands eventually came within the dominion of Norway in or about the 9th century. Even after the Lord of the Isles took control, the Norse language lingered on for a considerable time. The Orkney and Shetland Islands had been part of Norway from a much earlier date and only became part of Scotland when they were annexed by the Scottish Crown in 1471. The vast majority of Scottish island names end in '-ay', which means 'island' (-øy) in Norse and tends to illustrate the strong historical influence of this language.

English. Although English (or a Scottish form of it) is the language of most of Scotland today, having been widely established since the 12th century, there are areas of the Western Isles where Gaelic is still the native tongue and the language of choice. The English language was late in reaching the islands and it has had very little influence on most Scottish island names.

Many of the Western Isles have a local Gaelic name as well as the normal Norse-derived or Anglicised-Gaelic name. The Gaelic names are usually, but not always, closely related to the common-usage name given on the Ordnance Survey maps. I have for simplicity given only the 'Ordnance Survey' name (with occasional necessary corrections such as Rum instead of Rhum) but the Gaelic or Norse name is sometimes referred to in the notes on derivation.

The following abbreviations have been (loosely) applied:

B	Brythonic	E	English
EI	Early Irish	G	Gaelic
OE	Old English	ON	Old Norse, Norse, Norn.
S	Scottish	Sc	Scandinavian

PRONUNCIATION

In a few cases pronunciation is given in square brackets after a name. There are wide variations so this is no more than a very rough guide to normal-usage. The following simple key has been used:

Pronunciation of Vowels

ë	=	th**e**, m**o**ther	o	=	l**o**t
a	=	s**a**t	u	=	h**u**t
a:	=	f**a**ther	oa	=	b**oa**t
ay	=	d**ay**	oo	=	sch**oo**l
e	=	f**e**d	aw	=	cr**aw**l
ee	=	w**ee**k	ow	=	f**ow**l
i	=	f**i**t	a-oo	=	as **ow** but longer
Y	=	**i**sle or b**y**	oy	=	b**oy**
oe	=	approximately French **oe**ufs or German G**oe**the			

Most consonants similar to the English but for Gaelic pronunciation there are the following approximations:

s	=	**s**ee	b	=	nearly **p**
g	=	**g**et but nearly **k**et	d	=	nearly **t**
ch	=	German Ba**ch** or i**ch**	l	=	variable
gh	=	as **ch** but voiced			

When an island's name ends in '-ay' the ending is often pronounced either as [-ay] or as [-ë]. For example, Berneray is either Berneray [-ay] or Bernera [-ë], and usually the latter. This may have originated because the Old Norse '-øy' [oe-i] was a sound which was neither [-ay] nor [-ë].

An exception is Islay which is always [Y-lë], and never [Y-lay].

MAP REFERENCES

References are given for the Landranger series of maps at a scale of 1:50000 (2cm to 1km) and the Pathfinder series at a scale of 1:25000 (4cm to 1km) both published by the Ordnance Survey and readily available. Bartholomew maps can be of equal assistance. References are also given for the applicable Admiralty Charts.

AREA

Shakespeare defined England as 'this scepter'd isle... this precious stone set in a silver sea, which serves it...as a moat defensive'. This is inspiring stuff, but untrue because the moat is interrupted when it reaches Scotland. England is not an island and nor is Scotland. Britain is an island.

Scotland is for our purposes here, the mainland. It has an overall area of roughly 7,800,000 hectares (30,000 square miles).

How big is an island? As the tide goes in and out an island varies in size which leads to many wild suppositions and few hard facts. So, once again, a definition is required but the requirement here is different from the definition of an island given in the Preface. The part of the island that matters is the part that is more-or-less always dry land. Quoting an overall area which included vast tracts of sand, mud, and rocks only accessible at low tide would not be realistic. So I have come up with an arbitrary restriction:

An island's area is the total surface area lying above sea-level at Mean High Water Springs.

I have used averaged planimeter readings to estimate the area of each and every island within its MHWS perimeter as there is no consistent record elsewhere. With digitalised map data it will soon be possible to programme a computer to provide this information. In the meantime I have been as accurate as possible but I certainly do not plead infallibility!

The tables include every Scottish island (or linked group of islands) which totals forty hectares or more in size. Not only is this a nice round figure, as forty hectares is roughly equivalent to one hundred old-fashioned acres, but if this limit is lowered the number of islands requiring inclusion grows rapidly out-of-control. The disadvantage in being so definitive is that it leads to the omission of some very small islands which are of notable interest: Staffa for instance. Such islets have therefore been included as appendices or within the foreword to the relevant Section.

Where applicable the areas of small tidal islands have been included in the total area for the main island even where this is not specifically mentioned.

HEIGHT

I have included a separate table of heights for interest. The Admiralty and the Ordnance Survey use different sea-level data to suit their differing requirements and even these can change as surveying techniques improve. For example my old edition of the Admiralty Pilot quotes Holy Island as 312.4m in height, the latest Admiralty metric chart shows 311m height whilst the latest edition of the Ordnance Survey gives 314m as the correct height. I have used the most up-to-date Ordnance Survey heights for consistency. There is, in any case, a large margin of error as all the heights are in round-figure metres without decimal fractions.

CANNA'S CELTIC CROSS (4-4)

OWNERSHIP

Some islands have been under one ownership for generations but many change hands with astonishing frequency.

Islands are often bought on impulse. They come on the market. The sun is shining, the seas are calm. This brings out three main categories of buyer: those who buy, visit a few times, intend to return, but never do; those who are hooked and change their entire lifestyle to suit the island; and those who get bored and quickly trade on to the next impulsive dreamer.

As there is a fairly quick turnover of some Scottish islands it is impossible to keep up-to-date on ownership. Furthermore, some islands are bought relatively incognito under a company name or that of a bank, or even as an unspecified small part of a large estate. However, ownership is obviously of interest for a variety of reasons and I have tried to establish it where I can. As the information has come from a variety of sources its accuracy cannot be guaranteed.

POPULATION

Historic figures – pre-1830 – have been gleaned from a number of sources such as travellers' accounts and old gazetteers. These are therefore uncertain and unreliable. More recent figures are taken from the ten-yearly National Census. Some of the small 'uninhabited' islands are still occupied occasionally during the summer by herdsmen or fishermen or, in a very few cases, by an owner.

GEOLOGY

Although matters of individual interest have been covered in the text a general history of island formation gives a better overall picture. Most of the life-forms of today only appeared on the islands after the last ice age, a mere 10,000 years ago. Prior to this, island development was almost entirely a geological phenomenon.

The First Three Thousand Million Years...

About 2500 million years ago, in an area of the earth which is now the far South Atlantic, there was a large slab of proto-continent. The Earth was no longer molten but its crust was still hot and in a state of violent geological upheaval. Great tectonic plates ground against each other and parts of them, often composed of common rocks rich in quartz and feldspar and mica, were forced deep down beneath the crust and subjected to enormous pressures and intense heat. The rocks folded and melted and twisted, separated into layers and were intruded by other igneous rocks. After a long time the activity slowly subsided and the metamorphosis was complete. The reconstituted rock started to cool down, taking æons to do

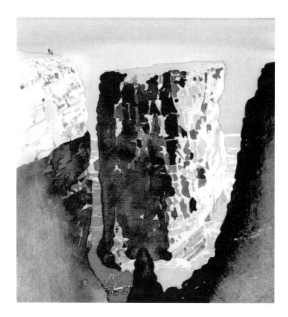

THE GREAT STACK OF HANDA (6-9)

so, and forming a coarsely crystalline structure. We call this rock – gneiss (pronounced, nice [nYs]. It comes from an old German word meaning 'sparkling').

Through most of the subsequent 2500 million years the gneiss stayed deep beneath the crust, almost un disturbed, until it surfaced in comparatively recent times in the middle of the Outer Hebrides (**North Uist**, **Benbecula** and part of **South Uist**). This partially explains why the rocks there, although ancient, look so freshly-scrubbed and clean: they have been kept under wraps until now. They have no fossils because they were formed before there was any recognisable life on earth.

There was a further similar period of upheaval in an adjacent part of the proto-continent about 2000 million years ago. This created gneiss of a different composition which forms the rest of the Outer Hebrides and patches of the Inner Hebrides. It is generally referred to as Lewisian gneiss.

The chunk of proto-continent was on the move, sliding slowly over the Earth's mantle in a northerly direction. By some 800 million years ago it had reached the latitude of South Africa. It had an upland region (which was eventually to become part of Greenland) eroded by rivers which spread alluvial deposits over a plain and into a shallow sea. These deposits built up increasing layers of red and grey sandstones, conglomerates, and shales. They are to be found today in the Torridon district of Wester Ross after which they have been named. Micro-fossils show that plankton and minute primitive life-forms were present in the shallow sea. Islands such as **Handa**, the **Summer Isles**, **Scalpay**, **Soay**, and parts of **Skye**, **Rum** and **Raasay** have all been sculpted from this dull red

Torridonian sandstone.

The shallow sea grew and became the Cambrian Sea and the land which contained Scotland and its islands sank beneath it and lay there for 150 million years. During this time the north-western seashore suffered further deformation and metamorphosis due to the vast weight of some five kilometres thickness of sand and mud which was deposited over it. Siltstone became schist, mudstone became slate, limestone became marble and quartz sandstones became quartzites. The crushing and overlapping of strata formed a zone which runs from the north coast of Sutherland to the Sleat peninsula on **Skye** and forced outcropping on **Jura**, **Islay** and in the **Shetland Isles**. There were small outcrops on **Arran**, **Gigha**, **Skye** and **Mull** and, possibly, **Colonsay**. Much of Jura still has 5 kilometres thickness of quartzite which was laid down at this time in the form of clean river sand. Large extrusions of granite also occurred, particularly in Shetland and the Ross of Mull.

During at least one stage, while still far south of the Equator, the land and sea were covered with ice which deposited a bed of glacial boulders. Part of this bed can be clearly seen today at Port Askaig on **Islay**.

The remorseless northern movement of the plate of proto-continent continued until, about 430 million years ago, it came up against another rigid plate. The collision squeezed up a colossal mountain range which equalled the present-day Andes in size. This was the Caledonian Mountain Chain. It extended across the continental slab from the area which was to become Scandinavia, through Scotland and Greenland, into Newfoundland and southwards down the east coast of North America. Only remnants of this chain still exist, as erosion, continental drift, and old age have steadily worn it down so that it no longer has the height and grandeur of the more recently formed mountain ranges – the Himalayas, the Andes and the Alps.

As the sliding plate approached the equator the violent upheavals caused by the collision waned, although volcanic activity was widespread. A huge lake stretched over the area of the future Orkneys and Caithness, sometimes extending as far north as Shetland. Layers of sand and limey mud were deposited in this lake forming sandstone strata. Fossils in the sandstone show that the lake was well-stocked with fish. This Old Red Sandstone, as it is known, is particularly thick on **Hoy**, forming sea cliffs 350m high. The Old Red Sandstone of the Old Man of Hoy sits on top of a layer of volcanic ash and basalt.

A split in the plate similar to the San Andreas fault in California started to form at this time, part of which eventually became the Great Glen.

About 350 million years ago the plate crossed the equator. Desert sand was compressed into sandstone on **Arran**. There was volcanic activity along an incipient rift zone forming between Great Britain, Norway and Denmark which was eventually to become the North Sea. The North Atlantic began to open up causing a number of rifts, one of which started to split the British Isles away from Greenland and North America. As the gap between Greenland and Europe opened up at the rate of about 2cm per year there was intense igneous activity down the west coast of Scotland. Vast quantities of basalt lava poured out of fissures and volcanoes and piled up at intervals along the centre line between the two plates. This is still going on today but the centre of activity has now moved over to Iceland.

Basaltic lava poured out and rapidly cooled on **Canna**, **Eigg**, **Muck**, **Skye**, **Raasay** and **Mull**. On Mull the lava layer is 1.8 kilometres thick! As the magma reached the surface it cooled fairly quickly forming the well-known columns to be seen at their best on **Staffa** or the **Shiant Isles**. Other activity became concentrated around intrusive centres on **Skye**, **Rum**, **Mull**, **Arran**, the **St Kilda** group and **Rockall**. These centres often have nearly circular outlines of 10-15km diameter. Most of them are of gabbro and peridotite, but some are of granite. Coarse crystalline gabbro is formed from magma which has cooled slowly, deep in the earth's crust. Other intrusions into cracks were later eroded to form dykes, stone 'walls' which can look almost man-made and maintain a constant thickness over long distances. There are dykes crossing Mull which continue all the way to the north-east coast of England.

All this violent volcanic activity died down about fifty-five million years ago as the fault centres moved elsewhere. It was at this time that another plate collision started the formation of the Alps in Europe which tended to uplift Scotland.

For most of geological time the earth has been ice free, even at the poles. There have been three major exceptions. There was the Ice Age in Precambrian times which incidentally formed the boulder bed on Islay. Then there was an Ice Age during the Carboniferous period, but as Britain was near the equator she was unaffected. It is the most recent Ice Age which has had a profound influence. Ice sheets formed over the whole country, and glaciers carved out many features in the landscape. For example, Loch Coruisk on Skye was gouged out to a depth of 30m below present sea-level.

The last glaciation finished only 10,000 years ago, a mere blink of the eye in geological time. The immense weight of ice had squeezed the land downwards. When it melted the land rebounded raising beaches and sea-caves far above sea level. Particularly on **Jura**, but throughout the Inner Hebrides, the effect of this change of level is very obvious. It is as though a giant has pulled the plug and partly drained the sea. The same effect is not to be seen in the Outer Hebrides, nor Orkney as very little ice covered these areas.

After the great glaciers of the last Ice Age had receded about 10,000 years ago and while Britain was still linked to the European land-mass, the forests moved north with the improving climate. Man followed and about 6,500BC small Mesolithic kinship groups of hunters, fishers and food-gatherers settled in the area south of Oban. They spread from there to **Arran**, **Jura**, **Oronsay**, **Rum**, **Skye** and **Lewis**. Evidence of their settlements are to be found in shell heaps, and the remains of their tools – antler mattocks, harpoons and fish-hooks, stone hammers and flints. Although the number of settlers at this time must have been very small they left a remarkable range and variety of artefacts. These show possible cultural links with earlier relics from the Basque and Baltic regions.

About 4,000BC immigrants arrived in Scotland in larger numbers. These were Neolithic farmers and fishermen. They were skilled seamen who brought their seed-grain, planted crops and kept domestic livestock. They spread up the west coast using the sea and lochs as their highway to the Great Glen, on through the Glen to the north-east and across the sea to **Orkney**. Later they reached **Shetland**. They were an intelligent and hard-working people and their way of life was so successful that they found time to build communal and religious structures. These became progressively more sophisticated. There were chambered cairns and communal tombs of a variety of types and complexity culminating in the splendour of Maes Howe in Orkney. The spectacular village remains at Skara Brae with canopied beds and stone cupboards show how advanced even their domestic

structures were. It should be remembered that the best-preserved and largest number of Neolithic remains in the whole of Europe are to be found on the Scottish islands and many of these structures predated the Egyptian pyramids.

Soon after Maes Howe was completed work began on the henges of Brodgar and Stenness. Hundreds of standing stones and stone circles were erected at this time to various mathematical models and apparently using a standard unit of measurement. Their purpose is still a matter of conjecture, probably religious, possibly astronomical, possibly both, but the engineering and geometric skills are clear to see.

THE BRESSAY STONE (11-8)

Callanish on **Lewis** is, of course, a supreme example.

By 2,500BC new groups of people had arrived. They are called the Beaker people because of their distinctive pottery but their area of origin is uncertain. For some time they maintained a separate culture but eventually we find them adapting the tombs and structures of the earlier settlers for their own requirements. They introduced basic metallurgy, stone-carving, textiles, and new concepts of social structure and political power. One of their prime settlements was the Crinan Plain in Argyll which strangely enough is also where the very first incomers to Scotland are thought to have settled. In due course the Beaker people introduced techniques for working in bronze, learnt from Southern Europe, heralding the demise of the Stone Age.

Between 1,500BC and 700BC the climate, which had been mild and pleasant for many centuries, deteriorated. Wet, cold weather made arable farming less productive, causing economic and social change. In due course the old religions were abandoned and cremation became favoured instead of burial of the dead. Peat moss accumulated around the deserted monuments. The people had attractive jewellery but bronze weaponry and the building of hill-forts indicate that these were troubled times. Jarlshof in **Shetland** has the best-preserved example of a Bronze Age settlement dating from about 1,000BC. There was also the development of timber-reinforced structures. Forts were built with timber posts sandwiched between stone skins (sometimes leading to vitrification) and timber, stone and soil were employed to build crannogs – artificial islands – in the lochs.

The strange and beautiful buildings called brochs were built between *c*. 200BC and 100AD. Fine examples are on **Mousa** and Carloway on **Lewis**. There are hundreds of them and they are found nowhere else in the world. Little is known about their purpose – were they really fortresses or watch-towers as has been claimed? – and, anyway, who built them? The Picts?

This mysterious race produced a wealth of beautiful stone-carvings with many strange, repetitive symbols. For a few centuries they dominated Scotland north of the central belt, but were eventually engulfed by the Scots and the Norsemen and disappeared from the world stage. Where they came from, what they looked like and what language they spoke is all conjecture. They are one of the mysteries of our past.

About this time there was a great influx of newcomers from the south of Britain. Between 600BC and 500AD Celts came over the Channel in large numbers and steadily drifted northwards, bringing their language and culture with them. They had a stratified matriarchal society and a great love of warfare. The Romans said that in spite of cold, wet weather the Celts always fought stark naked, wearing only golden ornaments, a sword belt and sporting an elaborate hair arrangement. Because they were so quarrelsome among themselves they were often easily outwitted by a disciplined force. The Romans also said that even the women enjoyed a fight and were built like Amazons. Celtic priests, the druids, held great authority in society. They worshipped in oak groves and had no connection whatsoever with ancient Neolithic stone circles. Celts were skilled craftsmen who understood the technology of iron-working and were adept at carving stone. The Romans suppressed them in the south of Britain but they held their own elsewhere. Generally speaking, the Roman occupation of Britain had little or no influence on any of the Scottish islands or their inhabitants.

The pre-Celtic or Brythonic or, maybe, Pictish language which was prevalent at the time was displaced in northern Ireland – Dalriada – by the Celtic-speakers that settled there. These were Gauls, or Gaels, of Indo-Aryan origin fleeing from the Roman invasion of Central Europe. Modern Welsh is derived from the earlier tongue (known as P-Celtic) whilst modern Gaelic as spoken in the Western Isles is derived from the Irish version.

In the 4th century AD the Romans adopted Christianity and about the 5th century, after the legions had left Britain, a mission was set up by Ninian in the kingdom of Strathclyde. He had studied in Rome and he was followed by Patrick, another Romanised Briton from Ayrshire. Patrick could write Latin and spoke Brythonic (or Welsh). He went to Ireland where he learnt Gaelic and then spread the word in western Scotland. He was followed by Colum Cille O'Neill – the Dove of the Church and prince of the royal Irish house of O'Neill – better known as St. Columba. Concurrently, Fergus Mòr, king of the Scots of Dalriada moved the seat of his kingdom from Antrim to Dunadd on the Crinan Plain of Argyll. In this way the Gaelic language, the Scottish name, and the Christian religion were introduced to the islands of **Arran**, **Bute**, **Islay**, **Jura** and mainland Argyll. Incidentally, the name of the Scots kingdom of Dalriada came from Cairbre Ruadh (G – red-haired Cairbar), nicknamed 'Red', who slew Oscar son of Ossian, and became king. Dal-ruaidh means the land of 'Red'.

In 563AD St Columba landed on **Iona** and founded the famous monastery which gained international recognition. Missionaries from Iona spread the Christian faith to many of the most remote islands, and scholars came from far across Europe to study at this famous seat of learning.

Around the year 800AD, the murderous Viking invasions began. The Danes mainly concentrated on England, but Norsemen could reach Shetland in thirty-six hours, or less, and spread south from there. The first Vikings were wealthy adventurers, expert seamen with good ships, weapons made of the finest Swedish iron, no respect for culture and an interest only in piracy. They plundered the

monasteries including Iona and destroyed most of the historical records of the time. Where there was no treasure they could always carry the people off to slavery or hold them to ransom. The tender Scoto-Irish civilisation centred on Iona and recognised by Charlemagne as one of the most learned in Europe was virtually destroyed. Following the first waves of pure piracy a few of the marauders chose to stay and the Norse settlers who followed were better behaved. In due course this brought a modicum of peace to some areas.

In Orkney and Shetland the Pictish culture was all but wiped out before the islands gained a new economic significance as a springboard for raiding parties travelling south. In 1098 another wealthy adventurer, King Magnus, sailed over from Norway on a campaign to plunder **Lewis**, the **Uists**, **Skye**, **Mull**, **Iona**, **Tiree**, **Islay** and the mainland of Argyll. He obtained an agreement from the King of the Scots confirming his ownership of all the islands. An island was defined as any piece of land which a boat could circumnavigate so he gained the Kintyre peninsula by having his men carry him across the Tarbert isthmus sitting in a boat.

He went on to pillage Ireland and came to a violent end in 1103.

In 1117 on the island of Egilsay, a different Magnus, Earl Magnus of Orkney, grandson of Thorfinn the Mighty, was murdered by his cousin, Earl Haakon. Earl Magnus was something of a pacifist and pilgrims to his tomb later claimed they had experienced miracles, so he was canonised and Kirkwall's beautiful cathedral was dedicated to him.

Although Shetland was under direct Norwegian rule and Orkney was a Norse earldom, all the Western Isles were a Norse sub-kingdom controlled from the Isle of Man by a king who was subordinate to the Norwegian sovereign. A Scots prince of the kingdom of Argyll, Somerled (the name means 'summer-sailor' in Norse), married a daughter of King Olaf, King of Man. In 1130, Somerled, who had built a fleet of ships of improved design and shown himself to be much more than a 'summer-sailor', succeeded to the throne of Argyll. He first drove the

TEAMPULL NA TRIANAID, NORTH UIST (7-16)

MIDHOWE BROCH, ROUSAY (10-20)

Vikings out of Morvern and in due course outmanoeuvred and defeated them in a brilliant sea-battle in 1156. He then set about restoring the monastery at Iona and founded the House of Islay. He, and the next five generations of his family called themselves 'King of the Isles', but changed this to 'Lord of the Isles' in deference to the King of the Scots. Somerled had three sons. He gave the Lordship of Bute and Arran to his son Angus, Kintyre and the Isles to Ranald, and Lorn to Dughall. His grandson, Donald, gave his name to the Clan Donald which became the most powerful clan in Scottish history. The MacDonalds supported Bruce and the victory at Bannockburn confirmed their powerful position in Argyll and the Isles. In the end however they overplayed their hand and after repeated rebellions they had their inheritance forfeited in 1493. The Campbells then took over.

The Norwegians did not give up easily. They still held the **Northern Isles**, **Lewis**, **Skye**, and the Isle of Man. A son of the King of Man, Leod, inherited Lewis, Harris and Skye and made his home on Dunvegan rock. The King of Scots offered to purchase the Hebrides from King Haakon of Norway but he refused to sell. Furthermore, in 1248, Haakon shrewdly invited Ewen, Somerled's descendant, to Norway and formally accepted his status as King of the Isles. He thus gained Ewen's allegiance, but the Scots started raiding the Hebrides which put Ewen in a difficult position as he also owed allegiance to the King of Scots for his lands in Argyll.

In 1263, King Haakon IV, an old man by then, decided to demonstrate his authority. He gathered a large fleet and sailed down the west coast of Scotland. Ewen refused to join him, but to be honourable he relinquished his Norwegian title of King of the Isles. There was an inconclusive Scottish-Norwegian skirmish between Largs and the Cumbraes when bad weather persuaded the Norwegians to withdraw. This was a disastrous decision and returning northwards their ships were battered by severe storms. Soon after they reached the haven of **Orkney** King Haakon died and, within two years, sovereignty of all the Western Isles and the Isle of Man had passed to the Scottish Crown.

Alexander III of Scotland offered his daughter's hand in marriage to the new Norwegian King as a diplomatic gesture of friendship which was accepted. But twenty years later Alexander died in an accident with the result that the sole direct heir to the Scottish throne was the King of Norway's baby daughter, Margaret – the Maid of Norway. Unfortunately, on her way to Scotland in 1290, she died at **Orkney**, just as King Haakon had done, and this gave Edward I of England an excuse to claim the vacant Scottish throne. The consequence was Scotland's lengthy war to maintain its independence.

Shetland and **Orkney** remained Norwegian possessions for two more centuries until Margaret, daughter of King Christian of Denmark and Norway, was betrothed to James III, King of Scots, in 1468. The islands were pledged as security for an agreed dowry of 60,000 golden florins. Christian could not find the dowry money so the Scottish Crown foreclosed and took over the islands instead.

Although the Lord of the Isles lost his mini-kingdom during the Haakon intervention the MacDonald clan continued to exercise a powerful and peaceful influence on island affairs from **Islay** where they held councils of Hebridean chieftains once a year. Their territory encompassed the **Uists**, **Benbecula**, and Sleat on **Skye**. The complex history of the isles at this time saw the formation of vassal clans through marriages and treaties which eventually became interlaced with skirmishes and treachery. The Clan Iain held most of **Jura** and part of **Islay** and **Mull**; The McLeans of Duart held **Coll**, **Tiree** and most of **Mull**; Clan Neil held **Barra**, **South Uist** and **Gigha**; the McPhees held **Colonsay**; the MacLeods held **Lewis**, **Harris** and a large part of **Skye**; the MacKinnons also held parts of **Skye** and **Mull**. All these clans disliked and often disobeyed the Norman feudal system of lords and vassals which was being imposed by the Scottish kings; they preferred the Celtic (and Norse) system of lords and freemen. Eventually an exasperated Stewart King, James IV, broke the last remnants of Donald overlordship: but this only resulted in a lack of adequate leadership and a widespread breakdown of law and order. Clan fought clan, churches were burnt down, and the islanders suffered appalling cruelty and hardship.

James VI was ashamed of his lack of control of this troublesome territory when he succeeded to the English throne in 1603 and decided to prove his authority. So he invited the Hebridean chiefs to a friendly meeting on Mull, imprisoned them all on his flagship and brought them to Edinburgh. They were released a year later but only after having agreed to specific conditions of behaviour. Remarkably, this rough and ready method worked. Relative peace returned to the islands although there were still some minor feuds in one of which the Campbells wrested control of **Islay** from the MacDonalds. Generally speaking, however, this was a time of reasonable prosperity.

EARL PATRICK'S PALACE, ORKNEY MAINLAND (10-10)

Many of the clans joined forces in a common cause in 1745 when Prince Charles Edward Stewart landed on **Eriskay** to lay claim to the British throne. By the following year, the collapse of his cause at Culloden effectively broke the power, and the wealth, of the clans for ever. Some distressed clan chiefs sold land which in ancient Celtic terms had belonged communally to the members of the clan as a whole, others looked to other means of raising money. By the early 19th century new absentee landlords, and some of the less scrupulous chieftains, were turning their land over to the new, profitable business of sheep-farming. The crofters, who had occupied their own land for centuries but held no written title, were mercilessly evicted. The Clearances had begun and huge areas, and many islands, were depopulated.

Crofters' rights of tenancy were only safeguarded by law in 1886 – too late – for by this time thousands of families had emigrated or been shipped off to Canada, Australia and the United States. Further depopulation was caused by potato blights, the decline of the fishing industry, two world wars and mainland attractions for the young.

WILDLIFE

The Scottish islands have a particularly interesting and diverse natural history mainly due to wide variations in climate and geology. Lime-rich alkaline soils occur on areas of calciferous rocks and acidic soils are found with granite and gneiss. The soil and the climate dictate the plantlife and the ground cover – moorland, meadow, woodland, peat bog, bare rock or sand – and the ground cover dictates the wildlife habitat.

These are the main considerations but there are other factors such as the influence of man or the geographical position of the island. Most islands have the same common plant forms as the nearest mainland regions but islands which lie in the warmth of the Gulf Stream and which are well-sheltered, like **Gigha** or **Arran**, have varieties of primula normally only found in the south of Britain and other unusual plants such as the rare whitebeam of Arran.

Scottish islands have few endemic plant species but there are a number of interesting subspecies or specialities. The Hebridean orchid, a subspecies of the common spotted orchid *dactylorhiza fuchsii*, is found in the **Outer Hebrides**, **Coll**, **Tiree** and **Shetland**, and there is a unique sub-species of the heath spotted orchid *dactylorhiza maculata* found on **Rum**. One of the few endemic species is the gold and orange flowered hawkweed found only in **Shetland** in a number of varieties.

The outlying islands have the most difficult climatic conditions, yet **Hirta** has around 140 different botanical species and even **Rona** in the far north has nearly fifty species. This can be contrasted with Shetland which has over a hundred times the land area of Hirta yet supports only three times the number of native species. This is partly due to the presence of man, as grazing and burning of the scrub have been going on for over 5000 years. Peat digging has also had a serious effect on many Scottish islands as the top layer is rarely replaced and in the end the landscape is reduced to bog or bare rock. After the Ice Age most of the islands acquired woodland cover. Even storm-ridden St Kilda had sparse birch and alder scrub. Subsequent climatic changes upset the balance but man was the greatest culprit as trees were cut for buildings or fuel, land was cleared for planting and overgrazing, and erosion then took over.

Atlantic gales have been a mixed blessing to the west side of the 'Long Island', as the almost continuous line of islands in the **Outer Hebrides** is known. They flatten and tear up any vegetation which dares to stand above the rest but they also scatter shell sand from the beaches – a valuable lime fertiliser. Interestingly, early records show much of the west coast of the Long Island as a sandy

THE ORKNEY VOLE

desert. It was by ploughing in seaweed to bind the sand
and provide potash that man created the machair,
welcome evidence that our species is not always
destructive! In spring and summer the machair is a carpet
of tiny wildflowers and particularly in the areas which
have not been grazed by sheep this creates an unrivalled
spectacle. Level as a billiard table and framed by pink
thrift, white sand and deep turquoise sea the colours
change with each passing week – daisies, buttercups,
silverweed, birdsfoot trefoil, kidney vetch, white and red
clover, wild pansies, corn marigold, spotted orchids,
purple-tufted vetch and yellow pepperwort. And beyond
the machair in the desolate peat bogs are butterfly
orchids, bogbeam, pink ragged robin, mare's tail, marsh
cinquefoil, kingcups and cotton grass. Contrast all this
colour with the east coast which has little else but sedges,
grass, heather and sphagnum moss in peat pockets on the
bare rock.

Behind the sand dunes of **Orkney Mainland** there are
great drifts of white clover, eyebright and birdsfoot trefoil.
There are Arctic alpines in the Cuillin of **Skye** and in
some of the nearby islands such as **Soay** and **Raasay**
which are to be found nowhere else in Britain; while
Mull, **Orkney** and **Shetland** and the **St Kilda** archipelago have examples of mountain sorrel, mountain
everlasting catsfoot, white globe flower, purple saxifrage,
meadow rue, roseroot and moss campion. **Rum** has a rare
alpine saxifrage and both **Orkney** and **Shetland** support
the unique purple-flowering Scottish primrose. In the
peaty lochans of **Jura**, the **Uists**, and some of the smaller
islands a distinctive and beautiful subspecies of the white

waterlily *nymphaea alba* can be seen. Unfortunately, such
plants are at serious risk from thoughtless collectors and
common thieves.

The remaining natural woodlands are mainly thickets
of oak, hazel, birch, willow, pine, alder and rowan.
Examples can be found on **Soay**, **Raasay**, **Ulva** and (south)
Rona to name a few. Cultivated woodland in limited areas
can also be found on **Canna**, **Gigha**, and **Lewis**, and
Arran has large tracts of planted imported conifers.

In some ways animal life on the islands is as varied as
the plantlife which supports it. Most of the island mammals were first introduced by man. The Soay sheep of the
St Kilda group have been there for at least a thousand
years. They were domesticated by Neolithic man but their
place of origin is unknown. Their population fluctuations
are the subject of scientific study at present. There is
another Neolithic strain of short-tailed sheep, also of
unknown origin, to be found on **North Ronaldsay**. This
breed lives mainly on seaweed. Many islands have feral
goats which have been traced back to Middle Eastern stock
but how they were introduced to the Scottish islands is
entirely speculative. Red deer are fairly widespread and as
they can swim a considerable distance they may have
colonised some of the inshore islands by their own effort.
The original population was almost exterminated by
destruction of the forests and by hunting. But in the 19th
century landlords encouraged their reintroduction for
sporting purposes and the deer themselves have learned to
adapt to the lack of forest cover. On **Rum** the deer are
carefully protected and studied for ecological research.
Rum's own breed of ponies is used to bring the deer

carcasses in for examination. The breed is the result of the islanders crossing Highland mares with Arab sires. The **Shetland** pony is also the result of selective breeding in the distant past.

The common fox *vulpes vulpes* has never been native to the Outer Hebrides although a few misguided people still defy common sense by introducing the occasional specimen. Foxes would have a devastating effect if they gained a foothold, particularly on communities of ground-nesting birds such as greenshank, dunlin and tern. These have already suffered by the deliberate introduction of mink, hedgehogs, ferrets, and domestic cats.

There are no frogs, toads, or adders in the **Northern Isles** but the adder is very common in parts of the Inner Hebrides such as **Jura.**

Rabbits were first introduced to some of the islands as a source of meat and Boswell mentions in particular the warren on **Coll** in 1773. Rabbits are not indigenous to the British Isles and were originally imported by the Normans who enjoyed their tasty meat. They posed no problem initially as they were kept successfully in defined warrens, culled and savagely guarded by the gentry. Then came the Industrial Revolution and the Clearances; the warrens were left to fall into disrepair and the rabbits were left in peace to do what rabbits do best. Strangely, there are no rabbits on Coll's near neighbour, **Tiree** and thankfully **St Kilda**, **North Rona** and **Berneray** in the Sound of Harris are bunny-free.

Among the other small mammals there are a number of unique sub-species such as the **St Kilda** mouse, the **Rum** mouse, and the **Bute** mouse. Short-tailed voles are a general Hebridean sub-species and there is also an **Orkney** vole but bank voles are only found on **Mull** and **Raasay**. Otters are common in most of the islands and especially on some of the **Northern Isles**.

Many grey or Atlantic seals frequent the west coast of the **Outer Hebrides** and the Scottish Islands generally are home to about half the world's population of this species. The common seal is less common and tends to prefer east-facing coasts. Numbers of porpoises and dolphins were in decline for many years but quite recently there seems to have been some recovery and it is rare to sail any distance in these waters without seeing them. Schools of killer or minke whales may also be seen.

Insect life is probably no more and no less varied on the islands than it is on the mainland but thanks to a lack of use of insecticides on many of the islands some of the less common species have had a better survival rate. This is particularly true of butterflies. Flodday by **Sandray**, south of Barra for example, boasts a unique sub-species of the dark green fritillary, **Rum** and **Eigg** have a number of species, and the **Northern Isles** also have a good assortment.

Without doubt, though, the most memorable island insect is the midge. It has been suggested that the forced depopulation of the islands in the 19th century may have been partly responsible for an increase in these tiny, voracious creatures which can make life so miserable in the mid-summer months. Discounting chemical insect repellents, which are only effective for a very short time, there are only two recognised antidotes – wind and whisky. The former blows them away and the latter makes them bearable. It is probable that, when the population was removed and the land reverted to rough grazing and sporting estates, midges would have found the change to their liking. Bracken, for example, protects them from the wind while cultivation destroys their breeding grounds. Compare well-managed and relatively midge-free **Canna** with the clouds of man-eating midges on wild and boggy **Rum** or **Jura.**

For the birdwatcher the islands are unsurpassed. For seabirds in particular, the remote or uninhabited islands are perfect sanctuaries. About 70% of the world's entire population of razorbills nest on the Scottish islands. In the **St Kilda** group, Stac Lee is home to some 100,000 pairs of gannets which is probably the biggest gannetry in the

TIGH AN QUAY, 1938 (FROM A FRASER DARLING PHOTOGRAPH)

TIGH AN QUAY, TANERA MOR, 1994 (NO 6-7)

world. And this particular island archipelago has a greater number and more species of seabird than any other island group in Europe. A runner-up on a smaller scale is the **Treshnish** archipelago off Mull. Apart from also having magnificent seabird communities the **Northern Isles** are the birdwatchers' finest hunting-ground for rare migrants blown there from far-off places.

Two of Britain's rarest birds, the corncrake and the chough, are now only to be found in the Western Isles: proof, if such were needed, that this is a last corner of paradise.

ACCESS

Where there is any regular form of public transport to an island this information is given but all details should be verified before use. There are a number of excellent annual guides which give more detail than there is room for here and the Scottish Tourist Board can also be of assistance (0131-332 2433). Although all the larger and more populated islands are served by public transport my main interest is with the smaller, and mainly uninhabited, islands. These are never easy to visit and means of access are not covered by the normal tourist guides.

Most hotels and guest-houses on the larger islands, or the adjacent mainland, are very willing to make arrangements with a local boat-owner. But even if weather conditions are suitable be prepared for some uncertainty.

Anchorages

It is, of course, much easier to arrange an island visit if you have your own boat. For this reason I have tried to provide a comprehensive list of all recognised (and some unrecognised) island anchorages with a brief note of their advantages or shortcomings. This is intended solely as an aid to pre-planning. It provides a simple means of selecting an anchorage to suit one's purpose – a quiet night with the family aboard, a visit to some particular site, a quick run ashore, a sketch, photography, a stop for lunch, a safe haven, etc. Difficulty of access, poor holding, or excessive exposure, will all influence one's choice.

In my attempt to be comprehensive I have compiled the list from a variety of sources – from the authority of Admiralty Pilots to the comments of local fishermen. *Neither these notes, nor the illustrative maps in this publication, should be used for navigation – they are intended only for passage-planning.* Where anchorages are indicated on the maps in this book by an anchor-symbol it is usually because they are well-recognised anchorages for that island. Most of the listed anchorage positions are described but not shown for reasons of scale. The navigation charts should always be consulted.

British Admiralty Charts and the sailing directions of the CCC which include the Northern Isles (Clyde Cruising Club Publications Ltd, Suite 408, The Pentagon Centre, 36 Washington Street, Glasgow G3 8AZ (0141-221 2774), are virtually essential. The CCC also supplies the FYCA sailing directions for the East Coast, Martin Lawrence's excellent West Coast Pilots which I highly recommend, and Imray Yachting Charts (Imray Laurie Norie & Wilson Ltd, St Ives, Cambridgeshire).

Where an anchorage is labelled 'temp' or 'temporary' it must be approached with caution and only used in daylight and under ideal conditions (slack tides, gentle winds, etc). Always maintain an anchor watch and normally use a tripping line.

An 'occasional' anchorage is slightly better and in ideal conditions could be used overnight. However it may only offer shelter from a limited wind direction and if conditions change should be vacated promptly.

SKAW. THE LAST HOUSE

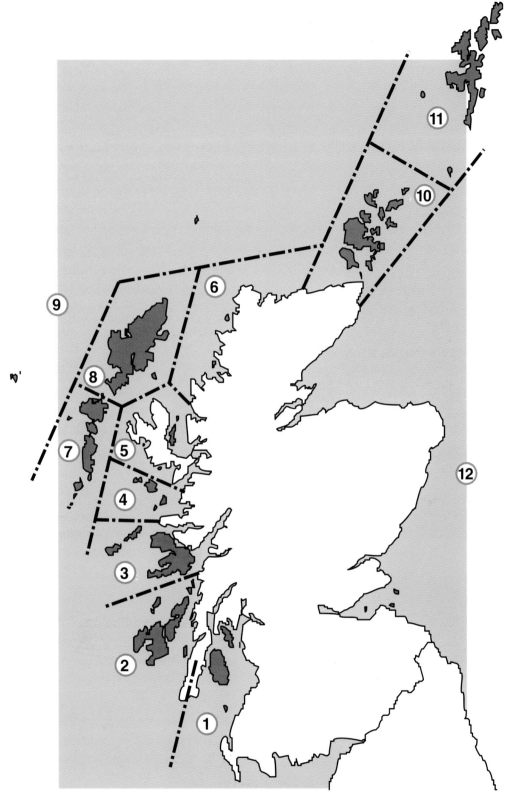

The Geographical Sections

The Solway Firth to the Firth of Clyde

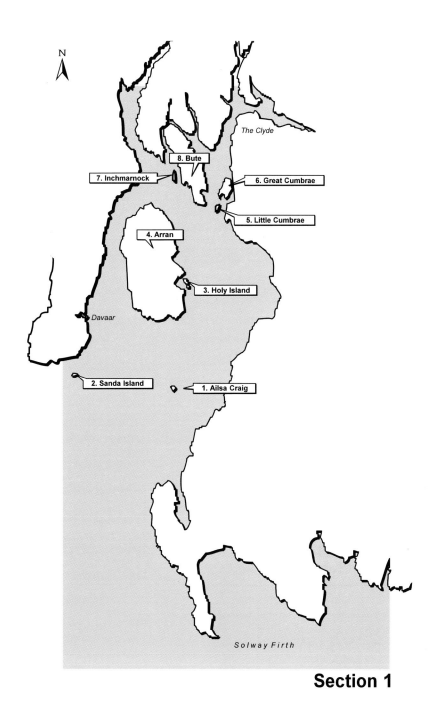

Section 1

Section 1, Table 1

No.	Name	Latitude	Longitude	Table 2* No.	Table 3** No.	Area in Acres	Area in Hectares
1.1	Ailsa Craig	55° 15N	05° 07W	114	19	245	99
1.2	Sanda	55° 17N	05° 35W	96	55	373	151
1.3	Holy Island	55° 32N	05° 04W	78	20	625	253
1.4	Arran	55° 35N	05° 15W	7	2	106750	43201
1.5	Little Cumbrae Island	55° 43N	04° 57W	67	54	773	313
1.6	Great Cumbrae	55° 46N	04° 55W	39	50	2886	1168
1.7	Inchmarnock	55° 47N	05° 09W	76	107	657	266
1.8	Bute	55° 49N	05° 06W	11	24	30188	12217

* Table 2: The islands arranged in order of magnitude
** Table 3: The islands arranged in order of height

Introduction

Here, within a short distance of Scotland's greatest conurbation, are eight fascinating and diverse islands. Turn left on the Clyde at Cloch Point and travel 'doon the water' to Bute, guard of the western entrance, with Inchmarnock tucked behind it. The eastern sentinels are the Cumbraes, Great and Little. Ahead and beyond, the towering serrated ridge of Arran dominates the entire Firth, dwarfing even the high peak of Holy Island. Further out, lonely and conspicuous in the southern reaches of the Firth, stands Ailsa Craig – familiarly referred to as Paddy's Milestone. On the horizon, a speck at the foot of the Mull of Kintyre, is mysterious Sanda Island.

This area, with its long sea–lochs offers a marvellous environment for inshore sailing. The longest of these lochs – longer than Loch Long – is Loch Fyne, stretching from the north of Arran to well beyond Inveraray. The fishing town of Tarbert is the main port on this loch and source of the world–famous Loch Fyne kippers. The larger 'islands' in the vicinity, Barmore and Eilean Aoidhe, are in fact peninsulas and the only islets possibly worthy of the name are **Eilean Buidhe** and **Eilean a' Bhuic** opposite Tarbert and **Eilean a' Chromhraig** just south of the entrance.

Halfway up the loch in Loch Gilp is **Duncuan Island** with, to the east of it, another drying island – Eilean Mór. However, alongside Eilean Mór is the strip of **Liath Eilean** with a pleasant anchorage in between.

In the upper reaches there is **Glas Eilean** off Port Ann with **Eilean Aoghainn** in the centre of the loch and overlooked by Minard Castle.

The islets of the Kilbrannan Sound are equally insignificant – two tiny islets on the coast of the Mull of Kintyre – **Thorn Isle** and **Island Ross**. **Davaar**, which guards the entrance to Campbeltown Loch is not by definition a true island as it can be reached at low water over a shingle causeway (dangerous when the tide comes in). It is worth a visit because there are seven caves and the fifth

conceals a famous mural of Christ crucified which was painted in secret by a local artist, Alexander MacKinnon in 1887.

On the Ayrshire coast by Ardrossan harbour five species of gull nest on low–lying **Horse Island** and, likewise, colonies of common, sandwich and arctic tern nest on **Lady Isle** off Troon. There are no other islets on this coast and the Solway Firth is also short of islands. The largest group is at Fleet Bay – **Murray's Isles**, **Ardwall Island** and **Barlocco Island**. At Kirkcudbright Bay **Little Ross** is off the Ross headland and **Hestan Island** is in the centre of shallow, tidal Auchencairn Bay. Little Ross supports a Stevenson lighthouse which has been automatic since 1961. Two lighthouse–keeper's houses are being renovated by the present 'laird', Dr S R Wild of Edinburgh. The islet was the scene of a nasty murder in 1960: but that's another story.

1.1 Ailsa Craig

(G. aillse creag – fairy rock). Referred to locally as Paddy's Milestone but sometimes known as creag Ealasaid (G. – Elizabeth's rock). In the old Irish tale of 'Buioe Suibne' it is called carraig Alastair (G. – Alastair's rock).

OS Maps: 1:50000 Sheet 76 1:25000 Sheet 490 1:10000 (NX 09)
Admiralty Chart: 1:75000 No.2126

AREA: 99ha (245 acres)
HEIGHT: 338m (1,109 ft)

OWNER: Marquess of Ailsa.

POPULATION: From 19th century to mid-20th century small population of quarrymen and families. 1881 – 29. 1891 – 27. 1931 – 11. 1961 – 10. 1971 – 3 (lighthouse keepers). 1981 – 3. 1991 – 0. (lighthouse automatic).

GEOLOGY: Mainly an acid igneous rock containing fine-

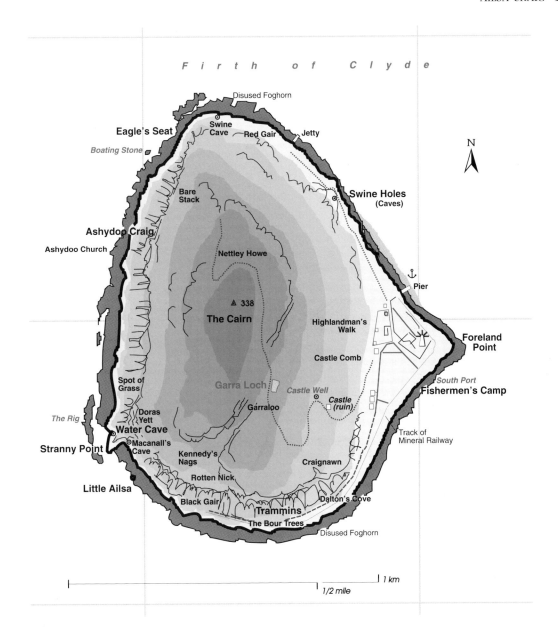

grained crystals of quartz, mica and felspar, known as microgranite. In the north-west corner there is a seam of reibickite, a red, fine-grained micro-granite, which was considered ideal for the manufacture of curling stones. These were cut on the island but polished on the mainland. The floor of the Chapel of the Thistle in St Giles Cathedral, Edinburgh, is made of this beautiful Ailsa Craig granite but the quarries are now disused. Much of the island is columnar basalt, sometimes forming columns four hundred feet in height.

HISTORY: An old square peel-tower on the island was al-most certainly built by the Hamiltons but there is no record of why it was built nor how long it was occupied. It is however said that the monks of Crossraguel Abbey (near Maybole in Ayrshire) eventually used it as a retreat. The Catholics also once held it on behalf of Philip II of Spain.

The lighthouse was built in 1868.

WILDLIFE: In relatively recent times Soay sheep from St Kilda (neolithic, dark-brown, small and hardy) were introduced. Rabbits were said to have been brought in by the quarrymen to supplement their diet. These have not been as big a problem, however, as the brown rats which ar-

AILSA CRAIG FROM DUNURE CASTLE, SEAT OF THE KENNEDYS.

plant, which is now sold in garden centres, is the Bass Rock (see appendix to Section 12).

AILSA CRAIG is the Lowland's answer to the Hebridean and Orcadian stacks, those great chunks of rock rearing out of the sea. Its basalt and columnar trap rises abruptly from sea level and soars to a height of nearly 340m – over 1100 feet. When its ethereal shape materialises out of the mist one can understand it being named fairy rock by some ancient Celt. Except on the east side which has an accessible slope it is so precipitous that even the sea birds are unable to nest on some of the cliffs. It is mentioned in the poetry of both Wordsworth and Keats but, strangely, not by Burns who grew up within sight of it.

Twenty-five thousand years ago when Scotland lay smothered under a thick sheet of ice, a glacier flowing down the Clyde valley broke off pieces of Ailsa Craig granite and carried them south to the English Midlands where they still lie around today scattered between Wales and the Pennines. Much more recently the same fine-grained granite was again distributed widely, but this time in the form of curling stones. For many years there was no other source.

An old anchor bedded in the pebble beach by the broken jetty marks the path to the group of white buildings clustered round the lighthouse.

A rusty narrow-gauge railway line runs from the pier and past the quarrymen's cottages to the abandoned quarry on the south side. A forge and disused foghorns are also in evidence and there are heaps of waste granite pieces from which the spheroidal curling stones have been cut leaving fascinating shapes like miniature Henry Moore sculptures. The Andrew Kay company still has the sole quarrying rights on Ailsa Craig.

A well-defined zig-zag path climbs to the top, starting near the lighthouse and passing the old square **peel-tower** about 100m up the slope [NX023995]. The three

rived in 1889 when ships were ferrying materials and supplies to the newly-built lighthouse. (The quarrymen later claimed that the rats and rabbits were interbreeding!)

Before the brown rats moved in there were at least 250,000 pairs of puffins on the island. An ornithologist, Robert Gray, reported in the 1860s that when he disturbed the puffins 'for a time their numbers seemed so great as to cause a bewildering darkness.'

By 1990 the rats had successfully driven many birds off the island by eating their eggs and young and not a single puffin had been seen since 1984.

Then in 1991 a rat eradication programme was instituted. Poison to kill the rats, three tons of Warfarin, was airlifted by helicopter from HMS Gannet, Prestwick, and distributed on the island in the Spring. 'Some of it was put in bait boxes and a lot went straight into the rat holes,' said an ornithologist member of the working group. The rats died in their burrows so there were no rat carcasses strewn about. The treatment seems to have worked but it only takes two happy rats to repopulate the island.

By the end of 1991 black guillemots and shelduck had already returned to nest and one lone puffin had been seen. If the experiment succeeds it may be repeated on other infested islands.

Ailsa Craig is noted for its immense gannet colony which has been there since at least 1526. In the early 1970s some 9500 breeding pairs were reported which is about 5% of the gannet population of the world. They are mainly on the south-west side. Numerous guillemots, kittiwakes and gulls are also to be found and blackbirds, song-thrushes, wheatears and willow warblers have been seen. Pipits may be found on the steep slopes above the smooth rock walls.

There is a wide variety of plant life. In places the cliffs are white with the scented flowers of scurvy grass spotted here and there with red lychnis. The rose-coloured flowers of the tree mallow, lavatera arborea, can be seen growing 2-3m high near the buildings. The only other natural Scottish site for this

THE JETTY ON AILSA CRAIG

stars of the Hamilton coat of arms are carved on a stone set in the walls.

Further up, the path passes over the shallow valley of Garraloo and beside the tiny **Garra Loch** with the cleft of Rotten Nick below before making its way to the top. Here the precipice plunges straight to the sea; **Bare Stack**, in the north-west, with two ferocious brown overhangs and **Ashydoo** cliff lying just south. Far below to the south-west is Spot of Grass, Doras Yett and the outcrop of Kennedy's Nags. And beyond the white lace of the surf lie the wide stretches of the Firth of Clyde with the long dark shape of Ulster on the south-western horizon.

It is possible to make an exciting and relatively easy two mile circumnavigation of the island beneath these cliffs. The only minor obstruction is at **Water Cave** in the south-west cleft. The exposed corner of Stranny Point has to be negotiated to reach this mini Fingal's Cave when coming from the east around the shore, past **Little Ailsa**. Try and time it for low water.

Climbers may prefer to go directly up the slope from the landing place on the east shore. There is no difficulty in the ascent but in places the route leads over steeply-inclined slabs. No rock-climbing routes on any of the dramatic cliffs have been recorded but this is just as well as the island is a bird-sanctuary.

ACCESS: Occasional boat trips are run from Girvan; or hire by arrangement, 01465 3219. Crossing time approx. 1 hour.

Anchorages:
1. A timber jetty or pier of sorts in the north-east beside the lighthouse at Foreland Point has only 0.6m at its head. Temp anchorage possible close N of jetty but beware ruins of old jetty close NW of existing jetty. Bottom of granite boulders shelves steeply. Use tripping line and do not leave yacht unattended.

1.2 Sanda Island

(ON. sandtange – sand spit) island. There is a large sand spit near the harbour called Oitir Buidhe (G. – yellow sand spit). According to the Ordnance Gazeteer Sanda was called 'Avona Porticosa' by the Vikings and known as 'Aven' in Gaelic, (?G. abhainn – river). But Dean Munro says the Danes called it 'Havin', i.e. anchorage, which makes much more sense.

OS Maps: 1:50000 Sheet 68 1:25000 Sheet 489
Admiralty Charts: 1:75000 Nos.2126 or 2199

AREA: 127ha (314 acres)
HEIGHT: 123m (403 ft)

OWNER: Formerly, Ellanveg Ltd of Douglas, Isle of Man. Now Mr John (?Richard) Gannon (formerly of Lundy Is-

'THE SHIP' LIGHTHOUSE, SANDA

land, Bristol Channel).

POPULATION: 1841 – 11 (1 house). 1871 – 32. 1881 – 14. 1891 – 36 (7 houses). 1931 – 14. 1961 – 7. 1971 – 9. 1981 – 3 (lighthouse keepers). 1991 – 0.

GEOLOGY: Lower Old Red Sandstone in red and yellow varieties, and undifferentiated schists.

HISTORY: In 1306 Bruce may have landed here. Angus II, fifth King of the Isles, sheltered him at Dunaverty Castle which stood on the headland at Southend overlooking Sanda Island [NR688076]. When the English fleet drew closer he slipped away to Ireland.

The end of the lighthouse promontory on the south of the island is called Prince Edward's Rock after Edward Bruce, Robert the Bruce's impulsive brother, who was, very briefly, King of Ireland.

At this time Sanda was part of the lands of the Priory of Whithorn in Galloway and remained so until the late 16th century when it became the property of the MacDonalds of Sanda with the Earl of Argyll holding the superiority.

In 1647, Dunaverty Castle again entered the history books when 300 MacDonalds of Kintyre, Catholic royalists and supporters of Montrose, made their last stand against the Covenanter general, Leslie. Among them were Archibald Mor, chief of the MacDonalds of Sanda and his son and heir Archibald Og. Sir Alexander MacDonald had left them to defend the castle when he withdrew to Ireland but they were besieged and short of drinking water. Leslie offered to spare them should they surrender. They did so whereupon he had every one of them massacred. The castle was razed to the ground, never rebuilt, and from then on it has been known as Bloody Castle.

The MacDonalds' estates were forfeited but in 1661 they were restored by Act of Parliament. Ronald MacDonald inherited Sanda but died in 1679 when his son, Archibald, became the 6th Laird of Sanda.

In 1946 the Campbeltown lifeboat *The Duke of Con-*

naught (brought out of retirement as the new boat was under repair) went to the assistance of the 7000-ton *By-ron Darnton* stuck on a reef on the south of Sanda. The skipper of the wrecked ship apparently considered it safer to stay aboard and keep below decks, but the lifeboatmen knew that the ship was bound to break up before long with the almost inevitable death of everyone on board. Unfortunately the old lifeboat had no radio. Conditions were appalling and communication with the ship was impossible as no one was on deck so the lifeboat sailed back round the island to the north harbour where one of the crew ran overland to the south side. There was a radio transmitter at the lighthouse by which he eventually persuaded the captain of the stricken ship to allow those aboard to be taken off. Once again the lifeboat set out into the violent storm, rounded the island, and in spite of a very unreliable engine risked going into the chaotic sea among the rocks. It took eighteen long hours of almost foolhardy bravery but all fifty-four passengers and crew (and even a dog) were saved. Just as the lifeboat pulled clear of the rocks the ship finally disintegrated. But the ordeal was not yet over for while struggling home, tired and overloaded, the old engine at last sputtered out. It seemed

a losing battle as they were blown out to sea but after an hour they managed to coax her into life again and at last reached the safety of the harbour.

WILDLIFE: Two of Sanda's small neighbouring islands, Sheep Island and Glunimore Island, are important breeding grounds for puffins in the Clyde area but many seabirds also breed on Sanda Island's crags.

Although **SANDA ISLAND** is a useful stopping-off point for a yacht waiting for the tide to round the Mull of Kintyre it is, surprisingly, only occasionally visited for its own sake. The farmhouse, which has been restored by the owner for his own occupation, is just beside the jetty and slipway. There are also various farm buildings and the old schoolhouse. This is a Site of Scientific Interest (SSI) and the Nature Conservancy Council have the seabirds monitored and ringed both on Sanda and on its two little neighbours, **Sheep Island** and **Glunimore Island**. Glunimore is a tiny lump of rock but Sheep Island is large enough to provide some grazing for sheep. It has a cave on it and a natural stone arch at its north end.

The road which runs round the bay and across the island to the lighthouse had been macadamed in the past and there are still patches of tar lying in the ruts. The roofless ruin of little **St Ninian's Chapel**, about 10.3m by 6.3m, is on the south side of a knoll within the burial enclosure [NR727046]. Fordun noted this building in the second half of the 14th century. The side walls, of local rubble dressed with local sandstone, are still standing to roof level, but the gables have partly collapsed. There is an intact wooden lintel over the entrance doorway. One of the three window embrasures is still in reasonable condition and it has a stone basin or piscina set in the wall beside it. A matching basin has not been seen since 1873. There is a stone altar slab with a rectangular slot in it – possibly used for relics and an inscription on a grave slab set in the floor refers to 'Archibald – son to MacDonald of Sanda' and 'Cirstin Stewart'. Cirstin Stewart was the widow of Archibald Mor MacDonald who died in the Dunaverty Massacre.

By the north-west corner of the chapel a worn Early Christian slab is incised with a cross and near the centre of the burial ground there is a large much-eroded cruciform-shaped stone nearly 2m high and a few scattered headstones. Heraldic memorials to the MacDonald lairds show that Archibald, the sixth laird, was alive in 1731.

Just west of the chapel are the footings of a small square structure. A 1630 record states – 'at the syde of that Chappell there is a litle well or compass of stones. . . And they say that the bones of certaine holie men that lived in that Illand is buried within that place.' The same record also refers to a 'spring of fresh water called St Ninian's Well' which had therapeutic powers but this has not been identified.

In the past there was an active fishing community living on Sanda. Apparently, by tradition, if there was a severe storm and the men were still at sea, the families would gather in the burial ground by a particular unmarked grave, say a prayer for the fishermen, and then solemnly pour a cup of fresh water on the grave. The origin of this ceremony is unknown.

Legend has it that St Ninian himself is buried on Sanda and that anyone who steps on his grave will die within a year. This dangerous spot once had an alder tree marking its whereabouts but that has long since disappeared.

The island had not been farmed since 1946 but in 1991 the new owner had neatly repaired the fences and sheep were grazing in the central valley. There are no trees but this was not always the case; the hill above the farmhouse is still called Wood Hill. The lighthouse, on a promontory on the south shore (called The Ship because it has that appearance from the sea), was built in 1850, and altered in 1881. The skerries here are littered with the wrecks of ships. There is a striking wide-span natural stone arch alongside the lighthouse and many cave-riddled crags and rock formations in the vicinity. On a sunny summer day there are few more enjoyable experiences than a walk across Sanda. The central valley traps the heat as it is sheltered from all the prevailing winds.

ACCESS: A boat trip can usually be arranged in summer from Southend, 1½M away on the S tip of Kintyre, or from Campbeltown – weather permitting.

Anchorages:
1. Off Sanda Roads just NE of slipway/jetty, 4-5m, sand. Strong nearby tidal stream requires care. On W side of anchorage a reef extends about ³/₄c N from Beinn a Theine marked by a beacon. Note sunken rocks in centre of the Roads. Some swell likely but well-protected from SW.
2. South Bay, small bight on S side of Sanda. Good temp. anchorage and shelter from NW winds about 3c ENE of The Ship light-tower. Rocks dry up to 2.5c E of SW point of the light-house promontory.

1.3 Holy Island

Formerly eilean Molaise (G. – Mo Las' island) corrupted to Lamlash. Was also known as Holy Island and this became its official name in 1830 when the village on Arran adopted the name of Lamlash.

OS Maps: 1:50000 Sheet 69 1:25000 Sheets 454 and 467
Admiralty Charts: 1:20000 No.1864

AREA: 253ha (625 acres)
HEIGHT: 314m (1,030 ft)

OWNER: At one time part of the estates of the Duke of Hamilton. Bought in 1991 by a group of Scottish Buddhists, the Samye Ling Tibetan Centre, for about £400,000 from Mrs Catherine Morris. The price was agreed on the understanding that there would be no commercial exploitation and that the archaeological and spiritual amenities, and the distinctive flora and fauna would be protected.

POPULATION: 1841 – no separate record. 1881 – 15. 1891 – 16 (3 houses). 1931 – 19. 1961 – 7. 1971 – 10. 1981 – 17. (These figures include the lighthouse keepers.) 1991 – 0. Uninhabited during 1989-91 but now populated by small community of Buddhists.

GEOLOGY: Mainly igneous rock of a rhyolite type in the north and basalt in the south. The steep patches on the west slopes are of porphyry and claystone.

HISTORY: The island's one-time resident and patron saint, St Mo Las was born in Ireland in AD 566.

In the 12th century Somerled established his dominion over the island and it was visited by King Haakon's Norsemen before and probably also after the Battle of Largs in 1263.

In 1548 the ship carrying the five-year-old child who was to become Mary Queen of Scots sheltered here on its way to France.

WILDLIFE: The island is now a nature reserve and there is evidence that it was once covered with trees. Wild rhododendrons have destroyed some of the habitat but the present owners are trying to correct this.

Wild goats, once common on Arran but now extinct there, still roam free on the high slopes of Holy Island apparently indifferent to human presence. They have occasionally been culled because of the restricted habitat. In Victorian times it was fashionable to drink their milk as it was thought to bestow longevity.

There are also about 100 Soay sheep, a small resident herd of Highland cattle, a dozen or so Eriskay ponies and thousands of rabbits on the island. Peregrines breed on the rocky cliffs and many birds, including eider duck, nest on the shores.

The 18th century traveller, Thomas Pennant, said that the island was 'infested with vipers' but this is certainly not true today.

HOLY ISLAND shelters one of the finest of naval anchor-

HOLY ISLE FARMHOUSE –
BEFORE THE
PROPOSED EXTENSION

ages and the large mooring buoys used by the great war-ships of the Royal Navy in the First World War are still in place. This was the home in the 7th century of St Mo Las, or St Molias (or St Luserian in some accounts). The saint lived and meditated comfortably in **St Mo Las' Cave** [NS059297] well-furnished with every 'mod. con.', a fire-place, a fresh water supply from a nearby spring, drainage carved out of the rock and, beside the front door, a large stone dining-table with stone seats which is known as the Judgement Stone because he sat there to settle local dis-putes. The saint was said to be a strict disciplinarian. The spring is called **St Mo Las' Well** and the cave contains ru-nic and early Christian inscriptions. The former are thought to have been carved by King Haakon's defeated followers returning home after the Battle of Largs. The lat-ter is a 'signature' thought to refer to Nicholas the 11th century Bishop of Man. It is marked with an episcopal cross. On my last visit there was an iron grille protecting the cave entrance and the (absent) owners' assistance would have been required to obtain access to the interior. In view of the damage that vandals have done to the King's Cave on Arran this is a sensible precaution.

St Mo Las is reputed to have lived to the ripe old age of 120 in spite of deliberately contracting thirty nasty dis-eases to expiate his sins. It is said that his bones were taken over to Arran, carried through the central valley and buried under a rough stone in a wall of the church at Shiskine, near Blackwaterfoot.

There are supposed to be a few traces of a 12th cen-tury fortress built by Somerled, Lord of the Isles, and in the 13th century a monastery was established in a posi-tion south-east of the present farmhouse. The small chapel was used for burials until 1790. The monastery is said to have been founded by Ranald, son of Somerled, but it was in a ruinous state by 1594.

Mullach Mór (G. – big top) is the descriptive name of the central peak and summit of the island at 314m, with Mullach Beag (G. – little top) to the north of it. This is the easiest route for a scramble up the mountain but avoid the precipitous east flank. Apart from the two lighthouses in the south of the island the farmhouse, outbuildings and known archaeological remains are all in the north. There are a few trees by the farmhouse, otherwise the island is bare.

The Buddhist community, the Samye Ling Tibetan Or-der, has a twenty-year plan to create Europe's biggest spir-itual sanctuary on the island. They hope to build a 'Potala-like' wall of retreat cells for a community of about 200 adherents. With the assistance of groups of volun-teers they have cleaned the shores of rubbish, restored a dry stone dyke around the one-time monks' orchard and started refurbishment of the existing farmhouse and the former lighthouse-keepers' cottages. Fresh water is ob-tained from springs. They hope eventually to replant the old monastery orchard with ancient varieties of fruit trees and to reafforest part of the island with Scottish tradi-tional species.

A coastal circuit, half by path and dirt road, makes an interesting and not too demanding walk. I have been un-able to discover the significance of the name of **Dorothy's Well** which is in the south-east [NS068292].

On the way back from such a walk, if the sun is setting over Goat Fell and Mullach Mór brooding in the evening light, rest for a while by the dry stone dyke near the farm-house and admire the view. Once upon a time, it is said, there was a farmer living there whose wife bore him fif-teen daughters. He was so disgusted at not having a son that he murdered her and buried her body under the stone-flagged kitchen floor. But no one has ever lifted the floor to find out if the story is true or not.

ACCESS: Summer boat trips from Lamlash but no regular service and casual visits are being discouraged by the new owners. 'People who wish to respect the island will be able to visit by agreement,' they say. It used to be considered 'macho' to swim across the channel from King's Cross Point (severe test for moderate swimmers due to the tidal current) to the lighthouse at the SE of Holy Island, but this is not to be recommended.

Anchorages:

1. Opposite the farmhouse in 6m to 8m, well SW of the jetty and as near the shore as reasonable. Weed on pebbles. Check that anchor well-bedded. Good shelter.

1.4 Arran

(B. aran – high place)

OS Maps: 1:50000 Sheet 69 1:25000 Sheets 441, 454 and 467
Admiralty Charts: 1:75000 Nos.2126 and 2131 1:36000 No.2220
Pladda to Brodick and No.2221 Brodick to Cock of Arran 1:25000
No.1864 Brodick 1:20000 No.1864 Lamlash

AREA: 43,201ha (106,750 acres)
HEIGHT: 874m (2,867 ft)

OWNER: Multiple ownership but the principal owners are
the heirs of the Duchess of Montrose, the Forestry Commission and the National Trust for Scotland (NTS). The
Duchess of Montrose's inheritance came when the direct
line of the Hamiltons ceased in 1895. Mary, Duchess of
Montrose died in 1957 and in 1958 her daughter, Lady
Jean Fforde gifted Goatfell and the neighbouring mountains to the National Trust for Scotland. At the same time
Brodick Castle was accepted in lieu of estate duty by the
Inland Revenue and transferred to the Trust by the Gov-
ernment.

Arran, oddly enough, appears to have three earldoms:
Earl of Arran (No 1), is the Duke of Hamilton – title
granted in 1389; Earl of Arran (No 2), title granted in
1467 and including 1000 acres and Lochranza Castle was
sold by Lady Jean Fforde to an anonymous purchaser in
1994; Earl of Arran (No 3), title originated in Ireland, is
held by the Gore family in Hertfordshire.

POPULATION: 1755 – 3646. 1792 – 5804. 1821 – 6600.
1841 – 6241. 1881 – 4730. 1891 – 4824. 1931 – 4506.
1961 – 3700. 1971 – 3564. 1981 – 4726. 1991 – 4453.

GEOLOGY: Arran is a geologist's paradise. It was described
by the eminent geologist Sir Archibald Geike as a complete
synopsis of Scottish geology and it was here that James
Hutton in the 18th century confirmed his theories of igneous geology. It is regularly visited by parties of students
to study the rock formations. Goat Fell is an igneous intrusion into the surrounding Devonian sandstones and
schists giving a ring of upturned strata around a granite
core – the dramatic high peaks and corries are a direct result of this. The early settlers used local pitchstone for
their artefacts and Cruttwell (18th century) claimed that
topaz were to be found in the area.

In the north-east of Arran there is a region of carboniferous limestone whilst the south is composed of new red
sandstone. Where there is hard granite the many basaltic
dykes have eroded to form fissures but in the softer rock in
the south of the island the dykes form conspicuous ridges.
There are many erratics – boulders which have been
moved a considerable distance from their source by Ice
Age glaciers, particularly in the south. In the west below
Dougarie Lodge there are interesting terraces of glacial
material while in the north great rockfalls on the coast
date back to the mesozoic and palaeozoic periods. The
northern tip is a large sandstone outcrop called the Cock
of Arran. A raised beach almost 8m above sea level virtually encircles the island.

HISTORY: Whoever the first inhabitants may have been
several thousand years ago, Arran was probably invaded
in 200BC by Britons speaking a Celtic language
(Brythonic) related to present-day Welsh. (Dunbarton,
meaning Fort of the Britons was another similar enclave
left by the Romans when they departed in 400AD. Scots
arrived from Ireland in the 6th century and included Arran in the Kingdom of Dalriada (roughly the extent of
present-day Argyll, but for a time stretching further
south). Norsemen then moved in about the 9th century
and separated the island from Dalriada but Somerled,
when founding the monastery at Saddell in Kintyre where
he was eventually buried, took it from the
Norse in 1156. After the Battle of Largs in
1263 Arran (still under the dominion of the
Lord of the Isles) became part of the Scottish
Kingdom but, as with Bute, it was considered
the personal property of the Stewart kings –
not Crown property. It was eventually awarded
to the Hamiltons by Royal Charter in 1503
and at the end of the 18th century the Duke
of Hamilton was still sole proprietor except for
five small farms. After 1745 villages and crofts
were deserted through massive emigration and
large areas were later laid waste by the introduction of sheep farming. The Gaelic life and
culture of the island was shattered. James
Hogg wrote: 'Ah! Wae's me, I hear the Duke of
Hamilton's crofters are a' gaun away, man and
mither's son, frae the Isle o' Arran. Pity on us!'

BRODICK CASTLE

Kilbrannan Sound

Ferry
Rubha Creagan Dubha
Cock of Arran
Lochranza
Newton
Ossian's Cave
Laggan
Castle
Catacol Bay
Catacol
Glen Chalmadale
Rubha Airigh Bheirg
Craw
Meal Mór
Fallen Rocks
Lenimore
Thundergay
Beinn Breac
Suidhe Fhearghas
Sannox
Sannox Bay
Beinn Bhreac
Caisteal Abhail
859
Pirnmill
Loch Tanna
Cir Mhór
Corrie
Whitefarland
Beinn Bharrain
Beinn Tarsuinn
△ 874
Goatfell
Imachar Point
Imachar
825
Glen Rosa
wood
Beinn Nuis
wood
Merkland Point
Glen Iorsa
Brodick Castle ☆
Dougarie Jetty
Auchencar
Brodick Bay
Ferry
wood
An Tunna The String
☆ Fort
BRODICK
Machrie Bay
Máchrie
☆ Stone Circle
Glaister
Glencloy
Strathwhillan
Corrygills
A' Chruach
w o o d l a n d
Machrie Water
Claughlands Point
Tormore
Stone Circles
Ard Bheinn
Beinn Bhreac
Benlister Glen
HOLY ISLAND
Chambered Cairns ☆
☆ Stone Circle
Ballymichael
Lamlash
☆ King's Cave
wood
Lamlash Bay
The Doon ↘ Fort
Shiskine
Fort ☆
w o o d l a n d
woodland
Dun ☆
1 ☆ Cairn
The Ross
Kingscross
Blackwaterfoot
Kilpatrick
Glen Scorrodale
Tighvein
1
Drumadoon Bay
☆ Chambered Cairn
☆ Carn Ban
Kiscadale
Whiting Bay
wood
Stone Circle
Glenashdale Falls
Corriecravie
Sliddery
Kilmory Water
woodland
Largybeg
Dippin Head
Lagg Kilmory
☆ Chambered Cairns
Kildonnan
Castle
8 km
4 miles
Bennan Head
Sound of Pladda
Pladda

N

WILDLIFE: Palm-lilies, a sub-tropical native tree of New Zealand, grow in the mild climate of the south and west. Most types of deciduous trees can be found and there are two unique protected species of whitebeam – *Sorbus arranensis* and *Sorbus pseudo-fennica*.

Some less common species of wildflowers flourish on Arran – alpine enchanter's nightshade in areas of deep shade and alpine lady's mantle which grows in Glen Sannox.

At present Arran has a population of about 2000 wild

red deer. This is a recovery from the end of the 18th century when the herds had been hunted almost to extinction. There are no foxes, grey squirrels, stoats, weasels or moles and both adders and badgers are now fairly rare.

The mountains are the domain of golden eagles and all the characteristic moorland birds are to be found.

Sheltering behind the Mull of Kintyre and sitting snugly in the busy Firth of Clyde, **ARRAN** has the blessing of a mild climate and easy access to populous Glasgow. There is an average annual rainfall of 1250mm (50 ins) in the west, and double that figure up in the mountains. This has been a popular holiday resort since the early 18th century – and tourism is still the main industry but agriculture, chiefly livestock and potatoes, runs a close second. This is also an island steeped in legends and ghosts, folklore and fairy tales.

A circuit of the island is about 92 Km (55 miles). The **Isle of Arran Heritage Museum** at Brodick is in an 18th century croft farm, complete with smiddy, stables, bothy and coach house. It has a tea room and demonstrations of local crafts.

To the north of Brodick Bay (ON *breidr vik* – broad bay) and beneath the highest mountain, Goat Fell (G. *gaoth* – wind, ON *fjeld* – mountain) (874m) stands **Brodick Castle**. The walled garden was started in 1710 and the woodland garden, with one of Europe's finest collections of rhododendrons including some propagated from the plants at Achamore Gardens on Gigha (No.2.3), was started in

1923. Both castle and mountain belong to the National Trust for Scotland.

Part of the Round Tower at Brodick Castle dates from the 13th century but the main building was constructed by the Hamiltons who started the work in 1558. In 1652 Cromwell's forces, normally renowned for destruction, built the Battery and an extra wing but the troops were later massacred by the islanders. In 1844 Gillespie Graham was the architect for the final work including the Great West Tower. He was commissioned by William, son of the tenth Duke of Hamilton, and his wife, Princess Mary of Baden who was a great-niece of the Empress Josephine. The castle is worth visiting as a fine example of Scottish baronial architecture with richly designed interiors, many art treasures, and a restored Victorian kitchen. The grounds are open throughout the year and the castle is open from Easter until late September.

There is a superb scenic hill-walk of 18km (11 miles) which starts near Brodick [NS004368] and goes up Glen Rosa, across the saddle at 460m (1500 ft) by Cir Mhór (G – big comb) then down through the wild landscape of Glen Sannox and the remains of old barytes mines (abandoned 1938) to **Sannox Bay** [NS016454].

North of Brodick is the pretty village of **Corrie** (G. *coire* – a cauldron-shaped hollow) with two tiny harbours. The quarry in the hills behind provided stone for the construction of the Crinan Canal. The road continues through Sannox to Lochranza but, if the weather's good, there is a fine 15km (9 mile) walk along the shoreline

LOCHRANZA CASTLE

passing Ossian's Cave and, the most northerly point, the **Cock of Arran**. The mountain side here once resembled an enormous crowing cock with its wings spread but its head has now eroded away. There is an alternative path at the mid-point, Laggan [NR979508], which goes over the hill ridge. Daniel MacMillan, founder of the publishing empire, spent his childhood here.

The little village of **Lochranza** spreads along the southern shore under the ramparts of ruined Lochranza Castle standing in the centre of the loch on a shingle spit. This is where Bruce is reputed to have landed in 1306 or 1307 on his return from Rathlin Island. His sister is also supposed to have sheltered here in a nunnery but no trace of one has been found. Fragments of Lochranza Castle are from an early fortification mentioned by Fordun in the 14th century but most of the existing ruin dates from the 16th century. In the early 15th century it belonged to John de Mentieth and it was then granted by James II to Alexander Lord Montgomery.

For the yachtsman the delightful anchorage of Loch Ranza has something of a reputation for anchor-dragging. I can recall one evening when the wind picked up to gale force and swung into the north-east and sudden violent squalls came down the glen. By midnight every one of the nine boats anchored in the loch was playing ring-a-ring-a-roses in the dark as they tried to find a sound bottom. We missed our normal visit to the excellent pub!

At **Catacol** (ON – ravine of the wildcat) south of Lochranza the terrace of cottages at the mouth of the glen is known as the Twelve Apostles [NR911497]. Loch Tanna, the largest loch on Arran, is at the summit of Glen Catacol in the wild landscape beneath Beinn Bhreac (G. – speckled mountain) – 711m high (2332 ft). Further south by the fine beach at Pirnmill [NR873445] pine bobbins or 'pirns' were made for the Paisley mills – until there were no more pines.

The road runs on past the palm trees of Whitefarland and Imachar to **Dougarie Lodge** where Iorsa Water tumbles into the sea. The lodge [NR884371] was built by the Hamiltons and the first island telephone was installed here in 1891.

At Machrie Moor (G. *machair* – low, level land) where the central valley opens out there is a feast of archaeological remains. Some of the standing stones were unfortunately turned into millstones but many undamaged stones remain as well as chambered tombs and cairns (3500BC-1000BC) both here and in the southern coastal areas [eg. NR9032 and 9132]. Bronze Age burial chambers or cists have been found inside one of the many stone circles on Machrie Moor and there is a 15-stone circle round a burial cairn in the woods above the road at Auchagallon [NR908351]. Arran has no less than ten such henges or stone circles.

An interesting walk above the shore from **Tormore**

MONOLITHS AT MACHRIE MOOR

leads to the **King's Cave**, a large, dry, sandstone cave, 30m deep and level with the raised beach [NR884309]. In the 18th century the Kirk Session met here and in the 19th century it was used as a school. The cave entrance (protected by a grille in 1995) can be seen when sailing in the Kilbrannan Sound. It was said to have been occupied by Fingal, Finn McCool, the legendary Irish King, who, to prove his manhood, rebuffed a Viking raid by Manos, heir to the Swedish King. The cave was excavated in 1902 exposing early Christian or Viking wall-carvings of hunting scenes but vandals have now covered these with graffiti and caused a lot of damage. Incidentally, this cave is also supposed to have been lived in by Robert the Bruce when he was inspired by the well-kent spider but the cave on Rathlin Island off the north-east corner of Ireland has better credentials.

In 1817 Thomas Telford built the road (B880) which crosses the island to Brodick Bay. It was named 'The String' by sailors because from the sea it looks like a piece of string laid across the bare moorland. South of Machrie Moor the village of Shiskine [NR913299] is reputed to be the burial place of St Mo Las of Holy Island (No.1.3).

A large cairn [NR891288] at **Blackwaterfoot** which was pillaged during the 19th century contained relics including a dagger and this was thought to show a link with the culture of Stonehenge. The double ramparts of an iron-age fortress, Drumadoon (G. – fort on a ridge) are on a steep slope west of the village [NR886294].

In the south-east, a picturesque minor road called The Ross, follows Sliddery Water and the Green Glen to Lamlash.

Arran's oldest hotel, an 18th century coaching inn, stands among the trees at **Lagg** (G – a hollow) [NR956216]. It is haunted by a laird who sold his soul to the devil. Below the village and by the sea is the ruin of a prehistoric tomb which once held the remains of four adults and two children [NR955211].

Torrylin by **Kilmory** is the home of Arran cheese. The whole of this rocky south coast was once the haunt of smugglers from Ireland and wandering through the woods above the village are the ghosts of a young couple who were mistaken for smugglers and shot by coastguards. There is extensive forestry in the area with many interesting woodland walks. **Carn Ban**, a well-preserved neolithic chambered cairn measuring 30m x 18m [NR991262] is by a burn in a high wooded valley – Allt an t-Sluice. It is 6½km (4 miles) up a forest track which starts just east of Kilmory and the site is 291m above sea level.

In the extreme south-east are the limited ruins of 14th century **Kildonan Castle** [NS036209] which was granted by King Robert III to his bastard son, John, in 1406.

Kildonan, a place reputedly visited by St Donan after his training at Whithorn, overlooks the small tear-shaped island of **Pladda** (ON – flat isle). Owned by Arran Estate it was up for sale in 1990 for £80,000, its first time ever on the market. Originally granted to the Hamiltons the lighthouse was rebuilt by Stevenson in the 1820s and was manned until the 1980s. In spite of being only 11ha in area, Pladda is lucky to have its own fresh water supply.

Glenashdale Burn enters the sea by the youth hostel at **Whiting Bay**. There is an easy walk [NS046252] through the woods one mile up the glen to see the dramatic waterfalls which have a 30m drop over a lava sill. Nearby are the ruins of a fort, two chambered cairns and the 'Giants' Graves'.

The substantial remains of a Viking burial mound and fort [NS056283] are at **Kingscross Point**, south of Lamlash Bay. It was here that Robert the Bruce waited for a bonfire to be lit on the Ayrshire coast as the prearranged signal that his supporters were ready for his final attempt to claim the crown. There was a false alarm and he arrived too early, but his claim was successful nevertheless.

The High School at **Lamlash** [NS024307] stands on the ground where Donald 'Tattie' MacKelvie developed the world renowned seed potatoes, *Arran Chief, Arran Pilot* and *Arran Banner*.

For anglers the salmon and trout fishing in both the Machrie and Iorsa Waters has a high rating and, for general recreational activities, Arran provides swimming, boating, pony-trekking, and seven golf-courses.

For the mountaineer Arran is noted for its four 'Corbetts': Goatfell, 874m; Beinn Tarsuinn (G. – transverse hill), 825m; Cir Mhór [keer vor] (G.- big comb), 798m; and, Caisteal Abhail (G. – Castle ptarmigan), 859m.

It is, I am reliably told, possible to traverse all the main tops in the east and central groups in one day – 'as the going is so easy'. This amounts to a total height of about 2600m to be climbed. Many of the excellent climbs, ridge-walks and hill-walks of Arran are listed in the publications of the Scottish Mountaineering Club.

Incidentally, the name of the mountain called Suidhe Fhearghas (G – seat of Fergus) [NR990455] recalls a day when the Fianna of Ireland were hunting red deer on Arran. They took time off to meet for a banquet on the mountain and to listen to their bard, Fergus of the True Lips.

ACCESS: Car ferry from Ardrossan, 01294-463470, to Brodick takes one hour. Train connections from Glasgow. Advance booking usually essential. Summer car ferry from Rothesay Bute to Brodick, 01770-302166. Tourist Information Office near Brodick pier, 01770-302140. Car ferry to Lochranza from Claonaig in Kintyre, summer only and subject to reasonable weather, 30 min. trip. There is a bus service on Arran and bicycles and cars can be hired. Local companies operate coach tours.

Anchorages:
Note: All anchorages except Loch Ranza and Lamlash Bay are exposed and only tenable in settled conditions.

1. North Sannox, between the southernmost measured-mile posts. Exposed temp. anchorage in 3m, sand, close inshore just N of the burn. Outstanding views.

2. Sannox bay, sandy bay at entrance to the Sannox River. Temp anchorage off old stone pier in 6-12m. Beware Sannox rock near centre of bay. Very exposed NE to SE. Beautiful view.

3. Corrie. Exposed temp anchorage in 4-8m off either of the old stone harbours N and S of Corrie Point.

4. Brodick bay. Visitors' moorings or good anchorage in light W'lies in 3-5m, sand, about 2c W of the pier. Anchor well off-shore to avoid moorings and ferry or, in NW winds, anywhere between Merkland Point and the Old Quay. Restricted temp shelter within inner pier subject to HM's agreement. (Access to Brodick Castle and grounds).

5. Clauchlands Point. Anchor in Lamlash Bay 4c W of the Point. Exposed to E.

6. Lamlash. Anchor in 4-6m, E of stone pier but many moorings and bottom steep. Swell in E winds. Squalls in strong NW winds.

7. Cordon to Kingscross. Anchor anywhere from SE of the Cordon shoal to Kingscross avoiding moorings, fish cages, and large unlit naval moorings in the bay.

8. Whiting bay, between Largybeg and Kingscross Points, sheltered from W'lies only. Anchor in 4-6m, well off-shore. Visitors' moorings N of stone slipway.

9. Pladda. Anchor on E side of island close in-shore just N of lighthouse jetty, in 5-8m, sand with thick weed. Sheltered N to W and partly from SW. Many dangers in channel between Pladda and Arran.

10. Blackwaterfoot (Drumadoon Bay), very exposed to S and W. Anchor in 4m near burn mouth but beware rocks.

11. Machrie bay, mid-W side, temp anchorage in 3-7m anywhere in bay but avoid Iorsa Patch at N end. Depths increase suddenly. At Machrie burn the bay dries out about 1½c and shore shoals for about 1c for ½M on either side. Exposed SW to NW.

12. Whitefarland bay, temp anchorage in 6-12m, protected from S winds. Bay shoals for 2c off shore for about ½M N.

13. Catacol bay, temp anchorage at S of bay in 12m, some shelter from S.

14. Loch Ranza, small sea loch which dries about 2c from head. Ferry pier extends N from Coillemore point (the S entrance point). Exposed W through N to NNE. NE to NW winds cause considerable swell and there can be violent squalls. Enter closer to ferry pier. Visitors' moorings or anchor in centre of loch, off the ruined castle. Bottom soft mud with poor holding.

1.5 Little Cumbrae

Probably, (B. cymri – Brythonic Gaelic people) i.e. the place of the Brythonic or Welsh-speaking Gaels. Formerly known as Little, Lesser or Wee Cumray.

OS Maps: 1:50000 Sheet 63 1:25000 Sheet 428
Admiralty Chart: 1:25000 1907 or 1:36000 2221

AREA: 313ha (773 acres)

HEIGHT: 123m (403 ft)

OWNER: Purchased in 1960 by Little Cumbrae Estate Ltd for £24,000 from the trustees of Ian Robertson Parker of Cheshire. Prior to 1913 was the property of the Earl of Eglinton and Winton. Three acres with the lighthouse are under separate ownership.

POPULATION: 1841 – 8. 1881 – 23. 1891 – 17. 1931 – 21. 1961 – 8. 1971 – 14 (includes lighthouse keepers). 1981 – 7. 1991 – 6.

GEOLOGY: Mainly Carboniferous basalt and spilite.

HISTORY: Until 1515 the hereditary keepers of the island were the Hunters of Hunterston. During the 14th century Kings Robert II and Robert III used the island as a deer forest.

Cromwell's men landed and caused some damage to the castle in 1653.

WILDLIFE: In the 19th century over 5000 rabbits a year were 'harvested'. Rabbits are still the most numerous inhabitants.

An attractive large house, **Cumbrae House**, overlooks the castle ruin and the bay but there are a number of forbidding notices such as 'Wildlife Reserve. No access', and 'No access without permission', which tend to detract from the view. The bay has some rocky outcrops on the north side known as **Broad Islands**.

Castle Island is linked by a drying strand to Little Cumbrae's east coast with **Trail Isle** lying alongside like a moored ship. The present square keep on Castle Island [NS152513] was erected in 1527 apparently to control deer poaching. It was wrecked by Cromwell's army but still stands as an imposing ruin. It is a twin to the keep on the mainland at Portencross. A short distance north of it [NS148518] are the remains of **St Vey's Chapel** and various antiquities which are worth inspection. St Vey, sometimes known as St Beya, was an obscure missionary.

The ancient lighthouse tower at the summit of the island [NS143515] is the type that had a fire of coals, or 'cresset', burning in an open grate. Presumably a fairly large fire had to be maintained. Imagine the effort of shipping coal to the island, carrying it up the hillside, hoisting it onto the open platform and keeping it burning during gale-lashed rainstorms! This particular light-tower was built in 1750 and is similar to the original design on the Isle of May (See No.12.1). The modern lighthouse and landing place stands below it on the west shore. There is a path leading over 'Rest and Be Thankful' and skirting Tom's Loch before descending to Cumbrae House on the east side by the castle.

The main house and farm buildings are possibly being used as a holiday retreat. The island, which is easily accessible but infrequently visited, is rugged, with many rock outcrops and caves on the raised beach at the south end.

ACCESS: No normal public access but a boat may be hired at Millport on Great Cumbrae. It would be advisable to obtain permission before exploring the island.

Anchorages:
1. Give N end of island a wide berth because of shoals. Anchor on E coast in 2-4m between Castle Island and Broad Island to the N. Avoid moorings and jetty. Uncomfortable in S and E winds. Landing is discouraged.
2. There is a landing place for the lighthouse on the W shore.

1.6 Great Cumbrae

Probably (B. cymri – Brythonic Gaelic people) i.e. the place of the Brythonic or Welsh-speaking Gaels. Formerly known as Great or Greater Cumray.

OS Maps: 1:50000 Sheet 63 1:25000 Sheet 428
Admiralty Charts: 1:25000 No.1907 or 1:36000 No.2221

AREA: 1,168ha (2,886 acres)
HEIGHT: 127m (417 ft)

OWNER: Principal owner is Bute Estates (Marquess of Bute).

POPULATION: 1793 – 509 (108 families). 1841 – 1413. 1881 – 1856. 1891 – 1784. 1931 – 2144. 1961 – 1638. 1971 – 1296. 1981 – 1611. 1991 – 1393.

GEOLOGY: Most of the island is old red sandstone but the area round Millport is carboniferous limestone. There are many igneous dykes such as 'The Lion' near the southeast corner opposite Largs.

HISTORY: King Haakon is reputed to have set up his camp at Tomont End, the northern tip of Great Cumbrae, before the Battle of Largs in 1263.

In the 17th century Great Cumbrae was owned by a family called Montgomery.

Millport was popular with trippers in the heyday of holidays on the Clyde but in 1906 the steamer companies boycotted the island because of excessive harbour dues. The island nearly died until Lloyd George stepped in and settled the dispute – just in time for the annual Glasgow Fair holiday.

WILDLIFE: The marine life round the island is very rich and has been studied since the 1840s. At that time David Robertson, the 'Cumbrae Naturalist', after many visits to the island established a floating laboratory in Kames Bay. In 1896 the headquarters of the Scottish Marine Biological Association were built to the east of the town at Kepple Pier but this was transferred to Dunstaffnage near Oban in 1970. The University Marine Biological Station controlled by Glasgow and London Universities then took over the buildings. They have diving facilities, research vessels and a decompression chamber. There is also a well-stocked aquarium which is open to the public.

It was in Millport Bay in 1812 that the roseate tern, *Sterna Dougalii*, was first identified as a separate species by Dr MacDougal.

At the start of the 19th century the Rev. James Adam, a local minister, always prayed for the people of **GREAT CUMBRAE** and 'the adjacent islands of Great Britain and Ireland', which gives some indication of this island's importance in the eyes of its inhabitants.

A ridge of green hills stippled with rose-red rocks runs

Firth

of

Clyde

Tomont End

White Bay

Stinking Bay

Monument

Cairn

Aird Hill

Cairn

Ferry

Skate Point

w o o d

Portrye

Water Sports
Training Centre

Gavin's
Glen

Downcraig Ferry

Horse
Hill

N

Bell Bay

Figgatoch

Tonnel
Hill

Well

Ballochmartin

*Ballochmartin
Bay*

Glaid Stone △127

Barbay
Hill

Fintry Bay

Sherriff's Common

Standing Stone

Clashfarland
Point

1

Craigengour

Gowk
Stone

Ballikillet

Reservoirs

Hosp.

Farland Hill

Butter Lump

Sheriff's Port

Breakough

Ninian Brae

MILLPORT

Cathedral

Kirkton

Sch

The Lion

*Doughend
Hole*

Aird
Hill

Pier

w o o d

*The
Eileans*

Keppel Pier

Marine Station

The Spoig

Millport Bay

Farland Point

Fairlie Roads

The Clach

Portachur Point

The Tan

down the centre with the highest point (127m) marked by the **Glaid Stone** [NS167570]. Alongside this ridge is a hill road with unrivalled views over the Clyde and, below it, a coastal road of about 20 Km (12 miles) which encircles the island. In summer it can almost rival Amsterdam with numerous holidaymakers on hired cycles in search of exercise and fun.

Millport spreading round the south-facing bay is a typical small seaside resort with fun-fair, cinema, museum

and sandy beaches. It was developed as a resort by the Victorians before they turned their attention to Rothesay. The solid residences look out on the bay to one of the loveliest views of Arran. The rocky islets in the middle of the bay are known simply as **The Eileans** (G. – islands).

The 'city' boasts the smallest cathedral in Britain – the **Episcopal Cathedral of Argyll and the Isles**. It was started in the 1840s by the 6th Earl of Glasgow under the influence of the Oxford Movement and the stone was

MILLPORT

quarried from the site, forming terraced gardens. The architect was William Butterfield. The mini-cathedral has a 37m spire, a starkly simple nave and a highly ornate brightly-coloured tiled chancel. One feels it has a foot in both camps, Presbyterian and Catholic. The Earl ran out of funds but the project was completed and consecrated in 1886 by Bishop Chinnery-Haldane of Argyll and the Isles.

The village of **Kirkton** in the south-west, which is now almost a suburb of Millport, was the first centre of population on the island. There has been a chapel there since the 13th century or earlier.

Norsemen who died in the Battle of Largs in 1263 are thought to be buried at **Tomont End** which is the northern tip of the island.

Both freshwater and sea fishing can be arranged from Millport and the Scottish Sports Council's **National Water Sports Training Centre** near the ferry terminal in the north-east teaches sailing, sub-aqua and canoeing.

The golf course on Sheriff's Common, near the reservoirs, provides spectacular views as well as a stimulating game and for climbers the rock outcrops on the hill behind Millport and the basaltic dykes of Lion Rock and The Deil's Dyke near Keppel Pier can be fun. Millport also has facilities for bowling and horse riding.

ACCESS: Car ferry from Largs (10-min crossing time) to Cumbrae Slip, 01475-674134. Round-island bus service to Millport timed to meet the ferry. Train connections from Glasgow to Largs. Tourist information, 01475-673765.

Anchorages:
1. Millport Bay. HIE buoys in the anchorage near the pier or anchor clear of the moorings E of the northmost of The Eileans in a suitable depth. Church tower in line with pier head bearing 333° between the Eileans and The Spoig leads to the anchorage. Bottom shelves gradually. Tripping line advised.
2. Keppel Pier with a T-head, on SE coast about 4c NE of Farland point, the SE extremity. Least depth of 4.9m alongside head of pier.
3. Ballochmartin or Balloch Bay N of Clashfarland Point on E coast has a T-headed pier at the N entrance point of bay. Anchor near Grey House in 8m.
4. National Water Sports Training Centre at N end of Balloch Bay. Suitable moorings may be available. If not anchor N of the slip but well off-shore.
5. Tomont End (Monument), White Bay. Good holding and well-sheltered from SW winds, 5-9m, sand. Bay dries out 1c.

1.7 Inchmarnock

(G. innis Marnoc – island of Marnoc)

OS Maps: 1:50000 Sheet 63 1:25000 Sheets 414 and 428
Admiralty Charts: 1:25000 No.2383 or 1:36000 No.2221

AREA: 253ha (625 acres)
HEIGHT: 60m (197 ft)

OWNER: Purchased in 1988 by an Englishman, Ian Branson, who is often resident in Northpark farmhouse. (The Marquess of Bute is the feudal superior.)

POPULATION: 1871 – 30. 1881 – 17. 1891 – 10 (3 houses). 1931 – 14. 1961 – 6. 1971 – 6. 1981 – 4. 1991 – 0.

GEOLOGY: Mainly Dalradian schistose grit similar to north Bute.

HISTORY: After the days of St Marnoc the Cistercians of Saddell in Kintyre owned the island.

It is a widely-held belief that, in the 19th century, the people of Bute left their alcoholics here to cure them 'by deprivation and isolation' but this has not been verified.

WILDLIFE: Inchmarnock has the largest herring-gull colony on the Clyde and there is prolific bird-life. It is a popular wintering haven for greylag geese.

A derelict 'landing-craft' for ferrying material across to the island is beached beside the anchorage off Midpark Farm on **INCHMARNOCK**. The farm buildings are picturesque with hawthorn hedges on each side of the farm road and bluebells in the long grass verges. The view from the low ridge running down the centre of the island is panoramic encompassing a great sweep of water stretching from the lower reaches of Loch Fyne to the high peaks of Arran. The hazy blue hills of the Mull of Kintyre are the back-drop. There is an overwhelming sense of peace and it is al-most impossible to believe that the great city of Glasgow is only a few miles away as the crow flies.

MIDPARK, INCHMARNOCK

Legend has it that there was a cheeky young Scots lad who pestered and interrupted St Columba with questions when he was preaching on the mainland. The monks were irritated and tried to silence him but St Columba chided them and prophesied that young Marnoc would become a great teacher. He had recognised a lively mind. The prophesy came true and Marnoc, later St Marnoc, settled on this island and built himself a chapel. People came from near and far to hear him preach.

A very few remains of the ancient 7th century **Chapel of St Marnoc** can be seen just north of the **Midpark** farm buildings [NS024596]. Several stone fragments of Celtic crosses have been uncovered near it and also other sculpted stones including one commemorating the Viking, Gutlief. These are now in Bute Museum. The church existed until the 18th century but a farmer, Alexander McDonald, used the stone from it to build Midpark farmhouse in 1718. Only when the work was complete did he decide to play safe with eternity so he sent £10 to the Church Session and asked for atonement.

A century later the gravestones from the cemetery were used by another farmer to build a cowhouse. No Christian atonement was requested in this case but it is recorded that his cattle all died. The farmer decided the devil was to blame so he made a burnt offering of one of the carcases on the beach at dead of night.

The farmyard is reputed to have been laid out over the burial ground which was adjacent to the chapel, but **The Women's Burial Place** could still be distinguished in 1860 in a field adjoining the church.

In the extreme north of the island the skeleton of a young woman was found in one of three stone burial cists which were uncovered during archaeological excavation of a Bronze Age cairn [NS020612]. She was wearing a necklace consisting of 139 jet (lignite) beads, which can be seen in Bute Museum, and at her hand lay a flint knife. The tomb of the **Queen of the Inch**, as she is known, is close to Northpark, the owner's house. After the 3500-year-old skeleton had been radio-carbon dated it was returned to its original tomb with a glass panel fitted to al-

low it to be seen. This was considered the best way to preserve the remains, rather than letting them moulder in a museum store. But walking past the tomb by torchlight at night requires a very steady nerve, says the owner. It is dark, it is quiet, it is lonely, and the shadows in the skull's eye-sockets follow every movement.

The island is divided into three farms – Northpark, Midpark and Southpark – although the latter buildings are now untenanted. The semi-derelict **Southpark** farm buildings adjoin Midpark.

Towards the end of the 19th century a tenant of Southpark was draining a 'moss' when he found in the peat a layer of preserved hazelnuts three feet thick. Investigation showed, that although the island had been farmed for several thousand years, at one time it was covered with luxuriant oak and hazel forest.

The Inchmarnock islanders were evacuated during the Second World War to enable a commando training area to be created. A considerable amount of damage was done and a large area is still covered with craters. The land is generally fertile but largely uncultivated. Visitors to the island should try to obtain permission first or at least keep to the shoreline as the owner is understandably keen that the island should be disturbed as little as possible.

ACCESS: No regular access but it should be possible to arrange boat hire from Tighnabruich or to find an accommodating fisherman on the coast of Bute.

Anchorages:
1. Anchor near the middle of the E side of island off Midpark Farm in 5m, sand. Sheltered from NW and W but subject to swell.

1.8 Bute

Probably (B. budh -corn, Sc -aer – island), or, less likely, (ON bot – patch of land). For centuries, however, the island was called Rothes-ay (Roth's or Roderick's island) and the main town was called Baile Bhoid (G. – the town of corn). The Chronicle of the Scots, 1482-1530, says Bute is named after St Brandan but this is doubtful.

OS Maps: 1:50000 Sheet 63 1:25000 Sheets 400, 401, 414 and 428
Admiralty Charts: 1:75000 No.2131 1:25000 Nos.1906 and 2383

AREA: 12,217ha (30,188 acres)
HEIGHT: 278m (912 ft)

OWNER: Principal owner – Bute Estates (The Marquess of Bute).

POPULATION: 1755 – 3220. 1792 – 4759. 1841 – 7147. 1881 – 10998. 1891 – 11735. 1931 – 12112. 1961 – 9793. 1971 – 8423. 1981 – 7733. 1991 – 7354. There are about one million visitors each year.

GEOLOGY: Loch Fad which cuts across the centre of the

island is a continuation of the Highland Boundary Fault. To the south is old red sandstone ('red pudding rock'), some basaltic lavas, and fertile undulating arable land; to the north is Dalradian schistose grit and hilly terrain.

A fine example of a raised beach can be seen from the road at Tormore Hill.

HISTORY: Bute has been continuously inhabited for at least 6000 years.

After the Roman period Bute, and Arran, may have been Brythonic (Welsh-type language) kingdoms. Nearby Dunbarton means the 'Fort of the Britons'. Later, the Erse, or Gaelic language of the Scots spread into Bute.

How early Bute was personally acquired by the royal Stewart family is uncertain although Robert the High Steward owned the island in 1334. They were known as Sheriffs of Bute and Keepers of Rothesay Castle and Roberts II and III used the castle as a holiday home. Rothesay became a Royal Burgh in 1403 with a further charter by James VI in 1584. Many of the Provosts of the

EILEAN DUBH AND CALADH BAY IN THE KYLES OF BUTE

Burgh have been members of the Bute family and much of the island's history centres on Rothesay Castle.

In the 19th century before the advent of tourism herring-fishing brought prosperity to the island and as far back as 1779 the first cotton mill was built in Rothesay. Robert Thom, an early mill-owner realised that more water was needed for the cotton mills and built a canal to bring water from the W side of the island to Rothesay. The dry canal can still be seen below the road at Tormore Hill.

The island peaked in popularity in the Victorian and Edwardian era as a tourist centre providing holidays 'doon the water' from Glasgow.

WILDLIFE: Bute has a unique long-tailed field-mouse which is a sub-species of the mainland variety. A trial re-introduction of the European beaver (extinct in Britain since the 13th century) took place on Bute in 1875 but the animals only survived until the 1890s.

Bird-life is not particularly noteworthy due to the amount of cultivation but there are some areas of pleasant mixed woodland habitat which encourage a variety of species.

With bog cotton in the marshes and heather on the upper slopes, all the common botanical species are in evidence but there is little in the way of distinctive plant life. However, Bute Natural History Society in the Bute Museum, Rothesay provides excellent information on nature trails, paths, plants and birdlife, and there is much of interest.

BUTE is first and foremost an island catering for the needs of visitors and there are many recreational facilities. Coarse fishing for pike and perch, sea angling, cycling, sailing and pony trekking are only a few of the many popular diversions.

The existence of **Rothesay Castle** was first recorded in 1230 when it was besieged and taken by the Norsemen. The breached east wall can still be seen in the massive, circular sandstone structure surrounded by a moat. The English took the castle on one occasion and it was taken in about 1334 by Sir Colin Campbell for Edward Balliol. It was also attacked by the Lord of the Isles in the 15th century. James IV and James V used it as a base for their campaigns to subdue the Hebrides and it was then that the great tower was built (1541). In 1498 the Bute family were appointed hereditary keepers of the castle and the present Marquess still holds that office. The rebel Master of Ruthven attacked the castle in 1527 but failed to take it so he destroyed the surrounding burgh. In 1544 the Earl of Lennox had more success when he took it for the English. Cromwell kept a garrison here but when it withdrew in 1659 much of the building was dismantled and during the Duke of Monmouth's rebellion in 1685 the rest of the castle was burned down by the Duke of Argyll.

The story goes that shortly after this the Duke of Argyll married off one of his daughters to a Bute. When the newly-wed bride reached the island the first thing she did was to complain bitterly to her husband that he did not have a castle fit for her to live in.

The 2nd Marquess of Bute began restoring the castle in 1816 and further work was done by the 3rd Marquess. The great hall was renovated by the 6th Marquess in 1970 and the government now maintains the property. The castle is open daily and well worth a visit.

The harbour at Rothesay was constructed in the 17th century and eventually rebuilt and extended during the heyday of holidays 'doon the water' from Glasgow. The bay was a naval anchorage from 1940 to 1957. Nearby, the Victorian Winter Garden on the sea front, at one time the haunt of music hall performers and comedians, has recently been restored.

This is the only Scottish island which had a tram service. This was electrified in 1902 but buses eventually took over in 1936.

The ancient **Church of St Mary's**, which was once part of the Bishopric of Man, is on the road just south of Rothesay at the foot of Loch Fad [NS086637]. It contains two canopied tombs.

Most of the north of the island is wild, hilly and unpopulated. The road runs up the east side to **Rudhabodach** with its ferry to Colintraive on the mainland. It passes Kames Bay where there is a tower house, **Kames Castle**, which had its origins in the 14th century [NS064675]. And sitting below Kames Hill, is **Wester**

MOUNTSTUART – HOME OF THE MARQUESS OF BUTE

Kames, a 17th century keep which has been restored [NS062680]. A scramble up Kames Hill (267m) is rewarded by a striking view across to Arran, and a short distance further to the north-west is **Windy Hill** (278m), Bute's highest point.

The bare northern tip of Bute which divides the Kyles is aptly named **Buttock Point** with, opposite it, the delightful little anchorage of Caladh Bay (G. *caladh* – haven) tucked behind **Eilean Dubh** (G. – black isle). On this islet [NS006757] is the small grave of the previous owner's young son who was drowned in a boating accident.

Just south at the head of the East Kyle are three more attractive islets, the **Burnt Islands**, one of which has the remains of a vitrified fort on it.

At the north-west extremity and south of Rubha Dubh there is a fort [NR995713], the ruins of little **Kilmichael Chapel** which was destroyed by the Norsemen [NR993706], and the chambered burial cairn of Glenvoidean in the hills above [NR997706]. Further south there are two more chambered cairns.

All these can be seen on a pleasant but long walk (about 20 Km total, there and back) along the quiet, narrow and wild coastal road from **Ettrick Bay**. There are beautiful views down the Kyles, and mature woods of birch and oak below the shapely ridge of Barlia Hill (105m).

Near Ettrick Bay there is a stone circle [NS044668] about 1 Km north-east of the shore and a Celtic cross near St Colmac [NS045672]. At the bridge over Glenmore burn concrete frames built for the army exercises on Inchmarnock (See No.1.7) represented practice landing craft for D-day.

A ruined chapel [NS035613] just north of St Ninian's Point was excavated in 1953. Standing stones can be seen in the north-west corner of St Ninian's Bay with another chapel 1 Km north of them [NS036626].

Although tourism is the main industry, dairy farming and cheese-making are also of major economic importance. The agricultural part of the island is south of the 'rift valley' between Rothesay Bay and **Scalpsie Bay**. This valley is partly filled by **Loch Fad** (G. – long loch) with its wooded shores, and Loch Quien which has a crannog in it. Several duns and forts are near Scalpsie Bay and where the road winds round Tormore there are some of the finest viewpoints on the island.

A stone circle stands starkly on the narrow neck of land near Kingarth [NS092556] beyond the cemetery on the south side of the road. Across the golf links on the other side a row of standing stones looks like stunted exclamation marks [NS084553].

At the extreme south of the island, which

culminates in Garroch Head, St Blane's Hill rises steeply 124m (403ft) above the shore. Here a path leads to **St Blane's Chapel**, a 12th century Norman church [NS095534]. Its green garth is set in a wooded glade amid the well-preserved ruins of a 6th century Celtic monastery established by St Catan but named after his nephew St Blane who died in 590. The circular stone building is known as the Devil's Cauldron. Remains of the monks' cells are still visible. On a promontory to the west and above a secluded cove with a beach of clean sharp sand is the vitrified Dunagoil fort dating from about 100BC [NS086531]. The whole of this area of tumbled landscape, bristling with antiquities and surrounded by the great expanse of the Firth of Clyde, is a rambler's delight.

On the east coast, approaching Rothesay and the rustic-English style 19th century village of Kerrycroy from the south the road passes **Mountstuart**, home of the Marquess of Bute and the family residence for over 250 years. It is hidden from the road and is now open to the public. The church and cottages at **Ascog** [NS108633], a few miles further north, were designed by David Hamilton in 1845.

ACCESS: Car ferry Wemyss Bay to Rothesay (30 mins), 01475-520521. (Train connections Glasgow-Wemyss Bay. Also car ferry Colintraive to Rhubodach (5 mins), 0170084-235. Tourist information, 0170050-2151.

Anchorages:
1. Rothesay bay. Visitors' moorings (pay) off sailing club or anchor anywhere in bay, clear of moorings, holding generally good. W side of bay is best. Considerable swell with NE winds.
2. Rothesay harbour. Pontoon berths (pay, 01700-503842).
3. Kames Bay, Port Bannatyne. E gales can cause heavy swell. Visitors' moorings (pay, 01700-503842) or anchor clear of moorings.
4. Eilean Mór, Burnt Isles. Good anchorage E of S extremity of En Mór in 4m, sand. Avoid rocky patch to N.
5. Balnakailly Bay. Anchor S of Eilean Mór and clear of Wood Farm Rock in 3m to 4m.
6. Wreck Bay. Anchor between Beere Rock (off Bear Craig) and Buttock Point in 3-4m.
7. Black Farland bay, about 1¹/₂M SW of Buttock point, good anchorage about midway between entrance points in 4-7m. Protected from S winds. The coast on both sides of entrance to bay is foul.
8. Ettrick bay is seldom used as open SW and W. Head dries out 2c and depths of less than 5.5m extend about 2c farther offshore. Underwater obstructions reported.
9. St Ninian's Bay, well-sheltered except SW. Head of bay dries out 3¹/₂c. There is a broad sandy beach. Avoid spit S of St Ninian's Point. Anchor in 6-8m.
10. Scalpsie Bay. Give Ardscalpsie Point a very wide berth. Anchor about 2c off farm on NW side of bay.
11. Stravannon Bay. Many rocks so keep well offshore. Very exposed but depths and holding reasonable.
12. Dunagoil Bay. Exposed, but temporary anchorage in light E'lies. (Useful for visit to Dunagoil fort and St Blane's).

WESTER KAMES – A 17TH CENTURY KEEP

13. Glencallum Bay (Callum's Hole). NE entrance marked by white beacon. Avoid rocks slightly NE of centre of bay. Temporary anchorage clear of SW shore in 2m to 6m. Exposed to S winds.
14. Kilchattan Bay. Visitors' moorings (pay, 01700-503842) or anchor NW of disused pier in 4m to 6m. Head of bay dries out about 4c. Exposed SE to NE.

The Mull of Kintyre to the Firth of Lorn

Seil

13. Luing

14. Eilean Dubh

15. Garbh Eileach

12. Eileach an Naoimh

10. Shuna

11. Lunga

8. Eilean Righ

9. Scarba

7. Eilean Macaskin

6. Colonsay

5. Jura

Eilean Mór

4. Islay

3. Gigha

1. Texa

2. Cara

Kintyre

N

Section 2

Section 2, Table 1

No.	Name	Latitude	Longitude	Table 2* No.	Table 3** No.	Area in Acres		Area in Hectares
2.1	Texa	55° 37N	06° 08W	154	124	119		48
2.2	Cara	55° 38N	05° 45W	137	112	163		66
2.3	Gigha	55° 41N	05° 45W	35	71	3447		1395
2.4	Islay	55° 45N	06° 16W	5	7	153093		61956
2.5	Jura	55° 58N	05° 50W	8	5	90666		36692
2.6	Colonsay	56° 04N	06° 12W	21	46	10067	4074	
	Oronsay	*56° 01N*	*06° 14W*			1342	543	4617
2.7	Eilean Macaskin	56° 08N	05° 33W	151	100	124		50
2.8	Eilean Righ	56° 09N	05° 33W	119	114	213		86
2.9	Scarba	56° 11N	05° 43W	34	10	3642		1474
2.10	Shuna	56° 13N	05° 36W	58	80	1114		451
2.11	Lunga	56° 13N	05° 42W	77	73	628		254
2.12	Eileach an Naoimh	56° 13N	05° 48W	145	85	138		56
2.13	Luing	56° 14N	05° 38W	32	77	3534	1430	
	Torsa	*56° 16N*	*05° 37W*			279	113	1543
2.14	Eilean Dubh Mór	56° 14N	05° 43W	139	115	161		65
2.15	Garbh Eileach	56° 15N	05° 46W	100	61	351		142
2.A	*Seil*	*56° 18N*	*05° 37W*			3283		1329

* Table 2: The islands arranged in order of magnitude
** Table 3: The islands arranged in order of height

Introduction

The islands to the west and north of the Mull of Kintyre have a long history as they were possibly the very first Scottish islands to be colonised by man. (In fact they may have been settled before anyone dared to colonise the mainland.) In medieval times the area gained particular importance when the Lord of the Isles established the 'capital' of his island empire at Finlaggan on Islay.

The Sound of Jura is a natural highway up the west coast as it is protected from the worst fury of the Atlantic gales. After passing Gigha on the route north, the Kintyre peninsula is broken by a succession of sea-lochs which give some shelter even although they are aligned to the prevailing wind coming from the south-west. The first of these – West Loch Tarbert – has an islet at its head, **Eilean dà Ghallagain**, and likewise the second, Loch Caolisport, has **Eilean Fada**. The latter loch also has two islets nearer the entrance – **Liath Eilean** (G. – grey island) and **Eilean nam Muc** (G. – isle of the pigs).

It is the next loch north, Loch Sween, which has more of interest. Long and narrow, it runs past forbidding Castle Sween and into the wooded hills of Argyll. Here in the creeks among the trees beyond an inhabited islet called **Eilean Loain** (G. – pack-of-hound's isle), are some colourful patches of mossy rock known affectionately as the **Fairy Isles**.

Apart from **Taynish Island** halfway up Loch Sween all the other islets are gathered around the entrance to the loch and the large bridged and tidal island of **Danna**. They are known as the MacCormaig Isles and consist of **Carraig an Daimh** (G. – isle connected to the rock), **Liath Eilean**, **Eilean nan Leac** (G. – island of the grave), **Eilean Gamhna** (G. – island of the farrow cow), **Corr Eilean** (G. – tapering island) with a prehistoric cairn, and the most important island in the group, **Eilean Mór** (G. – big island) which has the distinction of being owned by the Scottish National Party.

Scots-born John Paul Jones sailed in these waters during the American War of Independence and visited Eilean Mór. In ancient times this holy island was the retreat of St Abban mac ui Charmaig, otherwise known as St Cormac, who founded a monastery at Keills and who died in 640. It is a fascinating place to explore. A tiny inlet and anchorage on the north side has a submerged rock in it but it is snug and well-sheltered in all except northerly winds.

The medieval chapel, dedicated to St Cormac, is close to the anchorage. It is relatively well-preserved although it was once used as an ale-house and illicit still. The saint was buried nearby. To the south beyond the two standing crosses, one of which is a replica, there is a cave which was an anchorite's retreat. This deep, damp grotto has two 8th century crosses incised on its rock walls. Outside are the ruins of a second chapel proving the veneration in which this little island was held.

North again past **Eilean nan Coinean**, another rabbit

island, **Eilean Fraoch**, another heather island, and **Eilean Dubh**, another black island, brings one to **Carsaig Island** with a delightful anchorage behind it. On a visit there, while a young seal was showing off in front of its admiring elders, I was lucky to see a chough. This area is possibly the last Scottish home of the chough, an attractive member of the crow family – rather like a raven with a red beak. It is thought that there are only about one hundred breeding pairs left.

Eilean da Mhèinn sits in the centre of crowded Crinan Harbour surrounded by so many moorings that it is no longer possible to anchor to the south or east of it, but Crinan is such a pleasant spot that one can understand its popularity.

2.1 Texa

(EI tech – house, ON -øy – island). Thought to have been the island referred to as Oidecha insula by Abbot Adomnan. An alternative possibility is a monastic seminary – (G. oideachd – instruction).

OS Maps: 1:50000 Sheet 60 1:25000 Sheet 439
Admiralty Chart: 1:75000 No.2168

AREA: 48ha (119 acres)
HEIGHT: 48m (157 ft)

OWNER: In 1614 'Ilantasson' (Island Texa) was chartered by the crown to Sir John Campbell of Cawdor (see No.2.4) and confirmed by Act of Parliament in 1626. The Ramsays of Kildalton had ownership from 1855 to 1915, Philip Morel from 1915 to 1951, followed by Ian Hunter and then Elizabeth Williamson of Laphroaig who sold the island in 1983. (The island was up for sale in 1995 for offers over £80,000.)

POPULATION: 1625 – 29. Late 18th century – 8. Still populated in early 19th century but uninhabited since then.

GEOLOGY: Mainly interstratified quartzose-mica-schist, grit, and some hornblende.

HISTORY: Adomnan refers to the 'island of Oidech' as a stopping place for St Cainnech on his journey from Iona to Ireland in the 6th century and most scholars think that this refers to Texa. Cainnech, or Kenneth, was said to have left his pastoral staff on Iona. Columba found it, blessed it, and cast it into the sea and Kenneth later discovered it washed up on the shore of Texa.

It is assumed that Texa's present chapel, which may be on the site of an earlier one, was built in the late 14th century by Reginald, son of John of Islay. It was dedicated to St Mary the Virgin and generously endowed and the well, Tobar Moireig, was similarly dedicated.

The earliest sculptured stone portrait of a member of the house of Somerled was part of the shaft of a cross which stood east of the chapel. It was removed in the early 1900s for safe keeping and can be seen in the National Museum of Antiquities in Edinburgh. It is of Ragnald, eldest son of John the Good and progenitor of the MacDonalds of Clanranald. The inscription reads, 'This is the cross of Reginald, son of John, of Islay'. It was Ragnald's younger brother, Donald, who succeeded his father as Lord of the Isles. Ragnald inherited some of the Western Isles and also Castle Tioram beside Loch Moidart and it was there that he died. About the same time (1385) Fordun mentioned 'the monks' chapel' on 'Helan Hexa'. Early 16th century records show that the church was generously endowed with the lands of Texa, Cragabus and 'two Kilbrides.'

In 1608, Andrew Knox, Bishop of the Isles, wrote from 'Ilintexa' to King James VI asking to be retired – '..seeing my ould aige dayle crepis on..'.

Strangely, a report dated 1614-15 lists only six active churches in the parishes of Islay and there is no mention of Texa. In 1625 Father Cornelius Ward, a Franciscan missionary, also fails to mention the church when he landed on Texa and found that most of the inhabitants were Catholic. He converted the six who were not.

A century and a half later the *Statistical Account 1791-99* records that the inhabitants were 'formerly wont to bury those who were of the popish religion' in the chapel, '. . .but the whole inhabitants now belong to the Established Church, so that there are none now buried. . .'. But, even so, there is a burial enclosure beside the chapel which appears to date from the 19th century.

WILDLIFE: In early summer the rough ground is so covered with bluebells that it is like a mist collecting in the hollows. Groups of the eighty or so feral goats watch visitors warily and woodmice and otters are other resident mammals.

WILD GOATS BY THE RUINED CHAPEL

TEXA is a wee rocky hump of an island with many caves, good pasturage and a small white concrete beacon at the highest point, Ceann Garbh (48m) (G. – rough headland). It is part of the Islay parish of Kildalton. The traditional monastic islands sited round Islay are thought to have been – Texa to the south, **Nave** with **Eilean Beag** to the north and **Orsay** to the west. All three are tiny in size, Texa being the largest, but they all have religious relics.

On the slope overlooking **Caolas an Eilean** (G. – the island channel, or kyle) and some distance beyond the jetty there is a renovated cottage. On terraced ground about 100m north-east are the walls of an ancient chapel, built of rubble but with ashlar sandstone trimmings

[NR391438]. There is evidence that this formed the centre of an area of continuous agricultural settlement. There is also a burial ground with the footings of at least five buildings and an enclosure to the south and another structure to the north. None of these buildings is thought to be of an early date but they have not been examined in detail. Detailed investigation is needed to establish whether or not a monastery or seminary ever existed but at least this tiny island could support a population for it is fortunate in having its own water supply, **Tobar Moireig** (G. – Mary's well).

The early Celtic church had no parochial organisation. Any small Christian community could build a chapel for the purpose of mutual worship. There would be a lay custodian, but no resident priest, although occasionally one might attend from a neighbouring monastery. It is possible that this was no more than just a primitive 'clachan' church, although it seems unlikely that Texa would support a large enough lay community of farmers and fishermen to undertake such a building.

There are some minor landing places – An Laimhrig (G. – the landing place) in the east, and Port an t-Sruthain (G. – tidal port) and Port Bàn (G. – fair port) in the southeast bay. Texa also has a number of caves including Uamh nam Fear (G. – the men's cave).

Across Caolas an Eilean at the entrance to Port Ellen on Islay is tiny **Eilean nan Caorach** (G. – sheep island). In the 12th century Somerled's fleet anchored in nearby Lagavullin Bay beside Dunyvaig Castle. Loch an t-Sàilein provides a better anchorage beyond Lagavulin Bay. It is sheltered by tidal **Eilean Imersay** and the rocks of **Iseanach Mór** while, standing well out to sea like a sentinel, is **Iomallach**. Further up the coast are the lovely Ardmore Islands. They are treeless **Eilean Craobhach** (G. – tree-covered island), **Eilean a' Chuirn** (G. – heap-of-stones island) with a light beacon on it, **Eilean Bhride** (G. – Bridget's isle), and the long reef of **Eilean Mhic Mhaolmhoire**.

ACCESS: No regular access. Possibly by arrangement at Port Ellen on Islay.

Anchorages:
Note: Approach with caution, preferably 1¹/₂c clear of E end of island, and then keep nearer to S side of the Kyle. Note submerged rock about 3c WNW of En na Nighinn off W extremity of island. All anchorages are exposed.
1. Fionn Phort on the N face of the NE extremity in 5m.
2. Bàgh na h-Eaglaise (G. – Church Bay). Off the quay and chapel ruins near the centre of the N coast in 5-6m, sand. This is the traditional anchorage.
3. Port an t-Sruthain, in centre of open bay on SE coast. There are a number of offshore rocks and a large 7c reef extending S from the SW extremity.

2.2 Cara

Various possible derivations. (G. carr ON -øy – island of the projecting rock or rock ledge), or (G. cor ON -øy – island of the rounded hill), or (ON Kari-øy – Kari's island), Kari was a Norse hero. A (B. caer – fort) derivation is improbable.

OS Maps: 1:50000 Sheet 62 1:25000 Sheet 426
Admiralty Chart: 1:25000 No.2475

AREA: 66ha (163 acres)
HEIGHT: 56m (184 ft)

OWNER: For centuries Cara has been part of the Macdonald estate of Largie on the Kintyre peninsula. It is not part of the Gigha estate. The Macdonalds of Largie claim direct descent from the Lord of the Isles.

POPULATION: Alexander Macdonald of Largie married Jane McNeill in 1798 on Cara according to the parish register and there were several families living on the island at that time. 1881 – 4. 1891 – 3. 1931 – 3. Last person to be born on the island was Mrs Charlotte McAlister who was living on Gigha in 1991. Last farmed by Angus McGuigan in 1932 and uninhabited since the 1940s but a Londoner was renovating Cara House in 1991, possibly with a view to living on the island.

GEOLOGY: Cara is a continuation of the geology of Gigha (No.2.3).

At the south end, below the Mull of Cara, there are two interconnecting caves each about 12m deep which show signs of human – and goat – habitation. The strata have also created a number of rock shelters under overhangs, such as at Poll an Aba.

HISTORY: As King Haakon's huge fleet was anchored in Gigalum Sound for two or three weeks in 1263 it would be surprising if the Norsemen had not landed on Cara Island. But no definite evidence has been found.

In 1615 Sir James Macdonald escaped from a Crown prison and enlisted many islanders to help him free his lands from Campbell (Argyll) control. Hector MacNeill of Taynish and Gigha, Chief of the Southern Clan Neill, was thirled to Argyll and the rebels were keen to capture him. The rebels set up their base on Cara as this belonged to their ally, Macdonald of Largie, whilst their army of about 1000 men camped on the Kintyre coast opposite Gigha. MacNeill sent a raiding party to Cara but the Largie servants warned the rebels by beacon and they thwarted the attack. They were however generally undisciplined and Argyll's forces soon had them all in retreat. An uncorroborated story says that the MacNeill and Campbell lords then had a dinner in the Cara mansion-house and finished it by hanging eight captured rebels in front of the house. The corpses were later buried in the chapel.

These were strange times, for only three years later, in 1618, it was Argyll who was disgraced 'for open defection from the true religion' and 'suspicious dealings' with Sir James Macdonald. He was proclaimed a traitor whereas Sir James Macdonald was pardoned and given a pension.

Flora Macdonald was related to the Macdonalds of Largie and some time after the events of 1745 she stayed at Largie for a year before emigrating to Carolina. Her brother was also a guest at Largie but he was mortally wounded in a shooting accident on Cara.

WILDLIFE: Rabbits (particularly noted for their numbers by Dean Monro), otters, goats, nesting seabirds and peregrine falcons are Cara's specialities. In the days of falconry the Macdonalds would collect chicks from the cliff nests – 'but never more than one chick from a nest having two or more' according to an octogenarian whose grandfather used to collect them. Shags, guillemots and terns with a few razorbills, and herring, common, and great black-backed gulls breed on the coasts. Elsewhere are nests of ringed plovers, rock and meadow pipits, mute swans and buzzards.

The herd of wild goats is quite large and a considerable number of goat skeletons are scattered about, but the goats themselves can be difficult to see when the bracken is high.

There are many wildflowers but no trees.

Poll an Aba 'is always good for a sea trout near the white shore' says a local man.

The peaty ground below the house on **CARA** in the month of June is a sea of wildflowers. The marshy nature of the soil here keeps the bracken at bay. Cara House itself is a dour two-storey stone building, with a slated roof standing lonely and conspicuous, staring across the Sound towards Kintyre. It was built about 1733 as a residence for the tacksman. There is a well-preserved corn-drying kiln close by.

CARA HOUSE – LONELY AND CONSPICUOUS

Behind the house is the ruined chapel which could easily be mistaken at first for a sheep pen [NR640443]. It is about 9m long by 5m broad. It originally had a lancet-shaped window with splayed ingoes near the east end of each side wall as well as the west gable, and the door on the north side was Gothic-arched. It is said that the chapel was used for burials and that a priest is buried in the north-east corner where there is a broken greenish stone slab which was originally part of the pulpit. There is no record of a burial ground. The chapel fell into disuse in the late 18th century and was used for a time as a kitchen for the house.

According to a record dated 14th June 1456 it was called 'the chapel of St Finla in the island of Kara beside the Monkshaven'. St Finlay (G. *Fionnlugh* – fair hero) was a contemporary of St Columba and evidently the patron saint of the House of Islay. It appears that the chapel was built about this time by the Macdonalds although in the Latin 'Scotia Sacra' there is the entry – 'Insula Carray, where there is a shrine of the Most Holy Trinity. It is doubtful who first founded it.' Dean Monro said the chapel belonged to Icolmkill (Iona) with the island being used as a monks' retreat. This may be corroborated by there being a pleasant round pool on the south-east shore called Poll an Aba (G. – the pool of the abbot) and an anchorage called Monkshaven.

It was at Poll an Aba in later times that the Macdonalds rolled their fishing boats up the beach during the winter months as there was no shelter for them over on Kintyre. The men would stay in huts below the brow of the hill while carrying out maintenance work on the boats. The Brownie's Well close by provided fresh water and it has never run dry.

East of the main house there is another well which serves the house. A track leads from the chapel ruin to Port an Stòir (G. – stormy port) at the north extremity where there are some ruined enclosures. About two hundred years ago the track also extended southwards to a large building of unknown purpose according to an old map.

During the Second World War a newly-built P & O ship with a cargo of copra on board was hit by a German bomb which went straight down its funnel. The blazing hulk drifted for two days before coming to rest in the bay on the west side of Cara where she burned for a further six weeks.

At the south-west corner, Maol à Mhór-ràin, a cleft in the rock conceals part of a lifeboat and an embedded anchor, and the bay on the south side seems to attract all the flotsam and jetsam in the area. This was the area that was always searched first for the bodies of sailors drowned in the vicinity.

In the autumn of 1756 there was, according to the *Statistical Account of Scotland – 1791-99*, a great storm in this area. Lightning struck the southern headland called the Mull of Cara breaking off large pieces of rock, 'which has a lot of iron ore in it', and the shock was felt in all the islanders' houses. The sea rose so high on the west side that the waves swept right across the island. All the houses – which may have been of turf construction – were severely damaged and the stacks of corn were ruined. The people 'were obliged to take shelter in the only slated house on the island, which fortunately suffered no damage.' Other reports claim that it was not lightning but a meteor which struck just below the southern cliff on the Mull of Cara. This seems more probable. If the bulk of the meteor hit the sea to the south-west, this could account for the freak wave. The broken cliff face can still be seen.

The Brownie's Chair is a huge stone 'armchair', with only one arm, set on a ledge above the sea on the east side of the highest point – the Mull of Cara [NR639434].

The Brownie of Cara is said to be the ghost of a Macdonald murdered by a Campbell. Tradition says that he inhabits an attic room in Cara House, and that the laird and minister have always raised their hats to him when they step ashore on Cara, and so should everyone else. The Macdonald's gallery in the church at Ardminish on Gigha built in 1780 was known as the Brownie's gallery. The *Observer* reported in 1909 that Morton Macdonald of Largie claimed that the Brownie was often seen, or heard, moving about in his room, 'A neat little man, dressed in brown, with a pointed beard.'

The Brownie has a characteristically impish sense of humour. One story tells how the Laird of Largie sent two of his men over to fetch a cask of wine from the big cellar in Cara House. Whilst they were arranging a gangplank to roll the cask up from the cellar they were joking about the Brownie. They then found they were unable to move the barrel so, in the end, they offered a sincere apology for the remarks they had made. Suddenly the barrel ran up the plank by itself, bounced and rolled across the ground to the sea and came to a stop beside their boat.

There are many stories telling how the Brownie would wash the dishes and tidy up the kitchen to help the house-wife and maids – yet couldn't resist an occasional practical joke.

It was essential that the main house had a good view of the mainland because Cara was the centre of smuggling activity for Gigha, Jura and Islay. In 1786 the *Prince of Wales* revenue cutter dug up eighteen casks of foreign spirits at Poll an Aba. No wonder that twinkling lights were often to be seen on dark nights in the window of the Brownie's room!

ACCESS: Boat trips may be arranged with a local fisherman through McSporran's Store at Ardminish on Gigha (but not for anyone with Campbell blood in their veins!).

Anchorages: There are no permanent anchorages but Gigalum Sound is fairly close and sheltered from the E by Gigalum Island (see Gigha No.2.3).
1. Port na Cille or Monkshaven on E coast. Temp anchorage. in 9m, sand, with the house bearing approximately 240°. Exposed NNE to SSW.
2. Port an Stòir at the N extremity. Used as a landing place but local knowledge essential.

2.3 Gigha

*[**gee**-ē:] (ON Gud-øy – God's island or the good island) This is the normally accepted derivation but possible alternatives are, (ON gja-øy – island of creeks or geos) or, (ON – Gydha's isle). Gydha was a woman's name.*

OS Maps: 1:50000 Sheet 62 1:25000 Sheet 426
Admiralty Charts: 1:75000 No.2168 or 1:25000 No.2475

AREA: 1,395ha (3,447 acres)
HEIGHT: 100m (328 ft)

OWNER: Bought from David W Landale by English property developer Malcolm Potier's company, Tanap Investments, for £5.4m in 1989. This purchase included all Gigha's main businesses and a fish farm. In 1992 it was attached by Interallianz Bank of Zurich and then bought by Holt Leisure Parks (owners of Kip Marina on the Clyde) for £2m. Derek Holt, the new Baron of Gigha, promised 'no dramatic plans, just business as usual.'

POPULATION: Including Cara: 1755 – 514. 1792 – 614. 1801 – 556. 1821 – 573. 1841 – 550. Gigha only: 1881 – 378. 1891 – 398. 1911 – 326. 1931 – 240. 1951 – 190. 1961 – 163. 1971 – 174. 1981 – 176. 1991 – 143.

GEOLOGY: Some of the best examples of glaciated rock in Scotland are on Creag Bhan (G. – white or sacred rock). The summit appears to have escaped being covered with ice during the Ice Age. The island has a long spinal ridge and hummocky hills of epidiorite with basalt intrusions. In the north and west the rock is clean and less riven – like the Cuillin and there are many caves along the coast,

some at sea-level, some at old raised beaches. Sloc an Leim (G. – squirting pit) is a long subterranean passage through which the sea rushes violently during westerly gales and jets up to a great height. The south and east coast are of quartzite and grit and this stratum continues through Gigalum and Cara.

HISTORY: Occupancy stretches back five thousand years as proven by the archaeological remains. Gigha's key position on the sea route down the Mull of Kintyre had a profound influence on its history.

One of the earliest recorded visits was in the autumn of 1263 when King Haakon's fleet of more than 100 ships anchored in Gigalum Sound on the way to the Battle of Largs and were delayed there for some time by bad weather. On board the King's longship was Ewin, Lord of the Isles (called King John in the Haakon Saga). He had come on board at Oban to ask to be excused taking up arms against the Scots' King Alexander. Haakon eventually agreed and Ewin returned to the north. While on the island Haakon received the allegiance of Murdoch and Angus of Kintyre – the Lairds of Gigha, a peace mission from the Abbot of Saddell, and a request from the Irish for his assistance against the English. He sent a cutter to Ireland to investigate.

The King's return to Gigalum Sound after his defeat was not so triumphant. He still considered assisting the Irish but his men wanted to return home to Norway without further delay.

In 1309 the 'island of Gug' was made over by Bruce to the Earl of Mar. In 1335 Edward Baliol formally granted Gigha to John, Lord of the Isles and this grant was 'confirmed' by Edward III when he occupied Scotland in 1336. When the Kings of Scotland had regained their position in 1343 David II also confirmed the grant of the 'island of Githey' to John, Lord of the Isles and Chief of the

A GABLE OF OLD KILCHATTAN

Cairn
Jetty
Port Mór
Eilean Garbh
Bagh na Doirlinne
Cairn
Rubh' a' Chairn Bhain
Kinerarach
Bagh Rubha Ruaidh
West Tarbert Bay
East Tarbert Bay
Eilean na h-Airde
Standing Stone
Port Ban
Tarbert
Well
Cross
Cairnvickuie
Rubh' an Stearnail
Highfield
N
Creag Bhan
Druimyeon Bay
Sgeir Nuadh
Port an Duin
Dùn
Dùn
Sgeir Bheag
Watermill (ruin)
Cave
Mill Loch
Sgeir Mhór
Cnoc Loisgte
Dùn
Upper Loch
Ardminish Point
Acairseid na h-Uamhaidh Móire
Cave
Tarr an Tairbh
Dùn
Rubh' a' Phuirt Allaidh
Cave
Achamhinish
Port nam Faochag
Ferry jetty
P.O.
Jetty
Ardminish Bay
Carraig Mhór
Ardlamey
Hotel
Moorings
Ardminish
Ogam Stone
Chapel (ruin)
Eilean a' Chuil
Caolas Craro
Dun
Ferry
Craro Island
Eun Eilean
Achamore House
Port an Sgiathain
Sgeir Gigalum
Druimachro
Eilean Liath
Cath Sgeir
Port a' Gharaidh
Airstrip
Dubh Sgeir
Rubha Dubh
Leim
Pier
Caolas Gigalum
Eilean na h-Uilinn
Wee Rocks
Grob Bagh
Gigalum Rocks
Dearg Sgeir
Cave
Dùn
Gigalum Island
Slocan Leim
Eilean Leim
Corr Eilean
Sound of Gigha

2 km
1 mile

△100
1

Macdonalds. In 1449 Alexander, Earl of Ross and Lord of the Isles died having granted part of the island to Torquil MacNeill of Taynish and 'two merklands' to the Monks of Paisley. In 1493 the whole island came into the hands of the MacNeills of Taynish, but a pirate, Allan McLean (Allan-na-Sop), plundered Gigha in 1530 and slew Neil MacNeill of Taynish and many of the inhabitants. However, James V conferred the title on MacNeill's son, also called Neil, and elevated Gigha to a Barony. In 1542 the title deeds of the Thaindom of Gigha were 'lost' when eleven Gigha gentlemen were slain by unknown assailants. Dean Munro wrote in 1549 that 'the auld thane of Gigay should be Laird of the same, call it MacNeill of Gigay and now it is possessed by Clan Ranald' (i.e. the Macdonalds). Sure enough, by 1554 the deeds had reappeared in Macdonald hands. The following year Neil MacNeill was restored as Lord of Gigha by Mary, Queen of Scots, but he then sold the island to the Macdonalds of Islay. They in turn sold Gigha to Sir John Campbell of Calder but McNeill of Taynish repurchased most of it in 1590 for 3000 merks (£170 sterling).

William of Orange landed on Gigha in 1689 and had the support of MacNeill of Gigha. MacNeill also remained loyal during the 1745 uprising but this is not altogether surprising as the Duke of Argyll was his overlord.

ACHAMORE HOUSE

About 1779 MacNeill of Taynish sold out to John MacNeil of Colonsay, probably a relation, who became the first resident owner. The remaining part of Gigha was owned by another member of the MacNeill family of Taynish.

In 1865 J Williams Scarlett of Thryberg in Yorkshire bought Gigha for £49,000. This was the first time that the entire island had been under single ownership and it remained in the Scarlett family until 1919 when it was bought by Major John Allen. He sold it to R J A Hamer in 1937 and his son-in-law Somerset de Chair sold it to Sir James Horlick in 1944. David W Landale purchased it from the Horlick estate in 1973.

WILDLIFE: Gigha has an abundance of wildflowers. In late spring the Achamore woods are a sea of bluebells and the rocks and ridges are crowded with dwarf whin scented like honey and competing with the honey-scented flowers of the Grass of Parnassus. Apart from the main woodland at Achamore, Gigha has more trees than many small Scottish islands, with scrub willow, prostrate juniper, sycamore, thorn, alder, birch and hazel.

When the Scarletts were the proprietors from 1870 to 1919 they regularly stocked the Mill and Upper Lochs with trout – but these are now very scarce. Deer, weasels, stoats, moles and foxes apparently never reached the island but there are many rabbits. There were hares but they became extinct in the 19th century, probably due to the great black-backed gulls.

Over 70 species of bird have been recorded on Gigha including great northern and black-throated divers, mute and whooper swans, snipe, eider, fulmar, and shelduck by Eun Eilean in Craro Bay on the west coast. There is a gullery on Eilean Garbh in the north-west with eider and guillemot nesting on the western ledges. Hen harrier nest in the central moorland.

GIGHA is a fertile and hospitable island with good arable land on 25% of its surface area (about six separate farms) and a mild climate. In fact the rich soil produced such beautiful potatoes that the Irish used to buy them to place on top of their own potatoes on the way to market. This wonderful island supports a stable, balanced and partly Gaelic-speaking community, a relaxed way of life, and a nine-hole golf course.

When William James Yorke Scarlett, owner in the 1890s, was away on the mainland and his servants were taking time off for a round of golf on the island's course, a fire unfortunately burned down most of the Mansion House. It was eventually rebuilt and renamed **Achamore House** [NR642479].

Sir James Horlick (of the well-known beverage) purchased Gigha in 1944 and is remembered by the islanders as a very fine and generous benefactor who did a lot to make the island viable and stop depopulation. He modernised the farms and built-up dairy production to 250,000 gallons of milk a year. He converted some deciduous woodland around Achamore House into one of the finest gardens on the west coast of Scotland planted with many rare species which he had collected for his garden near Ascot. Apart from the varied deciduous trees there are rhododendron (including the famous Horlick hybrids), azalea, laburnum, *Primula candelabra*, and various subtropical plants such as palm lilies (*Cordyline australis*), palm trees and flame-trees (*Embothrium longifolium*). Sir James used to drive through his gardens in a dragon-caparisoned motorized tricycle. He died at Achamore House in 1972.

The beautiful gardens of Achamore, (the plants were gifted to the National Trust in 1962), are open to the public from April to September inclusive. May is probably the best month to see them.

The scattered little village of **Ardminish** is the main centre for the island. There is an attractive hotel (which won an architectural award) and the island's only policeman, Mr Seumas McSporran, also runs the island's only general store and post office. He is also Registrar of births, marriages and deaths and has numerous other official duties.

The parish church, whose congregation includes all denominations, has several good stained-glass windows, one dedicated to Kenneth MacLeod who was born in 1872 on Eigg (No.4.2). He composed, among many other songs, the 'Road to the Isles'.

The red and yellow sandstone ruins of the 13th century **Kilchattan** (St Catan's Chapel) are south of Ardminish [NR643481]. St Catan was an Irish missionary of the 6th century who settled in Bute but travelled widely. There are a number of interesting carved graveslabs in the church and churchyard dating back to the 14th century. The original octagonal stone font has been moved into the Parish Church at Ardminish for safe keeping. Opposite the lower end of the graveyard and south of the road is St Catan's Well.

The ogam stone near the church ruins is the only example of its kind in the west of Scotland. Ogam is an ancient Celtic writing which is still largely undeciphered. There are also some unusual standing stones and 'cup' stones at different parts of the island.

The beaches at Ardminish, and in the many attractive coastal bays and inlets, are of fine white sand. The pier in the south-east corner at Caolas Gigalum was the only ferry pier until the ro-ro ferry access was constructed at Ardminish in the 1980s. Gigalum Island, which gives its name to the kyle, is tiny but has a modern house in the dead centre. The two largest lochs, **Mill Loch** and the **Upper Loch**, are very ancient artificial lochs and the small islands in the latter may be crannogs.

Gigha is rich in folklore. At the north end of the island is Raven's Rock where it is believed that Noah's raven (not a dove) landed after the Flood.

Just south of East Tarbert Bay is Tobar a' Bheathaig (G. – Beathag's well). If a sailor wants a fair wind he must throw the well-water in the required direction and leave some payment by the well. A Viking Burial is thought to have taken place in East Tarbert Bay.

The very narrow loch west of and above North Ardminish, Tarr an Tairbh (G. – the tail of the bull), hides a shy bull-like monster reputedly seen by the islanders.

There are a number of interesting caves around the coastline. **Uamh Mhor** (G – big cave) [NR633495] is on the coast to the west of Tarr an Tairbh and difficult to approach from the land. It was probably occupied in prehistoric times and was also a favourite hide for smugglers. It has the same well-worn legend as other Hebridean islands; that a dog disappeared down it and reappeared, not as usual on the other side of the island, but on the mainland. This cave has never been fully explored. South of it is a large bay, full of rocks, skerries, and two islets, **Craro Island** in the centre, and tidal **Eun Eilean** (G. – bird island).

In 1991 the Russian factory ship *Kartli* was hit by a freak wave off Islay. Her crew was rescued but the wreck drifted on to the rocks off the coast of Gigha where it still lies. Although the islanders had to live with the smell of rotting fish for several months after the disaster, with their customary generosity they collected a substantial sum to assist the injured captain.

ACCESS: Vehicle ferry from Tayinloan, Kintyre. 20 minutes crossing time, about four crossings daily, 0188073 253. Cycles can be hired from McSporran's store near the ferry pier.

Anchorages:
1. Gigalum Sound (Caolas Gigalum). Approach is easy provided all visible rocks are identified and given a reasonable berth but best avoid S approach in fresh S'lies. The shore is foul. Anchor off the pier, sand.
2. Ardminish Bay. The most popular anchorage. Extensive reefs on both sides of the bay. Kiln rock, 1c off the jetty covers. HIE buoys available or anchor clear of the moorings, sand. Can be very unpleasant in E'lies.
3. Drumyeon Bay. Much obstructed by a fish farm. Sand and weed.
4. East Tarbert Bay. Occasional anchorage avoiding rocks and shellfish floats in middle of the bay.
5. Port Mór. Pleasant occasional anchorage if breeze is southerly and weather settled.
6. Eilean Garbh, N of the sand and shingle spit. Good anchorage 100m from the beach, sand, but exposed to N. Royal Yacht Britannia's favourite picnic spot.
7. West Tarbert Bay. Approach is clear. Exposed W. Reasonable in E'lies but swell likely. Anchor in 4-8m, sand and shingle.
8. Craro Bay. Temp anchorage in settled weather, best approached from due W. Anchor about 2½c W of the centre of Craro Island in 8m.

2.4 Islay

[Y-lë] Possibly, (ON Yula-øy or Jle-øy – Yula's isle). Yula was a Norse princess who is reputed to be buried under a standing stone on the east side of Port Ellen.

OS Maps: 1:50000 Sheet 60 1:25000 Sheets 397, 398, 410, 411, 424, 425 and 439
Admiralty Charts: 1:75000 No.2168 Sound of Islay 1:25000 No.2481 Port Ellen 1:15000 No.2474

AREA: 61,956ha (153,093 acres)
HEIGHT: 491m (1,610 ft)

OWNER: Multiple ownership.

POPULATION: 1755 – 5344. Pennant estimated 7000-8000 in 1772. 1792 – 9500. 1841 – 15772. 1881 – 7559. 1891 – 7375. 1931 – 4970. 1961 – 3860. 1971 – 3816. 1981 – 3997. 1991 – 3538.

GEOLOGY: Complex. In 1798 it was recorded that 'Ila has mines of lead mixed with copper: there is a strata of iron called Bog Ore, veins of emery, and some of quicksilver'. Lead and silver were being mined in the 19th century near Port Askaig, with copper and manganese also present.

The northern part of the Rinns is calcareous Torridonian sandstone with good loamy agricultural soil, whilst the southern part is Archaean gneiss with patches of hornblende; rough, rocky and treeless. The far north of the island is Cambrian quartzite with Dalradian limestone belts running through it. A strip of mica schist with limestone cuts right across the island from Port Askaig to the Mull of Oa. South-east of this is a continuation of the geology of Jura with a similar landscape, and in the extreme south-east coast between Port Ellen and Ardtalla there is mica schist and hornblende creating a beautifully shattered coastline backed by woodland and scrub.

HISTORY: The island was formerly the 'capital' of the Western Isles. Written records go back further in time for Islay than for any other Hebridean isle. The Irish settled

here in the 3rd century and for some 300 years the island was part of the Scots kingdom of Dalriada. The Norse were in charge from about 850 to 1150 then Somerled, King of Argyll, defeated them in a sea-battle off Islay, took over the southern Hebrides, made the island his home and his headquarters and founded the immensely powerful Clan Donald. His main MacDonald stronghold, Dunyvaig Castle, overlooks Lagavulin Bay where his war-galleys would lie at anchor.

Islay, as the seat of government of the Lord of the Isles, thus became an autonomous principality powerful enough by the 14th century to have made its own treaties with

England, France and Ireland, sometimes against the Scottish interest. New chiefs were proclaimed at the administrative headquarters at Loch Finlaggan near Port Askaig. This continued until 1493 when King James IV stripped John of the Isles of his titles and forced him to spend the rest of his days as a pensioner at the Stewart court.

In 1598 there was a vicious clan battle commemorated by a stone at the road junction south-west of the head of Loch Gruinart. James VI had granted land in Islay to the quarrelsome Sir Lachlan Maclean of Duart on Mull. The local Macdonalds understandably would not accept this so about four hundred Macleans, with their chief, invaded the island. Nearly all of them, including Sir Lachlan, were slain. About thirty took sanctuary in the ancient church of Kilnave (G. – church of the saints) by Loch Gruinart but the Macdonalds set fire to the church and they were all burnt to death.

In 1614 the Scots King granted Islay to Sir John Campbell of Cawdor but he had to fight for more than four years to gain possession from the MacDonalds. Sir John then gave Islay to his son as a wedding present, but his son was declared insane in 1639, and his grandson died young. All this strife and unrest devastated the island and impoverished the islanders. It was not until the early 18th century that the island was bought by a Daniel Campbell and his family who did a great deal to restore it to its former glory and make it a 'leader and model of the other isles'. This testimonial was actually given by a MacDonald and with widespread agreement.

By 1847 the owner's philanthropy had bankrupted him. His son, John Francis Campbell (1822-85), spent his life recording Gaelic traditions, poetry and folklore for posterity and there is a monument to him overlooking the house at Bridgend on the island that he never inherited.

WILDLIFE: Otters can often be seen on the shores of Loch Gruinart. There are red deer in the south-east and wild goats in the Oa. Many of the hedges are of fuchsia.

Islay has the richest bird life in the Hebrides with over 180 recorded species, and over 100 breeding on the island including the rare and elusive chough. Although it is particularly noted for its geese – about 20,000 barnacle geese and 6,000 Greenland white-fronted geese have been recorded – there is much more of interest. Some sites noted by the RSPB are:

Loch Gruinart: Geese, waders, and black and red grouse. Occasionally golden eagle, peregrine, hen harrier and merlin can be seen hunting.

Ardnave Loch: Oct-May. Mute swan, wigeon, teal, mallard, pochard and tufted duck.

Bowmore: Many sea-fowl including scaup, eider, common scoter and Slavonian grebe can be seen from the pier. Glaucous and Iceland gulls frequent the rubbish tip. Dabbling duck and waders are in the shoreline shallows.

Head of Loch Indaal: Shoveller in the small saltmarsh lagoons. Marvellous spectacle of barnacle geese at dusk coming in to roost. Pintail in the river channel.

Bruichladdich Pier: Rocks at distillery for purple sandpiper in winter and many divers and sea-duck.

Frenchman's Rocks: Sooty shearwater, gannet, storm petrel, Leach's petrel sometimes, arctic and great skua, kittiwake galore.

Saligo Bay-Sanaigmore coast: Seabirds, buzzard, golden eagle, merlin, kestrel, hen harrier, peregrine, red grouse, stonechat, chough, raven, twite. Also whinchat and wheatear.

The Oa: Snow bunting in winter. Many breeding seabirds on the cliffs.

Loch Ballygrant: for wildfowl and common woodland species.

Claggain Bay: for great northern divers Oct-May.

Port Ellen: for gulls and sea-fowl.

In 1993 Duich Moss, – Eilean na Muice Duibhe, – was made a National Nature Reserve by Scottish Natural Heritage.

ISLAY is probably better known for its whisky than for its birdlife. There are extensive peat deposits which are used as fuel and whose dark waters are used for the preparation of malt whisky. There are eight distilleries, all famous for their distinctive individual flavours – Ardbeg, Bunnahabhain, Bruichladdich, Bowmore, Lagavulin, Caol Ila, Laphroaig and Port Ellen. About 180 years ago many of the illicit stills were legalised but no duty was payable on local whisky. As a result there was such widespread drunkenness that the parish ministers demanded government action. Today Islay produces about four million proof gallons of whisky each year, most of which is ex-

BOWMORE PARISH CHURCH

ported overseas. Even so, the duty collected by the Government from sales on the home market alone is the equivalent of a generous income for every man, woman and child on the island.

The climate is relatively mild but it is difficult to avoid the Atlantic winds which constantly funnel through Loch Indaal. The landscape is generally undulating except where the line of Jura mountains cross the Sound of Islay and peter out in the south-east corner. The island has quite a prosperous farming industry and there is rich machair grassland on the west coast.

Historically Islay was once the most important of all the Scottish islands and it has much of archaeological interest. The elegant, 2.4m high Celtic cross at Kilchoman on the Rinns south of **Loch Gorm** was erected by John, first Lord of the Isles in the 14th century in memory of his second wife, Margaret. The wishing stone beneath it in a worn stone basin has to be turned by any mother who wishes to have a son. The legendary pipers, the MacCrimmons of Skye, are thought to have originated from near here.

On the west coast peat-bog of the Rinns (G. *rinn* – promontory. 'Rhinns' is the incorrect spelling) between Loch Gorm and **Saligo Bay** is an area where thousands of barnacle, greylag and Greenland white-fronted geese winter every year. The birds cause considerable damage to surrounding farms and peat-cutting is essential for the whisky industry so there was a rousing disagreement between islanders and conservationists in 1985. The area, **Duich Moss**, or Eilean na Muice Duibhe, was eventually made a National Nature Reserve in 1993 after agreement was reached with the distillers to use peat from an alternative site. This has safeguarded a rich variety of wildlife associated with peatland. United Distillers actively assisted Scottish Natural Heritage in measures such as damming drainage ditches to allow the water table to rise to its normal level.

At the head of Loch Gruinart which separates the Rinns from the rest of Islay a bloody battle between the MacLeans of Duart and the MacDonalds of Islay in 1598 was won, according to the MacDonalds, thanks to the magical intervention of the black elf, *Du-sith*.

The north-east part of the island has sporting estates well-stocked with deer, pheasants and trout streams and very few roads. This is hill-walking country. **Sgarbh Breac** (364m) is a good climb reached by way of Beinn Thrasda's summit (260m) with a stunning view down the Sound of Islay and over to West Loch Tarbert on Jura.

Port Askaig is a tiny indentation which just avoids the fierce tides in the Sound of Islay. Its attractive hotel dates from the 16th century. Ferries call here from Kennacraig on the mainland and Feolin on Jura. To the south is a wild and trackless mountain region with sport for the climber and hill walker and wonderful views for the artist or photographer from the slopes of Beinn Bheigier (491m), Glas Bheinn (471m) and Beinn Bhàn (471m).

A main road cuts across the island from Port Askaig to Bridgend on Loch Indaal. Each of several lochs near Ballygrant has its own crannog. **Loch Finlaggan**, north of the village, was the Lord of the Isles' headquarters and is one of Scotland's most important archaeological sites, although little attention was paid to it before 1989. There are two islands in the loch, Eilean Mór (G. – big island) and Eilean na Comhairle [co**a**-oorloo] (G. – council island), both covered with ruins [NR389681]. In among the profuse wildflowers are the remains of at least 28 buildings of this ancient centre of Scottish Gaelic culture and administration including the Great Hall of the Lords, the chapel, scattered carved gravestones, buildings which held the 'parliament' of ecclesiastics and chiefs, living quarters, and many other crumbling ruins still to be identified. Excavation continues and the Finlaggan Trust is setting up a visitor's interpretive centre on the site.

Bridgend is the home village of the former laird's mansion – Islay House, which is carefully screened from view by trees [NR334628]. The road on the north pebbled shore of **Loch Indaal** runs round to Bruichladdich with its distillery and on to the charming little fishing village of Port Charlotte, known as the **Queen of the Rinns**. This was built at the turn of the 18th century by a local minister, Rev. Maclaurin. Every house is of identical plan and measures 9m x 7m. In the old Free Kirk is the Museum of Islay Life with a lot of interesting exhibits.

At **Nerabus**, two ancient burial grounds contain some of the finest medieval graveslabs to be found in Scotland and 3km further on there are exotic wildfowl ponds at the Rodney Dawson Memorial collection of birds. The main

THE HIGH CROSS IN KILDALTON CHURCHYARD

90 m
300 ft

N

■ Assumed to date to the Lordship (c14thC)

■ Timberwork defences (pre-14thC ?)

■ Assumed to date to 16thC or later

Causeway
to the shore

Timber round tower
or entrance gate?

EILEAN MOR (Main Island)

Timberwork Fortification

Timberwork Fortification

Enclosure

Barn & Storage
Cooking Place

Towerhouse (?)

Dwelling House (?)

Jetty

ditch

Dwelling House (?)

St Finlaggan's Chapel

The Great Hall

Burial Ground

The Lord's Residence (?)

Causeway

**Islands of Loch Finlaggan ...
where the Lords of the Isles held council**

Jetty

Dwelling Houses (?)

EILEAN NA COMHAIRLE (Island of the Council)
This is a crannog or artificial island

Jetty

road ends at **Portnahaven** which faces the islands of **Mhic Coinnich** and **Orsay** with its ancient chapel and Stevenson lighthouse. This was once a fishing village but is now mainly a collection of holiday homes. About 9km north of Portnahaven on a very rural road **Kilchiaran** (G – cell of St Ciaran) was founded by St Columba in honour of his Irish tutor who had died in 548. **Eilean Liath** forms a reef beside the bay.

Turning south from Bridgend brings one to **Bowmore**, the present-day 'capital' of Islay, with a population of about 900. It was founded by the laird, Daniel Campbell, in 1767. The rounded church of Kilarrow here [NR312596] was designed 'so the devil could find no corners to lurk in'.

Between Bowmore and Port Ellen a 10 km shell-sand beach borders **Laggan Bay** with the airfield and a golf course on the machair at its southern end.

Port Ellen is the largest centre of population. The port construction was started in the 1820s by Walter Campbell, 4th of Islay, who named it Port Elinor after his wife. To the east of the town is the vestigial ruin of a chapel dedicated to St Lasar, an obscure 6th century Irish nun, marked by two curious upright stones with holes cut through them. A pub near the harbour has several walls covered with excellent murals of island scenes and depicting local people. These were painted by an Irish artist, each character being placed in the composition in return for a dram – or two – or maybe three. I understand the poor chap died of drink – but he has left a fascinating memorial.

To the west of Port Ellen is **The Oa –** pronounced 'oh' – and on the Mull of Oa is an American Memorial [NR270415] commemorating US servicemen lost when the *Tuscania* was torpedoed in February 1918 and the *Otranto* was wrecked in a gale the following October. Many bodies were washed ashore beneath these cliffs. This is a storm-lashed area which overlooks the grey Atlantic but mountaineers appreciate the cliffs. A clean granite arête from sea-level to the cairn of Beinn Mhor provides an exciting 150m climb. Other good ridges are nearby to the east and also beyond the Memorial.

The southern road from Port Ellen to **Ardbeg** runs through one of the most archaeologically interesting parts of the island. It passes the Laphroaig distillery overlooking the island of Texa (No.2.1). Further east, by Lagavulin, are the ruins of 14th century **Dunyvaig Castle** (G. – fort of the little ships) [NR406455], built either by Donald I or John of Islay, Lord of the Isles. This castle has a long and bloody history very similar to another MacDonald stronghold, Dunaverty Castle, on the Mull of Kintyre overlooking Sanda island (No.1.2). Further on, **Kildalton House** in a woodland setting is beside magic Loch a' Chnuic. This estate was owned by John Ramsay MP who deported all his tenants to America in the 19th century. He was cursed by an old woman as she was dragged away and before long both he and his wife died and the estate fell into financial ruin.

Three kilometres further, the renowned **Kildalton High Cross** stands by a ruined chapel (G. *cille daltan* – the church of the disciple) [NR458508]. Carved in *c.* 800 out of bluestone by a sculptor from Iona, it is considered by many to be the finest Celtic cross in the whole of Scotland. Beside it are some magnificent carved grave slabs of the 15th century. The road dwindles to a track by Trudernish Point near a vitrified dun and standing stones.

Apart from the beautiful scenery, beaches, birdlife, and prehistoric and medieval remains, Islay also offers the visitor golf, riding, hill-walking, sea angling, freshwater fishing, diving, and any amount of subject matter for the artist. And although the island attracts many visitors in the summer months it never appears crowded.

ACCESS: Car ferry from Kennacraig on West Loch Tarbert (Mull of Kintyre) to Port Ellen. Crossing 2¼ hours. Several services daily, 01880-730253 or 01496-302209. Air service from Glasgow, Mon.-Sat., 0345-222111. There are regular island bus services, 01496-302131. Tourist Information, 01496-810254.

Anchorages:
Note: The tidal range here is less than two metres and sometimes only 60cm – less than anywhere else in the British Isles. The movement at neaps is barely distinguishable.

1. Port Ellen. Hazards at entrance and west of harbour pier. Visitors' moorings, or anchor in 4m S of the pier, close N of innermost islet. A busy harbour; keep the approach clear. Bay shoals steeply. Holding moderately good but shelter indifferent. Kilnaughton bay W of harbour has better shelter from southerly swell or W winds. Anchor N of Carraig Fhada lighthouse in 6-9m.

2. Lagavulin. Various hazards on approach. Visitors' moorings at distillery or anchor in 3m in middle of pool, mud. Subject to swell.

3. Loch an t'Sailen. Approach to Lagavulin then follow a course 2c off the coast and pass above-water Ardbeg rocks. Anchor NNE of Sgeir Dubh in 3m, rock and sand, good holding. Well-sheltered.

4. Loch a' Chnuic (Kildalton Bay). Only suitable if no chance of winds from E to S, and in any case subject to heavy swell. Hazards on approach. Anchor near above-water rock in 3m, hard sand.

5. Ardmore Islands. A fascinating hideaway teeming with wildlife. Anchor SW of Eilean Craobhach or, with care, in the rocky but snug Plod Sgeirean behind a submerged reef.

6. Port Mór. Avoid N side and give S entrance point a wide berth. Head is shoal. Anchor in SW where depth suitable, sand. (Best for visit to Kildalton Church and Cross.)

7. Clas Uig. N of Ardmore Point, between Port Mór and Aros Bay. No dangers outside but a number inside the anchorage. Exposed to E and subject to swell. Anchor in 3m, rock and weed, some sand areas.

8. Aros Bay. A wide sandy bay with no offlying dangers. Exposed N and E. Anchor in 3m in centre. (Useful for visit to historic Kildalton Church and Cross but longer walk than No.6 above).

9. Port Askaig. Anchor close inshore in 4m, but strong tide makes this uncomfortable. Alongside ferry pier sometimes possible.

10. Caol Ila distillery. Better holding than Port Askaig but avoid obstructing pier.

11. Bunnahabhain Bay. Temporary anchorage in 4m ½c N of pier.

12. Tràigh Baile Aonghais bay near Gortantaoid point. Exposed. Occasional anchorage in suitable weather.

13. Nave Island. Anchor SE of island, sand, good holding but very little shelter. Temp anchorage in suitable winds, also possible in several nearby sandy bays.

14. Portnahaven (Orsay). Well-sheltered channel. North entrance foul with rocks. Approach from S but beware strong tides across the entrance. Anchor NW of Portnahaven quay, sand.

15. Port Charlotte, Loch Indaal. Temporary anchorage.

16. Temp anchorage off pier at Bruichladdich, Loch Indaal, in suitable weather. Pier has 3m depth at head.

17. Bowmore, Loch Indaal. The loch head dries out about 7½c and shores are shoal. Indifferent shelter. Anchor well-offshore N of the N'most of the two beacons.

2.5 Jura

(ON jur-øy – udder island) – to a Viking sailor the Paps of Jura would be the obvious identification. All expert sources, however, give the derivation as (ON dyr-øy – deer island) and one 7th century document refers to the island as 'Doiradeilinn'.

OS Maps: 1:50000 Sheet 61 1:25000 Sheets 365, 376, 386, 398 and 411

Admiralty Charts: 1:75000 Nos.2168 and 2169 Sounds of Islay and Jura 1:25000 Nos.2481, 2396 and 2397 Gulf of Corryvreckan 1:25000 No.2343

AREA: 36,692ha (90,666 acres)
HEIGHT: 785m (2,575 ft)

OWNER: Multiple ownership. In 1938 a large part of the island was sold to five separate purchasers and most of these estates are still intact. Mr C. H. Fletcher of Ardlussa owns the north; the central portion around Loch Tarbert is split between Viscount Astor and Lindsay C. N. Bury; Lord Vestey owns the area overlooking Craighouse Bay; A. W. A. Riley-Smith owns the south of the island around Jura House and north to Craighouse, and Sir William J. Lithgow's family own the western area centred on Feolin.

POPULATION: 1755 – 1097. 1794 – 929. 1831 – 1312. 1841 – no separate census figures. 1881 – 773. 1891 – 619. 1931 – 364. 1961 – 249. 1971 – 210. 1981 – 239. 1991 – 196.

GEOLOGY: This is the largest area of metamorphic quartzite in the Highlands producing poor soil and a lot of peat. A narrow strip of schist runs along the east coast and no other coast has so many arches, caves and raised beaches as the west side of Jura. The rocks are mainly white and red granite with fine blue slate and micaceous sandstone in the north. Iron ore is plentiful and the good silica sand deposits on the west coast were once used for glass-making. There are about fifty very large caves – some were used as mortuaries for the dead before the bodies were shipped to Iona or Oronsay for burial.

HISTORY: About 678AD, in Dalriadic times, there was a great battle fought on Jura between the native Picts and the Scots from Ireland.

During the time of the Lords of the Isles and MacDonald power, Jura's importance was due to its proximity to the headquarter territory of Islay. This lasted until the Clan Donald sold Jura to the Campbells of Argyll in 1607.

In 1647 during the Wars of the Covenant the MacLeans of Jura were attacked by Campbell of Craignish and there was a fierce battle. 'MacLaine saved his lands with the loss of his reputation' according to Sir James Turner. General David Leslie arrived from Islay and Maclean promptly gave him his castle, his son, and 'fourteen prettie Irishmen who had been all along faithful to him' as hostages. Leslie had the fourteen hanged.

Walter Campbell who inherited Islay in 1777 sold his lands in Jura to concentrate his assets on Islay. About this time the island was divided into twenty-seven separate farms. In the 18th century and the early 19th century Jura was a centre for breeding Highland cattle. There was also a small number of hardy little sheep with a particularly fine wool, a lot of wild goats and some horses. In 1812 experiments were conducted on Beinn An Oir to determine the boiling point of water in relation to altitude.

In 1767 fifty islanders sailed from Jura to settle in Canada and islanders continued to do so during the next seventy years. After 1840 there was widespread introduction of sheep and the crofters were cleared from the land. The grassy glens deteriorated in consequence and much of the ground is now only of use for deer stalking.

WILDLIFE: By the end of the 18th century the deer population had declined seriously but numbers have slowly increased again with encouragement from the hunting fraternity and today there are about 5,000. There are also some wild goats.

It is dangerous to wander about after mid-August when the stag shooting season has begun and at any time it is sensible to request permission. Enquire at the Isle of Jura Hotel at Craighouse, 01496-820243. There are many

THE PASSAGE TO INNER LOCH TARBERT

adders so wear sensible footwear. During a 3km walk on a hot summer day, I passed seven different rocks with adders sunbathing on them.

North along the beach from the ferry landing at Feolin is the largest heronry on the island. At least fifteen pairs of golden eagles are resident in the hills and hen harriers can be seen sweeping over the lower ground. At the end of the 18th century it was reported that the 'many eagles. . . are very destructive to the lambs.' West Loch Tarbert is a fa-

vourite haunt of mergansers and divers. Common seals frequent the skerries, mainly on the south shoreline.

The wild terrain is almost too coarse to encourage a great botanical variety but there are unexpected finds to be made. Many of the marshy pools are covered with water-lilies and an interesting variety of alpine plants thrive on the higher slopes. Palm trees grow around Craighouse as a reminder of the mildness of the climate when sheltered from the wind.

JURA is the wildest island in the Inner Hebrides. It is a vast area of rock and blanket bog, most of it without roads or habitation of any kind and the haunt of deer and wild goats. Crossing this terrain of rough ankle-twisting rock and scree, or knee-high grass, heather, and bracken, is painfully slow. But this gives it added fascination. On Jura it is easy to believe that there is no such thing as the human race and that exploration of this remote environment is bound to yield some earth-shattering discovery. And scattered along the west coast of the ragged lonely landscape are spacious caves with dry floors and lofty vaulted roofs, great natural stone arches and pillars, and raised beaches which are almost artificial in their perfection.

West Loch Tarbert nearly bisects the island. South of the first narrows, Cumhann Mór, there is a raised beach possibly ³/₄km in length and about 15m above sea-level with a lochan beside it. It is clean, with no weeds and the surface looks as though a gardener has just finished raking the smooth round pebbles. And yet it has been lying there for some 10,000 years!

Exploring West Loch Tarbert by boat for the first time is an exciting experience. Negotiating the outer loch past the **Eileanan Gleann Righ** (G. – islands of the royal glen), through the narrow Cumhann Mór into the large middle loch with **Eilean Ard** to the north and finding, and passing through, the concealed entrance to the dog-leg passage leading to the inner sanctum. This entails slipping past rocks and tidal eddies, squeezing past little **Eilean an Easbuig**, and then, at last, the shallow inner loch opens up with its one deep patch in the centre.

Some of the many large caves include rudimentary altars which were built by the islanders when they stopped there while transporting their dead to Iona or Oronsay for burial, and there is one cave in **Bàgh Gleann Righ Mór** (G. – large bay of the valley of the king) in West Loch Tarbert which has a royal connection and an ancient history, but is the subject of conflicting scholarly argument [NR518824].

The **Paps of Jura** are almost as high as Goatfell and almost as famous as the Cuillin – painted by McTaggart and many artists. There are, strangely, three paps: **Beinn an Oir** (a Corbett) at 785m (2575 ft) (G. – the mountain of gold), **Beinn Shiantaidh** at 755m (2476 ft) (G. – the holy mountain), and **Beinn a' Chaolais** 734m (2408 ft) (G. – the mountain of the kyle). North-west of Beinn an Oir is Sgriob na Caillich (G. – the witch's broom) – a large rock scar. A causeway was erected on Beinn an Oir by the Ordnance Survey in the mid-19th century.

For climbers, who want to conquer all the Paps, there is a favourite steep scramble up Beinn Shiantaidh from the river outlet of Loch an t-Sìob, down to the pass and lochans to the north-east and then a steep ascent of Corra Bheinn (575m) and a 5km round trip back to Shiantaidh: down the west ridge and across the 450m col and up to Beinn An Oir. Then descending the south spur, avoiding the steep ground overlooking Na Garbh-lochanan corrie to the col at 370m, and on up to Beinn a' Chaolais, the lowest of the Paps: after this a descent to Feolin on the west coast via Cnocbreac or to Keils near Craighouse via the shoulder above the head of Glen Astaile, under the east slope of Glas Beinn. Finish by passing the St Earnadail graveyard – if you are still able.

The west coast has always been underpopulated. It is now deserted but there used to be a small settlement at **Glengarrisdale** and another at **Ruantallain** at the entrance to West Loch Tarbert which was only abandoned about 1947. At Glengarrisdale Bay, in the far north-west, **Maclean's Skull Cave** contained a human skull and bones mounted on a cairn [NR647970] but about twenty years ago the skull was removed. This gruesome relic was alleged to be the remains of a Maclean who was slain when Jura was attacked by Campbell of Craignish in 1647 during the Wars of the Covenant.

Nowadays all the inhabitants of Jura live on the east coast, mostly in the vicinity of **Craighouse**. The distillery was built in 1963 and bottled its first malt in 1974. It replaced one built by the Campbells in the mid-19th century. Craighouse also has a post-office, shop, hotel, school and doctor. One of the two piers was built in 1814 by Thomas Telford. A string of islets known as the Small Isles form a breakwater to the bay. They are **Eilean nan Gabhar** (G. – island of the goats), **Eilean Diomhain** (G. – idle island), **Eilean nan Coinean** (G. – island of the rabbits), **Pladda** and **Eilean Bhride** (G – Bridget's isle).

At the south end of Jura, by the road running round from the ferry on the Sound of Islay, Jura House stands in a woodland estate. Offshore is the small island of **Am Fraoch Eilean** (G. – the heather isle) on which are the ruins of Claig Castle [NR471627], a Norman-style square tower with 3m-thick walls built in 1154 by Somerled to defend the Sound of Islay and also used by his descendants as a prison. The MacDonald clan slogan is still 'Fraoch Eilean'. To the east of Am Fraoch Eilean by the Sound of Jura is **Brosdale Island** and to the west, in the Sound of Islay, are the sharp rocks of **Glas Eilean**.

In this area and up the east coast standing stones prove that early man also favoured the east of the island.

Jura's one and only public road continues north from Craighouse and passes the crofting hamlet of Keils with its **Chapel of St Earnadail** [NR524687] who was a little-known early Celtic missionary from Iona. Although he lived on Islay he insisted that he should be buried on Jura, and that a ball of mist would guide his mourners to a suitable burial place. A gravestone in the churchyard commemorates Gillouir MacCrain who died in 1645. Another MacCrain, Mary, died aged 128 in 1856 and is buried at Inverlussa. The tombstone inscription says that she was a 'Descendant of Gillouir MacCrain who kept One Hundred

Hotel   Distillery   Shop

CRAIGHOUSE HAS LIFE'S BARE NECESSITIES. . .

ACCESS: Cal-Mac car ferry from Kennacraig to Port Ellen, Islay, 0188073 253. Bus from Port Ellen to Port Askaig, 01496-302131. Car ferry from Port Askaig, Islay to Feolin, 01496-840208. Summer boat excursions by arrangement with MacLachlan, Luing, 0185-24282. BA/Loganair air service, Glasgow to Islay, 0345-222111.

and Eighty Christmasses in his own house. And died in the reign of Charles I.'

The road continues up the east coast passing a wide stretch of beach at the head of **Loch na Mile**. Then it climbs and crosses a stretch of moorland before entering an area of attractive woodland at **Lagg**. Tarbert Bay, at the narrow low-lying neck of land adjoining West Loch Tarbert, has a small enclosed beach, standing stones and a ruined chapel and, a further 6km on, the road runs out at **Inverlussa**. Ardlussa estate, of about 6900ha, was once the only independent property on Jura. The present house was built by Lord Colonsay about 1840. A track continues up the coast from here to the north of the island passing Barnhill [NR705970] where George Orwell stayed when he wrote his famous novel *1984*.

From the most northern point of the vehicle track there is a fairly undemanding 3km hill-walk to a point above the clifftops overlooking the notorious **Corryvreckan** (G. *coire bhreacain* – the speckled cauldron). This is a marvellous vantage point to watch the swirl of the waters 100m or more below, although the finest view point is on Scarba (No.2.9) on the opposite side. The most dramatic sight is when a spring tide is in flood (i.e. running westwards at a speed of up to 10 knots) against a strong west wind. There have been many shipwrecks and disasters and Orwell recorded how he also nearly lost his life here in 1949 when trying to circumnavigate Jura.

It is often said that the tidal race was named after Breacan, a Norse Prince, who foundered with his entire fleet of fifty ships. But from Adomnan's *Life of St Columba* it would appear that this calamity occurred in the tidal race between Rathlin Island and Antrim. Nevertheless, Breacan is reputed to be buried in the 55m-deep cave [NM685005] on the south side of Bagh nam Muc (G. – bay of the swine), at the north-western tip of Jura and guarded by **Eilean Mór** and **Eilean Beag**. Martin Martin reported in 1695 that 'Breacan's stone', a tomb, and an altar, were in the cave.

Anchorages:

1. Craighouse. Avoid Goat Rock, E of Eilean nan Gabhar, and enter bay centrally between beacon and perch. HIE visitor moorings, or anchor in 3m off old stone pier. Alternatively, in E'lies anchor as close as depth permits to the centre of the W side of Eilean nan Gabhar. Sand and thick kelp in both cases and holding poor.

2. Loch na Mile, N end. Sand and kelp, but cleaner than Craighouse. Subject to swell.

3. Drumnatuadh bay. Small bay at W side of entrance to Lowlandman's Bay. Occasional anchorage in SW winds. Anchor in centre when the small islet off its point closes with the point, hard sand.

4. Lowlandman's Bay. Good shelter in W winds, but exposed to S and N winds which bring fierce squalls and a swell. Head dries out 1c and shoals a considerable distance. Best near E side, off stone jetty, thick kelp.

5. Lagg Bay is a shallow bight 3³/₄M NNE of Lowlandman's Bay. Temp anchorage. Avoid central cable, and anchor near W side. Kelp and subject to swell.

6. Tarbert bay, 1¹/₂M NNE of Lagg bay is small inlet with central reef. Enter close to Liath Eilean on W side of inlet and anchor just N of it in 2-3m, sand. Everywhere else is dense kelp. Can be subject to swell.

7. Lussa bay, temp. anchorage with good shelter from N. Avoid reefs about ³/₄c from W shore. Anchor in centre, 2-4m, kelp. Subject to swell.

8. Ardlussa bay, 1M NNE of Lussa bay, temp. anchorage midway between En Traigh and Ru an Fhaing, kelp.

9. Kinuachdrachd harbour in NE of Jura. Temp anchorage, close off N shore, in depths of 4-7m, cabbage kelp. Subject to swell.

10. Port an Tiobairt, at NE extremity, good occasional anchorage except for NE winds. Anchor centrally in 2-5m, sand and kelp. Subject to swell.

11. Bàgh Gleann nam Muc, in NW next Gulf of Corryvreckan, pleasant and safe, but with rocky shoals off both entrance points. Anchor at head of the larger bay off the small headland to port, firm sand. No swell except during NW wind at slack water.

12. Glentrosdale bay, the next bay SW of Bàgh Gleann nam Muc and 9¹/₂c NNE of Bàgh uamh nan Giall. Temp anchorage, open NW.

13. Bàgh uamh nan Giall, about 8¹/₂c NE of E entrance point of Glengarrisdale bay, is free from dangers, 4-6m.

14. Glendebadel bay and Glengarrisdale bay, 6¹/₄M and 8¹/₄M respec NE of Shian bay are small but easily accessible. Temp anchorages when wind suitable.

15. Shian Bay, 3¹/₂M NNE of Loch Tarbert, small, shallow with several rocks in it, exposed and often with a heavy swell but possible in fine weather.

16. *Rubh' an t-Sàilein, rocky headland at N entrance point of Loch Tarbert has small rocky cove on E side and bight close E again which are good landing points but poor anchorage.*

17. *Bàgh Gleann Righ Mór is an indentation E of Eileanan Gleann Righ, N side of outer Loch Tarbert. Easy access and good holding in 3-4m off W side of bay. Bay shoals. Heavy swell with W'lies but reasonable in N'lies.*

18. *Bàgh Gleann Righ Beag, a bight immediately ESE of Bàgh Gleann Righ Mór and NE of Aird Reamhar, gives occasional anchorage except in W'lies.*

19. *Cuan Mór Bay in outer West Loch Tarbert immediately NW of the Cumhann Mór (the narrows). Approach using leading lines in fair visibility. Anchor in centre avoiding reef on E side, mud, holding and shelter good.*

20. *Through the Cumhann Mór, anchor 5c E of the 4m high islet in the narrows, in 4-6m. Reasonable shelter in most conditions.*

21. *Cruib Lodge (bothy). Anchor well offshore on N shore of the centre loch, S of lone cottage and drying rocks in the bay, mud.*

22. *Eilean an Easbuig pool. Hazardous entry through the Cumhann Beag using several leading marks but good anchorage slightly N of centre of the pool, out of strong tidal currents.*

23. *Inner Loch Tarbert. Further fairly hazardous passage to remote inner loch. Anchor in a suitable depth avoiding shoal water on all sides. 2¹/₂km track from boathouse to the east coast of Jura.*

24. *Glenbatrick bay between Sgeir Agleann and Rubh' a' Bhaillein on S shore of Outer Loch Tarbert. Anchor in suitable depth, near Sgeir Agleann, sand. Sheltered SW. Mouth of river shoals 2c.*

25. *Whitefarland Bay. Opposite Caol Isla distillery in Sound of Islay. Clean, open bay out of main tidal stream. Anchor N of anchor-painted boulder in 3m. The boulder has a mooring ring.*

26. *Am Fraoch Eilean. Approach with care as many foul areas. Occasional anchorage NNW of Am Fraoch Eilean and W of the nearby boathouse and pier on Jura in 3-4m, sand and weed.*

2.6 Colonsay

(ON – Columba's island)

Oronsay

(ON – Oran's island). Normally this is the Gaelic name for a tidal island but here the name derives from St Oran who founded the island monastery in AD 563.

OS Maps: 1:50000 Sheet 61 1:25000 Sheet 375
Admiralty Charts: 1:75000 No.2169 Scalasaig Harbour 1:12500 No.2474

AREA: 4,617ha (11,409 acres)
HEIGHT: 143m (469 ft)

OWNER: Colonsay, with the exception of the church, the ferry pier, and the Priory on Oronsay, has been in the family of the one-time Minister of Defence, Lord Strathcona and Mount Royal, since 1905. 'I have to try to run it as a financially viable enterprise,' he says. Oronsay was also owned by the Strathconas but was sold to Adam Bergius for about £100,000 in the 1970s.

POPULATION: Approximate figures for Colonsay and Oronsay combined: 1792 – 718 (134 families). 1841 – 987.

	1881	1891	1931	1961	1971	1981	1991
Colonsay	387	358	232	164	137	132	98
Oronsay	10	23	6	2	2	5	8
	397	381	238	166	139	137	106

GEOLOGY: Lower mudstone strata with Torridonian sandstone containing lime which breaks down into good soil. There are some basalt dykes, white limestone at the north end of Bheinn Bhreac, and a particularly fine raised beach north of Kiloran Bay which is worth a visit.

HISTORY: The Macphees or MacDuffies, archivists to the Lords of the Isles, were the islands' owners from at least the 15th century but they were dispossessed by the MacDonalds soon after 1615. The Campbells of Argyll then ousted the MacDonalds. Malcolm MacNeil of Knapdale acquired the islands (i.e. both Colonsay and Oronsay) from the Campbells in 1700 for an agreed exchange of land. This was one of the few Hebridean islands which was fortunate enough to escape the 19th century clearances as the laird at the time, John MacNeil, had a liberal approach. Even so, many families had already emigrated to America in the summer of 1791 and the *Statistical Account* lamented, 'Pity it is that such numbers should bid farewell to their native country, when there is so great a demand for useful citizens'. By 1904 debt had forced the MacNeils to put the island up for sale and it was bought by Lord Strathcona in 1905.

WILDLIFE: There are many seals, particularly among the skerries of the grassy Ardskenish peninsula on the west coast, and also on Eilean nan Ron (G. seal island) which is a nature reserve. Rabbits were introduced 200 years ago to provide fresh meat. They have no predators and thrive enthusiastically.

When Lord Strathcona bought Colonsay he was able to take advantage of the woodland planted in Kiloran valley by the MacNeils. He cultivated many rhododendrons, magnolia and azalea, and extended the tree cover with acacia, maple, poplar, sea-buckthorn, and eucalyptus. The woods include sycamore, beech, elm, ash, spruce, aspen, hazel, willow, larch, silver birch and pine. The sheltered valley is almost sub-tropical and peaches and figs ripen in the sun but, sadly, much is now overgrown.

In late summer at Garvard by the Strand field gentians bloom and rock samphire hide in the clefts. Colonsay has, possibly, the greatest variety of flora in the Hebrides – some 500 species.

Loch Fada, and the lesser lochs in the centre of the island, have a great variety of birds. Decorative wildfowl such as flamingos and black swans were introduced by Lord Strathcona. The lochs also provide good fishing (Permits from the hotel). Around the coast eider are so common that they are known locally as 'Colonsay duck'. Kittiwakes, guillemots and razorbills breed on the west coast and Oronsay is a wintering ground for barnacle geese.

COLONSAY and **ORONSAY** are separated by a wide expanse of shell sand called The Strand which can be walked across when the tide is out, following a defined route. Halfway across is the sanctuary cross: any Colonsay fugitive who reached it was immune from punishment provided he stayed on Oronsay for a year and a day.

These islands have been inhabited for 7000 years. On the south side of **Kiloran Bay**, in Uamh Uir (G. – the cave of the gravedust) the bones of domestic animals and neolithic flint tools have been excavated. There are many pre-Christian and early Christian relics. A Viking warrior who had been given a ship burial in 855 with his weapons, horse and coins, was uncovered in the sand dunes here in 1882. Although it was a pagan burial two crosses incised on stone slabs were included as an additional guarantee.

Both islands have deeply indented coasts with numerous rocks and reefs and the west coast backed by machair.

Colonsay is generally of good soil although the higher ground is moorland and scrub. Raised beaches on the west coast and sea beach debris in the interior mark a time when the land was lower in the sea and these were four separate islands. The economy depends on crofting, farming, a little fishing and some limited tourism. Visitors may wander freely throughout the island.

In the extreme north, in a low valley of sand-dunes running down to a fine beach, the remains of **Kilcatrine** (G. – Catherine's chapel) are marked by a standing stone and cross [NR 421999]. This may have been the site of a 13th century convent.

According to legend the MacNeils first came to the island with their cattle in an open boat. MacNeil's wife gave birth during the voyage and to keep her and the baby warm they slaughtered a cow so that they could lie inside the carcass.

Palm trees and bamboo now grow in the mild and sheltered Kiloran valley where Malcolm MacNeil built Colonsay House in 1722. He is said to have salvaged stones from an old church or abbey which was nearby. The gardens were once considered equal to Inverewe, Crarae, and Gigha (No.2.3) but Colonsay House is now partly converted to holiday flats and the gardens generally need maintanance.

The inevitable Piper's Cave where a piper and his dog went to hunt for hell is on the coast at Port Bàn. Only the dog reappeared but from a cave four miles south with his hair burned off. (One wonders why this legend occurs on so many of the Scottish islands, see Barra, Gigha, etc.)

The ferry pier was built at **Scalasaig** in 1965. This is the main village and two other centres of population are Kilchattan and Kiloran. The island has a junior school, a minister of the church and a resident doctor, but no policeman. There is a hotel, some summer cottages and bed-and-breakfast accommodation. The hotel at Scalasaig provides all the local tourist information. By the road between the hotel and the harbour is the Well of the South Wind where fishermen used to pray for a south wind and overlooking the village is an Iron Age fort, the most important of many on the island, called **Dùn Eibhinn** [NR 382944]. There is another one just to the north-east on Beinn nan Gudairean and this is also possibly the best viewpoint on the island [NR 388950].

On the west coast opposite Scalasaig between **Tobar Fuar** (G. – cold well) and **Port Lobh** (G. – the port that smells of seaweed) is an 18-hole golf course. This stretch of Colonsay coastline has many skerries and off-shore islets – **Eilean nam Ban** (G. – women's isle), **Eilean Dubh**, **Eilean a' Chladaich** (G. – shore isle), **Eilean na Bilearach** (G. – sea-grass isle), **Eilean Leathan** (G. – broad island) and the inevitable **Glas Eilean** (G. – pale grey-green isle). This is in contrast to the east coast which boasts only one islet – **Eilean Olmsa**.

Across the sea from the old burial ground at **Balerominmore** [NR 384914] in the south-east of Colonsay, which has a cross and carved slab, the Paps of Jura glow in the evening sun. Nearby at Garvard, overlooking the Strand, are the foundations of a cell or chapel, with a dun, and a standing stone.

ORONSAY has a very fine ruin, possibly second only to Iona in importance, of an Augustinian **Priory** built in *c.* 1380 which is probably on the same site as St Oran's original monastery of 563 [NR 350890]. This is a fascinating group of buildings in a reasonable state of preservation although, unfortunately, part of the stonework was removed by the MacNeils to build the adjacent farmhouse.

THE AUGUSTINIAN PRIORY ON ORONSAY

Some human bones from the neighbouring graveyard are kept by the high altar in the chapel and beautifully sculpted medieval tombstones are protected in a roofed building beyond the delightfully-proportioned miniature cloisters. Outside there is a remarkable 3.7m high Celtic cross on a mound. Oronsay is suffused with a feeling of tranquillity and it is easy to understand why St Oran chose it for a retreat (Columba is said to have rejected it because it was within sight of Ireland).

Archaeological excavations on Oronsay have shown evidence of a Middle Stone Age settlement and there are a number of Mesolithic shell mounds. The grass airstrip by the monastery fights a losing battle with the rabbits.

A reef of islets, **Eilean Ghaoideamal**, **Eilean an Eoin**, and some skerries, lies parallel to the east coast of Oronsay creating a channel, Caolas Mór, which is the only partially sheltered anchorage in the area. A small sandy beach called Tràigh Uamha Seilbhe (G. – beach of the caves used as stock-pens) faces the kyle.

On Eilean nan Ron (G. – seal island) at the most southern tip, beyond the sheep and ponies grazing on the landing strip, is the ruin of an old kelp-gatherer's cottage. The huge expanse of skerries round this islet is a favourite breeding ground for the grey Atlantic seal. A thousand or more converge here in the autumn each year and the roar of battling bulls can be heard for miles.

ACCESS: Cal-Mac vehicle ferry from Oban three times a week, 01631-66688. Ferry excursions arranged from Kennacraig and Port Askaig on Islay in the summer on Wednesdays allowing several hours stopover on Colonsay while the ferry calls at Oban, 01880-730253. There is an island post-bus and bicycles can be hired at the hotel.

Anchorages: There are no good anchorages.
1. Caolas Mór, Oronsay. Occasional anchorage in the bay opposite Eilean Ghaoideamal on a line between N extremity of En Ghaoideamal and boathouse on Oronsay. Beware reef Leac nan Geadh to the N which covers. Better shelter N of Leac nan Geadh in Port na h-Atha. Keep slightly to right of a line between the dyke on the Oronsay skyline (which reads vertically) and N tip of En Ghaoideamal and anchor when Leac nan Geadh is about abeam. There is a further bight N of En Ghaoideamal behind the reef extending S from Eilean Treadhrach which is sometimes favoured. 4-6m in all cases, bottom sand, but swell from S and E.
2. Eilean Treadhrach. Occasional anchorage sheltered from SW but negotiate with care, preferably at LW.
3. Loch Staosnaig. Anchor near head of bay towards S side, sand. Avoid line of submarine cable. Subject to swell but more room than Scalasaig.

4. Scalasaig harbour, anchor N of pier, but space very limited, sand. Or tie alongside N side of pier at the wave screen, if there is room. Open to E and subject to swell.
5. Kiloran Bay. Temp. anchorage off sandy beach. Subject to severe swell at times and dangerous in W'lies.
6. Port Mór, a bay central on W coast. Keep at least 5c clear of coast until line of the road passing the cemetery is completely open, then approach carefully on this line. The head shoals about 2c. Good shelter from E but subject to heavy S'ly swell.

2.7 Eilean Macaskin

(G – Macaskin's Island)

OS Maps: 1:50000 Sheet 55 1:25000 Sheet 377
Admiralty Chart: 1:25000 No.2326

AREA: 50ha (124 acres)
HEIGHT: 65m (213 ft)

OWNER: Mr David P G Sillar of Winscombe, Somerset.

POPULATION: 1841 – no separate census figures. 1881 – 6. 1891 – 0. No permanent habitation since.

GEOLOGY: Metamorphic epidiorite with some Dalradian quartzite at the south end.

WILDLIFE: Many wildflowers although not as prolific as on Eilean Righ (No.2.8).

EILEAN MACASKIN lies at the entrance to Loch Craignish and has a narrow rock-strewn but easily navigable channel up the east side. The island consists of a long ridge running parallel with the loch, 65m high at its highest point, steep on the west side but with a strip of relatively level ground on the east. It is comparatively well-wooded and comfortably sheltered except for the southern end which can catch the blast of the prevailing

THE ANCHORAGE BY GOATS ISLAND

EILEAN RIGH

Eilean nan Gabhar

Sheepfank

25·

wood

65·

woodland

Limekiln

Loch Craignish

N

1 km
1/2 mile

Eilean nan Laogh

Liath-sgeir Bheag

MAINLAND

Liath-sgeir Mhór

wind rushing up the Sound of Jura. A reef of skerries extends further south towards an islet called **Eilean nan Coinean** (G. – isle of the rabbits).

Eilean nan Gabhar (G. – island of the goats) lies between Eilean Righ (No.2.8) and Eilean Macaskin giving shelter to a pleasant little anchorage. It is steep, with patches of scrub cover, and more suitable for goats than sheep although the latter seem to cope quite well. The landing place for Eilean Macaskin is on a rocky grey sand beach at the north extremity which fringes some swampy

ground. Beyond, old wooden sheep pens stand in a bed of foxgloves. Well-built dry-stone dykes run along the ridges and the patches of woodland and scattered mature trees give the settled appearance of parkland.

To the south-west of Eilean Macaskin is the powerful tidal race of the Dorus Mór (G. – great door) which tumbles with force through the gateway between Craignish Point and the small island of **Garbh Rèisa** (G. – the rough one in the tidal race). At 43m height this could almost be considered a doorpost. Adjoining Garbh Rèisa is

Eilean na Cille (G. – chapel island). West of Craignish Point is **Rèisa an t-Sruith** (G. – the tidal-race island in the current) and north of it is **Rèisa Mhic Phaidean** (G. – McFadyen's island in the tidal race). These little islands are all fairly insignificant rocks but they are worthy of respect when the tide is in full flood.

ACCESS: No regular access but enquire at Ardfern on Loch Craignish.

Anchorages:

1. Eilean nan Gabhar (G – goat island), N of En Macaskin. Anchor in limited space between the N end of the skerry and the reef which lies alongside the E side of Goat Island, 3-4m, firm sand and clay.

2. Temp anchorage in small bay at NE corner but restricted swinging space and bottom falls away rapidly.

2.8 Eilean Righ

[elan ree] (G. – royal island) May have been named after the Danish sea-king Olaf who is reputed to have died in this region, or one of the early Scottish kings who were crowned in mid-Argyll.

OS Maps: 1:50000 Sheet 55 1:25000 Sheet 365
Admiralty Chart: 1:25000 2326

AREA: 86ha (213 acres)
HEIGHT: 55m (180 ft)

OWNER: Bought by Viscount Chewton (a Somerset farmer and brother of the government minister, Mr William Waldegrave) in 1992 for £250,000. 'I couldn't resist it,' he said. Having spent all his childhood holidays on Scot-

Eilean Righ

S

tish islands he wanted his sons to have the same experience. He grazes sheep.

POPULATION: 1841 – no separate census figures. 1881 – 0. 1891 – 5 (2 houses). 1931 – 7. Uninhabited since but occasional occupation.

GEOLOGY: Mainly epidiorite and allied metamorphosed igneous rocks.

HISTORY: Once belonged to Sir Reginald Fleming Johnston, ex-tutor of Pu Yi, the last emperor of China. He was the author of *Twilight in the Forbidden City* and he was portrayed by Peter O'Toole in the film, *The Last Emperor.*

WILDLIFE: A fairly large area of mature woodland with oak, ash, rowan, alder and hawthorn spreads along the east shore. There is rich pasture for sheep, scattered with buttercups, ragged-robin and yellow flag, with clumps of reeds and ubiquitous bracken but very little heather. Wintering divers and wildfowl can be seen here from October to March.

There are wild mussel beds by the shoreline.

EILEAN RIGH is snugly situated in Loch Craignish between Eilean Macaskin (No.2.7) to the south-west and the tidal **Eilean Mhic-Chrion** (G. – MacNiven's Island) to the north across the loch.

Although it is a fairly small island it was evidently of some importance in ancient times for it has the remnants of two Iron Age duns and a name with royal connections. It is not known if the forts were contemporaneous or not but there is a further fort on the tiny Eilean na Nighinn which is part of **Eilean Dubh** on the north side of the loch. These would have controlled access to the head of the loch.

On Eilean Righ, the most northerly dun is 650m NNE of the house, set on the grassy summit of the ridge. It is oval-shaped and a number of minor artefacts were uncovered during excavation in 1982 [NM804022]. The second dun is south-west of the house at the summit of a flat-topped ridge. It is rectangular in plan with an oval structure in the south corner [NM800014].

The south side of the highest point, Dun Righ, has an interesting example of a large cup-mark on the lichen-covered rock [NM798010].

The former owner, Sir Reginald Johnston, modernised the island's two houses in 1934 and the farmhouse buildings were again being renovated in 1993. The road from the jetty climbs steeply through a dense belt of mixed woodland, stippled with primroses amid a tangle of brambles, before reaching the attractive group of buildings which are set round a courtyard with a central flagpole. They were said to contain a Buddhist temple and lantern built by Sir Reginald.

It is also said that when Sir Reginald died valuable porcelain and china were thrown into the loch, but I have been unable to establish any reason for this strange behaviour or even whether the story is true or not.

ACCESS: No regular access but enquire at Ardfern on Loch Craignish.

Anchorages:
1. Good anchorage centre of E coast of the island, below the farmhouse, 5m. Anchor at S end of the bay, NNE of the jetty, as N end is foul with weed. Shoal runs out for 50m in line with 2-storey gable of farmhouse.

2.9 Scarba

(ON skarpoe – sharp, stony, hilly terrain). Alternatively, but less likely,
(G. sgarbh, or ON skarf – cormorant, ON -øy – island)

OS Maps: 1:50000 Sheet 55 1:25000 Sheet 365
Admiralty Charts: 1:25000 Nos.2326 or 2343

AREA: 1,474ha (3,642acres)
HEIGHT: 449m (1,473 ft)

OWNER: The family of Lord Duncan Sandys, one-time Minister of State. Formerly owned by the late Mrs Yvonne Studd-Trench-Gascoigne of Leeds.

POPULATION: 1794 – 50 (14 families). 1881 – 19. 1891 – 9. 1931 – 5. 1961 – 5. Only occasional habitation since the 1960s.

GEOLOGY: Schist and slate in the east and quartzite in the west. A conglomerate of quartzite, limestone, and shale lies between, known as 'Scarba Conglomerate'.

HISTORY: This was the site of an early Christian settlement. At the end of the 18th century the island was divided into two farms.

WILDLIFE: There are many red deer, some wild goats, and otters live among the rockfalls below the coastline cliffs. Sheep and the famous breed of Luing cattle are grazed here. Although drainage channels have been recently cut and new fencing erected to improve the grazing, the ground is still very rough with heather, bracken and tufts of boggy grass and sphagnum moss. Ragged-robin and at least two different varieties of orchid give vivid splashes of colour among the tussocks.

Natural oak woodland and scrub are scattered over parts of the east coast below the 50m contour. Together with some patches of planted conifers at a higher level, these attract a variety of birdlife.

SCARBA is a single mountain top which rises straight out of the sea to a height of 449m. It is set between two notoriously dangerous tidal races, the Corryvreckan to the south and the Grey Dogs to the north. Its coasts are bleak and rugged with many great caves. The west flank is the most precipitous, the heather slopes tumbling steeply to the shore rocks with many unstable boulders covered by vegetation. Cut into this face is an exceptionally high raised beach – over 30m above sea level.

Above **Port nan Urrachann**, a bay on the west coast, the faint remains of Iron Age dwellings have been reported at the top of an ancient path which zig-zags up the steep slope.

The east side is gentler, with a small patch of land fit for cultivation, and some scattered woodland. **Kilmory Lodge**, the main house, is situated here and it is occasionally occupied by members of the owner's family. Below the Lodge and by the eastern shore, south-west of Port a' Chaibeil, is an ancient chapel ruin, **Cille Mhoire an Caibel** (G. – Mary's Church of the family graveyard) [NM718057]. The walls are still 1½m high but the only

recognisable feature is the doorway. This was almost certainly the 'chapel of the Blessed Virgin, where many miracles occur' – mentioned by John Fordun in 1380 or thereabouts. The burial ground was abandoned in the mid 19th century. There are reports of nearby remnants of rudimentary beehive cells but I have been unable to confirm this. If true, then – who knows? – Scarba may have rivalled Eileach an Naoimh (No.2.12) as a favourite retreat for the monks of Iona. Just south of the chapel is a cave [NM718055] which had associations with the early Christian community and beyond it and above the coastline trees is **Blàr nan Sìth**, which could be freely translated from the Gaelic as the Elysian Field!

Beside the road which leads from the pier to the Lodge there is an empty cist with a dislodged capstone. The islanders' village settlement was north of the Lodge.

Like so many of the Hebridean islands, Scarba had a reputation for healthy living and longevity – Martin Martin reported in the 17th century that an old woman had just died on Scarba aged 140, still having possession of all her faculties – but it also has its share of myths. The ghosts of evil sailors walk Scarba's cliffs as a penance. Others are chased by the Grey Dog which was drowned between Scarba and Lunga and which had belonged to Prince Breacan of Lochlann. To escape the dog's drooling fangs the phantoms must confess their crimes and these cries can be heard after dark on moonless nights.

There is a small cottage above the anchorage in **Bàgh Gleann a' Mhaoil** (G. – bay in the cleft of the mull) which is used in the summer by an adventure school. School children are given training in survival techniques after which they are taken by boat to various uninhabited islands and abandoned for a few days (see No.2.14). They live in caves and off the land – even when on Scarba itself – for the cottage is used only by the wardens. It sounds tough, but the wardens assured us that the children often come back again for more punishment!

The bay has a beach of large, multi-coloured pebbles. There is an interesting trudge up the ridge beside the bothy, then the next ridge and the next again. The going is rough: tufts of ankle-twisting grass, heather, and bracken with boggy patches between. Behind the ridges there is a small loch – **Loch Airigh a' Chruidh** (G. – loch in the horseshoe-shaped pasture) beside a vestigial path. Only a narrow earth barrier stops this loch emptying itself nearly 300m down the mountain-side. Following the path round the contours until it disappears brings you to the head of a steep gully which falls dramatically down to Camas nam Bàirneach (G. – limpet creek) and a deep-set cave. Beyond the creek is the main Corryvreckan whirlpool – a thrilling viewpoint! Deer spy on you from every rocky height.

THE BOTHY IN GLEANN A' MHAOIL

The footpath, which encircles part of the mountain, starts from the sheep fank above Kilmory Lodge. The easiest climb to the peak, **Cruach Scarba** (G. *cruach* – stack), and the low spine of rock at the top is from this path where it traverses the east side of the mountain. From the sheep fank it is also possible to reach the rough vehicle track which leads to Bàgh Gleann a' Mhaoil.

The tides run though the **Corryvreckan** (G. *coire bhreacain* – the speckled cauldron), west on the flood and east on the ebb, at speeds of up to ten knots. Beneath this channel is the rock-strewn record of some great primaeval cataclysm. There is a ridge running out from Camas nan Bàirneach on Scarba with a solitary rock stack on the end of it which rears up 44m and comes within 29m of the surface of the sea. When a westerly blows against the flood during a spring tide the noise of the violent overfalls can be heard many miles away. Local fishermen call the whirlpool which forms at these times over this submarine rock pinnacle, the Cailleach, (G. – the old woman). According to legend a hag controls the maelstrom and decides which ships will sink and which survive. There are also enormous breakers and violent eddies elsewhere. Another submerged rock stack is in the centre of the Gulf and beside it a great narrow pit like a gateway to hell which descends 100m below the surrounding seabed to an overall depth of 219m.

The early writers' descriptions are interesting. Martin Martin declared: 'The sea begins to boil and ferment with the tide of flood, and resembles the boiling of a pot; and then increases gradually, until it appears in many whirlpools which form themselves in sort of pyramids and immediately after spout up as high as the mast of a little vessel and at the same time make a loud report.' And John MacCulloch said: 'Impossible to be engaged in this place without anxiety. . .danger is always impending. The error of a few minutes might have been the price of as many lives. . .'.

There is a short period at slack water when it is safe to sail through the Corryvreckan but the timing has to be accurate. Even then, the turgid eddies, sudden movements and whorls sucking at the surface as the water spills over the irregular rock formations deep below create a palpable sense of menace.

ACCESS: Summer excursions by arrangement with MacLachlan, Luing, 0185-24282 or try Craobh Haven, 0185-25222.

Anchorages:
1. Bàgh Gleann a' Mhaoil, at the SW corner of Scarba. Occasional anchorage out of the tidal currents in 9m, sand with some weed. Exposed to S and SE

and can be subject to swell. Avoid approach when tide is running strongly or conditions adverse.

2. Port a' Chaibeil. Temporary anchorage due W of Kilmory Lodge in 8-10m.

3. Poll na h-Ealaidh and jetty. A very restricted little landing-place on N side of promontory by Kilmory Lodge.

4. An Gleann. Temp anchorage in quiet conditions off centre of inlet. (Interesting walk to see the 'Grey Dogs')

5. Port nan Urrachann, on W side. Approach from N using chart to avoid rocks and shallows, and anchor in 10-12m, sand. Exposed SW-N-NE, out of the tide but can be subject to swell.

2.10 Shuna

Possibly, (G. sidhean – fairy, ON -øy – island), but probably of Norse origin.

OS Maps: 1:50000 Sheet 55 1:25000 Sheet 365
Admiralty Charts: 1:25000 Nos.2326 or 2343

AREA: 451ha (1,114 acres)
HEIGHT: 90m (295 ft)

OWNER: Dowager and Viscount Selbey.

POPULATION: 1841 – 69 (10 houses). 1881 – 14. 1891 – 11. 1931 – 12. 1961 – 3. 1971 – 3. 1981 – 8. 1991 – 1.

GEOLOGY: Shuna was one of the small group of islands cut off from the mainland by the Firth of Lorn glacier in the last Ice Age. Unlike neighbouring Luing there is no workable slate on Shuna, the rock is mainly phyllite and mica-schist, but on the west side a band of attractive blue crystalline limestone used to be worked.

HISTORY: A small rectangular enclosure just north of Shuna farmhouse holds a tombstone commemorating John McLean of Shuna and his wife Mary Campbell. This was probably the John McLean who died in 1787 and whose son, Alexander, was the last of the McLeans to own the island. The McLeans' original liferent was granted by Lord Neil Campbell in 1679.

When the owner, James Yates, died in 1829 he bequeathed Shuna to the City of Glasgow with the stipulation that the income should be 'devoted to benevolent purposes'. The Corporation preferred the capital value and sold the island to a private purchaser.

WILDLIFE: The very thick growth of alder, birch, hazel and scrub oak attracts a variety of birds and woodland plants.

SHUNA lies between Luing and Craobh Haven. Shuna House, a castellated mansion stands at the north-west corner of the island with a view towards Loch Melfort. It is now partly ruinous but one of the owner's sons occupies a nearby estate house.

The island is grazed by sheep and there is a fish farm on the north-east side with a resident manager. Some of the estate cottages have been renovated and are let for holiday use.

In the north bay there is an old stone quay on the west side at **Rubh' an Aoil** (G. – lime-plaster headland), no doubt named when limestone was being quarried on the island. Over on the east side is **Rubha Salach** (G. – foul headland). By an inlet which floods at high water, the wreck of an old wooden ferry *The Maid of Luing*, with a turntable and a livestock hold, lies on the rocks. It is a difficult walk round the shoreline which requires scrambling over hard vertical slabs of grey aerated rock like petrified Dunlopillo. Striking inland is no easier as sheep tracks mysteriously disappear and the tangled growth of alder, birch and undergrowth in the mossy humps and ravines is almost impenetrable.

Round the corner, on the west coast, is **Port na Cro** (G. – the sheep-pen port) which is too small and shallow for anything but a dinghy.

Shuna House is more distinguished and substantial when seen from a distance. Its scale is misleading. An estate road runs diagonally across the island connecting it with **Shuna Cottage** (which is actually a solid two-storeyed house rather than a cottage) in the south-west.

Roughly in the centre of the island it passes **Druim na Dubh Ghlaic** (G. – The ridge by the black hollow) which is the highest point at 90m. A burn runs down the 'black hollow' to Port an t-Salainn (G. – the salt port) on the east side. South of this is further dense woodland in the Coille Mhór (G. – the big wood), and Poll na Gile (G. – clear pool), a little cove on the east coast.

The southern extremity, called Shuna Point, is marked by a prehistoric cairn, and there are two more cairns at **Rubh an Trilleachainn** (G. – oystercatcher point) behind Shuna Cottage [NM759075]. One of these is a chambered cairn which has been extensively robbed at some time in the past.

A remarkable hoard of three bronze swords, possibly dating from the 8th century BC, was discovered on Shuna sticking point-down in the peat. They may have been placed in this way as a votive offering.

There are several islets near Shuna – **Eilean Gamhna** (G. – farrow cow island) and **Eilean Creagach** (G. – craggy island) to the north east; **Eilean Buidhe** (G. – yellow island) and **Eilean an Dùin** (G. – island of the fort) to the east now form part of the Craobh Haven marina breakwater. Together with **Eilean Arsa** (G. – ancient island) they used to be known as the Craobh islands. The old fort on Eilean an Dùin was, regrettably, virtually demolished when the breakwater was built. Craobh, incidentally means a tree in Gaelic but it can also refer to bubbles on a glass of whisky – a much more poetic interpretation.

ACCESS: No regular access but enquire at Craob Haven.

Anchorages:
1. Bay at N of Shuna with remnants of a stone quay on its west side. Anchor no further in than abreast the quay, 3m, mud and sand. There is a drying reef on SW side and a large part of the bay is shoal. Note submerged rock about 3/4c N of the E point of the bay.

2.11 Lunga

(N langr-øy – isle of the longships) or (G long – ship, N -øy – island)

OS Maps: 1:50000 Sheet 55 1:25000 Sheet 365 and 354
Admiralty Charts: 1:25000 2326 or 2386

AREA: 254ha (628 acres)
HEIGHT: 98m (321 ft)

OWNER: Colin Lindsay MacDougall (who can claim direct descent from Somerled).

POPULATION: 1794 – 29 (6 families). 1881 – 17. 1891 – 15 (3 families in 1 house). 1931 – 5. 1961 – 0. 1971 – 0. 1981 – 33. 1991 – 2.

GEOLOGY: Schist and micaschist run northwards towards the small 'slate' island of Belnahua, but the west, and part of the 'drying-islands' to the north, are of 'Scarba con-glomerate' (see No 2.9).

WILDLIFE: Grazed by domestic sheep and Luing cattle. Golden eagles can often be seen over Bidein na h-Iolaire.

LUNGA is an untidy island, all humps and bumps, rocks

and bogs, and a misshapen coastline which disintegrates into smaller tidal islands in the north – **Rubha Fiola** (G. – eagle point), **Fiola Meadhonach** (G. – middle eagle) – these are sometimes called North and South Fullah, **Eilean Iosal** (G. – humble island) and **Fiola an Droma** (G. – eagle ridge). It is fortunate to have a reasonable anchorage sheltered from the prevailing wind just north of the skerry in Poll nan Corran (G. – the sickle-shaped pool) where there is a pebble beach. Golden eagles circle slowly above the dominant hill, Bidein na h-Iolaire (G. – pinnacle of the eagle) and seem to be acting a part – keen to prove that this really is eagle territory.

Walking on the island is not easy but the Luing cattle which graze there have trampled a number of muddy trails through the scrub. There are rock formations which could be mistaken for standing stones from a distance and many wildflowers in the crevices.

Tobar a Challuim-Chille (G. – the well of St Columba's church), a fresh-water spring bubbling into a mossy rectangular trough of ancient flagstones, is beyond the central ridge in the north-west [NM704090]. This has never run dry and in times of drought was used by the slate quarry workers from Belnahua. There are three houses on the main island, all of which have been renovated.

One of the tidal islands, Rubha Fiola, is run as an adventure centre. It has a timber chalet for accommodation built beside the remains of an old blackhouse.

The graves of some of the past inhabitants of Lunga are to be found in the burial ground of Kilchattan on Luing (No.2.13).

The channel between Lunga and Scarba is the famous **Bealach a' Choin Ghlais**, (G. – the pass of the Grey Dogs). This can be almost as dangerous as the Corryvreckan as a sly tide pounds through at over 8 knots. The channel is narrow and divided by **Eilean a' Bhealaich**. When the tide is at full flood the water south of the island is at two distinct levels with a spectacular downhill torrent. There is another dangerous overfall at the narrowest point after which the race rushes westwards for another two miles passing **Guirasdeal** rock (32m high).

Ormsa islet lies directly north of Lunga and beyond it is the slate island of **Belnahua**. Belnahua has a very extensive drying reef to the north-west. The visible part of the island is tiny and yet it supported a major slate industry. Now all that remains is the shattered quarry cutting deep into the heart of the island and the grey, deserted slate-workers' cottages. Beside Belnahua the islet of **Fladda** with its lighthouse is a well-known sea-mark in the Sound of Luing.

ACCESS: Summer excursions by arrangement with MacLachlan, Luing, 0185-24282.

Anchorages:
1. Poll nan Corran (Puill a' Charrain). A bay on the E side. Approach from NE and anchor N of the Sgeir, off centre of pebble beach, 8-9m, mud. Partially exposed to E, otherwise reasonably sheltered.
2. Camas a' Mhór-Fhir. S-facing bay on W side of Lunga, outside Grey Dogs. Anchor near head of bay according to depth, 4-10m. Exposed S to W.

2.12 Eileach an Naoimh

*[**el**-uchĕn **noe**:v] (G. – rocky place of the saint). According to Watson the correct name is* na h-Eileacha Naomha *(G. – the Holy Rocks).*

OS Maps: 1:50000 Sheet 55 1:25000 Sheet 354 and 365
Admiralty Charts: 1:75000 2169 1:25000 2386

AREA: 56ha (138 acres)
HEIGHT: 80m (262 ft)

OWNER: All the monuments are in the care of the Secretary of State for Scotland.

POPULATION: Uninhabited for many centuries.

GEOLOGY: The strata, mainly of limestone and Dalradian calcareous slate but with some sandstone, are severely tilted up to the north-west where they are exposed as steep cliffs falling directly to a continuous rock-platform at sea-level. The south-east slopes are sheltered and fertile.

HISTORY: This is generally agreed to be Hinba [**een**-ba] the island mentioned by Adomnan: 'Inba' in early Gaelic means 'Isle of the Sea' and 'Hinba' is the plural. However Watson, in *Celtic Place Names of Scotland*, disagrees and considers that Jura has a much better claim to the title.

A monastery was founded here by St Brendan of Clonfert in AD 542, twenty-one years before St Columba founded Iona. Although continuing to enjoy some significance as a religious shrine, the island appears to have remained unpopulated ever since the monastery was destroyed by Norsemen, probably in the early 10th century.

WILDLIFE: The soil bedded on limestone gives an ideal growing medium and the verdant hillsides all face south. Provided no sheep have been grazing on the island, the grassy slopes and rocky crevices are covered with scarlet pimpernel, primrose, blue pansy, spotted orchids, spring cinque-foil, yellow iris, meadow-sweet, honeysuckle and many other species.

The rare corncrake may still nest here.

If the wind is very light, and the portents good, one could be tempted to risk an overnight stop although as a West Highland friend once claimed: '. . . only a very brave man would spend the night on **EILEACH AN NAOIMH**, it is so peopled by ghosts.'

The original Celtic monks searched for communion with God in the lonely deserts of the ocean, emulating the devotion of St John the Baptist. It was in the spirit of this search for solitude that St Brendan established his monastery here. Later it is supposed to have become the favourite retreat of his nephew, St Columba, who loved it as much as Iona and who came here for peace and contemplation. His mother, Eithne, Princess of Leinster, is also supposed to be buried here. A small upright slate slab roughly incised with a cross marks the spot near the top of a little hillock south of the monastery ruins [NM639096].

The landing place is inside a lagoon formed by a line of skerries, **Sgeirean Dubha**. **Port Chaluim Chille** (G. – the port for Columba's church) – a tiny creek with a shingle beach, and a fresh-water spring in a stone basin overgrown with watercress is at the foot of a gully which leads up to a shallow amphitheatre below the slope of **Dun Bhreanain**, the spinal ridge. The hollow shelters the low, broken walls of the **Monastery** and **Church** [NM640097].

These are thought to date from the 9th century as St Brendan's earlier structures would almost certainly have been of wood. It has been suggested that the stone ruins might not have been the monastery at all, but a monk's farmhouse and byre although it is probably older than the church with its chancel and mortared walls.

Just north of these ruins is a small cell structure and beyond it the **Chapel**. Its walls are nearly 1m thick and it measures about 6.7m by 3.7m with only one indecipher

...SEMI-DETACHED BEEHIVE CELLS

able carved slab inside. There is open space by the chapel with a low vallum or rampart at the foot of the hillside.

Among other artifacts in the area are the remains of a stone oven or kiln with a fireplace and flue in which the monks baked their bread, or maybe dried corn. This is north of the chapel and to the east is a structure that may have been a winnowing barn.

A natural rock 'pulpit' stands by the landing-place near the shore and on the slope above it (about 90m east of the chapel) there are two partly-reconstructed 'semi-d' beehive cells [NM641097]. These are the finest Scottish examples of the ancient structures and only some cells on a cliff ledge of Skellig Michael Rock off Southern Ireland are better preserved. One of the cells of the Clochain – as this double cell is called – could have been an oratory with an underground cell beside it, like a Pictish souterrain, which may have been a wine cellar.

West of the landing place are two enclosures, the further being a herb garden. The burial ground beside it has a number of upended slabs, one of which bears a cross. It was reported in 1824, when the ruins were rediscovered, that there were many carved tombs, ornamented stones and crosses but through the years these have all been stolen.

The north end of the island sports a splendid natural sandstone arch, **An Chlàrsach** (G. – The Harp), gouged out at the time when the raised beaches were being formed. This can be reached by an interesting but rough walk along the shore. Beyond the skerry of **Sgeir Leth a' Chuain** is the islet of **A' Chuli** (G. – the retreat) on which there was once a chapel. St Brendan is reputed to have been buried here. A bracing walk back to the landing place on the springy turf along the top of the ridge is rewarding. On one side – larks singing above the lush grass; on the other – the sea frothing at the foot of the cliffs.

ACCESS: Summer excursions by arrangement with MacLachlan, Luing, 0185-24282.

Anchorages:
1. Occasional anchorage on SE side between island and line of skerries and islets. Approach from E through SW side of main gap in the skerries, or

from SW keeping parallel to, and fairly close to, the line of skerries. Anchor off the old landing-place, or E of drying/submerged rocks in NE pool. Too exposed for overnight stay except in very settled conditions.

2.13 Luing

[ling] (G. long – ship) or, (ON lyng – heather)

OS Maps: 1:50000 Sheet 55 1:25000 Sheets 354 and 365
Admiralty Charts: 1:75000 No.2169 1:25000 No.2326

AREA: 1,543ha (3,813 acres)
HEIGHT: 94m (308 ft)

OWNER: Multiple ownership but most of the agricultural land is owned by Cadzow Brothers of Kilpunt Farm, West Lothian.

POPULATION: 1841 – no separate census figures. 1881 – 527. 1891 – 632. 1931 – 312. 1961 – 187. 1971 – 151. 1981 – 183. 1991 – 180.

GEOLOGY: Predominantly graphitic schists and slate. The north end has large partially-quarried slate deposits but the north part of the central ridge is of hornblende-schist.

WILDLIFE: There are no rabbits but there are stoats. The birdlife is similar to the adjacent mainland and pipistrelle bats can be seen at Ardinamir on summer evenings. Wild boar were once common on the Scottish mainland but Luing is one of the few islands on which remains have been found.

LUING is an easy island to reach from the mainland as there is a fast and regular vehicle ferry service across the 200m wide Cuan Sound which separates it from the island of Seil (Seil in turn is linked to the mainland by the famous Clachan Bridge.) The spring tides rush through the Cuan Sound at nine miles per hour creating a 'step' in the water as the flood builds up a difference of level.

Slate was the principal industry on Luing and was still being quarried here beside the main village of Cullipool until 1965. 150 skilled men were employed and 700,000 slates were produced each year. Iona Cathedral is roofed with Luing slates. Now livestock farming is the principal activity, in particular the famous and unique herd of prize beef cattle bred by the island's owners.

Luing's other claim to fame is as a lobster-fishing centre. The lobster pond between **Eilean Loisgte** and **Fraoch Eilean** (G. – heather island) is one of the largest in Scotland.

Cullipool (G. – boat pool) is a pretty village of white-washed cottages. These were the slateworkers' houses but most are now holiday homes or have been purchased by retired couples. In the evening the old slate workings to the north have a sculptural quality with subtle colours in the strata and to the west, across the many tiny islets in the Sound of Luing with Lunga and the Isles of the Sea beyond, there are the most magnificent Atlantic sunsets.

The secure little anchorage of **Ardinamir** (G. – headland by the bed of the river) is very popular but the entrance has to be negotiated with great care. Until 1991 its popularity owed much to Irene McLachlin who lived alone in her croft beside it – with her cat, McElvie. She kept the leading mark freshly painted and should a yachtsman run aground she would offer friendly advice in a voice which could be heard on the mainland. As an honorary member of the Clyde Cruising Club she had a register of every visiting yacht since the 1940s and prided herself on never forgetting a name. Irene spent many happy hours sitting at the open window admiring the West Coast Drizzle. McElvie, a very big cat with pink eyes, always occupied the single armchair.

On the hill above Ardinamir, just north of Irene's house, is a large Iron Age fort, **Dun Ballycastle** [NM752121], and further south on the next hill is another one, **Dun Leccamore**, which has the remains of a stairway and several rooms [NM751108].

Above the attractive village of **Toberonochy** beside the bay and overlooking Shuna (No.2.10) stands the bleak well-tended ruin of Kilchatton chapel which was abandoned after 1685 [NM745091]. It is surrounded by slate gravestones including the grave of Covenanter Alex Campbell who 'digged my grave before I died'. On his tombstone he advises against '. . .women that wear Babylonish garments. . .men that have whiskers. . .Quakers, Tabernacle folk, Haldians, Independents, Anabaptists. . .' and so on.

At the centre of the island, near the ruined water mill, is the Fairy Knoll where visitors (who can spare one) are expected to place a hair on top to please the sprites.

The island's highest point, **Binnein Furachail** (G. – the outlook pinnacle) is 87m (285 ft). It lies on the central axis midway between Ardinamir and Poll Gorm (G. – the azure pool).

Luing has a number of satellite islands linked to each other or Luing itself when the tide is out. **Eilean Mhic-Chiarain** and **Glas Eilean** in the west, **Rubh' Aird Luing** in the south, and, in the north-east, **Torsa** (ON – Thor's island) and **Torsa Beag** which are permanently joined by a narrow strip of land. The sole habitation on Torsa is a farmhouse on the south side by Ardinamir which was occupied until the 1960s but is now only occasionally inhabited. On the north side the ruined 16th century fortress of **Caisteal nan Con** (G. – castle of the dogs) [NM766136] was the site of a hunting lodge for the Lords of the Isles and may also have given the Cuan Sound its name, although (G. *cuan* – ocean inlet) is more probable.

ACCESS: By car ferry from Seil, across the Cuan Sound. Frequent, daily service. Five minutes crossing time.

Anchorages:
1. Kilchatton Bay (Toberonochy) on E side about 2M N of Rubh' Aird Luing, good anchorage in 5.5m to 11m; sheltered except from SSW winds. Bay shoals rapidly all round and head dries out about ³/₄c. Avoid disturbing scientific research buoys.
2. Ardinamir bay, between NE side of Luing and SW bend of Torsa. Small shallow cove. Very narrow entrance channel between a rock drying 0.3m and an extensive rock ledge and shoal off Torsa shore with similar rock drying 1.5m opposite on Luing shore. Holding sometimes poor due to weed.
3. Cuan Sound. More secure than Ardinamir in S winds. Anchor off boat house slipway on Luing, SW of the Cleit Rock, 5m, sand and rock, but avoid drying reef just N of boathouse and foul ground near the islet.
4. Port Mary, a small creek on the W side, about 2³/₄c SW of Cuan point. Fairly shallow and exposed but useful temp anchorage between the shore and the closer of two off-lying islets.

IRENE'S HOME AT ARDINAMIR

5. Cullipool. An interesting anchorage provided sailing directions are followed carefully. Least depth in narrow N channel is 3.3m. There are leading marks for the W approach.
6. Glas Ford and Back o' the Pond, S of Cullipool. Needs careful negotiation at the right state of the tide. Secure anchorage but follow directions carefully.
7. Black Mill bay on W side, about 2M NNW of Rubh' Ard Luing. The head of the bay shoals ¹/₂c. Pier on S side of bay. Exposed to W.
8. Bàgh na h-Aird (Ard Bay) at SE corner. Temp anchorage 1c off-shore but very exposed.

2.14 Eilean Dubh Mór

(G. – big black island) and Eilean Dubh Beag [bek] (G. – little black island)

OS Maps: 1:50000 Sheet 55 1:25000 Sheet 365
Admiralty Charts: 1:75000 2169 1:25000 2386

AREA: 65ha (161 acres)
HEIGHT: 53m (174 ft)

POPULATION: No census records and uninhabited.

GEOLOGY: Graphite schist with some quartzite interspersed with 'Scarba conglomerate'.

WILDLIFE: Droppings and bones would indicate that deer occasionally swim over from Lunga. There are many nesting herring gulls with black-backed gulls waiting to pirate their nests and fledglings.

Among the numerous wildflowers are large patches of the low-growing Burnet rose (*rosa pimpinellifolia*).

There are a few rocks in the sea to the north-east of the anchorage between **EILEAN DUBH MOR** and Eilean Dubh Beag which must be avoided so boats normally approach from due north or round the top of Eilean Dubh Beag. The amount of swinging room is misleading. I have been told that the Highland Yacht Club sometimes uses this location for musters and that on one occasion forty boats anchored here!

Eilean Dubh Mór is composed of a single mound-shaped hill, 53m high connected by a saddle to a promontory on the north-east side which also has a small hill on it. The terrain is heather, rocks, peaty bog-land and bracken. There is a very small raised beach in the central saddle, just a patch of pebbles which is bare of heather. On the south-west side of the saddle is a cove with cliffs round it and a cave. Further south another cave has a raised platform within it. A large quantity of dry bracken on the platform showed that it sometimes served as a bed. The shoreline is rocky with small cliffs and indentations

summed up by the name of the headland on the west side, Rubha Mosach (G. – the mean and nasty headland).

Eilean Dubh Beag (15ha) is almost a miniature replica of its big brother (or sister?) but it lacks the extra appendage. It is just a simple hump, 40m high, surrounded by lichen and seaweed covered rocks. The narrow channel between the two islands could almost be a man-made canal and is said only to dry out at the very lowest of tides.

These islands are used sometimes by the adventure schools of Lunga (No.2.11) and Scarba (No.2.9). Children are left on them to survive for a week. They have to swim ashore, live in the caves and catch rabbits or crabs for food. Whatever the rigours there are, no doubt, compensations. It is surprising how often in these beautiful surroundings one will awaken to a clear still morning with air like a sparkling wine. What promise of excitement and adventure!

There are, by the way, poles set on every eminence. Their purpose, in case you wonder, is that the children are expected to tie something to them should they need help. . .

ACCESS: Summer excursions by arrangement with MacLachlan, Luing, 0185-24 282.

Anchorages:
1. E end of the channel between the islands. Approach from N keeping ¹/₂c off En Dubh Beag. Anchor as near the channel as convenient, off E side of Dubh Beag, or N of the promontory between the two foul bays on Dubh Mór, 4-10m, good holding when the weed can be avoided. Exposed N to E and occasional swell.

2.15 Garbh Eileach

*[ga:rv **el**uch] (G. – rough rocky mound)*

OS Maps: 1:50000 Sheet 55 1:25000 Sheet 354
Admiralty Charts: 1:75000 2169 1:25000 2386

AREA: 142ha (351 acres)
HEIGHT: 110m (361 ft)

POPULATION: No census records. Uninhabited.

GEOLOGY: This archipelago includes two members of the Dalriadan sequence, a white or pale limestone and a group which is largely quartzite and could be called the Boulder Beds. The strata are in a succession of sharp folds with white limestone at the core.

Garbh Eileach

VIEW FROM THE LANDING PLACE

summit of the ridge. The highest point is difficult to locate, but is at the most northern extremity with almost vertical cliffs tumbling down to the sea below. For rock-climbers the limestone ledges are like the Dolomites in miniature.

ACCESS: Summer excursions by arrangement with MacLachlan, Luing, 0185-24 282.

Anchorages:

1. Occasional anchorage in small bay in middle of SE side. There is a drying rock approx 1/4c directly S of the islet, Sgeir a' Phuirt, on E side of the bay. Anchor E of concrete slip, thick weed over sand. There are mooring points on the islet, N of the islet and on the slipway.

HISTORY: Signs of the past which prove that Garbh Eileach had its place in history alongside its better known neighbour are the remains of an ancient fort near the landing place and a small burial ground, Cladh Dhuban (G. – Duban's graveyard), with rough tombstones.

WILDLIFE: A small herd of red deer is resident and the scattered patches of birch woodland attract a variety of birds.

The largest of the Isles of the Sea, **GARBH EILEACH** has not the same historical interest as Eileach an Naoimh but is still worth exploring. Just north-east of it, separated by a navigable channel, there is the small island of **Dùn Chonnuill** (G. – Conal's castle) with a ruined 13th century castle probably built by the Macdougalls or by MacLean of Duart when he was given the island by Robert III about 1400. This is reputed to stand on the site of an earlier fortress built in the 1st century by a minor Ulster king, Conal Cearnach.

The Isles of the Sea form a small archipelago of violently tilted rock-strata. As with the others, Garbh Eileach's north-western side is steep cliff whilst its south-eastern side has a grassy slope. The island is split almost centrally by a deep cleft, **Bealach an Tarabairt** (G. – the pass at the isthmus), where there is a small burn of clear water which has filtered through the limestone.

On the south side by the landing place, a stone bothy is still maintained in reasonable condition for occasional use as living quarters. Sheep and cattle ferried over from Luing graze on the lush green grass, and occasionally one of the herdsmen will stay for a day or two, but apart from that the island is only inhabited by memories.

There are magnificent and extensive views from the

2-Appendix Seil

Derivation uncertain but possibly derived from the Indo-European root sal-meaning stream, flowing water, current (eg. R. Shiel, Loch Moidart).

OS Maps: 1:50000 Sheet 55 (and 49) 1:25000 Sheet 354 (and 343)
Admiralty Charts: 1:75000 No.2169 1:25000 No.2386

AREA: 1,329ha (3,285 acres)
HEIGHT: 146m (479 ft)

OWNER: Multiple ownership.

POPULATION: 1881 - 661. 1891 - 548 (122 houses). 1931 - 367. 1961 - 303. 1971 - 326. 1981 - 459. 1991 - 506.

GEOLOGY: Large deposits of slate at the southern end of Seil were quarried extensively until 1965. Most of the island is a slatey schist with a patch of hornblende-schist in the south and basaltic tuff bordering the Sound of Insh.

WILDLIFE: The joints of the mossy old masonry of the Clachan Bridge support a rare and tiny fairy foxglove, *erinus alpinus*, a native of the mountains of central Europe.

SEIL is proud of its insularity but it has been very much a part of the mainland ever since 'the Bridge over the Atlantic' was built. The **Clachan Bridge**, as it is correctly called, was designed by Thomas Telford and built in 1792/93. It spans the narrow, shallow, and tidal Clachan Sound which can only be navigated at high water by shallow-draught craft. Whales fail to appreciate this fact. In 1835 a whale of 78 feet in length was stranded in the sound and two years later a school of 192 pilot whales was also trapped.

At the north end of the Clachan Sound there are some islets which form the popular anchorage of Puilladobhrain (G. - pool of the otter). Unfortunately, the 'yachters' have frightened away the otters. At the end of a line of drying islets, **Eilean nam Beathach** (G. - isle of the brutes or beasts), **Eilean nam Freumha** (G. - isle of the roots) and **Eilean Buidhe** (G - yellow or pleasant island) - which give good shelter from the west, is **Eilean Dùin** (G. - fort island) which has a central rock outcrop like a small fort.

A well-trodden footpath leads over the hill from Puilladobhrain to the famous pub, Tigh na Truish (G. - the house of the trousers), by the Clachan Bridge. When Highland dress was banned by law after the Jacobite Rebellion, shore-going islanders swapped their kilts here for a pair of breeks.

Seil is noted for its slate which has been quarried for nearly three centuries. The fourth Earl of Breadalbane, who was the landowner, built picturesque villages for the workers. The main quarry on the south side went deeper and deeper into the ground as the men chiselled out the slate. Gunpowder was then used for blasting and by 1880 the pit was 75m deep (nearly 250 feet below sea-level) with only narrow walls of slate keeping out the sea. In November 1881 the inevitable happened. There was a violent storm and the sea broke through. Luckily it was night and the pit was unmanned but 240 families lost their only means of support and severe poverty ensued. The place where the sea breached the wall can still be clearly seen.

Easdale harbour with its disintegrating pier is now a rather desolate place but in the 19th century it was a major port of call for ships collecting slate for transport through the Crinan Canal. 526 ships, including 245 steamers, used the harbour in 1825 alone.

The delightful village of trim white slate-workers' cottages was featured in the film *Ring of Bright Water* and now supports a thriving artists' colony. It is generally called Easdale although its correct name is **Ellanbeich** as it was an island separated from Seil by a narrow channel which was eventually filled in with quarry waste. On the slope above the east end of the village is **An Cala** (G. - haven or refuge) - a five-acre garden started in 1930 by Lord Elibank and his wife, the actress Faith Celli. Sweeping terraces provide dramatic views, and shelter belts of trees with an undercover of escallonia protect the garden from the prevailing sou'-westerlies. A burn tumbles over rocks and a high wall draped with clematis gives further shelter. The present owners, the Downies, open the garden to the public from April to September.

Seil's particular saint was St Brendan of Clonfert in Galway. He died in 577. The Kilbrandon Parish Church, with an interesting graveyard of ancient carved slabs, is south of **Balvicar** on Seil Sound. **Eilean Tornal** is the islet in the centre of Balvicar Bay.

The broken-off outlier, **Easdale** (G. *eas* - waterfall, ON *dal* - valley) is owned by Clive Feigenbaum, a former chairman of Stanley Gibbons, the stamp dealers. He bought it for a six-figure sum in 1987 and introduced his own postage stamps. The population of this crowded piece of slate was 78 in 1931, only 16 in the 1961 census, but had risen again to 34 by 1981 although most of the whitewashed slate-workers' cottages have been converted to holiday homes. There is a regular ferry service across the harbour and an interesting folk museum which is worth visiting.

Rocky **Insh** (G. *innis* - island), also known as Sheep Island, lies west of Seil and separated from it by the Sound of Insh. It is reputed to be owned by a Londoner who occasionally occupies the cave.

ACCESS: Follow the B844 over the Clachan Bridge. Tourist Information, 01631-63122.

Anchorages:
1. Balvicar Bay. Perfect shelter but restricted by moorings where it does not dry out. Approach by mid-channel S of Eilean Tornal.
2. Easdale Sound. Anchor off the slate wharf which is N of the ruined pier. Navigation in the Sound requires care and close adherence to the sailing instructions. Reasonable shelter in moderate winds.
3. Ardencaple Bay. Occasional anchorage off Ardfad Point in settled weather. No difficulties if approached carefully from due N. Exposed N. Mud and weed.
4. Puilladobhrain. Very popular anchorage and often crowded. Careful identification of all hazards and beacons is required on approach.

CLACHAN BRIDGE – THE 'BRIDGE OVER THE ATLANTIC'

Mull and the Surrounding Islands

Section 3

Section 3, Table 1

No.	Name	Latitude	Longitude	Table 2* No.	Table 3** No.	Area in Acres		Area in Hectares
3.1	Iona	56° 20N	06° 25W	45	72	2167		877
3.2	Kerrera	56° 24N	05° 33W	38	37	3000		1214
3.3	Mull	56° 27N	06° 00W	3	1	216299	87535	
	Erraid	56° 18N	06° 22W			462	187	
	Calve Island	56° 37N	06° 02W			178	72	87794
3.4	Inch Kenneth	56° 27N	06° 09W	146	123	136		55
3.5	Little Colonsay	56° 27N	06° 15W	118	105	217		88
3.6	Eorsa	56° 28N	06° 05W	109	74	301		122
3.7	Ulva	56° 29N	06° 13W	29	21	4917	1990	
	Gometra	56° 29N	06° 17W			1050	425	2415
3.8	Lunga	56° 29N	06° 26W	123	67	200		81
3.9	Lismore	56° 30N	05° 30W	30	51	5809		2351
3.10	Tiree	56° 30N	06° 52W	14	47	19358		7834
3.11	Gunna	56° 34N	06° 43W	134	140	170		69
3.12	Shuna	56° 35N	05° 23W	95	93	383		155
3.13	Coll	56° 37N	06° 34W	15	66	18990		7685
3.14	Carna	56° 40N	05° 53W	85	42	526		213
3.A	*Staffa*	*56° 26N*	*06° 21W*			82		33

* Table 2: The islands arranged in order of magnitude
** Table 3: The islands arranged in order of height

Introduction

With Mull in the geographical centre, most of the classified islands in this section are easily-accessible and well-known. Mull itself has such good communication with the mainland that it would be easy to forget that it is an island while its next-door neighbour Iona attracts tourists and pilgrims from all over the world.

There are a few tiny islets in the mainland firths which have not been mentioned elsewhere. **Eilean an Ruisg** (G. – bare island) in Loch Feochan, and **Eileanan Mór** and **Beag** at the entrance to lovely Loch Etive beside the castle, chapel and marina at Dunstaffnage. On the loch itself are the **Abbot's Isles** which are little more than scattered rocks with hardly a grassy foothold. **Eilean Choinneich** and **Eilean Munde** in Loch Leven are not much bigger but the latter islet, at the foot of Glencoe, has a clan graveyard on it.

Eriska (G. *ùruisg* – water-nymph island) is a flat tidal island at the entrance to Loch Creran with a bridge over the drying channel linking it to the mainland road network. It has a hotel and pleasant wooded grounds.

Staffa with its world-famous Fingal's Cave is well below the size limit of forty hectares which I have set for classification but it is much too remarkable to be ignored and is therefore included as an appendix to the section. The name of the legendary Irish hero, Finn McCool, was given to the cave by Sir Joseph Banks because, so it was reported twelve years later, the local name for the cave was *An Uamh Bhinn* (G. – the melodious cave) and his interpreter mistook this for the Gaelic genetive form of Fingal – *Finn*. A plausible story, but not entirely convincing.

The traditional Gaelic term for a Norseman who had settled in the Hebrides was, and still is, *Fionnghall*, meaning a fair-haired stranger. (This is in contrast to *Dubhghall*, a dark stranger, for a Teuton or a Dane). Most Gaelic place names tend to be practical rather than poetic, so is it possible that the cave was simply known locally as the Norseman's cave?

3.1 Iona

In very early times called I [ee], IO, HII, HIA or IOUA – possibly from the Norse Hiöe [ee-ë] meaning island of the den of the brown bear. Later named ICOLMKILL (G. I Chaluim cille – island of Calum's monastery). Columba is a Latinised version of calaman *(G. – dove), but the saint's given name was Calum. IOUA became corrupted to IONA in the 18th century through a typographical error.*

OS Maps: 1:50000 Sheet 48 1:25000 Sheet 341
Admiralty Charts: 1:25000 No.2617

AREA: 877ha (2,167 acres)
HEIGHT: 100m (328 ft)

OWNER: The sacred buildings and sites were presented to the Church of Scotland's Iona Cathedral Trust in 1899 by the 8th Duke of Argyll. The island as a whole was purchased from the Duke of Argyll by Sir Hugh Fraser in 1979 and given to the National Trust for Scotland.

POPULATION: 1841 – 1084. 1881 – 243. 1891 – 247. 1931 – 141. 1961 – 130. 1971 – 145. 1981 – 268. 1991 – 130.

GEOLOGY: Although Iona lies close to Mull it has a different geological composition. Much of it is Lewisian gneiss but on the east side there are clayey Torridonian beds, minor igneous dykes and glacial erratics from the Ross of Mull; raised beach deposits of late-glacial and post-glacial periods make up the western machair. 300m north-east of Dun Bhuirg is the quarry for the original 'Iona marble' – actually a Lewisian gneiss with a large limestone content. The communion table in the abbey is made of it. The 'Iona marble' which is now sold on the island, and elsewhere, comes from Connemara in Ireland.

HISTORY: Iona was inhabited at least as far back as the Iron Age and it was a religious centre long before St Columba. It was then known as Innis nan Druinich (G. – the Isle of Druidic Hermits). The Druid symbol of Bel – a circle – was later incorporated with the Christian Cross to become the well-known Celtic Cross.

Columba, an Irish prince accompanied by twelve companions, arrived in the year 563 when he was forty-two years old. He probably made his approach up the west coast of Islay in a large currach with a lug-sail. During the next thirty-four years he founded a monastery and turned Iona into a place of pilgrimage and Christian learning which was renowned throughout Europe. He died on the island in 597 having achieved his goal of conversion of the Picts to Christianity at a time when St Augustine had only started conversion of the English.

St Columba was not the earliest Irish missionary to reach Scotland and may not even have been the greatest but he was a strong man with the confidence of a royal upbringing. When the king of Dalriada died Columba consecrated one of his relatives, Aiden, on the throne. With such powerful connections his fame grew and after his death it became established for posterity by the publication of no less than three biographies.

In 795 the first Norse raid on Iona took place with widespread destruction and pillaging. There was no defence. The monastery, which was built of mud, wood, wattle and thatch with an earthwork vallum and ditch to keep livestock out of the sanctuary area, was razed to the ground. It was rebuilt but the Norse struck again in 798 and 802, each time burning and levelling the buildings. Once more it was rebuilt. In 806 the Vikings yet again returned and destroyed the monastery and on this occasion they murdered sixty-eight monks at Martyrs' Bay (200m

2 km
1 mile

N

Eilean
Annraidh

Eilean Chalbha

Caolas Annraidh

Sand Hills

Port Chlacha
Dubha

Lagandorain

Traigh
Bhan

Carraig an Daimh

Ardionra

A' Chorr-sgeir Muigh

Dùn I

△ 100

Auchabhaich

En Liath

Port an Duine
Mhairbh

Boineach

⊙ Memorial Cross

Cliffs

Port a' Ghoirtein
Bhig

Dùn Cùl Bhuirg

□ Cladh an Diseart

Eilean
nam Ban

51
Fort

◇ ABBEY

Eilean Didil

Culbuirg

Baile Mór

MacLean's Cross

Eilean nan Slat

Maol

Nunnery

St Ronan's
Bay

Stac Liath

PO
Cross

Jetty

Camas Cuil
an t-Saimh

Shian

Port nam
Mairtir

1

Ferry

Sligneach

Ruanaich

Tràigh Mhòr

Cnoc
Druidean

Spouting Cave

Sound of Iona

Port Beul-mhòr

Eilean Maol
Mhàrtuin

Eilean
Carrach

M U L L

Stac an
Aoineidh

Cave

Loch Staoineig

Sgeir Ruadh

Druim
Dhughaill

Druim an
Aoineidh

Cave ⊙

Mounds

Dubh Sgeir

An t-Aird

Eilean
Musimul

Rubha na
Carraig-géire

Port an Fhir-bhrèige

Port na Curaich

Port
Goirtean Iar

Eilean na
h-Aon Chaorach

south of the ferry jetty). Following this, and much too late, the few remaining treasures were moved to Kells in Ireland for safety including, it is thought, at least part of the beautifully illustrated *Book of Kells*, now in Dublin, and the Breccbennoch, a reliquary, now in Edinburgh. St Columba's remains were also moved to Kells after which they apparently disappeared although it is possible that they were later returned to Iona and reburied in St

Columba's Shrine next to the cathedral. Kells proved to be no safer than Iona and was ravaged seven times by the Vikings. There were further murderous raids on Iona in 825 and again in 986 when the abbot and fifteen monks were killed at the White Strand in the north of the island. It is little wonder that so few relics of this ancient seat of European culture have survived.

Queen Margaret is said to have rebuilt the monastery

IONA ABBEY

in stone and also built St Oran's Chapel in 1074 (Oran was one of Columba's followers). It again fell into ruin but in 1203 Reginald or Ragnald of Islay, son of Somerled, founded a new monastery and abbey for the Benedictines on the site of Columba's (and Margaret's) monastery and also an Augustinian convent or nunnery whose fine pink granite ruins still remain. His sister became the first Abbess of Icolmkill. The greater part of the present cathedral was built on the foundations of Reginald's Benedictine abbey in the 1500s.

From the 14th century the Mackinnons of Mull were the hereditary Abbots of Iona. In 1507 the Benedictine church on Iona, which was the seat of the Bishopric of the Isles, was given cathedral status until the dissolution after 1570. The island was seized by the MacLeans of Duart in 1574 but it was taken over by the Duke of Argyll in 1688 and he replaced the Mackinnon abbot with a Campbell. During the Reformation most of the ecclesiastical buildings were destroyed, the priceless library vanished and around 360 stone crosses were smashed and thrown into the sea. In 1609 the Hebridean chiefs swore loyalty to the Stuart kings in the church on Iona (documented as the Statutes of Icolmkill) and agreed to measures which curbed their powers but which were designed to improve island life. Unfortunately, later statutes were repressive and led to severe restrictions on Gaelic culture. In 1617 the church on Iona was annexed to the Protestant Bishopric of the Isles.

The roofless old abbey church was restored by the Church of Scotland in 1902-1910. The general restoration and maintenance of all the monastic buildings is now in the hands of the Iona Community, a body founded by a Govan minister, the Rev. George Macleod (later, Lord Macleod of Fiunary).

WILDLIFE: Until recently, corncrake could be heard near the Abbey, although rarely seen. Fulmar, shag and kittiwake breed here and also rock dove and jackdaw. Linnet, twite and yellowhammer can be seen and both the common and Arctic terns.

'That man is little to be envied,' said Dr Johnson, 'whose patriotism would not gain force upon the plain of Marathon, or whose piety would not grow warmer among the ruins of **IONA**!' He was referring to the island cradle of Scottish Christianity and learning, a place of pilgrimage with religious associations stretching far back into antiquity. Sir Walter Scott may have found it 'desolate and miserable' but it inspired Wordsworth in 1835 to compose three sonnets.

The island is austere and windswept yet remarkably fertile. The coastline has a magic and mysticism which, to me, rivals or even surpasses that of the acknowledged religious sites. The shell-sands are clean and white, the rocks have subtle colours tinged with rose and the sea ranges from deep violet to translucent emerald green. There is a sparkle and clarity in the air which is unique to this island and which has proved a challenge and delight to many artists.

The lone and distinctive hill in the north standing above the cathedral has the pre-Columban name of Dùn I, [doon-ee]. In this case the 'dùn' probably refers to the mound-like shape rather than to a fort. It is an easy ten-minute climb to the top of this mountain in miniature which has its own 'north face' and rock chimney. From the top, at 100m (328ft), there is a marvellous view of coastline and islands stretching from Islay to Skye.

To the north is machair and the notorious but beautiful White Strand of the Monks with **Eilean Chalba** and **Eilean Annraidh** and, beyond, the islands of Staffa and the Treshnish Group.

The east coast, facing peacefully across the narrow Sound to the pink granite rocks of Mull, has a violent past. **Martyr's Bay** near the ferry jetty is where sixty-eight monks were massacred. The cathedral, solid and square, sits below the hill like a great supporting boulder. Further down the sound beyond Sligneach the white sands of Tràigh Mhór (G. – big beach) reach out to **Eilean Mór** and **Eilean Carrach**.

The south coast has cliffs and bays and green serpentine pebbles on the beaches. **Port na Curaich** (G. – port of the coracle), or St Columba's Bay, was the saint's traditional landing place when he arrived from Ireland and it lies beside Port an Fhir-bhréige (G. – port of the manlike prehistoric mounds). Entrance to the port leads past **Soa** (ON – sheep island) and between **Eilean Musimul** and **Eilean na h-Aon Chaorach**.

On the west, facing the Atlantic, there are fine farms and crofts on the machair while, out to sea, **Stac Mhic Mhurchaidh** stands proudly beside little **Réidh Eilean** (G. – levelled island). This is where tourists rarely go although there is a golf course overlooking Camas Cuil an t-Saimh (G. – the bay of the twin's hiding-place). South of this is Spouting Cave, beside an overhanging cliff. The bays here have semi-precious stones among the shingle.

The village, **Baile Mór** (G. – big town), facing the Sound of Mull sees half a million tourists a year tripping through it and like many tourist traps it is nothing to 'write home about'. However all the sacred sites are within easy walking distance of the ferry jetty.

Close to the jetty the first site to be reached, and the most beautiful, is the **Nunnery of St Mary** [NM284241]. It is of lovely mellow pink granite and the ruins, which are quite well-preserved, include the church and choir, the Lady Chapel, cloister court, chapter house and refectory. Beside it the Romanesque **Church of St Ronan** (14th century) serves as a museum for some of the tombstones including that of the last prioress who died in 1543.

Carrying on towards the cathedral you pass the 3m high MacLean's Cross dating from the 15th century [NM285242]. **Reilig Odhrain** (G. – graveyard of Oran) is on the right-hand side. A ridge in this simple cemetery was the burial place of all the Scottish kings up to the time of Duncan and Macbeth in the 11th century. Many of the West Highland chieftains in the Middle Ages are also buried here. The cemetery is said to hold the graves of forty-eight Scottish, four Irish, eight Norwegian and two French kings but, sadly, the gravestones have long been defaced or destroyed and only weathered stone slabs remain.

The little Norman-style **St Oran's Chapel** built by Queen Margaret in 1074, and the oldest building on the island, has been restored [NM285244]. Margaret was canonised in 1250.

Crossing the meadow in front of the cathedral and beneath Dùn I is the **Street of the Dead** – a 13th century pavement of red marble along which kings were borne for burial.

The 10th century **St Martin's Cross**, 4.3m high, is opposite the west facade and to the left of it is a concrete replica of the 9th century **St John's Cross**. Near the well is the broken shaft of **St Mathew's Cross**. St Columba's remains may be within **St Columba's Shrine** at the north-west corner of the nave or they may be in **Tor Abb**, the mound just west of the cathedral.

The **Abbey** or **Cathedral** [NM286245] is built of a rosy granite quarried from Tormore on Mull. It has a heavy square tower 21m high centred over arches on a cruciform plan. Much of the building dates from the late 15th century when Reginald's abbey of 1203 was rebuilt but there have been many additions and alterations since then. In the north the Sacristy doorway of golden sandstone from Carsaig on Mull dates from 1500. The **Cloister**, entered through Norman arches in the north transept, contains two medieval pillars. Several of the monastic buildings have been restored such as the **Chapter House** (1955) with Norman doorway, the **Refectory** and the **Undercroft** (1949), the **Reredorter** (1944) and the **Caretaker's House** (1950) which has a gable of the old Abbot's House. **Michael Chapel** (rebuilt 1960) and the **Infirmary** are built on the original Celtic foundations.

ACCESS: Regular passenger (no cars) ferries from Fionnphort on Mull, 01688-2017. Day cruises by Caledonian MacBrayne from Oban, 01631-66688. There is one taxi and no bicycles on the island.

Anchorages:
1. Martyrs' Bay S of pier. Temporary anchorage in suitable weather in 3m, sand.
2. Bull Hole, between Eilean nam Ban and Ross of Mull N of Fionnphort. Good, sheltered, but restricted anchorage in depths of 3-4m. Approach from S. Anchor near Limpet Rock if there is room or off ruined pier in entrance channel. 1M distance by dinghy to Martyrs' Bay.
3. Tinker's Hole. Popular restricted anchorage between En Dubh and W side of Erraid in Sound of Iona. Alternative is large pool immediately N of Tinker's Hole. Too far from Iona for dinghy contact but useful hideout in poor weather.

3.2 Kerrera

(ON Kjarbar-øy – Kjarbar's island) or (ON ciarr-øy – brushwood island)

OS Maps: 1:50000 Sheet 49 1:25000 Sheets 331, 343 and 344
Admiralty Charts: 1:25000 No.2387 1:10000 No.1790

AREA: 1,214ha (3,000 acres)
HEIGHT: 189m (620 ft)

OWNER: Principal landowner, Mrs C H E MacDougall of MacDougall. 270 acres at north end were put up for sale by Lord Lovat in 1994.

POPULATION: 1841 – 187. 1861 – 105. 1881 – 103. 1891 – 92. 1931 – 79. 1961 – 42. 1971 – 27. 1981 – 46. 1991 – 39.

GEOLOGY: The island is of secondary basalt, graphitic schists and red sandstone.

HISTORY: Kerrera has belonged to the MacDougalls since Somerled founded the clan in the 12th century. Alexander

II and his fleet of ships anchored in Horseshoe bay in 1249 to enforce suzerainty on Ewen of Lorn who was paying homage to King Haakon of Norway. Alexander died on the island before achieving his object. A few years later, in 1263, King Haakon's fleet also mustered in the bay on its way to the Battle of Largs. The remnants of his shattered fleet again gathered here after the battle before returning home to Norway by way of Orkney (where King Haakon died).

In 1647 during the Covenanting wars General Leslie's army destroyed Gylen Castle, the MacDougall stronghold at the south end of the island. The Protestant minister, John Neave, persuaded the troops to slaughter every MacDougall defender – there were no survivors.

WILDLIFE: Wild thyme, wild roses, meadow-sweet and honeysuckle festoon the hill tracks.

Mute swan, eider duck, black guillemot and white-winged gulls inhabit Oban Bay all the year round. Rare red kites have been seen circling over the island.

KERRERA is compact, rural, generally unremarkable, and forms a natural breakwater for the important harbour of Oban. Although it is so close to this bustling tourist centre it is a world apart, with lovely views, and many quiet and gentle walks. An easy climb up Càrn Breugach (G. – the false rocky hill) through shrub woodland is rewarding for its magnificent view of the Lorn coast. The island's main function for many years was as a stepping-stone for transporting cattle from Mull to the mainland.

The ferry channel leads between **Maiden Island** and the north end of Kerrera. Here there is a prominent memorial commemorating David Hutcheson who was one of the founders of the ubiquitous Caledonian MacBrayne ferry service. Maiden Island, by the way, is one of many such islands around Scotland which were so-named because they were used by chieftains as refuges for their womenfolk in time of war.

In **Ardantrive Bay** there are moorings, a boatyard, jetty and old slipway. The hillock south of the bay is called Mount Pleasant and **Heather Island** lies close by in the Sound of Kerrera. Across Kerrera, on the north-west coast, is Oitir Mhór (G – big shoal) – a large bay facing Lismore with several small islets on its west side. The largest of these is **Eilean nan Gamhna** (G. – island of the stirks). (A stirk is a year-old calf.)

The schoolhouse and church overlooking the Sound of Kerrera were built in 1872 and the post office was established in 1879. There is a lobster packing factory beside **Horseshoe Bay** where lobsters from the storage pond at Cullipool on Luing (No.2.13) are packed for market. The ferry jetty is just north of the bay.

When Alexander II's fleet anchored in Horseshoe Bay in July 1249 Alexander slept aboard ship. In the morning he mentioned that he had dreamed that St Columba had come aboard and told him to return home immediately. Alexander's nobles felt he should heed the warning but Alexander scoffed at the idea and went ashore. As soon as he landed he stumbled and before he could be carried back on board he died. The land behind the bay is still called Dalrigh (G. – the field of the King).

A road or track, which at times is little more than a footpath, runs from Horseshoe Bay in a loop encompassing most of the southern half of the island. Càrn Breugach, the highest point, sits above **Little Horseshoe Bay** and there is a pleasant walk past the hill to the wild rocky site on the south coast with the fairytale turreted ruins of **Gylen Castle** (G. *caisteal nan geimhlean* – castle of the springs) [NM805265]. It was built in 1587 by Duncan MacDougall of Dunollie, the 16th Chief, on the site of an earlier fortification. The natural springs beneath the castle provided ample fresh water for the inhabitants. The building was besieged and burned in 1647 by General Leslie during the Covenanting Wars. The castle, which can look formidable on a gloomy day poised above the steep and rocky coastline, has an interesting passage underneath it. Carved heads can still be seen on the walls and an inscription which may have read – 'Trust in God and sin no more'.

Gylen Castle was the repository for the MacDougalls' famous Brooch of Lorn. This is an 11cm (4½in) disc of Celtic silver with filigree ornament and a central dome concealing a cavity for sacred relics and supporting a large rock-crystal circled by eight jewelled obelisks. It is said to have belonged to Bruce.

When all the castle's defenders had been massacred,

GYLEN CASTLE – SCENE OF A MASSACRE

the Brooch was looted by one of Leslie's officers, Campbell of Inverawe. The castle was then burned down and for two centuries the MacDougalls believed their famous Brooch had been destroyed in the fire; that is, until 1825, when General Sir Duncan Campbell of Lochnell, who had inherited it, chose to present it to his neighbour, MacDougall of Dunollie, at a public ceremony.

The peninsula lying west of Gylen Castle which runs down to Rubha Seanach (G. – the venerable headland) has a number of caves in it and to the west is Ardmore Bay and the tiny tidal **Eilean Orasaig**. Lying off the western extremity and well into the Firth of Lorn is **Bach Island** (G. – windward island).

Another road and track leads directly across the centre of the island past Slatrach Bay on the west coast. Further south is Barr-nam-boc Bay (G. – billy-goat bay) and on the steep headland between these bays are two interesting caves – Uamh Fhliuch (G. – wet cave) and Uamh nan Calman (G. – the doves' cave) [NM802294].

ACCESS: Frequent passenger ferry (except Sundays) from Gallanach 3km S of Oban. Crossing 5 minutes, 01631-63665.

Anchorages:

1. Little Horseshoe bay about 4¾c NNE of Sgeirean Dubha light-beacon, 2.7-5.5m, good holding. Avoid shoal area marked by buoy and drying reef off S point. (Best anchorage for walk to Gylen Castle).

2. Horseshoe Bay, 4c NE of Little Horseshoe bay, sheltered with good holding. Anchor between central covering rock spit and cable beacon on S point.

3. Heather Island. Possible anchorage off the bight on Kerrera and N of Heather Island. Use trip line.

4. Ardantrive bay, opposite Oban Bay. Visitors' moorings and pontoon berths (pay, 01631-565333). Well-sheltered with good holding but many moorings. Beware drying reef at S point with wreck which covers.

5. Oitir Mhór bay, on N coast, affords reasonable shelter in moderate weather. Straightforward approach from NW. SW side of bay dries 1c.

6. There are no suitable anchorages on the W coast and the S coast is very exposed. Temporary anchorage in suitable weather S of Gylen Castle in centre of cove, 7-8m, sand and shingle. (Useful for a short visit to Gylen Castle).

7. Sgeirean Dubha lightbeacon. Possible anchorage about ³/₄c W of Sgeirean Dubha lighthouse but beware drying rocks.

3.3 Mull

(G. meall – a lump or a rounded hill) This might refer to the rounded shape of Ben More. Alternatively, (G. maol – bald).

OS Maps: 1:50000 Sheets 47, 48 and 49 1:25000 Sheets 301, 302, 315, 316, 317, 329, 330, 341, 342, 343 and 353
Admiralty Charts: 1:75000 Nos.2169 and 2171 1:25000 Nos.2386, 2387, 2390, 2392, 2617, 2652 and 2771 1:10000 No.2474 Tobermory Harbour

AREA: 87,794ha (216,939 acres)
HEIGHT: 966m (3,168 ft)

OWNER: Multiple ownership but with sizeable areas controlled by the Scottish Office (mainly the Forestry Commission). In the early decades of the 18th century the Kilninian and Kilmore parishes were controlled by the house of Argyll, and the Duke of Argyll still has considerable land-holdings in these parishes.

POPULATION: 1755 – 5287. 1794 – 8016. Overpopulation by 1821 – 10,600 inhabitants – led to some voluntary emigration before the Clearances. 1841 – 8121. 1881 – 5229. 1891 – 4691. 1931 – 2903. 1961 – 2154. 1971 – 2024. 1981 – 2605. 1991 – 2648.

GEOLOGY: Most of Mull is Tertiary basalt (trap) on top of Moine schist. In the mountain areas the basalt – volcanic lava flows of fifty million years ago – is weathered into terraces. These giant stepped formations are clearly seen round Loch Scridain and Loch na Keal. Ben More is the highest example of Tertiary basalt in Britain stepping down to a final 370m drop into the sea – the cliff at Wilderness on the Ardmeanach peninsula. Basalt cliffs at Ardtun have Tertiary leaf-beds petrified by liquid mud from the ancient volcano. Recognizable varieties are oak, hazel, plane, Ginco or maiden-hair tree, and various conifers – mainly Mediterranean varieties. The collapsed vent cores of volcanic eruptions centred on Beinn Chàisgidle and Loch Bà formed circular granite dykes 100m thick

and some five miles in diameter. Columnar basalt is to be found near Tavool on Ardmeanach and also at Bunessan and Carsaig in the south. A sill of sapphires can be seen near the famous Carsaig arches. In this area the basalt sits on a chalk layer beneath which is an expanse of lias washed by lime-laden water.

North Mull is a basalt plateau with a volcanic plug at 'S Airde Beinn. On the headland overlooking the Treshnish Isles there is a fertile pre-glacial raised beach and raised beaches are also to be found on the east coast of Mull.

Between the masses of basalt there is a thin spread of Cretaceous and other sediments. This, and the friable rock, has given Mull well-drained and fertile soil.

Glen More, which has many glacial features and a terminal moraine, defines the southern part of Mull. Loch Spelve and Loch Buie in the south-east are at the end of the Great Glen fault.

The butt of the Ross of Mull is pink granite, with the largest mass of the mountain gabbro extruded in screes, or small outcrops and crags. The gabbro on Mull does not form the spectacular shapes it has on Rum and Skye and some of it contains olivine which gives it a sombre colour. Ben Buie has extrusions of breccias and ryolites (volcanic granite). The south crags of Creach Beinn are granophyres (almost granite but interwoven with quartz and felspar).

HISTORY: As with so many of the islands, Mull is rich in prehistoric remains – standing stones, circles, cairns and many large crannogs of both stone and timber construction in the fresh-water lochs. The island was known to the classical Greeks and Ptolemy referred to it in the 2nd century AD as Maleus. In the same century the Irish Celts appeared on the scene. One can infer from the visible remains of forts and duns (about thirty-five of them) that there were many battles and skirmishes. For a time Loch Spelve, Glen More and Loch Scridain are said to have formed the boundary between the kingdom of the Picts and Dalriada, kingdom of the Scots. Christianity was introduced after St Columba's arrival on Iona in 563.

The Norwegians exercised tenuous control from about the 8th century but, even so, King Magnus plundered the island in 1100. The Lord of the Isles gained suzerainty in 1266. In the following century the MacDougalls, the senior clan descended from Somerled, supported Balliol instead of Bruce and this misjudgement led King Robert to transfer control to the MacDonalds, the junior branch which had given him support at Bannockburn. Thus the MacDonalds became Lords of the Isles and the most influential clan, and it was not until 1543, after an abortive revolt, that the Campbells gained ascendancy. The Mackinnons of Mull and the Macleans of Duart, although party to the uprising and allied to the MacDonalds, managed by various subterfuges to maintain status with the Campbells.

James VI (James I of England) was determined to destroy Gaelic culture which he thoroughly detested. In 1608 he sent Lord Ochiltree and the Bishop of the Isles to Aros Castle on Mull. All the Hebridean chiefs were summoned to meet there for a conference. An inaugural service was conducted by the Bishop on board a ship in Salen Bay whereupon the chiefs were all imprisoned in the ship and then sent to Edinburgh.

In Charles I's reign the Protestant Earl of Argyll chose to lead the Army of the Covenant. There were religious stresses throughout Mull as, for instance, the Maclaines of Lochbuie were Catholic while the Macleans of Duart were Protestant. Maclean however refused to join Argyll only to find that Argyll bought up all his debts compelling him to

sign away his castles of Duart and Aros. To enforce this, Argyll invaded Mull with 2000 men in 1674 and occupied the castles amid reports of needless barbarity. The Campbells rampaged through Mull and destroyed most of the priceless Gaelic library held by the Beatons of Pennycross.

Thomas Pennant observed in 1772 that although a Campbell lived in Aros castle and government troops occupied Duart castle, the Macleans still retained about half the island. About this time the talented 5th Duke of Argyll, a very different man from some of his predecessors, was looking to the improvement of his estates. He instituted a system of nineteen-year leases for his tenants with fair rents related to means and as Governor of the British

DUART CASTLE – ANCESTRAL HOME OF THE MACLEANS

Fisheries Society he established the enchanting little port of Tobermory.

WILDLIFE: There is not much heather on the island due to the good soil but flag and meadowsweet and luxuriant fuchsia abound. The remaining patches of natural woodland are mainly oak, ash, birch and hazel. Carsaig is one of only two places in the western Highlands where watercress grows in the chalky streams, as it does in southern England.

Heavyweight stags can be seen in the mountain corries but red deer stalking in September and October restricts safe access to the hills. At least one family of otters feed on the brown trout in Loch Poit na h'I on the Ross of Mull.

Ptarmigan nest on Ben Buie's slopes at under 700m – a lower altitude than they require in the Central Highlands. There is year-round interest for ornithologists with a wide variety of bird habitats and many interesting species. A few sites worth visiting are:

Glen More, 16km from Craignure. Upland species: hen harrier, short-eared owl, golden eagle, kestrel, raven, buzzard. Also breeding curlew, cuckoo, whinchat. stonechat, and wheatear. Snow bunting in winter.

Mishnish Lochs near Tobermory: Little grebe, heron, goosander and red-throated diver. Hen harrier, buzzard, short-eared owl and golden eagle hunt in the vicinity. Whooper swan and goldeneye in the winter.

Loch Don has resident heron, mute swan, eider, red-breasted merganser, redshank, buzzard and hen harrier. Common and Arctic tern in summer. Red-throated diver, little grebe, cormorant, greenshank, wigeon, teal, mallard, goldeneye and shelduck in winter. Passage waders such as grey plover, knot, sanderling, bar and black-tailed godwits and whimbrel. Pectoral sandpiper, ruff, spotted redshank and green sandpiper have been seen.

Loch Na Keal: Excellent viewing of divers and the vel-vet scoter is sometimes seen. Also the Slavonian grebe.

Fionnphort and 1½km S at Fidden: Many migrant waders and passerines with Greenland white-fronted geese in winter. 1½km east at Loch Poit na h-I there are little grebe and, in winter, white-fronted geese, tufted duck and pochard.

Loch Scridain: In winter, red-throated, black-throated and great northern divers.

The main body of **MULL** is mountainous, rising to 966m at Ben More – the highest peak and the only Munro in all the Scottish islands. (Skye has twenty-two Munros but no longer qualifies for island classification since it is linked to the mainland by a bridge). Ben More from the west and Beinn Talaidh from the north are very shapely mountains. The non-mountainous areas had good agricultural potential but much of this was lost when large-scale sheep farming was introduced in the 19th century. The island is so heavily indented with sea lochs that there is about 500km of coastline but, due to good drainage, inland lochs are comparatively few – even though Mull suffers the wettest weather in the Hebrides. (May is the driest month.)

The vehicle ferry from Oban has its terminal at **Craignure** pier (built in 1964). On the way over it passes close by **Duart Castle** (G. *dubh ard* – black height), a much-photographed and perfect example of an island warlord's homestead [NM749353]. This has been the MacLeans' ancestral home since about 1250 although it was burned by the Duke of Argyll in 1691, and confiscated after Culloden. The 26th Chief, Sir Fitzroy Maclean, bought it in 1911 and with Sir John Burnett as his architect, carefully restored it. It is presently occupied by the 27th Chief and is open to the public.

Eilean Rubha an Ridire (G. – island at the promontory of the knight) is across on the Morvern shore, where the **Glas Eileanan** (G. – grey-green islands) guard the entrance to the Sound of Mull. During a gale on the 19th October 1690 the Royal Naval frigate *Dartmouth* dragged her anchor in Duart Bay and was wrecked on this islet. The wreck, which is now protected, was discovered by divers in 1973. There have been many such accidents. Until recently the mast of a wrecked 'puffer' could be seen, but it has now disintegrated.

Lady's Rock lies opposite Duart Castle and is marked by a white beacon as it covers at high water. Long ago, a MacLean chieftain married the Earl of Argyll's sister. The marriage was a failure (he claimed his wife had twice tried to poison him!) so in 1523 he tied her up and marooned her on the rock. The next morning, seeing from the castle that she had been washed away by the tide, he sadly reported her death to the Earl. Argyll wanted her to be buried at Inveraray so in due course MacLean and his retinue appeared with a sealed coffin. He was shown into the dining hall where he was astonished to see his wife (who had been rescued by a passing fisherman) sitting at the top table next to her brother. Nothing however was said, the meal went ahead with pleasant decorum, and after this subtle torture MacLean was even allowed to leave. But, needless to say, some time later he was discovered murdered in his bed in Edinburgh.

A relatively modern Scottish Baronial castle, **Torosay**, is also in the vicinity and open to the public [NM728353]. David Bryce was the architect in 1856 and the building has beautiful terraced gardens designed by Sir Robert Lorimer in 1899 with a walk bordered by nineteen life-sized Venetian statues. It can be reached from Craignure by the Mull & West Highland Railway, a 10.25 gauge miniature line.

North of Craignure, beyond **Scallastle Bay**, is the terminal for the small Lochaline-Fishnish vehicle ferry which crosses the Sound of Mull and connects Mull with Morvern. Approaching the foot of Glen Forsa at **Pennygown** there is the ruin of a medieval chapel with the shaft of a Celtic cross in it [NM604432]. This area was once the haunt of benevolent fairies who would complete small tasks for people. Then someone left a twig with instructions to turn it into a ship's mast and the fairies have been on strike ever since.

Nearby is the island's airstrip which was built in 1966 in only fifty-four days by the 38th Engineer Regiment as a military exercise. The road leads on to the small village of **Salen** which lies in the 'waist' of Mull, the narrow strip between Salen Bay and Loch na Keal. On the north side of Salen Bay are the ruins of 13th century **Aros Castle** built on the site of the first Norman-style castle to be completed by Somerled and last occupied in 1608 [NM563450]. One of the **Eileanan Glasa** (G. – grey-green islands) in the centre of the Sound of Mull opposite Salen, called **Dearg Sgeir** (G. – red rock), was hit by the cargo ship *Rondo* in 1935. The collision wrecked the ship and demolished the original lighthouse.

Tobermory (G. *tobar Mhoire* – Mary's well) is one of the loveliest and best-known small towns in Scotland. It was planned and built by The British Fisheries Society in 1788 and had burgh status from 1875 to 1975. The fine stone houses on the main street are brightly painted and form a cheerful backdrop to the beautiful harbour. Further up the hillside and among the trees is more recent housing. The town is well-served with facilities. There are hotels, boarding-houses, a youth hostel, shops, bank, post-office, library, schools, museum and a tourist information office. The 1862 courthouse now serves as a police station and council offices. There is an attractive wooded public park and a nine-hole golf course. The eponymous St Mary's Well is at the top of the hill just west of the town beside a ruined medieval chapel. This was the original village in which Dr Johnson and Boswell stayed in 1773 in a 'tolerable inn'. As Boswell reported, 'Tobermorie is an excellent harbour. An island lies before it, and it is surrounded by a hilly theatre. The island is too low, otherwise this would be quite a secure port; but, the island not being sufficient protection, some storms blow very hard here. Not long ago, fifteen vessels were blown from their moorings'. Boswell's comments are correct but **Calve Island**, separated from Mull by a shallow tidal channel, is a fairly effective barrier nevertheless.

The famous wreck of a galleon of the Spanish Armada, possibly *Almirante di Florencia*, is in the bay. Fleeing from the battle in 1588 she anchored here and took on provisions but when Donald MacLean went on board to ask for payment he was locked in the magazine and the Spaniards prepared to set sail. MacLean managed to escape but started a fire which blew up the ship. It was alleged that the ship carried thirty million ducats, and there have been many attempts to recover the treasure. These have probably been unsuccessful although there were rumours that part of the treasure was recovered and buried at Aros Castle. The wreck has now sunk deep in the mud and clay below the harbour.

Bloody Bay, between the lighthouse at Rubha nan Gall and Ardmore Point, was the setting for a sea battle between John, the last Lord of the Isles, and his son Angus. Ardmore Forest Walk, just north of the bay, is a popular cliff path with splendid views.

Dùn Urgadul, a vitrified fort, lies west of Tobermory [NM494553]. The minor road leading past it wanders through forests to **Glengorm Castle** [NM439572] in the north-west of the island looking across the sea to Ardnamurchan point. There was such an attractive haze in the air when the new owner arrived in the 19th century that he named it Glengorm (G. – the blue glen). He had not realised that the haze was caused by the smoke of burning crofts which were being 'cleared'. South-

GLENGORM CASTLE

west of Tobermory the main road runs to Dervaig past the Mishnish lochs, well-stocked with trout, and on through open moorland.

Dervaig (G. *doire beag* – little grove) is a beautiful village built by the MacLeans of Coll in 1799. Kilmore Parish Church has an Irish style pencil-shaped steeple [NM431518]. Next door, the Mull Little Theatre, seating thirty-eight, was founded in this village. In the summer there are often boat excursions from here to Staffa and the Treshnish Isles. The minor road running south to Salen passes groups of standing stones and **Eas Corrach** (G. – steep waterfall) at the end of Glen Aros. Dervaig is at the head of Loch a' Chumhainn (G. – loch of the narrows), which has a narrow passage connecting it to the sea. The anchorage of **Port Croig**, where cattle from the outer isles were landed on their way to market, is in a rocky inlet.

A basalt dyke on its north side gives **Calgary Bay** its name (G. *caladh garaidh* – the haven by the dyke). In 1883 Col J. F. MacLeod of the Royal North-West Mounted Police, after an enjoyable holiday at Calgary House, gave the Canadian city the same name. (The bay is also incidentally noted for a 12lb lobster caught here in the 1920s.) On the moor to the south stands the lonely ruin of Reudle schoolhouse and beyond the hills on the peninsula to the west – overlooking the Treshnish Isles (No.3.8) – is the extensive deserted village of Crackaig. Two hundred people were cleared from here in the 19th century and a villager hanged himself from the ash tree in the walled garden beside the burn. Still Cave, where the local whisky was made, is further down the burn. Ruined **Dùn Aisgain** which dates from 1BC stands on a headland to the east [NM377453] while **Dun Bàn** is nearer the road [NM387453].

The road wends its way along the side of Loch Tuath (G. – north loch), the wide sea loch between Ulva and Mull through patches of natural woodland. In **Kilninian** burial ground [NM397457] there is a very fine medieval slab showing a kilted chieftain, and Torloisk (G. – burnt hill) was the home of Alan of the Straws, a famous pirate. Many ancient artefacts are along the way and at Ballygown there is a broch, Dùn nan Gall, [NM433431] and an ancient fort [NM441431]. One kilometre further on is Mull's most spectacular waterfall, **Eas Fors** (G. *eas* – waterfall, ON *fors* – waterfall). At the head of Loch Tuath a group of tiny islets cluster in the narrow Sound of Ulva – **Eilean a' Bhuic** (G. – buck island), **Eilean Garbh** (G. – rough island), and **Eilean a' Chaolais** (G. – kyle island) are the largest. The road passes the turn-off to Ulva Ferry and carries on round the sides of **Loch na Keal** (G. – loch of the cliff) to Gruline where a mausoleum is maintained by the National Trust of Australia for Major General Lachlan Macquarie (1761-1824) of Ulva, the first Governor of New South Wales and 'father of Australia'. **Ben More**

dominates the southern side of Loch na Keal and the easiest point to scramble up it is by Abhainn na h-Uamha (G. – river of the caves), 1½km NE of Dhiseig [NM507368]. Beyond its slopes the road skirts the cliffs overlooking Inch Kenneth (No.3.4) and turns southwards through the giant rockfalls at Gribun. One of these huge boulders, lying beside a stone wall, fell and crushed the entire cottage in which a young couple were enjoying their wedding night.

Opposite **Eilean Dubh Cruinn** (G. – round black island) the road swings across country to **Loch Scridain** (G. – loch of the screes) cutting off the wild and trackless Ardmeanach peninsula. A 2km path from the turn-off to Balmeanach farm leads to the renowned **Mackinnon's Cave** which was visited by Dr Johnson [NM440323]. Some 30m high and probably the largest cave in the Hebrides it can only be entered at low tide. As usual there is the well-worn legend of a piper and his dog entering the cave. The variation on this occasion is that a witch living in the cave killed the piper and the entire party which he was guiding through the cave to the other side of the peninsula. Only the piper's dog, scorched and hairless, appeared on the southern shore.

The most remote part of **Ardmeanach**, which Americans would call the Badlands but is known locally as the Wilderness, can be reached on foot from Balmeanach (a long and very strenuous walk) or partly by rough vehicle track from Tiroran above Loch Scridain followed by a 3km scramble with arrival timed for low water. The southern part belongs to the National Trust for Scotland and includes **MacCulloch's Tree**, a dramatic fifty million year-old fossil which is 12m high and a metre in diameter [NM402208]. Another lies toppled in a cave to the north. They can be located by two waterfalls on the cliff but ask for directions at Burg Farm. This area has a marvellous selection of wildlife and was given to the Trust in 1932 by A Campbell Blair of Dolgellau.

THE STURDY TOWER OF MOY CASTLE

NATURAL SCULPTURE – THE CARSAIG ARCHES

East of Tioran, at the head of the loch, the road meets the main Craignure-Fionnphort road which is the route to Iona.

Mull has many attractions for the sportsman whether in hunting, fishing, shooting, pony trekking, riding, camping, exploring caves, wildlife expeditions or hill-walking. For the mountaineer, apart from the 'Munro' – Ben More (966m), and numerous sea-cliffs, there are also two 'Corbetts': Beinn Talaidh (G. – hill of Valhalla or allurement) (761m) and Dùn da Ghaoithe [doo:n da: goo-i] (G. – castle of the winds) (766m).

South of Craignure and Duart Castle a road runs down to the old ferry terminal at Grass Point by shallow **Loch Don**. This was the ancient pilgrims' way to Iona and also the drove road when island cattle were shipped from here to the mainland. On the coast between it and Loch Spelve is Port Donain, a small cove with a cave [NM741293] and chambered cairns above it.

Loch Spelve has two arms, a few skerries, and one islet, **Eilean Amalaig**. A minor road runs along the north side through mixed woodland and rhododendrons beneath the basalt heights of Creach Beinn and on past little Loch Uisg to Lochbuie. This valley is exceptionally fertile and used to be called the Garden of Mull. The sturdy tower of **Moy Castle** – near Mull's only example of a stone circle [NM618251] – overlooks the loch. The castle (now closed to the public) was built above a natural spring in the 14th century by the MacLaines of Lochbuie. It has a bottle-necked dungeon filled with water and a stone in the centre on which the prisoner sat in darkness.

The brother-in-law of the 21st MacLean of Duart was Solicitor General in 1894-5 and the tiny island east of the mouth of Loch Buie is named after him – **Frank Lockwood's Island**. Lord Lovat's bay at the entrance to Loch Buie has Lord Lovat's cave close north of it. On the east side of the loch is a medieval chapel reconstructed as a mausoleum for the MacLaines in 1864 [NM626236]

and on the west side an 8km coastal path leads to Carsaig.

The main road runs beside the Lussa River in Glen More through a barren, glaciated landscape until one sees conifer forests on the way down to the head of Loch Scridain. At **Pennyghael** a cairn commemorates the Beatons, hereditary doctors to the Lords of the Isles. A minor road south meets the coast at the fertile farmland of **Carsaig**. This was a setting for the film *I Know Where I'm Going* which also featured the Corrievreckan whirlpool off Jura (No.2.5). Yachts find shelter behind the islet Gamhnach Mhór (G. – big cow) in Carsaig Bay. A long coastal walk to the west of Carsaig leads first to the **Nun's Cave** (G. – Uamh nan Cailleach) [NM524205] which has early Christian carvings and where nuns from Iona are reputed to have hidden during the Reformation. This is where sandstone was quarried in 1500 for dressing Iona Abbey and the masons' bankers with chips of stone beside them are still lying around. A further two hours walk beyond, at Malcolm's Point, are the spectacular rock formations of the Carsaig Arches [NM494185], one in the form of a very high pyramidal mass with arches in the middle and a solitary basaltic column on top. The arches are eroded sea-caves adjoining 220m-high cliffs lined with huge basalt columns.

The Ross of Mull is primeval moorland with scattered clumps of trees and a coast with many fine beaches and bays. **Bunessan** (G. – foot of the waterfall) on Loch na Làthaich provides a busy anchorage for fishing boats behind the shelter of **Eilean Bàn** (G. – pale island). The road finishes at **Fionnphort** [fina:foart] (G. – fair or holy port), the ferry terminal for Iona. Close by to the north, **Bull Hole** has a derelict stone jetty [NM301241] which was in use until the late 19th century when the beautiful pink granite was quarried here for the construction of the Holburn Viaduct, Blackfriars Bridge and the Albert Memorial in London. The stone was also used for several lighthouses.

At the southern corner of the Sound of Iona, the tidal island of **Erraid** is accessible across the sands for two hours at low water. It featured in Robert Louis Stevenson's book, *Kidnapped*, which he is said to have written when staying on the island. This was the lighthouse shore station for **Dubh Artach** and **Skerryvore** until 1967 and the iron observatory at the summit of Crioc Mór {NM296203] was once used for signalling to the lighthouses. Erraid is surrounded by rocks and islets, including **Eilean Ghòmain**, **Eilean nam Muc**, **Eilean Chalmain**, **Eilean na Seamair** and, of course, the inevitable **Eilean Dubh** (two of them!).

South of Erraid lie the infamous **Torran Rocks** (G. torrunn – loud murmuring or thunder) which are scattered over a wide area like dragons' teeth. They lurk menacingly just beneath the surface, occasionally showing themselves in a froth of white spittle.

ACCESS: Vehicle ferries from Oban to Craignure and Tobermory, from Lochaline to Fishnish, and from Kilchoan on the Ardnamurchan Peninsula to Tobermory, 01631-66688. Oban Tourist Information, 01631-63122. Tobermory Tourist Information, 48 Main Street, 01688-2182. Island bus services, 01688-2220.

Anchorages:

1. Dòirlinn, Tobermory. Good anchorage in basin about 2c NW of the Narrows between Mull and Calve Island. Use anchor light.

2. Aros Bay, Tobermory. Far S corner of Tobermory harbour, by waterfall. Anchor between boathouse and fish farm in suitable depth.

3. Tobermory Bay. Busy popular anchorage, convenient for access to the town. HIE moorings, but rarely vacant. Anchor off the stone pier or in deeper water (20m-40m). Bottom can be foul. Exposed NE; swell after N'ly gales; otherwise protected.

4. Ardmore bay. Temporary anchorage W of Ardmore point, affords shelter from S winds.

5. Loch Mingary. Temporary anchorage in quiet conditions. Tricky but worthwhile.

6. Loch a' Chumhainn (Loch Cuan), between Rubha an Aird and Quinish point. Head dries out 9^1/$_2$c and both sides rocky and foul. Good shelter but a trap in onshore winds. Approach with care.

7. Calgary bay. Temporary anchorage only suitable in N and E winds and when no onshore swell. Less attractive than Lochs Cuan and Mingary. Head dries out 2c. Keep 5c off coast to the N when approaching the bay and when rounding Rubha nan Oirean.

8. Port Rainich (56°31N 06°12W), behind Eilean Rainich reef, half-way down N side of Loch Tuath, about 7c beyond Traig na Cille, the sandy bay at Kilninian and almost SSE of Torloisk House. Limited room but useful in N'lies.

9. Sound of Ulva (56°28.5N 06°08W), S of the ferry, WNW of Sgeir Beul a' Chaolais, can be squally. Alternatively, in settled weather, E of this anchorage in the bay on the Mull shore beyond the drying reef.

10. Scarisdale, Loch na Keal. Useful anchorage but submerged rocks to negotiate. Subject to squalls.

11. Dhiseig. Shore of Loch na Keal, SE of Eorsa. Temporary anchorage 5c ENE of the Dhiseig burn (direct access to Ben More).

12. By Inch Kenneth. Temporary anchorage 4c SSE of Samalan Island in suitable depth near Mull shore. Exposed, subject to fierce squalls, holding poor.

13. Kilfinichen Bay, N side of Loch Scridain at foot of glen. Pleasant in settled weather. Head dries out 3c. Keep 1c clear of W side.

14. Loch Beg at head of Loch Scridain is shallow but there is anchorage in 3.5m just within the entrance. Subject to swell and squalls.

15. Sgeir Alltach, S side of Loch Scridain. Good but restricted anchorage 1^3/$_4$c SE of Sgeir Alltach, between Sgeir Chailleach and Sgeir na Rad. Complete shelter from W'lies but only enter near LW when the Sgeir are visible. Careful attention to sailing directions required.

16. Bun an Leoib, on S shore of Loch Scridain entrance, E of Rubha Dubh. Anchor behind Sgeir Leathen and Sgeir Mór but not in N and NW winds as there is a heavy swell. Many drying rocks and reefs.

17. Loch na Làthaich (Bunessan). Well sheltered inlet on N side of Ross of Mull but busy and space restricted. Safest anchorage in this part of Mull. Visitors' moorings (pay, 01681-700435) at boatyard.

18. Bull Hole, between Eilean nam Ban and Ross of Mull. Good, sheltered, but restricted anchorage. Approach from S avoiding Little Bull and Limpet Rock. Anchor near Limpet Rock or off ruined pier in entrance channel.

19. Fionnphort. Occasional anchorage in suitable conditions midway between ferry jetty and entrance to Bull Hole, sand. Avoid obstructing ferry.

20. Tinker's Hole. Popular restricted anchorage between Eilean Dubh and W side of Erraid in Sound of Iona. Well-sheltered. Alternative is large pool immediately N of Tinker's Hole.

21. Ardalanish (56°16N 06°17W). Small inlet on W side of Rubh' Ardalanish, S coast of Ross of Mull. Restricted but attractive in settled weather. S side is steep-to.

22. Carsaig bay. Occasional anchorage close N of Gamhnach Mhór, a reef of islets opposite the pier or at a suitable depth off the beach in the bay.

23. Loch Buie, exposed and not safe except in fine weather.

24. Loch Spelve, E coast of Mull. Croggan pier, depths of 2.7m at head. Best anchorage is in bight on W side of head of N arm of the loch off Lussa River. Gusty in W'lies particularly in S arm of the loch.

25. Loch Don, narrow and shallow, with many rocks and shoals. Head dries out 8c but there is a pool within. Shelter from SW to NW winds can be obtained off the entrance, in 11m.

26. Duart Bay. Dries nearly 4c then deepens quickly. Occasional anchorage near Torosay slip, or temporary anchorage in settled weather near Duart Castle jetty.

27. Craignure bay, sheltered S thro W to NW. HIE buoys available. Anchor in 4-5m NW of pier, sand; or off the old pier N of the Craignure Inn if shallow-draught.

28. Scallastle bay (56°29N 05°44W). Good anchorage in offshore winds but approach requires care.

29. Fishnish bay. Occasional anchorage near head of bay on 5m line. Head dries off 3c.

3.4 Inch Kenneth

Kenneth's island, named after Cainnech, follower of St Columba.

OS Maps: 1:50000 Sheet 47 1:25000 Sheet 328
Admiralty Charts: 1:25000 No.2652 or No.2771

AREA: 55ha (136 acres)
HEIGHT: 49m (161 ft)

OWNER: Dr Andrew D. Barlow of Kensington, London. Owned for a time by Sir Harold Boulton, composer of the 'Skye Boat Song'.

POPULATION: 1841 – no separate census record. 1881 – 8. 1891 – 2. 1931 – 10. 1961 – 13. 1971 – 2. 1981 – 0. 1991 – 0.

GEOLOGY: Different from Mull as the rocks are sedimentary. Triassic conglomerates and limestone outcrops have been eroded and broken down into good soil.

Geasgill Mór

Maol an
Domhnaich

Sgeir
Bhuidhe

Samalan
Island

Sgeir na
Laimhrige Móire

Sgeir a' Chèirde

Sgeir Leathan

An Fhearsaid

Port an Fharaidh

Aodann gun Nighe

Cairn

Poll na Sgeire Ruaidhe

25

Wells

Inchkenneth.
△ 49   House

Chapel &
Burial Ground

Sgeir nan Damh

A' Chrois an Iollaich

Bàgh an
Iollaich

Port an Ròin

Rubha Baile
na h-Airde

MULL

Bogha Leathan

N

Bogha Crom

Boghachan Ruadha

HISTORY: Named after Kenneth, contemporary of St Columba who is said to have saved the great man from drowning solely through the power of prayer. Kenneth became abbot of Achabo, in Ireland, and died in 600. The Prioress of Iona owned the island in 1569. It was considered second only to Iona in ecclesiastical importance.

WILDLIFE: The Statistical Account of 1845 reports that this was one of the main centres for kelp burning as the alkaline content of the ash was very high. The best sea-

weed was not the tangle, although this added bulk, but 'button wrack' which was prolific in the area.

In 1569 Dean Munro reported that rabbits were present in great numbers on Inch Kenneth so they have a long history here.

The island is popular with barnacle geese in winter. Shag, eider, red-breasted merganser, oystercatcher, curlew, redshank, razorbill and black guillemot are resident here all year round.

INCHKENNETH
CHAPEL,
WITH EORSA
IN VIEW

Like Tiree, **INCH KENNETH** is exceptionally fertile, and it once provided grain for the monks of Iona. There is a fine 19th century mansion house and an attractive single-storey farmhouse intended for the farmer who leases the land for crops and grazing.

Sir Alan MacLean, 22nd chief of Duart, was host here to Boswell and Johnson and entertained them in the low-roofed stone building which is still standing but no longer occupied. Boswell considered Inch Kenneth 'a pretty little island'.

There is no trace now of the original monastery but there is an ancient ruined chapel of the First Pointed period, 12m x 6m (40' x 20'), with deeply splayed lancet windows [NM437354]. There are also the remains of a Celtic cross and many sculptured tombstones including that of Sir Alan MacLean who was Dr Johnson's host. It is the most elaborately carved slab in the Mull area and shows the Chief in armour with his dog at his feet. Many of the tombs are of Highland chiefs who were buried here when conditions were too wild to allow a crossing to Iona.

All the buildings are grouped centrally on the east side of the island.

Much of the island's economy is now provided by fish farming. Landing can be a problem unless the weather conditions are suitable as there is no ideal anchorage. The normal approach is close by the **Geasgill Islands**, avoiding **Maol an Domhnaich** (G. – Sunday rock, but see No.7.5 Muldoanich derivation), and then between **Samalan Island** and **Sgeir na Laimhrige Móire** (G. – the rock of Mary's landing place). Inch Kenneth is encircled by wide areas of drying rocks, islets, reefs and skerries except for the west side where there is a 25m high cliff above tumbled boulders. Just north of this is a low escarpment called **Aodann gun Nighe** (G. – the dirty face).

ACCESS: No regular access. When the owner is in residence he has his own means of transport from Mull.

Anchorages:
1. Red Skerry Pool (Poll na Sgeire Ruaidhe). E and N sides of the island are foul so approach with caution from N on given bearings. Anchor in bay on E side of island in 6-8m, holding poor. Subject to fierce squalls and landing can be tricky.
2. SE of Port an Ròin. Hazardous approach round the end of reef which extends SE of S extremity of island. Preferably only for shoal-draught vessels at mid-tide in quiet conditions.

3.5 Little Colonsay

(ON koln-øy – Columba's island) or (ON – Kolbein's island)

OS Maps: 1:50000 Sheet 47 1:25000 Sheet 328
Admiralty Chart: 1:25000 No.2652

AREA: 88ha (217 acres)
HEIGHT: 61m (200 ft)

POPULATION: 1841 – no separate census record. 1881 – 0. 1891 – 2 (1 house). 1931 – 2. 1961 – 0. 1971 – 0. 1981 – 0. 1991 – 0.

GEOLOGY: Columnar basalt formations.

HISTORY: Between 1846 and 1851 Little Colonsay was cleared of its inhabitants by the owner F. W. Clark who also owned Ulva and Gometra. In the early 20th century the island was farmed by John McColum (known as 'Johnny Colonsay'). He had occupied the Victorian house for most of his life but he and his family were forced to abandon it because of a plague of rats.

WILDLIFE: Countless primroses, wild violets and celandine – no doubt due to the absence of sheep. A few seabirds nest on the cliffs and outcrops. We saw no wild goats but they were reported in the 1930s.

The anchorage on the north side of **LITTLE COLONSAY**

is approached from the east through the channel between Sgaigein and **Garbh Eilean**, a tidal island south of Ulva. **Sgaigein** is a large rock which only just shows at high water (0.6m high) and is about 1¾c north of the island. The householder keeps a lobster fishing boat on a private mooring. A path leads from the landing place through rocks covered with orange lichen. The house is surprisingly large and spacious with dormer windows and a slated roof. It is tucked into a hollow and protected from the prevailing sou'-westerlies by Torr Mór (G. – big hill), 61m high. It has recently been restored and an extensive water catchment system installed with storage tanks in a corrie on the hillside. Windbreaks of rowan tree saplings have also been

planted but unfortunately many have not survived the gales.

This is a nice little island in a stunning setting with Ulva and Gometra close to the north, Inch Kenneth and the mountains of Mull to the east, **Erisgeir** islet and Iona to the south, and Staffa and the Treshnish Isles to the west. On a calm sunny day it is easy to be enthralled until you remember that the south-west is entirely exposed to the Atlantic with no sheltering land-mass between Little Colonsay and the shores of America.

The columnar basaltic rock formations of nearby Staffa are also to be found here, although in a considerably less dramatic form. The best examples are probably on the east side near **Rubha Meall nan Gamhna** (G. – humpy head-

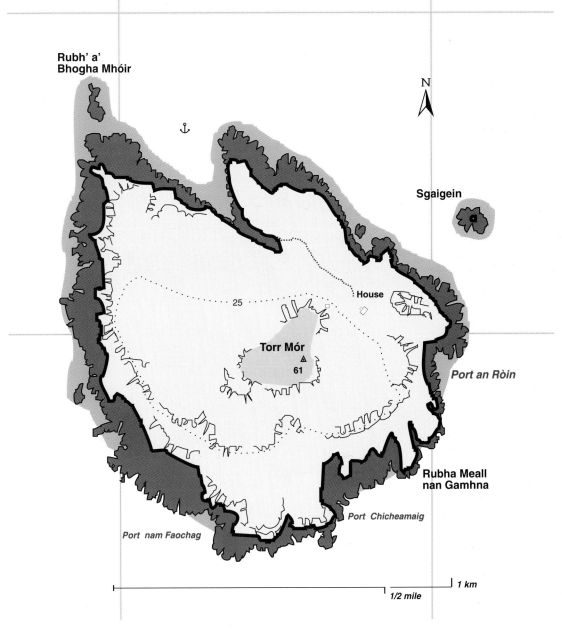

land of the stirks). There are several small inlets called 'ports' in Gaelic, because it is possible to beach a small boat there. Two of them, **Port nam Faochag** (G. – port in the centre of the brow) directly south of Torr Mór, and **Port an Ròin** (G. – port of the seal) just north of Rubha Meall nam Gamhna may afford restricted anchorage in light northerlies but this has not been tested.

ACCESS: No normal access.

Anchorages:
1. Temporary anchorage on N side about 1½c W of Sgaigein in 8m off the narrow geo and near a private mooring.

3.6 Eorsa

Derivation obscure. Possibly, (ON Jorulf-øy *– Jorulf's island) or a corruption of (G.* àrsaidh *– ancient).*

OS Maps: 1:50000 Sheet 47 1:25000 Sheet 329
Admiralty Chart: 1:25000 No.2652

AREA: 122ha (302 acres)
HEIGHT: 98m (321 ft)

POPULATION: No census returns and uninhabited.

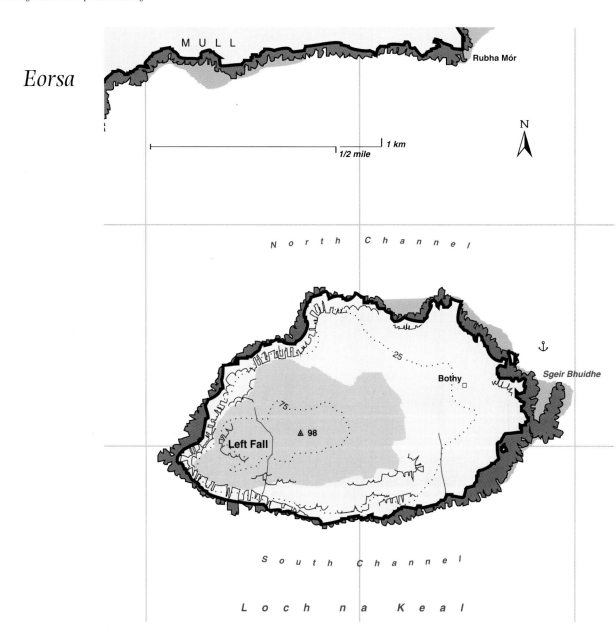

GEOLOGY: Tertiary basalt bedrock.

HISTORY: Eorsa, together with Inch Kenneth, once belonged to the Priory of Iona.

WILDLIFE: The shores are sometimes the haunt of Great Northern, red-throated and black-throated divers. Very occasionally, velvet scoters may be seen and some Slavonian grebe in early spring.

EORSA is a compact island in the centre of Loch na Keal (G. – loch of the cliffs). The west half of the island has a shoreline of high cliffs which were once frequented by wild goats but these moderate towards the east where a ruined bothy has a dramatic view of Ben More and the cliffs of Mull along the southern shore of the loch. There is the site of what may have been a hermit's monastic cell but there are no other features of note.

The island provides reasonable grazing for sheep.

Eorsa served as a natural barrier across Loch na Keal during the First World War when the loch was used as a deep-water naval anchorage. There were a number of visits by the Grand Fleet and it also provided a rendezvous for Atlantic convoys.

ACCESS: No regular means of access.

Anchorage:
1. Anchor ENE of the island on the 5m line. Loch na Keal is subject to squalls and westerlies cause a swell. Beware extensive reef S of anchorage.

3.7 Ulva
(ON ulv-øy – wolf island) or (ON – Ulfr's island)

Gometra
Derivation obscure

OS Maps: 1:50000 Sheet 47 1:25000 Sheet 328
Admiralty Chart: 1:25000 No.2652

AREA: 2,415ha (5,968 acres)
HEIGHT: 313m (1,027 ft)

OWNER: Owned by the Clark family from 1835 until sold to Edith Lady Congleton in 1945. Her daughter, the Hon. Mrs Jean Howard, now owns Ulva and her son, Jamie Howard, manages the estate. They also owned Gometra but sold it in 1983. Gometra had previously belonged to Captain Ian Henderson of Sussex who bought it from Lady Mary Evelyn Compton Vyner in 1947. Gometra was again put on the market in August 1991 for offers in the region of £650,000 and bought by Mr Roc Sand*ford.

POPULATION: 1841 – 859 combined population of Ulva and Gometra but in 1848 the potato famines followed by clearances reduced the population to 150.

	1881	1891	1931	1951	1961	1971	1981	1991
Ulva	53	46	25	19	33	23	13	30
Gometra	30	31	37	10	15	10	4	0
	83	77	62	29	48	33	17	30

GEOLOGY: Basalt domes reminiscent of the Pyramids and sea cliffs of columnar basalt but generally a dark, fine-grained igneous rock. The columnar formations on the south coast are particularly striking. There is no peat of any consequence.

HISTORY: Ulva belonged to the MacQuarries from the 10th century or earlier whereas Gometra belonged to the monastery of Iona before it came into the possession of the Duke of Argyll.

In 1543 Donald Dubh, aged sixty, recognised chief of the Clan Donald and heir to the Lordship of the Isles, escaped from captivity in Edinburgh Castle after a total of fifty-five years incarceration. This had been with the connivance of the first Earl of Argyll who was quick to exploit the situation after King James IV had decided to abolish the title of Lord of the Isles. It was the start of the Campbell takeover. The islanders rose to Donald's support – the Mackinnons of Mull, the Macleans of Duart, the MacLeods from Lewis and Skye, the MacDonalds of Clanranald and the MacQuarries of Ulva. They held a Council at Finlaggan in Islay in 1545 in the traditional manner but Donald Dubh, weak from a lifetime in prison, died of a fever. He was duly buried with the honours of a Lord of the Isles and then the islesmen sadly returned home. 'It is no joy without Clan Donald, It is no strength to be without them. . .' said a Gaelic bard.

At one time the MacQuarries had a bright young piper called MacArthur who had been trained by the legendary MacCrimmons of Dunvegan in Skye. He founded his own piping college on Ulva which became renowned in its own right.

It has been recorded that by 1800 every family on Ulva owned at least one boat and there was a surplus crop of potatoes for export, so the islanders must at least have enjoyed, for a time, a reasonable standard of living.

Later, MacQuarrie, may have had to sell Ulva to pay off his debts. Gometra was at that time in the possession of the MacDonalds of Staffa, and both islands were put up for sale simultaneously in 1845. They were thus able to be purchased jointly by the notorious Mr F. W. Clark. In just four years, 1846 to 1851, the ruthless new owner deported over two-thirds of the total population. His factor and men turned families out of their cottages without warning by setting fire to the thatch. The islanders were not even given time to collect their few possessions and their livestock was forfeit.

WILDLIFE: A first impression of Ulva is of bracken galore and lots of rabbits. But there are hares, otters and red deer. Oysters are cultivated in the west. Gometra has goats, a deer farm, and a small hardwood plantation on the east side.

Birdlife on both islands is varied, including buzzards, ravens, woodcock, snipe, occasional grouse and pheasant, common and Arctic tern, gannet, eider, oystercatcher, curlew, redshank and red-breasted merganser.

Dr Johnson and Boswell visited **ULVA** in October 1773. In Boswell's own words:

'. . .a servant was sent forward to the ferry, to secure the boat for us: but the boat was gone to the Ulva side, and the wind was so high that the people could not hear him call; and the night so dark that they could not see a signal. We should have been in a very bad situation, had there not fortunately been lying in the little sound of Ulva an Irish vessel . . . (which) ferried us over.

'M'Quarrie's house was mean; but we were agreeably surprised with the appearance of the master whom we found to be intelligent, polite and much a man of the world. Though his clan is not numerous, he is a very ancient Chief. . . He told us his family had possessed Ulva for nine hundred years; but I was distressed to hear that it was soon to be sold for payment of his debts.

'M'Quarrie insisted that the *Mercheta Mulierum*. . . did really mean the privilege which a lord of a manor had to have the first night of all his vassal's wives. Dr Johnson said the belief . . . was also held in England . . . by which the eldest child does not inherit, from a doubt of his being the son of the tenant. M'Quarrie told us that still on the marriage of each of his tenants, a sheep is due to him. I suppose Ulva is the only place where this custom remains.

'Being informed that there was nothing worthy of observation in Ulva, we took boat and proceeded to Inch Kenneth. . .'

There is actually a great deal 'worthy of observation' on these islands although possibly not to Boswell's taste. The MacQuarrie's 'mean' house was later rebuilt by the new owner to an Adam design and it was visited and praised by Sir Walter Scott. The present Ulva House stands in pleasant woodland on the site of the Adam masterpiece which unfortunately was destroyed by fire. Virtually all the present dwellings on Ulva are grouped at the east end of the island in the neighbourhood of the ferry and there is also a small chapel.

Thomas Campbell (1777-1844), in his famous poem 'Lord Ullin's daughter', told the sad story of an eloping Chief of Ulva and his bride who drowned when fleeing from her parents. They are reputed to be buried on the Mull shore in a grave between Oskamull Farm and Ulva

Ferry. The channel where the ferry crosses from Mull to Ulva is very narrow and is even narrower where the islets **Eilean a' Chaolais** (G. – isle of the kyle) and **Eilean Garbh** restrict the passage, but it is navigable with care.

A rough farm road leads up through the trees by **A' Chrannag** (G. – the pulpit), a hill lying west of Ulva House. This road leads along the north side overlooking Loch Tuath (G. – north loch) all the way to the causeway crossing **Am Bru** (G. – the gut), a narrow tidal channel, between Ulva and Gometra. **Beinn Chreagach** (G. – rocky mountain), the summit of Ulva and almost in the middle of the central ridge, is 313m (1027ft) high. Gometra's highest point which is in line with this ridge is 155m (508ft) high.

After the farm road has left the wooded area by Ulva House there is a track to the left which leads down to and along the south coast of Ulva. This passes a beautiful little ruined water mill with its lade connected to the burn tumbling down Glen Glass and the many sad ruins of the 'cleared' village of Cragaig. Some of the cottage doors still have their lintels in place. Beyond this point are standing stones beside the charming anchorage of Cragaig Bay, sheltered by tidal **Eilean Reilean** amid a peppering of skerries. A maze of sea-passages twist between the islets, **Eilean an Righ** (G. – royal island) and **Eilean na h-Uamh** (G. – cave island), and the many offshore rocks. The track deteriorates further at this point but on the headland to the west are the remnants of **Cille Mhic Eoghainn**. A string of tidal islands, **Eilean na Creiche**, **Garbh Eilean**, and **Eilean Bàn** form a natural breakwater for Cragaig Bay. In the west a dun on Ulva continues the chain of three duns stretching across Gometra.

General Lachlan MacQuarie (1761-1824), the 'father of Australia' was born on Ulva. He instituted liberal penal reforms in Australia while serving as governor of New South Wales. This made him so unpopular with the settlers that he was recalled. His mausoleum is at Gruline on Mull, by Loch na Keal.

Ulva was also the birthplace of some of the ancestors of the missionary and explorer, David Livingstone.

There is now a small restaurant on Ulva – the Boathouse – which sells delicious fresh oysters from the home farm, and visitors are encouraged by an interpretive display to enjoy the island's many attractions with its beautiful walks and nature trails.

GOMETRA was at one time, like Inch Kenneth, known as the granary of Iona. The land sheltering the tiny bay, Lòn Mór, in the south-west corner is still called Rhubha Maol na Mine (G. – flour-meal headland. The large low-lying skerry, **Màisgeir** (ON – seagull skerry), is almost a continuation of this headland. There are the remains of at least three duns and signs of old settlements. A Roman coin was found here in 1958. Gometra House with its six bedrooms has been unoccupied since 1983 and is in need of restoration (1991). It has extensive outbuildings and a walled garden. The old schoolhouse still stands near the shore and the most easterly of the cottages near Gometra House is called Teacher's Cottage. It has occasionally been occupied by a resident caretaker and his wife and family. The four dilapidated cottages beside Gometra harbour were formerly occupied by MacBraynes' Staffa boatmen who used to row passengers out to the steamers which were unable to come alongside. Behind these cottages is an old graveyard.

Hugh Ruttledge, the Himalayan explorer, once had his home on Gometra.

A popular but shallow anchorage, Acairseid Mhór (G. – big anchorage) at the north-west corner has the never-failing attraction of a secret hideaway – a narrow passage past the rocks of tidal **Eilean Dioghlum** leads into an enclosed pool.

ACCESS: Ulva Ferry – a service run by the owners on request during normal hours, 01688-2165. Crossing time about five minutes.

Anchorages:
1. Sound of Ulva (56° 28.5N 06° 08W), S of the ferry, WNW of Sgeir Beul a' Chaolais, can be squally in S'lies, 3m, sand and mud. Alternatively, in settled weather, E of this anchorage in the bay on the Mull shore beyond the drying reef.
2. Cragaig Bay. Pleasant sheltered (except for strong S'lies) anchorage NE of Little Colonsay among rocks and islets on S coast of Ulva.

GOMETRA HOUSE

3. Gometra Harbour. Sheltered anchorage between Ulva and Gometra entered from S. Well protected except S'ly gales. Anchor off E shore, mud and weed.

4. Acairseid Mhór, N coast of Gometra. A very snug but restricted anchorage behind Eilean Dioghalum. Anchor in 4m off E shore, sand and weed.

5. Soriby Bay (56 29N 06 11W), at SE of Loch Tuath. Good shelter except N'lies. Several hazards so follow sailing directions with care. Anchor at S end of W side of bay, or at inlet in SE corner.

3.8 Lunga

(ON langr-øy – longship island) or (G. long – ship, ON -øy – island). This is the largest of the Treshnish Isles, although Bac Mór, popularly known as the Dutchman's Cap, is much more prominent from a distance.

OS Maps: 1:50000 Sheet 46 or 48 1:25000 Sheet 315 1:10000 Sheet NM 24 SE
Admiralty Charts: 1:75000 No.2171 1:25000 No.2652

AREA: 81ha (200 acres)
HEIGHT: 103m (338 ft)

OWNER: The explorer and naturalist Col. Niall Rankin bought the Treshnish Isles in 1938. They were put up for sale by the Rankin family trust in 1994 for offers over £600,000. Permission to land should be obtained from House of Treshnish, Calgary, Mull.

POPULATION: 1800 – about 20. Year-round occupation ended in 1824 when Donald Campbell and his family left the island but regular summer occupation continued until 1857. Uninhabited since then.

GEOLOGY: All the Treshnish group are of volcanic origin with the distinctive hat shape of Bac Mór being an ancient volcano with a lava platform brim. On Lunga the volcanic flows have eroded to form a lava plateau.

HISTORY: When the Lord of the Isles acquired the Treshnish Isles in 1354 they were on the frontier between the Nordreys and Sudreys – the Northern and Southern Isles. There is more Treshnish history on Lunga's northern neighbours than on Lunga itself. Cairn na Burgh More has the remains of a castle on the site of an earlier Norse building. The castle is thought to have belonged to the Lord of Lorn, Chief of the Clan MacDougall. Beside the fort are the remains of a small chapel and the Well of the Half Gallon. It is claimed that during a clan feud MacLean of Lochbuie was imprisoned in the castle on Cairn na Burgh More with only the ugliest woman in Mull for company but

Lochbuie rose to the occasion and gave her a son who eventually won back his heritage. At the Reformation of 1560 it is said that the monks of Iona buried their priceless library on Cairn na Burgh More for safety but it has never been recovered.

In 1680 after a prolonged attack by Argyll against the Macleans of Mull they retreated to the Treshnish Isles and held out for a long time but eventually had to surrender when Argyll obtained the King's support for his cause.

The ruins of a smaller castle or fort used during the 1715 Jacobite rising are on the smaller island of Cairn na Burgh Beg. But on Lunga itself, below Cruachan's north slope, there are only the well-preserved walls of a small village of black houses last occupied in 1857.

WILDLIFE: Primroses, violets, birdsfoot trefoil, buttercups, daisies, bluebells, orchids, sea campion, sea pinks, wild rose, honeysuckle, brambles, scotch thistles, cotton grass, yellow flags, tormentil, silverweed, dandelion, and the scarce oyster-plant are all to be found on this delightful island. It is a designated Site of Special Scientific Interest.

This is a popular and important breeding ground for grey seals but only three land mammals have been recorded – mice, rabbits and domestic sheep. The mice may be descendants of the house mice that lived in the village in the mid 18th century according to Dr Fraser Darling who stayed for

BAC MÓR AND HARP ROCK FROM CORRAN LUNGA

Sgeir na h-Iolaire

Sgeir an Eirionnaich

Sgeir an Fheòir

Tighchoie

Sgeir a' Chaisteil

Corran Lunga

Sgeirean na Giusaich

Bn⊙

Village (ruin)

Dùn Cruit

Cruachan
Bn⊙100

Sgeirean Mór

1 km

1/2 mile

An Calbh

three months on Lunga in 1937. The mice ate his notes.

A thousand or more barnacle geese fly in each winter and there are hundreds of thrushes, blackbirds and starlings in the summer. Guillemot, razorbill and puffin breed on Lunga in large numbers, also fulmar, shag, kittiwake and other gulls. From May to September one can see Manx shearwater, storm petrel, gannet and Arctic skua and occasionally, pomarine, great skua, and great and sooty shearwater.

LUNGA has been described as 'a green jewel in a peacock sea,' which sounds an extravagant description until one lands and realises the truth of it for Lunga has a fresh and distinctive beauty all its own.

This is the largest island in the Treshnish group with a rounded hill called **Cruachan** (G. – conical hill) of 103m (338ft) and a magnificent view from its summit. To the south-west is the most conspicuous landmark of the Treshnish Isles, **Bac Mòr** (G. – the big bank), or the Dutchman's Cap, which is an eroded volcanic cone encircled by a grassy rim of lava. It is only possible to land in the quietest of sea and weather and there is no safe anchorage either here or on nearby **Bac Beag**. This did not concern our ancestors for amid the wildflowers round the Dutchman's Cap can be found the remains of summer shielings.

Looking across the many rocks and skerries on Lunga's north-east side the smaller islands of **Fladda** (ON – flat island)', **Cairn na Burgh Beag** and **Cairn na Burgh More** (G. *carn* – rock pile, ON *borv* – fort, – rock of the big fort) can be seen. Landing on both 'Carnburgs' is difficult and strong tidal streams don't help. It is easy to see how defensible they were. The larger Carnburg has its fortifications on the flat grassy top with a massive wall infilling a natural rock buttress on the perimeter. A further wall and stone gateway protects the castle and chapel.

On Lunga itself, **Dun Cruit** – Harp Rock – is a distinctive feature on the west side. It is a piece of sharply-angled cliff, almost a stack, with a narrow chasm beside it into which the sea surges 30m (100 ft) below. The shape is reminiscent of Boreray in the St Kilda group although the comparative scale is tiny. The grassy summit, and the edge of the surrounding cliffs are pitted with puffin burrows. During the nesting season these friendly little birds will walk close up to visitors, study them seriously, and pose for their portraits.

In the past when sea-birds' eggs were an important item of diet, fishermen used to carry a mast up to Dun Cruit. They would lay this over the chasm and crawl across to collect the eggs and young birds (puffin mainly). There is only one record of a man falling to his death.

North of Lunga at the end of a drying spit of tumbled boulders – Corran Lunga – is **Sgeir a' Chaisteil** (G. – castle rock), a castle-shaped rock. This is a popular area for nesting gulls and oyster-catchers. The boulder beach is also the most direct landing place for a dinghy from a yacht in the anchorage. Overlooking Corran Lunga there is a plateau beneath Cruachan with the ruined village on it and what appears to have been a walled vegetable patch. A fresh-water spring in fairly close proximity is quite difficult to find as it is under the shelter of a secluded overhanging rock on the hillside south of the village.

A rudimentary path runs round the entire island from Corran Lunga in the north to **An Calbh** (G. – the headland) at the southern extremity. Almost central there is a cave, or 'gloup' [NM276415] which leads from a hollow to the western seashore, with rough man-made steps leading into it. There are ferns in this mysterious, silent cavern which is shaped like a circular pit with a narrow dark passage through to the sea. The ravine nearby is called the Dorlinn (G. – drying gravel beach). On the east side in the same area is a landing place for a dinghy.

Mountaineers may enjoy the challenge of a climb on Harp Rock and the cliffs on either side of it. There is a possible line of ascent up a crack on the north side of the rock which is about 4m wide near the top – at a height of some 30m above the water. Remember, however, that this must never be attempted when the seabirds are breeding.

ACCESS: Frequent summer boat trips are run from Fionnphort and Dervaig on Mull (weather permitting).

Anchorages:
1. E of Corran Lunga. The approach is from N or S but both directions require great caution. Anchor SE of Sgeir a' Chaisteil off the boulder beach in about 4m, sand. Subject to swell.

3.9 Lismore

(G. lios-mór – big garden). As well as 'garden' the Gaelic word lios *can also mean a residence, palace, fortified place or enclosure.*

OS Maps: 1:50000 Sheet 49 1:25000 Sheets 318, 330 and 331
Admiralty Charts: 1:25000 No.2378

AREA: 2,351ha (5,809 acres)
HEIGHT: 127m (417 ft)

POPULATION: 1798 – 900. 1841 – 1399. 1881 – 621. 1891 – 561. 1931 – 280. 1961 – 155. 1971 – 166. 1981 – 156. 1991 – 140.

OWNER: The Duke of Argyll is the main landowner.

GEOLOGY: Mainly Dalradian limestone. Until the Second World War this was quarried at An Sàilean, a cove on the west coast. Lismore soil is exceptionally fertile.

HISTORY: There are a number of duns, forts and cairns which testify to the long period of settlement on Lismore.

St Moluag was an Irish contemporary of St Columba. For many centuries after he founded his monastery here in 561-564 the island was an ecclesiastical centre.

About the year 1200 John the Englishman, Bishop of Dunkeld and Argyll, appealed to the Pope to disjoin the Argyll see because he was unable to learn to speak Gaelic. The Pope complied and Lismore was chosen as the seat of a separate diocese of Argyll and continued so until 1507 when the centre moved to Saddell in Kintyre. The bishops were called *Episcopi Lismorenses*. A manuscript collection of Gaelic and English poems which are of value as a guide to the works of Ossian, the *Book of the Dean of Lismore*, was compiled here in the 15th century.

MAINLAND

Kingairloch

Loch Linnhe

N

Sgeir nan
Tom

Eilean Ramsay

Eilean nan Caorach

Eilean nam Meanh

Rubha Bàn

Inn
Island

Eilean
Loch Oscair

Ferry

Port
Ramsay

Port na Moralachd

Fennachrochan

Achuaran

Castle Coeffin

Clachan

Baileouchdarach

Càrn
Mór

Cross

Port Moluag

ERISKA

Sloc a' Mhuilinn

Balure

Tirefour Castle
(broch)

Killandrist

PO

Loch Baile
a' Ghobhainn

Eilean
Dubh

An Sàilean

Quay

Balliveolan

Port an Dreadhain

Killean

MAINLAND

Quarry

Achnacroish

Benderloch

Ferry Pier

Baligrundle

Lynn of Lorn

Achadun Bay

Frackersaig

Dùn
Mòr

Dùn Cuilein

Kilcheran
Loch

Bernera
Island

Achinduin

Achadun
Castle

△127

Kilcheran

En na
Cloiche

Barr Mór

Bernera Bay

Loch Fiart

En
nan
Gamhna

En Dubh

Cairns

Broch

Pladda

Bàgh Clach
an Dobhrain

Rubha na Gaoith
Miller's Port

Creag

Rubha
Fiart

Dalnarrow

Dùn Chruban

Ferry

Eilean Musdile

5 km
3 miles

WILDLIFE: There are many fine trees and shelter belts, mainly sycamore, ash, lime and chestnut, but little natural woodland although in 1596 the whole island was very thickly forested with oak. Thanks to the rich soil, wild-flowers grow to larger than normal proportions; field gentians, rock rose (Helianthemum), mimulus, tutsan, ivy-leaved toadflax, wild orchids, yellow monkey-flower, cranesbill, brooklimes, water mints and speedwells are all to be found.

There are gulleries on the islets, Eilean nan Gamhna, and linked Eilean na Cloiche and Eilean Dubh in the Lynn of Lorn.

For delightful walking country **LISMORE** is supreme – a long narrow island with an undulating landscape of fertile soil in shallow longitudinal valleys. The highest hill is **Barr Mór** (G. – big tip), a modest 127m, but right in the centre of the southern area with a stunning panoramic view from its summit – north to the mountains of Ardgour, Lochaber with Ben Nevis to the north-east, Port

Appin and Lochs Creran and Etive to the east, Oban, Kerrera and the Firth of Lorn to the south, Duart Castle and Mull to the south-west and the mountains of Morvern to the west. The walk along the ridge, over the summit of Barr Mór and down by the reed-fringed lochan to the south must be one of the finest walks in Scotland with views which are unequalled anywhere.

The lighthouse on **Eilean Musdile** at the southern extremity was built by Alan Stevenson.

Lime was quarried on the west coast and lime kilns and quarrymen's cottages can still be seen on **Eilean nan Caorach** (G. – sheep island) among the skerries at the extreme north end opposite Port Appin and alongside **Inn Island** (?G. *innis* – island). The boats carrying the lime operated out of Port Ramsay in the north. This sheltered anchorage between **Eilean Ramsay** and **Eilean nam Meann** (G. – kid island) is now used as an overnight stop by the occasional workboat from the giant quarry at Glensanda on the Morvern coast opposite Lismore. To the north is **Eilean Gainimh** (G. – island of fine sand) and **Eilean Glas** (G. – grey island). Port Ramsay is overlooked by two neat rows of limeburners' cottages most of which are now holiday homes.

The main road runs down the spine of the island with connections to the crofts and farms. In the 18th century the main crops were oats and barley but nowadays cattle and sheep are more popular. Most of the dwellings are in the north. The ruin of a tall galleried broch called Tirefour Castle, about 4km from the north-east end of Lismore, lies on the summit of a 50m high grassy knoll close to the east coast [NM867429].

Almost opposite Tirefour, on the north-west coast, **Coeffin Castle**, a ruined 13th century structure, was probably built by the MacDougalls of Lorn on the site of a Viking fortress [NM853437]. The MacDougalls were defeated by Robert the Bruce. There is an ancient tidal fish trap on the shore below the castle and above it are the remains of the largest cairn in Argyll [NM859435].

The ferry pier is at **Achnacroish**, near the centre of the east coast where there is a general store and a junior school. Lismore has no mains water supply. All the water comes from wells and springs and these can run dry at times.

The disused lime quarry at An Sàilean (G. – the creek), across the island from Achnacroish, is sadly deserted today with its ivy-covered kilns and roofless cottages. Carthorses from far afield used to be landed at the old quay as the Lismore men were noted for their ability to break them in.

Much of the shoreline is low sea cliffs with a few pleasant shingle beaches. The cliffs in the south-east opposite Eilean na Cloiche are only some 25m high yet they can present a severe challenge for mountaineers. **Eilean na Cloiche** (G. – island of the stone) is a boldly-shaped rock rising almost straight out of the

sea for about 21m with **Eilean nan Gamhna** alongside and a dumbell-shaped islet formed by linked **Pladda** and **Creag**. **Eilean Dubh**, further north in the centre of the Lynn of Lorn is worth a visit but not for climbing as it is very loose rubble.

The man who built the great folly on the hill above Oban, John Stuart McCaig, was born on Lismore. He was a banker, essayist and art critic.

Bernera on the west coast is more of a peninsula than an island and was once known as Berneray of the Noble Yew, a tree under which St Columba was said to have preached. The ancient yew was felled in 1850 to make a staircase in Lochnell Castle on the mainland and the remains of the small island chapel have disappeared. **Achadun Castle**, – the Bishop's Castle, – overlooks Bernera [NM804393].

The bishop lived at some distance from the small cathedral which was founded at the start of the 13th century. The ancient monastic site is known as **Kilmoluaig** (G. – St Moluag's cell or church). It is on the main road near Clachan [NM860434]. Unfortunately there are few remains of the cathedral which was burnt during the Reformation but in 1749 the walls of the cathedral choir were reduced in height and roofed to create the present tiny parish church – one of the earliest parish churches still in use. There are some fine medieval tombstones in the graveyard which is also reputed to be the burial site of St Moluag (523-592). **Eilean Loch Oscair** is in the bay to the north.

The story goes that two competitive saints, St Moluag and St Mulhac, had a boat race across the Lynn of Lorn after agreeing that the first to touch Lismore would be entitled to found his monastery on the island. St Moluag realised at the last minute that he would not reach the land first so he cut off his finger and threw it ashore. It landed on the beach just north of the broch at Tirefour. This gained him the title and he duly founded his monastery in AD 564. His pastoral staff, a thorn stick nearly one metre long, is still held by the Livingstones of Bachuil, hereditary keepers for the parish.

ACCESS: Two ferries serve the island. Port Appin, about every two hours, is passenger only: crossing time 10 minutes, 01631-73217. Oban, car ferry, 01631-66688.

TIREFOUR BROCH GUARDS THE LYNN OF LORN

Anchorages:

1. Port Ramsay, close E of Eilean nam Meann at N end of Lismore, a well-sheltered anchorage, bottom sand and shells. Use the north approach.

2. Port na Moralachd, at NW corner, reasonable shelter except for winds SW-W which can cause a swell. Anchor close in at S side of the bay. Only approach is from SW.

3. An Sàilean, middle of W coast. Shallow inlet. Moderate draught in neaps or small craft able to take the ground.

4. Achadun Bay, occasional anchorage NE of Bernera in S'ly winds.

5. Bernera Bay, by the SE side of Bernera Island, occasional anchorage in N'ly winds. Keep near the E shore to avoid rocks 1c from SE side of Bernera.

6. Achnacroish is the Oban ferry terminal; a stone causeway and pier extend from the shore; least depth of 3m alongside the pier.

3.10 Tiree

[tY-ree] (G. tir iodh – land of corn). Watson disputes this derivation and suggests the name may be pre-Celtic.

OS Maps: 1:50000 Sheet 46 1:25000 Sheet 314
Admiralty Charts: 1:100000 No.1778 Sound of Gunna 1:25000 No.2475

AREA: 7,834ha (19,358 acres)
HEIGHT: 141m (462 ft)

OWNER: The Duke of Argyll owns most of the island.

POPULATION: 1755 – 2200. 1794 – 2555. 1830 – 4450. 1841 – 4391 (805 houses). 1881 – 2730. 1891 – 2449 (537 houses). 1931 – 1448. 1961 – 993. 1971 – 875. 1981 – 780. 1991 – 768.

GEOLOGY: A flat fertile island with a bedrock of Archaean gneiss (a schist known as paragneiss). A limestone outcrop known as Tiree marble – pink flecked with green – was quarried at Balephetrish from 1791 to 1794 and briefly again in 1910. (Stones now sold as Tiree marble come from Connemara in Ireland). East of the quarry is Clach a' Choire (G. – ringing stone) – a glacial erratic which originated on Rum (No.4.3).

HISTORY: Pottery and tools of 800 BC have been uncovered at Dùn Mór Vaul where there is a broch. St Columba sailed into Gott Bay on his way to visit the monastery founded by his cousin, Baitheine, at Sorobaidh. Apparently, on arrival, he struck a rock which nearly sank his boat, so he cursed it. Most sailors still follow this tradition.

St Comgall, a Pict and an associate of St Columba, also founded a monastery on Tiree.

In 672 the Vikings burnt down the monastery, but some decided that they liked the island and settled. This however did not stop King Magnus of Norway – twenty-five years old and a born arsonist – plundering the island

THE MEDIEVAL CHAPEL AT KIRKAPOL BESIDE THE LONG BEACH, TRÁIGH MHÓR

at the end of the 11th century and setting it alight. According to one of his skalds, Bjorn Cripplehand, 'The glad wolf reddened tooth and claw with many a mortal wound in Tiree. . .' Control passed to the Kingdom of Man and then to Somerled, King of the Isles, and his heirs in 1164. After the Battle of Largs in 1263 Alexander III granted ownership to the MacDougalls but they were indecisive owners and there were continual disputes. By 1390 Lachlan MacLean was Bailie of Tiree and Coll which led to his descendants claiming ownership. Eventually however, in the latter part of the 17th century, the Duke of Argyll took control.

It was at this time that much of the arable farming began to be replaced by cattle grazing, although barley was still grown for whisky. Tiree was exporting up to three thousand gallons of whisky a year at the end of the 18th century.

The population which had been 4450 in 1830 had dropped to 2700 fifty years later due to evictions and potato famines. In 1885 the Duke of Argyll prevailed on the Government to send fifty policemen and 250 marines on the *Ajax* and *Assistance* to evict the crofters. The crofters resisted and although the marines arrested and held five crofters for a token period they were generally sympathetic towards the islanders. The matter was settled in 1886 with the passing of the Crofters' Act which split the land into 270 crofts.

WILDLIFE: Tiree has hares, but no rabbits, foxes, stoats or weasels.

The machair has a dense cover of meadow flowers, particularly where there is restricted access for sheep. There is very little actual grass, the cover is mainly daisy, dandelion, red and white clover, buttercup, blue speedwell, hop and birdsfoot trefoil, eyebright, harebell, yellow and blue pansy, silverweed, wild thyme, and the common spotted orchid sub-species, *O. fuchsii hebridensis*.

A mat of sea thrift rings the coastline with marram grass tying down the dunes.

Tiree has great interest for bird watchers all the year round and in spring and summer wildfowl, waders and

seabirds breed there: skylark on the machair: sedge warbler, corncrake and reed bunting in denser vegetation. Exceptional sites are:

Loch a' Phuill: mute and whooper swans in autumn
and winter. Oct-April Greenland white-fronted geese.
Greylag geese all year. Wigeon, teal, mallard, pintail,
shoveller, pochard, tufted duck, goldeneye, red-breasted
merganser in winter.

Loch Bhasapoll: Pochard, tufted duck and much more.

The Reef: The centre of the island. Greenland white-
fronted geese.

Balephetrish Bay: ringed plover, sanderling, dunlin, purple sandpiper and turnstone. Great northern diver, eider
and long-tailed duck in winter.

Salum and Vaul Bays: good for feeding waders.

Ceann a' Mhara: Breeders: fulmar, shag, kittiwake, guillemot and razorbill. Starlings nest in the caves.

TIREE is sometimes referred to as *Tir-fo-Thuinn* – the land
beneath the waves. There are only two high points, **Ben
Hynish** in the south (141m) with its 'golf-ball' radar station and **Ben Hough** in the north-west (119m). Over
two-thirds of the island has been covered with wind-
blown shell sand which has created a fertile, plough-deep

and well-drained machair. It was this rich soil which
earned Tiree the title of the land of corn. Tiree is virtually
unique among Scottish isles in having no peat-bog. The
rainfall is low and from May to September the climate is
the sunniest in Britain, but the wind that brought the rich
soil blows constantly and there is no natural shelter from
it. This is the windiest place in the United Kingdom with
an average annual wind speed of 17mph. No wonder that
every October it is the venue for the world-renowned International Windsurfing Championships.

This is still a thriving crofting community (unlike its
sister island Coll) maintaining a stable and viable population, although the smallness of the land-holdings make
many of the crofts barely economic. Cattle and sheep are
grazed, the arable farming being mainly for winter feed.
The black houses (G. – tigh dubh) with dry-stone walls up
to nine feet thick, rounded corners, a fire hearth in the
middle of the floor and thatched roofs within the outer
walls for wind-protection are still here but most have been
'modernised' and are now white houses (G. – tigh geal),
so-called because the original walls have been cemented
and whitewashed. Thatched roofs have been replaced with
felt or corrugated iron and the houses now have fireplaces
with chimneys.

In Gott Bay a fine sweep of sand (G. *Tràigh Mhór* – long beach) leads round from the tidal island of **Soa** (ON – sheep island) to the ferry terminal at **Scarinish**. Here there is a post-office, shops, hotel, and an old stone harbour (built 1771), now only frequented by the lobster boats, while on the beach lies the wreck of the *Mary Stewart*, one of the last sailing ships to trade in this area. West of Scarinish, in the flat centre of the island – called **The Reef** – is an airfield built by the RAF in 1941 for Squadrons 218 and 518 flying Warwicks and Halifax bombers. It is now used for commercial flights. The weather station here, which contributes to the shipping forecasts, was started by the Head Teacher of Consignor School who began keeping records in 1926.

At the southern tip, **Hynish** has granite houses and a small pier built for the workers on the **Skerryvore** lighthouse which is ten miles out to sea to the south-west. It was built by an uncle of R. L. Stevenson in 1838-43. It is 42m (138ft) high and sits on a rock only three metres above Mean High Water Springs. The 4000 tons of granite used in its construction came from the Bull Hole quarry on Mull. It has been unmanned since it was damaged by fire in 1954. The granite tower at Hynish was used to send signals to the lighthouse, and is now a museum.

Tiree's largest loch, **Loch a' Phuill**, is near the west coast amid extensive areas of dunes which are grazed by sheep and cattle. The knuckle in the south-west corner, **Ceann a' Mhara** [kenë-va:rë] (G. – head of the sea) is littered with ancient relics while at the north-west corner numerous offshore rocks and skerries surround the shell-sand bays.

Loch Bhasapoll is also in the north-west, with its two crannogs, marshy fringes, and wintering geese. A village called Baile nan Craganach (G. – place of the clumsy people) is said to have once stood on the loch's north shore, so called because the villagers all had six fingers on each hand. Further east, in the centre of the north coast, **Balephetrish Bay** (G. *baile pheadairich* – the place of the storm petrel) was the original source of Tiree marble.

Dun and broch remains (more than twenty of them), stone circles, standing stones, cairns and crannogs are scattered right across the island. **Dùn Mór Vaul** by Vaul Bay in the north-east is of particular interest [NM042492]. It was started as a timber structure in the 6th century BC and was later turned into a stone broch about the 1st century BC. Galleries are still visible in the 4m thick walls. The brochs of Tiree are the furthest south of all the island brochs.

The Ringing Stone, west of Vaul [NM027487], is covered with cup-marks and clangs eerily when struck. It should be treated with care as it is prophesied that if the stone is broken Tiree will sink forever beneath the waves.

ACCESS: Vehicle ferry from Oban to Scarinish, 3 to 4 times weekly, 01631-66688 or 0187-92337. Air service from Glasgow, 0345-222111. The Post Bus serves most of the island. Cars can be hired locally, 018792-469 or -555, and bicycles, 018792-428.

Anchorages:

1. Scarinish. Both creek and drying harbour can occasionally be used if no swell is coming in. Near HW, or at neaps, temp. berth at old pier possible, or anchored in middle of creek.

2. Gott Bay concrete pier has a depth of 3.4m (11') alongside. Landing slip on inner side. Foul ground extends 6c SE from pier.

3. Gott Bay. Exposed but affords moderately good anchorage in settled weather or light W'lies in 4-5m, sand, N-NE of pier on SW side of bay. Several dangers both sides and in the fairway.

4. Clach Chuirr (Port Ruadh) off Gunna Sound affords some shelter from S and W. Anchor on either side of the power cable in 3m, sand.

5. Hynish pier. Some limited shelter from S in very settled conditions. Pier and dock dry out.

3.11 Gunna

(ON Gunni-øy – the island of Gunni the Dane)

OS Maps: 1:50000 Sheet 46 1:25000 Sheet 300
Admiralty Charts: 1:75000 No.2171 Sound of Gunna 1:25000 No.2475

AREA: 69ha (168 acres)
HEIGHT: 35m (115 ft)

POPULATION: No census records.

GEOLOGY: A bedrock of paragneiss schist with a light sandy soil. Metasediments in the west grade into undifferentiated gneiss in the east.

WILDLIFE: Gunna has many varieties of birds but is noted particularly for the arctic tern, little tern, and possibly also sandwich tern, which nest here. Three common species of large gull also have colonies, but all these ground-nesting birds periodically suffer serious losses when brown rats, *rattus norvegicus*, invade the island. Barnacle geese use the island for winter bed-and-breakfasting while fairly large numbers of white-fronted and greylag geese occasionally appear. Shelduck are prolific in the spring.

This is a grey seal nursery and about fifty calves are born here every autumn.

Lying in the sound between Tiree and Coll, **GUNNA** was possibly once inhabited by an anchorite. It is now only grazed by cattle or sheep. It is separated from Coll by a shallow rock-strewn passage. Gunna is a narrow little wind-blown island, no more than 500m wide for most of its length, and with few prominent features. There is an

Calgary Point

COLL

Creagan a'
Chaolais Bhàin

Soy
Gunna

Eilean nam Maidean

Caolas Bán

Bo maoil nam
Faoileag

Eilean Frachlan

Sloc na Faing

Bàgh
Frachlan

Uamh Mór
(cave)

McNeil's
Bay

35
25

Well

Port
na Cille

Eilean nan
Gamhna

Seabed Cables

Eilean Bhoramuil

Gunna Sound

Sgeir Dubh

1 km
1/2 mile

Gunna

Placaid Bogha

old well beside Port na Cille (G. – port of the chapel), a name which provides a clue to possible early habitation, and a distinctive cave in the centre of the north coast which could have served as a hermit's shelter [NM099514].

The sea passage, Gunna Sound, between Coll and Tiree is a relatively shallow stretch of water. The area in the immediate vicinity of Gunna is scattered with rocks and there are more rocky patches off the Tiree shore. Islets near Tiree include **Creachasdal**, **Librig**, **Eilean Liath** and **Eilean Ghreasamuill**, while **Eilean Bhoramuil** lies off the southern extremity of Coll.

ACCESS: No regular means of access.

Anchorages: No recommended anchorages, but temporary anchorage possible, in quiet conditions and best near low water, about 3/4c E of the S extremity of Eilean na Gamhna.

3.12 Shuna

Uncertain derivation, probably Norse but possibly (G. sidhean – fairy hill, ON -øy – island).

OS Maps: 1:50000 Sheet 49 1:25000 Sheet 318
Admiralty Chart: 1:25000 No.2379

AREA: 155ha (383 acres)
HEIGHT: 71m (233 ft)

OWNER: Col Thomas R Craig of Invergare, Rhu (?Present owner, Mr Stephen Newall, Deputy Lord Lieutenant of Dunbartonshire).

POPULATION: 1881 – 8. 1891 – 6. 1931 – 4. 1961 – 0. 1971 – 0. 1981 – 0. 1991 – 0.

GEOLOGY: Mostly Dalradian limestone giving a good soil.

HISTORY: A document of 1577-1595 says that the island belonged to John Stewart, Laird of Appin. A further description in 1630 says that Shuna, property of the Laird of Appin is 'the most profitable and fertilest in all these Countries'.

SHUNA is sometimes rather needlessly called Shuna Island but this is probably to distinguish it from the other Shuna (No.2.10) which lies alongside Luing. It is a compact island separated from the mainland by the narrow Sound of Shuna and rising to a table-topped hill near the north-east end. In a hollow near the hill is a lochan with a stream running past some clumps of conifers. The view from here is dramatic, looking up Loch Linnhe to where the great flank of Ben Nevis can be seen beyond tiny **Eilean Balnagowan**.

Shuna is run as a farm by the owner, and the pleasant white farmhouse faces southwards towards Lismore

(No.3.9) and Appin. At the southernmost extremity are the substantial ruins of **Castle Shuna**, a small square building about 10m high [NM915483]. This is actually a domestic tower house rather than a castle. It was probably built near the end of the 16th century by John Stewart, who died in 1595, or his son, Duncan Stewart. The building was abandoned in the late 18th century or early 19th century.

Across the sound is another island fortress, **Castle Stalker** in Loch Laich. It was built about 1500, also by the Stewarts of Appin, and James IV used it as a hunting lodge. It was a ruin for many years but has now been restored.

In 1958 near Tom an t-Seallaidh (G. – the knoll of the vision) a rock-shelter on Shuna was excavated and deposits of limpet shells, stone-scrapers, deer horn and flints were found.

Unfortunately, on our first visit, both the anchorage in the Sound of Shuna and the beautiful setting were spoilt by the unpleasant odour from a poultry processing plant on The Knap, a piece of ground projecting into the Sound. I am happy to report that on our last visit this was no longer a problem.

ACCESS: No regular means of access.

Anchorages:
1. In Shuna Sound, SW of Knap Point. Alternatively, more sheltered but further from the island, in Dallens Bay (Shuna Cove), E of Knap Point.

3.13 Coll

(G. coll – a hazel). Adomnan calls it 'insula Coloso' from which Watson infers a pre-Celtic origin.

OS Maps: 1:50000 Sheet 46 1:25000 Sheets 286 and 300
Admiralty Charts: 1:100000 No.1796 1:75000 No.2171 Sound of Gunna 1:25000 No.2475 Loch Eatharna (Arinagour) 1:10000 No.2474

AREA: 7,685ha (18,989 acres)
HEIGHT: 104m (341 ft)

OWNER: The Stewart family, owners of Coll since 1856, sold about two-thirds of the island estate to Coll Properties Ltd in 1964 (the Dutch businessman, Jan de Vries), but Kenneth and Janet Stewart continued farming the rest until 1991 when they sold the remainder of the estate and retired to the mainland. Four square miles of coastal grassland were bought by the Royal Society for the Protection of Birds from de Vries some years ago and the remainder of the estate (3,210 acres) is being sold by his widow (1996) for £375,000.

POPULATION: 1740 – about 400. 1755 – 502. 1794 – 902. By 1841 it had reached 1442 (271 houses) which was greater than the island could support according to the

laird, Maclean. He cleared half the population to Australia and Canada. 1881 – 643. 1891 – 522 (111 houses). 1931 – 322. 1961 – 147. 1971 – 144. 1981 – 153. 1991 – 172.

GEOLOGY: Until comparatively recent times in geological terms, Coll and Tiree were one single island. Coll consists of low hummocks of a weathered rock called paragneiss, a schist metamorphosed from sedimentary rock, sticking through the grass and heather like currants in a bun particularly in the eastern half. The south-western area around Gorton and Breachacha is of ancient sediments containing quartz and marble. High dunes and machair stretch along the west coast with raised beaches at Arnabost and Arinagour. Lead was mined in the south of the island in early times.

HISTORY: Coll and Tiree have a very similar early history. Angus Og of Islay, King of the Isles, was granted Coll by Bruce when MacDougall forfeited it around 1314. He was probably then responsible for building Breachacha Castle using the latest defensive techniques known to the MacDonalds.

The Maclean chieftains of Coll were an interesting and enlightened family. The 4th Chieftain, who died in 1560, was a bard who composed verse in both Gaelic and Latin. The 11th Chieftain, Lachlan Maclean, a renowned soldier, was drowned in an accident in 1687. His grandson, Hector, 13th of Coll, had a personal in-house harper at his new residence at Breachacha. He kept most of his clansmen from becoming embroiled in the 1745 rebellion and received a royal charter to his property so that he was not a vassal to the Campbells. He had two successive Campbell wives yet when the Duke of Argyll tried to lease two of his farms on Coll Maclean vowed that he would never let a Campbell move in. Neither of his Campbell wives gave him an heir, so his brother Hugh took over when he died in 1754.

Hugh maintained Neil Rankin, the last hereditary piper to the Macleans, in his household and constructed a mausoleum for his brother's remains. He subsidised a spinning school and the development of linen manufacture on the island. His son Donald, 'young Coll', embarrassed Boswell in 1773 by having to share his bed for the night when they met as guests on Inch Kenneth.

'He was a lively young man,' Boswell reported. 'We found he had been a good deal in England, studying farming, and was resolved to improve the value of his father's lands, without oppressing his tenants, or losing the ancient Highland fashions.' The young man tragically drowned the following year. His brother Alexander, who succeeded as 15th Chieftain in 1790, had many of the same ideals as his brother. He was Lieutenant Colonel of the Breadalbane Fencibles, a regiment which gave employment to many of his clansmen.

By 1841 the population had grown rapidly to over

Cairns of Coll
Sùil Ghorm
Eilean Mór
Acairseid Mhór
Rubha Mór
Bousd
Sorisdale
Sorisdale Bay
A' Chròic
Meall na h-Iolaire
Burial Gd
Church
Cists
Loch Fada
Loch na Cloiche
Sloc na Gamhna
Gallanach
Druim Fishaig
Arnabost
Eileanan na h-Aornan
Rubha Hogh
Fort
Grishipoll
Loch Cliad
Crannogs
Bàgh Feisdlum
Clabhach
Cairn
Loch an Duin
Meall nam Muc
Hogh Bay
104
Ben Hogh
Arinagour
Rubha nan Uan
Cnoc na Moine
Cairns, Crannogs & Standing Stone
Loch Ronard
Pier
Loch Eatharna
Ferry
Acha
Eilean Ornsay
Feall Bay
Ben Feall
Fort
Airstrip
Breachacha Castle
Port na h-Eathar
Dunes
Grave
Loch Gortan
Friesland Bay
Calgary Point
Crossapol Bay
Port a' Mhurain
Loch Breachacha
Eilean Iomallach
Gunna
N
TIREE

Bàgh an Traillaich
Cliad Bay
Grishipoll Point

5 km
3 miles

1400 which was more than the island could support. The laird impoverished himself trying to feed the islanders during the potato famine and paying the fares of those who wished to go to Australia and Canada, and finally had to sell the island to John Lorne Stewart in 1856. The new owner, despite the crofters' protests, raised the rents so in 1861 the 'great exodus' took place. Virtually all the tenants, overnight, left their crofts and moved from the arable south-east to the rock-bound north-west of the island. This area was under Campbell ownership and the promised rents were reasonable but the families had to improvise shelter while they built their new homes. Unfortunately overcrowding led to many families leaving the island in the ensuing years.

Towards the end of the 19th century the Stewarts decided that they now had to repopulate the land and offered crofts at attractive rents to Ayrshire dairy farmers. This resulted in the production of the famous Coll cheese – a favourite delicacy at the House of Lords up to the time that the market for dairy produce collapsed near the start of the First World War.

WILDLIFE: In 1939 botanists were surprised to discover the Irish lady's tresses orchid growing on Coll. It grows in a few Irish localities but is actually a native of North America. Since then a few have also been found on Colonsay. The subspecies, *hebridensis*, of the common spotted orchid also grows here.

It is estimated that, due to modern intensive farming, less than 500 pairs of corncrakes now survive in Britain, mostly in the Outer Hebrides. The birds, which are more often heard than seen, like rough uncultivated conditions. There are about 120 pairs on Tiree and the RSPB has created a corncrake reserve for the twenty or so pairs on Coll.

Boswell gives an interesting account of the natural history (in 1773): 'There are no foxes; no serpents, toads, or frogs, nor any venomous creature. They have otters and mice here; but had no rats till lately that an American vessel brought them. There is a rabbit-warren on the northeast of the island, belonging to the Duke of Argyle. Young Coll (the laird) intends to get some hares, of which there are none at present. There are no black-cock, moor-fowl, nor partridges; but there are snipe, wild-duck, wild-geese, and swans, in winter; wild pigeons, plover, and great number of starlings; of which I shot some, and found them pretty good eating. Woodcocks come hither, though there is not a tree upon the island.' He also mentions the great variety of fish in the brooks and trout and eel in the lochs. Coll has no stoat or weasel and today the Duke of Argyll's rabbits have become a serious pest.

Little lochans scattered over the north end of the island, covered with white water-lilies in the summer months, are the home of red-throated divers and the heather conceals red grouse.

Most of **COLL** is bleak with gnarled lumps of rock protruding through a thin skin of grass and heather. But the trim whitewashed cottages of **Arinagour** (G. *airigh na gobhar* – shieling of the goats), lying beneath two churches on the hill, are welcoming. They were built by Maclean, laird of Coll, about 1800 in an attempt to modernise the island. They are now mainly holiday cottages with most of the 'Collachs' (the local inhabitants) occupying the council houses. Arinagour is alongside **Loch Eatharna** (G. – loch of the small fishing boats). There is an old stone pier and a new ferry pier which was built in 1969. The Isle of Coll Hotel (018793-334) overlooks the loch. It is a pleasant building owned by a past master of the Magic Circle; it has bicycles and mopeds for hire and is the most useful information centre on the island.

Across the island from Arinagour is **Arnabost** where the ruined school was built over a medieval earth house with the entrance under the school porch [NM209600]. The islanders had used this as a hiding place during Viking raids and a gold brooch was found there in 1855.

East of Arnabost the land is virtually empty – low-lying, rocky, and peppered with lochans but the road runs up the northern coastal strip which was the most densely populated part of the island in the 19th century. The area was de-serted by choice, not by forced clearance and the vacant townships of **Bousd** and **Sorisdale** are there to be seen. Along this northern coast, the machair is so rich and fertile that there was an experiment to grow tulips in competition with the Dutch. The climate is mild, Coll is one of the sunniest spots in Britain, and the flowers were a great success but the cost and difficulty of transportation defeated the project. The road passes a cemetery and the remnants of a medieval chapel – **Cille Ionnaig** – where Young Coll, host to Dr Johnson and Boswell, lies buried [NM221618]. He was drowned the year following the visit when sailing from Inch Kenneth to Mull.

Off the northern extremity of Coll are some dangerous rocks and islets although the space beside **Eilean Mór** is known as Acairseid Mhór (G. – big anchorage). **Eag na Maoile** (G. – cleft bare rock) is north of Eilean Mór and **Sùil Gorm** (G. – blue eye) with a light tower on it.

Turning south-west at Arnabost the road passes **Grishipoll**. In the 15th century MacNeill of Barra set up a garrison at this farm when he chose to annex Coll. But Iain Garbh, his stepson and hereditary owner of the land, raised the Collachs, took the garrison and regained his inheritance. His descendants have owned part of Coll until the present time. The road turns into a track beside **Ben Hogh** (104m), Coll's highest hill. On it is a huge boulder balanced on three small ones which according to folklore was placed there by a giant. It is worth following Boswell's footsteps up this hill as the views south are worthwhile. (Dr Johnson chose instead to sit down and read a book).

From Arinagour there is a pleasant road leading to an airstrip on the sand dunes and **Breachacha** (G. – the field speckled with wild-flowers). Here, on the shore of the loch, stands ancient Breachacha Castle which dates back to the 15th century and probably earlier. It has been carefully restored by the Project Trust, a training scheme for young people to give voluntary service in underdeveloped countries. Near it is the attractive new castle built in 1750 by Hector MacLean and visited in October 1773 by Boswell and Dr Johnson. The irascible Johnson 'relished it

BREACHACHA – WHERE MACLEAN FOUGHT MACLEAN

much at first, but soon remarked. . .that. . .it was a mere tradesman's box.' It was later enlarged and mutilated by a Victorian owner and it is now used for holiday homes.

When the Duarts invaded Coll in 1593 they were mown down by the MacLeans and the burn that flows into Loch Breachacha was choked with the heads of the Duart clansmen. It has been called ever since Struthan nan Ceann (G. – the stream of the heads).

There are a number of prehistoric remains in this southern area – standing stones, cairns, traces of brochs and crannogs, and **Dùn an Achaidh**, an ancient fort beside the road from Arinagour [NM183546]. West of Loch Breachacha there are two large attractive bays, Crossapol Bay, with the offshore islet of **Soa** almost linked to **Eilean Iomallach**, and Feall Bay, separated by marram dunes. The neglected shell of the 13th Maclean's Mausoleum is on the peninsula between the southerly bays [NM149524].

ACCESS: Car ferry from Oban, 01631-66688, linking with Tiree. Air service from Glasgow to Tiree continuing to Barra, 0345-222111.

Anchorages: These anchorages are only suitable in favourable conditions and are all open to any directional swell.

1. Loch Eatharna (Arinagour). Popular but exposed. Head dries out about ³/₄M. Divided into two parts by Eilean Eatharna 13.4m high. W part most used but open to S and only suitable for occasional anchorage in summer. Bottom sand. There are HIE visitors moorings. Stone slip and pier off Arinagour village has depth of 2.7m (9') alongside it at HW springs.

2. Hogh Bay on N coast. Occasional anchorage. Sheltered NE-E-S. Approach from N, head for break in sand-dunes. Anchor in 3m, firm sand.

3. Feall Bay on N coast. Occasional anchorage. Sheltered NE-E-S. Approach from N, slightly W of centre line, and anchor in 2-6m, sand with some rock patches (usually visible).

4. Loch Breachacha. Approach requires care. Rocks on both sides. Head shoals gradually. Visitors moorings on W side.

5. Loch Gortan. Narrow sandy bay 1M E of Breachacha. Anchor in 3m, sand.

3.14 Carna

(G. càrn – cairn, heap of stones, rocky mound, ON -øy – island)

OS Maps: 1:50000 Sheet 49 1:25000 Sheet 303
Admiralty Chart: 1:25000 No.2394

AREA: 213ha (526 acres)
HEIGHT: 169m (554 ft)

POPULATION: 1881 – 7. 1891 – 10 (2 houses). 1931 – 3. 1961 – 2. 1971 – 3. 1981 – 0. 1991 – 4.

GEOLOGY: Mainly a Moine schist bedrock of quartz-feldspar constitution, except for the west coastal strip which is mixed schists and mica-schist.

WILDLIFE: An interesting variety of habitat for, among others, willow warblers, redstarts, wheatears, whinchats, twites, ravens and kestrels.

Look east from Loch Drumbuidhe (G. – loch at the yellow ridge) and the dinosaur back of **CARNA** rears up behind the tidal island of Oronsay. It straddles the mouth of remote Loch Teacuis dividing the entrance into two narrow kyles which are a rock-dodging test for any yachtsman. But Loch Teacuis is one of the most fascinating lochs on the West Coast and worthy of its awkward entrance from Loch Sunart. **Eilean nan Gabhar** (G. – goat island), usually covered with basking seals and not a goat in sight, is in the loch just south of Carna's southern headland.

For those approaching by land, Rahoy on Loch Teacuis is a beautiful spot in the heart of Morvern reached by a very minor road from Loch Aline. A walk up the lochside to the shore by Carna passes a fascinating example of a vitrified fort set in oak woodland above the narrows [NM633564].

The west side of Carna is steep and unwelcoming. Wet, slippy and boggy with abrupt rocky slopes covered in a profusion of flag irises, tufts of sphagnum moss, bracken, grass and scrub birch.

There is a central peak, **Cruachan Chàrna** (G. – the conical hill of Carna), which is the highest part of the knobbly north-south ridge dividing the island. South of it is Cruachan Buidhe (G. – the yellow stack). The eastern slopes are sheltered from the prevailing winds and are much gentler than the west side. As on neighbouring **Oronsay** the inevitable lonely little ruined cottages are scattered south of a stream which trickles down the mountain and into Caol Chàrna at Rubha na h-Eaglaise (G. – headland of the church). But at least Carna still has a token population with three occupied houses and one being renovated at the time of writing. There is not much in the way of level ground but there is a mellowness in the landscape with a stand of conifers and a small copse of deciduous woodland. A few rowan and birch trees are sprinkled over the higher ground. In 1845 Carna was considered to be more fertile and productive than the larger and less mountainous Oronsay, although there is a fish trap on Oronsay which must have made a big contribution to its larder. Interestingly, the northern part of Carna is called **Bac à Mhathachaidh** (G. – the cultivated bank).

In the centre of Loch Sunart between Oronsay and Carna there is the steep little island of **Risga** with **Eilean a' Chuilinn** and **Garbh Eilean** further up the loch.

ACCESS: No regular means of access. There may be a helpful boat-owner at Salen or Glenborrodale on Loch Sunart.

Anchorages:

1. W side, immediately N of narrow entrance to Loch Teacuis, in the shallow bay opposite Eilean nan Eildean. 9-10m, sand with some mud and weed. Sheltered except NW-N.

2. E side, in the channel leading to Loch Teacuis in the pool immediately S of Drochaid Chàrna (G – Carna's bridge). Rather awkward entrance but good shelter.

3. E side, in the entrance to the channel leading to Loch Teacuis, N of Drochaid Chàrna in 4-5m. Reasonable shelter but approach with care.

3. Appendix Staffa

(ON stafi-øy – stave or pillar island) The basalt columns resembled the vertical log staves used by the Norse for house construction.

The town of Stäfa on Lake Zurich in Switzerland was named after this little island by a monk from Iona.

OS Maps: 1:50000 Sheet 48 1:25000 Sheet 328
Admiralty Charts: 1:25000 No.2652 or No.2771

FINGAL'S
CAVE

AREA: 33ha (82 acres)
HEIGHT: 42m (138 ft)

OWNER: National Trust for Scotland. The island was
bought and donated to the Trust in 1986 by Mr John
Elliott of New York as a birthday present for his wife Elly
who has been appointed 'Steward of Staffa' by the Trust.

POPULATION: 1772 – 1. 1784 – 16. Uninhabited since 1800.

GEOLOGY: Cliffs over 40m high are riddled with caves and
the regularity of the basalt columns is such that it is
sometimes difficult to realise that these are natural formations. At parts the columns have been twisted into dramatic and contorted shapes. This is a result of the same
volcanic activity which created the Giant's Causeway in
Ulster. The rock is an almost-black fine-grained Tertiary
basalt surmounted by amorphous lava. Slow cooling
caused the lava to split in a pattern forming regular hexa-
gons or, occasionally, pentagons.

HISTORY: In the 3rd century Finn MacCool, the Irish hero
who was known to the Scots as Fingal (G. *fionn na ghal* –
chief of valour) is said to have defended the Hebrides
against early raids by the Vikings and to have died in battle in Ulster in 283. It is not known whether he ever visited Staffa but the beautiful cave on the island is now
named in his honour.

   On 13th August 1772, Sir Joseph Banks, President of
the Royal Society, not long returned from the famous voyage with Captain James Cook and *en route* to Iceland, 'discovered' Fingal's Cave. His ship had been driven by bad
weather into the Sound of Mull. There he met an Englishman, a Mr Leach, who told him of this extraordinary island and he went to see it for himself. In spite of spending
the night in the house of the island's sole inhabitants and
becoming infested with lice as a result (his companions
used a tent), Banks waxed lyrical about Staffa and following his report when back in London, tourists started to appear in droves. Among them in subsequent years were Sir
Walter Scott, John Keats, Felix Mendelssohn, J W M
Turner, William Wordsworth, Queen Victoria and Prince
Albert, Jules Verne, Dr David Livingstone and Robert Louis
Stevenson.

WILDLIFE: In 1788 barley, oats, flax and potatoes were
grown and in 1800 there were three red deer on the island. In 1801 one deer became dangerous and had to be
shot and the other deer started following boats which left
the island and on one occasion went too far and drowned.
Goats replaced the deer and were followed by a small herd
of black cattle which were resident for many years. These
in turn gave way to sheep. Seabirds nest on the island but
not in any great number.

We anchored off **STAFFA** very early on a morning in May.
The sea lay like molten lead and it was warm in the sun.
We were exceptionally lucky to have such favourable conditions and we had the island to ourselves. The landing
place, which has now been 'improved', is beside **Am
Buachaille** (G. – the herdsman), a dramatic tidal islet
composed of gracefully bent stone columns in a curious
pyramid about 10m high [NM326351]. Nearby, across a
narrow channel is Clamshell Cave which has an entrance
portico of twisted columns resembling a giant scallop.
Shags give eery warnings from their nests in the shadows.

   A path across the natural hexagonal paving, called The
Causeway, leads along the beautiful colonnaded cliff-face
and round the corner to **Fingal's Cave** which is spectacular and quite unique. It is lined with glossy black hexagonal columns which on the west side rise symmetrically
12m out of the sea: the roof, like a complicated Gothic
vault, is 20m high and the cave is 75m long. A rough
path runs among stumps of column to the back of the
cave (a torch is needed) and below it is a 20m deep arm of
seawater which sighs with the swell. This may give the
cave its Gaelic name, An Uamh Binn (G. – the melodious
cave).

   It is possible to reach the back of the cave by dinghy.

   Mendelssohn visited the island in 1829 and was inspired to write his Hebrides Overture (Die Fingalshöhle). *If*
conditions allow you to visit the island, and only *if* you
can avoid disturbing other visitors, then for an experience
that you will remember for the rest of your life play a recording of the *Overture* inside the cave and afterwards sit
in silence and listen to the music of the sea.

   Crowds can destroy the magic so try to visit the island
out of season. May and June are the best months.
Wordsworth was disgusted at being accompanied by too
large a crowd of fellow travellers in 1833:

Eilean Dubh

N

Port an Fhasgaidh

Refuge
Hut

Cormorant Cave
Mackinnon's Cave

Clamshell
Cave

Landing Place

Am Buachaille

The Great Face

The Causeway

Boat Cave

Fingal's Cave

25

25

△ 42

1 km

1/2 mile

We saw, but surely in the motley crowd
Not one of us has felt, the far-famed sight;
How could we feel it? Each the others blight,
Hurried and hurrying volatile and loud.

Round the southern end of the island and west of
Fingal's Cave is the Colonnade, otherwise known as The
Great Face, – a vast expanse of columns reaching up 17m
towards the sky with Boat Cave below them. In May 1945
a vagrant mine exploded here and the marks can be seen
on the cliff face. Opposite this southern tip is a strange formation known as the Wishing Chair. Further round on
the west side Mackinnon's Cave (named after Abbot
MacKinnon of Iona who died in 1500) is almost as grand
as Fingal's and has a tunnel connection through to Cormorant Cave.

The bay on the west side, fully exposed to the wild Atlantic, is called, strangely, Port an Fhasgaidh (G. – the port
to clean off vermin) though a slightly different emphasis
makes it the more probable, Port of Refuge.

ACCESS: Excursions from Oban but no landing. Boats sail
from Dervaig, Ulva Ferry, and Fionnphort on Mull, landing
only when conditions allow.

Anchorages:
No adequate anchorage and landing only possible in very settled conditions.
1. Off the landing-place at N end of Buachaille but many unmarked rocks.
Approach carefully from SE with Erisgeir astern.
2. Possible but risky spot 2c NNE of landing-place between the rocks. Bot-
tom weed.
3. Small beach at NE end suitable for dinghy landing but no anchorage.

The Small Isles

N

S k y e

4. Canna

3. Rum

Oigh-sgeir

2. Eigg

1. Muck

Shona

A r d n a m u r c h a n

Section 4

Section 4, Table 1

No.	Name	Latitude	Longitude	Table 2* No.	Table 3** No.	Area in Acres	Area in Hectares	
4.1	Muck	56° 50N	06° 15W	57	49	1381		559
4.2	Eigg	56° 54N	06° 10W	24	14	7534		3049
4.3	Rum	57° 00N	06° 20W	13	3	25854		10463
4.4	Canna	57° 04N	06° 33W	36	32	2792	1130	
	Sanday	57° 03N	06° 29W			455	184	1314

* Table 2: The islands arranged in order of magnitude
** Table 3: The islands arranged in order of height

Introduction

The four islands in this section are not particularly small but they are generally known as the Small Isles, or Sma' Isles, because that is the name of their parish. The total number of parishioners in 1755 was 943 and in 1794 it was 1339. Unfortunately it is not possible to find out separate figures for each island.

When sailing 'over the sea to Skye' from Ardnamurchan each island shows a very distinctive profile – the long stretch of Canna, the high cloud-wreathed mountains of Rum, the almost-primeval Sgurr of Eigg, and Muck creeping past like a grey-green submarine.

Far to the west lies lonely **Oigh-Sgeir** (G. – maiden or virgin rock) with **Garbh-Sgeir** (G. – rough rock) alongside and a neat little anchorage in between. These rocks are only about four hectares (10 acres) in area, formed of hexagonal basalt columns – like Staffa, and rising to 10m above sea-level. In the 19th century cattle from Canna were taken there to graze on the lush grass. The lighthouse on Oigh-Sgeir was built in 1902 and, until it became automatic, the keepers grew vegetables and flowers in a walled garden and played golf on a miniature golf course.

Tucked away in the corner of the Ardnamurchan peninsula, Loch Moidart is split in two by tidal **Shona**. This lovely island of 525ha was sold in 1995 by Richard and Anna Stead to Robert Devereux of London for a price believed to be about £1.5m. It has high and precipitous hills, natural woodland, exotic trees and a large house and grounds. The house overlooks South Loch Moidart with a densely wooded islet called **Riska**, and romantic Castle Tioram (G. tioram – dry, or fair) on its own drying islet, the home of Ranald, son of Somerled, Lord of the Isles.

Shona's old schoolhouse, now occasionally occupied as a holiday home, is on the opposite side of the island from the main house. It is reached by walking nearly two miles along a well-constructed stone track which follows the beautiful shore of North Loch Moidart. In the last century, I was told, the lady of the house ordered the school to be built as far from the house as possible so that she would not be disturbed by the children's voices! The schoolmaster's house, renovated by a professor from the USA, has a stunning view over the Small Isles with sunsets that have

the sort of magic no photograph can ever capture. Otters frequent this lonely place, herons pose on the shores of the loch, golden eagles nest in the heights, and civilisation is light-years away.

The entrance to North Loch Moidart from the sea is fairly straightforward once the skerries beside **An Glas Eilean** (G. – the grey island) and **Eilean Coille** (G. – wooded isle) have been located. **Eilean a' Choire** (G. – corrie isle) lies below the mountain slopes of Shona. The South Loch Moidart entrance is more devious and entails crawling past **Eilean Raonuill** (G. – Ranald's island) and then slipping round a rock pimple called **Eilean Corra** (G. – peaked island) with a few skerries in between providing interesting diversions.

North of Moidart the Sound of Arisaig is divided into Loch Ailort and Loch nan Uamh (G. – loch of the caves). **Eilean nan Gobhar** (G. – goat island) and **Eilean a' Chaolais** (G. – channel island) are at the entrance to Loch Ailort. Halfway along the loch are **Eilean nam Bairneach** (G. – isle of the limpets), **Eilean Buidhe** (G. – yellow isle) and **Eilean Allasaigh** (G. – tilted isle) and at the head of the loch are some very tiny islets – the Black Islands or **Eileanan Dubha**.

On the north shore of Loch nan Uamh the **Borrodale Islands**, a string of skerries, give partial shelter for a yacht to anchor in attractive surroundings. The best spot is north of **Eilean nan Cabar** (G. – island of the rafters or poles). **Eileanan Sgurra** (G. – rocky isles), **Am Fraoch Eilean** (G. – the heather isle), and **An Glas Eilean** are to the south-west surrounded by rocks. At the head of the loch there is another anchorage to the east of **Eilean Gobhlach** (G. – forked island), an islet with a cleft between two hillocks.

In the middle of the entrance to the Sound of Arisaig a treacherous group of skerries, **Eilean an t-Snidhe**, can be a hazard in poor visibility. By the coast to the north **Eilean a' Ghaill** (G. – stranger's isle) has the remains of a fort on it.

Loch nan Ceall, which is the harbour for Arisaig, is guarded by a minefield of rocks, islets, and skerries. There are perches to mark the passage through but many yachtsmen claim that either the perches swim about or the rocks do. If nothing else, a visit by sea to Arisaig is a memorable experience. Virtually all the offshore hazards are tidal with **Luinga Mhór** and **Eilean Ighe** being the largest.

A rather shabby little islet, **Eilean na h-Acairseid** (G. – harbour island), lies off Mallaig near the entrance to the harbour.

4.1 Muck

(G. eilean nam muc – isle of pigs). Fordun called it Helantmok – isle of swine. (G. muc-mhara – porpoise) is a kind but improbable option. In 1582 Buchanan referred to it as insula porcorum. When Dr Samuel Johnson met the Laird of Muck he was told that 'Muck' (Lord Muck) was the incorrect title. With a touch of wishful thinking the Laird asked to be called 'Monk' as he claimed that his property's original owner was a hermit from Iona.

OS Maps: 1:50000 Sheet 39 1:25000 Sheet 274
Admiralty Charts: 1:100000 No.1796 1:50000 No.2207

AREA: 559ha (1381 acres)
HEIGHT: 137m (449 ft)

OWNER: Purchased by the MacEwen family in 1896. Lawrence MacEwen is principal shareholder.

POPULATION: Early 1800s – 280. 1841 – 68. 1861 – 58. 1881 – 51. 1891 – 48. 1931 – 48. 1961 – 29. 1971 – 24. 1981 – 21. 1991 – 24. The laird advertises at intervals for young families to settle on the island.

GEOLOGY: Mostly Tertiary sheet basalt with typical terraced cliffs, grassy ledges and flattened crowns. Dolerite dykes run NW to SE. Very fertile soil composed of glacial drift and sea-blown shell sand which produces appetising potatoes as early as May.

HISTORY: In 1588 when a Spanish galleon was wrecked in Tobermory bay, Sir Lachlan Maclean of Mull, encouraged by the Campbells, employed the surviving Spanish sailors as mercenaries and let them loose on several islands belonging to the MacDonalds. Consequently Muck was burnt, plundered, and left in a desolate state.

By 1773 when Boswell and Dr Johnson were passing by the island it was again reasonably prosperous, thanks to a considerate laird and the production of kelp (which was used to make potash). Boswell reported that the Laird had 'seven score of souls' on Muck. 'Last year he had eighty persons inoculated, mostly children, but some of them eighteen years of age. He agreed with the surgeon to come and do it, at half a crown a head. – It is very fertile in corn, of which they export some; and its coasts abound in fish. A taylor comes there six times in a year.' Almost Utopian, but some fifty years later, in 1828, the kelp market collapsed and 150 islanders were shipped off to Nova Scotia. Then in 1854 Muck was purchased by Captain Thomas Swinburne RN, who started a fishing industry but also rented the land for sheep farming causing further depopulation. Only today is the island recovering once again – or at least surviving – thanks to the enlightened and benevolent policy of the owners.

WILDLIFE: Some alpine plants grow here 600m below their usual altitude – dwarf juniper, crowberry, club moss, rose root sedum, mountain cats-paw and pyramidal bugle. In early summer the fields are covered with the flowers of marigold, iris, cornflower and bluebell. The only heather is in Glen Martin. There are a few acres of woodland mostly planted in 1922 but there are plans to plant more trees.

A small number of Rum ponies are bred on the island. There is no stallion so the mares are occasionally ferried over to Rum. Otters can be seen in Gallanach Bay and there are a number of small rodents but, luckily, no rabbits.

Gallanach Bay is also a popular playground for porpoises which may have been a factor in the naming of the island as they are called 'sea-pigs' in Gaelic.

Over eighty species of birds nest here with the seabirds favouring isolated Eilean nan Each. There are also many visiting species.

MUCK is a peaceful, low-lying island with attractive beaches but exposed to the Atlantic gales. This brings in the shell sand which keeps the basalt soil fertile. Most of the coast is rocky and near the west end are cliffs 15m to 18m high. There are some springs of good water.
This is the most fertile of the Small Isles and Lawrence MacEwen, the laird, runs the main farm at **Gallanach** (G. – full of young trees), with his wife Jenny and some additional help. It is a mixed farm with cattle, sheep, a small dairy herd, and crops of potatoes, oats and root crops. There are also two small tenant farms and the island is self-sufficient in milk, eggs and vegetables with the islanders having a communal vegetable patch for

PORT MÓR

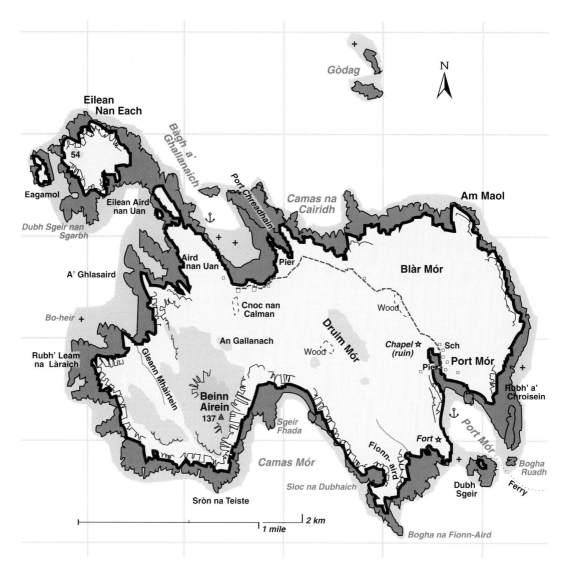

Gòdag

N

Eilean
Nan Each

Bàgh a'
Ghallanaich

Port Chreadhain

Camas na
Cairidh

Am Maol

54

Eagamol

Eilean Aird
nan Uan

Dubh Sgeir nan
Sgarbh

Aird
nan Uan

Pier

Blàr Mór

A' Ghlasaird

Cnoc nan
Calman

Wood

Bo-heir

An Gallanach

Wood

Druim Mór

Chapel ☆
(ruin)

Sch

Port Mór

Pier

Rubh' Leam
na Làraich

Gleann Mhàirein

Rubh' a'
Chroisein

Beinn
Airein
137 △

Sgeir
Fhada

Fionn-aird

Fort ☆

Port Mór

Camas Mór

Sloc na Dubhaich

Dubh
Sgeir

Bogha
Ruadh

Ferry

Sròn na Teiste

1 mile   2 km

Bogha na Fionn-Aird

their own use. There are no cars, the farm tractor being the only powered transport, but then there are only two kilometres of road. As there is no peat, all fuel, apart from driftwood, has to be imported.

Jenny's father was in the colonial service in Africa and bought a croft in Soay (See No.5.1) which he saw advertised in *The Times*. He never reached it but his twenty-year-old daughter took up the challenge and it was there that she met Lawrence MacEwen when he sailed over to help ship the island cattle to market.

There is only one Gaelic-speaking family on the island.

The island children were taught in a corrugated iron shed with an outside lavatory until 1992 when Highland Regional Council approved the building of a new school costing over quarter of a million pounds with an indoor lavatory and a wind-powered electricity generator. Four children were of primary school age at the end of 1993.

Port Mór in the south-east corner is the main harbour

with a small settlement of houses and an all-important telephone box. Camping is allowed with permission and a guest house is run by Lawrence MacEwen's younger brother, Ewen. Freshly-baked bread and rolls for breakfast and lobster are often on the menu. A graveyard and ruined chapel [NM421795] are on the hill above Port Mór and on the south side of the harbour entrance a few remnants of Dùn Bàn (G. – white fort), an old Bronze Age fortification, are still visible [NM422787].

Livestock names tend to be a feature of Muck's topography. In the north-west two drying islands form a peninsula, **Eilean nan Each** (G. – horse island) and **Eilean Aird nan Uan** (G. – island of the headland of the lambs). In **Gallanach Bay** to the east of the peninsula sea-beans from the West Indies are sometimes washed in by the Gulf Stream. They are looked on as lucky charms. Two long reefs form the east side of Gallanach Bay and between them is tiny **Port Chreadhain** with a small jetty. Beyond that is another small bay called **Camus na Cairidh** (G. – bay of the weir), possibly used for trapping fish in the past.

From the top of **Beinn Airein**, which is an easy climb from Gallanach, the whole island reveals itself – with the Sgurr of Eigg as a backdrop. For a climber it may be more of a challenge to ascend the steep cliff on the west side of Camas Mór (G. – the big bay), but Muck is not really for such strenuous pursuits. It is much better just to ramble about and explore, and to revel in the ever-changing aspect of sea and sky.

ACCESS: Calmac passenger ferry from Mallaig. 7½hrs round trip of the Small Isles but does not always call at Muck, 01687 2403. Occasional local service between Eigg and Muck. Sailings from Arisaig to Eigg, Rum, and Muck, 01687 5224.

Anchorages:
1. Port Mór, on the SE side lies between two extended reefs. Entrance reasonably easy, with care. Anchor inshore on NW side clear of moorings. Rather exposed to S'lies.
2. Bàgh a' Ghallanaich, on the N side of Muck, 4c SE of the E extremity of Eilean nan Each. Potentially dangerous entrance and untenable in N'lies. Anchor 1c S of Bo Haund in 4m, sand.

4.2 Eigg

[eg] (G. eag – a notch) – from Rum the silhouette shows a deep groove framed by the two humps of An Sgurr and Beinn Bhuidhe. Until the 16th century called Eilean Nimban More (G. – island of the powerful women) – note 'Loch nam Ban Móra' beside the Sgurr.

OS Maps: 1:50000 Sheet 39 1:25000 Sheet 261
Admiralty Chart: 1:50000 No.2207

AREA: 3,049ha (7,534 acres)
HEIGHT: 393m (1,289 ft)

OWNER: Ownership was the subject of a long, tortuous Court of Session action by the Hon. Margaret de Hauteville Udny-Hamilton – now Mrs Margaret Williams – but formerly the wife of Keith Schellenberg, Yorkshireman, entrepreneur, farmer and sportsman. The couple had bought Eigg jointly for £265,000 in 1975 but following divorce and remarriage Mrs Williams wanted to sell her share on the open market. This required Schellenberg's co-operation which was withheld and the matter went to court. Finally in 1992 Mr Schellenberg, who had continued to visit Eigg in the meantime, lost the case and was forced to put his half-share up for sale. But having done so, he then bought the whole island for just under £1 million.

In 1995 he sold Eigg for a reported £1.5m to Eigg Island Ltd, a company owned by a German artist, Marlin Eckhard, who prefers to be known as 'Maruma'.

POPULATION: 1798 – about 500. 1841 – 546 (peak). 1871 – 290. 1881 – 291. 1891 – 233. 1931 – 138. 1951 – 115. 1961 – 74. 1971 – 69. 1981 – 79. 1991 – 69. This is approximately half the total population of the Small Isles Parish.

GEOLOGY: An Sgurr (G. *sgùrr* – conical hill) or (G. *sgòrr* – sharp point, buck tooth) – the huge sugarloaf crag which dominates the island – is the largest residual mass of columnar pitchstone lava in Britain. It rests on an old riverbed in which there are driftwood fossils. The southern moor and north plateau are basalt which has weathered to a good soil. Eilean Chathastail in the south-east is of columnar basalt. The northern cliffs are sandstone which has eroded into fascinating shapes at Camus Sgiotaig where the beach is renowned for its Singing Sands – when dry the grains of white quartz drone eerily underfoot and when damp they squeak like blackboard chalk. Sometimes when the wind blows the sand can sound like an Aeolian harp. Also north of the Bay of Laig are limestone nodules trapped in rock cages and rattled by the waves. At the north extremity fossilised fish and reptiles are to be found in shale at Eilean Thuilm just above the low-water mark. In 1840 the fossilised remains of a Plesiosaur, a 180-million-year-old swimming dinosaur with paddle-shaped legs and a long neck and tail, were found on Eigg.

HISTORY: St Donan or Donnan, who had been trained at Whithorn and may have stayed for a time at Loch Alsh (Eilean Donan), eventually set up a sizeable monastery on Eigg but was murdered together with fifty-two of his monks in 617 according to the Irish annals.

The island was part of the Norse empire but was seized by the MacDonalds, Lords of the Isles. Robert the Bruce granted official title to MacDonald of Clanranald in 1309.

The earliest recorded meeting of island chiefs seems to suggest that it took place on Eigg – although Islay may be the correct interpretation: '. . .at Kildonnan in Eigg, where the staff of Lordship of Clanranald was given to one who was nominated Macdonnall and Donald of Isla. . .'

One story runs that in the winter of 1577 some MacLeods from Skye were sent home castrated after being caught raping MacDonald girls on Eigg. The MacLeods retaliated in force. Three hundred and ninety-five MacDonalds hid in Uamh Fhraing (G. – St Francis Cave) but were eventually discovered by the MacLeods who tried to smoke them out by lighting a brushwood fire in the entrance. Every MacDonald is said to have suffocated in the smoke and the cave is still known as 'Massacre Cave'. Some bones were removed from the cave for burial in the 19th century.

The population seems to have recovered quickly for eleven years after this incident Sir Lachlan Maclean and his Spanish mercenaries burnt and plundered the island.

The Reformation had left the islanders uncertain which

religion it was safe to follow. At that time they were part of the Protestant parish of Sleat in Skye but their minister, Reverend Mackinnon, never visited them. A missionary priest, Father Ward, landed in 1625 and soon renewed their Catholic faith. Mackinnon was furious and sent soldiers to seize the priest but the people refused to yield. Mackinnon retreated and was looking for additional support when MacDonald of Clanranald, (a Catholic), offered to pay Mackinnon one-third of the island's tithes if he left the islanders in peace. Mackinnon readily accepted.

The MacDonalds of Eigg supported the Catholic Jacobites in the 1745 rebellion so Captain John Ferguson of the King's ship, *Furnace*, was sent to arrest the leader John MacDonald. He surrendered and handed over all arms on the promise that there would be no reprisals against his clansmen but as soon as he was in custody Ferguson sacked the island and deported the young men.

In 1829 the MacDonalds sold Eigg to Dr Hugh MacPherson, Professor of Greek at Aberdeen University, for £15,000 and several minor clearances followed. The

GALMISDALE, CROUCHED BENEATH AN SGURR

next owner, Robert Thompson, a wealthy shipbuilder, bought the island in 1893 and spent a lot of money on improvements. It was a time of comparative prosperity for the crofters. Thompson died in 1913 and his grave is on Eilean Chathastail. Eigg then drifted until in the 1920s it was bought by the Runciman brothers, James a writer and Walter a shipowner. They created the home farm, planted a semi-tropical garden of palms, bamboo and lush woodland and ploughed back profits. Relative prosperity was regained until a Welsh farmer, Robert Evans, bought the island in 1966 and resold it in 1971 to a Christian charity with some rather impractical and illogical ideas.

It was something of a relief for the islanders when the Schellenbergs took over in 1975 but, later, the relationship between them deteriorated.

WILDLIFE: Campion, golden rod, a variety of heathers, thyme, willow, remnant hazel scrub, and even some imported eucalyptus trees grow in the mild, damp climate which also encourages a wealth of saxifrages. A number of wild goats frequent the heights.

The owner forbids any shooting or fishing and the island is managed as a wildlife reserve supervised by the Scottish Wildlife Trust. There are a few rare species of butterfly.

A fairly large and noisy colony of Manx shearwater burrows into the soil on An Sgurr, and there are some colonies of puffins on the sea cliffs. Until about 1900 white-tailed sea-eagles had eyries on the cliffs of Eigg before disappearing from the list of native British birds.

For an island the size of **EIGG** it is unfortunate to have no harbour. There are several bays and inlets but none gives satisfactory shelter. Although most of the population lives in the cluster of village houses at **Cleadale** in the north-west the ferry can only call in at the south-east at **Galmisdale** where the ocean swell surges through the gap between the jetty and rocky little **Eilean Chathastail** (G. – castle island).

Above Galmisdale is 'The Lodge' – the laird's house – a white Italian-style residence of 1920s vintage set in a garden of crazy-paving, catmint and carnations. Gorse overhangs the garden wall and thickets of bramble and wild roses invade the woodland surrounding the house.

At **Kildonnan**, (G. – Donnan's cell) just north of the anchorage an ancient Celtic cross-slab is near the ruins of a 14th century church which was built on the site of a monastery founded by St Donan in the 7th century [NM489854]. The saint and his fifty-two monks were massacred in 617, some say by pirates, others by a band of warrior women who lived on a crannog in **Loch nam Ban Móra** (G. – loch of the mighty women) [NM455852]. The loch and several little lochans are in a sheltered hollow high in the hills behind the Sgurr. The women apparently disliked missionaries but it was Norsemen who destroyed the monastery buildings.

Macdonald's Cave and **St Francis Cave**, both of them worth a visit, lie half a mile southwest of the pier. Walk up the road marked 'Private' and climb the first stile on the left. Follow the path to the cottage, then a sheep track to the cliff fence. Follow the fence to a zig-zag track leading down to the shore beside a small burn. Turn left to Massacre Cave (St Francis Cave) [NM476834] and right to Cathedral Cave (Macdonald's Cave). Cathedral Cave is still sometimes used for Catholic services, a custom dating from the persecution following the 1745 rebellion. A stone wall in the cave may have been an altar.

A strip at the extreme north end of the island is low-lying but ½km in from the shore steep cliffs rise to about 250m clearly marking, there and on the east coast, the change in sea-level since the Ice Age. Cliffs nearly encircle the island with the dramatic **Sgurr of Eigg** rising a further sheer 150m above the southern plateau. When the clouds are low, there is a touch of mystery; when the sky is blue, throw in some imaginary palm trees (there are real ones at the Lodge) and it could be Tahiti.

Kenneth MacLeod, composer of many beautiful songs including the 'Road to the Isles' was born on Eigg in 1872. Nowadays Eigg has the largest population among the four Small Isles and is thus the centre of the parish.

Fishing as a sport may be banned but there are many enjoyable exploits for experienced climbers. On The Sgurr there is Collie's Cleft in the South Wall rated as severe; Eagle Chimney – hard severe; The Flue – very severe and Botterill's Crack – severe. The latter has a fossilised coniferous tree trunk at the foot. On the cliffs overlooking Cleadale, called the Cleadale Face, there is Laig Buttress – severe, and the Pod – very severe.

Less dangerous, but equally thrilling, is the fine hillwalk from An Cruachan (G. – the rounded hill) to Beinn Bhuidhe (G. – pleasant or yellow mountain) with the inspiring sight of Rum's dark mountains, Ainshval and Askival, towering into the clouds beyond the wind-swept sound.

ACCESS: Passenger ferry about four times weekly from Mallaig by Cal-Mac, 01687 2403. Bruce Watt summer excursions from Mallaig, 01687 2320. Services from Arisaig, 01687 5224. Information from Fort William Tourist Board, 01397 3781. Air charter, details from Eigg Estate, 01687-82413.

Anchorages: There are no sheltered anchorages.

1. South of Galmisdale Point. Approach from SSW well-clear of En Chathastail. Anchor in the NW part at least 1c off-shore and out of the tidal channel in 3-6m, sand. Exposed to SW and swell.

2. SE of N extremity of En Chathastail. Beware 1¹/₂c reef just S of this. Anchor ³/₄c off the island. Exposed to E'lies and can be uncomfortable.

3. NE of Galmisdale Point. Approach through the narrows or from NE between the perches – with care. Restricted anchorage in moderate weather between Sgeir nam Bagh and En Chathastail avoiding moorings, reef and ferry channel. Bottom foul. Subject to swell. Shoal-draught boats may snug in N of pier.

4. Poll nam Partan, within Rubha na Crannaig, for moderate weather only. Tidal pool can take medium-sized craft, but only ¹/₂m surrounding depth at LW. Anchor on sand.

5. N of Rubha na Crannaig. Depths shallow enough for anchorage up to 2c from shore of Eigg but very exposed. Useful in perfect conditions or in emergencies.

6. Bay of Laig. Occasional anchorage in quiet weather or E'lies. Keep about 2c off S shore on approach.

4.3 Rum

[room] Probably pre-Celtic but possibly (ON röm-øy – wide island) or maybe (G. i-dhruim – isle of the ridge).

(Note: Sir George Bullough changed the spelling to Rhum. 'Rh' is not a Gaelic form and in 1991 the Nature Conservancy Council of Scotland after consultation with the School of Scottish Studies at Edinburgh University asked for the spelling to be corrected.)

OS Maps: 1:50000 Sheet 39 1:25000 Sheets 233 and 261
Admiralty Charts: 1:100000 No.1796 1:50000 Nos.2207 and 2208

AREA: 10,463ha (25,854 acres)
HEIGHT: 812m (2,663 ft)

OWNER: A Lancashire family, Bullough, were owners from 1888 to 1957. The Government purchased the island on behalf of the Nature Conservancy Council from Sir George Bullough's widow, Monica Lady Bullough, Countess of Durham, in 1957 for £26,000. The castle contents were donated to the nation by Lady Bullough.

Ownership has now passed to Scottish Natural Heritage.

POPULATION: 1794 – over 400. 1831 – 134. 1841 – 124. 1881 – 89. 1891 – 53. 1931 – 32. 1961 – 40. 1971 – 40. 1981 – 42. 1991 – 26. The population is mostly made up of employees and families of Scottish Natural Heritage and a schoolteacher.

GEOLOGY: A square platform of purple-red Torridonian sandstone, 150m to 300m high, fringed with sea-cliffs, some of the formations on Rum are geologically unique. The range south of the Kinloch-Harris divide is called the Cuillin and includes the peaks, **Askival** (812m) (ON – mountain of the ash trees), **Hallival** (723m) and **Trallval** (702m) (ON – mountain of the trolls) composed of rock allied to gabbro but with fewer basalt dykes than usual. Hallival has escarpments of allivalite, its own pale variety of gabbro and the slopes between are of peridotite, a dark variety which weathers to orange-brown. **Ainshval** (781m) (ON – hill of the strongholds) and **Sgurr nan Gillean** (764m) are capped by quartz-felsite overlying Torridonian sandstone. On the south and western cliffs there is granite. The strongest gravitational pull in the British Isles has been recorded one kilometre north-east of Harris, below Ard Mheall.

Rum was a centre of violent volcanic activity some fifty million years ago. During the last ice age it had its own independent glaciers, one of which carved out Kinloch Glen. There is a raised beach at Harris and long raised terraces cut by the sea into the spectacular western precipice which is now being carved by the Atlantic breakers at a lower level.

Only a few patches of arable land exist – at Harris, Kilmory and Kinloch.

HISTORY: In spite of its somewhat inhospitable climate today, Rum was one of the earliest places of human settlement in Scotland although little is known of its early prehistory.

Norse names of the various features extend beyond those merely of navigational benefit but no evidence of Norse settlement has yet been found.

Rum passed from the Norwegian to the Scottish Crown in 1266 and early records show that Rum was chartered to John of Islay in 1346. It was attacked and plundered by Sir Lachlan Maclean and his mercenaries in 1588, and in 1695 became part of the lands of the MacLeans of Coll. The main industry – fishing – was damaged by the Salt Tax, and yet in spite of the difficult conditions the population steadily increased. By the beginning of the 19th century there was overcrowding and extreme poverty. A clearance was arranged and over 300 islanders were persuaded to emigrate to Canada and the United States, leaving less than fifty inhabitants behind. MacLean leased the island for sheep-farming and 8000 sheep were introduced and some shepherds. They were joined by some families of crofters who emigrated from Skye and settled at Port nan

Caranean in 1827. By 1831 the population had risen to
134 but eventually stabilised at about ninety. In 1845
MacLean sold the island to the Marquis of Salisbury as the
sheep-farming was unprofitable. The Marquis converted
Rum to a sporting estate by stocking the burns with trout
and bringing in red deer before he too sold out.

There was a further unsuccessful attempt at sheep-
farming by the Campbells of Oronsay and then in 1888 a
Lancastrian MP, John Bullough of Oswaldtwistle, stepped
in. He had made a fortune from the design and production
of milling machinery. Rum became his holiday retreat and
sporting estate and according to his widow he wrote poetry when out shooting while enjoying his after-luncheon
cigar 'by some bonnie burn'.

His wealthy and eccentric son, George Bullough, aged
twenty-one, took over in 1891. After sailing round the

world he built Kinloch Castle in 1900-02. He imported
London architects (Leeming and Leeming), red Arran
sandstone, and Lancashire stonemasons to build a home
on the island fit for a laird. The workmen were paid extra
to wear kilts and tuppence a day for tobacco (midge
money). Even the garden soil was imported from Ayrshire.
This was a prime example of extravagant Edwardian opu-
lence – live turtles and alligators in heated tanks; birds of
paradise in the conservatory; a large mechanical
'orchestrian' with trumpets and drums for military
marches and operettas; central heating, double-glazed
stained glass, a baronial hall, a billiard room with air-con-
ditioning (to remove the cigar smoke), and a Victorian
'jacuzzi' bath. Guests were brought to Mallaig by a private
train, taken by steam yacht to Scresort and met by Albion
motor cars which were kept on the island. Grapes, figs,

peaches and nectarines were grown in the glass-houses.

Sir George was married on Rum and stayed there for three weeks every year.

WILDLIFE: In 1957 Rum was declared a National Nature Reserve and Biosphere Reserve.

The entire ecology is being carefully managed by Scottish Natural Heritage, successors to the Nature Conservancy Council, to maintain it in a controlled isolated state. The existing woodland of alder, rowan and Corsican pine at Loch Scresort was planted by the Bulloughs about 1900. Native trees and shrubs are now being planted and open heathland preserved to allow study and conservation of the natural flora and fauna in a unique environment. An excellent little SNH leaflet is available by the pier (booklet on sale at the post-office).

Plant life is prolific and some is undisturbed since the last ice age. Rare arctic sandwort and penny-cress can be found, the spotted orchids, *dactylorhiza maculata*, are of a sub-species unique to Rum, and there are three unique micro-species of eyebright. The moors are studded with blue heath milkwort, sundew, tormentil, butterwort, black bog-rush and bog asphodel, and thrift, roseroot and Scots lovage grow on the cliffs. Nineteen species of butterfly have been recorded.

Rum ponies are sometimes claimed to be descended from ponies saved from a wrecked Spanish galleon, or sometimes the offspring of Eriskay ponies. They actually originate from a cross between an Arab sire and a West Highland mare but stand only 14 hands high (1.4m). Sir George introduced a pure white Arab stallion to improve the bloodstock.

Highland cattle are kept to maintain, by controlled feeding, the herb-rich pastures of Glen Harris and a small herd of feral goats favour the south-western cliffs.

The biology and habits of both the wild and the hand-reared red deer are closely studied. One surprising discovery was that they are occasionally carnivorous – eating live young seabird nestlings, presumably to compensate for mineral deficiencies. (See Foula No.11.6 for carniverous sheep). Rum ponies are used to bring the deer carcasses in for study after they die naturally.

The peak season for ornithologists is April to October with many varieties of upland species. In all, over 150 species of bird have been recorded. Corncrakes still breed on the farm at Kinloch and there are seabird colonies on the south and north-east coasts – mainly kittiwake, puffin, razorbill and guillemot. Nearly 120,000 pairs of Manx shearwater breed in mountain top burrows. Their ghostly sounds in the night probably gave Trollaval its name (a midnight ascent in May is unforgettable). Golden eagles are to be seen over the glens. Rum's great success story has been the reintroduction of the white-tailed sea eagle

KINLOCH CASTLE

using chicks taken from Norwegian nests. The last Scottish bird was seen on Skye in 1916. It is hoped that this magnificent creature will one day be found again in all its old haunts.

RUM is by far the largest island in the Small Isles group but because it is so mountainous and its climate is less mild it has never been able to support a population relative to its size. The average annual rainfall at Kinloch is 240cms but in the mountains above it is over 300cms. Before the 15th century most of the island was cloaked in native woodland but slashing and burning by man destroyed it all except for a few stray trees on rocky cliffs. The present bleak moorland slopes are a direct result of this systematic destruction.

A roadway connects the three 'settlements' of Kinloch, Harris and Kilmory and there is also a rough track running south from Kinloch to Dibidil and on to Papadil.

Kinloch on Loch Scresort is the main settlement centred round **Kinloch Castle** which is filled with remarkable 'objets d'art' collected by Sir George in the Far East. (Sadly, if understandably, this unique monument is deteriorating. SNH is doing its best but obviously does not have the resources of a benevolent landlord.) The **Post Office** is the oldest inhabited building on Rum. It used to house the kitchen for Kinloch House – the original laird's house which was near the site of the present Castle. The beech and sycamore trees behind the Post Office were planted about 1830 when Kinloch House was being built.

Although there is a stone pier at **Loch Scresort**, it is only readily accessible at high water, so everything must normally be trans-shipped ashore. A whole year's supply of coal is delivered once a year by a puffer and stored in the coal store by the jetty. Electricity is from a small hydro-electric turbine.

A prehistoric site at Kinloch was discovered during ploughing in the summer of 1983. Excavations were carried out between 1984 and 1986 which revealed extensive mesolithic and later activity dating from 7000BC providing the best evidence to date of the early settlement of Scotland. A vast number of artifacts were recovered, mainly stone tools made of Rum bloodstone and flint.

On the south side of Loch Scresort is the schoolhouse, built in 1962 in front of the previous schoolhouse, and further east on the headland are the remains of an old village, **Port na Caranean**. It lies across Gleann Carn nan Dobhran (G. – glen of the cairn of the otters) and otters can still be seen here in the early morning. The village population was twenty-seven in 1841 but by 1861 it was abandoned.

Harris in the south-west has the lowest rainfall on Rum (140cms). The main feature there is the Bullough mausoleum – as eccentric as everything else – built in the style of a Greek temple [NM336957]. It contains the tombs of John, George and Monica. John (Sir George's father) was first laid to rest in a burial vault but a friend said it looked like a public lavatory for London Underground so Sir George built a new mausoleum and blew up the vault with dynamite.

The track from Kinloch to **Dibidil** (ON *djup-dalr* – deep valley) on the south-east coastline passes Creag a' Wealishech (G. – Welshman's rock). Some Welsh slate quarriers widened the precipitous path near here. The track leads on round the southern extremity to **Papadil** (ON *papa-dalr* – valley of the hermit), romantically lonely and attractive with a loch backed by a wood of mixed trees. The Lodge was built by Sir George but Lady Bullough disliked it and let it fall into ruin [NM366922].

At the opposite extreme in the far north **Kilmory** has a very fine beach, the remains of quite a large village settlement, an old burial ground [NG361036], one inhabited cottage and the original Kinloch Castle laundry. The area is often closed for deer research.

For the mountaineering fraternity, both Askival and Ainshval are classed as 'Corbetts' but a permit must be obtained for climbing and it can only be with an organised party. Furthermore, the estate staff can take no responsibility for rescue. Many interesting climbs have been listed – easy, moderate, difficult and severe. Allivalite is similar

to the black gabbro of the Cuillin on Skye, rough, but firm. A traverse of the main ridge involves little actual climbing yet is a classic expedition, and walking the ridges of Hallival, Trallval and Sgurr nan Gillean, down Glen Dibidil, and back along the coast to Scresort is a memorable experience.

There is also spectacular hill-walking (again, permission first required). For one walk, take the Dibidil track starting at a gate in the deer fence close to the pier at Loch Scresort, $8\frac{1}{2}$km over a 230m ridge (easier than crossing the tussocky moor) to Dibidil then an indistinct 4km to Papadil. From Papadil and across Glen Harris, 6km, keeping roughly to the 200m contour to avoid the sea-cliffs.

The west coast may be reached from the road junction point. From there a stalker's path goes to the 370m bealach at the top of Glen Guirdil, then under the basalt summit cliff on Orval, across to 388m Bloodstone hill and the fine sea cliffs of Sgòrr Mhór. An alternative track leads down Glen Shellesder past waterfalls to the shielings at Guirdil. Both these walks are 6km there (and 6km back) and only the man-eating midges can spoil one's pleasure; but remember also that this is a big rough island, hard-going at places and distances are misleading.

Fishing may be allowed by the warden (free) but there are no boats and all catches must be reported. Deer stalking can also be arranged (for a price). The only vehicles permitted are SNH's own jeeps.

ACCESS: Cal-Mac passenger ferry about 4 times weekly, 01687 2403. Occasional summer cruises from Arisaig, 01687 5224. Day visitors welcome but please ensure that there is no damage and no rubbish. No dogs allowed. Apart from the hotel, limited accommodation is usually available and camping allowed but prior permission to stay overnight required from the Reserve Office, White House, Rum PH43 4RR, 01687 2026.

Anchorages:

Generally, the bottom is rock off S and W sides, mud off E side with irregular depths, and sand off N side. Landing permitted at Loch Scresort only.

1. Loch Scresort affords good anchorage but subject to squalls in W'lies and swell from E'lies. It is shallow, and the head dries out about 2c. S shore moderately steep-to, except for reef extending 2c N from Rubha Port na Caranean. Pier dries and concrete slip has a least depth of 0.6m at outer end. Anchor well off the slip or NE of the pier in sufficient depth, stiff mud.

2. Kilmory Bay, near N extremity, has depths of 1.8m to 5.5m, sand, but is not recommended. Several rocks on both sides of bay.

3. Camas na h Atha, on NE side of A' Bhrideanach, the W extremity, is a small sandy bay with a rock off each entrance point. Temp anchorage only when conditions ideal.

THE BULLOUGH MAUSOLEUM – A GREEK TEMPLE IN REMOTE GLEN HARRIS

4.4 Canna

(EI cana – wolf-whelp) island, or (ON kne-øy – knee-shaped island) or, possibly (G. cana – little whale or porpoise) island

Sanday

(ON sand-øy – island with a conspicuous sandy beach)

OS Maps: 1:50000 Sheet 39 1:25000 Sheet 232
Admiralty Charts: 1:100000 Nos.1795 or 1796 1:50000 main anchorage and western part No.2208

AREA: 1314ha (3,247 acres)
HEIGHT: 210m (689 ft)

OWNER: Ownership donated in 1981 to the National Trust for Scotland by Dr John Lorne Campbell, who had owned it since 1938.

POPULATION:

	1841	1881	1891	1931	1961	1971	1981	1991
Canna		57	40	40	24	22	11	20
Sanday		62	62	20	0	11	7	0
	255	119	102	60	24	33	18	20

GEOLOGY: A lava platform of terraced Tertiary basaltic rock which has formed a rich and fertile soil with only a few small areas of peat bog. The basalt columns on the south coast are up to 6m in height. Compass Hill (139m) at the north-eastern corner is undifferentiated tuff with a sufficiently high iron content to distort ships' compasses helped by a vein of iron ore which continues under the sea to the north.

HISTORY: Canna belonged to the Benedictine Monastery of Iona followed by Norwegian suzerainty although the monks continued to cultivate it until the Reformation. Piracy was such a problem however that the Abbot of Iona appealed to the Pope to threaten excommunication if the raids did not cease. Canna became part of the Kingdom of Scotland in 1266 under the nominal rule of the Lord of the Isles which passed to the Macdonalds of Clanranald. As with the other Small Isles, Canna was subjected to fire and plunder by Sir Lachlan Maclean's mercenaries in 1588.

Macdonald of Clanranald found himself short of income when the kelp boom collapsed so he sold Canna in 1827 to Donald MacNeil.

Severe clearance followed the death of MacNeil in 1848. His natural son, Donald, was still a minor at the time and therefore not responsible. In 1881 he sold the island to Robert Thom, a Glasgow shipowner, for £23000. Thom brought in a much more benevolent regime which continued until 1938 when his family took the trouble to look privately for the right sort of understanding purchaser. This they found in the Gaelic scholar, Dr John Lorne Campbell, historian, folklorist, farmer and 'bonny fechter', who was sold Canna for just £9000 and took up residence on the island with his American wife. Campbell had founded the 'Sea League' with Sir Compton Mackenzie when they both lived on Barra in the 1930s – a pressure group to try to protect the West Coast fishing industry from external incursions. He has worked for most of his life on the preservation and encouragement of Gaelic culture and has, in Canna House, the world's biggest library of Celtic language and literature. He has also fought to keep Canna as a viable community although, 'I'm not a laird,' he says, 'I'm an owner-occupying farmer'. In 1981,

ESCARPMENT NEAR TARBERT BAY

laird,' he says, 'I'm an owner-occupying farmer'. In 1981, when he gave Canna to the National Trust for Scotland, he also gave them his large and invaluable library and collections of Gaelic songs for safe-keeping. The hope of this conscientious custodian is that the Trust will fully understand the needs of this small community and not allow it to become depopulated and a mere tourist attraction.

WILDLIFE: Woodland of natural rowan and hazel interspersed with introduced sycamore, ash, elm, oak, birch, willow, elder, beech and some Sitka spruce, Corsican pine, Austrian pine and Japanese larch on the hillsides above the harbour. Hedgehogs were introduced by the Campbells – for better or for worse – and thistles are encouraged to support several species of butterfly and moth.

The western cliffs are a superb sea bird sanctuary which includes colonies of Manx shearwater and puffin, and several varieties of duck frequent the shores. Occasionally white-tailed sea eagles fly over from Rum – they were once indigenous here.

Viewed from due north or south, each end of **CANNA** appears to terminate in a bluff with the middle sinking to a low neck or knee. Compass Hill is at the eastern extremity and the highest point **Carn a' Ghaill**, (G. – rocky hill of the storm) about 1km west of it, is 210m high.

SANDAY, close south, joined by a bridge and a drying

reef, rises to 44m height at its east end where there are several detached rocks in the sea. Two of these lie close to the cliff – a small one like a steeple and the other like a large tower (31m).

The space between Canna and Sanday forms the only well-protected harbour and has the only ferry pier (improved in 1992) in the Small Isles. The harbour is entered by rounding a graffiti-covered rockface – originally the names of fishing boats and early traders from the Baltic States, but now those of day-trippers seeking immortality.

The principal house on this idyllic island is **Canna House** [NG273056], surrounded by thick woodland overlooking the harbour. This is the home of Dr Campbell and his wife, the American writer Margaret Fay Shaw. Close by is the main farm. With no high mountains to south or west, the clouds usually slip past Canna and the climate is pleasant and sunny. The fertile soil gives a rich and unusually early yield with particularly delicious early potatoes. Fields lying fallow are cropped by pedigree Highland cattle and Cheviot sheep.

The islanders are Catholic but there is a carefully maintained and charming little **Protestant Church**, built like early Celtic churches with a conical bell tower, on the east side of the harbour [NG277054]. This was constructed in 1914 as a memorial to Robert Thom. On Sanday and facing it is the much more ornate **Catholic Church** built by

Lady Bute in memory of her father [NG275048]. It has fallen into serious disrepair and the islanders now worship in a simple building near the main farm. The proud title of **Post Office** is given to a tiny creosoted wooden shed and the adjacent telephone box was painted blue when I first saw it.

A' Chill (G. – the cell or chapel), north-west of the harbour and above the main farm, was the site of the original township, cleared by MacNeil in the 19th century. There are some remnants of the early 7th century St Columba's Chapel [NG270055] at present being excavated by archaeologists and a Celtic cross. A standing stone probably proves that this is another case of the early-Christian policy of building on important pagan sites, although a small hole at head height in which an offender's thumb could be jammed has led to this being called a pillory stone.

An Coroghon, on the coast east of the harbour [NG280055], is a medieval prison tower on top of an isolated stack where a Clanranald chief imprisoned his wife to keep her from her lover, a MacLeod from Skye. Sir Walter Scott wrote a sensible warning:

> Seek not the giddy crag to climb
> To view the turret scathed by time:
> It is a task of doubt and fear
> To aught but goat or mountain deer.

Tarbert Bay is almost central on the south coast, defined by the islet **Hàslam** like a punctuation mark. A ruined fort is on the bay's western shore and the remains of a very ancient nunnery or 'cashel' are on a grassy terrace beyond the bay, 4km along the road from the harbour [NG230043]. The site overlooks **Sgòrr nam Ban-naomha** (G. – sharp rock of the holy women) and, 5km away to the south-west, the isolated basalt rock of **Humla.**

A very well-preserved Viking ship burial was uncovered near Rubha Langanes in **Camas Thairbearnais** on the north side of the central neck. Signs of Viking occupation can still be seen and a rectangular outline of boulders is known as **Uaigh Righ Lochlainn** (G. – the grave of the King of Norway). On adjoining Sanday signs of Norse burials have also been discovered but unfortunately the graves had been rifled in the distant past.

A fairly long, but interesting, hill-walk to Garrisdale Point at the western extremity brings you to Dùn Channa (G – Canna's fort). This distant end of Canna was fortified by a wall and there is another fort about ½km to the north-east.

ACCESS: Cal-Mac passenger ferry from Mallaig about four times weekly. 7-8hrs round trip, 01687 2403. No accommodation but camping allowed with permission. NTS Resident Warden, 01687 2477.

IN THE SCOTS KIRK

Anchorages:

1. Canna harbour. One of the best and most popular anchorages on the west coast. Beware reef N of Sanday on approach and rocks by pier. Bottom is kelp on thick mud – good holding if anchor is well bedded-in.

2. Tarbert Bay. W of Sanday and SE of the central dip on Canna. Approach W side of bay keeping well clear of the islet called Hàslam then anchor in NE side 2c offshore, 4-6m. Worthwhile in fair weather. Exposed S and subject to swell.

3. Boat harbour. Temp anchorage between S side of Canna and W end of Sanday in settled weather. Many rocks to be avoided. Anchor in 3.7m N of Sgeirean Dubha with landing on sandy beach in SE corner.

Islands Surrounding Skye

Ascrib Islands

9. Rona

8. Isay

7. Raasay

6. Eilean Mór
(Crowlin Isles)

5 . W i a y

S k y e

4. Longay

3. Scalpay

2. Pabay

1. Soay

N

Section 5

Section 5, Table 1

No.	Name	Latitude	Longitude	Table 2* No.	Table 3** No.	Area in Acres		Area in Hectares
5.1	Soay	57° 09N	06° 13W	41	48	2560		1036
5.2	Pabay	57° 16N	05° 52W	107	157	301		122
5.3	Scalpay	57° 18N	05° 58W	28	15	6135		2483
5.4	Longay	57° 19N	05° 53W	149	98	124		50
5.5	Wiay	57° 20N	06° 30W	97	106	366		148
5.6	Eilean Mór (Crowlin I)	57° 20N	05° 50W	75	60	477	193	
	Eilean Meadhonach	57° 21N	05° 51W			190	77	270
5.7	Raasay	57° 25N	06° 03W	17	11	15397	6231	
	Eilean Fladday	57° 29N	06° 02W			297	120	
	Eilean Tigh	57° 31N	06° 00W			133	54	6405
5.8	Isay	57° 31N	06° 39W	140	155	148		60
5.9	Rona	57° 33N	05° 59W	43	52	2298		930
5.A	Skye	57° 22N	06° 11W			409259		165625

* Table 2: The islands arranged in order of magnitude
** Table 3: The islands arranged in order of height

Introduction

I must admit to having misgivings about omitting Skye from a comprehensive book on the Scottish islands. But rules are rules, and having decided that a bridge destroys insularity there was no other option. So, by my definition, Skye, which has always been the very essence of a Scottish island, no longer qualifies for inclusion. With the construction of a bridge it has now joined the mainland. Just as Seil took the same step many years ago.

To fend off criticism, however, I have compromised and included Skye as an appendix to this section. As with all the large islands, the description is necessarily brief. There are, after all, many excellent guides and books about Skye already available and my interest here is to pay more attention to the somewhat smaller islands which are given inadequate coverage elsewhere.

Apart from the nine classified islands in the vicinity of Skye, each of which has its own unique story and its collection of satellite islets, there are the other tiny islands hugging the mainland coast which at least deserve a mention.

North of Mallaig, at the entrance to sombre Loch Nevis, **Glas Eilean** (G. – green island) and **Eilean Dearg** (G. – red island) add an imaginative touch of colour and, further north, **Airor Island** shelters the small bay by the village of Airor in Knoydart.

Loch Hourn is a lovely loch to explore, stretching deep into mountain wilderness. **Eilean Ràrsaidh** with adjoining **Eilean a' Chuilinn**, just within the entrance of the loch and by the north bank, provide a delightful anchorage under the wooded crags of Beinn Mhialairigh. There is another anchorage south of **Eilean a' Phìobaire** (G. – the piper's island), on the south-west bank where there is

a navigable channel between the island and the shore. At the first narrows a wide shoal and several tidal islets are beyond **Corr Eileanan** at Barrisdale Bay and beyond the second narrows – Caolas Mór – a central islet, **Eilean Mhogh-sgeir**, supports some twisted pines and a very active heronry.

Eilean Chlamail is just north of the entrance to Loch Hourn, and projecting into the Sound of Sleat are the **Sandaig Islands**. These are all tidal with the exception of the largest, Eilean Mór, which has a light beacon on it.

Sailing through Kyle Rhea at mid-tide is like having a jet-engine attached to the hull. In the middle of Loch Alsh (which is a millpond compared to Kyle Rhea) **Glas Eilean** is little more than a permanent shoal covered with grass – a large flat expanse of grazing land. **Eilean Tioram** (G. – drying island) is tied to the land by a muddy tidal isthmus and beyond it another tidal island, **Eilean Donan**, linked by a bridge to the mainland, is the site of one of Scotland's most photographed castles.

The entrance to Loch Alsh is named after King Haakon, Kyle Akin. Some islets off Kyle of Lochalsh, **Eileanan Dubha**, lie in the navigable channel. Beyond is the site of the newsworthy or notorious, depending on your viewpoint, **Skye Bridge** which makes use of Eilean Bàn (G. – white or unused island), a Government property, for support. Eilean Bàn is a double islet with a drying channel between and there are lighthouse keepers' houses beside the lighthouse on the western half. It was in one of these houses that Gavin Maxwell wrote his best-selling novel, *Ring of Bright Water*. Otters are resident on many of the islets in this area, most of which belong to the National Trust for Scotland. The larger of these islands are

Eilean a' Mhal, **Black Islands** and round the corner by Duirinish – still all Trust property – **Eilean Dubh Dhurinish**, **A' Ghlas-leac**, **Eilean na Bà Mór** (G. – isle of the big cattle), and **Eilean Dubh**.

Eilean a' Chait (G. – cat island) has a disused light beacon on it at the entrance to Loch Carron. The largest of the **Strome Islands** in the loch is **Eilean an-t-Sratha**. Plockton – that little gem of a Highland village – snuggles into a corner of the southern shore wrapped in its own private Mediterranean climate. **Ulluva** is the name of the little island which appears in every photograph of Plockton – a few lone pines standing to attention on warm-grey rocks covered with orange and yellow lichen. A similar island near the shore, **Eilean na Creig Duibhe**, is tidal.

Off the peninsula dividing Loch Carron from Loch Kishorn are a number of rocks and skerries dominated by **Kishorn Island** and **An Garbh-eilean**.

Very much further north, there is a tiny islet of no particular significance, **Eilean Chuaig** (G. – twisted island), where the mainland turns away to make room for Loch Torridon.

On the south side of Outer Loch Torridon, **Eilean Mór** shields a deep pool which is a pleasant but limited anchorage as the bottom drops away fairly steeply. Loch Torridon divides into three distinct parts but the middle section has a change of name – Loch Shieldaig. There are two little islets in this part, **Eilean an Inbhire Bhain** and **Eilean Dùghaill**, and one distinctive larger island of about thirteen hectares, **Shieldaig Island**, which sits in tree-covered splendour opposite the sleepy whitewashed village of Shieldaig. Shieldaig Island was bought by the National Trust for Scotland in 1970 as it represents a small surviving sample of the ancient Caledonian Forest which used to spread over this entire region. The Scots pine regenerate because there are no sheep or deer to destroy them and they provide a refuge for many species of bird. There is a heronry at the north end of the island. In 1974 the cost to the NTS was reimbursed in full by Mr and Mrs Armistead Peter III of Washington DC who 'adopted' the island.

Kent doctor, Nicholas Martin, bought the island for £100 in 1980 but he thought this included the crofting-rights and there were long and expensive Land Court hearings. Dr Martin had a home on Soay and owned the common grazing land but in 1993 'Tex' Geddes bought the island from him for an indisclosed sum.

POPULATION: 1821 – one family. 1841 – 113. 1851 – 158 (the peak). 1861 – 129. 1881 – 102. 1891 – 78. 1931 – 64. 1953 – most of the population moved voluntarily to Mull. 1961 – 11. 1971 – 5. 1981 – 9. 1991 – 14.

GEOLOGY: Mainly Torridonian sandstone alternating with greywacke traversed by a fine-grained igneous rock.

HISTORY: Soay was the property of the MacLeods of Dunvegan from the 13th century. They sold it to Gavin Maxwell in 1946. The island was very lightly populated until the Clearances on Skye in the mid-1800s when more than one hundred of the dispossessed crofters chose to settle on this infertile little island rather than go to America.

After the Second World War, the islanders petitioned the government for evacuation, mainly because communications were so poor. So on 20th June 1953 with a great deal of publicity and a lone piper playing a lament the *SS Hebrides* evacuated the crofters and took them to Mull where land had been purchased for them by the government at Java Lodge, Craignure. Only one family refused to leave – that of Mr Geddes, the present owner. The affair had some overtones of the sad evacuation of St Kilda (No.9.1) in 1930. In recent years the island has seen a small increase in population, mail and stores are landed on a regular monthly basis, and there is irregular contact with Elgol on Skye.

WILDLIFE: Not very fertile land but there is a profusion of deciduous bushes and trees such as birch, oak, and rowan in the low saddle near the centre with a consequent variety of birdlife. Herons nest near the harbour and ravens cross the sound from Skye.

Unfortunately, in spite of his espousal of the cause of conservation, Maxwell's shark oil venture on Soay contrib-

5.1 Soay

[so-ay or soy] (ON so-øy – sheep island)

OS Maps: 1:50000 Sheet 32 1:25000 Sheet 217
Admiralty Chart: 1:50000 No.2208

AREA: 1,036ha (2,560 acres)
HEIGHT: 141m (462 ft)

OWNER: The author, Gavin Maxwell, bought Soay in 1946 for a shark-fishing venture and Joseph 'Tex' Geddes, his harpooner, had crofting rights to twenty-one of the twenty-five crofts. A

MAXWELL'S DERELICT SHARK-OIL FACTORY

uted to a serious reduction in the numbers of basking sharks in West Coast waters. These inoffensive and harmless creatures may have been saved by the drop in value of shark oil in 1949 but they have never really recovered from the onslaught and are rarely seen. Maxwell wrote a book about his experiences – *Harpoon at a Venture*.

A dumb-bell shaped island with a narrow isthmus almost cutting it in half, **SOAY** is dwarfed by the Cuillin mountains which tower over it. **Acarsaid Soa** (G. – Soay harbour) is the northern part of the central gut.

When Maxwell bought Soay in 1946 he founded the Island of Soay Shark Fisheries Ltd and built a factory for processing shark oil beside the harbour. But the venture only ran for three years and, although there is a small, active community on Soay, the harbour today has a deserted

aspect. One or two fishing boats are moored or beached but there are abandoned fish cages and the old shark-oil factory buildings now form an attractive group of derelict structures [NG451151]. Blackbirds nest in the broken boiler stoke-hole, the generator base is covered in rust and the original two-storey house (built about 1849) has only half its slated roof remaining. It was first constructed to help the fishing industry with curing facilities at ground floor level and accommodation for visiting fishermen upstairs. At least some of Maxwell's corrugated-asbestos roofed buildings are still in use as stores for fishing gear. A dry 'mill lade' runs from a brick and concrete tank to an 'oven' by the house. The area is littered with the brass cases of rifle cartridges, presumably used to scare the herring gulls away.

A well-constructed cobbled pathway, constructed in the

early 1900s with government funding, runs through birch, rowan and alder woodland in the central cleft and on past the solar 'telephone exchange' [NG453144]. This was the first in the world of its kind and powers nine telephones. The path leads on down to a settlement of pleasant, well-maintained houses, **Mol-chlach**, (G. – village by the pebble beach) on the west shore of **Camas nan Gall** (G. – bay of the strangers, or Norsemen), a deep indentation on the southern side of the central isthmus. When the islanders were evacuated to Mull in 1953 only Tex Geddes, Maxwell's harpooner, and his family stayed on but the settlement has now grown again to a thriving small community although some of the houses are in effect holiday homes.

Two bright, fresh-faced and well-spoken boys (eleven or twelve years old when we met them) are the only pupils at the island school. They have a full-time schoolmaster who is, they said, 'really quite good'.

The north-eastern part of the island is smaller and higher than the south-western area. It contains **Beinn Bhreac** (G. – speckled hill), almost central, 141m high and with wooded patches on its eastern slopes. It was more thickly wooded in the past and the area on its south side is still known as Doire Mhór (G. – the big oak wood). Two small lochs nestle directly north of Camas nan Gall – Loch Doire an Lochain, and Loch Mór which contains a small islet.

In October 1868 a schooner, *Woodman of Berwick on Tweed*, with a cargo of slate from Easdale, foundered on the east coast of Soay. Her skipper, Thomas Weatherhead, and his wife were drowned but the crew of two men and a boy were swept ashore and rescued by the islanders. The off-lying rocks have always been a hazard in this area, particularly off the south-west side of the island.

South of Mol-Chlach is rough hilly ground with a number of lochans. Once again the names recall ancient woodland – Loch na Doire Buidhe (G. – loch of the pleasant copse), Loch Coire Doire na Seilg (G. – corrie loch of the hunting thicket) and the whole area is called Doire Chaol (G. – thin woodland).

ACCESS: Special arrangements through Arisaig Marine, 01687 5224. Boat hire sometimes from Mallaig, Bruce Watt Cruises, 01687 2320. Also sometimes from Elgol, Skye – Mackinnon, 014716 213 or 235.

Anchorages:
The tidal stream in Soay Sound appears to run continuously W.
1. An Dubh Chamas (G. – the black bay), a small bay on the N side of Soay, about 8c ENE of Soay harbour. Good shelter in S'lies. Anchor in centre, 4-8m, good holding.
2. Soay Harbour is a narrow creek with a shingle bar drying 0.6m at the entrance. Access after half flood along inconspicuous leading line. Anchor W of pier, 3-4m, black mud, good holding and good shelter.
3. Harbour entrance, temp anchorage in light S'lies, outside the entrance,
8-10m, but beware drying reef.
4. Camas nan Gall on S coast. Exposed S-SE. Poor holding on shingle.

5.2 Pabay

(N pap-øy – hermit or priest island)

OS Maps: 1:50000 Sheet 32 1:25000 Sheet 204
Admiralty Charts: 1:50000 No.2209 1:25000 Nos.2498 or 2534

AREA: 122ha (301 acres)
HEIGHT: 28m (92 feet)

OWNER: A resident farmer.

POPULATION: 1841 – 21. 1881 – 10. 1891 – 7. 1931 – 3. 1961 – 7. 1971 – 5. 1981 – 3. 1991 – 0.

GEOLOGY: The island is formed of lias – a Lower Jurassic limestone interspersed with many fossils – and intersected by numerous dark fine-grained igneous dykes. The soil is very fertile.

HISTORY: Possibly the holy man who originally occupied this island was never canonised because his name is not on record. But in the early days of Christianity Pabay obviously had some significance.

However, in the 16th century pirates and so-called 'broken men' were using Pabay, which was then well-wooded, as a base for their nefarious activities. Dean Monro in 1549 described it as 'full of woods, good for fishing, and a main shelter for thieves and cutthroats.'

A century and a half later much of the woodland must have been cleared because Martin Martin wrote; 'It excells in Pasturage, the Cows in it afford near double the Milk that they yield in Skie. In the Dog-Days there's a big Fly in this isle, which infests the cows, makes them run up and down, and discomposes them exceedingly.'

WILDLIFE: Pabay was riddled with rabbits until myxomatosis took its toll in 1969.

The island plateau of **PABAY** with its neat fields of agriculture draped over it like a brightly coloured tablecloth lies almost straight ahead as one sails through the Kyle of Lochalsh. At low water the island grows before your eyes as extensive drying reefs appear from beneath the surface of the sea.

The east and west coasts rise steeply to about 12m and there is then a very gradual slope to the highest point (28m) near the west coast. A road runs across the island from the concrete jetty in the south west to Shell Beach in the north. The main farmhouse is not far from the jetty and looks south across Caolas Pabay to Broadford Bay on Skye. An ancient ruined chapel and burial ground are east of the jetty [NG674265].

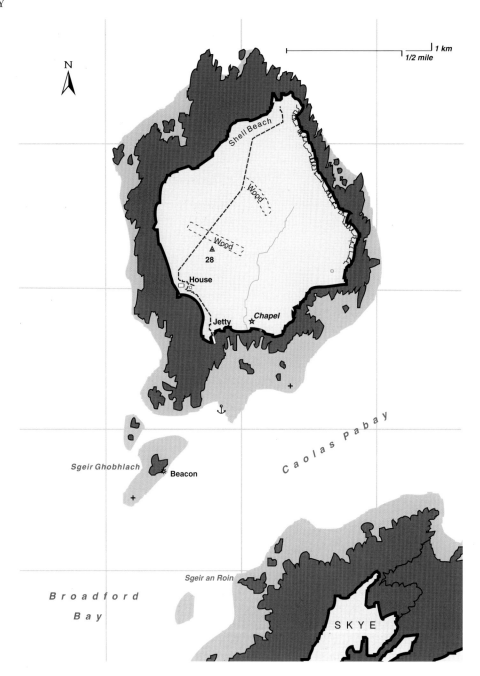

The owner, who is a working farmer, has planted large areas of mixed native deciduous woodland and also extended some of the small existing stands of timber. There are some holiday cottages to let.

Pabay is one of the few islands which is licensed to issue its own postage stamps. This is because it is uneconomic for the post office to provide a boat. Deliveries are left at Broadford for collection.

ACCESS: No regular access. Enquire in Broadford.

Anchorages:
There are extensive drying rocks 2½c on W side, 3c on NW side, 1½c on E side and 2c from S side and foul ground extends 6½c to the SSW so it is important to study the charts carefully.
1. The landing place is a concrete jetty at the SW extremity of the island, the outer end of which is marked by an iron perch. Anchor 1c S of the perch, sand with weedy patches, 4-6m.

5.3 Scalpay

Possibly, (ON – cave island). Although there is no notable cave there are many small ones on the coast. Alternatively, (ON skalpr-øy – scallop island).

OS Maps: 1:50000 Sheet 32 1:25000 Sheets 187, 188, 203 and 204 or Outdoor Leisure Map 8
Admiralty Charts: 1:50000 No.2209 or 1:25000 No.2498

AREA: 2,483ha (6,135 acres)
HEIGHT: 392m (1,286 ft)

OWNER: Trustees of J. G. Walford's settlement.

POPULATION: 1841 – 90. 1881 – 37. 1891 – 49. 1931 – 27. 1961 – 2. 1971 – 5. 1981 – 11. 1991 – 7.

GEOLOGY: Almost entirely of Torridonian rocks – red and grey sandstones, conglomerates, siltstones and shales which were deposited about 800m years ago. Part of the west coast is granite and the ground by Scalpay House is on a patch of fertile lias.

HISTORY: Dr Johnson, in 1773, wanted to buy the island and to 'found a good school, and an episcopal church, ..and have a printing-press, where he would print all the Erse that could be found' but thought better of it after discovering that ownership carried an obligation to spend at least three months every year on the island.

In the 19th century Sir Donald Currie constructed the first roads and planted trees.

RUINED CROFT AT CAMAS NA GEADAIG

WILDLIFE: The hill slopes are covered with heather, mainly *calluna vulgaris*, *erica carnea* and *erica tetralix*.

The island's herd of red deer is carefully managed and there are good trout in the mountain lochs.

SCALPAY rises abruptly from its south and west coasts to **Mullach na Càrn** (G. – cairn hill) its highest peak of slightly more than 392m. It is rough and hilly, other main peaks being **Beinn Loch a' Mhuilinn** (G. – mountain of the mill loch), 291m, and **Beinn Reireag Bheag**, 225m. Mullach na Càrn stretches in a ridge across the centre of the island with a lochan-studded plateau and two minimountains, An Ailldunn (G. – the castle rock) and Sithean Glac an Ime (G. – the fairy hill in the butter bowl). Below lie the Mill Loch, the Black Loch, and the much-larger **Loch an Leòid**. The north-east coast is rocky and fringed by a reef but the mountain slopes here are more gradual.

Scalpay is separated from Skye by the narrow and shallow Caolas Scalpay. **Scalpay House** in the south-east corner of the island looks over a small tidal harbour with, beyond it, **Guillamon Island**, 24m-high, rocky and speckled with seabirds. To the west of Scalpay House are the remains of a chapel, **Teampuill Fraing** (G. – St Francis' Chapel), built on the site of an ancient Celtic cell [NG628281]. The area around Scalpay House is well-cultivated and there are patches of woodland.

A road runs from the harbour along the west coast, through extensive conifer plantations to a holiday cottage at **Corran a Chinn Uachdaraich** (G. – the upper projection), facing Skye. The track leads on from there up towards the summit of Beinn Reireag Bheag.

Some 1600ha is fenced off in this north-east area for red-deer farming which was developed with the support of the Highlands and Islands Development Board (now Highlands and Islands Enterprise). Venison was successfully exported to Germany where it is a very popular meat, but, unfortunately, with access to Eastern European venison this is no longer such a profitable enterprise.

A recently ruined croft in the north of the island is beside the aptly named **Camas na Geadaig** (G. – bay at the patch of lazybeds) because the lazybeds beside it can still be clearly seen beneath a layer of buttercups.

The heathery hillsides provide pleasant walking as, being sheltered by Skye from the wettest winds, the ground is not too boggy, but from whatever direction you approach you can still expect rough going to reach the bouldered summit of Mullach na Càrn. However, the views from the top make the exercise worthwhile, and be sure to rest for a while by Loch Dubh where you can see the waterfall tumbling down the hill behind Loch an Leòid and listen to the skylarks.

Scalpay offers good camping and fishing but it is important first to obtain permission from Scalpay House.

ACCESS: No normal public access. Private charter of a boat may be arranged from Broadford or Portree.

Anchorages:

1. Camas na Geadaig, at NW extremity. The head of the bay dries out about

1¼c. Beware reefs both sides of entrance. Occasional anchorage in the centre, 5-7m, sand. Sheltered from S'lies but squally in strong winds.

2. Loch na Cairidh (G. – weir loch). NW of the narrows. Anchor anywhere in suitable depth.

3. Caolas Scalpay. E of narrows, midway between narrows and Sgeir Stapaig. Can be squally.

5.4 Longay

(ON long-øy – longship island). Note also (G. long spùinnidh – pirate ship)

OS Maps: 1:50000 Sheet 32 1:25000 Sheet 188
Admiralty Charts: 1:50000 No.2209 1:25000 No.2498

AREA: 50ha (124 acres)
HEIGHT: 67m (220 ft)

POPULATION: Uninhabited and no census records.

GEOLOGY: Longay is the southern end of a reef, Sgeirean Tarsuinn (G. – the traverse or oblique reef), running parallel with the east side of Scalpay. It is formed of large slabs of volcanic rock but with a considerable area of red sandstone.

HISTORY: Longay is one of the group of islands in this area which was frequented by pirates in the 16th century. It would have been covered with Caledonian Forest trees at that time giving added cover. The thieves and cutthroats, with no clan or territorial attachments, must have concentrated their attacks only on 'foreign' ships – Dutch, Lowland Scottish, Flemish and English commercial and fishing craft which ventured into the Inner Minch; otherwise the local clan chiefs would certainly have suppressed them. They had ample power to do so. The pirates probably paid insurance to MacLeod of Raasay in the form of

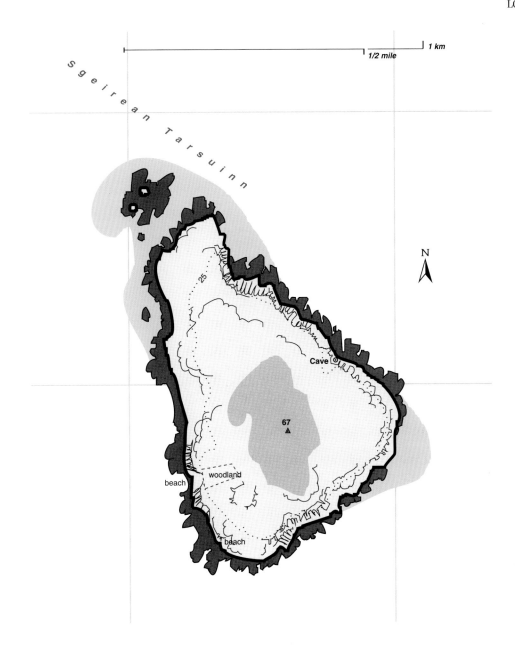

Sgeirean Tarsuinn

N

Cave

67

woodland

beach

beach

a proportion of the plunder but in any case their depredations helped to protect the local fishing grounds.

WILDLIFE: Sheep are occasionally pastured here.

A fair number of nesting seabirds take advantage of the lack of human habitation.

There is little of note to report about the compact little island of **LONGAY**. It could be considered a good example of a desert island, but not an ideal one on which to be marooned.

We found no adequate anchorage. The chart shows a possible area of suitable depth on the east coast but we were unable to find less than a dubious 15m of possibly boulder-strewn bottom so we landed by dinghy while *Jandara* stood off. The island is covered with rough scrub making walking uncomfortable. It rises to a single central ridge with its peak 67m above sea-level. Crossing the ridge, the west slope has scattered patches of rowan and alder but the terrain is mainly heather, bracken and coarse boggy turf. In the extreme south-west corner a patch of beach made up of red sandstone pebbles lies above tongues of semi-submerged rock. Further north there is the impression of a wide cleft or cove with a copse above a narrow gravel beach. This may be a suitable spot for temporary anchorage but I have had no opportunity to test it.

At our landing place on the east coast directly below the crest of the hill there was a narrow rocky beach of tumbled volcanic slabs and a small cave [NG660313] with fresh water trickling down the back of it – a useful pirates' den.

ACCESS: A boat-owner at Broadford or Plockton may be persuaded to co-operate.

Anchorages:
There is no recommended anchorage but temp anchorage may be possible in depths of 12-15m clear of the reef on the S or E sides, or in less depth off the small beached 'cove' on the W side near the S corner. Be sure to use a tripping line.

5.5 Wiay

(G. bhuidhe – yellow or pleasant, ON -øy – island). Sometimes written in the past as 'Vuiay', or 'Buia' (Martin Martin).

OS Maps: 1:50000 Sheet 32 1:25000 Sheet 186
Admiralty Chart: 1:100000 No.1795

AREA: 148ha (366 acres)
HEIGHT: 60m (197 ft)

OWNER: MacLeod Estates.

POPULATION: 1841 – 6. 1881 – 4. 1891 – 0. Uninhabited since 1890.

GEOLOGY: Basaltic lava.

HISTORY: One might assume that Boswell and Johnson visited the island of Wiay since Boswell reported:

'In the afternoon, Ulinish carried us in his boat to an island possessed by him, where we saw an immense cave. . . It is one hundred and eighty feet long, about thirty feet broad, and at least thirty feet high. This cave we were told had a remarkable echo; but we found none. They said it was owing to the great rains having made it damp. Such are the excuses by which the exaggeration of Highland narratives is palliated.'

WILDLIFE: Two large colonies of herring gulls nest on the cliff tops near the lochans above Geodha nan Faochag.

WIAY is the largest island in Loch Bracadale. Most of the coastline consists of vertical cliffs and the southern bluff is a striking overhanging cliff 59m high and covered with yellow lichens & seabird droppings. There is a large sea cave [NG296356] at its base which amplifies the sound of the surf breaking in it and another large cave on the north-east side of the island [NG301370]. I have been unable to establish if either of these caves was the one referred to by Boswell but it seems probable as there are no other prominent island caves close to Ullinish where they were staying. Johnson's account was written from memory in London. He too mentions visiting a sea-cave by boat at low water but he could be describing a cave on Idrigill Point.

The beach in **Camas na Cille** (G. – church bay) is composed of round pebbles many of which are so large that they are better described as boulders. A pleasant green valley stippled with yellow irises, reeds and patches of bracken leads up from the bay to a plateau area of rough bog and coarse grazing for sheep. The derelict remains of at least three dwellings are near the beach, one of which was a black house [NG292366]. There was also a church in this area in bygone times although we saw no obvious trace of it. Flax was once grown here, and Seton Gordon mentions that Donald MacLeod of Ose had a table-cloth spun of Wiay flax, but the arable land has long since disappeared. The central summit (60m) is almost at the geometric centre of Loch Bracadale and the view is all-encompassing. To the east is the dramatic 'castle' of tidal **Oronsay**, great cliffs rising abruptly from the sea like a fortress. To the north are the lesser cliffs of **Tarner Island** and **Harlosh Island**, but **Macleod's Maidens** – three large rock stacks realistically sculpted by the sea – can only be seen from the southern part of the island as they are concealed by Idrigill Point.

In this area there are several tiny lochans and the entire south-western portion is almost isolated by a very deep cleft forming the **Geodha nan Faochag** (G. – narrow creek of the periwinkles). The cliffs here are the steepest and most cave-riddled on the island.

ACCESS: No regular access. Enquire at Portnalong, Loch Harport.

Anchorages: Admiralty Pilot says landing only possible in two places, one being the small bay on NW side. Shores clean to within 1½c.
1. Camas na Cille. Temp anchorage. Rocks on NE side but clear in middle and towards SW side of bay. Approach centrally and anchor off the pebble beach in a suitable depth, shingle.

5.6 Crowlin Islands

[**kroa**-lin] Probably (G. crò linne – eye-of-a-needle channel).

Eilean Mór

(G. – big island)

Eilean Meadhonach

[meeoo-unuch] (G. – middle island)

Eilean Beag

(G. – little island)

OS Maps: 1:50000 Sheet 24 or 32 1:25000 Sheet 188
Admiralty Charts: 1:50000 No.2209 1:25000 No.2498

AREA: 270ha (567 acres)
HEIGHT: 114m (374 ft)

OWNER: Applecross Estate Trust (Captain Fred H. Willis).

POPULATION: 1841 – 40. 1881 – 9. 1891 – 9. 1931 – 0. Uninhabited since.

GEOLOGY: This is a group of three eroded chunks of Torridonian sandstone with volcanic rock intrusions.

WILDLIFE: Common seals seem to be particularly fond of Eilean Beag.

The largest island in this tight-knit group is **EILEAN MOR**. It is 170ha in area and rises to a height of 115m. There are some ruined cottages in the north-east corner near **Camas na h-Annait** (G. – church bay). In the north-west corner by the anchorage a rock shelter has provided storage for visiting fishermen [NG690353] and on the east coast there is an interesting cave [NG695352]. The islands have been denuded of trees and grazing sheep prevent regeneration. A small loch, Loch nan Leac (G. – tombstone loch), in the undulating central plateau of Eilean Mór overflows into a small burn leading down to Camas na h-Annait.

Eilean Mór is separated from Eilean Meadhonach (50ha) by a narrow cleft which is only about 50m wide. Boats can enter from the north at a suitable state of the tide, and there is a pool in the centre which forms a snug little harbour, but reaching it can be a bit like threading a needle. A reef fringes the south coasts of both Eilean Mór and Eilean Meadhonach.

When approaching or leaving the anchorage at high water it is important not to cut the corners. To the west is a submerged reef and on the east a narrow rocky beach which covers, as one poor man discovered when he grounded his hired yacht on it. We arrived at low water to find him high and dry but unhurt. His blushes shone like a beacon in the driving rain.

The smallest island, Eilean Beag (3ha) has a light beacon on its summit and there are many small caves on the rocky shoreline. A reef extends northwards from this islet.

North of the Crowlin Islands is the grassy expanse of **Eilean na Bà** (G. – island of the cattle) and, north again,

sheltering the anchorage of Poll Creadha is **Eilean nan Naomh** (G. – island of the saints) which has a lot of seaweed-covered rock, but hardly enough dry land to support a single saint.

ACCESS: No regular access. Try a private arrangement with a boat owner at Plockton on Loch Carron or, possibly, Broadford on Skye.

Anchorages: Give S coast a wide berth and, similarly, N coast of Eilean Beag.

1. North entrance to harbour. Occasional anchorage just within the mouth of the gut between the two larger islands, 6-8m.

2. Harbour. Access above half flood through narrows. Safe anchorage in N of first pool. Reef projects from W shore at centre of pool.

5.7 Raasay

Possibly, (ON raa-s -øy – roe-deer island) or (ON ross-øy – horse island)

OS Maps: 1:50000 Sheet 24 1:25000 Sheets 171 and 187 and for the extreme north Sheets 154, 155 and 172
Admiralty Charts: 1:50000 Nos.2209 and 2210

AREA: 6,405ha (15,827 acres)
HEIGHT: 443m (1,453 ft)

OWNER: The entire island was purchased by the Government in 1922. Raasay House and some other key properties on the island were sold for a low price in the 1960s to Dr John Green – a Sussex pathologist – who visited the island once and never returned. After considerable pressure over many years and the payment of a high price he was eventually 'persuaded' to sell out to the Highland and Islands Development Board in 1979. Highlands and Islands Enterprise (the successor to HIDB) still owns farmland, a hotel and other property on the island which is rented out at commercial rates. The rest of the island is in Government ownership. The Government offered to transfer all the crofts it owns to a local trust but the crofters did not favour change.

POPULATION: Figures include the tidal island of Eilean Fladday. 1780 – over 400. 1803 – over 900. 1841 – 676. 1881 – 532. 1891 – 489. 1931 – 377. 1961 – 223. 1971 – 163. 1976 – ferry service introduced. 1981 – 182. 1991 – 163.

GEOLOGY: The south is mainly Torridonian sandstone and shale but with two large areas of granite. Iron ore was mined here by Baird & Co using the labour of German prisoners-of-war during the First World War, but it became uneconomic and was closed in 1919. Some of the Torridonian shales on Raasay contain the oldest fossilised plant remains yet found. There is unique loam at the Glam in the centre of the island at the 200-300m level which is evidence that this part of Raasay for some reason probably escaped glaciation and therefore still has its rare and ancient living flora. The extreme north of the island is Archaean gneiss.

HISTORY: The first MacLeod on Raasay was Calum Garbh, younger son of Calum, the 9th Chief of Lewis. In 1518 he was granted title to Raasay, Rona and some estates on Skye and he had a lucrative line in piracy which he mastermined from Brochel Castle. He founded the cadet branch of Mac Gille Chaluim which survived mainly by avoiding involvement with his relatives, the Macleods of Lewis and Dunvegan. In fact the MacLeods of Raasay often preferred to support the MacDonalds of Sleat. Calum son of Gille Chaluim was a poet who was awarded a further charter to his estates by James VI. The next Calum, the 4th Chief, accepted the feudal superiority of Mackenzie of Kintail after Mackenzie had wrested Lewis from the Macleod Clan but there was family tragedy when his son, the much-loved Iain Garbh, met his death by drowning.

Although the MacLeods were Protestants and the Skye Macleods supported the Government, the MacLeods of Raasay, in their usual contrary way, chose to support the Catholic Jacobites, possibly for purely chivalrous reasons. The islanders followed their Chief wholeheartedly and thus tiny Raasay provided one hundred men and twenty-six pipers at Culloden. Later, when Skye was being searched, they secretly rowed the Young Pretender over from Portree at dead of night. Government troops had already burned down the Laird's house and almost every dwelling on the island in reprisal for their Jacobite sympathies but Prince Charles was nevertheless hidden in a shepherd's hut and fed oat-bread and whisky. He was then smuggled over to Loch Broom where he hoped to be rescued by a French ship.

Raasay's support of the Stuarts proved catastrophic. Homes and boats were destroyed, men murdered, women raped, and 'there was not left in the whole island a four-footed beast, a hen or a chicken.'

The MacLeods spent their family fortune on reconstruction and consequently within thirty years the island appeared to have made a remarkable recovery.

By the early 1800s, however, the population was increasing rapidly and poverty became widespread. Emigration began and the Laird, John MacLeod, did what he could to help but by 1843 he was so deeply in debt that he had to sell the island before he too emigrated (to Australia). George Rainy of Edinburgh bought Raasay for 35,000 guineas and genuinely tried to improve conditions on the island for a time, but having failed he turned to sheep farming which resulted in the inevitable eviction of over one hundred families. Raasay's world-renowned Gaelic poet, Sorley MacLean, has immortalised in haunting verse this sad period in Raasay's history.

After Rainy's twenty-seven-year-old son and heir died in 1872 there was a succession of unsympathetic owners

RAASAY HOUSE (WHERE DR JOHNSON STAYED)

until a commercial mining company, Baird & Co, bought the island in 1912 to extract iron-ore. This brought jobs and housing until mining ceased in 1919. The Government eventually bought the island in 1922 for £37,000 after the episode of the Rona Raiders (See Rona, No 5.9).

Raasay is famous for its pipers, the finest being John MacKay (b.1767) who was sent as a child to Skye to study. He and his son Angus – first piper to Queen Victoria – are

remembered for their exceptional talent and for recording and preserving much pipe music which would otherwise have been lost.

But the sound of music died in 1893 when Raasay became the centre for a strict and repressive sect of the Free Church introduced by a Mr Macfarlane. All pleasure was frowned upon and music, dancing and poetry were banned. Although there has been some adjustment of attitudes

THE STABLES WHERE THE CLOCK STOPPED. . .

with the passing years, religious observance on the island, and particularly on the Sabbath, is still very strict. Raasay folk are friendly but they expect their beliefs to be respected.

WILDLIFE: Since Raasay partially escaped glaciation, extensive rare and ancient flora can be found on the steep grassy slopes of the east coast, particularly below the long Druim an Aonich (G. – steep sloping ridge) escarpment. There are many varieties of alpines, saxifrages, orchids, ferns and mosses. Sea aster and bog asphodel flourish beneath Dùn Caan. It is worth the effort of going to Hallaig in the south or Screapadal in the north to see the variety of the wild flowers and the island also has several areas of pleasant mixed woodland.

Animal life includes red deer, alpine hare, otter, water shrew and a unique sub-species of bank vole, darker and twice the weight of the mainland vole; this may not in fact be a sub-species, but an ancient survivor of an original Scandinavian species. Raasay is the only Hebridean island on which the pine marten still survives.

Rabbits were introduced by a thoughtless proprietor, Herbert Wood, in the 19th century and they almost destroyed the agricultural economy.

Birdlife is more varied than usual and golden eagles can be seen circling over the rocky landscape in the north.

The long stretch of **RAASAY** is separated from Skye by a narrow sound and sheltered by it from the prevailing winds. Its east coast is steep with **Dùn Caan** near the centre, 443m high and very conspicuous – like a truncated Fujiama – with the same appearance from all sides except the north-east. The view from the top is one of the most inspiring in the Western Isles. The southern half of the island is mountainous, with gentle gradients to the west and cliffs to the east while the northern portion is comparatively low except for **Beinn na h-Iolaire** (G. – hill of the eagle) about 3km from the northern extremity.

The main village is **Inverarish**, 2km north of the ferry

terminal at Suisnish where the remains of Baird & Co's ore trans-shipment station are still to be seen. Inverarish was also partly built by the mining company. A roadway leads from it to the east coast bypassing the disused mine [NG567367], then on past a 3½km track leading to a waterfall by the shore at Hallaig, before reaching **Fearns** where the Rona Raiders seized land in 1919. Inverarish is set in pleasant woodland which is best experienced by taking a forest walk up the Inverarish Burn.

Dùn Borodale is an ancient broch with part of the walls and galleries remaining, in woodland just north of the village [NG555363].

Churchton Bay, overlooked by Inverarish, is named after the 13th century chapel [NG548367] dedicated to St Moluag (who founded the monastery on Lismore. See No 3.9). Its ruins stand on an ancient burial ground, together with two other buildings, the smaller of which may be 11th century. Boswell considered there was 'something comfortable in the thought of being so near a piece of consecrated ground', when he and Dr Johnson were guests at Raasay House. In the north of the bay is **The Battery** [NG545363], a cannon emplacement on a knoll, built in 1807 and guarded by two busty stone mermaids. A shallow tidal harbour behind the knoll is not obvious from the sea.

Raasay House standing above the Battery and looking towards the mountains of Skye is on the site of the family home of the MacLeods. The original house was burned down by Government troops in reprisal for the help given to the Young Pretender during the Jacobite Rebellion. All the cottages on the island were also destroyed. Raasay House was rebuilt a few years later by the MacLeods but the Regency frontage was added in the early 1800s by John MacLeod and there have been subsequent additions since Dr Johnson stayed there. Raasay House was run as a hotel between 1937 and 1960 when it was bought by Dr Green. He allowed both it and the land to fall into serious disrepair but refused to sell it, even when vandals wrecked the house and stole the contents including the library books. Nor would he sell a small piece of land needed for a ferry pier to serve the island. After years of acrimony and Government inaction the property was eventually purchased for a high price by the Highland and Islands Development Board. The Board converted Borodale House into the Isle of Raasay Hotel but failed to restore Raasay House. The ferry pier was never built – it is Baird's original pier which is still in use. Beautiful old Raasay House is now run as an outdoor centre and volunteers have made a valiant attempt to save the building. The wooded grounds are still derelict but with delightful surprises – mossy pieces of sculpture and an overgrown fountain.

The road passes beneath the clocktower of the **Raasay House Stables**. In 1914 the thirty-six able-bodied men of

Raasay assembled here to go to war and only fourteen returned. The day they left the clock stopped and it has never been satisfactorily repaired. Beyond lies **Temptation Hill** with an incised Pictish Ogam-stone, possibly dating from the 7th century. Temptation Hill is supposed to have been named by the MacLeod who was first tempted by the magnificent outlook to become the island's owner.

Another Pictish stone in front of Raasay House has a cross of unique design incised on it and these stones may have been part of a number historically marking an area of sanctuary.

To the south of the flat summit of Dùn Caan, on which James Boswell danced a reel 'in sheer exuberance', is **Loch na Mhna** (G. – the loch of the woman). A water-horse which haunted this loch devoured the daughter of a local smithy according to legend. The father trapped and killed the monster and found to his surprise that it was made of jelly. **Loch Storab** to the west is named after a Norwegian prince whose grave is beside it.

The tarmac road overlooks **Holoman Island** in Holoman Bay on the west coast – it is tidal and connected to the shore by a pebble strand – before it ends in the north at **Brochel Castle**, the pirate stronghold of the MacLeods of Lewis in the 15th century. Iain Garbh who died in 1671 was the last inhabitant. The fantastic fairy-tale ruin sits on a pinnacle of sheer rock and originally stood three storeys high. A track runs 2km south through east coast woodland to the shielings of Screapadal, scene of the George Rainy clearances. This area has been immortalised in the poems of Sorley McLean (b.1911), a Raasay man and one of Gaeldom's greatest poets.

The road running 2km north from Brochel to **Arnish** was built by Calum MacLeod, a postman. His entire Arnish community of eight families was proposing to leave because there was no road access but the council refused to help. So in 1966, armed with a four-shilling book on roadbuilding, Calum constructed the road himself with a pick, shovel and wheelbarrow. He was awarded the BEM when he eventually completed the work but by then he and his wife were the last remaining inhabitants and he died soon after in 1988.

A track leads on round the shore of Loch Arnish through Torran, where the school was closed in 1960, and branches off to the tidal island of **Eilean Fladday** which used to accommodate four families with their own school. The houses there are now holiday homes. Continuing to the northern tip of Raasay is more than an hour's further walk. Remote **Eilean Tigh** (G. – home island) can be reached by crossing a rock ledge which is exposed at low water.

ACCESS: Caledonian MacBrayne vehicle ferry from Sconser, Skye to East Suisnish, Raasay, 01478 612075. Several crossings daily except Sunday. 15 minutes crossing time. Summer excursions from Portree. Note that there is no petrol for sale on Raasay.

Anchorages:

1. Churchton bay, SE of Eilean Aird nan Gobhar. Anchor either side of Perch Rocks, holding good. Head dries off one cable and SE of bay is foul. HIE moorings available. Pier on NW side of the knoll affords good shelter but it dries.

2. Oskaig Point. Some shelter during W or N winds, S of Oskaig point.

3. Fladday harbour, on E side of S end of Eilean Fladday, is a narrow inlet. Secure anchorage in 5-10m. Approach from SW between Ard an Torrain and Fraoch Eilean following sailing directions carefully.

4. Caol Fladda, on E side of Eilean Fladday with easy approach from N avoiding Bo na Faochag. Holding can be poor due to kelp.

5.8 Isay

[**ee**shĕ] (ON ise-øy – porpoise island)

OS Maps: 1:50000 Sheet 23 1:25000 Sheet 153
Admiralty Charts: 1:100000 No.1795 1:25000 No.2533

AREA: 60ha (148 acres)
HEIGHT: 28m (92 ft)

OWNER: Bought in the mid-1960s by Donovan, the folk singer.

POPULATION: 1841 – 90. There was a final clearance of the last twelve crofter families in 1860. 1881 – 0. Uninhabited since.

GEOLOGY: Basaltic lava with shale and quartzite covered with a reasonably fertile soil.

HISTORY: In the early 16th century Roderick MacLeod of Lewis, whose daughter had married twice, decided to eliminate two entire families so that his own grandson should inherit the island of Raasay (See No.5.7) and the lands of Gairloch. He invited the families to a banquet on Isay promising that they would hear something to their advantage. They all turned up and during the meal Roderick said he wanted the private and personal views of everyone present on a matter of great importance. He left the hall and each guest was summoned in turn to a room where Roderick had them stabbed to death.

WILDLIFE: On a June visit there were dozens of pairs of nesting wrens around the ruins and near the headland south-west of the laird's house a large colony of gulls was nesting on the grass. Eider and shelduck paddled along the shores with their young. Wildflowers were in bloom everywhere – marsh marigold, campion, thrift, common spotted orchids, and forget-me-not to name a few – but the many grazing sheep have obviously taken their toll.

Grass-covered **ISAY** with its two lesser companions, **Mingay** and **Clett**, lies peacefully in Loch Dunvegan. The south-western headland forms a vertical bluff over 20m high but the rest of the coast is generally low.

'. . .There is a beautiful little island in the Loch of Dunvegan, called Isa.' recalled Boswell in 1773. 'M'Leod said he would give it to Dr Johnson, on condition of his re-siding on it three months in the year; nay one month. Dr Johnson was highly amused with the fancy. I have seen him please himself with little things, even with mere ideas like the present. He talked a great deal of this island; – how he would build a house there, – how he would fortify it, – how he would have cannon, – how he would plant, – how he would sally out and take the isle of Muck; – and then he laughed with uncommon glee, and could hardly leave off. . . M'Leod encouraged the fancy of Dr Johnson's becoming owner of an island; told him that it was the practice in this country to name every man by his lands; and begged leave to drink to him in that mode: "Island Isa, your health!"'

At that time Isay was a populous and industrious island and by the early 1800s it was a big fishing station with its own general store. The evidence of human activity is still there but the people have long since gone.

A 'street' of more than eighteen cottages and black house ruins lines the east shore where there are also the remnants of a crude stone jetty. At the south end of this village is the main house [NG220567]. Its west gable has a large 'arched' hole through it giving it the appearance of the west gable of a church. This is evidently where the fireplace for the main hall on the first floor used to be. The main entrance to this hall is from the higher ground level on the south side by way of a fine stone staircase with splayed stone balusters. The ground floor appears to have been divided into three rooms and there is an outhouse on the east gable – possibly the kitchen. One of these ground floor rooms was presumably the site of the notorious 16th century murders.

The soil is fertile but the land is now only used for grazing sheep.

South of Isay at the head of Loch Dunvegan the famous MacLeod castle is sheltered by **Gairbh Eilean**. **Eilean Grianal** and **Garay Island** are two tiny reefs or skerries alongside a double island, **Eilean Dubh** and **Eilean Mór**, linked by a drying channel.

On the other side of the Waternish Peninsula in Loch Snizort are the basalt **Ascrib Islands** – **Eilean Iosal**, **Eilean Creagach**, **Eilean Garave** and **South Ascrib**. These were purchased in 1985 by Peter Palumbo, property developer and past-Chairman of the Arts Council, as a site to build a subterranean residence for himself. This is an unusually considerate approach. 'Not a nuclear shelter,' he insisted, '- but there are after all already traces of underground 18th century monks' cells and being below ground will cause the least disturbance to a beautiful environment'. However, I believe his family were not so enthusiastic.

ACCESS: Summer excursions from Dunvegan.

Anchorages:

1. Anywhere in the S part of the narrow channel between Isay and Mingay island. Well-sheltered from all winds, but winds from the E and SE can sometimes raise an unpleasant sea. Best anchorage possibly in shallow bay with village ruins opposite the S extremity of Mingay Island but N of the chapel-like ruin of the main house, weed and mud.

2. About the centre of the E side of Isay there is an iron stepladder giving access to a landing platform.

5.9 Rona

Probably (ON hraun-øy – rough island), but possibly (G. ròn – seal, ON - øy – island)

OS Maps: 1:50000 Sheet 24 1:25000 Sheet 155
Admiralty Chart: 1:500000 No.2210

AREA: 930ha (2,298 acres)
HEIGHT: 125m (410 ft)

OWNER: Department of Agriculture and Fisheries until 1992 then sold on the open market to a private buyer for, possibly, £250,000.

The new Danish owner, Mrs Dorte Christiansen, has a right of pre-emption over 142 acres at the north extremity owned by the Ministry of Defence.

POPULATION: (In 1763 the Laird of Raasay kept a cowman and 160 head of cattle on the island). 1841 – 165. 1851 – 115. 1861 – 147. 1881 – 176. 1891 – 181. 1922 – 14 tenants and their families. 1931 – 16. 1961 – 49. 1971 – 3. 1981 – 11: these were all Royal Navy personnel at the NATO station at the north end. 1991 – 0.

GEOLOGY: The rocks, some of the oldest in Scotland (and western Europe), are of glaciated Archaean gneiss which is loosely described as Lewisian gneiss. This is a complex group containing dark masses of amphibolite and crystalline veins of pink pegmatite. The earliest metamorphosis – the Scourian – took place about 2,500 million years ago.

HISTORY: In 1518 the first MacLeod to have taken up residence in Brochel on Raasay, Calum Garbh (Lusty Malcolm), younger son of Calum, the 9th Chief of Lewis, established the line of Mac Gille Chaluim, with the lands of Raasay, Rona and parts of Trotternish, Vaternish and Assynt. He came to an arrangement with the pirates and so-called 'broken men' hiding on the islands and raiding ships as they passed through the Sound of Raasay and the Inner Sound. Rona's perfectly concealed natural harbour of Acairseid Mhór (G. – big harbour) was known at that time as Port nan Robaireann (G. – the robbers' port) because it was the centre for piracy in the area. So, like that other island chieftain, MacNeil of Barra, who carried out piracy on a much bigger scale, MacLeod and his descendants, prospered. But in 1745 they made a grave misjudgement by backing the Jacobites and for this they paid dearly.

Although MacLeod entertained Boswell and Johnson royally, he was deeply in debt. So when the Duke of Argyll, Governor of the new British Fisheries Society which was planning the construction of a number of fishing stations (see Nos.6.4 and 6.7), sent a questionnaire to him in 1787, MacLeod speedily replied:

'There is a part of my property (an island called Rona) which is allowed by the best judges to be one of the most advantageous places on this coast for a fishing station. It

Na Gamhnachain

Cow Rock

Sgeir Shuas

Sgeir na h-Iolaire

Loch a' Bhràige

Ob an Dreallair

Port na Ba Brice

Sgeirean
Buidhe Bhorlum

Geodha Chùil-tairbh

Sheilings

Rubha
Chùil-tairbh

Ob nam Feusgan

Beinn 110
na h-Iolaire

Loch
Braig

Inner Sound

Port an Fhearainn

Sgàth a'
Bhannaich

72

Village
(ruins)

Wood

Acairseid
Thioram

125△
Meall
Acairseid

Rona
Lodge

Church
Cave

Wood

Eilean
Garbh

Acairseid Mhor

Sound of Raasay

Doire na Guaile

An Dubh Chamas

Rubha Dubh Chamais

Sheilings
(ruins)

An Teampull

Caol Rona

Port an
Teampull

Garbh Eilean

Eilean
Tigh

Eilean
Seamraig

Sgeir nan Eun

2 km
1 mile

RAASAY

Eilean an
Fhraoich

is surrounded with numbers of banks which are daily discovered by the country people who come to fish from the mainland, which makes me think there is an inexhaustible fund of them about the island. It is likewise supplied with the best harbours at every creek, both for large vessels and small boats.'

But finance was not forthcoming and in the end the imposition by Whitehall of a salt tax stopped the enterprise and crippled the Hebridean fishing industry. Salt was needed to preserve the fish on the way to market.

By 1843 the MacLeod debts were so great that Raasay and Rona had to be sold. They were bought by George Rainy who was something of a philanthropist and in 1850 he did his best to negate the effects of the potato famine. But the population of Raasay had been rising and instead of turning to fishing the people tended to spread on to the more unproductive land such as on Rona. Rainy then started the inevitable sheep farming and evicted over one hundred families. Some of these also settled on Rona – an island already much less able to support them than Raasay. Rainy died in 1863 and his eighteen year-old son and heir took over. He did his best for the islanders but died only ten years later. The next owner George Mackay was a ruthless Gael who forced up the rents and within three years sold the two islands for a handsome profit to an Englishman, William Armitage. He in turn sold them on after eighteen months to another Englishman, Herbert Wood, whose only interest was sport. He imported deer, pheasants and rabbits and cleared the best agricultural land on Raasay which put even more pressure on Rona.

Throughout the Western Isles islanders were at last provoked into retaliation and there was the episode of the 'battle of Braes' on Skye in 1882, just across the water from Raasay House. Parliament responded with the Crofter Act, which was passed in 1886, and which protected the crofters' existing holdings although it failed to return their dispossessed land.

Meanwhile the struggle for survival continued among dwindling numbers on rocky Rona. The small settlement in the north at Braig was abandoned in 1889. Then the Great War gave the chance to travel and see new horizons. In May 1921 seven of Rona's demobilised ex-servicemen and their families staked a claim to their own ancestral land at Fearns on Raasay. They built homes and had prepared ground for planting when they were arrested and given prison sentences. This created a public outcry which resulted in Raasay and Rona being purchased by the Government (Scottish Board of Agriculture) in 1922.

At this time there were fourteen tenants and their families still remaining on Rona at Doire na Guaile, Acairseid Mhór, and Acairseid Thioram, but by 1930 the numbers had dwindled to only two tenant families. The last of these, the Macrae family, left the island in 1943.

The Department of Agriculture stocked the island with fifty-five Highland cows and 150 Blackface ewes and let it as a grazing farm in 1946. There were a number of different tenants until 1987 when the sheep were removed and the island was put up for sale in 1992. The new owner must be given credit for renovating the house by the harbour, planting native trees, improving paths and tracks and installing a water supply without, thankfully, destroying Rona's wonderful ambience.

WILDLIFE: There are no deer on Rona. There were a few wild goats but no sightings have been reported for several years.

The small patches of mixed woodland with some fine Scots pines provide cover for a variety of bird species.

RONA, which is sometimes called South Rona to distinguish it from its namesake which lies well north of Cape Wrath (No 9.4), has a bare, rugged appearance from the sea. There are several hills of 60-90m in height which form a broken ridge and most of the eastern side of the island falls steeply to the sea. The highest hill, **Meall Acairseid** (G. – harbour hill), is 125m high and roughly central.

Rona has been part of the Raasay Estate (See No 5.7) for over 600 years. Martin Martin described it as '..the most unequal rocky piece of ground to be seen anywhere,' and the description in the Gazateer of 1844 is also graphic as it shows the changing perception of beauty:

'. . .To an ordinary observer its aspect is quite repulsive; presenting no picturesque features and but little verdure to chequer its grey and sterile surface. . . Nearly all its arable ground lies round a scattered village which is situated at the head of a bay and contains most of the population.'

Unlike so many of the islands there is still some woodland on Rona but at one time it was entirely covered with trees and was used as a source of timber for neighbouring islands. One remaining patch of about two or three hectares, which is on the north side of **Acairseid Mhór** (G. – big harbour), is mainly oak, birch, and hazel but interspersed with some fine Scots pine. Another patch to the north is mainly alder.

A path of sorts runs from the newly-renovated house known as Rona Lodge at Acairseid Mhór beneath Meall Acairseid which has a triangulation beacon on it. The path carries on to the lighthouse in the extreme north passing through the settlement at **Acairseid Thioram** (G. – dry anchorage) and then meandering between Sgàth a' Bhannaich (110m) and the long rib of gneiss to the east of it and by little Loch Braig. A path also runs south from Acairseid Mhór to the remains of the southernmost village, **Doire na Guaile**, and the ruins of An Teampull at the southern tip.

In the days when the lighthouse was manned, Callum MacLeod BEM, of Arnish on Raasay (See No.5.7), was the Rona postman (this was before he built his famous road

THE OLD SCHOOLHOUSE AT ACAIRSEID THIORAM

from Brochel to Arnish). He used to collect the mail at Brochel Castle, walk to Eilean Tigh, row across Caol Rona, and then walk the entire length of Rona to the lighthouse, deliver the mail and retrace his steps, a total distance of 34km! Only when you have tried to follow in his footsteps for a few tortuous kilometres can you start to appreciate his dedication.

The lighthouse is now automatic but 142 acres next **Loch a' Bhràige** at the north tip of the island are used as a deep-sea listening post by the Ministry of Defence. To the west of it is **Ob an Dreallaire** (G. – the loiterer's creek) and a tidal pond which was probably used as a fish trap.

The three settlements on Rona boasted two schools and a church. The largest settlement was at **Acairseid Thioram**. A derelict church with a slated roof which was built about 1912 is still there together with the old school-house [NG622580] and a number of ruined cottages. I understand the owner intends to convert the schoolhouse into a house.

Some of the crofters evicted from Raasay in the 19th century settled at **Doire na Guaile** in the south-east of the island. This is fairly close to the ecclesiastical site known as **An Teampull** (G. – the temple) [NG617544] which is thought to have been an early Christian monk's cell. A stone wall surrounds the ruin of a small chapel and there is one gravestone for a man called Graham. He is reputed to be the only person actually buried in Rona's stony ground, everyone else being buried on Raasay.

Caol Rona is a relatively narrow stretch of water dividing Rona from Raasay and the tide can run through briskly past **Eilean an Fraoich** (G. – heather island) in the centre of the kyle. **Eilean Seamraig** (G. – shamrock island) is a narrow islet on the north side of the kyle beside tidal **Garbh Eilean**.

On the east coast almost directly across the island from Acairseid Mhór is **Church Cave** [NG626572]. Before the island church was built in 1912 the islanders worshipped in this cavern and even after they had a church it was still a tradition to have babies baptised in the cave. The entrance is like a large Gothic arch and there is a low stone pillar which was used as a pulpit. Beside it is a depression in the stone fed by drips of water from the cave roof and this served as a font. Rows of stones were used as pews by the congregation. The last service was held in 1970 by the Very Reverend Dr James Matheson attended by thirty members from the Portree Parish Church.

This cave is well worth a visit but it is not marked on the Ordnance Survey maps. Take the path from Acairseid Mhór, follow it north from the junction with the south-going path and at the head of the rise turn right (2 o'clock), across a flat boggy patch, over a small ridge and further boggy patch. The next ridge has a small cairn on its rocky top – cross it and carry on down the hill through thick heather (approx. SE direction). There is a flat depression with four small birch trees (and a narrow cleft running down towards the sea). Turn right (approx S) up a rise into a shallow valley with old peat cuttings. This leads down and round the side of a cliff in which the cave is located. Tough going, but even grannies used to do it!

There is a story which keeps cropping up but which I am unable to verify. It claims that in times of drought water had to be fetched from Skye. The boat coming back with water from Skye sank and the boat-owner, Mr Macrae, drowned. This left his widow as the last inhabitant on the island. She was never sure what had happened to her husband so for thirteen years she kept a light in the window of her house, Rona Lodge, to guide his boat back into the harbour. She was eventually given a pension of £40 a year and persuaded to live with relatives in the Braes district of Skye.

ACCESS: Occasional summer excursions arranged from Portree. Enquire at Isle of Skye Tourist Board, 01478 612137.

Anchorages:
1. Acairseid Mhór. A popular and excellent anchorage. Entrance concealed by Eilean Garbh and care needed in the approach. Shingle or mud, holding varies.
2. Loch a' Bhràige. Anchorage used by Admiralty. Well lit and good shelter but unattractive.

5-Appendix Skye

[sky] Probably, (Early Celtic *skitis*, or G. *sgiath* – winged) isle. Interpreted by Norse as ?(ON *skuy* – misty) isle.

OS maps: 1:50000 Sheets 23, 32 and 33 1:25000 Sheets 127, 137, 138, 152, 153, 154, 169, 170, 171, 186, 187, 202, 203, 204, 217, 218, 219, 234, and 235
Admiralty Charts: 1:100000 No.1795 1:50000 Nos.2208, 2209 and 2210

AREA: 16,5625ha (409,259 acres)
HEIGHT: 993m (3,257 ft)

OWNER: Multiple ownership but the Scottish Office (Government) has sizeable holdings.

POPULATION: 1755 – 11252. 1794 – 14470. 1821 – 20827. 1841 – 23082 (peak). 1881 – 16889. 1891 – 15705. 1931 – 9908. 1951 – 8537. 1961 – 7478. 1971 – 7183. 1981 – 8139. 1991 – 8695.

GEOLOGY: The dramatic Cuillin mountains in the south were formed by volcanic activity some fifty million years ago. Narrow tilted strata of brittle rock run through the iron-hard gabbro which has been shaped by ice into great jagged and irregular teeth. The Red Cuillin on the other hand are of granite (gabbro which flowed out of the ground and cooled quickly) and this by comparison is soft enough to have eroded into more rounded shapes. The oldest rock on Skye, gneiss, is found south of Isle-Ornsay on the Sleat [slayt] peninsula.

There is a wealth of geological variety on Skye. Marble is quarried near Torrin, there are coral beaches on Loch Dunvegan, and north of Trotternish there is a beach of green sand (due to the presence of olivine). Gold has also been found on the island.

HISTORY: St Columba visited Skye in 585 AD. From the 8th century until 1266 – three years after King Haakon's defeat at the Battle of Largs – the Norse were in control. Later the land was divided between the MacDonalds, the Mackinnons and the MacLeods who were constantly feuding and fighting.

In 1745 twenty-four-year-old Flora MacDonald helped Bonnie Prince Charlie, with a price of £30,000 on his head, to escape capture. With the Prince disguised as a maid and called Betty Burke Edinburgh-educated Flora brought him by boat from Benbecula 'over the sea to Skye', landing at Kilbride Bay, where he hid in caves and cattle byres. Then he crossed to Raasay (See No 5.7) by night and arrived there just after the staunchly Jacobite island had been sacked by government troops from *HMS Furnace*. His French rescue ship failed to appear so he returned to Skye and then crossed over to Knoydart on the mainland. On the 19th September 1746 he was picked up from Loch nam Uamh by the French and escaped to France. He died in Rome in 1778. Flora was arrested and taken to London but she was freed in 1747 after the passing of the Indemnity Act by Parliament and became very popular with London society.

Many families were forced to leave Skye after the unsuccessful Jacobite Rising and between 1840 and 1880 a further 30,000 people were evicted from their crofts by landlords and forced to emigrate to the New World. Yet more left when bad harvests struck the island in 1881-85. The ruined houses and empty glens can still be seen as testimony of this misery.

WILDLIFE: Skye has a rich diversity of flora with a number of rare species. On the east side of the Trotternish ridge a relative of the sorrels which are native to Iceland was discovered in 1934. Mountain avens, guelder-rose and helleborine can be found in the birchwoods behind Broadford and rock whitebeam and red broomrape flourish on the cliffs and slopes above the sea.

'There are in Skye neither rats nor mice; but the weasel is so frequent that he is heard in houses rattling behind chests or beds as rats in England,' according to Dr Johnson, whose natural history was not always accurate.

The white-tailed sea-eagles nested on Skye until 1907, and the last sighting was recorded in 1916.

The 'capital' of **SKYE** is **Portree**. It was called Kiltragleann (G. – the church of St Talarican in the glen) until the 16th century or thereabouts. It is said to have been renamed in honour of a visit in 1540 by King James V (G. port-rìgh – King's port) but some say the derivation is (G. *portrigheadh* – port on the hillside). The Royal Hotel is on the site of McNab's Inn where Bonnie Prince Charlie bade fond farewell to Flora MacDonald but there is little of historical interest. The building which used to be the courthouse and jail for the whole island now houses the tourist office. Highlighting Skye's recent insularity it is noteworthy that until 1949 the only electricity on the island was produced by a diesel generator in the Portree Hotel.

The road north to Trotternish passes by the **Storr** (G. – buck tooth) 719m high, with its conspicuous 50m high rock-needle called **The Old Man of Storr** – first climbed in 1955. **Holm Island** lies off-shore to the south-east.

On the beach north of **Rigg** a church-shaped rock –

Eaglais Bhreagach marks the place where the Clan MacQueen is said to have raised the devil using an ancient ritual which involved roasting live cats. A small carpark at **Lealt** is the start of an interesting climb down a ravine with a view of several spectacular waterfalls and further on, at **Lonfearn**, are the remains of early Christian beehive cells [NG526626]. These are known as druids' houses in Gaelic. High on the ridge above, near the summit of Beinn Edra (611m), a Flying Fortress bomber crashed in 1945.

Beyond Kilt Rock [NG507665], a piece of natural black basalt with folded strata, is **Staffin**, scene of the alleged wreck of a galleon of the Spanish Armada. Offshore are **Staffin Island** and **Eilean Flodigarry** where according to local tradition the owner once had his corn harvested for him in two nights by 150 fairies. Above Staffin is the **Quiraing**, a fantastic group of awesome rock formations. A short walk north-east from the highest point of the Staffin-to-Uig road [NG443682] leads to The Table, The Prison, and the 36m-high Needle.

As the road turns west at the head of the peninsula there is a striking viewpoint at **Bàgh nan Gunnaichean** (G. – bay of the cannons). To the north is **Eilean Trodday** (G. and ON – island of the trolls) which once supported a settlement and a chapel. At the extreme north-west of Trotternish the ruin of 15th century **Duntulm Castle** [NG410743], last occupied in 1732, overlooks **Tulm Island**. Further out to sea are a group of slab-shaped islands, – **Lord Macdonald's Table**, **Gearran Island**, **Gaeilavore Island**, and **Fladdachùain** with a ruined chapel in which, it is said, Sir Donald MacDonald of the Isles hid his title deeds before the 1715 Rising. The cell was founded in Columba's time by a giant of a monk called O'Gorgon and, strangely, the last man to live on the island was also of huge stature and known as Muileach Mór (G. – the big man from Mull).

About 2km south is a **Cottage Museum** in four restored black houses, and the burial place of Flora MacDonald. The original MacDonald mausoleum was slowly dismantled by souvenir-hunting tourists and the present memorial replaced it [NG400719]. West of **Balgown** a marshy loch with beehive dwellings and a nunnery on its islands was drained in 1824 [NG377689].

The ferry terminal of **Uig** (ON *vik* – a bay), with services to Harris and North Uist, is in a large cove sheltered by basaltic cliffs.

Travelling south to Loch Snizort Beag, ruined **Caisteal Uisdean** (G. – Hugh's castle) overlooks **Eileanan Mór** and **Beag**. It was built about 1580 by Hugh MacDonald of Sleat with stone quarried from the Ascrib Islands (See No.5.8). Hugh's clan chief found that he had been plotting against him so he entombed him alive in Duntulm Castle with a piece of salt beef and an empty water jug [NG381583].

A broad valley runs from Portree to Loch Snizort containing the village of **Skeabost**. A tiny island in the river below the Skeabost bridge has associations with St Columba [NG418485] and it was in this village that the poet Mairi Mhor Nan Oran (Mary MacPherson) was born. Above **Clachamish** are the remains of **Dùn Suladale** [NG374526], one of the best-preserved brochs on Skye.

The village of **Stein** on the Vaternish peninsula nestles on the side of Loch Bay overlooking the islands of Isay (No.5.8), Mingay and Clett. Further on, at the end of the road, the windswept ruin of **Trumpan Church** [NG225612] above Ardmore Bay was the scene of one of the bloodiest episodes in Scottish history. In 1578, while the MacLeods were at worship, the MacDonalds of Uist decided to avenge the massacre of Eigg (See No.4.2) so they barred the door and set fire to the church. One young girl escaped, although she severed one of her breasts while struggling through a small window, but all the rest were burned to death. The girl raised the alarm and the MacLeods quickly gathered a force together. Carrying their famous Fairy Flag they rushed down on the MacDonalds as they were leaving in their galleys. Every MacDonald was slaughtered and the bodies were buried in a dyke. The battle has been remembered ever since as the 'spoiling of the dyke'.

The grave of Lady Grant is in the churchyard. She was exiled to St Kilda (No.9.1) for eight years by her husband and died in 1742, three years after returning to Skye.

By the **Fairy Bridge** [NG278513] on Bay River the road travels south to **Dunvegan Castle** [NG247491], seat of the Clan MacLeod since 1200. This is the longest continuous occupation of any Scottish castle although much of the present castle was built in the 19th century. On Skye, by the way, the *sìthiche* [shee-huch], the fairies or little people, have often played a prominent part in clan history. They were said to live in the rounded grassy mounds called *sithean* [shee-hen] and enjoy many mischievous pranks.

Duirinish, the area west of Dunvegan, is dominated by twin peaks called **Macleod's Tables**, **Healabhal Bheag** which is the highest (488m) and **Healabhal More**, larger but lower (469m). Much of this area is wild moorland, but there are several villages in the north including **Boreraig**, home of the hereditary pipers to the MacLeod chiefs, the world-renowned MacCrimmons. The Piper's Cave is in the cliffs below the reputed site of their piping college. The MacArthurs founded the first piping school on Skye but they moved to Islay (No.2.4) as hereditary pipers to the Lords of the Isles.

PORTREE

Through the valley to the west is **Glendale** with its restored 200-year-old dry-stone grain mill. Further west still there is a well-made path running out to the lighthouse on Neist Point where the view is panoramic. For memorable scenery try the bumpy road to Ramasaig, followed by a walk down the track to **Lorgill**. On 4th August 1830 every crofter in Lorgill was ordered to board the *Midlothian* in Loch Snizort or go to prison. (Those over the age of seventy were sent to the poorhouse instead). Experienced hill-walkers could take the cliff-top route from here to Idrigill Point but a safer bet is to drive to Loch Bharcasaig at Orbost and take the 6km track from there. Idrigill Point overlooks Loch Bracadale and **Macleod's Maidens**, three dramatic stacks like Victorian statues standing in the sea. They were named to commemorate the drowning of the wife and two daughters of a MacLeod chief.

Loch Bracadale is a fascinating loch with many inlets and small islands. Dr Johnson stayed at Ullinish and visited **Dùn Beag**, an interesting ruined broch beside the road at Struan [NG339386]. At the entrance to Loch Harport which opens off the southern end of Bracadale there is the small fishing village of **Portnalong** which was founded by crofters from Lewis and Harris in 1921, and the famous Talisker Whisky distillery is further south at **Carbost**. A narrow road connects Carbost to **Loch Brittle** in the south-west of Skye with its sandy beach, a campsite for climbers, and the cruel but beautiful spiked ridges of the Cuillin Hills towering above the glen.

The road south from Portree meets the junction at **Sligachan**. There is a track from here [NG487298] which climbs over the mountains to **Loch Coruisk** (G. *coire uisge* – cauldron of water). The approach to Loch Coruisk by sea is from Loch Scavaig into Loch Cuilce (G. – reedy loch). The anchorage behind **Eilean Glas** and beneath a high cliff with a waterfall is one of the most dramatic on the West Coast. There is not much swinging room but there is an alternative spot by **Eilean Reamhar** (G. – fat island). Loch Coruisk – fresh water, only 10m above sea level, and one of the most awe-inspiring places on earth – is only a short walk away. The deep dark loch, 30m deeper than sea-loch Scavaig, is set in a giant amphitheatre of lonely, primaeval mist-shrouded mountains. It was painted by Turner and visited by Sir Walter Scott.

Sgurr Alasdair, on the west side of Loch Coruisk, is Skye's highest peak at 993m (3257ft), while one of the longest rock climbs in Britain is the ascent of Sgurr a' Ghreadaidh (G. – peak of torment) from the head of Loch Coruisk.

The road from Sligachan runs through **Sconser**, ferry terminal for Raasay, round Loch Ainort with a folk museum at Luib and on to Broadford Bay. **Broadford** lies under Beinn na Caillich (732m) and its eastward continuation is called Waterloo because many of the veterans of the 1815 battle made their homes here. The road to Elgol, a little settlement which overlooks Soay (No.5.1) by Loch Scavaig, runs through a broad valley south of Beinn na Caillich. On the way it passes close to **Coire-chatachan** [NG621227] where Mackinnon entertained Dr Johnson and Boswell during their tour of the Hebrides in 1773. Just beyond are the ruins of Cille Chrìosd (G. – Christ's church) and further on, past the **Torrin** marble quarry by Loch Slapin, the village of **Kilmarie** was once the home of the Mackinnon chiefs. A track from here leads over the hills to Loch Coruisk via 'Bad Step' while the view to the east is up lovely Loch Eishort with **Eilean Gaineamhach Boreraig** and **Eilean Dubh** dotted on either side of the narrows like the Morse code.

Sitting on the headland at **Suidhe Biorach** (G. – pointed seat) south of Elgol is reputed to make childless women fertile. There is a marvellous walk along the rocky shore at **Elgol** with its strange honeycomb cliffs facing gloomy Loch Scavaig. The east side of the Strathaird promontory has equally fine views of Sleat and, at Glasnakille, Spar Cave with its stalactites is worth a visit [NG538128].

The **Sleat** [slayt] peninsula between Loch Eishort and the Sound of Sleat is served by a road from Broadford. Opposite dour Loch Hourn on the mainland, lies the pretty little village and anchorage of **Isleornsay**. Unfortunately, the bottom is thick with weed and anchors easily drag. On the tidal island of Ornsay (ON *örfiris-øy* – ebb island) there is a ruined chapel and an automatic lighthouse beside Eilean an Eòin (G. – isle of birds).

Further south the pier at **Armadale** for the Mallaig ferry shelters the Skye Yacht Club's anchorage. Above the road stands Armadale Castle [NG640047] which was built in 1815-19 for the second Lord MacDonald. It is surrounded by tree specimens from all over the world and is now the **Clan Donald Centre**. There are estimated to be three million MacDonalds in the world.

The southernmost tip of Sleat – the lighthouse at Point of Sleat with **Eilean Sgorach** (G. – scollop isle) beneath it – can be reached on foot by a track. On the west side of the peninsula ruined **Dunscaith Castle** [NG595120] is between the villages of Tokavaig and Tarskavaig. According to legend this was the home of the Queen of Skye who taught the art of war to Cuchulainn, an Irish hero. It was last occupied in 1570. **Eilean Ruaridh** (G. – Rory's island) is off-shore.

Kyle Rhea, north of the Sound of Sleat, with its privately-operated ferry from Glenelg is the traditional ferry crossing to Skye, although until 1906 cattle bound for market were tied nose to tail and made to swim across the narrows. The modern ferry terminal is at Kyleakin, or King Haakon's kyle, commemorating his visit in 1263. Four miles west is the Skye airstrip and at the end of the runway a row of graves contain the dead from the cruiser *HMS Curaçao* which was cut in two by the *Queen Mary* when she was escorting her in 1942.

ACCESS: Road access (A87) by toll bridge at Kyle of Lochalsh linking Skye and the mainland. Vehicle ferries, 1) Glenelg to Kylerhea, crossing 5 minutes, 01599 81302, and 2) Mallaig to Armadale, crossing 30 minutes, 01687 2403 or 014714 248.

Anchorages:

1. Camas Daraich, at Point of Sleat. Keep in centre. Occasional anchorage more than 1c off shore in 6-10m. Exposed S and subject to swell.

2. Port na Long, Sound of Sleat. Temp anchorage well off shore.

3. Port a' Chuil, Sound of Sleat. Temp anchorage well off shore.

4. Armadale. Beware rocks S of Armadale. Restricted space but good holding in sand. HIE buoys available. Subject to swell from NE.

5. Knock Bay, Sound of Sleat. Anchor 1 1/2c SE of castle ruin. Protected from NE swell but holding poor. W side of bay is foul. Beware sudden change of depth.

6. Loch Camas Croise. Temp anchorage, N side and not too far in, clay.

7. Isleornsay harbour. Easy access, good shelter except NE, but head dries out a long way and holding poor due to weed. Best holding due W of N beacon on Isle Ornsay.

8. Camas nam Mult, opposite Duisdale Hotel. Better holding than Isleornsay, and nearer shore.

9. Loch na Dal. Head dries nearly 5c. Open SE but better than Isleornsay in N'lies.

10. Bagh Dunan Ruadh, S of Kyle Rhea. Occasional anchorage 2c S of river mouth, 2c off shore, good holding. Squally in NW'lies. Beware 2c drying bank at river mouth.

11. Sgeir na Caillich, N of Kyle Rhea. Anchor 1 1/2c WNW of the beacon, or closer to shore if using large-scale chart.

12. Loch na Béiste. Narrow shelf on NW side is suitable depth but loch is foul with old moorings and wrecks. Exposed E.

13. Ob na Partan. Mainly foul with cables but possible anchorage 1/2c from W side in 7m. Use tripping line.

14. *Kyleakin. Temp anchorage in restricted space and depth, or temporary lie alongside fishing boat at pier. Bottom foul and poor holding. Visitors' moorings proposed (1995).*

15. *North of Kyleakin village, off King's Arms Hotel. Beware cables E of hotel. Occasional anchorage, blue clay. Subject to swell from traffic and N'lies.*

16. *Corry Pier, Broadford. Anchor off pier on W side of bay clear of moorings and drying rock SE of pier or temp alongside pier. Exposed N.*

17. *Caolas Scalpay, E of narrows. Anchor where convenient. Can be squally. Beware Sgeir Stapaig off Scalpay.*

18. *Loch na Cairidh, W of narrows. Anchor where convenient. Can be squally.*

19. *Loch Ainort. Anchor off Luib or in either corner at head. Can be very squally.*

20. *Loch Sligachan. Narrow entrance with several hazards. Anchor less than 1/2c W of ruined slip at Peinchorran or towards head of loch in not less than 5m. Can be very squally.*

21. *Balmeanach Bay, S of Raasay narrows. Anchor clear of cables. Holding good.*

22. *Camas a' Mhór-bheòil, N of Raasay narrows. Beware drying rock in middle of bay. Uncomfortable in N'lies.*

23. *Portree. Restricted by moorings. Anchor NE of pier in 7-10m, soft mud, doubtful holding. HIE buoys available but uncomfortable in S'lies. Temp stay alongside pier when tide and space suitable, but be ready to move off. Alternative anchorage at Camas Bàn, but subject to 'whirlies' in S'lies.*

24. *Staffin Bay. Enter from NE. Bay is clean but exposed NE and squally in W'lies. Anchor on W side of Staffin Island or SW corner of bay.*

25. *Kilmaluag Bay. Beware drying reef at entrance and submerged rock off N shore. Fierce squalls in strong W'lies. Exposed E. Anchor in 5-10m, sand and pebbles, good holding.*

26. *Duntulm Bay. Approach mid-channel by S entrance. Anchor close to NE side of Tulm Island but N of mid-point, or under cliffs at NE of bay. Some swell at turn of tide, but sheltered.*

27. *Uig Bay. Restricted space behind pier but bottom foul and most of the bay dries. Temp lie alongside pier may be possible in daylight. Camas Beag on S side of bay suitable in S'lies but deep until close to shore.*

28. *Poll na h'-Ealaidh (Port na Ella). Beware drying rocks N of entrance. Anchor close E of Dùn Maraig islet on S side. Sheltered except W'lies.*

29. *Loch Snizort Beag. Keep mid-channel on approach up the loch. Anchor just within the middle arm, SW of Skerinish Quay, 4m, mud, good holding and good shelter.*

30. *Loch Treaslane on W side of Loch Snizort Beag. Keep mid-channel. Head dries off for 4c. Good shelter.*

31. *Clachamish Bay, first bay on W side of Loch Snizort Beag. Suitable anchorage.*

32. *Loch Greshornish. Approach and enter loch on course midway between Eilean Mór and Greshornish Point and keep mid-channel up loch. Anchor SW of Borve. Excellent shelter.*

33. *Loch Diubaig. Head dries off 3c. Occasional anchorage. Exposed N.*

34. *Aros Bay. Clean and open. Occasional anchorage.*

35. *Ardmore Bay. W side shoal. Shelter from N'lies but holding doubtful.*

36. *Stein. HIE moorings but usually occupied by local fishing boats. Uncomfortable in S and W winds.*

37. *Dunvegan Castle. Visitors' moorings or anchor between Gairbh Eilean and castle, clear of rocks. (Visit Dunvegan Castle).*

38. *Head of Loch Dunvegan. Follow approach directions and anchor beyond pier as depths allow.*

39. *Loch Erghallan. Follow approach directions with care. Anchor less than 1c from S of Eilean Mór.*

40. *Loch Mór. Follow approach directions and anchor in centre of basin or, for best shelter, ESE of Colbost slip.*

41. *Loch Pooltiel. Occasional anchorage near head which dries off several cables, 3-5m, mud, good holding. Exposed NW but small boats might gain shelter between pier and Sgeir Mór, bottom stony.*

42. *Loch Bharcasaig, Loch Bracadale. Best anchorage in this area other than Loch Harport. Anchor in SW corner in 4m.*

43. *Loch Vatten. Anchor near bay in NW corner. Fair shelter but exposed to SW swell. Beware Harlosh Skerry on approach. Shallow-draught boats can enter Poll Roag at HW but not recommended.*

44. *Loch Caroy. Occasional anchorage exposed to S'ly swell with various hazards on approach. Anchor near jetty on E side.*

45. *Tarner Island. Approach from S and anchor close to NE side of island in 9m. Reasonable shelter.*

46. *Oronsay, bay on NW side is clean. Restricted but suitable for small yachts, 4m.*

47. *Loch Beag, Loch Harport. Occasional anchorage if no sea from S. Holding poor, dries out halfway and obstructed by moorings.*

48. *Gesto Bay. Fair anchorage except in SW'-W'lies.*

49. *Carbost. Visitors' moorings or anchor near shore between pier and distillery. Beware extensive shoal at burn. Head of loch dries. (Visit Talisker distillery).*

50. *Port na Long. Anchor off jetty, good holding and fair shelter except from E. Bay obstructed with moorings and fish cages.*

51. *Fiskavaig Bay. Temp anchorage off burn on W side, 7m.*

52. *Loch Eynort. Occasional anchorage. Exposed W but some shelter beyond bend. Holding uncertain. Head dries 8c. Subject to squalls.*

53. *Loch Brittle. Temp anchorage if no swell.*

54. *Loch Scavaig, Eilean Reamhar. Approach 1/2c E of Eilean Reamhar and turn towards shore when midway between Eilean Reamhar and Sgeir Doigich (which sometimes covers). Anchor NW of Eilean Reamhar. Reasonable shelter but subject to squalls.*

55. *Loch na Cuilce, Eilean Glas. Follow sailing directions carefully for approach to anchorage on NW side of Eilean Glas. Good holding in mud and sand but subject to violent squalls. (Access to Loch Coruisk).*

56. *Loch Slapin. Keep mid-channel on the approach until Rubha Cruaidhlinn is abeam on W side, then keep W of mid-channel. Best anchorage near S shore of Bgh nam Faoilean, 4-6m, mud. Fish cages and occasional swell.*

57. *Loch Eishort, Heast Island. Follow sailing directions carefully for difficult approach. Anchor E of island, clear of moorings and N of fish cages, mud, good holding.*

58. *Bagh an Dubh Ard, SW of Loch Eishort narrows. Follow directions for approach. Occasional anchorage in suitable weather. Bottom shelves steeply.*

59. *Tokavaig. Occasional anchorage in very settled weather.*

60. *Tarskavaig. Occasional anchorage in very settled weather.*

61. *Acairseid an Rubha, on W side of Point of Sleat has a jetty for servicing the lighthouse. Not recommended.*

Gairloch and the North Coast

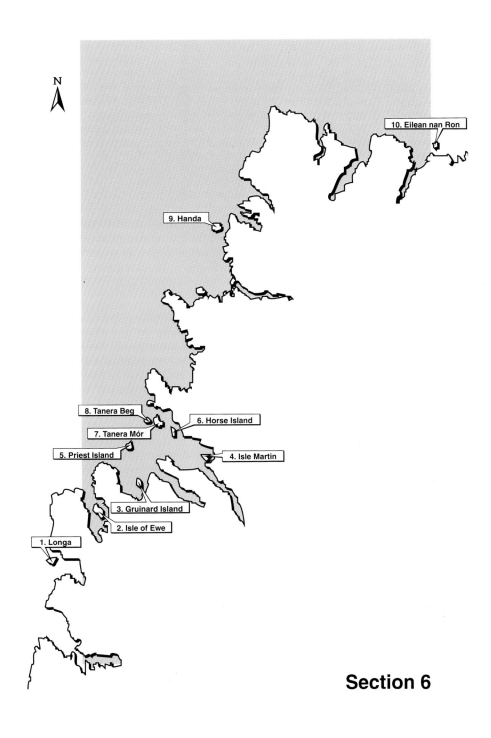

N

10. Eilean nan Ron

9. Handa

8. Tanera Beg

6. Horse Island

7. Tanera Mór

5. Priest Island

4. Isle Martin

3. Gruinard Island

2. Isle of Ewe

1. Longa

Section 6

Section 6, Table I

No.	Name	Latitude	Longitude	Table 2* No.	Table 3** No.	Area in Acres	Area in Hectares
6.1	Longa	57° 44N	05° 48W	103	94	311	126
6.2	Isle of Ewe	57° 50N	05° 37W	71	92	764	309
6.3	Gruinard Island	57° 53N	05° 28W	89	64	484	196
6.4	Isle Martin	57° 57N	05° 13W	94	57	388	157
6.5	Priest Island	57° 58N	05° 30W	108	87	301	122
6.6	Horse Island	57° 59N	05° 20W	148	108	131	53
6.7	Tanera Mór	58° 01N	05° 24W	69	56	766	310
6.8	Tanera Beg	58° 01N	05° 27W	137	83	163	66
6.9	Handa	58° 23N	05° 12W	70	53	764	309
6.10	Eilean nan Ron	58° 34N	04° 20W	101	90	341	138

* Table 2: The islands arranged in order of magnitude
** Table 3: The islands arranged in order of height

Introduction

There are no large islands off the north-west coast of Scotland from Skye to Cape Wrath but there is a surfeit of little ones.

What is the collective noun which best represents a collection of small islands? A cluster, a scatter, an accumulation, an agglomeration? How about a swarm or an assembly? A clutter or a hotchpotch? Anyway, some such term is badly needed for the medley of assorted islets scattered in patches along this coastline.

Seen as part of a vast primaeval landscape with its reedy pools, patches of heather, and enormous expanses of smooth pink rock, the islets are almost indistinguishable in the random mix of land and water. The land dominates. The sea is a mere intrusion.

That is the view from the land but, as always, the view from the sea is very different. Now the islets create a patchwork of fascinating channels, each one different, each turn revealing new vistas and tempting further exploration. The scale is more human and immediate, each discovery more exciting, possibly because speed is limited and distances are restricted. The sea is in control and there are no hill-top views of distant horizons to give a foretaste of things to come.

The region prospered during the herring boom of the late 18th century. **Isle Ristol**, a tidal island near the **Summer Isles**, was the site of a fishing station founded in the later 18th century by Morison and Mackenzie. Close beside it is **Eilean Mullagrach** while **Eilean Ghlais** gives its name to a bay to the north. The Summer Isles, by the way, were so named because they were, and still are, used for summer grazing.

The huge Inverpolly Nature Reserve abuts Enard Bay with the islets of **Eilean Mór**, **Eilean Mòineseach** (G. – diffident isle), **Fraochlan** (G. – heather island), and

Green Island immediately offshore. There are anchorages by Lochan Sàl and in Loch an Eisg-brachaidh east of these islets. Loch Inver, with its busy fishing harbour, is a few miles to the north with **Soyea** (ON – sheep island) marking its entrance and **A' Chleit** (G. – the reef) nearby.

In the next huge bay to the north, Eddrachillis Bay, there are many islets. **Oldany Island** is larger than Isle Ristol but is also linked to the mainland by a drying channel. **Eilean Chrona** (G. – faulty island) is to the west of it and **Eilean nan Uan** (G. – lamb island), **Eilean an Achaidh** (G. – field island), and **Cùl Eilean** (G. – island at the back) are the larger of the tight group of islets to the east.

The islets in the centre of Eddrachillis Bay, **Meall Mór** (G. – big lump) and **Meall Beag** are almost a continuation of the line of a proto-peninsula formed by Calbha Mór which is part of the mainland, and **Calbha Beag** (G. – little headland), an independent island in spite of its name. They are at the entrance to Loch a' Chàirn Bhàin which is spanned by the beautiful Kylesku Bridge. **Eilean a' Ghamhna** (G. – isle of the stirks) is west of the bridge and **Eilean na Rainich** below the bridge on the east side. The bridge itself is built on the tidal islet of Garbh Eilean.

There is another **Eilean na Rainich** (G. – isle of the ferns) in the **Badcall Islands**. If any group of islets needs a suitable collective noun, this is it. A 'school' is too orderly, a 'gaggle' sounds better. The larger islets are **Eilean a' Bhreitheimh**, **Ceannamhór** (G. – bighead), **Ox Rock**, **Eilean na Bearachd** (G. – island with the pointed snout) – the largest of the gaggle, **Glas Leac**, **Eilean Riabhach** (G. – grizzled island), and **Eilean Garbh** (G. – rough island).

Lochs Laxford and Dùghaill, between Handa Island and Kinlochbervie also have their share of 'wee ones.' **Eilean**

Ard (G. – high island) is the largest. And there are also **Eilean a' Mhadaidh** (G. – isle of the dog), the inevitable **Eileanan Dubha**, **Eilean an Sithein** (G. – isle of the fairy mound), Eilean Meall a' Chaorainn (G. – island hillock of the rowan tree) and **Eilean Port a' Choit** (G. – isle of the small boat harbour) beside Weaver's Bay.

Loch a' Chadh-Fin which opens off Loch Laxford, and which is the magnificent setting for John Ridgeway's adventure school, has **Eilean an Eireannaich** at the entrance and **Eilean a' Chadh-fi** in the centre.

At Loch Clash by Kinlochbervie, barren **Eilean a' Chonnaidh** (G. – island of the faggot of firewood) has a thought-provoking name. Could this have referred to driftwood or was there a shipwreck there in some bygone age? About one and a half miles away two islands **Eilean an Ròin Mór** and **Beag** (G. – large and small seal island) are linked together with only a narrow channel separating them from the mainland. From the sea they look like a peninsula and as with so many of the islets in this part of the world, they have little vegetation and the rock faces are worn into smooth, rounded shapes.

With the exception of one tiny group of rocks a mile off the remote and beautiful Sandwood Beach, the biggest descriptively named **Am Balg** (G. – the belly), the coast is now devoid of islands all the way to wild Cape Wrath (ON *hvarf* – turning point).

6.1 Longa

(G. long, ON -øy – ship island)

OS Maps: 1:50000 Sheet 19 1:25000 Sheet 128
Admiralty Charts: 1:50000 No.2210 1:15000 No.2528

AREA: 126ha (311 acres)
HEIGHT: 70m (230 ft)

OWNER: (?) Gairloch Estate.

POPULATION: 1841 – 35 (6 houses) 1881 – 0. Uninhabited since then.

GEOLOGY: Mainly sandstone.

LONGA is covered with grass and heather and attains a height of 70m at **Druim an Eilean** (G. – the island ridge). The west side, which has its own mini-peak called Carr Mór (G. – the big pap) and inlet, Camas nam Faochag (G. – bay of the whirlpools), is almost divided from the rest by a low neck of land between two bays. The north bay, **Camas nam Rainich** (G. – bracken bay), has a small sandy beach backed by a bracken-covered slope. It is the favourite place to anchor provided the wind is not in the north. The south bay, which is rockier, is called **Eag Mhór** (G. – the big notch). Longa is separated from the beach and village of Big Sand on the mainland by Caolas Beag (G. – little channel).

There is one tiny lochan almost in the centre of the island and directly south of it a rocky promontory with a hooked silhouette descriptively called **Sròn na Caillich** (G. – the old woman's nose). Further along the coast is Uamh nan Gabhar (G. – cave of the nanny-goats).

On the south side of Loch Gairloch and opposite Longa the small and crowded harbour of Badachro is sheltered by **Eilean Horrisdale**. Although unkempt with wild irises and bracken, the centrally-situated owner's house creates the impression from a distance that the island is an informal private garden. This tiny islet, less than one-third the area of Longa, supported twenty-seven people in four houses in 1841 and the population had risen to thirty-one islanders in five houses by the end of the 19th century. This was surely overcrowding, but they would be fishing folk so the area of land would be of little consequence.

Glas Eilean is a useful sea-mark when sailing up the

A HERRING DRIFTER IN THE 1930S

loch to the pier by Charlestown and **Fraoch-eilean** (G. – heather isle) marks the entrance to Gairloch's Loch Shieldaig, which is a pleasant anchorage when you want to avoid being crushed by fishing boats at the pier.

ACCESS: No normal access but a boat from Charlestown or Badachro may be co-operative.

Anchorages: The W coast of the island is foul for about 3/4c offshore and a reef fringes the island. Note that the mainland shore dries for 2c at Caolas Beag and there is a fairly shallow spit NE of the island.
1. Occasional anchorage in centre of bay on N coast, 5-8m, sand.

6.2 Isle of Ewe

Island of Loch Ewe. (EI eo – yew tree) but Watson thinks (G. eubh – echo) from place-name on adjoining mainland.

OS Maps: 1:50000 Sheet 19 1:25000 Sheet 119
Admiralty Charts: 1:100000 No.1794 1:12500 No.3146

AREA: 309ha (764 acres)
HEIGHT: 72m (236 ft)

OWNER: Leased to the two families of Grant (the only inhabitants) for a peppercorn rent by a whisky company.

Longa

The Grant family have lived on the Isle of Ewe since the middle of the 19th century.

POPULATION: 1841 – 34. 1881 – 43. 1891 – 39. 1931 – 37. 1961 – 10. 1971 – 10. 1981 – 10. 1991 – 12.

GEOLOGY: Torridonian sandstone with acidic soil in the north and a more fertile soil on New Red Sandstone (Permian or Triassic) in the south.

HISTORY: Loch Ewe was an important naval base during the Second World War and is still a scene of NATO activity.

WILDLIFE: Dean Munro recorded in 1549 that the island was wooded. Nowadays, most of the island is a working farm with the type of flora and fauna to be expected in such an environment but a visit to Loch Ewe provides the added bonus of access to the world-famous Inverewe Gardens – more than 2000 acres of magnificent landscaping and plantlife now under the care of the National Trust for Scotland. Loch Ewe may be remote and at the same latitude as Hudson Bay or Siberia but these Gardens are visited every year by more than 100,000 people who revel in their subtropical splendour.

The **ISLE OF EWE** looks steep and rocky when approaching by sea from the north but from Aultbea (G. – the birch-lined stream), the nearby village on the mainland, it can be seen that much of the island is gently undulating farmland. The highest point (72m) is in the north-west above a cliff, **Creag Streap** (G. – climbing cliff), which has a large rock, Sgeir a' Bhuic (G. – rock of the roe-buck), in the sea below. North of it is Uamhag nan Gobhar (G. – rock shelters of the goats). The high ground (68m) on the north-east peninsula is called **Sitheanan Dubha** (G. – the black fairy hillocks) and the soil here is peaty with a thick cover of coarse grass, heather and sphagnum moss.

The anchorage at **Camas Angus** is echoed by a bay on the opposite side of the island, **Camas Beithe** (G – birch-tree bay). A hummock between the bays called **Cnoc na Gaoithe** (G. – windy knoll) shelters the anchorage from the prevailing wind.

A small copse of trees on **Druim nam Freumh** (G. – ridge of roots) defines the northern limit of the arable land.

The Families: Roddy Grant is a fisherman. He was born on the island and his family has lived here since the middle of the 19th century. He is married to Marion and their life revolves round work, family and church. Their two children enjoy a carefree life. Neil, the elder, was born in 1987.

Roddy's cousin Willie is married to Jane, a Somerset girl who met him when she was a ship's engineer in the Merchant Navy. For ten years they sailed the world together but now Willie farms the island croft. Jane has built a landing stage, has helped Willie build their house, and she cares for their two young children – but she would probably prefer to be stripping diesels instead. She dives for scallops as recreation.

There were more families living on the island in the past but they left during the Second World War.

Schooling for the children means sailing across to the mainland each day followed by a thirteen-mile bus trip; and the same return journey each evening. The education authority want the children to board at school but both mothers insist that island life is an essential part of their education in spite of the difficulties of daily transport. There is no doubt that children given a mainland education will rarely settle for island life when they are adults.

There is a direct telephone link to the island which is an invaluable lifeline. Its installation was agreed by British Telecom before the company realised that the connection would cost them £30,000!

ACCESS: No regular access, but enquire at Aultbea. Ullapool Tourist Information, 01854-61 2135.

Anchorages:

1. Camas Angus (Acarsaid Mhór), in NE, 3c S of N extremity. Beware unlit buoys, and partly submerged reef to SE. Good shelter in W'lies.

2. The Sound. Off the island's SE jetty in 7m or more, good holding but exposed.

3. Acarsaid Beag, 2c SE of Acarsaid Mhór. Poor holding on kelp.

6.3 Gruinard Island

(ON groenn fjordr – green firth) island

OS Maps: 1:50000 Sheet 19 1:25000 Sheet 110
Admiralty Charts: 1:100000 No.1794 1:25000 Nos.2500 or 2509

AREA: 196ha (484 acres)
HEIGHT: 106m (348 ft)

OWNER: (?) Gruinard Estate.

POPULATION: 1881 – 6. 1891 – 0. Uninhabited since the 1920s.

GEOLOGY: Mainly Torridonian sandstone with laminated shales and micaceous sandstone in the north-east.

HISTORY: Gruinard Island has a notorious recent history.

During the Second World War some scientists decided to use this 'useless' uninhabited Scottish island as a test ground for biological warfare.

Anthrax was the chosen weapon but, as there was no satisfactory antidote at the time, it was a ridiculous choice. It is a particularly deadly and indestructible bacillus for, even forty years after it was sprayed over the island, up to 385 viable spores per gram of soil were found when the Chemical Defence Establishment carried out one of its periodic tests. In 1986, after many protests from environmentalists, the Ministry of Defence decided to disinfect the island by soaking the entire surface area in formaldehyde and sea-water. Sheep and rabbits were then introduced to test whether the treatment had been satisfactory.

In April 1990 Gruinard Island was declared free of anthrax. It was opened to press and public and returned to its pre-war owners with a 150 year Government indemnity. However Dr Brian Moffat, an archaeologist involved in the investigation of a medieval hospital at Soutra, claimed in a radio broadcast that anthrax spores had survived for 500 years on that site. Vegetation he claimed brings them up to the surface of the soil and certainly nothing on earth would persuade him to risk landing on Gruinard! The Ministry of Defence replied that this was an unfair comparison. Soil samples had shown that the island was clear of danger although no one could say there may not still be a few spores around; the sheep were fit and healthy and so were twelve wild rabbits.

WILDLIFE: In 1549 Dean Munro recorded that the island was wooded. The peak seabird-season in Gruinard Bay is October to May. This is a prime area to see the great northern diver.

GRUINARD ISLAND rises gently to a rough rounded summit (106m) which is called simply **An Eilid** (G. – the hind). The island is covered with rough grazing – grass, heather and bracken and fringed by a rocky shore and occasional pebbly beach.

One good result of the Microbiological Research Establishment's unfortunate experiment on Gruinard was the development of an effective vaccine against anthrax for both animals and humans. But it is a pity that animals had to be introduced so quickly after the clean-up, as it would have been an excellent opportunity for botanists (wearing suitable clothing, of course!) to study the effect of forty-five years of sheep- and rabbit-free existence.

For the committed island-hopper keeping below the high water mark should present no danger. Going above it is a matter of personal choice!

It is probable that historically the island has always provided useful pasturage, the flocks and herds being swum across the narrow kyle near Gruinard House. Certainly the headland beside the long spit at the southern extremity is called **Aird nan Caorach** (G. – sheep or livestock point).

ACCESS: No normal access.

Anchorages: Reefs extend up to 1c off the island at places and the bottom is generally rocky. There are no regular anchorages but there are moderate depths SE and E of the island with some mud and sand.

6.4 Isle Martin

Named after Saint Martin to whom the island chapel was dedicated.

OS Maps: 1:50000 Sheet 19 1:25000 Sheets 102 and 111
Admiralty Charts: 1:100000 No.1794 1:25000 No.2500

AREA: 157ha (388 acres)
HEIGHT: 120m (394 ft)

OWNER: Bought in 1965 by Mrs Monica Goldsmith who restored the four houses. She then presented it to the Royal Society for the Protection of Birds to manage as a nature reserve.

POPULATION: 1841 – 45. 1881 – 42. 1891 – 47 (8 houses). In 1901 – 33. 1931 – 3. 1961 – 0. 1971 – 0. 1981 – 2. 1991 – 1.

GEOLOGY: The island is a rounded hill of Torridonian sandstone.

HISTORY: In the late 18th century the British Fisheries Society built a curing station on the east side overlooking Loch Kanaird. This was still standing in a ruinous condition in 1908 but now only the foundations remain.

WILDLIFE: Bird sanctuary.
Peak viewing November to May for wintering divers and gulls, especially Glaucous and Iceland. Otherwise, of

particular interest are the red-breasted merganser, oyster-catcher, ringed plover, heron, tern and eider.

Two ecology graduates from Edinburgh University run a tree nursery at Scourie (near Handa. No.6.9). Since 1982 they have been reintroducing native trees to Isle Martin – willow, oak, ash, hazel, rowan and pine. This has already created a young forest which has its own micro-climate and is a larder for native wildlife. Brambles, introduced by birds, are heavy with fruit. The woodland shelters farm animals, provides firewood, encourages wildlife, and generally improves the environment. They have, in fact, turned the clock back to the island's traditional landscape before it was denuded of trees many centuries ago.

Close to, but separate from, the Summer Isles group **ISLE MARTIN** lies beside the entrance to Loch Broom. From the sea it often merges with the background hills. It consists of a single rounded hill 120m high with rocky cliffs on the west and north coasts. The slope is gentle on the sheltered east side where there is a small bay. It is here that the restored houses and the remains of the old fish-curing station [NH096990] can be found but the scant remains of St Martin's chapel are further west. The small valley on the west coast is called **Bad an Ling** (G. & ON – tuft of heather).

The British Fisheries Society, with ample funds from the south, built the port of Ullapool in 1788, and several curing stations on key island sites such as Isle Martin. This was to take advantage of the vast herring shoals for which Loch Broom was renowned. These swept into the loch between the months of May and September every year. For hundreds of years the local boats had enjoyed a bonanza as the shoals were so dense that it was possible to scoop them out of the sea by hand. The Society curtailed the activities of the local boats, and netted fish for themselves in vast quantities. The boom lasted for fifty years and then this depredation took effect. By 1830 the shoals had thinned and by 1880 they had disappeared. The curing stations were abandoned and the local fishermen were left to search for alternative catches.

Isle Martin has its local legend. According to this a cooper once worked for the fish curing station and was ordered to cut brooms one evening. The little people took pity on him and miraculously transported him to the woodland on South Rona (No.5.9). In the morning he was back at work with all the brooms that were required.

ACCESS: Landing is prohibited without prior permission from the RSPB, 0131-557 3136. There are summer excursions from Achiltibuie and Ullapool.

Anchorages:

1. Good anchorage E of island in Loch Kanaird. N entrance to Loch is easiest. Anchor in bight, if possible, clear of fish pens and mooring buoys.

6.5 Priest Island

(G. Eilean a' Chléirich – island of the Priest or Cleric)

OS Maps: 1:50000 Sheet 15 1:25000 Sheet 101
Admiralty Charts: 1:100000 No.1794 1:25000 No.2509

AREA: 122ha (301 acres)
HEIGHT: 78m (256 ft)

OWNER: Royal Society for the Protection of Birds.

POPULATION: No census records and uninhabited.

GEOLOGY: The island consists of two main masses of Torridonian sandstone cut by a glen running from south-west to north-east. The southern mass is a ridge in which the strata have tilted to form rugged cliffs of fluted columns facing the glen to the north. The southern slope is less steep. The sandstone is smoother and redder than that on the mainland.

HISTORY: Three prehistoric stone circles are proof of early human interest and the name shows that this was a retreat or hermitage in the early Christian era, possibly associated with the monastery on Isle Martin (No 6.4). In the 18th century an outlaw banished from the mainland settled here and founded three generations of crofters but his descendants abandoned the island in the 1850s.

Dr Frank Fraser Darling stayed here during the late 1930s and wrote about it in his book, *Island Years*.

WILDLIFE: Heather is dominant south of the glen, but in the north and west apart from erica and calluna there are plantain and thrift, bog asphodel, bog cotton, crowberry, sheep's fescue and buckthorn.

Aspen, poplar, royal fern, honeysuckle, willow and the inevitable flag irises are widespread around Lochan Fada.

As with all the Summer Isles there are many birds. Shelduck, fulmar, heron, snipe and eider are common and merganser breed along the banks. Twenty-nine species of bird are known to breed here, the most notable being greylag geese and storm petrel, but according to Fraser Darling, forty-three species of bird which breed on Tanera Mór (No.6.7) do not breed on Priest Island – probably due to the wind.

LOCH FADA ON EILEAN A' CHLÉIRICH

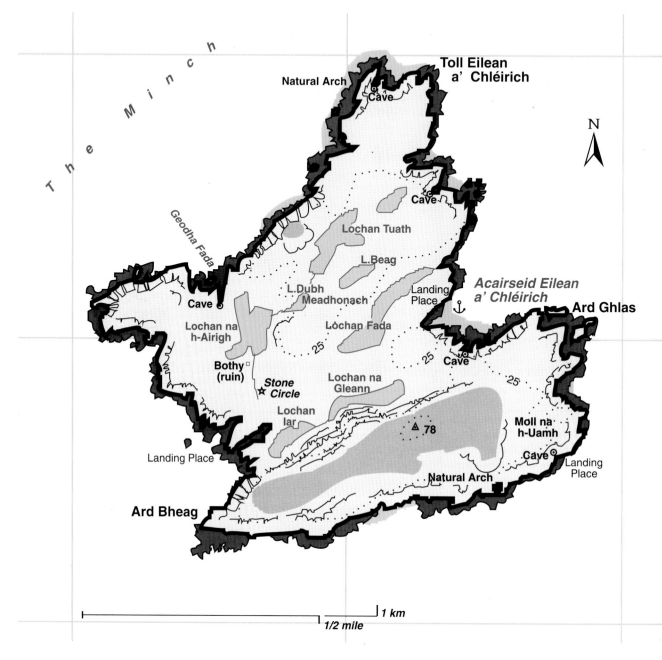

Grey seal, pigmy shrew (to be found near the caves in the south according to Fraser Darling) and otter, can all be seen. In particular the two lochans in the main glen are much frequented by otters. All the eight lochans are reputed to have excellent fishing.

The most westerly of the Summer Isles, 4 miles or 7km south-west of Tanera Mór, **PRIEST ISLAND** has no proper landing place and with its exposed position and a persistent heavy swell getting ashore at its one and only 'anchorage', a bay in the centre of the east coast, can be difficult. Getting off again can be harder still! The alterna-tive landing places depend on wind direction but none is comfortable or easy.

Approaching from due south the island appears to be smooth-topped with two summits near its east end, but from elsewhere its outline is rugged. As there are several small lochs providing a plentiful water supply this could account for the fact that in spite of its inaccessibility it has been inhabited off and on since pre-history.

The highest point (78m) is south of the anchorage at **Moll na h-Uamh** (G. – cave point). This particular cave [NB930017] is on the south-east coast below the ridge and is the one in which Fraser Darling dug up bones of pig, ox, deer, guillemot and fulmar petrel. Further interesting and fairly deep caves are to the north of the anchorage. One, at a little boulder beach, has signs of human habitation and was probably used by smugglers [NB927026]. Part of a whisky still was found near **Lochan na h-Airigh** (G. – shieling loch). The sea booms eerily as it enters **Toll Eilean a' Chléirich** (G. – Priest's Hole) in the north-east corner – a sea-cave with a fallen roof [NB927029].

The main glen runs right across the island from the anchorage to the west coast and contains two lochans. To the north of the glen there is a tumbled landscape with more lochans, several pools and patches of bog ending abruptly at the steep cliffs and fissures of the north-west coast.

Evidence of an ancient chapel has been uncovered on level ground on the south side of Lochan na h-Airigh [NB920021] which is also the site of the 19th century ruined bothy. The ground here has been cultivated in the past. A prehistoric stone circle is beside the burn which flows out of the loch. This was originally on the west side of the burn but the Victorian yachtsman and naturalist, Harvie-Brown, found after several visits that it had sunk into the boggy ground and disappeared so he dug it up and transferred it to the dry ground on the other side of the burn!

Between Priest Island and Tanera Beg is the small island (11ha) of **Glas-leac Beag** (G – little green slab). It is, as described, narrow and flat-topped, about 29m high, and on a fine day its covering of grass, gloriously fertilised by a colony of black-backed gulls, makes it appear bright green.

ACCESS: Landing is prohibited without prior permission from the RSPB. There are summer excursions from Achiltibuie and Ullapool, 01854-61 2008 or -61 2264.

Anchorages: All are subject to considerable swell.
1. Acairseid Eilean a' Chléirich, bay on E side. Occasional anchorage in settled weather, clean but bottom mainly boulders. Landing best on or near 'pier rock' on NW side of bay.
2. Landing point at cleft in bay on W side of island. Temp anchorage possible in settled weather 1/2c off-shore in 15-20m.
3. Landing point at cave on SE side of island. Temp anchorage possible in settled weather in 15-18m.

6.6 Horse Island

OS Maps: 1:50000 Sheet 15 1:25000 Sheet 102
Admiralty Charts: 1:100000 No.1794 1:25000 No.2501

AREA: 53ha (131 acres)
HEIGHT: 60m (197 ft)

POPULATION: Uninhabited and without census records but is reputed to have been inhabited in the 19th century.

GEOLOGY: Torridonian sandstone.

HISTORY: Treasure from a ship of the Spanish Armada is said to have been hidden here in 1588. The story is reinforced by a local record that a shepherd in the 19th century found a gold doubloon in his boot-top after stumbling in the heather. He rushed to the mainland and told his friends who immediately organised a treasure hunt but when they were on the island they could find nothing. One piece of heather looks much like another and the shepherd then wondered if he had remembered the correct spot where he tripped. The dejected group returned empty-handed. Unlike so many local legends, the unsatisfactory ending makes this story ring true!

WILDLIFE: Multi-coloured lichens, thrift, sea campion, lovage and scurvy grass grow on the ledges of the cliffs.

Only wild goats inhabit Horse Island nowadays but no one is sure how they came to be on the island. The first official record of their presence was in 1837. But there seem to have been resident goats in earlier times as the drying islet at the north end is called Meall nan Gabhar (G. – hillock of the she-goats).

HORSE ISLAND is separated from the mainland by a deep channel called Horse Sound. The highest point (60m) is **Sgùrr nan Uan** (G. – conical hill of the lambs) – near the south-east coast. **Meall nan Gabhar** (13ha) is at the northern extremity and connected to the main part by a reef which dries at low water. The opposite hill on the main island is **Meall an Fhithich** (G. – raven's hill). **Iolla Mór** (G. – big drying rock), lying off the south coast, is a flat rock which is extensive at low water.

Similar plants to those on Horse Island are to be found on **Carn nan Sgeir** – two small islands separated by a

HORSE ISLAND FROM THE SOUTH WITH ACHILTIBUIE BEYOND

Horse Island

shingle spit which lie to the south but, unlike the rest of the Summer Isles which are of Torridonian sandstone, these islets are of Hebridean gneiss.

It is natural that in this animal-farm region of horses and goats another nearby islet should be called **Meall nan Caorach** (G. – sheep hump)

ACCESS: Boat hire may possibly be arranged in Achiltibuie. Tourist Office, Ullapool, 01854-612135.

Anchorages:
1. Good anchorage in bight SE of Meall nan Gabhar but keep in N half as there is an uncharted reef in the S half, 3m, sand and some weed. Exposed to E.

6.7 Tanera Mór

(ON hawnarøy – island of the haven, pasture, G. – large) or, improbably,
(B or Gaullish Tanaros – thunder-god)

OS Maps: 1:50000 Sheet 15 1:25000 Sheet 101
Admiralty Charts: 1:100000 No.1794 1:25000 No.2501

AREA: 310ha (766 acres)
HEIGHT: 122m (400 ft)

OWNER: Sold by Summer Isles Estate to Mr Srampton in 1991. Up for sale again in 1995 for approximately £700,000.

POPULATION: 1745 – 21 families. 1841 – 99. 1881 – 119. 1891 – 95 (19 houses). 1901 – 70. The population had fallen to zero by 1931. 1961 – 6. 1971 – 2. 1981 – 8. 1991 – 0.

GEOLOGY: Torridonian sandstone mostly covered with peat, pasture and heather.

HISTORY: In 1784 Murdoch Morrison of Stornoway was installed as manager of the newly-founded fishing station at Tigh-an-Quay (between Ardnagoine and Garadheancal). As with the stations on Isle Martin (No.6.4) and Isle Ristol, this was built by the London-based British Fishery Society. It was a very prosperous enterprise while the her-ring stocks lasted. Up to 200 vessels at a time would an-chor in the bay and salted herring was even exported to the West Indian colonies.

After the fishing spree was over in 1820, and the com-pany was bankrupted, there followed a period of many changes of ownership and greedy tacksmen demanding high rents. So the resourceful islanders took up the distil-lation of illicit whisky. In 1900 another lucrative sideline was introduced when the island was acquired by Captain MacDonald, a local smuggler. There is a rumour that a cargo of rum was buried at Tigh-an-Quay and another story of buried treasure in the 'big park' between Tigh-an-Quay and Mol Mór.

WILDLIFE: The climate is mild and there are wild-flowers everywhere – heather galore, common orchids, forget-me-not, foxgloves, dandelions, clover and burnet rose. Near An Lochanach there are flag irises, honeysuckle, willow and aspen poplars which grow to 3-4m in height. Bluebells and primroses are sheltered by rowan and birch which grow on the slopes. Unlike Priest Island (No.6.5) the lochs here are almost lifeless except for tadpoles.

Gulls and arctic terns are common but few other sea-birds are to be seen. There is, however, a wide variety of general bird life including breeding heron, shelduck, buzzard and red grouse.

TANERA MOR is the largest of the Summer Isles, a small group of a dozen or so islands lying close to the mainland which were used for summer grazing. The highest hill, **Meall Mór**, (122m) has a flat summit when viewed from the south and below it is one of the best natural harbours in the north-west. It is known as **The Anchorage** and was a great favourite with the Vikings but they would not recognise it today as it is now packed with fish-farming cages.

The last permanent inhabitants left in 1931 but from 1938 to 1944, Frank Fraser Darling, the noted naturalist, farmed on the island and wrote his book *Island Farm*. There followed another period when the island was uninhabited and then in 1963 the new owners, Summer Isles Estate, restored and let many of the cottages and the schoolhouse as holiday accommodation and provided facilities for boating, sailing and fishing. (All the houses have drainage, water, and electricity and many are centrally-heated). This created the need for a small population to service the enterprise, and a few more connected with the fish-farm. Not only is there now a Summer Isles Post Office – situated in a tearoom which opens when a boatload of tourists arrive – but it is officially permitted to issue its own postage stamps. These are most attractive and popular with collectors.

Rock shapes on the coasts of Tanera Mór and Tanera Beag can take on exquisite colours in the changing light. There are two tiny islands in The Anchorage, **Eilean Mór** and **Eilean Beag** and a drying island, **Eilean na Saille** (G. – salt island), on the north-west coast sheltering **Acairseid Driseach** (G. – anchorage of thorns). Burns feed into this anchorage from three small lochs. In the south-west there is another cove, Mol Mór (G. – the big pebble-beach) while the north extremity of the island is called Cùl na Béinge (G. – the back of the bed-board or bench).

Between the two settlements, **Ardnagoine** and **Garadheancal** (G. – the cabbage-patch or kail-yard), are the remains of the herring fishing station at **Tigh-an-Quay**. The old building is now partly used for fish-farm storage purposes and also houses an electricity generator. Close north of it is a new house with a beautifully-maintained garden – the work of an enthusiast – beside the level area above the quay known as the 'Planestones'.

When Fraser Darling first purchased Tigh-an-Quay the ruin was much more extensive. The northern part of the stone structure was a three-storey building with an attic and slate roof – part of which was still intact. An alley-way had divided this building from the fish factory on the south side but an arcaded wall between the alley and the factory had collapsed in the 1870s leaving an enclosed unroofed area with two gables still standing. He called it the 'Walled Garden', removed much of the rubble, and demolished the top of the gables which were in a dangerous state. He also demolished the roof and upper floor of the residential buiding as the timbers were rotten and the wind turned the slates into dangerous missiles. He rebuilt some of the lower walls and reconstructed the quay to its original design.

The walled field between Tigh-an-Quay and the hill to the north, **Cnoc Glas** (G. – green knoll), is called 'Little Irish Park' because much of the soil came from Ireland as ships' ballast. The large field west of Tigh-an-Quay is the 'Big Park' with a rocky hillock in it called Cnoc an-t-Sidhe (G. – fairy knoll). Using coral sand from Tanera Beag (lime), and seaweed and boiler slag (potash), Fraser Darling reinstated this field as productive arable land. Clover provided the nitrogen content.

ACCESS: There are summer excursions from Achiltibuie and Ullapool. Tourist Office, Ullapool, 01854-61 2135.

Anchorages:
1. The Cabbage Patch. Between, and S of, the two small islands on the S side of 'The Anchorage'; best shelter and good holding but cluttered with moorings.
2. The Anchorage. Anchor between fish cages and old pier in SW corner of bay, or between fish cages and beach at N of bay.
3. Acairseid Driseach. (at NW corner of Tanera Mór). Enter from N and anchor between Eilean na Saille and Tanera Mór, but not further S than mid-island, 4m, sand.

'THE CABBAGE PATCH' BEYOND 'THE ANCHORAGE'

6.8 Tanera Beg

(ON hawnarøy *– island of the haven, pasture), (G. beag – little) or, possibly, (B. or Gaullish Tanaros – thunder-god)*

OS Maps: 1:50000 Sheet 15 1:25000 Sheet 101
Admiralty Charts: 1:100000 No.1794 1:25000 No.2501

AREA: 66ha (163 acres)
HEIGHT: 83m (272 ft)

OWNER: (?) Summer Isles Estate.

POPULATION: No census records and uninhabited.

GEOLOGY: Torridonian sandstone, mostly covered with peat, pasture and heather. There is a bank of coral sand

Sgeir Dubh

Sgeir Iasgach

Dorney Sound

N

Eilean a' Char

Sgeir nam Feusgan

Eilean Choinaid

Eilean a' Bhuic

56

38

Eilean Fada Mór

Sròn Slugain Uaine

Caolas a' Mhill Ghairbh

△ 83

Coral

Sand

Mol Beag

TANERA MÓR

Sròn Ghlas

1 km
1/2 mile

and on the shores unusual displays of pink coral can be seen at low water. Nearby Eilean Fada Mór which lies between Tanera Beg and Tanera Mór has similar coral.

WILDLIFE: Honeysuckle, irises, dwarf willow and aspen poplars flourish.

Merganser ducks breed along the water edge and gulls nest among the pink thrift on the shoreline rocks. Wheatears and pipits frequent the heathland and many other mainland varieties thrive.

Seals breed here but not in any great number.

TANERA BEG is separated from Tanera Mór (No.6.7) by a fairly narrow but easily navigable channel, Caolas a' Mhill Ghairbh (G. – channel of broken pieces).

Its coastline is very irregular with delightful little pebble coves sheltered between low cliffs overhung by green terraces. Beneath the summit of the central hill (83m) is a tiny pool, the only one on the island, and from there the heather-clad slope runs down to a bluff. Here a shallow valley crosses the island.

Tanera Beg's main claim to fame must surely be its bank of fine coral sand – something which is quite uncommon in this part of the world. It lies close to the best anchorages in the corner of the 'lagoon' but it is only visible at low water [NB972074].

The anchorages to the north are protected by several islets and many rocks and skerries. **Eilean Fada Mór** (G. – big long island) hides little **Eilean a' Bhuic** (G. – buck island) behind it and the larger **Sgeir nam Feusgan** (G. – skerry of the mussels). And directly north is **Eilean a' Chàr** (G. – island of seal-flesh) and **Eilean Choinaid** (G. – rabbit island). **Glas-leac Mór** (G. – big green slab), a fair-sized islet to the north-west with heather slopes and a small lochan, is almost part of the same group.

About two miles south of Tanera Beg there is an island, **Eilean Dubh**, which only just fails to meet my 40 hectare minimum size limit. It has probably never been permanently inhabited and there is no safe anchorage but a substantial log house now occupies the cove on the north-east side. Eilean Dubh is one of a group of islets and skerries. Two of these, **Carn Iar** and **Carn Deas** (G. – west and south rockpiles), are linked by drying rocks, and another has the suggestive name of **Bottle Island**.

ACCESS: Summer excursions from Achiltibuie and Ullapool. Tourist Information, Ullapool, 01854-61 2135.

Anchorages:
1. S side of Eilean Fada Mór. Good anchorage in bight, north of shoal, 4m, sand. Strong tide at springs. Beware semi-submerged fish-farm ropes and moorings.
2. Pool SW of Eilean Fada Mór. Anchor in 10m, sand.
3. Inlet in centre of NE side of Tanera Beg, 3m, sand. Beware reef of drying rocks N of the inlet.

6.9 Handa

(ON hund-øy – dog island) or (ON sand-øy – sand isle)

OS Maps: 1:50000 Sheet 9 1:25000 Sheet 61
Admiralty Charts: 1:100000 No.1785 1:25000 No.2503

AREA: 309ha (764 acres)
HEIGHT: 123m (403 ft)

OWNER: Major and Dr Jean Balfour of Scourie Estate, the owners, gave the RSPB a twenty-five-year lease in 1961 to run the island as a nature reserve. They extended the lease in 1986 for five years. However in 1991 Dr Balfour did not renew the lease as she felt that it was appropriate that a solely Scottish conservation body should run the island. The Scottish Wildlife Trust now manage the island, a body which did not exist when the original lease was signed. Dr Balfour is a founding member of the Trust and she is also a former chairman of the Countryside Commission for Scotland.

Handa is a Site of Special Scientific Interest.

POPULATION: 1841 – 65 (11 houses). 1851 – onwards, uninhabited. 1991 – no permanent inhabitants but about 5000 visitors each summer.

GEOLOGY: An outcrop of Torridonian sandstone separated by the Sound of Handa from the mainland of Lewisian gneiss.

HISTORY: In early times the island was used as a burial ground by people on the mainland so that wolves would be unable to scavenge the corpses. Later, seven families settled and started cultivating the rough pastureland. They were self-sufficient, living on a staple diet of oats, potatoes, fish and sea-birds. The population grew, they had their own 'queen' – the oldest widow – and the men held a daily parliament to decide the allocation of work. It was, in fact, a very similar form of society to that on St Kilda (See No.9.1).

But then in 1848 the potato famine struck and the islanders emigrated to America. Handa has been uninhabited since that time but the old cottages and lazy-beds can still be seen.

WILDLIFE: Handa is renowned for its birdlife.

Best bird-watching is from early-May to mid-July, by August the cliffs are deserted. Over 170 species have been recorded, with thirty regular breeders. Twelve species of nesting seabirds include large populations of guillemot (100,000 strong – the largest colony in Britain), razorbill, fulmar, and kittiwake. There are also four other gull species, shag, puffin, black guillemot and small numbers of Arctic and great skua.

No raptors breed here at present, but golden eagle, buzzard, peregrine falcon, sparrowhawk and merlin may be

Stac an t-Seabhaig
(The Great Stack)

Stachan Geodh Bhrisidh

Puffin Bay

Little Stack

Eilean an Aigeich

Am Bonair

Geodh' na Goibhre

106

Dorus Mór

Bo Iasg

Sithean
Mór
△ 123

Roinn
Dubh

Poll Ghlup

Bothy Loch

Footpath

Bothy

Chapel
(ruin) ☆

Tràigh an
Teampuill
Bodha
Morair

Village (ruin)

Tràigh Shourie

Bogha Mór

Glas Leac

Port an Eilean

Sound of Handa

N

1 km
1/2 mile

MAINLAND

seen. White-tailed sea-eagles last nested here in 1864.

Other interesting species include great northern diver, red- and black-throated diver, eider and shelduck, oyster-catcher, ringed plover, common and Arctic tern, and rock dove. Inland breeders include snipe, wheatear, stonechat and sometimes, red grouse, golden plover and reed bunting. Migrants include pink-footed and greylag geese, dunlin, greenshank, turnstone, sanderling, whimbrel, Pomarine skua, and Manx and sooty shearwater. A few barnacle geese turn up in winter.

A stuffed albino oystercatcher with a twisted bill can be seen in the Royal Scottish Museum in Edinburgh. It died on Handa in 1967 and was notorious for its eccentric habits.

216 species of plants have been recorded and more than 100 species of mosses. The only trees are small plan-

tations of lodgepole pine and alder. The island is home to thousands of rabbits.

Whales are fairly frequent visitors in this area and sometimes swim through the Sound.

HANDA is mostly heather, peat-bog and rough pasture on top of a large tilted block of Torridonian sandstone which rears sharply out of the sea to a height of over 100m on the precipitous north and west sides. Here the cliffs are dark-red and brown with horizontal strata sharply out-lined in white by seabird droppings. In the north-west and close to the cliffs is the higher of the two hills, Sithean Mór [shee-hen moar] (G. – the big fairy-hill). From the top the view stretches almost to Cape Wrath with the tall thin figure of the Old Man of Stoer on the far point of

Eddrachillis Bay. Directly north of Sithean Mór the cliffs form an amphitheatre, Am Bonair, with a natural arch [NC130488]. On the east side of this bluff in an inlet or 'geo' and separated by a gap only 24m wide, stands the **Great Stack**, a gigantic rock 115m high and balanced on three legs [NC132488].

The first recorded crossing from the clifftop on Handa to the flat top of the Stack was in 1876 by Donald MacDonald of Lewis swinging hand-over-hand from a rope. This terrifying narrow chasm has a sheer drop of over 100m down the wet sandstone face to turbulent ocean surf pounding the rocks far below.

In 1967 the original crossing was re-enacted by Dr Tom Patey of Ullapool except that on this occasion the traverse was made by a 180m nylon rope stretched from one side of the geo to the other and lying over the Stack. 'A thought-provoking experience,' he said afterwards.

For a different experience details of the route up the 'very severe' north face can be obtained from the Scottish Mountaineering Club.

Close to the east of the Great Stack is another stack, **Stachan Geodh Bhrisidh** (G. – stack of the broken chasm) in a cove which is usually referred to as Puffin Bay.

The Trust's hut is between **Bothy Loch,** one of Handa's six lochs all of which provide ample water but contain no fish, and the ruined chapel [NC147477] beside **Tràigh an Teampuill** (G. – temple beach) with its view south over the distant **Badcall Islands** and **Eilean a' Bhuic** off Scourie Bay.

From the landing place by the south-east promontory and **Port an Eilean** (G. – island port) a path runs along the south coast beaches, climbs slowly to the top of the high cliffs, chasms, stacks and natural arches of the west coast, and then turns south-eastwards across the centre of the island, sloping gradually down towards the Sound of Handa – the ocean channel separating Handa from the mainland. The path is partly paved with duckboarding to try to protect the fragile machair from the effect of 5000 pairs of tramping feet each year. A few shells of the old cottages are alongside the pathway before it reaches the burial ground. This has no walled boundary as on St Kilda or Tanera Mór but merely some rough weathered head-stones in the grass. This clockwise walk (6km), on an is-land that combines startling topography with a deep sense of history and an astonishing variety of birdlife, is a 'must'. And a fitting climax is to circumnavigate the island by boat and see the drama on the cliffs from sea-level. Dorus Mór – the big door – is on the north-east side facing the narrow horse-back ridge of **Eilean an Aigeich** (G. – stallion island).

ACCESS: Permission to camp is required from the Scottish Wildlife Trust, Edinburgh, 0131-312 7765, or from the warden who is resident from April to August. A private boat operates from Tarbet (unclassified road off A894 3M N of Scourie), and there are excursions from Scourie, 01971-2140. Overnight accommodation in a bothy is oc-casionally available.

Anchorages:
1. Port an Eilean. Approach from SSW. Avoid reef of drying rocks on west side. Good holding in sand, but some swell from S.
2. Tràigh an Teampuill. Beware Bo Morair in centre of Sound. Anchor off ruined chapel in 3m, weed. Beware dragging in strong current.

6.10 Eilean nan Ron

(G. – island of the seals)

OS Maps: 1:50000 Sheet 10 1:25000 Sheet 46
Admiralty Charts: 1:200000 No.1954

AREA: 138ha (341 acres)
HEIGHT: 76m (244 ft)

OWNER: (?) Tongue House Estate. (Countess of Sutherland.)

POPULATION: 1841 – 42 (7 houses). 1881 – 73. 1891 – 63 (8 houses). 1931 – 30. Now uninhabited.

GEOLOGY: Undifferentiated Permian or Triassic sandstone.

WILDLIFE: This is a National Nature Reserve. Hundreds of grey seals gather here in the autumn to pup and about 350 calves are born annually.

EILEAN NAN RON was well-populated for much of its history but, like so many of the Scottish islands, is now only populated with ghosts. The main island has an abrupt rocky shoreline, an irregular grassy surface and two similar hills in the northern part of almost identical height, **Cnoc an Loisgein** (76m) and **Cnoc na Caillich** (75m) (G. – hag's knoll). There are steep cliffs on the east side, north of a natural arch at **Leathad Ballach** (G. – spotted slope) and these continue round to the north coast. Here many broken inlets, another rock arch and a cave have been carved out by the sea. **Eilean Iosal** (G. – low or humble island) is a drying island connected at a narrow channel on the north-west side. It is steep – just over 50m in height – with a cave, **Uamh nan Ròn** (G. – the seals' cave) on its south side. Beyond lies a smaller islet called Meall Thailm (G. – sling shot) according to the Ord-nance Survey, or Meall Holm according to the Admiralty (G. and ON – blob of an islet).

The settlement of houses and ruins is in the waist of the island. To the west is **Mol Mór** (G – big pebble beach) and a rock-strewn bay. **Port na h-Innse** (G. – island port) is adjacent with a cave on either side – Night Cave to the north and Day Cave to the south.

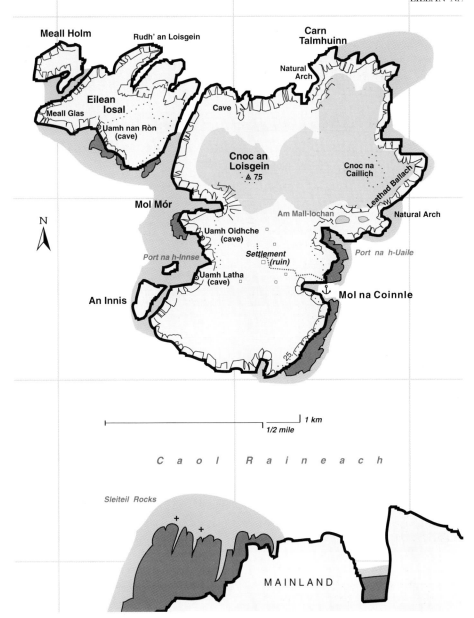

The **Rabbit Islands** in Tongue Bay can be seen from here. They are aptly named and worth a visit. A partly-sheltered anchorage is off the beach on the south side of the larger island.

Port na h-Uaile (G. – fake port) with a gravel beach and **Mol na Coinnle** (G. – oily-surfaced pebble beach) are east of the old settlement on Eilean nan Ron.

The island is separated from the mainland by Caol Raineach. East of it, lying just off the coastline, is **Neave Island** (G. *naomha* – holy), also known as **Coomb Island**.

West of the Kyle of Tongue **Eilean Hoan** (G. & ON – haven island) and **Eilean Clùimhrig** lie at the mouth of Loch Eriboll. Deep within the loch, **Eilean Choraidh**, otherwise known as Horse Island, was taken to represent the German battleship *Tirpitz* when it was used for target practice by wartime Mosquito bombers. The Census of 1931 recorded a population of one lonely male on Eilean Choraidh and one hopes he didn't stay on.

Beyond Faraid Head and near Cape Wrath is the very insignificant **An Garbh-eilean** (G. – the rough island).

ACCESS: No regular access but local boatmen usually arrange visits in the summer months.

Anchorages: Beware below water rock off NE extremity of island and W coast is foul. E and S sides clean to within ¹/₂c.

1. Mol na Coinnle. The most southerly small bight on SE side. Shelter from W and NW winds. Anchor opposite corrugated-iron roofed hut near shore.

The Outer Hebrides – South of the Sound of Harris

Section 7

Section 7, Table 1

No.	Name	Latitude	Longitude	Table 2* No.	Table 3** No.	Area in Acres		Area in Hectares
7.1	Berneray	56° 47N	07° 38W	87	36	504		204
7.2	Mingulay	56° 49N	07° 38W	55	25	1581		640
7.3	Pabbay	56° 51N	07° 35W	79	40	618		250
7.4	Sandray	56° 54N	07° 31W	60	33	951		385
7.5	Muldoanich	56° 55N	07° 26W	125	45	193		78
7.6	Barra	56° 59N	07° 28W	16	17	14517	5875	
	Vatersay	56° 56N	07° 32W			2372	960	6835
7.7	Flodday (E Barra)	56° 60N	07° 21W	164	131	99		40
7.8	Fuiay	56° 60N	07° 22W	122	63	208		84
7.9	Hellisay	57° 01N	07° 21W	99	87	351		142
7.10	Gighay	57° 01N	07° 20W	116	76	237		96
7.11	Fuday	57° 03N	07° 23W	82	81	573		232
7.12	Fiaray	57° 04N	07° 26W	162	151	101		41
7.13	Eriskay	57° 05N	07° 17W	50	38	1737		703
7.14	Eileanan Iasgaich	57° 09N	07° 19W	150	160	124		50
7.15	Stuley	57° 12N	07° 15W	158	134	111		45
7.16	South Uist	57° 17N	07° 20W	4	6	79136	32026	
	North Uist	57° 36N	07° 19W			74884	30305	
	Benbecula	57° 27N	07° 19W			20270	8203	
	Baleshare	57° 32N	07° 23W			2249	910	
	Grimsay	57° 29N	07° 14W			2058	833	
	Vallay	57° 40N	07° 25W			642	260	
	Kirkibost Island	57° 33N	07° 25W			507	205	
	Oronsay	57° 40N	07° 18W			210	85	72827
7.17	Wiay	57° 24N	07° 12W	61	68	927		375
7.18	Ronay	57° 29N	07° 11W	56	59	1391		563
7.19	Floddaymore	57° 30N	07° 09W	143	156	143		58
7.20	Ceann Ear (Monach Isles)	57° 31N	07° 37W	64	162	502	203	
	Ceann Iar	57° 31N	07° 39W			381	154	357
7.21	Hermetray	57° 39N	07° 03W	132	142	178		72
7.22	Tahay	57° 40N	07° 06W	148	101	131		53

* Table 2: The islands arranged in order of magnitude
** Table 3: The islands arranged in order of height

Introduction

Like Australia's Great Barrier Reef the chain of Outer Hebridean islands parallels and protects the mainland coast from ocean storms. The side facing the Atlantic is an almost continuous strand of sand-dunes and machair while the east coast is savagely indented and irregular with sea-lochs which disintegrate into a maze of inlets between reefs and tidal islets. For the yachtsman, all these lochs are fascinating to explore and there are anchorages to suit most conditions.

Loch Eynort, near the centre of South Uist, presents a navigational challenge where the wide outer loch suddenly channels through the dog-leg of Sruthan Beag (G. – little tidal streamlet). The tide tumbles through at seven knots with eddies and overfalls but with care it is possible to sneak through at slack water. Once through, the islet **Risgay** and a rocky patch are straight ahead, and to left and right there are many bays and secret inlets in which to anchor (some free of fish cages!).

Although few fish farms are locally owned there is no doubt that fish farming has brought limited, but welcome, employment to Scottish islands. Yachtsmen are aware of this and have accepted that some of the finest and safest anchorages are now filled with fish cages. Their only plea is that when fish farming ceases the cages should be removed. Some are being abandoned and left to disintegrate on the sea bottom, thus creating a hazard and effectively denying use of that anchorage for a century or more.

At the north end of South Uist where it meets Benbecula the land shatters into fragments. **Corr-eileanan, Eilean an Fhraoich Mia, Glas-eileanan, Eilean a' Bhogha, Glas-eilean na Creige, Eilean a' Mhadaidh** (G. – dog isle) and **Gasay** (G. – swept isle) are only some of the many islets and skerries in the area.

The east shore of Benbecula continues this broken landscape. North of the island of Wiay (No.7.17). **Greanamul Deas** (G. – south Greanamul) and **Greanamul** (ON – green hump) itself act as eastern markers. **Maaey Riabhach** (ON & G. – grizzled seagull island), **Maragay Mór** (G. – big pudding isle), and **Maragay Beag** stand guard at each side of Loch Uiskevagh. **Bearran** islet is in the centre of the loch.

In the channel between Benbecula and Grimsay two islets **Calavay** and **Eilean Leathan** are linked by a long tidal strand.

Loch Eport, in North Uist, is another lengthy sea-loch. Shallow Loch Langass which connects with it near the head can be explored for miles by dinghy and is an alternative route to see the chambered cairn on Ben Langass. Most of the islets in Loch Eport are tidal except possibly **Treanay** at Bay Sponish and **Eilean nam Mult** (G. – island of the castrated rams) in the centre of the loch.

7.1 Berneray

(ON bjarnar-øy – bear island) or (ON – Bjørn's island). As the southernmost island of the Outer Hebrides Berneray is often referred to as Barra Head.

OS Maps: 1:50000 Sheet 31 1:25000 Sheet 260
Admiralty Charts: 1:100000 No.1796 1:30000 No.2769

AREA: 204ha (504 acres)
HEIGHT: 193m (633 ft)

OWNER: Barra Head Isles Sheepstock Company (a syndicate of Barra crofters). Bought from Mrs Peggy Greer, an Essex farmer, in 1955.

POPULATION: In the 18th century the population was over fifty. 1841 – 30. 1881 – 72. 1891 – 36 (9 houses). The three lighthouse keepers and their wives were the only occupants of the island from 1931 until the lighthouse became automatic in the late 1970s.

GEOLOGY: The granite to build the island's own (Barra Head) lighthouse in 1833 was quarried on the island. Most of Berneray consists of gneiss.

HISTORY: In 1992, sponsored by Historic Scotland, Berneray was surveyed by archaeologists from Sheffield University and Prague and eighty-three sites and monuments were noted and recorded. Less

than forty were thought to be of post-medieval date.

WILDLIFE: In early May the hillside is a riot of colour with primroses, celandine, wild violets and yellow flag iris – luckily not the chosen diet for the 200 or so breeding ewes which are kept here.

The cove east of the landing place is much frequented by grey seal and the cliffs support large numbers of kittiwake, guillemot, auk and some puffins.

Martin Martin (1695) recorded that Berneray 'excels other islands of the same extent for cultivation and fishing. The natives never go a-fishing while Macneil or his steward is in the island, lest seeing their plenty of fish, perhaps they might take occasion to raise their rents.'

BERNERAY has a wedge-shaped appearance when approaching from the north-east or south-west. The south coast consists of rugged cliffs which have a least height of about 40m at the east end. Barra Head lighthouse is a white stone tower on top of **Sròn an Dùin** (G. – fortress promontory) above the western cliffs.

This is the most southerly point of the Outer Hebrides. The magnificent cliffs of 190m height (623ft) on the west side at Skate Point take the full force of gigantic seas because there is no shallow water to impede them. Small fish are often found in the grass at the top of the high cliffs after severe gales. Even if one might suspect that sea gulls dropped them the lighthouse keepers said that this was not so and as proof of the ferocity of the gales it was reliably reported in 1836 that a forty-two ton rock was moved almost two metres (five feet) during a violent storm.

A vehicle track climbs up the hill from the landing place to the lighthouse at the summit. A 'chalybeate spring' (water with traces of iron in it) is about halfway up, at the side of the track, with a pumphouse to provide water for the lighthouse. A helicopter pad near the top allows maintenance teams to service the lighthouse now that it is automatic.

Two duns or fortified mounds are situated near the summit of the island. One is called **Dùn Briste** (G. – the

BARRA HEAD LIGHTHOUSE – OVER 200M ABOVE THE SEA

broken fort) [NL549805]. Unfortunately, the other one, a galleried dun of the Iron Age, was largely destroyed when the lighthouse was constructed. This will be the fort that Martin noted – 'having a vacuity round the walls, divided in little apartments'. A gateway now leads through the ancient wall from the lighthouse yard onto a cliff-top area completely surrounded by a parapet of natural stone slabs and boulders. From here the cliff drops vertically to the surging waves 200m below. Alongside, there is a great chasm – **Sloc na Beiste** (G. – ravine of the monster) – 100m long by 200m deep leading to a cave, but to explore it would require considerable expertise in mountaineering. The roar of the sea breaking into the chasm far below forms a bass chorus to the cries of thousands of seabirds wheeling past the cliffs.

Apart from the site of a chapel (near the landing place) [NL567803], Berneray has five cists, five suspected burial cairns and four megalithic chamber tombs so the island appears to have been well occupied in the Neolithic/Bronze Age, possibly less intensively settled in the Iron Age but followed by renewed activity in the Christian and medieval period.

Fresh water can be scarce, and in dry summers the islanders had to ship water over from Mingulay.

ACCESS: There is no regular means of access but it is possible to make arrangements at Castlebay on Barra.

Anchorages: Landing on the slippery jetty from an inflatable dinghy can be difficult and potentially dangerous due to the swell.

1. On N side, except in heavy seas, anchor off the concrete jetty and storehouse, 7-8m, good firm sand. This is out of the tidal stream and sheltered from S through W to N. Very heavy squalls sometimes during S and SW gales but very little swell.

7.2 Mingulay

(ON mikil-øy – big island)

OS Maps: 1:50000 Sheet 31 1:25000 Sheet 260
Admiralty Charts: 1:100000 No.1796 1:30000 No.2769

AREA: 640ha (1,581 acres)
HEIGHT: 273m (895 ft)

OWNER: Barra Head Isles Sheepstock Company (a syndicate of seven crofters). Bought from Mrs Peggy Greer, an Essex farmer, in 1955.

POPULATION: 1841 – 113 (18 houses). 1881 – 150. 1891 – 142 (29 houses). 1901 – 140. In 1908 many of the islanders claimed land on neighbouring islands, some becoming known as the Vatersay Raiders (See No.7.6) and after this the remaining population dwindled rapidly. The last inhabitants left in 1912.

GEOLOGY: Almost entirely of gneiss but with some granite.

HISTORY: Mingulay must have been first settled long ago as the island is covered with potential archaeological sites. Crois an t-Suidheachain (G – cross of the sitting-place), was a structure on a level area of ground above the road

THE CHAPEL HOUSE AND MACPHEE'S HILL

at Aneir. Nothing remains but it has been variously de-scribed as a standing stone, a stone circle, or a group of three 'cells or chests'. There may be some Viking graves but the record of Viking influence is in the topographical names such as Hecla, Skipisdale and, for that matter, Mingulay.

When the MacNeils of Barra owned Mingulay they took a paternal interest in their tenants, arranging new husbands and wives for widows and widowers, helping to feed the children, or making good the loss of a milking cow. The community thrived. The laird's annual rent was mainly *fachaich* – shearwater chicks collected from the precipices. As on St Kilda, life here depended on the seabirds, although fishing also played its part. The famous Mingulay boat song was never sung on Mingulay. It is a West Highland air with words written in 1938 by Hugh Roberton for his Glasgow Orpheus Choir to sing.

WILDLIFE: Sorrel and wild celery grow on the hillsides and nettles frame the village ruins. This is a place of an-nual pilgrimage for ornithologists as it is a principal breed-ing station for guillemot and kittiwake. A boat trip around the awe-inspiring western cliffs, virtually inaccessible and covered with seabirds, is an unforgettable experience. A re-ally close approach is difficult except on the rare days of calm water. In the breeding season the granite stacks and very high cliffs are festooned with nesting kittiwakes, ra-zorbills and guillemots and there are also large colonies of puffins and black-backed gulls.

About 500 breeding ewes are kept on the island throughout the year and more or less fend for themselves.

The islands south of Barra and Vatersay used to be known as the Bishop's Isles and **MINGULAY** is the largest of the group. It is almost an inshore Hirta (No.9.1) with its St Kilda-like stacks, its towering cliffs and even its village bay. It shows several rounded summits when viewed from the sea, **Carnan** the highest at 273m, **Hecla** (219m) (ON – hooded shroud) close south-west of it and **Macphee's Hill** (224m) in the north. Between them is **Tom a' Mhaide** (G. – hillock of the stick), a smaller peak of over 150m. The west coast has precipitous cliffs but the south and east coasts slope gradually down to a rugged fore-shore. Mingulay Bay (or Village Bay) is centrally situated on the east coast with a half kilometre of sandy beach and the extensive remains of the deserted village above it.

The **Schoolhouse** is at the south end of the cart road and the bay [NL568825]. It was built in the 1880s by the Free Church Ladies' Association but has been used as a bothy and sheep fank since the first sheep-farmer, Jonathan MacLean, took over in 1912. It was reroofed with corrugated iron in 1986 to allow the shepherds to use it on their annual visits. At the opposite end – to the north – stands the Catholic priest's house, which had a chapel on the upper floor [NL564834]. It is known as the **Chapel House** and was built in 1898. The ruined village lies below it.

One island story relates how, in the time of MacNeil of Barra's ownership, a rent collector, Macphee, was landed on the island and found everyone dead. He rushed back to the boat and called to the men to take him off quickly as there was 'plague' on the island. On hearing this the men rowed away and left him to his fate. For a whole year he had only the corpses for company. Every day he would climb the hill to the north of the village and signal franti-cally to passing ships but they would wave back and pass on. He survived and eventually MacNeil decided it was safe to have the island resettled. He made a special grant of land to Macphee by way of compensation and since then the hill has always been known as Macphee's Hill.

This north part of the island has an additional prom-ontory with a small hill on it called **Tom a' Reithean** (G. – hillock of the ram). It has a number of large detached rocks and islets clustered round it including the remark-able stack, **Red Boy**, on the north-west side and on the opposite side, **Solon Mór** (G. – big gannet) which is al-most detached by a deep cleft. The Big Gannet has a fledg-ling called **Solon Beag**.

The sea cliffs on the west side towering up to 215m in height are among the most dramatic in the British Isles and have many fantastic rock formations. The greatest sheer drop is at **Biulacraig**, below Carnan. ('Biulacraig' is the MacNeils of Barra war-cry). There are large colonies of seabirds on the treacherous cliffs and the islanders used to scale them to collect the eggs and young birds.

Normally these great rock-faces can only be seen clearly from the sea but an interesting and not too de-manding walk westwards up the valley from the derelict village arrives at a point above **Bàgh na h-Aoineig** (G. –

bay of the steep promontory), a gigantic cleft cutting deep into the island. From here it is possible to look across the cleft towards Carnan and see the utterly breath-taking height of the precipice rising straight out of the sea and soaring towards the sky. Near the top it leans further and further out in a great rock cornice which looks as though it might overbalance at any moment. Every little horizontal crack, ledge and crevice is stippled white – each insignificant dot another nesting bird.

Sheep were grazed on the grassy tops of the two famous stacks, **Arnamul** (ON – erne mound) and **Lianamul** (ON – flax mound), which stand close to the cliffs on either side of Bàgh na h-Aoineig. For many years Lianamul, which has a sea-cave, was reached by a rope bridge spanning the chasm but this had disappeared by 1871. Before the bridge was constructed the *Statistical Account* of 1794 described how the people would climb to the top of Lianamul 'at the risk of their lives, and by means of a rope carry up their wedders to fatten'.

A huge natural arch at **Gunamul** is on the southern side of Arnamul where the cliffs are over 150m in height [NL547824]. It is possible to sail a small boat through it on the very rare occasions when conditions are suitable. South again there is an island-like promontory called **Dùn Mingulay** [NL545821], which was the site of an Iron Age fort.

Two rocky islets, **Geirum Mór** and **Geirum Beag** break into the Sound of Berneray and further east a burn runs down the south side of Hecla through **Skipisdale** (ON – ship valley) and discharges into the sound. This is sometimes the best spot to land from a dinghy and it was so used by the people of nearby Berneray when collecting water in times of drought.

ACCESS: No regular access. Enquire at Castlebay (distance 10 miles).

Anchorages:

1. Mingulay Bay. Occasional anchorage off middle of beach, sheltered from W and NW winds. There is usually a considerable swell which can make landing -and leaving! – difficult. Sometimes easier to land at rocks at Aneir – S end of beach.

2. Skipisdale. Occasional landing place but no anchorage.

7.3 Pabbay

(ON papa-øy – priest or hermit island)

OS Maps: 1:50000 Sheet 31 1:25000 Sheet 260
Admiralty Charts: 1:100000 No.1796 1:30000 No.2769

AREA: 250ha (618 acres)
HEIGHT: 171m (561 ft)

OWNER: Barra Isles Sheep Stock Company (a group of seven Barra crofters). Bought from Mrs Greer, an Essex farmer, in 1955.

POPULATION: 1764 – 16. 1794 – three farming families, about 20 people altogether. 1841 – 25 (3 houses). 1881 – 26. 1891 – 13 (3 houses). 1901 – 11. 1911 – 7. Uninhabited since.

GEOLOGY: The shell sand is extremely rich in lime and frequent rains have broken this down to produce beds of impure limestone. Otherwise the island mainly consists of gneiss.

HISTORY: In early Christian times Pabbay, as its name would infer, had a hermitage or cell located on it and there is an ancient symbol stone and cross slabs on the slope above Bàgh Bàn.

Martin Martin wrote (*c.* 1695): 'the natives observe that if six sheep are put a-grazing in the little island of Pabbay, five of them still appear fat, but the sixth a poor skeleton, but any number in this island not exceeding five are always very fat.' This possibly refers to Lingay (N of Pabbay). Martin's map shows Pabbay and Mingulay interchanged. Today, Pabbay supports about 100 breeding ewes.

On 1st May 1897 every able-bodied man was lost in a fierce storm at sea while out fishing. The Mingulay boat survived the same storm. The island never fully recovered from this disaster and the population dwindled. Within fifteen years no one remained.

WILDLIFE: Heather is scarce, possibly due to the areas of alkaline soil but the rough grazing is full of daisies and celandine, and sundew and flag irises grow in the damper areas.

There are many rabbits and ground-nesting seabirds. Cliff-nesters are almost absent.

PABBAY is another member of the Bishop's Isles and another one of the many 'Priest's Isles'.

The summit, **The Hoe**, rises to a height of 171m at the south-west extremity where there are steep sea cliffs and a massive arched overhang. The settlement which reached a peak population of twenty-six in 1881 was on the eastern side above the blinding-white shell-sand beach in **Bàgh Bàn** (G. – white bay). A cottage still stands on the small central promontory of Sumula. Between Bàgh Bàn and the ruined settlement is an artificial-looking mound about 5m high. The mound may be a burial ground as human bones have been uncovered by the drifting sands. Three cross-marked stones may be gravestones and a fourth marked with a crescent, a cross and a lily is probably Pictish as it is of a design quite different in style to the interlacing Celtic patterns usually found in the Outer Hebrides [NL607874]. Visible traces of an ancient chapel were reported in 1915 beside the nearby rivulet.

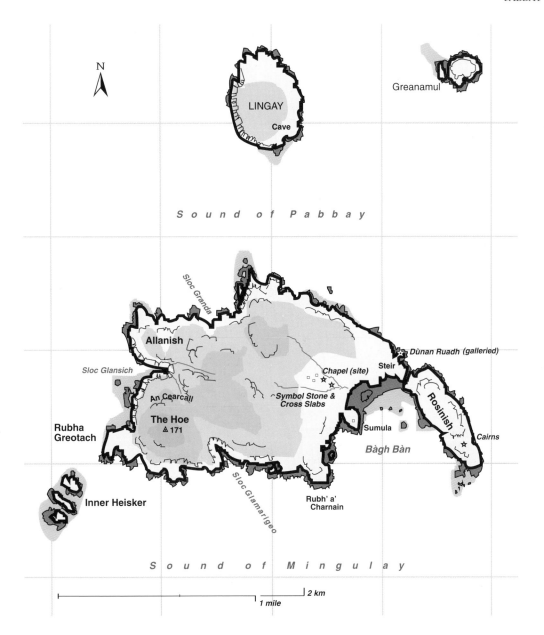

The **Rosinish** peninsula, really a drying island, forms the east side of Bàgh Bàn and rises to 43m where it juts into the waters of the Minch. Near the junction – a narrow cleft – is **Dùnan Ruadh** (G. – the red fort) [NL613876], a ruined galleried broch which looks across the Sound of Pabbay to its opposite number on Sandray (No.7.4).

Dark, narrow vertical fissures intersect the cliffs on the south-west coast by The Hoe where they tower over the islets of Inner and Outer Heisker. These lie in the Sound of Mingulay. To the north is the Sound of Pabay with the small hump of **Greanamul** (ON – green mound) in it and the larger island of **Lingay** (ON – heather isle). Lingay is steep but is occasionally used for grazing sheep. It has a cave in its south-east side.

ACCESS: No regular access. Enquire at the Tourist Office, Castlebay, Barra, 08714-336.

Anchorages: There is no recommended anchorage.
1. Bàgh Bàn is mainly rocky but there is a 4.1m charted sounding off the small headland called Sumula which is sand and affords temporary anchorage in calm conditions. Approach with caution.

7.4 Sandray

(ON sandr-øy – sand island). Old charts have it as Soundray, Sanderay or Sandera.

OS Maps: 1:50000 Sheet 31 1:25000 Sheet 247
Admiralty Charts: 1:100000 No.1769 1:30000 No.2769

AREA: 385ha (951 acres)
HEIGHT: 207m (679 ft)

OWNER: Government owned (Department of Agriculture).

POPULATION: 1835 – population cleared for sheep. 1841 – 14 (2 houses occupied by shepherds' families). 1861 – 9. 1881 – 10. 1891 – 4 (1 house) 1901 – 3. Temporary influx of evicted people in 1909 so, 1911 – 41. 1930 – 20. 1931 – 0. Uninhabited since.

GEOLOGY: Mainly gneiss bedrock.

HISTORY: Neolithic settlements and tombs were identified

SANDRAY FROM THE SOUTH-EAST

by Sheffield University archaeologists in 1991. The Iron Age dun which is still some 2m in height is prominent above a steep ridge on the west side of Cairn Galtar [NL638913] facing Dùnan Ruadh on Pabbay. The ruin of another dun was reported on the east coast, and various Iron Age dwellings.

Faint traces of the old chapel site, Cille Bhride (G. – Bride's or Bridget's cell) were reported in 1915 to be partly covered by a sheep dip [NL650918]. The chapel served the nine crofts into which the island was divided in the early 18th century.

The SS Fair Branch from Sunderland was wrecked on Sandray in 1882.

WILDLIFE: According to Dean Monro, who visited it in 1549, Sandray was 'inhabit and manurit, guid for corne and fishing', and Martin Martin in 1695 claimed that 'it is designed for pasturage and cultivation. . . fruitful in corn and grass'. Today, this is no longer true as the landscape is deserted and fairly barren.

There are no trees, although hazels have been recorded in the past, and the commonest mammals on Sandray are, without doubt, rabbits.

SANDRAY is a fairly circular island with a central peak, **Cairn Galtar** (207m). A lesser hill to the east of Cairn Galtar is called Carnach (179m) (G. – heap of stones) and, again, to the east of Carnach there is a huge sand dune 52m high. This has always been a well-known seamark as it clearly identifies Sandray's east coast. MacCulloch said: 'At a distance the island appears as if covered with a coating of snow.' My own impression is that the sand is possibly no longer as striking as it once was. Maybe there is more marram grass covering it nowadays.

This island, as with the other Bishop's Isles, is used as grazing land by an association of Barra crofters. There is a reasonable supply of fresh water from two good streams, one in the big glen, Gleann Mór, and one flowing from a small loch, **Loch na Cuilce** (G. – loch of the reeds).

A Gaelic tale recorded in Barra in 1859 told how the wife of a herdsman on Sandray had her kettle borrowed every day by a woman of peace (a fairy). Before she would let go the kettle the wife would say: 'A smith is able to make cold iron hot with coal. The due of a kettle is bones, so bring it back again whole.' The kettle was returned every day with fresh meat and soup bones in it.

One day, as the wife was leaving by boat to visit Castlebay on Barra, she warned her husband to say the same words when the fairy came to borrow the kettle. But when the woman of peace came to the door the husband took fright and refused to open it. Then the kettle started jumping and it jumped right through the smoke hole in the roof. When the housewife returned the husband confessed that he had lost the kettle.

So the housewife went to the fairy hill and found her kettle there with flesh and bones in it. She had just picked it up when two vicious fairy dogs started chasing her. She held them at bay by throwing them the contents of the kettle and managed to reach her home unharmed. But the fairy never returned to borrow the kettle.

This story is a fairly typical fireside tale. According to tradition fairies always feared iron and it is of course particularly mentioned in the wife's rhyme. Some scholars suppose that these fairy stories originated in the time when the new Iron Age immigrants met the wild and shy Neolithic settlers.

About one nautical mile west of Sandray the interesting little island of **Flodday** is 43m high, with black cliffs on its west coast and a natural rock arch in the centre. This is a small, but popular, grey seal nursery. There is no shelter whatsoever and the island is constantly windswept by Atlantic gales yet, remarkably, Flodday has its own unique subspecies of butterfly – a tiny pale-coloured form of the dark green fritillary Argynnis aglaia scotica.

ACCESS: No regular access. Enquire at the Tourist Office, Castlebay, Barra, 08714-336.

Anchorages: There are no recommended anchorages but, proceeding cautiously, temporary anchorage in suitable conditions is possible at the following locations:

1. Small bay directly SW of Meanish. Occasional anchorage off centre of sandy beach in 4-5m, sand. Subject to swell.

2. Wide bay in E between Meanish and Eilean Beg. Temp anchorage in 7-8m, sand. Avoid N end of bay. Subject to swell.

7.5 Muldoanich

(G. – Duncan's mound) or (G. mul Domhnach – Sunday island). Dean Munro in 1549 seems to refer to it as Scarp and it is Scarpa on Blaeu's 1654 map, (ON scarfr – cormorant) – island, or (ON – sharp, stony, hilly terrain) but in 1695 Martin Martin called it 'Muldonish'.

OS Maps: 1:50000 Sheet 31 1:25000 Sheet 247
Admiralty Charts: 1:100000 No.1796 1:30000 No.2769

AREA: 78ha (193 acres)
HEIGHT: 153m (502 ft)

POPULATION: No census records. Uninhabited.

GEOLOGY: A hill of gneiss with a light covering of soil.

HISTORY: The island was part of the domain of the MacNeils of Barra. Dean Monro claimed in 1549 that 'Scarp' once had a chapel on it and that it was 'full of pastures and very guid for fishing'.

WILDLIFE: In 1695 Martin Martin said that, 'Muldonish is high in the middle, covered over with heath and grass, and is the only forest here for maintaining the deer, being commonly about seventy or eighty in number'. (A deer

MULDOANICH FROM
THE SOUTH-WEST

forest, of course, does not require trees.) I presume in Dean Munro's time it was cattle that were pastured on the island but that MacNeil of Barra had at some stage stocked it with deer to provide his family with a regular source of venison.

Botanists have found the pyramidal bugle growing on Muldoanich.

The sea eagle nested here before it was exterminated in the early 20th century.

This distinctive dark rounded island lies two miles east of Vatersay and clearly marks the entrance to Castlebay on Barra.

It was MacCulloch who suggested that the name **MULDOANICH** came from St Duncan. The chapel, if it ever existed, may have been dedicated to this important saint but MacCulloch's idea is generally considered to be incorrect.

Muldoanich has no level ground and rises fairly steeply on all sides to a central rounded summit of 153m – **Cruachan na h-àin** (G. – midday hill). As there is no regular water supply, if anyone ever did live on the island life would have been difficult. The east side has the highest cliffs with two deep clefts defining **Creag na h-Iolaire** (G. – eagle crag). This probably referred to the once-common white-tailed sea-eagle which became extinct in Scotland but is now being reintroduced (See Rum No.4.3). The rudimentary inlets on this coast are **Sloc an Lus a' Chorrain** (G. – spleenwort hole), **Sloc na Uillean** [oylun] (G. – honeysuckle hole), and **Sloc na Calaman** (G. – pigeon hole).

On the north side there is a detached rock called **An Laogh** (G. – the calf) and on the north-west is another detached rock off **Rubh' a' Mhorbhuile** (G. – miracle point).

The southern headland called **Vanish** [vay-neesh] (ON – headland of the house or sacred place) may indicate past habitation of some kind.

ACCESS: No regular access. Enquire in Castlebay, Barra.

Anchorages: No recommended anchorages.
1. Temporary anchorage is possible in suitable conditions NE of Rubh' a' Mhorbhuile but beware foul ground north and west of this headland.

7.6 Barra

(ON Barr-øy – Barr's island). Barr was a 6th century saint (G. Finbar – St Barr). He was an Irish missionary and disciple of St Columba who is reputed to have been sent to Barra because his predecessor had been eaten by the inhabitants.

Vatersay

Probably (ON – fathers' island), priest island. (ON vottr-øy – glove island), from the finger-shaped peninsulas? or (ON vatr-øy – wavy island), have also been suggested.

OS Maps: 1:50000 Sheet 31 1:25000 Sheets 231 and 247
Admiralty Charts: 1:100000 No.1796 1:30000 Nos 2769 and 2770

AREA: 6,835ha (16,889 acres)
HEIGHT: 383m (1,256 ft)

OWNER: Barra is mostly owned by the MacNeil of Barra – Ian MacNeil, an American who teaches law at Northwestern University, Chicago, but who plans to retire to Scotland, his ancestral home. His annual income from the 275 protected crofts is less than £3000. The Scottish Office owns the crofts in the north of the island. 'There are some little patches of ground here and there which I actually own outright' says MacNeil. He owns Kisimul Castle and one commercial property (a bank) in Castlebay main street.

The Scottish Office owns Vatersay which the Scottish Board of Agriculture bought in 1909 for £6250.

POPULATION: Barra only: 1755 – 1150. 1794 – 1604.

	1841	1881	1891	1931	1961	1971	1981	1991
Barra	1977	1869	2131	2001	1369	1005	1232	1244
Vatersay	84	19	32	240	95	77	108	72
	2061	1888	2163	2241	1464	1082	1340	1316

GEOLOGY: The island, of heavily glaciated gneiss, has a rocky and broken east coast and fine, sandy bays on the west coast backed by machair. East of the central fault line the gneiss has been sheared to give a belt of mylonite, or flinty crush. The east side of Castlebay is gneissose granite.

HISTORY: Following the centuries of Norse domination Alexander, Lord of the Isles, granted a charter to Gilleonan MacNeil in 1427, and this was confirmed by James IV in 1495. Some say that MacNeil ownership actually goes back to 1030. The family is reputed to be descended from Niall of the Nine Hostages, the 4th century High King of Ireland. By the 16th century the MacNeils were using Castlebay on the island as a pirate base for raids on the ships of the English Queen Elizabeth. MacNeil explained to James VI (James I) that his actions were merely because 'that woman' had killed his mother (Mary Queen of Scots). The comment saved his life. The MacNeils were keen sailors and it is said by some that an invitation

from Noah to a MacNeil of Barra to sail with him on his ark was turned down by MacNeil because he had a boat of his own.

Martin Martin in the 17th century said that when the islanders were too old to work the MacNeil chief would take them into his household and provide for them. Boswell recounts the Earl of Argyll's comment on receiving a letter from MacNeil of Barra – 'His style of letter runs as if he were of another kingdom.'

By 1838 the then chief General Roderick MacNeil was so heavily in debt that he had to sell the island. It went for £38,050 to Colonel Gordon of Cluny who had also bought Benbecula, South Uist and Eriskay. Without any consideration for the islanders the colonel offered Barra to the Government for use as a penal settlement – an offer which was not accepted. Then in 1851 on the grounds of receiving insufficient rent he imported policemen to clear the island of its crofters, confiscate their stock and belongings, and send them penniless to the New World. These were some of the most cruel and shameful cases of inhumanity ever seen on the West Coast. In 1858 when the colonel died he was said to be the richest commoner in Scotland. Barra and its few survivors then passed to Lady Gordon Cathcart and her husband, who, in their dealings with both Barra and Vatersay, followed in the unlamented colonel's footsteps.

Most of Barra was bought back in 1937 from the Cathcart estate by the present Macneil's father, who had been recognised by the Lyon King of Arms as the Clan's 45th chieftain. In 1979 the laird offered to transfer the freehold of all the crofting land to the crofters for only £30,000 but the crofters for various reasons preferred to keep to the traditional arrangement.

WILDLIFE: Over 150 bird species and 400 plant species have been recorded. This is comparable with the rest of the Outer Hebrides but the island is particularly noted for the profuseness of both its wildflowers and its butterflies.

There are spectacular views from both of the highest hills on **BARRA**, **Heaval** (383m) and **Ben Tangaval** (333m). Little idea of the island's size can be gained at Castlebay but from the top of Heaval one can see great rolling hills to the north and the wide sweep of the Borve Valley dropping down to the sandy west coast. But take care when walking in these hills for the mists and sudden climatic changes have given rise to many ghost stories and mysterious disappearances. There are enjoyable walks from Garrygall to Brevig, **Ben Tangaval** to Tangasdale and Glen Dorcha to Northbay. **Northbay** is a second harbour for the island. It is beyond the **Black Islands**, which are south of **Lamalum** islet, and in a sheltered corner but it is a rather rocky, bleak, and uninspiring area.

A pleasantly energetic 18km hillwalk from Castlebay can include climbing the five highest summits (1040m or 3400ft of total ascent). Heaval – 396m ascent, Hartaval – 60m, Greanan and Corrabheinn – 76m, then west by **Dùn Bharpa** chambered cairn [NF672019] to Beinn Mhártainn – 122m, down to sea-level and 4km along the coast road before climbing Ben Tangaval, over the top, and back down to Castlebay.

PUFFER IN CASTLE BAY

Another interesting walk is from Cleat past Ardmhor with its seals and bird life to **Vaslane Sands**. There is reputed to be an underground passage running from Cleat to **Uaimh an Oir** (G. – cave of gold) on the east coast. Two hairless mad dogs which emerged from Uaimh an Oir were reported to have entered the Cleat cave with their masters several days before but the men were never seen again. (This is another example of the standard Hebridean cave tale.)

In the late-19th century, **Castlebay**, the principal town, was a very active and prosperous herring port with a fleet of over 400 boats using the harbour. This was started by James Methuen in 1869 with associated curing and packing industries to take advantage of the herring boom. Castlebay has shops, a post-office, tourist office, schools, hotels, a bank and a cottage hospital and its residents are cheerful and good-natured. In fact, Barra is full of friendly people.

The medieval fortress of **Kisimul Castle** which includes a keep, hall and castle is built below the town on a rocky island outcrop in the bay. The first fortifications were built in the 11th century but the present building dates from the 15th century. Beneath the castle there is a very convenient geological pipe which provides a supply of fresh water to a well. A herald used to proclaim from the Great Tower: 'Hear ye people and listen ye nations. The great MacNeil of Barra having finished his meal, the princes of the earth may dine.' The castle was burnt down at the end of the 18th century. The MacNeils had to sell Barra in 1838 due to debt but the 45th Chief of the Clan MacNeil, Robert Lister MacNeil, an American architect, bought back the ancestral home in 1937 together with almost half of Barra. He restored the castle which had been uninhabited for more than 200 years and turned it into a place of pilgrimage for MacNeils from all over the world. He died in 1970 and is buried in the castle chapel. A flag flies from the tower when his son, the 46th Chief, is in residence and the castle is usually open to the public on Wednesday and Saturday afternoons.

Cars can be hired in Castlebay but it is possible to walk round the island in an afternoon. One of the world's most exciting airfields, a great sweep of beach in the north of the island called **Tràigh Mhór** or the Cockle Strand is covered at every tide. In the 18th century as many as 200 cartloads of live cockles were collected from this famous beach every day during times of famine. Recently, the cockle-shells were being collected and sold for harling which provided some local employment but there was concern that their removal might eventually destroy the beach.

The 1745 Jacobite rebellion led to the chief of the Clan MacNeil being imprisoned for implication in the revolt although he had taken no active part. Two years later the clan moved its headquarters from Castlebay to **Eoligarry** in the extreme north of the island. A small cemetery here, **Cille-bharraidh** [NF705074], is the burial ground of the MacNeils. The only Hebridean example of a Norse sculpted stone (which is now in the National Museum of Antiquities in Edinburgh) was found here among the three ancient chapels and interesting tombstones dating back to the 14th century. Sir Compton Mackenzie, the famous novelist who made Barra his home, is also buried here in sight of Eriskay (See No.7.13), – the setting for his novel

Whisky Galore. It was on Barra that Sir Compton and John Lorne Campbell of Canna formed the Sea League in the 1930s to try to persuade the Government to protect local fishermen from over-fishing and trawling in the Minch.

A prehistoric galleried fort, **Dùn Scurrival** [NF695080], is beside a cave near Eoligarry.

An award-winning hotel with an emphasis on informality and a welcome for yachtsmen at **Halaman Bay** on the west coast was used as a hideout by the children of the Shah in the lead-up to the Iranian Revolution. Their nurse came from Barra. Across the sand dunes from it is fresh-water **Loch Tangusdale**, stocked with trout and with Castle Sinclair perched on an islet [NL648996]. Nearby is Barra's perfumery where visitors are welcome.

The island is predominantly Catholic and on the slopes of **Heaval** is a white Carrara marble statue of the Madonna and Child, sculpted by Hew Lorimer [NL679992].

The remains of a fine chambered cairn [NF677012] are further north on the west slope of Grianan, and there are a pair of standing stones [NF653015], said to mark the grave of a Norse warrior killed by a local champion, on the way to Borve Point. An old burial ground and black houses are nearby.

CASTLEBAY

VATERSAY, whose economy is based on sheep and cattle farming, and fishing, is linked to Barra by a long-awaited causeway which was completed in 1990 at a cost of £3.8m. To send the cattle to market they traditionally swam across the Sound of Vatersay to Barra to meet the ferry but when a prize bull, Bernie, drowned in 1986 the resulting publicity at last helped to persuade the Government to build the causeway.

In 1853 off the west coast of Vatersay the *Annie Jane* ran aground and capsized. The bodies of 450 emigrants bound for the New World were washed ashore.

Lady Gordon Cathcart owned Vatersay for a period of fifty-four years but only visited it once. Her tenants ran the island as a single farm. At the turn of the century the demand for land by the crofters of Barra was so great that pressure was put on her to sell land for crofting. She refused, so, in 1906, an ambitious crofter landed on Vatersay and laid claim to some land. Others copied him and these men became known as the **Vatersay Raiders**. They were brought to trial and imprisoned for a time. In 1909 a Government Board bought the island and divided it into fifty-eight crofts.

The highest hill on Vatersay is **Heishival Mór** at 190m. Entering the Sound of Vatersay by sea from the east you pass a small tidal island called **Uinessan** with the remains of a church on it [NL665956]. This is known as the Chapel of Mary of the Heads. (Apparently Mary was a short-tempered islander who beheaded anyone who upset her.) **Snuasimul** islet east of Uinessan marks a narrow but navigable shortcut between Vatersay Bay and Castle Bay. Avoid all other shortcuts.

ACCESS: Caledonian MacBrayne, Castlebay, 018714-306: car ferry from Oban to Castlebay – 5½hrs crossing time, 01631-66688: car ferry from Lochboisdale, South Uist – 1½hrs, 01878-700288. By air: (BA Express) Glasgow to Barra, and Stornoway, Lewis via Benbecula to Barra, 0345 222111. Private passenger ferry from Ludag, South Uist to Eoligarry – 40mins, 01878-700216. Island bus service, circuit includes airport and Eoligarry, 018714-286. Hotel accommodation available. Bicycle hire and fishing permits from Post Office. Tourist Office, Castlebay, 018714-336.

Anchorages:

1. Bagh Beag, Castlebay. Good shelter but tricky narrow channel with only 1.3m at half-tide and inadequate information on chart. Risky.

2. Castle Bay, NW of castle. HIE visitors' moorings, or anchor in 6m, mud, holding poor unless well bedded-in. Avoid obstructing ferry pier. Reasonable shelter except S'lies.

3. Castle Bay, NE of castle. Good shelter but very limited space between drying rocks and moored craft, 3.5-5m or close W of the castle in 7m, mud.

4. North Bay on E coast affords good shelter. Enter SW of Fuiay, pass mid-channel SW of Black Isles and anchor in inlet W of the Black Isles, or,

better still, continue into N part of Bagh Hirivagh and anchor 2c W of the jetty and factory. Not the most attractive anchorage.

5. Inner Oitir Mór, W of Greanamul, in the Sound of Barra. Best approach N of Gighay, leaving Greanamul 1c-5c to port and anchor S of E end of Orosay, clay and sand, with some weed. Safe in all winds but unpleasant in E'lies.

6. Eoligarry Jetty, about 6¼c NNW of N side of Orosay is a tidal harbour with pier where small craft might find shelter.

7. Sound of Fiaray could be used occasionally and anchorage obtained in 4m or more when sufficiently out of the swell.

8. W coast of Barra has no anchorages but the Admiralty Pilot records one landing place amongst the rocks 1M S of Greian Head.

9. Sound of Vatersay. There may be some useful shelter in the west end of the Sound which is now blocked by the causeway. Beware rocks at entrance.

10. W coast of Vatersay has no anchorages. Bàgh Siar has moderate depth and sandy bottom but no shelter.

11. Vatersay Bay – good anchorage. Enter passing 2-3c S of Muldoanich and then steer centrally for the bay. Anchor W of Sgeir Vichalea in suitable depth, sand.

12. Cornaig Bay, S of causeway and Orosay. Pipeline, cable and rocks to be avoided but well-sheltered from SW.

13. Causeway bay, between causeway and Orosay may be a useful anchorage well clear of the shore. There is a slipway.

7.7 Flodday

(ON floti – a raft or flat island) This island is east of Barra. There is another smaller Flodday south-west of Barra which does not appear to have ever been inhabited.

OS Maps: 1:50000 Sheet 31 1:25000 Sheet 231
Admiralty Charts: 1:100000 No.1796 1:30000 No.2770

AREA: 40ha (99 acres)
HEIGHT: 42m (138 ft)

POPULATION: 1841 – 7 (1 house). The island was cleared in the mid-19th century and has been uninhabited since then.

GEOLOGY: The bulk of the island is made up of gneiss with a sufficient covering of soil to provide good grazing.

WILDLIFE: The low-lying nature of the island gives encouragement to only a few seabirds but rock-pipit and twite can be seen and may even be resident.

FLODDAY rises gradually to a height of 42m and is covered with grass and heather, but Rubh' a' Chaolais (G. – the kyle headland) in the south-west is bare and rocky. Opposite it in the south-east is the equally barren Grey Rock. It is an easy island to explore but has few features of any particular interest.

The 1991 Census quotes Flodday as having a population of eight but this refers in fact to the tidal island

Sound of Hellisay

Colla

+ +
+ *Fuiay Rock*

Snagaras

N

Bò Bheanachan

Irishman Rock

+

△ 42

25

FUIAY

Grey Rock

+
Rubh'
a' Chaolais

+

1 km

1/2 mile

Rubha na Maighdein

which is part of Benbecula in the Civil Parish of South Uist and should not be confused with this Flodday. The name was very popular and applied freely to any flat island.

Flodday never appears to have supported more than one family and it was cleared for sheep by Colonel Gordon of Cluny in 1851. It has no reliable source of fresh water so water would have had to be brought in by boat when there were long dry spells.

A small, drying islet off the north extremity called

Snagaras lies at the end of a reef.

ACCESS: No regular access. Enquire at Northbay or Castlebay, Barra.

Anchorages:

1. The only recommended occasional anchorage is NE of Irishman Rock, W of the N extremity of Flodday, in 13-14m, mud. It may be possible to find a shallower spot (5-6m) in the channel S of Irishman Rock but the bottom is uncertain.

7.8 Fuiay

Probably, (G. bhuidhe, ON -øy – yellow or pleasant island)

OS Maps: 1:50000 Sheet 31 1:25000 Sheet 231
Admiralty Charts: 1:100000 No.1796 1:30000 No.2770

AREA: 84ha (208 acres)
HEIGHT: 107m (351 ft)

POPULATION: The island was populated with at least six households during the 19th century, possibly until about 1850, but I have found no census records. Uninhabited since.

GEOLOGY: Gneiss generally, but large dark slabs of volcanic rock with pronounced cleavage planes.

WILDLIFE: Rabbits, bracken and heather.

FUIAY is a bit of a puzzle.

Firstly, I have found no record of any population. And yet, **Rubh' an Aiseig** [ash-ug] (G. – ferry headland), has the ruins of a neat village 'street' [NF737027] laid out

RUINED HOUSES BY THE TIDAL LOCH

west with patches of sea-grass on it.

ACCESS: No regular access. Enquire at Northbay or Castlebay, Barra.

Anchorages: There is a tricky navigable channel through the reefs between Sgeirislum and Fuiay, except possibly at LW.

1. Off N coast. Anchor midway between Sgeirislum and Eilean Sheumais, 5m, mud. Good anchorage but partly obstructed by fish cages. If approaching from W keep close S of Garbh Lingay to avoid rocks N of En Sheumais.

2. W of Rubh' an Aiseig. Occasional anchorage about 1/2c off-shore and about 3c S of the N extremity of the headland opposite some rocks which form a natural 'jetty', 5-6m, mud.

along the side of the tidal inlet. There were at least six cottages and by comparison with similar ruins elsewhere they were probably occupied until the mid-19th century and possibly later. Of course, the ten-yearly census only started in 1831, and it was fairly sketchy to begin with, so the odds are that Fuiay's inhabitants were included somewhere but not specifically mentioned.

The second mystery, if such it is, is at the tidal inlet. We visited the island at high water and the sea was flowing downhill *into* the inlet. A stony shelf or bar crosses the entrance opposite the ruined cottages and there was about 300mm, or one foot, difference between the two water levels. The inlet is like a miniature sea-loch when full but is shallow and dries out at low water. Our conclusion was that when the tide ebbs and the outside sea-level falls below the 'floor-level' of the inlet the water in the inlet drains out through the rock strata, but when the tide rises the water cannot seep in fast enough to fill the inlet: the sea therefore floods over the 'bar' when it reaches the required level. This would seem to create a natural fish trap at the spring tides which the islanders must have found very convenient.

Fuiay has a prominent peak (107m) which is almost at the exact centre of the oval-shaped island. The headland in the south-east is called **Rubha na Maighdein** [myjun] (G. – maiden's headland) – a name which begs another intriguing question.

The sea to the north and north-west of Fuiay is littered with islets, skerries, and rocks. The nearest islets are **Eilean Sheumais**, **Colla** (G. – hazel island), and **Sgeirislum**. Beyond these lie **Garbh Lingay** and **Lingayfhada** (G. – rough heather-isle and long heather-isle).

To the south there are more rocks off Barra's Bruernish peninsula gathered around an islet called **Heilem**. The large lone rock, **Curachan**, is prominent in the south-

7.9 Hellisay

(ON – island of caves), but Blaeu's map of 1654 uses 'Hildesay' (ON – Hilda's island) which may be more acceptable as the number of caves is not excessive.

OS Maps: 1:50000 Sheet 31 1:25000 Sheet 231
Admiralty Charts: 1:100000 No.1796 1:30000 No.2770

AREA: 142ha (351 acres)
HEIGHT: 79m (259 ft)

OWNER: Government owned (Scottish Office).

POPULATION: 1764 – 56. 1841 – 108. 1851 – 7. 1861 – 20. 1881 – 9. Uninhabited since 1890.

GEOLOGY: Mainly gneiss with occasional quartz veins.

HISTORY: Clearances on the adjoining islands led to an influx of population in the early 1800s. Then in the 1840s the people of Hellisay were themselves evicted and by 1851 there were only seven inhabitants left. Most of the families cleared from Hellisay found refuge on Eriskay.

WILDLIFE: Every pocket in the rocks above sea-level is filled with sea-thrift. There are many grey seals and apart from sea-birds we saw falcon and a pair of golden eagles.

There are two distinct peaks on **HELLISAY**, **Meall Meadhonach** (G. – middle mound), in the south-east (79m) and **Beinn a' Charnain** (G. – cairn hill), in the north-west (73m). Meall Meadhonach has a vertical face over 60m high on its west side with distinctive orange lichen near the top. It is on a peninsula which finishes steeply at **Rubha na h-Uamh** (G. – cave headland). **Meall Mór** (G. – big mound) is on this peninsula and is virtually an extension of Meall Meadhonach [meeoo-unuch]. At 75m it is not as high, but its position is more prominent.

The most westerly part of the island is **Rubh' an t-Seana Bhalla** (G. – headland of the ancient wall). Most of the island is rocky and uneven and it is difficult to see how it could have supported over 100 inhabitants at one time, even with the advantage of good fishing in the Sound of Barra. The main settlement was on the lower ground at **Bualavore** [NF754046].

The easiest landing place by dinghy in Hintish Bay is in the south-east corner. On the outside of the neck of land

the sea surges into a narrow rock cleft with a noise like severe indigestion. From here there is a pleasant scramble up Meall Mór and Meadhonach with extensive views from the top.

Hellisay is an island rich in fairy tales and myths. The stories of Alasdair Alpin MacGregor tell of a magic land of strange happenings remembered by the old folk on winter nights by the peat fire.

ACCESS: No regular access. Enquire at Northbay on Barra or Haun on Eriskay.

Anchorages: The anchorages are in the sound between the two islands. Entrance to the sound is tricky and there may be uncharted rocks.
1. Hintish Bay. In the SE part of the sound, anchor NW of Charish. Excellent shelter, good holding, sand and mud.
2. Pool in W part of the sound, ENE of Beinn a' Charnain. Many submerged rocks.

7.10 Gighay

(ON – Gydha's island) Gydha was a woman's name in Old Norse.

OS Maps: 1:50000 Sheet 31 1:25000 Sheet 231
Admiralty Charts: 1:100000 No.1796 1:30000 No.2770

AREA: 96ha (237 acres)
HEIGHT: 95m (312 ft)

OWNER: Government owned (Scottish Office).

POPULATION: Dean Monro recorded that Gighay was inhabited in 1549, but there is no other information. The island was known to be inhabited at the end of the 18th century but it has been deserted for a long time and there are no census records.

GEOLOGY: Mainly gneiss. The Hebridean Fault Line runs approximately NE-SW at Eilean a' Ceud and Hintish Bay.

HISTORY: It is probable that the increase in population recorded for Hellisay during the Clearances in the mid-19th century overflowed on to neighbouring Gighay.

THE SECRET ANCHORAGE BETWEEN GIGHAY AND HELLISAY

WILDLIFE: Heather is fairly widespread – mainly calluna with very little erica. Banks of nettles surround the areas of former human habitation. The wet areas have marsh marigolds and yellow flag among the reeds and there are daisies and wild violets on the slopes.

Rats frequent the area near the sheep dip.

When we visited Gighay it was the month of May. Oystercatchers were busy on the shore, sky larks larking in the sky, and an eagle was being mobbed by falcons above Mullach a' Charnain's cliffs.

Like its sister island, Hellisay, **GIGHAY** is another magical place, no doubt given additional charm by the fairly difficult entry into its secret anchorage. Because *Jandara*, having achieved entry, was trapped until the tide rose again the feeling of isolation was exaggerated. We were marooned.

The easiest landing place was in the bay behind **Eilean a' Ceud** [ked] (G. – hundred island). Only the sheep and sheep pens beneath the bluff destroyed the impression that man had not set foot on the island for many years.

This is the area that was once inhabited because among the reeds, nettles and bracken there are still signs of the old habitations. Over a dozen are easily discovered – small, rude, stone dwellings giving an impression of desperate poverty; and on the opposite slope of the bay, to the northwest, there are the regular striations of old lazybeds.

A short visit here is delightful, particularly in fine spring weather but the islanders' existence must have been finely balanced. Gighay is barren enough in late spring – what must it be like during the long winter

1 km
1/2 mile

Outer Oitir Mhór

An Laogh

Fionnphort

Meall an Laoig

Ruadh-phort

Creag an Caora

Bualaveg

△ 95
Mullach a' Charnain

Eilean a' Ghamhna

Carnach

Clach Eagach

Settlement (ruin)

Eilean a' Ceud

Rubha na Muireart

Colla

HELLISAY

Creag an Teirm

Sound of Hellisay

N

++

+

Fuiay Rock

Snagaras

FUIAY

FLODDAY

months? Only the inland sea, the Sound of Gighay, sheltered between the islands, could tip the scales by providing all-weather fishing with nothing but seals for competition.

The highest peak **Mullach a' Charnain** (G. – cairn summit), 95m high, has a steep cliff on its south-west side above the anchorage. There is also a high flat point in the extreme north-east ending in a hummock called **Meall an Laoig** (G. – calf hill). The calf itself, **An Laogh**, is a miniature stack at the end of this promontory. Round the corner, on the exposed north-west coast there is an indentation with enough space to draw small boats ashore called **Ruadh-phort** (G. – red port).

Although the anchorage beside Eilean a' Ceud is excellent, if the wind is in the north or north-west squally gusts can come tumbling over the cliff. In that case it is better to cross the sound to the Hellisay side, but remember that at high water a large reef crossing most of Hintish Bay is not visible.

ACCESS: No regular access. Enquire at Northbay on Barra or Haun on Eriskay.

Anchorages: The anchorages are in the sound between Gighay and Hellisay. Entrance to the sound can be tricky, depends on the state of the sea and the tide, and there may be uncharted rocks.
1. In the small bay NW of Eilean a' Ceud, thick mud.
2. Pool in W part of the sound just S of the line between Mullach a' Charnain on Gighay and Beinn a' Charnain on Hellisay. Many submerged rocks.

7.11 Fuday

Possibly, (ON fut-øy – bailiwick or bailiff's island) or (ON ut-øy – outside isle)

OS Maps: 1:50000 Sheet 31 1:25000 Sheet 231
Admiralty Charts: 1:100000 No.1796 1:30000 No.2770

AREA: 232ha (573 acres)
HEIGHT: 89m (292 ft)

OWNER: Government owned (Scottish Office).

POPULATION: Walker's list for 1764 gives a population of 56 for 'Fuda' but doesn't mention the island of Hellisay

Fuday

(No 7.9). Yet in 1841 Hellisay had 108 and Fuday only 5. Francis Thompson says that Hellisay was sometimes known in Gaelic as 'An t-eilean Fuideach' which may be the cause of confusion. 1841 – 5 (1 house). 1861 – 7. 1881 – 6. 1891 – 7 (1 house). 1901 – 4. Uninhabited since.

GEOLOGY: The island is covered with grass on a core of Archaean gneiss and with a wide sand-based shelf on the west-side.

HISTORY: Fuday is supposed to have been the last retreat of those Norsemen, a small section of King Haakon's defeated forces, who remained in the Hebrides after the Battle of Largs in 1263. According to tradition, an illegitimate son of MacNeil of Barra wished to ingratiate himself with his family. He managed to attract the attention of one of the Norse maidens and courted her assiduously. She fell in love with him and through her he gained detailed information about the Norse defences. He then led a raid on the island and wiped out the entire population.

WILDLIFE: Seabirds nest on the southern headland, Rubha nan Eun (G. – headland of the birds) and among the sand dunes on the west coast. Otters have also been seen here.

Tradition says that **FUDAY** was a Norse burial ground. Certainly graves can still be seen in the sand, built of rounded stones. The Norse liked to have a quiet island for the dead to rest in peace although, if the MacNeil massacre actually took place, it is uncertain who buried the dead. At the north end of the island, **Ru Hornish**, there are two cairns which are evidence that the Norse were not the first inhabitants.

The Sound of Fuday which separates the island from the Eoligarry peninsula of Barra is full of rocks and shifting sandbanks and at low water it is sometimes only a few centimetres deep but it can be navigated with care at the right state of the tide.

The island rises to three rather flat hills. The central hill, **Mullach Neachel** (G. – lone summit) is 89m high with a slightly lower hill to the north. The westward slope runs down to a wide expanse of high sand dunes and a great stretch of beach, **Tràigh na Reill**, exposed by the low tide. South-west of Mullach Neachel and joined to it is a small hill called **Dùnan Ruadh** (G. – the red heap). A crystal clear burn runs from the saddle of this hill down to Cordale Beag on the south coast where it discharges into the sea. On the east side a rock-strewn sandy cove, **Cordale Mór** (G. and ON – the big tapering valley) is sheltered from the north by Rubha Carraig-chrom (G. – cliff-ridge point) and on the north coast there is a wide attractive beach, **Tràigh Bhàn**, or White Sand – a white chalk-mark on a blue ground when seen from across the Sound of Barra.

Greanamul is an islet which provides a useful point of reference when approaching Fuday from the south because navigating in this area of skerries and shifting sandbanks requires care.

ACCESS: No regular access but enquire at Eoligarry jetty on Barra where the ferry arrives from Ludag, South Uist.

Anchorages: No recommended anchorages.
1. Rubha nan Eun. Temporary anchorage off the headland in 6-8m, sand. Approach from N of Gighay, leaving Greanamul 1c-5c to port. After passing Greanamul 2-4c turn to starboard on course for Mullach Neachel 005° approx.
2. Cordale Mór. Temporary anchorage NNW Goose Rocks, 4-6m, sand. Follow sailing directions to NE of Fuday and turn SW to Cordale Mór. Goose Rocks cover so best to approach near LW.

7.12 Fiaray

(G. feur – grass or pasture, ON -øy – island)

OS Maps: 1:50000 Sheet 31 1:25000 Sheet 216
Admiralty Charts: 1:100000 No.1796 1:30000 No.2770

AREA: 41ha (101 acres)
HEIGHT: 30m (98 ft)

POPULATION: No census records and uninhabited.

GEOLOGY: Archaean gneiss with a sandy soil.

WILDLIFE: A favourite staging-post for barnacle geese.

Except for two small hillocks on the west side, **FIARAY** is a flat and featureless island. The most northerly hill is the highest at 30m. There is a distinctive sandy promontory at the east side called **Corran Bàn** (G. – white sickle-shaped tapering point) and a seaweed-covered headland on the other side of the island facing the Atlantic called **Gruagach** (G. – beautiful head of hair). The original shielings were at **Port a' Tuim Bàn** (G. – port of the white knoll) near Corran Bàn.

Fiaray boasts, which is remarkable for such a tiny island, two little lochans and it is entirely surrounded by a drying reef. Some local fishermen would swear that this is the home of a fairy woman, often seen by passing boats.

In a collection of folk stories the Rev. Fr. Allan McDonald (d.1905) recorded that towards the end of 1890 people on the shore of South Uist heard dreadful cries coming from **Lingay** (ON – heather isle). Lingay is the little islet in the middle of the Sound of Barra, east of Fiaray. A rescue boat put out for the island as it was assumed that sailors were drowning. The screaming suddenly stopped when they were close to Lingay and although they searched the area they could find nothing to account for the cries. Almost exactly eight years later, in October 1898, a boat from Eriskay was wrecked on Lingay

Fiaray

and the sailors cries brought help from South Uist. All were saved but the first incident was claimed by the islanders to have been a forewarning. (Nowadays it would be called, in science-fiction terms, a 'time-warp'.)

ACCESS: No regular access but enquire at Eoligarry Jetty on Barra where the ferry arrives from Ludag, South Uist.

Anchorages: No recommended anchorages.
1. Temp anchorage in Sound of Fiaray in suitable conditions, 3-4m, sandy
patches.

7.13 Eriskay

(G. ùruisg, ON -øy – goblin or water-nymph island). 'Eric's island' is sometimes given as the derivation but this is probably incorrect.

OS Maps: 1:50000 Sheet 31 1:25000 Sheets 216 and 231
Admiralty Charts: 1:100000 No.1795 1:30000 No.2770

AREA: 703ha (1,737 acres)
HEIGHT: 185m (607 ft)

OWNER: South Uist Estates.

POPULATION: 1841 – 80 (12 houses). 1881 – 466. 1891 – 454 (96 houses). 1931 – 420. 1961 – 231. 1971 – 219. 1981 – 219. 1991 – 179.

GEOLOGY: At very low spring tides, tree trunks are exposed in the sand off the Prince's Strand proving that the island was once forested. As with the rest of the islands in this region the base rock is mainly Archaean gneiss.

HISTORY: On 23rd July, 1745 on the beach of Coilleag a' Phrionnsa (G. – the Prince's cockle-shell strand) on the west coast of Eriskay Prince Charles Edward Stuart was put ashore from the French ship *Du Teillay*. This was the first time he had set foot on Scottish soil.

The MacNeils of Barra owned Eriskay at the time and this continued until 1758 when it passed to the MacDonalds of Clanranald. Colonel Gordon of Cluny bought the island in 1838, together with Barra, Benbecula and South Uist, and he allowed a few of the crofters whom he had evicted from Uist to settle there as the land was considered too poor even for sheep to survive. It was for this reason that the population of Eriskay increased dramatically as many crofters preferred destitution in Scotland to forced emigration. They built raised lazybeds of peat and seaweed on the rocky ground and grew meagre crops of barley, oats and potatoes for sustenance.

WILDLIFE: It was claimed at one time that the pink sea-convolvulus (*Calystegia soldanella*) grew only above the western beach on Eriskay, and nowhere else, and that it came from seeds dropped by Bonnie Prince Charlie when he first landed. It still grows there but it can also be found at several other places in the Hebrides including Vatersay (No.7.6). It blooms in June and has a small heart-shaped leaf and large trumpet.

Eriskay ponies stand 12 to 13 hands high and are possibly a distinctive Scottish breed although some doubt this. They were used to carry peat and seaweed but are now close to extinction.

ERISKAY is known for the lovely Eriskay Love Lilt and several other beautiful Gaelic songs. In a way, the music is more beautiful than the land for it is a barren island, the only soil being rocky moorland, and yet there is a relatively large population.

The main township, **Haun** (ON *havn* – harbour), is on the north coast with another small settlement beside the natural harbour in the east. The men are mostly fishermen for prawns, lobsters, herring and mackerel and the women knit fishermen's jerseys and gossamer shawls in distinctive Eriskay patterns.

Almost all are Roman Catholics. A former priest who was born on South Uist, Father Allan McDonald, is remembered for his valuable collections of Gaelic folk-tales (see Fiaray, No.7.12), his dictionary of Gaelic phrases and his poetry. In 1893 he built a new church at Haun. He died in 1905 at the early age of forty-six, a simple man and a dedicated scholar. Unfortunately, much of his literary work was mutilated by Ada Goodrich-Freer, a German woman, who befriended him, persuaded him to hand over his manuscripts and then published much of the material, incorrectly edited, under her own name. Luckily, what was left of Father Allan's work was rescued by John Lorne Campbell of Canna.

The church built by Father Allan, **St Michael's Church**, now has a bell which is the ship's bell from the German battle-cruiser *Derfflinger*, scuttled at Scapa Flow (see No.10.7), and the altar base is the bow of a lifeboat from the aircraft-carrier *Hermes*.

Others followed the lead of Father Allan. Hebridean songs and folklore were passed on orally so it was important that they should be recorded before they were lost. Unfortunately, some of these records are now the subject of controversy such as *The Songs of the Hebrides* (which included the famous Love Lilt) published by Marjory Kennedy Fraser. She, with the help of the Rev. Dr Kenneth

ACAIRSEID MHÓR

MacLeod of Skye, visited Eriskay in 1905 to record Hebridean songs.

The 12,000-ton steamship *The Politician* sailing from Liverpool and bound for New York, avoided striking the lone islet of **Hartamul** east of Eriskay, but foundered in the Sound of Eriskay near the islet of **Calvay** and broke in two. This was on the 5th February 1941, at the height of the Battle of the Atlantic when Hitler's U-boats were exacting a terrible toll on merchant shipping. The Harrison Line ship was unaccompanied and trying to avoid attention by sneaking through the Minch but she should not have ventured into the shallow Sound of Eriskay. Among her assorted cargo of plumbing fittings, motorcycle parts, art silks and Jamaican currency were 264,000 bottles of whisky. The story goes that as soon as the crew were safe the islanders naturally turned their attention to the precious cargo. Before long, nearly every living creature on the island, including the ponies, was blind drunk. During the ensuing weeks the cargo was steadily removed from the wreck. Then, to the islanders' surprise, Charles McColl and Ivan Gledhill of H M Customs & Excise appeared on the scene with some police and began searching the crofts. Most of the whisky miraculously disappeared into peat stacks, hot-water bottles and rabbit holes. The local police disliked the affair and withdrew but thirty-six islanders were sent to court by the excisemen, including a fourteen-year old boy. Nineteen were found guilty of illegal possession and imprisoned at Inverness.

Some years later Sir Compton Mackenzie based his hilarious book *Whisky Galore!* on the incident (but naturally omitted the sad fact that islanders had been prosecuted). The film was made by Ealing Studios on the adjoining island of Barra (No 7.6) in 1948.

In 1989 a company was formed to try to salvage any whisky remaining in the wreck. Customs & Excise agreed not to charge duty on any recovered spirit, possibly through remorse for their harsh action in 1941. However the whole expensive operation only yielded a few bottles. The stern of the ship, which contained No 5 hold and the whisky cases, can still be seen at low tide where it has drifted some distance north-west of Calvay but much of it is now bedded deep in the sandy bottom.

Strangely enough, Eriskay had always been a 'dry' island until its first public house was opened in 1988. Naturally it was called *Am Politician* and the Eriskay islanders can be found there happily drinking a dram with their friends. I first visited it on a Thursday, mid-afternoon. It was crowded, and the sweet smell of spirit and soft Gaelic voices encouraged dreams of secret treasure troves of golden liquid. Some bottles still occasionally turn up in unlikely hidey-holes. The islanders call them 'polly-bottles' and I was told by John Alan MacNeil of Barra that genuine ones can be recognised because they are stamped – 'No resale without Federal approval.' They were of course

originally destined for the United States.

The best anchorage for the island is unfortunately some distance from Haun. **Acairseid Mhór** (G. – big anchorage) is an inlet which cuts deep into the island between the two main peaks, **Ben Scrien** in the north (185m) and **Ben Stack** in the south (122m). Practically all the houses, brightly painted and with a distinctly Scandinavian flavour, are in the north clustered round the anchorage at **Haun**. This is a shallow little bay, but it is the terminal for the vehicle ferry from South Uist and therefore the lifeline for the community. Besides the church there is a well-stocked village store, an active primary school (with thirty-two pupils in 1994), a post-office and, of course, the pub.

Off the southern tip lie the **Stack Islands** where the ruin of Weaver's Castle can be seen on **Eilean Leathan**, the largest of the group. The castle was the base for a notorious MacNeil pirate and wreck-plunderer. The other islets in the group **Eileanan Dubha** and **Eilean a' Gheòidh** are linked together by drying reefs.

ACCESS: Vehicle ferry daily except Sunday between Haun, Eriskay and Ludag, South Uist, 01878-700216.

Anchorages:
1. Acairseid Mhór. Well-sheltered. Follow sailing directions to avoid drying rocks at entrance. There are HIE visitor moorings or anchor S of the pier and nearer the S shore. W of pier is foul with old moorings.
2. Haun. Not recommended. Very shallow and difficult approach through rocks and sandbanks in Sound of Eriskay. There are light beacons marking the car ferry route to Haun from South Uist.

7.14 Eileanan Iasgaich

(G. – the fish, or fishing, islands)

OS Maps: 1:50000 Sheet 31 1:25000 Sheet 216
Admiralty Charts: 1:100000 No.1795 1:12500 No.2770

AREA: 50ha (124 acres)
HEIGHT: 23m (75 ft)

OWNER: South Uist Estates Ltd.

POPULATION: No census records and uninhabited.

GEOLOGY: Gneiss bedrock with scanty areas of soil.

WILDLIFE: The many pockets and cracks in the rocks provide a home for prawns and lobsters and shelter for fish.

EILEANAN IASGAICH is an ill-defined group of low-lying islands in Loch Boisdale linked by reefs and skerries at low water. The largest of the group is the most easterly and it rises to a central hummock which is just 21m high. Vegetation is sparse due to the lack of soil and the high salt content. There is a channel in the centre of the group which has a sufficiently narrow entrance to form a natural tidal fish trap and it is possibly this that gave the islands their name.

Loch Boisdale is generally shallow and studded with tidal islands and rocks. The most conspicuous islets, both of which are in the entrance to the loch, are **Calvay** and **Gasay**. Calvay has a ruined castle on it which guarded the entrance in medieval times and the ubiquitous Prince Charles Edward Stuart spent a night in hiding there. To the west of Eileanan Iasgaich are **Eilean nan Imireachean** (G. – island of the processions), tiny at high water but extensive when the tide is out, **Eilean Mór** (G.

– big island), and **Pabbay** to the north-west. These are all tidal islands. It is out-of-character for a Pabbay, or priest island, to be tidal as it would allow the hermit to interrupt his isolation and walk ashore to meet his friends whenever the tide went out. This was obviously the abode of an extrovert anchorite.

ACCESS: No regular access. Enquire at Lochboisdale. Landing can be difficult due to seaweed-covered reefs.

Anchorages:

1. Rubha Bhuailt. In channel N of Eileanan Iasgaich. Fish cages block much of the anchorage. Holding reported to be poor.

2. Rubha Arinangallan. Anchor 1c NW of the ruined pier on S shore of

Loch Boisdale. Beware drying rock and shoal patch NW of the pier and Hut Shoal N of the pier.

7.15 Stuley

(ON – Stula's island) The peak on South Uist overlooking Stuley is Stulaval (ON – Stula's hill).

OS Maps: 1:50000 Sheet 22 1:25000 Sheet 201
Admiralty Charts: 1:100000 No.1795

AREA: 45ha (111 acres)
HEIGHT: 40m (131 ft)

POPULATION: No census records and uninhabited.

GEOLOGY: Intermediate and basic Lewisian rock with a distinctly greenish colour.

STULEY is made up of three low grass-covered hills with the highest point (40m) near the centre. Both the island and its grazing sheep have a leisurely unassuming appearance.

We approached the island from the north-east and then rounded the coastline between Stuley and Broad Rocks to enter the Sound. According to both the chart and the Pilot there is a shoal area at the north end of the sound fairly close to **Creag an t-Sagairt** (G. – priest's rock) but we failed to find it. The echo-sounder gave a steady reading of 20m right up to the point where the sound narrows in width although the depth certainly decreases south of this point. The original soundings, of course, were by leadline and date back to 1852. It is not a bad little anchorage, given suitable conditions, and landing is easy on the green, slatelike, slabs of rock.

Although I have found no written record of permanent human habitation the green ridges of old lazybeds and a few scattered sheiling ruins show that Stuley was probably yet another place where people, who were considered of less importance than sheep, fought to survive. The cleft in the north is called **Sloc Duilich** (G. – awkward inlet) and the cliffs facing the Priest's Rock are – according to one old map – aptly named **Creag na h-Oraíde** (G. – sermon crag).

Glas-eilean Mór (G. – big green island), south-east of Stuley, is, as its name suggests, covered with a sward of bright green grass.

ACCESS: No regular access. Try a Lochboisdale boat-owner.

Anchorages:
1. Stuley Sound between South Uist and Stuley. According to the Admiralty Pilot 'small vessels pass through or use it as an anchorage.' It is about ¹/₂c wide at its narrowest and a submerged rock is charted about midway but the channel appears to be clean if a course nearer to Stuley is maintained.

7.16 Uist

[yoo-ist] (ON – west)

Benbecula

Possibly (G. beinn a' bhuachaille, N -øy – herdsman's hill island) or (G. beinn bheag a' bh-faodhla – little mountain of the fords).

Baleshare

(G. baile ear – east town)

Grimsay

(ON – Grim's island)

Vallay

(ON – hill island)

Kirkibost Island

(ON – church farm)

Oronsay

(G. – drying or tidal island)

OS Maps: 1:50000 Sheets 18, 22 and 31 1:25000 Sheets 125, 126, 135, 136, 151, 168, 185, 201, and 216
Admiralty Charts: 1:200000 No.2722 Complete E coast 1:100000 No.1795 Sd of Barra & Loch Boisdale 1:30000 No.2770 E coast, L

Skiport to L Eport 1:25000 No.2904 Lochs on E coast 1:15000 No.2825

AREA: 72,827ha (179,956 acres)
HEIGHT: 620m (2,034 ft)

OWNER: South Uist is almost entirely owned by South Uist Estates.

The MacDonalds of Clanranald held Benbecula until 1839 when it was bought by Colonel Gordon of Cluny whose family were the owners until 1942. Most of Benbecula is now owned jointly by South Uist Estates, the Scottish Office and the Ministry of Defence.

The greater part of North Uist (including Grimsay, Vallay, and Baleshare) is owned by the family of Lord Granville (cousin of the Queen), as the North Uist Estate Trust 1990. The Scottish Office also has some sizeable holdings.

POPULATION: Approximate pre-census totals: 1755 – 4118. 1794 – 6668. 1821 – 11009.

	1841	1881	1891	1931	1961	1971	1981	1991
N.Uist	3870	3398	3250	2349	1622	1469	1454	1404
Benbecula	2160	1638	1787	1006	1390	1372	2009	1771
S.Uist	5093	3831	3708	2810	2376	2281	2223	2138
Baleshare	157	266	318	136	59	64	66	55
Grimsay	269	292	281	259	239	193	206	215
Vallay	59	29	34	19	0	0	0	0
Kirkibost	25	12	6	6	0	0	0	0
Oronsay	102	0	0	0	0	0	0	0
	11735	9466	9384	6585	5686	5379	5958	5583

GEOLOGY: North Uist, Benbecula and the northern half of South Uist is a 2.5 million years-old gneiss but the southern half of South Uist is younger gneiss – about 1.5 million years-old. During the last Ice Ages there were minor glaciers on Hecla (whose rocks are mildly magnetic) and Beinn Mhór in South Uist and on Eavel in North Uist with the result that the rocks in the bealachs (mountain passes) are ice worn but the summits are not. There was never a heavy all-enveloping ice-sheet as on the mainland. The 'long island' was in fact one long island at this time and it was only in the post-glacial era that the islands sank and the sea lochs broke through. Ancient peat and forests can be found below mean sea-level at Borve on Benbecula, and at Loch Eynort, Lochboisdale and on the west coast of South Uist.

HISTORY: In 1098 King Magnus III of Norway pillaged the Hebrides, 'gained much gold', and set the Uists on fire.
South Uist, which was ruled by the Clanranald chiefs after the Norse occupation, has many associations with Bonnie Prince Charlie. The Prince landed in Corodale Bay, directly beneath Beinn Mhór, on 14th May 1746 and hid in a forester's hut. From Prince's Cave he watched the navy patrolling the Minch in the search for him. Neil

MacEachain MacDonald who was helping him, introduced him to the twenty-three-year-old Flora MacDonald who had arrived from Skye on a visit to her brother, and it was he who suggested that when Flora returned to Skye she should take the Prince with her disguised as her servant girl. The island at the mouth of Loch Boisdale, Calvay, has the ruins of a 13th century castle on it where the Prince took refuge on 15th June 1746.

During the clearances which followed the purchase of South Uist and **Benbecula** by Colonel Gordon of Cluny in 1838 some crofters were chased into the hills by the police. More than 1000 destitute islanders were shipped from Lochboisdale to America on *The Admiral*.

After the Norse occupation the MacRuairidhs ruled **North Uist** but in 1495 the MacDonalds of Sleat were given official title by James IV.

About 1850 Lord Macdonald of Sleat brought police to the island and ruthlessly evicted many families, the minister of the local church having conveniently disappeared before the event. Although there were bloody fights and cottages were burned at Sollas it was a pointless exercise as only five years later Macdonald sold the island to Sir John Powlett Ord.

WILDLIFE: White and yellow water-lilies dapple the surface of the many fresh-water lochs. These are now scarce on the mainland due to disturbance and plundering by plant collectors. The small islands in these lochs have dense thickets of the native willow, aspen, birch, rowan growing on them because they are beyond the reach of hungry sheep. Originally these trees were the elements of widespread island afforestation. A patch still clings to a heathery rock-wall on Beinn Mhór, and a few other sheltered corries in the hills north of Loch Eynort. Here too are several varieties of fern, including the royal fern, *osmunda regalis*, and many alpine species.

SHORT-LIVED ORMICLATE CASTLE

But for sheer profusion and floral display nothing can compare with the machair in the spring and summer months.

Mute swans are sometimes seen on South Uist's shallow Loch Bee. The Uists have the highest density of breeding waders in Britain and many rare bird species. Some of the more interesting ones to be seen throughout the year are: corn bunting, reed bunting, twite, raven, wheatear, stonechat, black-headed and common gulls, black guillemot, rock dove, short-eared owl, rock pipit, greenshank, redshank, snipe, golden plover, hen harrier, buzzard, golden eagle, merlin, peregrine, red grouse, red-breasted merganser, eider, shoveller, teal, gadwall, little grebe and heron. Red-necked phalarope arrive mid-May. Also pink-footed goose, pintail, knot and bar-tailed godwit. In summer quail, knot, sanderling and ruff. Later, little stint, curlew sandpiper, dunlin and whimbrel. In winter, turnstone, purple sandpiper, scaup, water rail, jack snipe and woodcock, and many more.

The Loch Druidibeg National Nature Reserve on South Uist, lying astride the main road, is the most important breeding ground of the native British greylag goose; and the Balranald RSPB Nature Reserve in North Uist is an equally outstanding site.

Corncrakes, which can be heard from mid-April, benefit from this being an Environmentally Sensitive Area (ESA), allowing crofters to be paid for managing their land in ways which benefit corncrakes and conservation, even though the farming methods may be less efficient.

The coastline has many favourite havens for both the grey and common seal.

SOUTH UIST has a spine of mountains along its eastern side the highest being **Beinn Mhór** at 620m (2034ft).

Hecla is also conspicuous at 606m. The spine is broken by three sea lochs, Boisdale, Eynort, and Sheilavaig; and a fourth, Skiport, which slices right through the island by joining up with Loch Bee on the west coastal plain. The Atlantic coast, which is the populated side, is virtually a continuous stretch of white shell sand backed by dunes and flower-filled machair. Between the machair and the barren and mountainous east coast is a maze of lochans interspersed with peat moorland and deserted black houses. These lochs are well-stocked with trout but angling is strictly controlled.

South Uist is predominantly Catholic. **Lochboisdale** with a population of about 300 is the ferry port, and the only village on the east coast.

A chambered cairn, 26m diameter and 6m high, can be found about 2½km north-west of Lochboisdale and due west near **Kilpheder** on the west coast there is a wheelhouse dating from about 200AD which was excavated in 1952 [NF734203]. It has a circular plan with the hearth at the hub and stone piers at the rim supporting wooden rafters as spokes. It was probably a farmhouse. South of here at Garrynamonie School from 1890 to 1913 there was a headmaster, Frederick Rae, who would never allow Gaelic, the native tongue of the islanders, to be spoken in his school. Sadly, this practice was widespread at the time.

About 5½km north of Daliburgh and just north of **Milton** is the birthplace of Flora MacDonald. It was here, to the family home [NF741269], that she came to visit her brother when her chance meeting with the Young Pretender put her name in the history books. The house is now a ruin. In nearby **Loch Kildonnan** a Norse church and island settlement similar to that at Loch Finlaggan (see No.2.4) were recently investigated. A further 5½km brings one to the ruins of **Ormiclate Castle** built in 1701-8 by a French architect and burnt down in 1715 during a boisterous Jacobite party. It was the short-lived residence of the Clanranald Chiefs [NF740318].

Off the south shore of Loch Druidibeg and about 1½ km from the road is an islet with rectangular **Dùn Roauill** on it [NF778371]. This is perhaps the best dun on South Uist. **Caisteal Bheagram**, the ruin of a small 15th or 16th century tower, is on the other side of the road on an islet in Loch an Eilean [NF761371].

A road crosses from the **Loch Druidibeg Nature Reserve**, a waterfowl paradise, to Loch Skiport's decayed pier which was built for steamers in 1879 [NF829387]. South of the Usinish peninsula on the east coast is **Nicolson's Leap**. The story goes that Nicolson was found in bed with the wife of the Clanranald Chief. As he escaped he snatched the Chief's baby son as hostage and to escape the clansmen he leapt the 15m chasm on to the rock stack [NF864332]. From there he tried to bargain with his pursuers but ultimately jumped to his death into the sea below with the boy in his arms.

The Royal Artillery Missile Range which was built in 1961 is in the north-west corner of South Uist. The range is sandwiched between the main road and the Atlantic, and its missiles are tracked from Hirta (St Kilda.No 9.1) which is more than forty miles to the north-west. On the Hill of Miracles, Rueval, just east of the road, stands the great granite statue of **Our Lady of the Isles** sculpted by Hew Lorimer in 1957 [NF776408] and above the statue is 'space city' – the range control installation.

Just south of the causeway across Loch Bee there is a small loch to the west of the road with clear traces of a large dun – **Dùn Mór** [NF775415]. Loch Bee itself, a west coast loch, is like a Panama Canal cutting right through South Uist because it has a long arm with a flood gate which connects with an arm of Loch Skiport, an east coast sea-loch. Loch Skiport has a number of fascinating channels and anchorages. By **Shillay More** and **Shillay Beag** there are two popular pools, joined by a shallow but navigable channel, known as Wizard Pool and Little Kettle Pool. **Ornish Island** marks the entrance to Loch Skiport with **Luirsay Dubh** and **Luirsay Glas** on the north headland.

South Uist provides some excellent hill-walking and climbing. Ben Tarbert, Hecla, Feaveallach, Beinn Mhor, Ben na Hoe, Sheeval, Arnaval, Stulaval, Triuirebheinn, Roneval and some of the lesser peaks are all recommended. On the south wall of Coire Hellisdale by Beinn Mhór are 260m high cliffs with deep gullies.

BENBECULA, is the stepping stone between the Uists, not only physically but because it is here that the predominant religion changes from the Catholic south to the Protestant north. The island is mainly low and flat but has an almost-central solitary hill of 124m, also called **Rueval** like the adjacent peak on South Uist. There is a magnificent view from the top. The causeway which crosses the sands of South Ford and links South Uist to Benbecula was built in 1983. It replaces a wartime bridge built in 1943 to serve the airfield.

In 1896 a pier was built at **Peter's Port** [NF849457] in the narrows between Benbecula and the island of Wiay

(No 7.17). This was a typical Governmental folly as there was no road access and a hazardous approach by sea. A road and causeway were eventually built but the pier has never been of much practical use.

Beside the west coast road is the remnant of **Borve Castle** [NF773506]. The castle was a Clan Ranald stronghold which was burnt to the ground by clansmen who supported the king's stand against the Jacobites. Opposite it is the ruin of **Teampull Bhuirgh** [NF769503].

South-west of the airport is the island's main village, **Balivanich** with the army base built in 1970 to house the men servicing the rocket range on South Uist. This is a transient population but it is a great help to the economy of the island. Just south are the ruins of 14th century **Nunton Chapel** – a nunnery which was wrecked during the Reformation and the nuns massacred [NF766537]. It was from Lady Clanranald at Nunton House that Bonnie Prince Charlie obtained the clothing with which he disguised himself as Betty Burke, maidservant to Flora MacDonald. Nunton House was built by the MacDonald chieftains after Ormiclate Castle on South Uist was burned down but it has had alterations since.

The east coast has many small coves and rocky islands and it was in April 1746 that the Prince's party landed on the peninsula of Rossinish where they took shelter in an empty boat. It was also from here that he sailed 'over the sea to Skye' with Flora MacDonald.

North Ford causeway over **Oitir Mór** (G. – the big shoal) was opened in 1960. The strand can be crossed on foot in fine weather when the tide is out but the crossing can be dangerous.

NORTH UIST is low-lying and so sprinkled with lochs that half the total area is under water. The lochs teem with trout and salmon (this is one of the earliest salmon runs in Scotland). Loch Scadavay alone has an area of 8 sq.km. and a shore line of 83km. The highest hill is **Eaval** (347m) but hills are few and far between and the Atlantic winds blow over the island virtually unchecked. The Rev. Cruttwell wrote in 1798 – 'In the warm season of the year, no country in the highlands can exhibit a more delightful prospect but in bad weather when the wind blows the sea swells to a prodigious height and rolls with inexpressible violence against the shores, exhibiting a prospect awfully grand beyond description.'

Most of the crofts in North Uist are large enough to be economically viable.

In the south-east the drying island of **GRIMSAY** is linked to North Uist and Benbecula by a causeway which was completed in 1960. This is the centre for North Uist's fishing industry (mainly lobster) and there is an active processing plant. **Baymore** is an attractive spot for artists.

After crossing Oitir Mhór the road cuts straight through the middle of a stone circle with a chambered

WIZARD POOL – LOCH SKIPORT

cairn to be seen to the north-east [NF837603]. Just beyond in the hamlet of Carinish is the Ditch of Blood – where a battle between the MacLeods of Harris and the MacDonalds of Uist took place in 1601. Nearby is a curious ruin, **Teampull na Trionaid** (G. – Trinity Temple) with twin churches founded by Somerled's daughter, Beathag, in about 1200 on an earlier Celtic site [NF816603]. The churches were later rebuilt with a unique vaulted roof and fine carved stonework by Robert II's daughter, the wife of John, first Lord of the Isles. This is said to have been a seat of learning similar to Iona which was attended by Duns Scotus and is one of the most important archaeological sites in the Western Isles. Incidentally, because Duns Scotus (*c.* 1265-1308), who became a renowned teacher at the universities of Oxford, Paris, and Cologne, argued that religion depended on faith and not on reason, he was unpopular with the establishment. (Thereafter anyone with similarly 'stupid' views was labelled 'dunce'.)

The main road circles the island. At Ben Langass there is a chambered cairn, **Barpa Langass** (NF837657), 5½m high and 22m wide which is entered through a tunnel. After crossing a desolate central stretch of loch-strewn moorland the road then reaches **Lochmaddy**, the main ferry terminal and administrative centre for North Uist. Here there is a court house and jail, a cottage hospital, a bank, a garage and a comfortable hotel which particularly caters for the needs of anglers and sailors. Loch Maddy or **Loch nam Madadh** (G. – loch of the dogs) is named after

the two dog-shaped rocks, **Madadh Beag** and **Madadh Mór,** standing guard on each side of the entrance to the loch with a further one to the south called **Madadh Gruamach** (G. – the surly dog). In the 16th century this was a favourite pirate rendez-vous but a century later it was hosting a fleet of 400 fishing vessels and by the 18th century the port was frequented by many ships trading from Ireland, the west coasts of the English and Scottish mainlands, and as far afield as the Baltic. Sponish is the site of one of the local industries, a factory to process seaweed for alginates.

Loch Maddy is full of islands, many tidal or little more than skerries. It is worth mentioning **Glas Eilean Mór, Faihore**, **Ruigh Liath**, **An Glais-eilean Meadhonach, Hamersay**, **Flodday**, **Ferramas**, **Cliasay More** and **Beg**, and **Keallasay More** and **Beg**.

Northwest of Lochmaddy the road skirts the hill of **Blashaval**. On its western slope are three standing stones called Na Fir Bhreige (G. – the false men) [NF887717]. They are reputed to mark the graves of three traitors who were buried alive although another story claims that they are three men from Skye who were turned to stone for having deserted their wives.

Near here a minor road wanders eastwards through the broken land to the north of Loch Maddy. It passes through **Lochportain** with its small fishing pier and ends up at Cheese Bay in the furthest north-east corner.

After the main road has skirted Crogary Beag hill a secondary road runs north by **Newtonferry** to the jetty for a small car ferry to the island of Berneray (No.8.1) and a passenger ferry to Leverburgh (An t-Obbe) on Harris (No.8.15). The latter ferry route passes close to **Torogay**, a large islet with extensive reefs which shelter the ferry jetty in **Loch nam Ban**. Near Newtonferry is a lochan with a causeway to the remains of a broch last occupied in 1602 by Hugh MacDonald of Sleat [NF897777]. There is also a white house where W. S. Morrison, later Lord Dunrossil, was brought up. He was a Speaker in the House of Commons who became Governor General of Australia. A scramble up **Beinn Mhór** (190m) is rewarded by a superb view of the Sound of Harris and the fragmented landscape.

The main road crosses Loch nan Geireann where, on **Eilean-an-Tighe**, are the remains of the earliest neolithic potter's workshop yet found in Western Europe. The drying island of **ORONSAY** lies to the north in Vallaquie Strand – uninhabited since the Clearances – and further west the road passes **Sollas**, forever remembered as the centre of one of the most inhumane Clearances. The culprit was Lord MacDonald of Sleat.

Evidence of a Norse settlement has been found on the low sandy peninsula to the north of here.

The road now skirts Vallay Strand. **VALLAY**, another drying island, is like a long breakwater so that the Strand is virtually an enclosed sea-loch when the tide is in. When it is out a track fords the huge expanse of sand and stone to reach Vallay House which was built on the island by Erskine Beveridge, owner of linen mills in Fife. He wrote an authoritative book on the archaeology of the area. Vallay is crowded with antiquities – duns, standing stones, and chapel ruins. The house is now occupied by the family of Lord Granville who is the benign landlord for much of North Uist and has undertaken valuable experiments in land improvement on Vallay.

Loch Olabhat is near the road. Its tiny island, **Eilean Domhnuill**, is a crannog built nearly 5000 years ago – predating Ireland's earliest-known crannogs by 2000

ILL-FATED NUNTON CHAPEL

years [NF747753].

A 9m high natural rock arch is at **Griminish Point** at the north-west corner of North Uist. **Sloc Roe** (G. – the pit passage) is a cave with an entrance from both sides of the point and two holes opening to the surface. During gales, the water spouts through these to such a height that it can be seen from ten miles away at sea [NF727765].

Turning south through **Balmartin**, Loch Hosta is said to cover a drowned village, and across the road in the cliffs of Tigharry (G. – house on the rock) is another spouting cave, the Kettle Spout. A track leads east up South Clettraval where there are two chambered cairns and an impressive view of the loch-strewn landscape [NF749714]. The RSPB's **Balranald Nature Reserve** juts into the Atlantic at the next headland and includes the tiny off-shore islet of **Causamul**. An even smaller islet, **Deasker** (G. – south skerry), lies nearly three miles south. The churchyard of **Hougharry** holds the graves of many of the island's 'nobility' [NF708706].

Off the wide white sand beaches lie the drying islands of **KIRKIBOST** and **BALESHARE**. Kirkibost Island is now uninhabited whereas Baleshare (G. – east town), the first Hebridean island to gather kelp, has a small but thriving population. Baleshare's sister island, Baile-iar (G. – west town) – was swept away in a tidal wave in the 16th century (see Monach Islands No.7.20).

North of the road at this point a prominent hill stands alone among the moorland lochans. A 2½km cross-country trek leads to **Unival** chambered cairn or barrow – a large New Stone Age tomb [NF801669] – near a 3m high standing stone on the barren hillside.

There are many interesting walks among the hundreds of lochs, and some of the best fishing in the Western Isles, but always take a good map and a compass.

ACCESS: Bus services cover most of the island including Benbecula airport; Lochmaddy, 01876-503330; west of N Uist, 01876-505247; Lochboisdale and Ludag, 01878-700278. Hotel and bed & breakfast accommodation available, Outer Hebrides Tourist Board, 01851-703088 (Lochboisdale 01878-700286, Lochmaddy 01876-500321).

South Uist: Car-ferry, Oban to Lochboisdale, 01631-66688, and Castlebay-Barra to Lochboisdale, 01878-700288. Private passenger ferry from Eoligarry, Barra to Ludag, 01878-700216. Benbecula airport: British Airways from Glasgow, and Lewis-Benbecula-Barra, 0345 222111.

North Uist: Car-ferry, Uig-Skye to Lochmaddy, 01470-542219; and Tarbert-Harris to Lochmaddy, 01859-502444. Car-ferry from Newtonferry to Leverburgh, Harris, 01876-70230.

Anchorages:

1. South Loch Boisdale. Anchor 1c WNW of ruined pier. Beware dry-

ing rock and shoal patch NW of the pier and Hut Shoal N of pier. Alternatively, anchor E of the ruined pier, SE of the fish cages.

2. *South Loch Boisdale*. Anchor close SW of Gasay. Poor in W'lies or SW'lies.

3. *Loch Boisdale*, in channel W of Ru Bhuailt. Fish cages block much of anchorage and holding reported poor.

4. *Lochboisdale*. Visitors' moorings, or anchor in Bàgh Dubh SW of pier. Many moorings, very restricted, poor holding, soft mud. Swell in SE gales.

5. *Stuley Sound*, about ¹/₂c wide. Submerged rock is charted about midway, position uncertain.

6. *Cearcdal Bay, Loch Eynort*, SW corner of outer loch, NW of Eilean Eallan, sand. Clean and easy access but exposed E and SE swell. Or, occasional anchorage N side of loch due N of Eilean Eallan in 10m, mud. Holding good but open SE.

7. *Poll Craigavaig, Loch Eynort*, W of first narrows. Entrance difficult and subject to tides. Restricted by fish cages.

8. *Upper Loch Eynort*. Plenty of room for anchorage clear of rocks and fish cages, 2-10m, mud. Dramatic scenery, good shelter but seldom visited due to difficult entrance.

9. *Mol a Tuath*, bay on NW side of Usinish promontory, temporary anchorage with moderately good holding.

10. *Loch Skiport*, enter N of Ornish Island. Anchor S of Shillay Beag in Wizard Pool – squally in S'lies; or, in Caolas Mór (Little Kettle Pool); or Bagh Charmaig – not so good; or Poll na Cairidh – excellent shelter in S'lies; or Linne Arm – holding poor.

11. *Caolas Luirsay* just N of Loch Skiport entrance. Narrow, shallow, entrance behind Luirsay Dubh. Affected by swell in N'lies. Anchor in settled weather in 7-11m, mud.

12. *Loch Sheilavaig*, N of Loch Skiport. Fish farms and featureless but rocky challenge. Anchor SW of Canmore Island, 4m, rock. Inner loch obstructed by fish nets.

13. *Loch Carnan*, approach S of Steisay and along marked channel. Jetty for Uist power station and oil terminal is 55m long with 2.5m depth. HIE visitors' moorings, or anchor clear of fairway and moorings NW of quay, or 3c further NW beyond Direy. Beware rocks and shoals.

14. *Peter's Port*, 3¹/₄c W of SW extremity of Wiay, approach round N side of Lingay. Slipway at SE extremity of Eilean na Cille has depth 2.4m, rocky bottom. Alongside it and only 15m away is a parallel reef. If anchoring, keep clear of approach to slip.

15. *Loch a' Laip*. Enter between Wiay and Bo Carrach keeping ¹/₂c off Wiay until Bàgh a Bhràoige opens, then cross to N side and follow right through into NW arm beyond Keiravagh Islands. Anchor N or S of 0.6m drying rock. Good shelter.

16. *Loch Keiravagh*. Enter with caution and anchor anywhere suitable.

17. *Loch Meanervagh*. Approach with caution. Very restricted but possible anchorage for small craft.

18. *Loch Uskavagh*, between Maaey Riabhach and Greanamul. Intricate navigation required but well-sheltered anchorage. Anchor anywhere suitable. Neavag Bay is very soft mud. Scarilode Bay has many rocks.

19. *Caolas Wiay Beag*, W of Maragay Mór and Beag. Can be entered with caution. Anchor N of Ballagary.

20. *St Michael's Point*, opposite Sugar Bay on W side of Ronay. Anchor 1¹/₂c W to NW of Ru na Monach in 4-7m, sand. In summer there is seldom any swell. Or, 2c NNW of Ru na Monach and ³/₄c from W side of Ronay. Or small craft can anchor in bay surrounded by drying reefs N of

islet N of St Michael's Point. Pass 20m NE of islet.

21. *Kallin Harbour*, 2.5m depth inside but 1.7m at entrance, very restricted temporary space. Approach with care by Vallastrome W of Garbh Eilean Mór. Anchorage difficult as fairway narrow, rocks at the sides and strong tide. There is one HIE visitor's mooring.

22. *Acairseid Fhalaich* in Flodday sound between Ronay and Floddaymore. Tight entrance to restricted anchorage. Metric chart of rocks considered incorrect (see Martin Lawrence's Pilot).

23. *Upper Flodday Sound*. Beware mid-channel rocks SE of Haunaray if near LW. Anchor in pool SE of E end of Haunaray, or W of Floddaybeg, or in E side of Poll nan Gall.

24. *Moireag Bay or Harbour*. Concealed and awkward entrance about 3c N of Floddaybeg, but good, interesting anchorage. Follow directions carefully. (CCC List of Additional Anchorages).

25. *Loch Eport*. Follow sailing directions carefully for entrance to loch then possible anchorage E shore of Acairseid Lee or either side of Deer Island. Holding poor due to weed and soft mud, and subject to squalls. Better anchorage in Bàgh a' Bhiorain but narrow entrance to bay between reefs. Other anchorages can be found from Chart 2825 or anchor at head of loch (tricky approach) E of pier, 2m, mud, or N of Eilean a Cairidh, 4m, mud.

26. *Loch Maddy, Bàgh Aird nam Madadh (Ardmaddy Bay)*, on S shore 6c WSW of Rubha nam Pleac, anchor off S shore. Fish cages, holding poor and squally in S'lies.

27. *Loch Maddy, Ferry Terminal*. HIE visitors' moorings or anchor SW of pier and well clear of ferry approach. There is a narrow slot, 2m depth, on N side of the pier which can be useful in emergencies.

28. *Loch Maddy, south basin or Vallaquie*, in SW corner of Loch. Anchor between old mooring buoy and wreck but beware reef and squalls can be heavy. Fish cages.

29. *Loch Maddy, Charles Harbour*, NW of Hamersay, space confined, rocks, fish cages, and bottom soft mud or rock. Best NE of Eilean Fear Vallay or, if any space, in small pool by Oronsay.

30. *Loch Maddy, Sponish Harbour*, cleaner than Charles Harbour but poor holding. Enter between Flodday and Little Glas.

31. *Loch Portain (Partan)*, off Loch Maddy. Well-sheltered but holding uncertain in soft mud. All sides shoal. Careful approach required. Anchor where suitable but not more than 2c beyond pier.

32. *Bàgh Chaise (Cheese Bay)*, W of Groatay. Best holding and shelter in the area but care necessary. Anchor SW of central islet.

33. *The Caddy*, W of Orasay. Approach S of Righe nam Ban and beware Strome Rock. Anchor off concrete slip, WNW of Orasay.

34. *Lingay*, in large bay between Sound of Berneray and Caolas a' Mhòrain. Anchor close off the island's SW side in 5.5m, sand. Open to NW but very little swell. Note that Lingay strand connects E side of Lingay to the shore.

35. *Vallay*, a drying island midway between Griminish point and Aird a' Mhòrain. Anchorage in Vallay Sound is rock encumbered and difficult to enter. Depth inside 1.8m, sand, and protected from swell. Anchorage S of E side of Vallay has a bar to cross (0.6m depth at LW). Pool inside is 1.5-2.7m deep and sheltered from swell. Avoid shoals ³/₄c S of Vallay.

36. *West coast of N Uist, Benbecula and S Uist* has no shelter or safe landing places. Nor are there any sheltered anchorages on the S coast of S Uist.

37. *Hartavagh*, an inlet on W side of Meall an Iasgaich, WSW of Loch Boisdale. This is a muddy creek but offers temporary shelter in suitable conditions. Dangerous in NE gales.

7.17 Wiay

(G. bhuidhe – yellow or pleasant, ON -øy – island). Sometimes written in the past as 'Vuiay', or 'Buia' (Martin Martin).

OS Maps: 1:50000 Sheet 22 1:25000 Sheet 168
Admiralty Charts: 1:100000 No.1795 or 1:25000 No.2904

AREA: 375ha (927 acres)
HEIGHT: 102m (335 ft)

POPULATION: 1861 – 6. 1881 – 5. 1891 – 10 (2 houses). 1901 – 4. Since then, uninhabited.

GEOLOGY: Lewisian gneiss, similar to the west side of Benbecula.

WILDLIFE: Wiay is a bird sanctuary and home to a number of species of raptors together with a good selection of marsh and shoreline species.

WIAY is the largest of the many rocky islands lying to the east of Benbecula. Although it lies closer to South Uist it belongs to the Parish of North Uist.

The rounded summit of **Beinn a' Tuath** (G. – north peak) near the centre of the island is the highest point at 102m with **Beinn a' Deas** (G. – south peak) considerably lower at 56m. The island is thickly covered with heather and pasturage on fairly gentle slopes and has only a few rocky outcrops but quite a number of lochans. The largest of these is **Loch na Béiste** (G. – loch of the beast) which was once believed to shelter a monster. It has three small islands in it, one of which may be a crannog. North-west of the loch, in the valley between the two hills and over-looking Sruth a' Chomhraig are the remains of a small settlement. Although this is a relatively large island it never appears to have been densely populated.

In the south, **Meall an t-Sruith** (G. – the hillock by the tidal channel) shelters a shallow rock-strewn bay, **Bàgh na Haun** (ON *havn* – harbour) with a narrow channel through which the tides rush. The islets, **Lingay** and **Steisay** are to the south-west.

The north of Wiay is bounded by rocky Loch a' Laip (G. – spoon-shaped loch) with the tidal **Keiravagh Islands** to the north. The entrance to the loch is guarded by Rubha Cam nan Gall (G. – crooked headland of the strangers). On our first entrance into this loch, creeping tentatively between the reefs and islets we were hit by a violent squall which flattened the water and covered the rocks with spume. **Bàgh na Creige** was too restricted for shelter and **Bàgh a' Bhràoige** cluttered with fish cages. The squall was so strong that we left on a reciprocal course but, needless to say, as soon as we reached the open sea the wind dropped, the rain stopped and the sun appeared.

The western half of Wiay is puddled with lochans in the wide stretch between two small hills with **Lochan nan Lachan** (G. – little loch of the reeds) the most central.

Peter's Port on **Eilean na Cille** [NF849457] to the west of Wiay was completed in 1896 at a cost of £2000 in response to a demand for a new Hebridean port. Parliament wanted to be helpful, and the County Council gave assistance, but the result was a typical bureaucratic blunder. Not only was access by sea difficult but there was not even any access by land. Nevertheless the pier was built and extra expenditure of another £100 approved for the removal of a large rock which blocked access to the end of the pier. Although the sea approach was still considered hazardous, without a road the pier was, in any case, unusable.

At last a further grant of £1800 was obtained to construct a road which, if nothing else, helped communication between the local crofts. The 1931 edition of the *West Coast Pilot* dryly remarked '. . .the approach is so difficult, and there is so little room to turn, that it is not used by the local steamers. The port should not be entered without local knowledge. . .'

ACCESS: No regular access. Enquire at Loch Carnan, South Uist or Peter Port, Benbecula.

Anchorages:

1. Bàgh a' Bhràoige, Loch a' Laip. Enter Loch between Wiay and Bo Carrach keeping ¹/₂c off Wiay until Bàgh a' Bhràoige opens. Formerly best

anchorage SW of drying rock, now probably no room due to fish cages.

2. Bàgh na Creige, Loch a' Laip. Cross over to N side of Loch when Bàgh a' Bhràoige opens, then SW course for Bàgh ne Creige. Just enough room at bay entrance for smaller craft.

3. Loch a' Laip. Best anchorage is in far NW corner, N or S of 0.6m drying rock. Good shelter but ¹/₂M distance from Wiay.

4. Sruth a' Chomhraig, W side of Wiay, approached from S. Not now suitable as fish cages obstruct W side and too many rocks on E side.

5. Peter's Port approach. Beware drying rocks SSW of Wiay. Approach round N side of Lingay and anchor in 4m, sand on rock, leaving clear approach to slipway. Awkward anchorage, about 4c from Wiay.

6. It may be possible to find a temporary anchorage in suitable conditions W of Cleit Charmaig in 6-8m but the bottom is mainly rock.

7.18 Ronay

(ON hraun-øy – rough island) or, (G. ròn, N -øy – seal island)

OS Maps: 1:50000 Sheet 22 1:25000 Sheet 151
Admiralty Charts: 1:100000 No.1795 1:25000 No.2904

AREA: 563ha (1,391 acres)
HEIGHT: 115m (377 ft)

OWNER: North Uist Estate Trust 1990 (Lord Granville and family).

POPULATION: 1826 – 180 (Gaelic School Society *Moral Statistics Report*). Cleared in 1831, many settling on the neighbouring tidal island of Grimsay. 1841 – 9. 1861 – 4. 1881 – 6. 1891 – 6. 1931 – 6. Uninhabited since then.

GEOLOGY: Lewisian gneiss with some flinty crush and a peaty soil.

HISTORY: Ronay appears to have had a number of religious associations in its past. It has a priest's hill, a monk's headland, a Druid's hill, and it had a chapel according to Martin Martin. Archaeological investigation may prove interesting.

WILDLIFE: One of the few islands in the area which is home to the Atlantic grey seal – protected by a special Act of Parliament in 1921.

RONAY is a fairly large rugged island with an extremely indented coastline. It has a series of hills which are bare to the north but heather clad to the south. The northern peninsula, Ronaybeg, is joined to the rest of the island by an isthmus and encloses a large and very shallow bay in the north-west called **Bàgh nan Uamh** (G. – bay of the caves). South of this bay are the two highest hills, Beinn an t-Sagairt (G. – the priest's hill) at 104m and **Beinn a' Charnain** (G. – the cairn hill) at 115m.

Ronay is divided from North Uist by a channel on the west side which is an impenetrable morass of rocks and reefs although the island could be circumnavigated by an inflatable dinghy in suitable weather and at the right state of the tide (distance almost nine miles). **Garbh Eilean Mór** (G. – big rough island) is in the middle of the channel with **Eilean a' Ghobha** (G. – island of the dipper) to the north.

Martin Martin noted that there was 'a little Chappel in the Island Rona, called the Low-landers Chappel, because Seamen who dye in time of Fishing, are buried in that place.' This apparently refers to a pre-Reformation chapel. Fishermen from Ronay may have been buried at St

Michael's Chapel on Grimsay [NF882548]. The ruins are clearly visible only just across the water from **Ru na Monach** (G. – headland of the monks), Ronay's south-western tip, and Martin may have confused the geography. On the other hand there is a small rocky knoll near the west side of Ronay known as Cnoc nan Gall which can be translated as (G. – knoll of the Lowlanders) so maybe there was a 'Lowlander's chapel' actually on Ronay.

The hill in the centre of Ronay is called **Beinn nan Druidhneach** [drooi-niach] (G. – hill of the sorcerers). There was a Gaelic tendency to attribute anything an-

Floddaymore

cient, like a Neolithic ruin for instance, to Druids or sorcerers but the hill may well have been the site of pagan rites.

ACCESS: No regular access. Enquire at Lochmaddy or at Kallin on Grimsay.

Anchorages:

1. Off St Michael's Point, on W side of Ronay. Anchor 1¹/₂c W to NW of Ru na Monach in 4-7m, sand. In summer there is seldom any swell. Or, 2c NNW of Ru na Monach and ³/₄c from W side of Ronay.

2. Acairseid Fhalaich in Flodday Sound. Very tight entrance between two islets to restricted but snug anchorage. Metric chart of rocks may be incorrect (see Martin Lawrence's Pilot) as channel depth may be 4m.

3. Haunaray. Restricted temporary anchorage between Haunaray and Rubh' an Tairbh. Bottom mud but depth increases rapidly when clear of drying rocks.

7.19 Floddaymore

(ON floti, G. mór – big raft)

OS Maps: 1:50000 Sheet 22 1:25000 Sheet 151
Admiralty Charts: 1:100000 No.1795 1:25000 No.2904

AREA: 58ha (143 acres)
HEIGHT: 28m (92 ft)

OWNER: North Uist Estate Trust 1990 (Lord Granville and family).

POPULATION: No census records and uninhabited.

GEOLOGY: A low-lying slab of Lewisian gneiss.

WILDLIFE: Barnacle and greylag geese stop off here in winter.

FLODDAYMORE or Flodday Mór lies close off the north-east side of Ronay. **Floddaybeg** or Flodday Beag lies to the north of it.

It is a low and fairly barren island but it is not short of fresh water as it contains one large central loch with its own islets and two other lochans connected to a stream in the south. The eastern headland, which is almost discon-nected, is called **Rubha nan Caorach** (G. – the headland of the sheep or cattle). This may still be a landing-place for stock. In the north continuous skerries join up a number of small islets and only a very narrow channel separates Floddaybeg.

All these small islands such as Floddaymore offer rather poor quality grazing but they are popular with sheep farmers and crofters because no fencing is required. This largely compensates for the fewer sheep per acre and the difficulty of access.

To the north-west the definitive hump of **Haunaray** di-vides the channel between Floddaymore and Ronay at a deep pool. Among the shallows beyond here is **Eilean nan Gearr** (G. – isle of the hares).

Our landing on Floddaymore was abrupt. *Jandara* was temporarily anchored south of Haunaray and near the Ronay shore. Two of us had no sooner cast off the dinghy than the outboard cut out. The gusty west wind immedi-ately caught us and as we blew clear of Ronay's shelter we were thrown across the channel with almost hurricane force. Oars were useless and in a different situation there could have been nasty consequences. As it was we came to a comfortable stop at our intended destination cush-ioned on a heap of Floddaymore kelp.

ACCESS: No regular access. Enquire at Kallin on Grimsay.

Anchorages:
1. Acairseid Fhalaich in Flodday sound. Very tight entrance channel be-tween two islets to a restricted but snug anchorage. Metric chart of rocks may be incorrect (see Martin Lawrence's Pilot) as channel depth may be 4m.
2. Haunaray. Restricted temporary anchorage between Haunaray and Ronay, N of Rubh' an Tairbh (G. – bull point). Bottom mud but depth in-creases rapidly when clear of drying rocks.
3. Upper Flodday Sound. Beware mid-channel rocks SE of Haunaray if near LW. Anchor in pool SE of E end of Haunaray (off N point of Floddaymore), or W of Floddaybeg.

7.20 Monach Islands

(G. and E. – monk islands) Also known as Heisker.

Ceann Ear

[er] (G. – east head)

Ceann Iar

[eeur] (G. – west head)

OS Maps: 1:50000 Sheet 22 1:25000 sheet 135
Admiralty Charts: 1:200000 No.2722

AREA: 357ha (883 acres)
HEIGHT: 19m (62 ft)

OWNER: North Uist Estate Trust 1990 (formerly the fam-ily of Lord Granville). Grazing leased to Mr Norman MacAulay of Tigharry, North Uist.

POPULATION: In 1595 the islands were said to be able to raise twenty men of military age suggesting a population of about one hundred. 1764 – 70. In 1810 the population left because of the failure of the soil due to overgrazing which had exposed large areas of sand. Before the ground could recover there was a great storm which tore up the remaining turf and covered the islands with sand. By 1841, 39 people had returned (4 houses). Later, marram grass was planted to stabilise the soil and by 1861 the population had risen to 127. 1881 – 124. 1891 – 140 (17 houses). 1914 – 80. 1921 – 66. 1931 – 33. Everyone then moved to North Uist except the lighthouse keepers who were there until 1942 when they were recalled. Since uninhabited.

GEOLOGY: Schistose and granite rock covered with fine shell sand and uncultivated machair, but great changes in the surface take place from Atlantic storms acting upon such a light soil.

HISTORY: Human settlement goes back to before AD1000. In about the 13th century a nunnery or convent having connections with Iona was established on Ceann Ear, and the now-deserted lighthouse on Shillay marks the site of a monastery in which part of the monks' duties was to maintain a light as a guide for mariners. The religious as-sociations of the Monachs however failed to survive the Reformation al-though the islands continued to be well-populated until the 20th cen-tury.

Lady Grange (see Hirta.No.9.1) was held prisoner here for two years (1732-34) by MacDonald of Sleat before being transferred to St Kilda by MacLeod of Dunvegan. She had hidden be-

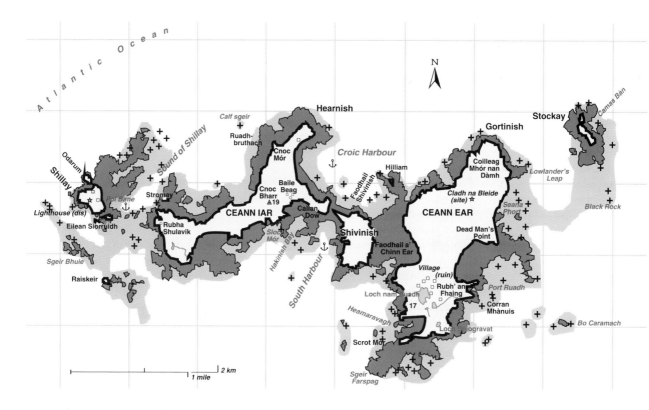

hind a sofa and overheard a Jacobite plot at her house in Edinburgh. Stupidly, she threatened to denounce the conspirators so, with her husband's agreement, she was sent to the Western Isles while Edinburgh society attended her 'funeral' at Greyfriars Church.

WILDLIFE: The Monachs are a National Nature Reserve and permission to land is required from the North Uist Estate at Lochmaddy.

There are no trees but there is good machair consisting of very little grass but a great deal of buttercup, red and white clover, dandelion, eyebright, blue speedwell, daisy, harebell, hop and birdsfoot trefoil, pansy, silverweed and wild thyme.

Fulmars which normally prefer high cliffs nest here in the sand dunes and herons nest in an empty house as there are no trees. Favoured for wintering by barnacle and white-fronted geese, common and little terns can also be seen.

The grey seal was one of the world's rarest seals with two-thirds of the total population of about 160,000 animals in the British Isles, and more than half that number in the Hebrides. Recently, however, numbers have been increasing rapidly. About 1000 pups a year come from the Monachs and the reefs of Stockay are a favoured breeding location in the last four months of each year. This is a comparatively recent phenomenon as the area was only colonised after the islanders had left. Grey seals are more cautious of man than the common seal. In the past, islanders found seals useful for food and clothing. They

were easily killed when breeding, so depopulation of the islands has been of some benefit to the species.

Five small islands and several drying rocks form the **MONACH ISLANDS** group which lie about five miles west of North Uist and Benbecula. The group is also known by the old Norse name of **HEISKER** (bright skerry). The three central islands are all interconnected at low water. **Ceann Ear** is the largest of the group (231ha), connected to **Shivinish** (28ha) which, in turn, is almost a part of **Ceann Iar** (134ha). There are difficult waters round about but these low-lying islands – little more than sandbanks – have wide sandy beaches and high dunes which offer shelter from the worst of the westerlies. Several sandy hillocks near **Gortinish**, in the north-east of Ceann Ear, reach their highest point of 18m at **Coilleag Mhór nan Dàmh**. To the east there is an islet called **Stockay**, and to the west one called **Shillay**.

History records that a great five-mile stretch of sand which was exposed at low water linked the entire group to North Uist. But in the 16th century an enormous tidal wave – the same titanic tsunami which formed the Sound of Pabbay (See No.8.3) – swept away the sand banks and the Monach Islands and their inhabitants have been isolated ever since. History does not record how many of the islanders, if any, survived this disaster.

The remains of some patches of grazing and cultivated land can still be seen in the vicinity of the small village in the south-west of Ceann Ear. This village is visible from

Croic harbour and lies between **Port Ruadh** (G. – red port) and **Loch nam Buadh** (G. – loch of virtues). The village had good amenities, a post-office and a school which was maintained by the Church until 1874 and thereafter by the School Board. There were no shops – but there was a resident missionary. Sadly, the deserted village is disintegrating although the old schoolhouse is still kept weatherfast for the accommodation of visiting lobster fishermen from time to time. The village houses were unusual for the Hebrides as they had grain-drying kilns built inside them instead of in out-houses. This arrangement is common to Shetland.

Port Ruadh is south of **Rubh' a' nam Marbh** (G. – dead man's point). To the north is the probable site of the old monastery and churchyard, **Cladh na Bleide** [NF644624].

As one of the duties of the ancient monastery and convent on Ceann Ear the monks were expected to maintain a fire on the small western island of **Shillay** to help ships avoid the many rocks in the area. Eventually a red brick lighthouse was built in 1864. This has been disused since 1942 but there are now plans to reestablish it. A dressed stone from this lighthouse is now built in to the church wall at Paible. On it the lighthouse keeper had carved – 'Eternity oh eternity.'

Although by the 1930s the last of the islanders had left the Monachs this was no St Kilda type of evacuation. It was merely that, as with so many of these isolated settlements, the young people had travelled 'abroad' and failed to return and numbers steadily dwindled away.

Hebridean sailors believed, and maybe still do, that if they drown the sea will always carry their body home. A cairn on Ceann Iar marks the grave of Lieut. R. N. R. MacNeill, who drowned off Northern Ireland when his ship, *H M A Laurentic*, struck a mine in 1917. His body was washed up on Ceann Iar which is part of the clan lands of the MacNeills.

ACCESS: Private charter can sometimes be arranged with local fishermen from Baleshare on North Uist.

Anchorages: Navigation around the Monach Isles requires great care as there are many hazards.

1. Croic Harbour. Good shelter except from NE, but uncomfortable swell in W to N winds. Good holding in sand or clay, 6m. Anchor middle of W side of bay, or in SE corner, clear of drying rocks.

2. Port Ruadh, on E side of Ceann Ear was the boat harbour for the village but it almost dries and has many reefs. It is well protected by high rocks and has very little swell but is rather open to SE winds.

3. South Harbour. Good shelter in N'lies, but scend may be uncomfortable. Beware drying rocks.

4. Shillay. Only approach from N, with stone beacons on Eilean Siorruidh [shioorooi] (G. – eternal island) in line. Anchor off lighthouse jetty, 5m. This is the best anchorage but ill-positioned for easy exploration of the islands.

7.21 Hermetray

(ON Hermundr-øy – Hermundr's isle). Hermundr was a man's personal name.

OS Maps: 1:50000 Sheet 18 1:25000 Sheet 126
Admiralty Charts: 1:100000 No.1795 1:20000 No.2642

AREA: 72ha (178 acres)
HEIGHT: 35m (115 ft)

OWNER: Government owned (Scottish Office).

POPULATION: 1841 – 8 (1 house). Uninhabited since mid-19th century.

GEOLOGY: Lewisian gneiss.

HISTORY: In 1633 Charles I founded a 'Company of the General Fishery of Great Britain and Ireland' with its 'registered offices' in Lewis. (He already had proposals afoot for the purchase of Lewis by the Crown). Lord Seaforth, who was owner of Lewis at the time, was invited to join the board so that his influence would 'keep the islanders in awe'. The corporation set up one of its fishing stations on Hermetray but the scheme collapsed in 1640 due to the start of the troubles which eventually led to the civil war. Charles II tried to revive it but it was seriously undercapitalised. In 1695 Martin Martin wrote that when he visited Hermetray he saw 'the foundation of a house built by the English in King Charles the First's time, for one of their magazines to lay up the cask, salt, etc, for carrying on the fishery, which was then begun in the Western Islands; but this design miscarried because of the civil wars which then broke out.'

In 1921, on the 16th March, following a savage storm, Alexander (Alex Beag) MacDonald was out checking his lobster pots when he saw two men waving on Compass Knoll, Hermetray. He found a ship broken apart on the rocks and three survivors in poor condition. Among the wreckage was a case of whisky so he first tried to persuade them to drink some but they refused. They were Norwegian and spoke neither English nor Gaelic. MacDonald had dry clothing aboard and after making them as comfortable as possible he took them home to Berneray where his wife and a neighbour fed them well and put them to bed. The following day, arrangements were made by the islanders for the men to travel to the mainland and thence to Scandinavia. Strangely, at no time did the men give any indication of gratitude or thanks to their rescuers and they were never heard of again. The name of the ship was the *Puritan* and to this day the islanders consider this must account for the men's inexplicable behaviour – their refusal to drink good whisky!

WILDLIFE: Strange humps near the shores like large goose-pimples have been created by generations of gulls' nests. The rough grass, scattered with ragged robin and bog cotton, provides good grazing. Adder's tongue fern grows in the wet turf and white clover where the soil is drier.

Buzzards make their home in the low cliffs and help to control the rat population. There are no fish in Loch Hermetray.

HERMETRAY is the southernmost island of a group which lies close to North Uist in the Sound of Harris. **Cnoc a' Chombaiste** (G. – compass knoll), the highest point, is only a mere 35m above sea-level. It is in the

north-east opposite Acairseid Mhór (G. – big harbour), which is a shallow and weedy inlet with a rocky shore. The east coast is moderately steep but Loch Hermetray in the centre of the island is low-lying and tends to pick up the sea-spray when the wind is in the east.

The irrepressible Martin Martin reported that Hermetray had '. . .a moorish soil, covered all over almost with heath, except here and there a few piles of grass and the plant milkwort. Yet, notwithstanding this disadvantage, it is certainly the best spot of its extent for pasturage among these isles, and affords great plenty of milk in January and February beyond what can be seen in the other islands'. Hermetray still provides good all-year-round pasturage, but for sheep – not cattle, and peats were cut here until quite recently. The island is on the North Uist/ Harris boundary and officially is part of Harris.

There are many small islands and skerries surrounding Hermetray, with **Greanem** (ON – green holm) to the north-east. Site Rock lies due north of State Rock and both cover at high water. About a century ago two Berneray men, with their guns and a dog were landed on Site Rock at low water to shoot sea-birds. A strong wind blew up and the boatman lost an oar when returning to take them off the rock. The wind and tide carried his boat away but, luckily, he landed back on Berneray. He immediately roused a rescue party. By then it was blowing a gale and night had fallen but in pitch darkness the rescuers managed to navigate through the reefs and reach Site Rock. The tide was still rising and by the time they reached the rock the fowlers only had their shoulders above water with the dog on one man's back.

Groatay [groa-ay], to the south-west, has a small drying islet between it and the North Uist coast on which can be seen the ancient ruins of **Dùn Mhic Laitheann** (G. – MacLean's fort). The fort was used as a herring magazine in the 17th century and has an artesian well for its water supply. The seaway between Groatay and Hermetray is part of the **Seolaid na h-Eala** (G. – channel of the swan), named after a famous 17th century Skye-built birlinn called *White Swan*.

Vaccasay (ON *vagr-øy* – island with a bay) lies immediately west of Hermetray and with extensive reefs linking it to **Hulmetray** provides valuable shelter for the Vaccasay basin. Martin referred to an island 'in Loch Maddy' called 'Vacksay' on which there 'is still to be seen the foundation of a house, built by the English, for a magazine, etc., for carrying on a great fishery.' It would seem likely that he was referring to Vaccasay (and not Loch Maddy) as the Hermetray fishery project would have used the Vaccasay basin for its anchorage. The full name for the drying islet forming the south barrier to the basin is **Fuam an Aon Fhoid** (G. – far-out isle of the one peat). It has shallow soil which only allowed a cutting depth of one peat.

To the north of Vaccasay is the large, almost circular 'Cabbage Patch' group which contains the Grey Horse reef, **Opsay**, and two islets, **Sarstay** and **Narstay**, sounding like the ugly sisters in a pantomime.

ACCESS: No regular access. Enquire at Loch Maddy or Cheese Bay.

Anchorages:
1. N of Fuam, Vaccasay Basin. Beware Stanley Rock 1c NNE of Fuam and drying reef between Fuam and Hermetray. Good anchorage NE of Fuam but uncomfortable in N'lies.
2. Acairseid Mhór, narrow inlet on NW side of Hermetray. Except for the entrance only really suitable for shallow draught boats, but reported deeper

and well-protected, but with very restricted space, beyond the bend. Bottom mainly weed.
3. Between Vaccasay and Hulmetray, Vaccasay Basin. Beware Dirt Rock 1c E of Vaccasay. Anchor N of Dirt Rock. Distance to Hermetray, 3-4c.

7.22 Tahay

(ON tagg-øy – island with a prominent hill)

OS Maps: 1:50000 Sheet 18 1:25000 Sheet 126
Admiralty Charts: 1:100000 No.1795 1:20000 No.2642

AREA: 53ha (131 acres)
HEIGHT: 65m (213 ft)

OWNER: Scottish Office.

POPULATION: 1841 – 0. 1851 – 34 (6 households). Uninhabited since 1855. Although close to North Uist, Tahay is part of the administrative district of Harris.

GEOLOGY: Lewisian gneiss.

HISTORY: Six families (five MacLeods, one MacAskill) – evicted from Pabbay in 1846 tried to make a home for themselves on Tahay. Although there is virtually no arable land they hoped to survive by fishing. They constructed houses and a boat harbour; the ruins are still visible and one of the old houses has been converted to a sheep fank. Several children were born on the island but conditions were appalling and in the mid-1850s the families gave up the struggle and emigrated to Australia with financial assistance from the Highlands and Islands Emigration Society.

WILDLIFE: A few small stunted rowan trees less than a metre in height support the only heronry in the Sound of Harris. A number of families of the birds like to group together for protection with their young of differing ages.

TAHAY is 65m high, easily the highest and most conspicuous island in the surrounding group. It has a regular – almost rectangular – shape and a central peak. There is a very narrow and shallow channel between tidal **Trollaman** and Tahay which is all that separates it from North Uist. Tahay has small inland cliffs and hilly tracts of heath and peat bog; the latter has always been a useful source of fuel for the Berneray islanders. The normal landing-place for the peat boats was at **Rubha Mòr Nighean Tormaid** (G. – promontory of Morag, daughter of Norman).

To the north and north-west are **Sursay** and **Votersay**. The ruined sheiling on the south side of Sursay is called Airigh na h-Aon Oidhche (G. – one-night sheiling) because in the late 19th century a lone shepherd had to stay overnight on the island but was awakened by screeching

seagulls and his terrified dog. He rushed outside and saw
with horror what he described as an enormous cartwheel
in the sky making a strange noise. As frightened as his
dog, he ran to his boat, and beat all records to reach
North Uist. He never returned to Sursay.

To the south of Tahay there is a group of three islets
with the curious name of **Righe nam Ban** (G. – ?sheiling
of the women) although they are better known locally as
Eileanan na Yacht.

ACCESS: No regular access. Enquire at Loch Maddy or
Cheese Bay.

Anchorages: There are no recommended anchorages for Tahay.

*1. Temporary anchorage is possible in suitable conditions due S of Tahay
hill and ESE of Trollaman in 7m, sand and shingle. Approach with care 1/2c
N of Righe nam Ban.*

*2. The Caddy. Off concrete slip on N Uist, 5c S of Tahay and WNW of
Orasay, 3-4m, subject to weed. Approach S of Righe nam Ban keeping
closer to Orasay. Beware Strome Rock and other rocks W of Righe nam
Ban.*

*3. Bàgh Chaise (Cheese Bay) on North Uist is 3/4M SE of Tahay but is the
best available anchorage in the vicinity. Anchor SW of central islet but beware drying rocks.*

The Outer Hebrides. The Sound of Harris and North

N

22. Little Bernera

21. Pabay Mór

Great Bernera

20. Vacsay

18. Eilean Kearstay

19. Vuia Mór

16. Lewis

17. Mealista Island

13. Eilean Iubhard

15. Scarp

14. Seaforth Island

12. Soay Mór

10 Garbh Eilean (Shiant Isles)

11. Taransay

9. Scotasay

8. Scalpay

6. Shillay

16. Harris

5. Pabbay

7. Stockinish Island

4. Ensay

2. Boreray

3. Killegray

1. Berneray

Section 8

Section 8, Table 1

No.	Name	Latitude	Longitude	Table 2* No.	Table 3** No.	Area in Acres		Area in Hectares
8.1	Berneray	57° 43N	07° 11W	42	78	2496		1010
8.2	Boreray	57° 43N	07° 18W	88	111	489		198
8.3	Killegray	57° 45N	07° 05W	93	126	435		176
8.4	Ensay	57° 46N	07° 05W	90	122	460		186
8.5	Pabbay	57° 46N	07° 14W	48	35	2026		820
8.6	Shillay	57° 48N	07° 15W	155	86	116		47
8.7	Stockinish Island	57° 49N	06° 49W	153	129	121		49
8.8	Scalpay	57° 52N	06° 40W	53	65	1614		653
8.9	Scotasay	57° 53N	06° 45W	152	110	121		49
8.10	Garbh Eilean (Shiant I.)	57° 54N	06° 22W	98	43	217	88	
	Eilean an Tighe	57° 54N	06° 20W			136	55	143
8.11	Taransay	57° 54N	07° 02W	33	27	3645		1475
8.12	Soay Mór	57° 56N	06° 58W	156	138	111		45
8.13	Eilean Iubhard	58° 00N	06° 26W	105	91	309		125
8.14	Seaforth Island	58° 00N	06° 44W	74	31	675		273
8.15	Scarp	58° 01N	07° 08W	40	22	2582		1045
8.16	Lewis/Harris	58° 03N	06° 40W	1	4	5384126	217898	
	Great Bernera	58° 13N	06° 51W			5243	2122	220020
8.17	Mealista Island	58° 05N	07° 07W	106	89	306		124
8.18	Eilean Kearstay	58° 12N	06° 46W	128	137	190		77
8.19	Vuia Mór	58° 13N	06° 53W	121	97	208		84
8.20	Vacsay	58° 14N	06° 55W	163	144	101		41
8.21	Pabay Mór	58° 14N	06° 56W	113	96	250		101
8.22	Little Bernera	58° 16N	06° 52W	102	134	341		138

* Table 2: The islands arranged in order of magnitude
** Table 3: The islands arranged in order of height

Introduction

The Hebrides are said to derive their name from the Norse word, *Havbrødøy* – meaning islands on the edge of the sea. On the other hand, long before the Norse era, Pliny called them the Hebudes – inhabited by the Ebudae tribe – and Ptolemy in the 2nd century wrote of the Eboudai islands above Ivernia (Ireland).

The great archipelago of the Outer Hebrides can look like a single island and is often spoken of as the 'Long Island'. Geologically it was, in fact, one long island in the distant past but, as the ground sank, the sea formed several shallow but distinctive interruptions. The most significant of these is the Sound of Harris. Lewis and Harris, north of the Sound of Harris, combine to form the largest offshore island of mainland Britain and Ireland. For comparison it is more than twice the area of the next largest island – mainland Shetland – and one-third larger in area than Skye. The Isle of Man is not much bigger than Harris alone and the Isle of Wight does not even enter the lists.

It is hard for the modern city-dweller to realise the importance of water transport in early ages. Without roads, or even satisfactory tracks, and with forests, bogs, rocky escarpments, wild animals, and possibly hostile tribes, the sea was the main thoroughfare. The smaller islands were every bit as important then as our townships are today and, by the standards of the time, island access was relatively simple.

From this viewpoint it is easy to see why Lewis and Harris were thought of as separate islands. They are divided by a forbidding mountain barrier and to get from one to the other required a long boat ride round an irregular coastline. Mankind has farmed this land for some 5000 years yet the sheer size of the land mass meant that, for centuries, human settlements clung only to the coastline. Inland was a large area of forest wilderness and swamp. Peat was scarce as the climate was warmer so timber was the primary fuel. Steadily the forests were cleared for fuel and to gain more land for subsistence farming. Such were the conditions 4000 years ago when the stones of Callanish on the west side of Lewis were erected on open meadowland. A thin layer of fine soil lay over the ashes and pollen grains of ancient forest.

Within a few more centuries only scattered patches of

scrub birch, hazel and rowan remained and it was about this critical time that the climate turned colder.

Tundra-type vegetation now took over the barren, treeless land. Heathers, sphagnum and other mosses, bog cotton and coarse grasses failed to decompose in the cold atmosphere and peat started to build up. When Callanish was excavated in 1856 the peat had reached a thickness of five feet (1½ metres) and in some areas it is as much as twenty feet deep (6 metres).

Magnus Barelegs, the Norse marauder, is usually blamed for burning down the forests in Lewis in 1098 but although he caused devastation virtually all the woodland had been destroyed by the islanders themselves long before Norsemen arrived in the area.

8.1 Berneray *or* Bernera

(ON bjarnar-øy – bear island) or, possibly, (ON – Bjorn's island)

OS Maps: 1:50000 Sheet 18 1:25000 Sheet 116
Admiralty Charts: 1:100000 No.1795 1:20000 No.2642 (part only)

AREA: 1010ha (2496 acres)
HEIGHT: 93m (305 ft)

OWNER: Part of the Bays of Harris estate. Bought by the Hitchcock family in the 1920s for £500 (but without crofting rights). The current laird is Rodney Hitchcock, an English businessman.

POPULATION: Until the early 18th century the island was occupied by a tacksman at one end and a community of crofters at the other. Later there was an influx due to evictions from Pabbay and Harris. 1841 – 713 (130 houses). A few families were cleared from Berneray in the 1850s. 1861 – 315. 1881 – 452. 1891 – 501 (96 houses). 1901 – 524. 1931 – 331. 1961 – 201. 1971 – 131. 1981 – 134. 1991 – 141. In 1992 the primary school role was about eighteen pupils compared to about four in the 1980s.

GEOLOGY: There are no workable peat deposits. The island is of gneiss covered with a fertile light sandy soil. In the 16th century a tidal wave removed the sandbank which at that time almost connected Berneray to Pabbay.

HISTORY: In 1614, when Tormod (G. – Norman), third son of Ruaridh Mór chief of the Clan MacLeod, was five years old he was settled with Berneray by his father. The remains of the home that he later built are still to be seen. He received a knighthood after the Restoration for his services to the exiled Charles II. Sir Norman, who died in 1705, was an ardent supporter of Gaelic art and literature and he gave a house on Berneray to Mary MacLeod, the famous Gaelic poet.

At this time the MacLeod Chiefs were reasonably good proprietors and keen to ensure satisfactory communication between the islands. In 1705 a boat was purchased by MacLeod of Harris for use as a ferry. Lauchlan MacLean as ferryman was instructed to maintain a regular service between Harris and Skye and also the islands of Berneray, Ensay, Killegray and Pabbay.

Sir Norman's settlement in Berneray had been a leasehold title but his grandson, Donald, lent money to the MacLeod chief to help him pay his gambling debts and, in return, gained a full feu charter. Donald borrowed the funds for this exchange from his second son, Alexander, who was a prosperous sea captain serving the East India Company. As Berneray had been by far the most fertile part of the MacLeod's Harris estate, when the destitute Clan Chief eventually put the estate up for sale he found it difficult to find a suitable purchaser. So in 1779 Captain Alexander stepped in and bought the entire estate.

In 1865 there were three schools on the island. – an SSPCK (Scottish Society for the Propagation of Christian Knowledge) school, a Gaelic School Society school and a 'female industrial school' supported by SSPCK and taught by a venerable Highland lady in receipt of a salary of £8 per annum. This school was housed in the 'oldest dwelling in the Long Island, at one time inhabited by persons of distinction' – in other words the original home of Sir Norman MacLeod of Berneray. The present primary school had ten pupils in 1993 and Gaelic is still the first language. English gained ground when television was first introduced, but Gaelic is now regaining its importance.

WILDLIFE: Martin Martin wrote in 1695: 'The west end of this island which looks to St Kilda, is called the wooden harbour, because the sands at low water discover several trees that have formerly grown there. Sir Norman MacLeod told me that he had seen a tree cut there, which was afterwards made into a harrow.'

There is very little heather and with no peat bogs there are few midges. The island is also fortunate to be free of rabbits. The soil structure is rich in shell-sand and the machair is particularly beautiful. About 200 different species of wildflowers have been identified which bloom in sequence giving rolling waves of colour throughout spring and summer.

For the local fishermen, the velvet crabs which were once thrown away or used as bait now fetch good prices in southern Europe.

The two hills on **BERNERAY** are both on the east side. The west is a wide stretch of low-lying machair, rough grazing and sand dunes and one of the loveliest stretches of white shell-sand beach in Britain – about four kilometres of perfection. **Beinn Shléibhe** (G. – mountainous hill), also known as Moor Hill, is 93m high and south of it is **Borve Hill** (ON – fort hill), 85m high. Between these two hills is a wide freshwater loch, **Loch Bhruist**, and a reef-ridden sea loch, **Bays Loch**, forming a deep indentation on the south-east coast.

Although Berneray lies close to North Uist it is part of the parish of Harris. All the habitation is on the south-east side. The village of Borve lies south of Borve Hill but the road which runs almost the full length of the east coast links this settlement with its northerly neighbour, **Ruisgarry**. In between, on Bays Loch, is the post-office, the harbour, the shop, and the church and manse (a rare example of church and manse under one roof). At one time there were three churches on Berneray.

It is a good little harbour, well-sheltered, built with EC funds in the late 1980s. Fuel and water are available although the nearest water tap sometimes produces more peat than water.

The harbour is particularly appreciated by visiting sailors after successfully dodging the rocks in Bays Loch. There is no reliable guide to the position of these rocks; the locals navigate entirely by instinct. One old islander bringing a visitor across from Harris ran his boat on to the rocks. 'But I thought you knew all the rocks!' cried the visitor. 'Aye,' said the old man, 'I do. And that is one of them.'

Even when the kelp boom was over Berneray survived on its potatoes. The light sandy soil, still manured with kelp, grows a generous and tasty crop and for many years most of the potatoes eaten on Harris were imported from Berneray. Nowadays, sheep farming and fishing are the main industries although potatoes are still grown. The fishing is for prawns, lobsters and velvet crabs. Berneray is a good example of how years of decline have been replaced by hope and a belief in a viable future. Trim new suburban bungalows, however incongruous in such a beautiful setting, are appearing among the deserted black houses.

In the late 1980s the Prince of Wales wanted to 'get away from it all' and experience life among these gentle and friendly people. He arranged to spend some time on Berneray, lodging in a typical household. The home of 'Splash' McKillop and his wife was chosen. It says much for Hebridean loyalty and respect for privacy that both during his stay and thereafter not a single man, woman or child breathed a word about their famous guest to the media. It was the Prince himself who revealed the facts four years later.

While there the Prince went lobster fishing, helped gather potatoes and dip the sheep. He planted some trees of which only a few have survived the gales but these have since been replaced and some are becoming established.

There are few prehistoric remains here but part of a stone circle [NF912807] stands on a hillock, **Beinn a' Chlaidh** (G. – hill of the churchyard), beside Loch Borve – a large shallow and circular sea-loch. And there is a souterrain west of Borve Hill [NF907816] near Little Loch Borve – a freshwater lochan.

Berneray was the birthplace of the 'Cape Breton Giant' – one of the world's tallest and strongest men. Angus MacAskill (1825-1863) was a well-proportioned 2.36m (7ft 9ins) in height and weighed 425lbs. He died in Canada.

The possibility of building a causeway to North Uist is under consideration.

ACCESS: Passenger ferry from Leverburgh (An t-Ob) on Harris and Newtonferry on North Uist, 01876-70230. There is also a small car ferry from Newtonferry.

Anchorages: Avoid Berneray in bad weather as navigation in these waters is not a science but an art.

1. North of The Reef. Temporary anchorage in settled weather off the sandy beach 2-3c N of the Reef beacons. Approach from Cope Passage, turn S from Buoy 12 and pass 1c off Massacamber.

2. Berneray Harbour. Excellent shelter but very restricted. Passage across Bays Loch best if taken very slowly on a rising tide. (See Martin Lawrence's pilot for instructions).

3. Bays Loch. Pass through the Reef keeping 5m E of both beacons, ease round to starboard and follow the deeper water about ½c off the shore. This approach is relatively easy. Visitor's moorings W of school, or anchor in N corner of bay, 3-4m, mud. Sheltered except from SE. No swell.

8.2 Boreray

[**baw**-rĕ-ray or **baw**-rĕ-rĕ] (ON borve, or burgh, -øy – fort island)

OS Maps: 1:50000 Sheet 18 1:25000 Sheet 116
Admiralty Charts: 1:200000 Nos.2721 or 2722

AREA: 198ha (489 acres)
HEIGHT: 56m (184 ft)

OWNER: Scottish Office and Bernera Common Grazing.

POPULATION: 1841 – 181. 1881 – 137. 1891 – 152 (37 houses). Evacuated by request in 1923 but one family stayed on with a land-holding of 87 acres. 1931 – 8. 1961 – 5. Uninhabited since the late 1960s.

GEOLOGY: Grey Lewisian gneiss with a light sandy soil.

HISTORY: Unlike neighbouring Berneray which is in the Parish of Harris, Boreray is in the parish of North Uist. It has been inhabited since prehistoric times. Coins dating from the reign of James IV have been found in its sands.

Boreray was MacLean territory and the MacLeans of Boreray – up to the 13th laird who died in 1821 – are all buried in the family graveyard on the east side of Aird a' Mhòrain, North Uist.

WILDLIFE: Barnacle geese fly in each winter from Greenland to the shores of Loch Mór and common seals collect round the coasts in high summer. Huge flocks of starlings can be seen and Boreray is at the southern limit of the range of the purple sandpiper.

BORERAY's highest point is **Mullach Mór** (G. – big top) which is 56m high and has a flattish summit. It is in the larger northern part of the island which is connected to the flat southern part by a strip of rocks and a low neck of land with sand dunes. The dunes continue on to the south-eastern shore while the north and west coasts are shelving cliffs.

The sand dunes curve round a wide bay bounded by **Tràigh na Lùibe** (G. – the bay beach). Ruins of an abandoned village are scattered on the flank of Mullach Mór and near a small burn which babbles down to the sea at Breivik (ON – broad bay). An archaeological site known as the **Nuns' Burial Chamber** lies north of the village [NF857816]. The marks of communal peat-cutting can still be seen and it is easy to imagine the sound of children's voices in the old schoolhouse. South of the dunes there are more blackhouse ruins by the shore and below the chapel and churchyard site with its cup-marked stones [NF856805] a lone standing stone marks the edge of the

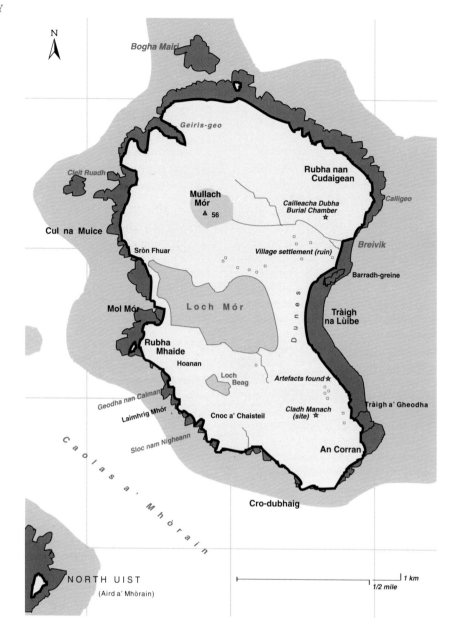

N

Bogha Mairi

Geiris-geo

Cleit Ruadh

Rubha nan
Cudaigean

Calligeo

Mullach
Mór
△ 56

Cailleacha Dubha
Burial Chamber
☆

Cul na Muice

Sròn Fhuar

Village settlement (ruin)

Breivik

Barradh-greine

Mol Mór

Loch Mór

D
u
n
e
s

Tràigh
na Lùibe

Rubha
Mhaide

Hoanan

Loch
Beag

Artefacts found ☆

Tràigh a' Gheodha

Geodha nan Calman

Laimhrig Mhór

Cnoc a' Chaisteil

Cladh Manach
(site) ☆

An Corran

Sloc nam Nigheann

C
a
o
l
a
s
a
'
M
h
ò
r
a
i
n

Cro-dubhaig

NORTH UIST
(Aird a' Mhòrain)

1 km
1/2 mile

rocks. **Cladh Manach** (G. – the monks' churchyard), or 'Monks' Field' was renowned in Martin Martin' time (1695) – 'for all the Monks that dyed in the Islands that lye Northward from Egg were buried in this little plot.'

In the centre of Boreray and almost cutting it in two is **Loch Mór**. The loch has its east side protected by the line of sand dunes but the Atlantic, when the mood takes it, breaks over the steep rocky reef closing the west side, or through a mysterious submarine passage (according to Martin) and consequently the water is salty. The rocky point beside the reef is aptly called **Sròn Fhuar** (G. – cold nose). Just south of Loch Mór is Loch Beag – a mere puddle by comparison – but fresh water.

Late in the 19th century, in an attempt to increase the area of fertile land, Loch Mór was drained for a time. It was proudly recorded that this action created '47 Scotch acres of good alluvial soil at a cost of only £125'.

A large vessel of the Spanish Armada (over 30m length) is said to have sunk in the area between Berneray's Rubha Bhoisnis and Boreray during a severe Atlantic storm. A collection of small boats brought survivors ashore at Port nan Long (G. – port of the boats) on North Uist.

ACCESS: No regular access but the local fishermen can be very cooperative. Enquire on Berneray.

Anchorages: There is no safe anchorage near Boreray and no large-scale charts available (Imray's C66 is 1:150000, only slightly better than the Admiralty Chart). The deeper water has a rocky bottom and where there is sand it is either shoal or exposed to swell, but on a rising tide and in quiet weather it is possible to find temporary anchorage among the sandbanks to the east of Boreray.

8.3 Killegray

(ON kjallard-øy – graveyard island)

OS Maps: 1:50000 Sheet 18 1:25000 Sheet 116
Admiralty Charts: 1:50000 No.2841 1:20000 No.2642

AREA: 176ha (435 acres)

HEIGHT: 45m (148 ft)

OWNER: Bought by Sir Harry Wolfe in September 1985 from the Campbell brothers of Leverburgh.

POPULATION: 1841 – 7 (2 houses). 1861 – 5. 1881 – 6. 1891 – 8 (1 house). 1911 – 3. 1921 – 3. 1931 – 5. 1951 – 0. 1961 – 0. 1971 – 2. 1981 – 0. House was being renovated in 1991. 1991 – 0.

GEOLOGY: As there is no suitable building stone in Leverburgh on Harris many of the black stone lintels used there have been brought over from Killegray.

HISTORY: This was one of the group of islands in the Sound of Harris served by ferryman Lauchlan MacLean in 1705 on the instructions of MacLeod of Harris.

The most expensive gravestone in the Rodel cemetery on Harris, apart from the MacLeod mausoleum, is in memory of John MacDonald, the MacLeod estate factor and former Army officer, who died on Killegray, his personal domain, after thirty-one years of service.

WILDLIFE: The shallow waters and many reefs in this area are a rich breeding ground for velvet crabs and lobsters.

KILLEGRAY is the most southerly of the two larger islands which lie opposite Leverburgh (An t-Obbe) – the small ferry-port on the south coast of Harris. **Killegray House** overlooks a shallow reef-rimmed bay on the northeast side with a pleasant beach and a small stone jetty. Behind the house a grassy hill 45m high has a conspicuous cairn on its summit. In 1991 the house, which is the only one on the island, was being renovated.

The island provides rich grazing for sheep in the summer months. On the north coast there are sand dunes between **Rubh' an t-Soithich** (G. – ship headland) and **Rubha Claidhe** (G. – churchyard headland) – the site of a ruined chapel, **Teampull na h-Annait** [NF975846]. This could be the churchyard site that gave its name to the island. Two tiny lochans sparkle in the machair on the west coast guarded by a small ruined fort to the south [NF975831]. Here, a small burn runs through a cleft which divides off the southern peninsula. An old dyke spans the island at this point and the ground south of it is uncultivated deep moss and a good source of peat which was worked for a time. There is an attractive sandy cove near Steisinish on the south coast, but the south-eastern extremity deteriorates into a confused group of drying islands, **Hestem**, **Vacam**, and **Eilean na Ceardaich** (G. – the tinker's island), and weed-covered skerries.

Both Killegray and Ensay have been visited occasionally by the Royal Family when cruising in the royal yacht.

To the south-east a group of tiny green islands guard the northern side of the Sound of Harris, **Groay**, **Gousman**, **Gilsay**, **Lingay** and **Scaravay** with an even tinier group beside them – **Langay**, **Gumersam Mhór** and **Bheag**, and **Dùn-aarin**. To explore these islets it is possible to anchor on the east side of Groay (north-west of Lingay). This is a sheltered spot but can be uncomfortable sometimes due to the swell.

ACCESS: No regular access but arrangements can usually be made on Berneray. Alternatively enquire at An t-Obbe (Leverburgh) Post Office.

Anchorages: There are no recommended anchorages.
1. Caolas Skaari between Ensay and Killegray can be reached by a narrow channel extending to the Groay group of islands. This requires considerable navigational care and is best attempted near low water when most dangers are visible. Occasional anchorage due NE of Killegray House but beware central shoal patch.

8.4 Ensay

(ON – John's island)

OS Maps: 1:50000 Sheet 18 1:25000 Sheet 116
Admiralty Charts: 1:100000 No.1795 1:50000 No.2841 1:20000 No.2642

AREA: 186ha (460 acres)
HEIGHT: 49m (161 ft)

OWNER: Bought by Simon Mackenzie of Leverburgh in 1933 from Donald Stewart, a Nairn landowner who also had property in Skye. Ensay is now run by Simon Mackenzie's three sons.

POPULATION: 1841 – 16 (2 houses). 1861 – 15. 1881 – 6. 1891 – 11 (1 house). 1931 – 8. 1951 – 2. 1961 – 2. 1971 – 2 (seasonal shepherds). 1981 – 0. 1991 – 0.

GEOLOGY: Gneiss bedrock.

HISTORY: A standing stone in the north proves that Ensay was of interest to prehistoric man. There are also two cupmarks on a small rock ridge lying parallel to the shore and about 100m north of the pier. The island, which is said to have been well-wooded up to that time, was raided by Norsemen about 1000 years ago. They slew the inhabitants and slashed and burned the woodland. It never recovered and much of the soil was lost. This, of course, was not the only Scottish island to have suffered soil erosion and in the end the Hebrideans developed the system of lazybeds to make up for the deficient soil.

Ensay was linked by the ferry service paid for by MacLeod in 1705 with Berneray, Killegray, Pabbay and Obbe (Leverburgh) on Harris.

In the 19th century MacLeod of Harris' factor, Donald Stewart, bought Ensay from him together with some other properties when the MacLeod was facing bankruptcy. The Stewart name is now of ill-repute in the area for Donald is said to have ruthlessly evicted the tenants and his son John Stewart of Ensay followed in his father's footsteps. But it is also said that the Stewarts were good farmers who, for instance, introduced a horse-drawn precision seeder on Ensay when dibbers were still being used elsewhere.

WILDLIFE: Stunted elder, fuchsia, and sycamore – almost laid flat by the wind – struggle with beaten veronica bushes to survive by the main house.

In summer sheep are grazed on **ENSAY** which is a verdant island and very similar in appearance to neighbouring Killegray. The ground rises to a maximum height of 49m. A small stone jetty juts into a cove near the southeast end of the island, and **Ensay House**, which was being renovated in 1991, overlooks a more attractive bay on the east side with a gateway and steps leading down to a crescent beach of white sand. The restored private Episcopal chapel near Ensay House [NF982866] has a fine oak door carved by Robert Thompson of Kilburn, North Yorkshire.

Toan, the north-west extremity and **Rubha nan Sgarbh** in the north are steep dark-coloured rocky points with a beautiful shell-sand beach, **Manish Strand**, between them. One of the tidal islands on the beach is the site of an old burial ground. A 12th century chapel [NF975868] was uncovered about 1970 which looks a bit like a half-buried nissen hut. The wall round the burial

ground is thought to date back to the 9th century, or even earlier, and there may be earlier remains at a lower level. A Stewart grave has also been exposed and Viking relics have been found nearby. Martin recorded in 1695 – 'there is an old chapel here, for the use of the natives; and there was lately discovered a grave in the west end of the island in which was found a pair of scales made of brass, and a little hammer, both which were finely polished.'

It was from Ensay that Martin set off on his later voyage to St Kilda, on 'the 29th of May, at Six in the Afternoon, 1697, the wind at S.E. . .'

As with Killegray, Ensay is surrounded by rocks and skerries. The only ones which might justify the title of islets are **Stromay** in the north-east, **Saghay More**, **Saghay Beg**, and **Suem** to the east, and **Sleicham** and **Coddem Island** to the south-east. **Sùnam** is beside the entrance to An t-Obbe (Leverburgh) harbour but the **Carminish Islands** on the coast of Harris are all tidal.

ACCESS: No regular access but arrangements can usually be made on Berneray. Alternatively, enquire at An t-Obbe (Leverburgh) Post Office.

Anchorages:
1. In bay on NE side off Ensay House, sand. Approach with caution following sailing instructions carefully. Sheltered except for N'lies and E'lies. Note reef on SE of bay.

8.5 Pabbay

(ON pap-øy – hermit or priest island)

OS Maps: 1:50000 Sheet 18 1:25000 Sheet 116
Admiralty Charts: 1:200000 Nos.2721 or 2722 1:50000 No.2841
1:20000 No.2642

AREA: 820ha (2,026 acres)
HEIGHT: 196m (643 ft)

OWNER: Oliver Plunkett. Bought from the Stewarts by the Campbells of Rodel (Harris) at a London auction in March 1934. Sold in 1974 to Mr David Plunkett – a Lloyd's broker. North Uist Estates Trust (Lord Granville's family) own the crofting rights and these are managed by Mr Kenny Campbell of Leverburgh.

POPULATION: In the early 19th century there were twenty-six families (about 100 people) living in comparative comfort. 1841 – 338 (61 houses). The island was cleared for sheep in 1846. 1861 – 21. By 1868 only a single shepherd's family remained. 1871 – 8. 1881 – 2. 1891 – 3 (1 house). 1931 – 3. 1961 – 2. 1971 – 4. 1981 – 0. 1991 – 0.

GEOLOGY: Gneiss bedrock with a fertile sandy soil and very little peat.

HISTORY: It is not known which priest or hermit settled on Pabbay and gave it its name. Columba never crossed the Minch and although the small chapel was dedicated to St. Moluag it is doubtful if he ever landed here.

In the early 15th century the MacLeods of Pabbay spotted a raiding party of MacDonalds approaching. All the islanders took cover so when the MacDonalds landed they found the village deserted and set about looting and burning the

houses. The MacLeods meanwhile set the MacDonald boats adrift and then rowed over to Berneray to summon help. A large party returned to Pabbay and found the MacDonalds now intent on dividing the spoils and rounding up the cattle. They hid by the shore and when the MacDonalds tried to escape to their boats they were trapped and slaughtered. The final battle probably took place between Seana-Chaisteal and the river, Abhainn Lingay, but the whole area has now been covered with sand dunes.

Pabbay was a favourite island of the MacLeod chiefs and some years after the Norsemen left they built a castle which, at the time, was equal in importance to Dunvegan in Skye. It was not until the 16th century that their interest concentrated on Dunvegan and the castle on Pabbay lapsed into disrepair. In 1467, Iain Borb, Chief of the MacLeods, died at the castle while fencing with his cousin. He apparently lost his temper and an old battle wound on his forehead could not be staunched when it started bleeding profusely.

It is recorded that in 1680 there were four 'townships' on Pabbay – Baile fo Thuath, Baile Meadhanach, Baile Lingay, and Baile na Cille – but in 1697 a violent storm destroyed Baile Meadhanach, stripped off the topsoil and buried the wrecked village in sand.

Pabbay once had a considerable population and most of the Stewards of St Kilda were Pabbay men. In 1705 a boat was purchased by MacLeod for use as a ferry to serve Pabbay, Berneray, Ensay, Killegray, Harris and Skye. Unlike the MacLeods of Berneray who had Jacobite sympathies, the MacLeods of Pabbay supported the Government in the 1745 rebellion.

There was a population of about one hundred at the start of the 19th century living in comparative comfort and producing, and even exporting, corn, barley and illicit whisky. Pabbay was then part of the 'quod sacra Parish of Bernera'. Numbers had risen to over 300 by 1841 before the island was cleared for sheep. It is known that there were still a few cattle because three of these won a prize for the heaviest Highland cattle at Smithfield – proof of the richness of the island machair. Some of the displaced population went to Canada and Australia, but many set-

MARY'S CHURCH ON PABBAY

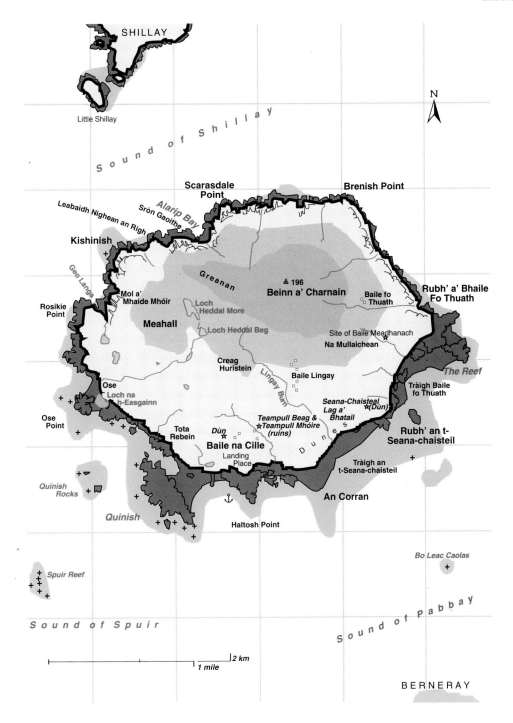

SHILLAY

Little Shillay

N

Sound of Shillay

Scarasdale
Point

Brenish Point

Leabaidh Nighean an Righ

Alarip Bay

Sròn Gaoithe

Kishinish

Geo Langa

Mol a'
Mhaide Mhóir

Greenan

△ 196
Beinn a' Charnain

Baile fo
Thuath

Rubh' a' Bhaile
Fo Thuath

Rosikie
Point

Loch
Heddal More

Meahall

Loch Heddal Beg

Site of Baile Meadhanach

Na Mullaichean

The Reef

Creag
Huristein

Lingay Burn

Baile Lingay

Tràigh Baile
fo Thuath

Ose

Loch na
h-Easgainn

Seana-Chaisteal
Lag a'
Bhatail

☆(Dun)

Ose
Point

Tota
Rebein

Dùn

Teampull Beag &
☆Teampull Mhóire
(ruins)

Dunes

Rubh' an t-
Seana-chaisteil

Baile na Cille

Landing
Place

Tràigh an
t-Seana-chaisteil

Quinish
Rocks

An Corran

Quinish

Haltosh Point

Bo Leac Caolas

Spuir Reef

Sound of Spuir

Sound of Pabbay

2 km
1 mile

BERNERAY

tled on Scalpay, Berneray and in the Bays area of Harris. But with the island clearance in 1846 the value of centuries of careful husbandry was lost to coarse grazing.

The island is now run as a single sheep farm.

WILDLIFE: Ancient birch tree trunks, roots and peat deposits are sometimes exposed by the wind and sea, particularly during abnormal spring tides, in the intertidal

zone at the north end of the Quinish reef and on the shore opposite. Marram-grass on the dunes struggles to hold down the windblown sand. It is also found in patches by the ruined main homestead at Baile fo Thuath – probably originally seeded from the thatched roofs.

A small resident herd of red deer, introduced in 1880, graze on Beinn a' Charnain. Shag and fulmar nest on the low north-coast cliffs but gulls and eider prefer the tidal reef at Quinish. Barnacle geese winter on Pabbay in large numbers.

The island of **PABBAY** was once rich and green and known as 'the granary of Harris'. But since clearance in the mid-19th century, drift, sea spray and lack of care have destroyed much of its former fertility and sheep now graze on the wildflowers of the machair. Nevertheless, it is still one of the most beautiful islands in the Hebrides with its white sands, rich machair and aquamarine sea. **Beinn a' Charnain** (G. – cairn hill), a sharp-peaked hill in the north is the highest point at 196m.

A pointed sandy hillock between two beaches on the south-west coast still shows traces of the walls of **Seana-Chaisteal** (G. – ancient castle). This is the site of the old MacLeod castle or dun [NF902871]. The wide beaches below the castle are backed by sand dunes.

West of the castle site and beyond Abhainn Lingay (ON and G. – heather burn) is the landing place of Haltois below **Baile na cille** (G. – Kirktown). A small cottage which is used by visiting shepherds faces the sea with a burn behind it dividing it from the ruin of **Teampull Mhóire** (G. – Mary's Church) in its old kirkyard [NF890870]. One gable and part of the walls remain. The age of the building is uncertain but it may be early 16th century. Only four metres to the west are the remains of an earlier chapel which was probably dedicated to St Moluag and between these ruins and the Lingay Burn is an old corn-drying kiln.

The stone from many of the old houses has been used to build a wall enclosing a Pairc Mhor (G. – big park) for the sheep at lambing time and within this area is a ruined Iron Age dun.

The lost village of **Baile Meadhanach** (G. – Midtown) lay to the north of Seana-Chaisteal but the houses of **Baile Lingay** are clearly visible beside the Lingay Burn. These form two groups – the MacNeill farm buildings, and the workers' houses higher up the hillside and above the arable land. West of the workers' houses is Creag Huristein – an odd collection of eroded erratic boulders likes pieces of imaginative modern sculpture.

Baile fo Thuath (G. – Northtown) is high on the western hillside with a T-shaped main farmhouse and a circular ruin behind it. Looking across the Sound of Harris from here the **Druim na Beisde** (G. – the ridge of the beast) can be seen as a pale shape across the water. This three-mile long sandbank shifts its position frequently and sometimes cuts off the passage to Pabbay.

The north coast consists of rugged cliffs which stand against the tide that sweeps through the Sound of Shillay. In the cliff-face at **Sròn Gaoithe** (G. – nose of the wind) is a cave known as Carn mhic an t-Sronaich after a notorious murderer who is said to have hidden there and the small plateau to the west of it is called, strangely,

Leabaidh Nighean an Righ (G. – the king's daughter's bed).

The lochs in this remote western side of the island have a few peat deposits near them and were probably, therefore, the site of the old illicit whisky stills.

Although there are the ancient remains of sacred buildings on Pabbay, in recent centuries folk usually crossed the Sound (weather permitting) to attend church on Berneray. The sand spit from Berneray was once said to be so close to Pabbay that a wife could throw her washboard across the channel between them.

ACCESS: No regular access. Enquire on Berneray.

Anchorages: Avoid the N coast as local fishermen say there are uncharted inshore rocks, the W coast is too exposed and the SW foul with skerries. On the E side the shoals and sandbanks move and must be navigated with great caution.

1. Temporary anchorage on S coast near Haltosh Point, E of drying reef in 4m, sand. Land, and re-embark, at or above half-tide, swell permitting.

8.6 Shillay

(ON selr-øy – seal island)

OS Maps: 1:50000 Sheet 18 1:25000 Sheet 116
Admiralty Charts: 1:50000 No.2841 1:20000 No.2642

AREA: 47ha (116 acres)
HEIGHT: 79m (259 ft)

OWNER: Scottish Office (Department of Agriculture). Borve Township, Berneray has the grazing rights.

POPULATION: No census records and no signs of past habitation.

GEOLOGY: Gneiss with a light sandy soil.

WILDLIFE: In 1695 Martin Martin said that he had found sheep on Shillay with the biggest horns he had ever seen.

Both storm and Leach's petrel breed among the boulders on Shillay and probably, also, Arctic tern, *Sterna macrura*.

Hundreds of grey seals, one of the world's rarer species, also breed here producing between 150 and 200 calves per year. They collect in huge numbers on the foreshore during the pupping season. When the weather is particularly bad seals which normally give birth on Haskeir join those on Shillay. The seals on Shillay were studied in detail when a special camp was set up in October 1961. Juveniles were branded to track their movements but as a consequence some of the seals moved over to Coppay to give birth.

The Sound of Shillay yields reasonable quantities of the edible crab, *cancer pagarus* and some of the tastiest lobsters in the Hebrides. Donald MacKillop of Berneray records that in 1946 a lobster found under a rock on the North Uist shore was 35ins long, 15½ins in circumference, with 7½ins of cutting edge on the scissors claw and an empty shell weight of 10¾lbs.

The water lapped gently under our hulls as *Jandara* lay alongside *Berneray Isle* in the Sound of Shillay. We had stopped for a chat with Angus MacAskill and his nephew Roddy who were out lobster fishing. The sunlight glinted off the wet seaweed on the rocks of Shillay. *Berneray Isle* is the boat in which Prince Charles, Lord of the Isles and Prince of Wales, went lobster fishing with all the long experience of Angus to assist him, (and it was Angus's wife, Mary, who cooked the Prince his favourite clootie dumpling).

SHILLAY has dark-coloured vertical cliffs at its northern end beneath a round-topped hill of 79m height. Vegetation is sparse but offers grazing for sheep. The southern part of the island slopes towards the **Sound of Shillay**, the channel between Pabbay and Shillay, and has a small bay with a sand and boulder beach on its south-east side where the grey seals gather in the autumn sheltered by **Aird an Laoigh** (G. – headland of the seal-calf). Although the gentle slopes make it easier for the seals to come ashore it also means greater infant mortality when there are storms and high seas. These sweep the young ones into the water before they can fend for themselves.

Little Shillay, lying south-west of Shillay, is a rocky outcrop that rises to a height of 30m. And some distance away in the opposite direction, guarding the north-west

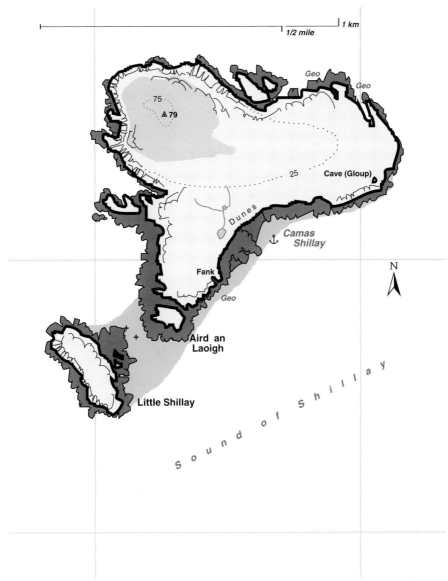

entrance to the Sound of Harris is the steep little island of **Coppay** (ON – cup-shaped island).

ACCESS: No regular access but arrangements can usually be made on Berneray.

Anchorages:

1. Temporary anchorage when winds are between NW and NNE off the centre of the sandy beach on the SE side in suitable depth. Bottom chiefly sand with patches of rock which can normally be seen and avoided.

8.7 Stockinish Island

(ON stakkr – stack, ON nes – promontory). Rock stacks guard the seaward approach.

OS Maps 1:50000 Sheet 14 1:25000 Sheet 108
Admiralty Charts: 1:100000 No.1795 1:50000 No.2841

AREA: 49ha (121 acres)
HEIGHT: 44m (144 ft)

Stockinish Island

OWNER: Bay of Harris Estate (Rodney M. Hitchcock).

POPULATION: No census records and uninhabited.

GEOLOGY: Lewisian gneiss similar to the geology of neighbouring Harris with small pockets of poor peaty soil.

Loch Stockinish is another of the many firths penetrating the frayed eastern edge of Harris – dark brown, barren, and beautiful. Where the Golden Road skirts the loch there is a youth hostel and a few houses scattered in the hollows. **STOCKINISH ISLAND** at the entrance to the loch is separated from the 'mainland' by a long, narrow, but navigable channel – **Caolas Beag** (G. – little channel). In fact, in spite of its narrowness (27m minimum), it is an easier route into the loch than **Caolas Mór** on the west side, which is wide but littered with rocks. A tiny islet, **Eilean Leasait**, snuggles by the west shore of Stockinish Island.

Stockinish has no habitation on it and matches the surrounding landscape – pink and grey glaciated rock with little pockets of dark-umber peat and a tangle of twisted heather. Its main feature is a large shallow central pool, Loch an t-Sàile (G. – saltwater loch), opening off an inlet from Caolas Beag which may once have served as a fish-trap but which is now permanently dammed and used by the local fishermen as a lobster pond. The island's highest point (44m) is a steep hillock beside this inlet.

At the southern end of the island there is a deep skirt of drying islets, rocks, reefs and stacks.

ACCESS: No regular access. The owner of a fishing boat at Kyles Stockinish or Poll Scrot may be helpful.

Anchorages: No recommended anchorage close to the island.
1. Loch Stockinish. Easiest access to loch is through Caolas Beag, E of Stockinish Island; best before half-tide. Very narrow (only 27m at one point) but clean if close-in to Stockinish Island. After passing Stockinish Island keep just NE of mid-channel. Anchor in mouth of westerly arm at head of loch, completely sheltered, 9m, sand. Beware rock off Ardvey Point & overhead cable to N (15m? clearance). Distance is slightly over 1M by dinghy to Stockinish Island.

8.8 Scalpay

(ON skalpr-øy – scallop island)

OS Maps: 1:50000 Sheet 14 1:25000 Sheet 108
Admiralty Charts: 1:100000 Nos.1794 or 1795 1:12500 No.2905

AREA: 653ha (1,614 acres)
HEIGHT: 104m (341 ft)

OWNER: John Taylor, a London architect. He has a cottage here and flies his personal flag (an anchor and lobster) over it when in residence. He bought the island in the early 1980s from North Harris Estate and thus 'gave it its independence'. Most of the island is under crofting tenure.

POPULATION: Scalpay was occupied by two or three tacksmen in succession before being 'crofted out'. 1841 – 31 (4 houses). The Harris factor settled twenty crofting families about 1843 and five years later added another twenty families – some evicted from Pabbay (No.8.3) in the Sound of Harris. 1861 – 388. 1881 – 540. 1891 – 517 (95 houses). 1921 – 624. 1931 – 636. 1951 – 541. 1961 – 470. 1971 – 483. 1981 – 461. 1991 – 382.

For fear of depopulation there was controversy in the early 1980s over a Council decision to transport the children across the Sound to school on Harris.

GEOLOGY: Irregular protuberances of gneiss. A steeply-angled bed of serpentine traverses a promontory at the eastern extremity.

HISTORY: Bonnie Prince Charlie stopped here on his way to Stornoway in 1746 after his defeat at Culloden. Donald Campbell, a farmer, gave him refuge and the use of his boat. The Free Church manse now stands on the site of Campbell's house.

By 1912 Stornoway had become the main centre of the Scottish herring industry and a thousand or more boats brought prosperity to the town. Many of these craft also called in to Scalpay and it was this which stimulated the local interest in fishing. The men began to acquire boats of their own and their principal markets were Ger-

NORTH HARBOUR.
SCALPAY

many and Russia. The interest continues and even today more than 60% of the working males earn a living from fishing. The women run a knitting cooperative which sells beautiful hand-knitted jerseys and other garments made of Harris wool. These have original and very fashionable designs.

WILDLIFE: There are large tracts of heather on the peaty soil shielding ground-nesting birds. The density of housing on the south-west coast limits the variety of wildlife.

> The ferry wades across the kyle. I drive
> The car ashore
> On to a trim tarred road. A car on Scalpay?
> Yes, and a road where never was one before.
> The ferrymen's Gaelic wonders who I am
> (Not knowing I know it), this man back from the dead,
> Who takes the blue-black road (no traffic jam)
> From by Craig Lexie over to Bay Head.

> A man bows in the North wind, shaping up
> His lazybeds,
> And through the salt air vagrant peat smells waver
> From houses where no house should be. The sheds
> At the curing station have been newly tarred.
> Aunt Julia's house has vanished. The Red Well
> Has been bulldozed away. But sharp and hard
> The church still stands, barring the road to Hell.
>
> *from 'Return to Scalpay' by Norman MacCaig*

SCALPAY is a thriving island – with change being the penalty for success. The Scalpachs have managed to maintain a vigorous community when many other islands have lost theirs. Although there is a reasonable agricultural base, which produces a good crop of oats from forty crofts, the land is poor and the main industry is fishing, principally for prawns. Many of the islanders own their own boats and there are also a number of trawlers.

All the settlements are on the south-western seaboard.

A CORNER OF SCALPAY

In the past with a large population having less interest in fishing there was extensive lazybed cultivation. But there were too many mouths to feed and fishing became an essential occupation which eventually led to relative prosperity. In recent years, such a large number of people on an island of this size has created an almost urban atmosphere and the excellent harbours, surrounded by crisp white-washed houses, are always busy.

Scalpay has a very irregular outline with deep indentations. On the east side is **Beinn Scoravick**, 104m high with Loch na Craoibhe (G. – loch of the tree) separating it from 58m-high Ben Scoravick South. The north-west is rough territory of rock and heather-covered slopes, pockets of peat bog, lochs running parallel to the coast – **Loch Cuilceach** (G. – loch of reeds), **Loch an Dùin** (G. – loch of the fort) and **Loch Tarsuinn** (G. – the crosswise loch) at right-angles to the others.

Eilean Glas lighthouse, on the east coast, was erected in 1788 by the Commissioners of Northern Lights. It was the first and for a long time the only lighthouse in the Western Isles and was placed strategically on the busy sea lane which existed at that time between Skye, Harris and the Baltic. A new tower was constructed in 1824 with an oil-burning light and this was converted to incandescent in 1907. The lighthouse is now automatic and the keepers' houses are holiday homes. They were built of Aberdeen granite by Robert Louis Stevenson's grandfather.

The road ends by the peat diggings beyond Kennavay but there is an interesting walk around or over Ben Scoravick – down past the east coast lochans to the lighthouse with its rented accommodation and small restaurant and then along an unmapped south coast path for the return journey.

The west side of Scalpay shelters behind a line of small islands, **Eilean na Praise** (G. – pot island), **Stiughay, Fuam an Tolla, Stiughay na Leum, Rossay, Hamarsay**

and **Greinem**: and across the deep channel called Bràigh Mór (G. – big neck) is a great cluster of islets and rocks with the largest being **Gloraig a' Chaimbeulich, Eilean Mhic Fhionnlaidh, Eilean na Gearrabreac** (G. – guillemot isle) and **Eilean na Sgaite** (G. – skate isle).

Scalpachs are renowned throughout the islands for their excellent seamanship. This was proven when, in December 1962, the trawler *Boston Heron* was in difficulties in a full sou'-westerly gale and was driven on to the rocks of **Stilamair** off the south coast of Scalpay. Stilamair is a tidal island near Greinem islet. As there was no time to spare six Scalpay men set out immediately in a small open boat to try to give assistance. In spite of the ferocious seas they managed to rescue three of the trawlermen, one of whom was clinging exhausted to the rocks. They were unable to save the other seven but their heroism was rightfully recognised by the RNLI.

ACCESS: A vehicle-ferry which serves the island across the Sound of Scalpay from Kyles Scalpay, 01859-540266, is to be replaced by a bridge. Frequent service. Crossing time 10 minutes.

Anchorages: Both harbours give better shelter than Tarbert.
1. South harbour, on SW side, enter between Hamarsay and Rossay. Keep midway between south-east shore and Raarem islet. When past Raarem turn north and keep $^1/_2$c off E side of Raarem and continue close to W shore at the narrows. Anchor SE of islet in inner loch. Beware drying rock $^1/_2$c SE of islet.
2. Temporary anchorage in inlet $^3/_4$c W of lighthouse. Study directions carefully.
3. North harbour, a fine natural harbour in a small bight at NW end, with depths of 1.8m to 5.5m but limited space. Beware MacQueens rock and a reef and wreck near the entrance.

8.9 Scotasay

Probably, (ON – Skati's island) but, possibly, (ON Skot's-øy – Scot's island)

OS Maps: 1:50000 Sheet 14 1:25000 Sheet 108
Admiralty Charts: 1:100000 Nos.1794 or 1795 1:12500 No.2905

AREA: 49ha (121 acres)
HEIGHT: 57m (187 ft)

OWNER: Mr John Taylor, an English architect, who also owns neighbouring Scalpay.

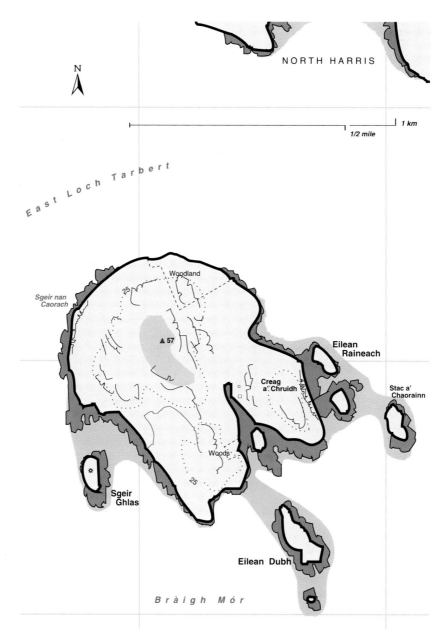

N

1 km
1/2 mile

East Loch Tarbert

NORTH HARRIS

Woodland

Sgeir nan
Caorach

△ 57

Eilean
Raineach

Creag
a' Chruidh

Stac a'
Chaorainn

Woods

Sgeir
Ghlas

Eilean Dubh

Bràigh Mór

POPULATION: 1861 – 14. 1881 – 0. 1891 – 18 (2 houses). 1901 – 15. 1911 – 20. 1921 – 19. Uninhabited since, except for summer visits by the owner and his family.

GEOLOGY: Banded gneiss bedrock.

Mainly covered with heather and rough grazing, **SCOTASAY** is in a central position in East Loch Tarbert and together with Scalpay provides valuable shelter for the ferry terminal at Tarbert. The croft house is in the cleft running up from the cove on the south-east side of the island while the highest point of 57m is towards the north. There is a fish farm on the north-east side.

The owner is well-liked by the local people because he 'leaves them alone,' I was told by a Scalpay ferryman.

The rowan tree on **Stac a' Chaorainn** (G. – stack of the rowan tree) no longer grows there, and **Sgeir Ghlas** (G. – pale grey-green skerry) with its beacon is more of an islet than a skerry. **Eilean Dubh** is part of the underwater reef which extends south of Scotasay while the islets, **Eileanan a' Ghille-bheid** and **Eilean Arderanish**, continue the parallel line of the Gloraigs opposite Scalpay.

ACCESS: Enquire at Harris Hotel, Tarbert or on Scalpay.

Anchorages: No recommended anchorages.

1. Temporary anchorage opposite the small bight on the NE side in 10m if if not obstructed by fish farm.

2. The cove on the SE side is full of rocks but has been called a 'small boat harbour'.

8.10 Shiant Isles

[sh-unt] (G. na h-eileanan seunta – the enchanted islands)

Garbh Eilean

(G. – rough island)

Eilean an Tigh

(G. – house or home island)
The largest separate island is Eilean Mhuire (G. – Mary's island)
The entire group of about a dozen islands and skerries is known locally as Eileanan Mora – the Large Isles.

OS Map 1:50000 Sheet 14 1:25000 Sheet 108
Admiralty Charts: 1:100000 Nos.1794 or 1795

AREA: 143ha (353 acres)
HEIGHT: 160m (525 ft)

OWNER: Sir Compton MacKenzie bought the group about 1925. He renovated a cottage on Eilean an Tigh and stayed there during the summer months when he wanted solitude for writing. He sold the islands to the publisher Nigel Nicolson in 1937 for £1500, and Nicolson still owned them in 1971. The grazing rights are let to a sheep farmer on Scalpay who keeps the cottage repaired and uses it during visits to tend the sheep.

POPULATION: There were five families living on Eilean an Tigh in the mid-18th century but by 1796 only one family was left, and it suffered a number of fatalities. By the 1820s Eilean an Tigh was uninhabited except for shepherds living in summer shielings but in 1845 one family was living on Garbh Eilean. The census shows that in 1881 there were two males and four females in the Shiants. 1891 – 8 (3m,5f) 1901 – 1 family (4m,4f) Since then, uninhabited.

GEOLOGY: Geologically the Shiants are outliers of Skye, although they are closer to Lewis. The rock formations are similar to Staffa, the Giant's Causeway in Antrim and parts of Mull – columnar (tertiary) basalt, forming spectacular cliffs of over 120m in height. The columns are almost 2m in diameter on Garbh Eilean's north face. This is geologically young rock; not like the ancient weathered gneiss of the 'Long Island'. There are fine natural stone arches on Eilean Mhuire's south-west shore and also a natural arch on Eilean an Tigh. Basalt is not generally a suitable rock for climbing.

Martin Martin said there was a blue stone in the Shiants and that he had seen a set of 'table men' carved from it.

HISTORY: In the 1820s two brothers, Alexander and Archibald Stewart of Park, Lewis, were notorious tacksmen who severely punished any fisherman who landed on the Shiant Islands, even in an emergency. It was always assumed that they were sheep-stealing (and occasionally they were). At that time the Shiants were part of the tack of Park, in Lochs, Lewis, whereas they are now considered to be part of Harris.

WILDLIFE: The common seal breeds here and basking shark used to frequent these waters. Porpoise and blue shark have been seen.

The islands were reputed to have become rat-infested from a shipwreck and Sir Compton Mackenzie imported cats to try to deal with them. The cats have died out (or been eaten by the rats!) and it is hoped that the brown rats, which live in the scree below the cliffs and steal the sea-birds eggs and young, will eventually be eradicated by the same method as that used on Ailsa Craig (see No.1.1). The naturalist, Dr Frank Fraser Darling, claimed that rats would only survive on an island if they had an accessible foreshore and shellfish. Very few rats are in fact to be seen but there have recently been worrying reports that mink have arrived.

Large numbers of puffins nest here in the turf at the top of the sea-cliffs. There is a colony of herring gulls, and oystercatchers, nesting eider, shag, snipe, lark, pipit, wheatear, golden eagle, greater and lesser black-backed gulls, rock dove, turnstone, hooded crow, blackbird, and many other species, can be seen.

Thousands of kittiwakes, guillemots, razorbills and fulmars nest among the huge fluted basalt columns on the northern cliffs.

According to legend the ghostly and menacing Blue Men of the Minch live in the Sound between the **SHIANT ISLANDS**. Some say they are storm kelpies who must be treated with great respect by sailors, and others that they are bad-tempered angels who fell into the sea when they were expelled from Heaven. The minister of Tiree from 1861 to 1891, the Rev. John Campbell, claimed that one followed his boat when he was sailing in the area – 'a blue-covered man, with a long, grey face, and floating from the waist out of the water.' The creature sometimes came so close that he could have touched him.

If you are accosted by a Blue Man it is important to have Gaelic. One skipper had to answer a Blue Man's questions in rhyming couplets on the threat of being dragged to the bottom of the Minch if his replies were not poetic.

Even if you don't see any Blue Men, the columnar basalt rock formations are every bit as spectacular. This is the back-street Manhattan of the Western Isles. A vast skyscraper city of seabirds, noisy and rank smelling. In *The Highlands and Isles of Scotland* MacCulloch (1773-1835) claimed that these '. . .form one of the most magnificent colonnades to be found among the Western Islands. But these islands are nowhere more striking than when viewed at a sufficient distance from the northward; the whole of this lofty range of pillars being distinctly seen rising like a long wall out of the sea; varied by the ruder forms of the others which tower above or project beyond them, and contrasted by the wild rocks which skirt the whole group.'

The well-known pillars of Fingal's Cave on Staffa are a mere 10m high, those on the Shiants are over 150m (500 ft). In comparing them MacCulloch said that they 'exceed them in simplicity, in grandeur, in depth of shadow, and in that repose which is essential to the great style in landscape'.

The Shiants are a group of two islands and several islets and outlying rocks. There is pasturage for sheep brought over from Scalpay (No 8.7) but there are no permanent inhabitants nowadays. **Eilean an Tigh** which is the southern part of the largest island of the group is connected with **Garbh Eilean**, the northern part, by a low narrow neck of polished pebbles. This isthmus covers at spring tides or during storms. Garbh Eilean is very steep; Eilean an Tigh is lower but has precipitous cliffs on its eastern side. Eilean Mhuire lies a short distance to the east of Garbh Eilean, so that the group almost forms a bay with a south-eastern exposure.

There is a cottage on the west side of Eilean an Tigh near the shingle link with Eilean Garbh [NG418976]. This is the cottage that was renovated by Sir Compton Macken-

zie when he owned these islands. Behind it is the ruin of an older dwelling and on the north side there are the remains of two more. A crystal clear spring of fresh water about one hundred yards from the cottage is hidden by lush green grass and wild flowers. The large scale Ordnance Survey map shows three wells or springs on Eilean an Tigh but only the one near the cottage has not been fouled.

L R Higgins, a writer who loved to camp on uninhabited Scottish islands, spent a fortnight here in the 1960s. He said that the only archaeological relic he could find on Eilean an Tighe was in the south hinterland. He called it the Pile. 'Near this Pile is the site of a church marked by a few stones but otherwise indistinguishable and ignored by the map.'

In the late 18th century there was only one family left on the island and it met with tragedy. Both the wife and the son of a shepherd fell to their death while chasing sheep above the steep cliffs. Not long after, one of his two daughters also fell to her death while collecting sea-birds' eggs, so this left only the shepherd and his younger daughter. After a short time he also died – but of natural causes, or possibly heartbreak – and so his daughter was left alone on the island. Ten days went by before the weather was settled enough for her to row the twelve miles to Harris. She never returned. (Then the story loses some of its drama when we learn that she had quite often rowed over to Harris to visit her boy-friend.)

Eilean Mhuire, Mary's Island, has also been inhabited and it is in fact the most fertile island in the group. There are steep cliffs on all sides and access is up a difficult rock 'stair' but the top is like the 'lost world' – a large plateau covered with arable land and ancient lazybeds, a fresh water lochan, and the remains of dwellings marked by clumps of nettles – a certain sign of human occupation. The ruin of a chapel is near the headland [NG430986]. This was dedicated to the Virgin Mary and was still in use at the time of the Reformation.

Martin Martin claimed that these islands were 'fruitful in corn and grass' and that the cows were much fatter than any he saw on Lewis. It must have been a hard life but at least the islanders were self-sufficient. There was seafood, potatoes, cabbages, milk, eggs, meat, seal-oil, peat, driftwood, and fresh water: all the essentials for a healthy existence – and the strength to row twelve miles to Harris and twelve miles back.

ACCESS: There are irregular sailings from Scalpay to tend the sheep. For boat hire during suitable weather try 01859-540225 or, alternatively, arrangements might be made for guests of the Harris Hotel, Tarbert, 01859-50 2154.

Anchorages: Tidal currents are strong in the vicinity of these islands and there are overfalls both N and S. Landing can be hazardous.

1. Approach from N or S for occasional anchorage between the islands in settled weather. Avoid reefs extending 1 1/2c W and 1 1/2c S of Eilean Mhuire. Anchor E of neck of gravel between Garbh Eilean and Eilean an Tigh but the bottom slopes steeply and holding may be uncertain. Exposed NE to SE but sheltered N through W to S. With SW winds a heavy swell sets in. Better holding has been reported in the NW corner of the Bay of Shiant in 10m, sand.

2. Temporary anchorage on W side of neck of gravel between Garbh Eilean and Eilean an Tigh. Sheltered N to E.

8.11 Taransay

(ON – Taran's island)

OS Maps: 1:50000 Sheet 18 1:25000 Sheets 98 and 107
Admiralty Charts: 1:200000 No.2721 1:50000 No.2841

AREA: 1,475ha (3,645 acres)
HEIGHT: 267m (876 ft)

OWNER: Purchased by John Mackay of Horgabost, Harris in 1967, or thereabouts, from Roddy Campbell. Mr Mackay has a transport company – John Mackay & Sons – and farms sheep on the island.

POPULATION: 1841 – 88 (16 houses). 1881 – 55. 1891 – 56 (12 houses). 1911 – 76. 1931 – 33. Last family left the island in 1942 but it was later reinhabited. 1961 – 5. 1971 – 5. 1974 – again abandoned.

GEOLOGY: Grey gneiss traversed by veins of granite with a grassy top-soil. The isthmus is mainly sand.

HISTORY: Eponymous Taran is an uncertain figure in Celtic history. According to Adomnan he was the son of a noble Pictish family who requested St Columba's protection. Columba agreed and asked Feradach, a rich man on Islay (No.2.4), to accept him in his retinue and treat him as a friend but Feradach chose instead to have him murdered. Columba was naturally outraged and condemned Feradach with a divine judgement.

Some scholars however consider that Taran was the Irish Saint Ternan or Torannan who had great influence on the Pictish mainland. As one of the chapels on Taransay was dedicated to St Taran this may be a more likely candidate.

Prehistoric man was well-established on Taransay and the Vikings may also have settled here judging by the wealth of Norse nomenclature.

In 1549 Dean Monro described Taransay as a place where people delved with spades, with good barley and corn and fishing.

WILDLIFE: The shoreline is magnificent in summer with brilliant white sands and the sea-thrift in bloom.

There is a small herd of red deer.

Unfortunately, mink – which are strong swimmers – are now reported to have reached Taransay from Harris and established themselves on the island. They are attacking ground-nesting birds, in particular the populations of puffin and shelduck.

TARANSAY is divided into two shapely hills by a low sandy neck of dunes. The village of **Paible** which is on the larger part of the island was the main settlement with a maximum population of seventy-six, but the school (next to the landing) closed in 1935 and numbers gradually dwindled until the last family left in 1942. Some of the original inhabitants are still to be found living on Harris, some within sight of their old home.

A mountain bothy on the island provides useful emergency accommodation for visitors. There is one big house which is maintained by the owner and used exclusively for accommodation by the farm workers during regular visits to tend the sheep, cattle and deer. They usually stay for ten days or so at a time.

Beinn Raah, 267m high, dominates the northern section with a ridge to the north and lesser peaks to the south-west where there are a number of small lochs. **Loch an Duinn** [NB022013] has a dun and probable crannog near its east shore. It is linked to Loch Shinnadale and then by Allt a' Mhuilinn (G. – the mill burn) to Loch Cromlach. The stream eventually reaches the sea beside Paible. North of Paible is the ruin of another Iron Age dun at **Corran Raah** [NB041005]. Little is known of the history of either of the two duns on Taransay.

The sites of two ancient chapels are at Paible, one dedicated to St Taran where only women were buried and the other to St Keith where only men were interred [NG030991]. This time-honoured method of segregation was upset, it is said, when a mixed burial took place in one of the graveyards. The following morning one of the

bodies was found lying on the surface of the ground beside the grave.

Loch na h-Uidhe (G – loch of the isthmus), the sea-loch which divides the island into two parts, is bounded by a magnificent stretch of shell-sand beach. **Aird Vanish** (ON *ve-nes* or *van-nes* – promontory of the sacred place or of Wane, the fertility god), the south-western part of the island, is a rough and lonely area, riddled with sea caves. It has twin peaks, Herraval and Bullaval.

Taransay is separated from Harris by the Sound of Taransay. At no point is the sea here deeper than 12m. The sandy spit of Corran Raah projects into the Sound and the bay on its north side is called Cealach na h-Atha (G. – the fireplace of the kiln). This presumably refers to the shape and should not give visitors a misleading impression of the temperature.

ACCESS: No regular access but arrangements can usually be made with a fisherman at Horgabost.

Anchorages:

1. South of Corran Raah and Bo Raah in Sound of Taransay. Close inshore, sand. Good shelter from NW but beware Bo Raah.

2. Cealach na h-Atha, on N side of Corran Raah. Anchor well in-shore, sand. Sheltered from SW winds by Corran Raah.

3. Loch na h-Uidhe. Beware Old Rocks and Langaraid on approach. Keep nearer E side of bay when entering to avoid rocks on W side. Reasonable shelter, except in S'lies.

8.12 Soay Mór

(ON so-øy – sheep island, G. mór – big)

OS Maps: 1:50000 Sheet 13 1:25000 Sheet 98
Admiralty Charts: 1:200000 No.2721 1:50000 No.2841

AREA: 45ha (111 acres)
HEIGHT: 37m (121 ft)

OWNER: The islands are leased by a fish-farming company who do not welcome visitors.

POPULATION: 1841 – no census record. 1881 – 0. 1891 – 15 (2 houses). No further record of any habitation.

GEOLOGY: Lewisian gneiss with some granite and quartz.

Soay Mór

The two islands, **SOAY MOR** and its associate **Soay Beag**, reach the same height of 37m and have few features of note. Reefs extend from both sides of the southern extremity of Soay Mór and drying rocks fill the passage between Soay Mór and Soay Beag. The fish farm is on the northeast side of Soay Mór facing Soay Sound.

West Loch Tarbert lies south-east of Soay Mór with small but steep **Isay island** (ON – porpoise island) in its centre.

ACCESS: Enquire in Tarbert.

Anchorages:
1. Occasional anchorage near centre of bay at N end of Soay Mór, facing Soay Sound if fish cages permit. An approach from direction of Soay Beag is safest.

8.13 Eilean Iubhard

[elan yoo-urt] (G. – yew-tree island)

OS Maps: 1:50000 Sheet 14 1:25000 Sheets 90 and 100
Admiralty Charts: 1:100000 No.1794

AREA: 125ha (309 acres)
HEIGHT: 76m (249 ft)

OWNER: Eilean Iubhard may be part of the Parc Crofters (Lewis) Estate.

POPULATION: No census records, uninhabited today and apparently uninhabited in 1746 – see below – but five families lived here in the early 19th century at Seanna Bhaile (G. – ancient settlement) and Tigh a' Gheumpail.

Eilean Iubhard

GEOLOGY: Gneiss bedrock with some basaltic intrusion.

HISTORY: On the 4th May 1746 Prince Charles Edward Stuart with two companions and a guide landed near the head of Loch Seaforth at Aribruach. They set off across country to Stornoway where Donald Macleod had arranged for a ship to take the Prince to France. The party lost its way during the night among the bogs of Arnish moor and only reached the outskirts of Stornoway in the late morning very wet and tired. They were sheltering under a rock when Donald Macleod reported to them that news of the Prince's approach had reached Stornoway and the captain of the ship now refused to sail. Mrs Mackenzie, a farmer's wife, provided overnight shelter and food for the party and at 8am on the 6th May the Prince, O'Sullivan, O'Neill, Donald and Murdoch Macleod, Ned Burke and four boatmen set sail in Donald Campbell of Scalpay's boat. They intended to cross the Minch to Poolewe but the wind was against them and ships of the Royal Navy could be seen on patrol. So they chose instead to land the Prince in the bay on the south shore of Eilean Iubhard and, as the boatmen refused to leave, the boat was possibly concealed on the north side of the island.

It was raining heavily and the party stretched a sail over a 'low pitiful hut' and spent four days there. Local fishermen used the island for drying their catches so Ned and the Prince cooked some of these fish for sustenance.

WILDLIFE: Dean Munro (1549) reported: '. . .guid to pasture and schielling of store, with faire hunting of ottars out of their bouries.'

EILEAN IUBHARD lies at the entrance to Loch Shell – or Loch Sealg – on the east coast of Lewis. It shelters an inlet and the village of Lemreway but it lies close to the coast and on approaching from the sea it can be difficult to recognise it as an island at all. It looks much more like a part of Lewis.

There are two minor peaks at opposite ends of the island, the one in the west being 62m high and the other in the east 76m high. The ground is very rough and irregular and there are several lochans and a number of small burns. Most of the coastline drops abruptly into the sea but there is a shallow bay at the west end called **Puill Chriadha** (G. – clay pool) and a cove in the centre of the south coast called merely **Bàgh** (G. – bay).

The eastern half of Eilean Iubhard is separated from Lewis by **Caolas a' Tuath** (G. – north channel) but at the western end this kyle becomes shallow and is obstructed by a number of rocks and islets.

ACCESS: No regular access. Enquire at Lemreway.

Anchorages:
1. Occasional anchorage on narrow shelf close to N shore of Eilean Iubhard, S of Sgeir Fraoich, but mainly obstructed by fish cages. Sheltered in S'lies. If winds change, move N into Tob Lemreway.

8.14 Seaforth Island

in Loch Seaforth

OS Maps: 1:50000 Sheet 13 1:25000 Sheets 89 and 99
Admiralty Charts: Only 1:100000 No.1794 covers Loch Seaforth but it is unsatisfactory.

AREA: 273ha (675 acres)
HEIGHT: 217m (712 ft)

POPULATION: No census records and uninhabited.

GEOLOGY: Lewisian gneiss bedrock covered with poor acid soil supporting rough grazing.

HISTORY: Seaforth Island belonged to the MacLeods until they were usurped by the Mackenzies in 1610. Francis Mackenzie, or Lord Seaforth, inherited the island in 1783.

Loch Seaforth is a long narrow loch wedged between high mountains and towering cliffs. The winds whisper through the peaks, build up their strength, meet in the corries, and then without warning sweep savagely down the mountain sides and flatten the waters of the loch with unpredictable ferocity. **SEAFORTH ISLAND** sits four-square in the centre of Loch Seaforth, six and a half miles from the entrance. It is a great heap of rough heather and bracken-covered slopes reaching up to a height of 217m above the loch. There are few signs of any human habitation or cultivation.

A couple of miles down the loch on the western shore is Loch Maaruig – where naval craft sometimes anchor near little **Maaruig Island**. The loch here forms the boundary between Harris and Lewis: Harris to the west, Lewis on the precipitous east side.

The loch entrance is guarded by **Rhenigidale Island** on the Harris side and three islets on the Lewis side, **Eilean Mór a' Bhàigh**, **Dubh a' Bhàigh** and **Beag a' Bhàigh** (G. – big, black and little island at the bay)

Francis Mackenzie (Lord Seaforth), who inherited the island in 1783, had four sons and two daughters. As one of the best recorded cases of Gaelic second-sight, a clansman named Kenneth Mackenzie, also known as the Brahan Seer, predicted that none of the sons would outlive the father and that the elder daughter would cause the death of her sister. This Gaelic prophecy became widely known and Sir Walter Scott recorded it in English before the events took place. Not only did the father outlive all his sons but while Lady Hood, his widowed elder daughter, was out riding in a carriage with her sister at Castle Brahan, the ponies shied and Lady Hood was unable to control them. The carriage overturned and her sister was killed in the accident.

ACCESS: It may be possible to arrange transport on one of

the local boats at the slipway at Bogha Glas on the main Stornoway to Tarbert road.

Anchorages:

1. Anchor off the N coast of the island ½M NE of Aline Lodge jetty in 7m, or off Aline Lodge jetty itself which is NW of the island. Good shelter and holding but can be subject to violent squalls.

2. Temporary anchorage where suitable depth can be found in the navigable channels W and E of Seaforth Island but beware squalls.

8.15 Scarp

(ON skarpoe – sharp, stony, mountain terrain)

OS Maps: 1:50000 Sheet 13 1:25000 Sheet 88
Admiralty Charts: 1:200000 No.2721 1:50000 No.2841

AREA: 1,045ha (2,582 acres)
HEIGHT: 308m (1,010 ft)

Seaforth Island

Map labels:
Duisker
Bo Leathan
Boghannan Cuil
Kearstay
Ostem
Slettnish
Cave
Geo an Fheòir
Waterfall
Rubha Ruadh
Cave
Sgeir Moil Duinn
Loch na Learga
Bula-charpach
△308
Sròn Romul
Glen Romul
Fladday
Geo Forse
Obe Rocks
Sròn Udemul
Abhainn Forse
Loch Rumalach
Alabost
Loch Bràigh an t-Sidhein
Loch Steisevat
Loch Uidemul
Beinn fo Thuath
177
Tràigh Mhellein
Tarta Geodha
Loch Beag a' Mhuilinn
Manish
Allt a' Mhuilinn
Rubha na Glaodhaich
Burial Gd
Geodha Islaca
Pier
Eilean na Moil Móire
Mol Mór
Bo Leire
Rubha na Creadha
Caolas an Scarp
Pier
HARRIS
(Hushinish)

Bràigh Mór
N

2 km
1 mile

OWNER: Sold by Mr Dewsbery to Mr Rolf Rothmayer in the early 1980s for £80,000. Rothmayer then sold Scarp to Mr Nazmu Virani, one-time owner of Belhaven Breweries and director of BCCI – the bank which held the title. BCCI collapsed and the property was resold in 1995 to Mr Anderson Duke Bakewell of Oxfordshire for £155,055.

POPULATION: Settled by eight farming families in 1810. About 1823, thirteen villages between Loch Resort and Bunabhainneadar were cleared and some of the displaced villagers settled on Scarp. 1841 – 129 (23 houses). 1861 – 151, the original eight crofts had been subdivided into smaller and smaller units. 1881 – 213. 1891 – 143 (29 houses). 1931 – 95. 1951 – 74. 1961 – 46. 1971 – 12. The last two resident families, seven people in all, left

Scarp in December 1971. 1981 – 2 (shepherds?). 1991 – 0.

GEOLOGY: Chiefly gneiss and gneissose granite but containing some soft asbestos-bearing rock which is geologically unique in this region. The asbestos content was discovered in the 1960s.

HISTORY: On 14th January 1934, attended by an eighty-five-year-old midwife in her home on Scarp, Mrs Christina Maclennan gave birth to a child. On the following day her condition was poor and as there was no telephone on Scarp an islander crossed to Hushinish. But the telephone there was out of order so the postman's son was sent to Tarbert to call the doctor. The doctor decided that Mrs Maclennan must go to hospital. The sea was rough but she was taken to Hushinish tied to a stretcher laid across a bouncing open boat. There she was laid on the floor of the local bus for the seventeen miles of bumpy road to Tarbert. She was then taken by car to the hospital at Stornoway where the cause of her distress was discovered. She gave birth to a second child, and felt much better for it! Thus the twins, both alive and well today, were born on different islands, in different counties and in different weeks.

This story, widely reported in the press at the time, came to the ears of a young German (who was later to become prominent in the German V2 rocket programme during the Second World War). So on the 28th July of the same year – which came to be known as 'Latha na Rocait' (G. – the day of the rocket) – Herr Gerhard Zucker, chose to demonstrate his rocket-mail invention on Scarp. Special stamps were printed for the occasion and a letter was written to the King. The one-metre-long solid-fuel rocket weighed 14kg and could carry several thousand letters at 1,000 mph but when Gerhard lit the fuse the rocket exploded prematurely scattering mail over a wide area. The local postmaster had the letters collected and he labelled each cover with violet ink reading – 'Damaged by first explosion at Scarp – Harris'. A second experiment with the same mail fired from Harris back to Scarp was successful but the project was abandoned, although a few letters addressed to Orkney actually reached their destination having travelled by rocket, ferry, automobile, mail-steamer, railway, and Highland Airways.

After the evacuation of St Kilda, **SCARP** was the most westerly inhabited island in Britain. Even in the 1940s the population was over one hundred but it was dwindling and only seven crofters were left to abandon the island in 1971. The postmaster, Mr Maclean, had finally shut the post-office in 1969, and no more Gaelic sermons were preached in the church. Angus Macinnes and his wife Margaret were last to leave with their son, Donald John, aged twenty-one. Donald John now lives in Dunbartonshire but his brother Murdo still crofts in Harris and visits Scarp frequently to tend his sheep.

The island is rocky and the north part is 308m in height, (over 1000ft) with a steep drop to the sea. The village, now used for holiday accommodation, is in the south-east corner and partly sheltered from the Atlantic winds by a low hill. The only land capable of cultivation is here on the east coast and it is easy to see how the island could not support a large population. Communication today is by boat between two stone jetties. The lack of an all-weather anchorage is a serious deficiency which must have contributed to the depopulation of the island. Latterly, the local economy was still very basic – potatoes, cabbages, oats, turnips, milk, fish, and some lobster fishing. There was no electricity and oil lamps were the only means of illumination but there was some piped water. The village

had one small shop and a telephone was installed in 1947.

Scarp has a proud educational record and it is claimed that more professionally qualified people came from the island than from any other island community of similar size. The Hebridean writer, Francis Thompson, tells of the Londoner who was amazed at the sheer isolation of Scarp and asked a Scarpach how he ever got the news from London. 'Well,' was the puzzled rejoinder, 'how do you get the news from Scarp?'

Although the **Kyle of Scarp** is a short crossing, landing at the pier can be difficult when there is any swell. The sea here is very shallow.

The islet beside Slettnish in the north, **Kearstay**, is divided from Scarp by a narrow channel less than 1m deep called the Sound of Kearstay. Another small island, **Fladday**, lies somewhat further offshore on the east and there is **Liongam** near the Lewis coast to the north-east. Low-lying **Gasker** is well-out in the Atlantic five miles south-west of Scarp and has an established seal colony. There are proposals that a lighthouse should be built on it.

ACCESS: No regular access but the owner of one of the boats at the Hushinish jetty facing Scarp may assist. Alternatively the Harris Hotel, Tarbert, 01859-502154, might make arrangements if they are given sufficient notice by their guests.

Anchorages:
1. Occasional anchorage in suitable weather just S of the bar in Caolas an Scarp, off Rubha na Glaodhaich.
2. Occasional anchorage in suitable weather in N entrance to Caolas an Scarp, N of the bar and SSW of Fladday.
3. Sound of Kearstay. Temporary anchorage in E entrance of the sound in 9-10m, sand.

8.16 Lewis

The derivation normally given is (G. leogach [loo-ach] – marshy). The entire area together with its offshore islands, once MacLeod territory, is referred to as 'The Lews.' (G. Eilean Leodhais [loo-is] – Leod's island). Leod or 'Ljod' is Norse for 'clan'. The Norse occasionally referred to the whole island as (ON Ljodusherad – Lewis Province).

Harris

(ON hearri – hills) or (G. na h-àirdibh – the heights)

Great Bernera

(ON bjarnar-øy – bear island) or (ON – Bjorn's island)

OS Maps: 1:50000 Sheets 8, 13, 14, and 18 1:25000 Sheets 42, 50, 51, 59, 60, 68, 69, 70, 71, 79, 80, 81, 88, 89, 90, 98, 99, 100, 107, 108, 116, 117 Admiralty Charts: 1:500000 No.2635 1:200000 No.2721 west coast 1:100000 Nos.1785, 1794 and 1795 east coast 1:50000 No.2841 south-west coast 1:20000 No.2642 Sound of Harris 1:12500 Nos. 3381 and 3422 Loch Roag 1:12500 No.2905 Loch Tarbert various scales No.2529 Loch Erisort and Stornoway

AREA: 220,020ha (5,389,369 acres)
HEIGHT: 799m (2,621 ft)

OWNERS: Lewis/Harris has multiple owners. They include the Stornoway Trust, Uig Crofters, Lord Thorneycroft, Barvas Estates, J. F. Robinson, Carloway Estate, Parc Crofters, and Major Hereward Wake. Amhuinnsuidhe Castle with its 50,000 acre estate was bought by Jonathan Bulmer, the cider heir, in 1994. His wife is the daughter of Earl Granville (of North Uist).

Great Bernera is owned by Captain Robin Mirrlees, Prince of Coronata, Comte de Lalanne, Freeman of London and Patrician of San Marino according to *Who's Who*. He bought it in the 1960s and has a house and fish farm there but he announced in 1992 that he intended to sell the estate.

POPULATION: In 1755 Harris had a population of 1969 and Lewis (excluding Bernera) 6386. By 1801 the equivalent figures were 2996 and 9168.

	1841	1881	1891	1931	1961	1971	1981	1991
Lewis	16988[1]	24876	27045	24685	21614	20047	21253	21737[2]
Harris	3058	3463	3681	3357	2493	2175	2137	
Bernera		596	535	514	317	276	292	262
Total	20046	28935	31261	28556	24424	22498	23682	21999

1 includes Bernera, Little Bernera & Pabay Mór 2 Lewis/Harris combined

GEOLOGY: Almost the entire island is gneiss, both ortho-gneiss and paragneiss, much of it overlaid with glacially deposited boulder clay; the orthogneiss is predominant. It has been metamorphosed from igneous as opposed to sedimentary rock and although it is complex and highly variable it is loosely known as Lewisian rock. It has a crystalline texture, is pink or grey in colour, and glitters with granules of mica or quartz. It does not weather readily and is unfortunately short of the minerals required to make a good fertile soil.

Exceptions are scarce. Near Stornoway there are a few small areas of New Red Sandstone; in Uig scattered areas of granite; a few linear basalt dykes; and, at Lingerbay in Harris, and two spots near the Butt of Lewis, anorthosite is predominant. This is the only anorthosite in Scotland – a mineral valued as a road aggregate for its reflective and skid-free properties.

The hills of South Lewis and North Harris have been shaped by glaciers emanating from a central ice-cap during the last Ice Age.

Central Lewis is a vast dark undulating plain of peat moorland which began to be laid down about 4000 years ago and continues to grow in thickness each year as the cold, wet, and acidic conditions delay decomposition of the previous year's layer of dead plants. So Lewis is reducing the 'greenhouse effect' by absorbing excess carbon dioxide! Peat is still the main fuel source for many of the islanders but the rate of growth exceeds the rate of consumption.

HISTORY: After Norwegian rule had ceased, Bruce's son, David II, granted Angus Og's son, John MacDonald, King of the Isles, many of the Hebridean islands including Lewis and Harris. That was in 1335. Lewis became one of the four regional administrative centres for the island kingdom. Later, having demoted himself to 'Lord of the Isles' in deference to Robert I of Scotland, MacDonald granted Lewis and Harris to the indigenous vassal clan Leod and thereafter the Macleods ruled the island.

Lewis/Harris was the last area of the western isles to adopt the Gaelic tongue and even today the spoken language of Lewis has many associations with Norse.

King James VI – the 'wisest fool in Christendom' – had no love of the Gaels. He promoted a company called the Fife Adventurers to plunder Lewis, if need be with 'slaughter, mutilation, fyre-raising, or utheris inconvenieties' and openly recommended genocide. Three raids on Stornoway were mounted – in 1598, 1605 and 1609 – but all were beaten off by Neil MacLeod and his

THE EAST SIDE OF HARRIS

Lewismen and the Adventurers eventually went bankrupt. James spitefully withdrew the MacLeods' charter and granted title to the Mackenzies of Kintail, who took over control of Lewis in 1610. The Mackenzies developed Stornoway and dominated the MacLeod clansmen, but their Chiefs – the Earls of Seaforth – never took up residence in the old MacLeod castle in Stornoway harbour. Their main interest in Lewis was deer hunting in Park, otherwise they chose to remain absentee landlords. The Seaforths lost their title following support of the Jacobites in 1715 but they quickly regained it by supporting the Hanoverians in 1745. Throughout, they retained possession of Lewis and from their residence in London supported an oppressive regime. Tacksmen, such as the notorious George Gillanders in the late 18th century, were permitted to charge extortionate rents and run what amounted to 'protection' rackets.

In 1778 the Earl of Seaforth raised a regiment to fight in the American War of Independence – the Seaforth Highlanders – for which he was paid a handsome Government levy but his soldiers received no pay until they mutinied in Edinburgh.

In 1783 a younger son of the Mackenzies inherited Lewis, was created Lord Seaforth, and proved a much more understanding landlord but although he had four sons they all predeceased him.

By the early 1800s Stornoway's fishing industry was booming. Mrs Stewart Mackenzie – Lord Seaforth's daughter – sold Lewis in 1844 to Sir James Matheson for £190,000. He then spent nearly £1/2m – earned from trade with China – on improvements. He also paid the costs of 1,800 people who wished to emigrate to Canada, for more than half the population had signed on with the Destitution Fund as this was the time of the potato famines.

Matheson's tenure was benevolent and there were no evictions. Nevertheless in 1887 crofters desperate for more land killed 200 deer in the Park area, roasted the venison, and held a feast for journalists in order to attract public attention to their cause. This was one of the last 'uprisings' in what became known as the Crofters' War. The leaders were later charged with mobbing and rioting and tried in court, but they were found not guilty.

In 1918 Lord Leverhulme, the soap magnate, bought the entire island, both Lewis and Harris, and spent nearly a million pounds trying to develop the fishing industry. In 1923 he gifted the 25,000 hectare parish of Stornoway to the people and offered crofts as free gifts although only forty-one tenants accepted. His plans were starting to bear fruit when he died in 1925 but his executors abandoned the project, split the island into several large estates and sold out. Poverty followed and more than 1000 young men emigrated to North America, although some returned during the years of the Depression.

The MacLeods of Harris had controlled the southern part of the island until 1779 when it was sold to Captain MacLeod of Berneray (No.8.1) who built the harbour at Rodel, constructed roads, restored Rodel church, planted many trees and developed the fishing industry. Unfortunately the Harris population was increasing rapidly and the demand on the land was excessive. Consequently the islanders were unable to meet their rent obligations.

In 1834 MacLeod sold Harris to the Earl of Dunmore, and unlike Sir James Matheson in Lewis he evicted islanders from their west coast crofts in order to lease the land to sheep farmers. However, he did attempt to carry out the evictions in a reasonably humane manner by giving three year's notice to quit. And his wife is to be remembered as the person who first popularised Harris tweed and thus created a new industry. The Earl's heirs sold North Harris to Sir Edward Scott in 1868 and South Harris directly to Lord Leverhulme in 1919.

Much of the recent successful development of Lewis and Harris is thanks to the efforts of the Highlands and Islands Development Board (HIDB), now Highland and Islands Enterprise (HIE), and a number of projects funded by grants from the European Community.

WILDLIFE: Some 4000-5000 years ago Lewis and Harris were covered with stunted forests mainly of alder, oak, pine, ash and elm. But with settlement by man the island was steadily denuded of trees. A change of climatic conditions dealt the final blow.

Lewis has relatively little machair as the west coast has many rocks and cliffs, but the central plain is rich in peat with ling and bell-heather, cross-leaved heath, bog-asphodel, sundew, cotton grass, bog-myrtle, blue moor grass, deer's hair grass and sphagnum moss.

Among the Harris mountains there is little heather but wild thyme, saxifrages and violets are everywhere. There are a few alpine willow and roseroot but no *silene acaulis* and *azales procumbens* as these prefer granite. When ferrets were introduced rabbits were almost exterminated and the ferrets also preyed on ptarmigan. But the rabbits survived and even pine martens have not succeeded in wiping them out in the treeless Forest of Harris.

Seton Gordon when writing *A Highland Year* found Clisham and its environment singularly devoid of animal and bird life. He mentions grouse and meadow pipits but no golden plover, curlew, buzzards or eagle.

In Stornoway a colony of grey seals inhabit the harbour and the woodland surrounding Lews Castle has been colonised by many species of birds and includes a large rookery.

On the west coast there is a wildfowl refuge at Loch Mór Barvas and corncrakes nest in the undisturbed old burial grounds.

Escapees from the mink farms of the 1950s are now unfortunately established predators threatening the endangered bird populations. They are virtually impossible to eradicate and as they are strong swimmers it is almost certain that they will eventually colonise adjoining islands and spread south to the Uists.

Although **LEWIS** and **HARRIS** are parts of a single island there is a natural six-mile barrier of high mountains and forbidding moorland between the great sea-lochs of Seaforth and Resort. This so effectively separated the two communities throughout history that they were considered entirely separate islands. Even today, although now connected by road, they speak Gaelic with a distinctly different dialect.

HARRIS, the southern part of the island, is itself divided into two parts, North and South Harris, where sea lochs nearly meet at Tarbert (G. *tairbeart* – a narrow isthmus). The west coast has dunes backed by machair which is so thick with wild flowers in early summer that milk from the grazing cattle is said to be perfumed. Here the white shell-sands are blown over the machair by the winds giving it a natural dressing of lime while the islanders spread seaweed as an organic fertiliser. The other traditional farming practice, lazybeds, is reserved for the barren east coast – strips of peat and seaweed built laboriously by hand on top of the rock strata and used for growing oats and potatoes.

At the time of the Clearances the population was larger than the land could support and the standard of living was low. Islanders were turned off their productive west coast crofts and many, loathe to leave their homeland, tried to eke out a living on the desolate east coast where the landowners had no interest in such an uneconomic region. To make matters worse families evicted from the neighbouring islands in the Sound of Harris also settled here and lazybeds consequently stretched far up the hillsides amid terrible poverty. In the end depopulation by emigration seemed the only answer.

From the ferry terminal at **Tarbert** there are connec-

tions to Skye and North Uist but the town itself, although the largest settlement on Harris, is small, consisting of a few shops, a hotel, a post-office, a small tourist office, and some stores and workshops for the fishermen.

The narrow, winding, road on the east coast south of Tarbert is called the **Golden Road** because it was so expensive to build. In this area, known as Bays, the bare gneiss is pockmarked with tiny lochs, the predominant colours are rich dark browns and greys, and the coastline is a broken conglomerate of inlets and islands. There are mere pockets of sodden charcoal-coloured peat and the ground is so rocky that the dead had to be taken to the west coast for burial. It is difficult to imagine a more desolate, yet awe-inspiring, landscape with human habitation limited to an intermittent smattering of neat little houses near the shoreline.

> The narrow bay
> Has a knuckle of houses and a nail of sand
> By which the sea hangs grimly to the land.
> *Norman MacCaig, 'Harris, East side'*

The Golden Road serves the scattered settlements around the bays. Every turn brings a new picture-postcard scene of white houses in rocky coves, moored boats, lobster pots and nets. There are two islets in Loch Grosebay – **Càiream** and **Eilean Dubh** and at the next firth, Loch Stockinish, a youth hostel overlooks Stockinish Island (No.8.7). Two more islets in bays further to the west are much smaller than Stockinish – **Eilean Mhànais** outside Loch Gheocrab and **Eilean Quidnish** in Loch Finsbay. The road winds and twists past Lingara Bay, and **Lingarabay Island** about which the pros and cons of a gigantic quarrying venture are being hotly argued at the time of writing and arrives at Rodel near Renish Point, the southern extremity of Harris. **Renish Island** is no more than a punctuation mark at the end of Renish Point.

The village of Rodel has an attractive little harbour which was built in the 18th century by Captain Macleod of Berneray. It was here that the Harris ferry would put passengers ashore by tender before the new terminal was built at Tarbert. Above the harbour stands **St Clement's Church** [NG0488832] which was built by Alasdair Crotach, the 8th MacLeod in about 1500 using sandstone imported from Carsaig on Mull (No.3.3). Its solid rectangular tower is a distinctive landmark which is unique in the Western Isles, and MacLeod's tomb within the church is beautifully carved and well worth a visit. The church was restored in 1787 and again in 1873. If locked, the key can be obtained from the nearby hotel.

Leaving Rodel and travelling parallel to the Sound of Harris one arrives at **Leverburgh**, a

ST CLEMENT'S CHURCH, RODEL

small, sad, rather down-at-heel port now restored to its original name of **An t-Obbe** (G. – the creek). It was named Leverburgh by Lord Leverhulme when he tried to make it a centre for the herring fishing industry after the First World War and spent a considerable sum on providing facilities. But the project languished and he sold out in 1923 and the township never really recovered from its growth pains. A small ferry runs from here to Berneray and North Uist.

Further to the north-west beyond **Northton** is the distinctive peninsula of **Toe Head**. Its dominant peak is Chaipaval (339m). From its summit on a clear day the St Kilda group (Nos 9.1, .2 and .3) can be seen to the west, and the Cuillin of Skye to the east. Between the road and Chaipaval is a vast stretch of perfect Hebridean beach, **Tràigh an Taoibh Thuath** (G. – beach on the north side) which continues on to **Tràigh Scarasta** (G. – beach, ON – the farm in the pass) with its sand dunes below the machair. The road here winds along the Atlantic coast and the scenery is dramatically different from the desolation of the east; wide open meadows, pale pink or cream shell sands, turquoise sea and white surf. At **Borve** (ON – fort) there is a standing stone and an ancient dun and the hills to the south conceal a large loch – Loch Langavat (ON – long water). Borve Lodge, surrounded by woodland planted by the Earl of Dunmore, was Lord Leverhulme's home on Harris. Opposite Taransay (No.8.11) there is another wide stretch of sand – Tràigh Seilebost with a spit of sand dunes separating it from the estuarine sands of Tràigh Luskentyre. Here the road turns eastwards through a long valley before returning to Tarbert.

The bare mountains of the Forest of Harris are north of Tarbert. Beneath them on the shore of West Loch Tarbert the remains of a whaling station, built by Norwegians before the First World War and abandoned in 1930, are a reminder of another age. There are dramatic views from the coast road as it runs west round Loch Meavaig and beneath the windows of **Amhuinnsuidhe Castle** [a:vin-soo-ee] (G. – river seat) beside Loch Leosavay [NB043084]. The castle was built by the Earl of Dunmore in 1868 beside stepped falls where the waters of Loch Leosaid tumble over smooth rock slabs and into the sea. Salmon jump these falls in June and July. It was here in 1912 that James Barrie, of *Peter Pan* fame, wrote the drama *Mary Rose*. He was inspired, it is said, by the islets in Loch Voshimid at the head of Glen Meavaig. This area of Harris has large herds of red deer and the lochs are rich with salmon and trout. There is a hydro-electric

AMHUINNSUIDHE CASTLE IN THE FOREST OF HARRIS

scheme hidden in the hills above which provides most of the electricity requirements for Harris.

The coast road comes to an end at beautiful **Hushinish Bay** with the island of Scarp (No.8.15) to the north and Taransay (No.8.11) to the south.

For anyone proposing to camp on Harris most sites are boggy and midgy, so be prepared. However, as compensation, there is rock-climbing for enthusiastic climbers on Clisham which is the highest peak in the Outer Hebrides at 799m (a Corbett), or Sgurr Scaladale, Cnoc a Chaisteil, Creag Mò, Glen Scaladale, Gillaval Glas, Sgaoth Ard, Toddun, Craig Stulaval, Oreval, Ullaval, Strone Ulladale and Taran Mór. There are also many fascinating walks along the hill-tracks which are marked on the Ordnance Survey maps; for example, Vigadale Bay on Loch Seaforth to Loch Voshimid, or Aline Lodge to Loch Langavat (a much larger loch than that of the same name in South Harris).

LEWIS has a mixed economy of weaving, fishing and crofting and occasional construction work for the oil industry. Although Harris tweed, known locally as *clò mór* (G. – big cloth), originated in Harris, the centre of production is now in Lewis, probably because the great majority of the population live there. The tweed is still produced on hand looms and the weavers have resisted any attempts to introduce power looms although spinning and dyeing is now done in a factory. The 650 weavers on the island produce about 4½ million yards of tweed each year. Unfortunately, with widespread central heating and a preference for light-weight clothing there was an inevitable decline in sales of this fine, warm, water-resistant, and almost indestructible material. But the fashion pendulum is swinging back in its favour as lighter-weight cloths of broad width are now available.

The road connecting Harris and Lewis runs from Tarbert to Stornoway skirting the shores of Loch Seaforth and Loch Erisort. Loch Seaforth is twelve miles long and the area between it and Loch Erisort is called Park (G. *pairc*), a 23,000 hectare estate of wild country with many herds of red deer. Much of this area is fairly inaccessible and the simplest method of reaching it is probably by boat from Loch Seaforth. This is a truly remote wilderness just waiting for exploration by hill-walkers although it should be avoided during the hunting season. It was on this sporting estate in 1887 that crofters killed 200 deer to draw attention to their desperate need for land.

At the head of Loch Erisort, another long sea-loch, by **Balallan** (G. – Allan's town) there are roads leading into the north-east of Park, the only area accessible by vehicle. At the loch entrance is a drying-island, **Eilean Chaluim Chille** (G. – island of Columba's church) having, as expected, an ancient ruined church dedicated to St Columba [NB386211] and a small burial ground next to what may have been a monastery. Macleod of Lewis kept an orchard on this island at one time and Murdo Mackenzie, 'Mac Mhic Mhurchaidh,' the first of Lord Seaforth's factors, lived here. **Eilean Cheois** is in the centre of the loch while **Eilean Thòraidh** and **Eilean Rosaidh** are east of the Cromore headland. The **Barkin Isles** are to the north at the entrance to Loch Leurbost; they comprise **Tabhaidh Mhór**, **Tabhaidh Bheag**, **Tannaraidh** and **Bhatarsaidh**.

North of Park is the parish of Lochs with its steep and rocky coastline cut deeply by sea-lochs. The dark peat moorland is spattered with lochans like pools of mercury gleaming under a cloudy sky.

STORNOWAY (ON *stjorna* – steering or anchor bay), is the only town of burgh status in the Hebrides and the administrative centre of Comhairle nan Eilean Island Council. It has a population of about 8,100 and the town is centred on its fine natural harbour. Strangely, it was the Dutch who first recognised the fishing potential of Hebridean waters and during the 17th century their fishing fleets were often to be seen in Stornoway harbour. Although cod and ling were caught, it was herring that proved the great attraction. In 1798 Cruttwell's Gazateer reported that '. . .the coast is annually visited by myriads of herrings. So immense are the shoals of dog-fish that pursue the herrings that their dorsal fins are sometimes seen like a thick bush of sedges above water as far as the eye can reach.' By the 19th century Stornoway had become a major fishing port and its architecture reflects the prosperity of this period. The local history is illustrated in the Stornoway Museum in Cromwell Street.

The oldest building still standing is possibly the 18th century net-loft on **North Beach Quay** while **St Columba's Parish Church** on Lewis Street was erected in 1794. At the upper end of Francis Street is **St Peter's Episcopal Church**, built in 1839, which has an ancient sandstone font brought from the Hermit's Chapel on the remote Flannan Isles (See Introduction to Section 9). Its Tower Bell of 1631 once summoned the burghers of Stornoway to civic meetings and David Livingstone's 1608 Bible which he carried in Africa is kept in the vestry.

Arnish Point, at the entrance to Stornoway Harbour, is the site of an oil fabrication yard. Near Arnish is a monument to the memory of Prince Charles Edward Stuart and on the opposite side at Holm Point is another monument to the 205 Lewis men who were drowned on New Year's Day, 1919 [NB445305]. They were returning home from service at the end of the First World War when their ship, the *Iolaire*, was wrecked on the Beasts of Holm, the rocks just north of the entrance to the harbour while their waiting families watched helpless from the pier. The last survivor of this terrible disaster died in 1993.

Sir Alexander Mackenzie, the explorer who made the first overland crossing of Canada, was born in Stornoway and **Martins Memorial** (1885) stands on the site of the house where he was born. West of the town is Sir James Matheson's **Lews Castle** [NB420332], built in 1856-63, which is now a thriving and popular technical college. It is surrounded by spacious gardens and mixed woodland which is a unique sight in the Outer Hebrides.

Although Stornoway lies on the periphery of Europe it is a remarkably cosmopolitan place with an unexpected bustle of activity quite unlike the rest of the Outer Isles. Some of the shops are run by Pakistanis who are said to speak fluent Gaelic.

To the east of Stornoway, beyond the airport, is the comparatively densely populated **Eye Peninsula**, known as Point (G. *an rubha*). On the north shore of the narrow isthmus is the 14th century St Columba's church and graveyard where nineteen MacLeod chiefs are buried [NB485322]. The church was last used in 1828.

West of Stornoway a road crosses the island to Loch Roag and another strikes north-west across the moors to Barvas. Much of Lewis is dark peat moorland with hundreds of shallow lochs and fascinating patterns created by centuries of peat cutting. In early summer 'going to the peats' is an important social occasion and the peat is still cut for fuel in the traditional way. It has been estimated that there are eighty-five million tons of peat on the island. An average family uses about 15000 blocks of peat each year, and this takes at least fifteen man-days to cut, dry and stack.

A road runs round **Loch Roag** crossing **Abhainn Grimersta** which is considered one of the best salmon rivers in Europe. The waters come from distant Loch Langavat through a tortuous succession of remote lochs before discharging into Loch Roag. A branch road leads to the large island of **GREAT BERNERA** (G. *Bearnaraidh Mór*) which lies in the centre of the loch. Its access bridge,

KIRKIBOST PIER, GREAT BERNERA

the first pre-stressed concrete bridge to be built in Europe, was constructed in 1953 after the islanders threatened to dynamite the hillside to form a causeway. Many of the islanders are called MacDonald and are said to be descended from a watchman who was given the island by the MacAulays of Uig as a reward for his services. Great Bernera is a lobster-fishing centre; the processing plant at Kirkibost was built in 1972.

Loch Roag is a fascinating area and one could spend weeks exploring its many islands and inlets. The freshwater lochs which surround it provide excellent brown trout fishing. The beaches and coves near **Valtos** are of particular beauty.

Beyond Loch Roag is **Camas Uig** (G. *camas* – bay, ON *vik* – bay) and the magnificent Sands of Uig. It was here that a 12th century Norse chess set probably carved from walrus ivory was found in the dunes behind the beach. The Uig sands are a remarkable sight – wide, clean, flat and virginal white with a viridian sea and heather-covered Mealisval and Tahaval behind.

The road carries on down the coast from here but it slowly loses importance and dwindles to a track at **Mealista** where there are the remains of an army camp adjoining the ruins of a Benedictine convent called Tigh nan Cailleachan Dubha (G. – house of the old women in black, i.e. nuns) and traces of a 'souterrain' [NA991241].

If camping by the white sands of Uig or Mangersta Bay with the big Atlantic breakers for company it is essential to have some shelter from the wind. There are fascinating hill walks and many good climbs in this region – Mealisval 574m, Cracaval, Tarain, Tahaval, Teinnasval, or Tamanaisval – to name a few.

Back at the head of East Loch Roag the main road from Stornoway reaches one of Britain's most famous landmarks – the ancient standing stones of **Callanish** [NB213330]. It was only in 1857, when the surrounding peat was excavated, that the true height of these stones was realised. This is the second greatest prehistoric stone circle in the British Isles, and some 4000 years old. The alignment of the stones appears to relate to astronomical observations of the moon, unlike Stonehenge which relates to the sun. The monoliths are laid out in an oblique cross, 123m from north to south and 43m east to west with a central circle and cairn in which the remains of a cremation were found. The tallest standing stone is 4½m high. Other small stone circles in the vicinity of Callanish are probably related to it. (Calanais Visitor Centre. Mon-Sat 10am-7pm.)

Local legend claimed that the standing stones of Callanish were giants petrified by St Kieran for refusing to be christened.

About 8km north of Callanish is **Doune Carloway** one of the best-preserved brochs [NB190413]. It is 15m in diameter, parts of the galleries and staircase are still intact, and the quality of the dry stone masonry is remarkable. The broch is on a height overlooking Loch Carloway. An islet, **Craigeam**, is concealed behind its northern headland.

Just north of the village of Carloway, **Garenin** has the last remaining street of black houses on Lewis. These are clustered above a shingle beach in a sheltered cove [NB193442]. The last inhabitants left in 1973 but the houses are now being restored and re-occupied as part of a far-sighted project to preserve the village in its original state.

This north-west Atlantic coastline is steeped in history. There is a folk museum at **Shawbost**, a 6m high whalebone arch at **Bragar** with the harpoon which killed the whale suspended from it and a Black House Museum at **Arnol** [NB311493]. This *tigh dubh* was occupied as recently as 1964 and with a peat fire kept burning in the centre it is possible to see an authentic interior with the original straw-lined box beds. It makes one realise how well these houses were suited to the climate. Walls 2m thick and thatch and turf roofs weighted with stones created a warm, dry interior no matter what the state of the weather outside.

At **Barvas** a road cuts across the moors to Stornoway with the rare sight of a petrol station at the junction. There are many prehistoric sites near the coast on the route north. For instance, the tallest standing stone in Scotland (over 6m) is at **Ballantrushal** [NB376537]; a 15m burial cairn and large enclosure is at **Shader** [NB396541]; and there are many brochs, duns and temple ruins.

The main road ends at **Port of Ness**. From here Lewis men sail every August to Sula Sgeir, forty-one miles to the north, to bring back *guga* – young gannet, which is considered a great delicacy but is certainly an acquired taste. Port of Ness is a delightful little harbour although it offers only limited shelter.

Near **Eoropie** (ON *eyrar-boe* – beach village), the most northerly settlement, is a natural stone arch and 'pygmy's isle' – **Luchruban** or Eilean nan Daoine Beaga (G. – isle of the little people) [NB508661]. A pygmy race was believed to have lived here and Dean Munro said that they had their 'ane little kirk in it of ther awn handey wark.' The chambered building is on the steep summit of the is-

CARLOWAY BROCH

land. In an excavation many small bones were found which were thought to be human but were later identified as animal bones.

Just north of Eoropie is the restored 12th century **Teampull Mholuidh** (G. – Church of St Moluag) [NB519653]. The key for access is kept in the local store.

A little more than another kilometre to the north the Outer Hebrides come to a dramatic end at the **Butt of Lewis**. The brick lighthouse overlooks a mist-shrouded tumble of stacks and rocky precipices: the sea boils in the chasms between and the eery sound of the fog-horn echoes from the cliffs. Apart from Sula Sgeir and Rona there is nothing now but wild sea until one reaches the Faeroes 200 miles to the north.

ACCESS: Vehicle ferries: To Stornoway, Lewis, 01851-702361, from Ullapool, 01854-612358: To Tarbert, Harris, 01859-502444, from Uig, Skye, 01470-542219. To Leverburgh, Harris from Newtonferry, N. Uist, 01876-70230.
British Airways: Glasgow or Inverness direct to Stornoway or Glasgow via Barra/Benbecula to Stornoway, 0345-222111
Tourist Information: Stornoway, 01851-703088; Tarbert, 01859-502011.

Anchorages:
1. An t-Obbe (Leverburgh). There is 4.3m depth alongside head of pier but anchor as convenient clear of pier and moorings. Sheltered and safe in channel 2¹/₂c SE of Rubh' an Losaid in 5.5m, very good holding, but very restricted and access difficult.
2. Carminish bay, has some shelter from NW for boats which can take the ground. Mostly dries.
3. Port Eisgein, Sound of Harris, 1M NW of Renish Point, small inlet noted in Admiralty Pilot. No other information.
4. Loch Rodel, Renish point. Exposed to S'lies but occasional anchorage at head of bay on NW side, or off boulder beach on NE side, W of church (conspic.). Beware Duncan rock.

5. *Poll an Tigh-Mhail, Rodel. Enter from Loch Rodel thro' Bay Channel (which dries 0.9m with large stones). When base of Pillar Rock perch is covered there is 3.4m depth. Pool is deep with perfect shelter. HIE visitor's moorings on N side of Vallay. Harbour by hotel dries completely. Anchor off jetty in NW corner of pool in 5m.*

6. *Lingara Bay, by Lingarabay island. Sheltered only in W'lies. Anchor just past S side of Eilean Collam in 5m. Go no further in.*

7. *Loch Finsbay. Little sea, good holding and perfect shelter in all winds. Beware rocks N of Finsbay Island, west of Eilean Quidnish and in loch at Ardvey. Anchor mid-channel N of Ardvey promontory in 4m, mud. Hard to recognise in misty weather but fairly easy entrance if directions followed carefully.*

8. *Loch Flodabay. Not recommended due to number of rocks but ³/₄c wide channel along NE shore is charted as clear.*

9. *Loch Gheocrab. Poor shelter except for pool at head of loch behind a drying reef but obstructed with fish cages.*

10. *Loch Beacravik, which is the W arm at the head of Loch Gheocrab is well-protected but has fish cages and E side is foul at entrance. Avoid rocky patches on bottom when anchoring.*

11. *Loch Stockinish. Access best through Caolas Beag, E of Stockinish Island, before half-tide. Very narrow (only 27m at one point) but clean if close-in to Stockinish Island. After passing Stockinish keep just NE of mid-channel. Anchor in mouth of westerly arm at head of loch, completely sheltered, 9m, sand. Beware rock off Ardvey point and overhead cable to N.*

12. *Loch Grosebay. Safe anchorage but poor shelter N of Sgeir a' Chais at head of loch in 9m, mud. Several hazards on approach.*

13. *Loch Scadabay, on N side of entrance to Loch Grosebay. Passage W of Eilean an Duine is shallow and only 30m wide. Keep to E side to avoid drying rocks. Pool depth less than 2m but soft mud. Perfect shelter.*

14. *Plocrapool, East Loch Tarbert, 57° 50.5N 06° 45W. Snug but shallow. Approach carefully by sailing directions. Pass W of rock at entrance, steer 210°. and anchor in suitable depth.*

15. *Ob Meavag, Loch Ceann Dibig, East Loch Tarbert. Many rocks but sheltered. Dries 2c from head. Approach from NW with head of inlet bearing 138°. Beware fish cages.*

16. *Bàgh Diraclett, Loch Ceann Dibig. Sheltered but beware drying rocks on approach.*

17. *Eileanan Diraclett, 57° 53N 06° 47W. N of entrance to Loch Ceann Dibig. Sheltered anchorage but no further than 1c into inlet on W side of islands.*

THE THRUSHAL STONE AT BALLANTRUSHAL

18. *East Loch Tarbert. Little space due to moorings and ferry access. Ferry needs space to turn on S side of pier. Anchor W of pier only if space permits.*

19. *Loch Maaruig, 2¹/₂M into Loch Seaforth on W side. Anchor W of Goat Point, mud. Beware rock awash SW of Goat Point. Well-sheltered. In places the shore is so steep that it is possible to moor to it and lie afloat.*

20. *Aline Lodge. Anchor off the jetty, or better, ¹/₂M farther NE in 7m. Sheltered but subject to squalls.*

21. *Loch Claidh. 1M into loch on E side, anchor NE of Eilean Thinngarstaigh (Hingarstay) in 5.5-7m, mud and sand. Space just over ¹/₂c width. Enter W and N of En Thinngarstaigh. Good holding and shelter and little swell.*

22. *Tob Smuasavig, inlet on NE side of Loch Claidh. Anchor at head of inlet, bottom stiff clay, shells and stones. Uncomfortable in S winds.*

23. *Loch Bhalamuis (Valamus). Approach with care only when loch well open and keep W of centre when in the loch. About ¹/₂M into loch on E side anchor ¹/₂c N of Transit Point if sufficient depth found clear of drying rock and boat mooring.*

24. *Loch Bhrollum. Tob Bhrollum on NE side of Aird Dhubh is well-sheltered but some swell sets in with S'lies. Skirt W and N sides of Aird Dhubh at a distance of 30m until Rubh' a' Bhaird is shut in by Aird Dhubh then anchor as convenient in 4-6m, good holding. This position is east of a sunken rock in the entrance.*

25. *Loch Bhrollum. Anchor at head of loch on E side of islet. Shallow but soft mud.*

26. *Loch Shell or Sealg. S side clean but there are rocks W of Eilean Iubhard. Anchor in Tòb na Gile Móire on S side, at head of loch, in Tòb Eishken (beware rock E of entrance) on N side, in Tòb Stiomrabhaigh (Stemervay) or Tòb Orinsay. All areas shoal or shallow, partly exposed and some may be foul with old moorings or obstructed with fish cages. Squalls possible.*

27. *Tòb Lemrevay (Limervay), Caolas a' Tuath. Follow directions for approach. Anchor off E side of inlet with just enough room to clear shoreline rocks. Good holding but subject to N squalls.*

28. *Loch Odhairn (Ouirn). Anchor towards the head, opposite N shore jetty, on S shore behind promontory. Bottom good, no sea in any wind, but heavy squalls in SW gales. Loch free from dangers.*

29. *Loch Mharabhig (Mariveg), 58° 05.4N 06° 23.5W. Tortuous entrance by Caolas na h-Acarsaid, S of Eilean Rosaidh, or S of Eilean Thòraidh, and several rock obstructions in loch. Best anchorages SE of Sgeir a' Bhuic or in NW corner. Well-sheltered.*

30. *Eilean Thòraidh (Torray), at entrance to Loch Mharabhig. Fairly tricky approach. Anchor between W side of Torray and mussel farm or in opposite bay off Aird Fhalasgair (beware drying rock off S point). Well-sheltered.*

31. *Camas Thormaid (Witches' Pool), NW of Aird Fhalasgair. Beware drying rocks at centre of approach. Approach on course 20m from S shore and anchor no further than SW of islet, clay. Well-sheltered.*

32. *Orasaidh, NW of Eilean Rosaidh. Anchor in the basin, S or SW of Orasaidh.*

33. *Comes Orasaidh, inlet W of Orasaidh. Straightforward entrance from N. Anchor near head.*

34. *Tòb Cromore, on SE side of Peacam, near entrance to Loch Erisort. Snug anchorage in 2-4m, clay, shoal near head and foul ground near shores. Note rock off NW shore.*

35. Peacam (Cromore) 58° 06.5N 06° 25W, E of Eilean Chaluim Chille. Anchor S of Sgeir Peacam.

36. Loch Thorasdaidh (Hurista), S of Eilean Chaluim Chille. Sailing directions must be followed with care. Anchor W of Toa peninsula in soft smelly mud. Alternatively pass S and E of the central islets and anchor S of Toa. Some swell in W'lies.

37. Keose, 58° 06N 06° 29W, on N shore of Loch Erisort. Anchor SW of jetty in 3m, mud.

38. Loch Erisort. Several bays with good anchorages. Some drying rocks but no serious navigational difficulty.

39. Loch Leurbost on N side of approach to Loch Erisort. Approach S of the Barkin Isles; Tabhaidh Mhór and Bheag, and Bhatarsaidh and beware drying reef 1c SW of Tannaraidh. Anchor in basin W of Risay at S side of loch entrance, 2-3m, soft mud. Enter basin from N.

40. Loch Leurbost, head is shoal for 3c. Anchor off jetty at Aird Feiltanish: or off slip by the Free Church at Crossbow: or in Tòb Shuardail on S side of loch but note Jackal Shoal (1.8m depth) on approach: or near head of loch S of Orasaigh.

41. Loch Grimshader, 58° 09N 06° 23W. Well-protected. Beware Sgeir a' Chaolais midchannel. Anchor either side of Buaile Mhor at head. Good holding. SW part of loch is soft mud. Beware power cable over Loch Beag.

42. Glumaig harbour, bay SW of Stornoway Harbour, is best anchorage but far from town and in industrial area. Reefs marked with beacons on W side of entrance and 1c N of Arnish Point. Bottom foul, anchor should be buoyed.

43. Stornoway Harbour. Poll nam Portan opposite commercial quays. Note drying rocks. Crowded with moorings and exposed to S'ly swell. Avoid swinging into fairway if anchored. North Beach quay, N of No 1 pier in Stornoway Harbour has over 2.7m depth on its W side and over 1.8m on its N side but going alongside amid traffic can be hazardous. Pontoon berths (pay, 01851-702688).

44. Bàgh Phabail (Bayble Bay) on Eye Peninsula. Occasional anchorage. Protected from SW winds. Concrete pier at head with 3.7m at HW at outer end.

45. Broad Bay, N of Eye Peninsula. Some shelter from SW at head.

46. Port of Ness (Callicvol), 2M SE of lighthouse. Small open bay free of dangers but subject to swell. Bottom sand, depths moderate. Exposed E'lies. Boat harbour on N side dries; enter after half flood but not in stormy weather.

47. Eoropie bay. Extensive sandy beach can be approached carefully but avoid Aird Dell vicinity. Temp. anchorage in suitable conditions. (2km walk to Luchruban.)

48. Loch Shawbost, small bay open N and subject to swell. Shoal with sandy bottom. Keep to centre. About 1c swinging room.

49. Loch Carloway. On approach avoid channel between N headland and Craigeam island. In the loch keep nearer N shore and note shoal patch 1c WSW of Dunan Pier. Anchor SSW of pier, 3-5m, sand and mud. (Slip on S shore convenient for access to famous Carloway Broch). Good holding but heavy swell in W'lies.

50. Port a' Chaoil, 58° 14N 06° 46.5W, on E shore of East Loch Roag. Sheltered. Several rocks to be noted. After entering midchannel anchor close to E shore near head of bay.

51. Tòb Breasclete, E of Keava. Anchor S of old jetty which is E of new pier, mud, good holding and no swell.

52. Callanish, 58° 11.5N 06° 45W. Anchor E of Bratanish islands which are drying islets E of Eilean Kearstay (No.8.18). (Callanish Standing Stones are close-by). Submerged rock S of Bratanish Mór, and another off E shore of anchorage. If going further S, beware power cables over Loch Ceann Hulavig entrance (only 5.7m clearance).

53. Dubh Thob, East Loch Roag, 58° 13N 06° 48W, between Great Bernera and Vacasay. A secure little anchorage but a number of hazards on entry. N entry easiest.

54. Loch Beag Breaclete, W of Loch Risay, narrow inlet in Great Bernera with 2-9m depth. Rocks on both sides at entrance. Too open to N for good shelter.

55. Kyles of Little Bernera, (Bernera Harbour). Good anchorage. Keep N of mid-channel on entering, then S of Sgeir a' Chaolais (marked with beacon) and anchor off ruin in NW side of inlet or 1c SW of beacon. Beware submerged rock 1c W of beacon near fish cages.

56. West Loch Roag. A large selection of interesting anchorages can be found with the aid of Chart 3381. Examples are; Aird Torranish opposite S of Great Bernera; Loch Drovinish; or Miavaig Bay between Floday and Carishader.

57. Loch Meavig, snug, little harbour, 3.7m to 9m, very soft mud. No rocks. Shoal beyond power cable.

58. Shiaram Mór, an islet in Kyles Pabay near Valtos pier. Anchor at NW or SE end.

59. Camas Uig. Occasional anchorage in pool behind two small islets off Carnish, 3m, sand. Dangerous to enter or leave in NW'lies.

60. Caolas an Eilean – temp. anchorage in settled weather or quiet W'lies off beach on E shore of Mealista Island (No.8.17), sand.

61. Loch Tamanavay (Hamnaway). Remote and scarcely inhabited. Keep close to south shore to avoid Bo Thorcuill in mid-entrance. Good, well-sheltered anchorage at head of loch or E of Aird Sleitenish.

62. Loch Tealasavay. Occasional anchorage at S side of loch head.

63. Loch Resort, 4M length, good and safe anchorage at loch head or about half-way along at Diriscal on S side, black smelly mud.

64. Loch Cravadale. Occasional anchorage at head of bay.

65. Caolas an Scarp. Anchor in settled weather N or S of the sandbar. Avoid passage between Fladday and Harris.

66. Hushinish bay, temp. anchorage in settled weather in 6m, sand.

67. Govick bay, close E of Rubha Bogha Sgeir. Temp. anchorage in 9m.

68. Loch Leosavay (by Amhuinnsuidhe), drying rock off NE shore, at steps S of jetty. Keep towards W side of loch and anchor in bay off mansion, 4m, mud. Sheltered.

69. Loch Meavaig, 2¹/₄M ESE of Glas sgeir, in 2m to 9m, soft mud and shells. Anchor half-way up the loch in 4-6m, beyond which shoals rapidly. Subject to swell.

70. Loch Bun Abhainn-eader (Bunaveneader), excellent shelter off whaling station. Anchor clear of fish cages to suit wind direction, mud. Landing can be difficult.

71. West Loch Tarbert, Anchor W of jetty on S side. (There is also a pier on the N side). No heavy seas, but squalls in S'lies and swell in NW'lies.

72. Traigh Nisabost. Occasional anchorage in sandy bay E of Aird Nisabost in Sound of Taransay. Beach landing can be difficult due to swell.

73. Camas nam Borgh, a sandy bay E of Toe Head. Drying reefs off W shore. Good shelter and holding in S'lies in SW corner of the bay, but beware windshifts to NW or N.

8.17 Mealista Island

(ON muli-staoir – promontory farm) – on the adjoining 'mainland'. Also spelt – Mealasta.

OS Maps: 1:50000 Sheet 13 1:25000 Sheet 79
Admiralty Charts: 1:200000 No.2721 1:50000 No.2841

AREA: 124ha (306 acres)
HEIGHT: 77m (253 ft)

OWNER: Uig Estate Ltd (Jonathan Bulmer and syndicate).

POPULATION: The island has been inhabited but there are no records. In 1861, at the time of the census, the crew of a fishing boat from Rosehearty near Aberdeen, including a female cook, was living in a tent on Mealista.

GEOLOGY: The bedrock is gneiss, some of which contains a reddish quartz.

HISTORY: The Celtic saint Catan, who is believed to have lived in the 6th-7th century and to have had a cell on the Eye Peninsula on the east side of Lewis, had a shrine dedicated to him at Mealista in Uig, just north-east of Mealista island. The extensive remains of a nunnery – the House of the Old Women in Black – is by the shrine. Knowing the love of isolation of the early saints, it would be surprising if the island did not feature at some time in the life of St Catan or one of his followers.

MEALISTA
ISLAND
FROM THE
LEWIS SHORE

WILDLIFE: Much of the island is covered with grass and grazed by domestic sheep.

MEALISTA ISLAND is about half a mile off the west coast of Lewis, after the road from Brenish has passed the ancient convent ruins and then disappeared into the confused shoreline where the mountains approach the sea. A clean sandy beach faces on to **Caolas an Eilean** (G. – the island kyle). The island is uncultivated but offers good grazing. The west coast is rocky and unwelcoming.

On the south coast **Sgeir Ghlas na Roinne** (G. – grey rock of the seals) is beside Rubh' an Dobhrain (G. – otter point). The west coast is dominated by a deep bay between rocky headlands called Camas Leirageo (G. – the bay with the obvious cleft). Cnoc Ard (G. – high knoll) is the highest point at 77m. At the northern extremity one can look north from Airighean a' Chràois (G. – shieling by the gaping inlet) to the skerries and scattered rocks near the Lewis coast and see the little island of **Greineim** – 19m high. Another islet, **Eilean Molach**, near the entrance to Uig Bay is hidden from sight by Aird Brenish.

There are some ruined houses on Mealista Island showing that it once supported a small community, but in 1823 the island was incorporated into a sheep farm and, although I have found no record, one could assume that the islanders were encouraged to leave the island at about that time. Certainly there is no record of any population in the 1831 or 1841 census. The small Lewis township of Mealista was itself cleared in 1838 with the majority of the inhabitants being sent to Canada.

Sheep are still grazed on the island and stock is ferried across at Leac na h-Aiseig (G. – ferry ledge) by Rubha Buaile Linnis on the Lewis mainland. This is where the south-going coastal track finally expires. The island collection point is **Laimhrig na Seoraid** (G. – landing place by the primroses).

There was always a desperate need for timber on the islands. Even driftwood was the property of the laird under the old laws and the tacksmen would sometimes ruthlessly enforce this by entering houses and even removing driftwood used for roof supports. In 1795 a boat from Mealista was bringing timber back from the Scottish mainland when it ran aground at Bàgh Ciarach in Park on the west coast of Lewis. Her crew was murdered for the precious cargo.

It was said at one time that anyone born on Mealista Island would eventually end up as an idiot. Maybe the landlords started the rumour to encourage the islanders to leave.

ACCESS: No regular access. A lobster fisherman from Loch Roag may assist although the distance is considerable. A boat from Hushinish, near Scarp (No.8.15), may be a better bet.

Anchorages:
1. Caolas an Eilean. Temporary anchorage in settled weather, or quiet W'lies, off the central beach on E shore of Mealista, sand. Holding may be unreliable.

8.18 Eilean Kearstay *or* Cearstaidh

Derivation uncertain. ?(ON Krist-øy – Christ's island). Munro called it 'Kertay'. Possible, but tenuous, connection with St Kieran, the local saint. There is another Kearstay north of Scarp.

OS Maps: 1:50000 Sheets 8 or 13 1:25000 Sheet 69
Admiralty Charts: 1:200000 No.2721 1:12500 No.3422

AREA: 77ha (190 acres)
HEIGHT: 37m (121 ft)

OWNER: Sold in 1990 by the laird of Great Bernera, Count Robin Mirrlees to two Australians, Rosemary Nicolson Samois (who has a Lewis family background) and Anne Inglis of Sydney, NSW. Price understood to be £20,000. Since resold to a purchaser who wished to build a house on the island but was refused Council permission in 1994.

POPULATION: No census records.

GEOLOGY: The Admiralty Pilot notes that there is a local magnetic anomaly in this area with the compass needle, unusually, being repelled from the centre of disturbance.

HISTORY: A party, attended by many notable Highlanders and Islanders, and the Australian Consul, was held in August 1990 to celebrate the new ownership of the island. An Australian gum tree was planted, supported by Gaelic prayers and classical pipe music. The new owners, who had a shop in Portree on Skye, said they planned to market a specially-designed handwoven tweed of local wool which would be called 'Cearstaidh' but by 1993 they had sold the island.

The seaward approach to **EILEAN KEARSTAY** is southwards through lovely East Loch Roag, between **Vacasay** and **Grèinam** islet and then through Kyles Keava beside the fairly substantial island of **Keava** after which the view

CALLANISH

of Callanish opens up. There is a narrow channel on each side of Eilean Kearstay, the west one being formed by Rubha na Sidhean (G. – headland of the fairy knoll) projecting from Great Bernera, while the shallow east channel is bounded by the Callanish peninsula.

Eilean Kearstay has few distinctive geographical features but there would seem to be a reasonable chance, in view of its proximity to Callanish, for the discovery of prehistoric associations. The island is smooth and grassy and rises to a low central plateau with a conspicuous cairn at the north end. This is at virtually the same height as **Cnoc Gasamail** (37m) in the south-west, which is the highest point and which overlooks **Eilean Scarista**, an islet tucked into a small bay on the Lewis coastline.

South-east of Eilean Kearstay, Loch Ceann Hulavig shelters **Eilean an Tighe** and **Eilean Trosdam**.

ACCESS: No regular access. Try Breasclete, or Port Mór on Great Bernera.

Anchorages: Temporary anchorage in suitable conditions can be found at several points around the island with the aid of the East Loch Roag chart (No 3422).
1. The nearest overnight anchorage is E of the Bratanish islands, S of Callanish. (Suitable spot for a visit to Callanish).

8.19 Vuia Mór

(G bhuidhe, ON -øy, G. mhór – big fair and pleasant island)

OS Maps: 1:50000 Sheet 13 1:25000 Sheet 69
Admiralty Charts: 1:200000 No.2721 1:12500 No.3381

AREA: 84ha (208 acres)
HEIGHT: 67m (220 ft)

OWNER: Uig Crofters Ltd. Part of the Uig (Valtos) grazings.

POPULATION: There were four families in 1807 and in 1841 there were seven houses on the island accommodating forty-six inhabitants. The island was then cleared and there has been no permanent habitation since.

GEOLOGY: Mainly Lewisian gneiss.

HISTORY: I was told that some of the local people are disinclined to discuss Vuia Mór because of the brutality of the clearances and that some are even reluctant to land on the island. Others, however, claim that this is a ridiculous notion.

VUIA MOR is yet another example of an island that once supported a thriving community, was cleared for sheep in the 19th century, and now lies deserted and uncared for. It is almost L-shaped with the northern leg, **Rubha Rollanish**, divided by a shallow valley and rising to a low hill (45m). There are caves in the rocky east coast of this headland. The main part of the island rises to a central hill, **Mullach na Beinne** (G. – top of the hill), with a cairn on the summit (67m). The south-west side of this hill falls abruptly to the sea at **Creag na h-Iolaire** (G. – eagle cliff) and in the words of the Admiralty Pilot this steep cliff '. . .is very noticeable from the vicinity of **Old Hill** (a remarkable islet about 89.9m high identifying the entrances to East and West Loch Roag)'.

The south coast has three headlands, Rubha na Mòine (G. – mossy headland), Rubha Liath (G. – grey headland) and in the middle, Rubha Eadar Dhà Thòb (G. – the headland between two coves).

Mr Norman Buchanan, a nonagenarian resident of Valtos, said he could still remember a neighbour, Mrs Kate Morrison, who was born on Vuia Mór. She died in Valtos in 1908 aged one hundred.

Mr Kenneth Smith, a crofter at Earshader, told me that during the clearances, 'one young married couple were evicted by the Bernera Ground Officer, and they went to Canada. The Ground Officer was later removed from office, and he went to Ontario, Canada, where he died as a tramp. One day he had gone to a certain door to beg for a piece of bread. The lady of the house recognised him at once, but he did not recognise her. She gave him a good piece of bread and never said a word until he had eaten it. She then asked if he was satisfied and he said he was and only then did she tell him that he had evicted her from Vuia Mór'.

There are many small islands in this corner of Loch Roag: **Eilean nam Feannag**, **Linngeam**, **Cliatasay**, **Garbh Eilean** in the entrance to Little Loch Roag, **Vuia Beag** – little sister of Vuia Mór, **Gousam** and **Floday**. Both Vuia Beag and Floday were inhabited until 1827 when they were cleared for sheep and became part of Linshader Farm.

ACCESS: No regular access. Try Valtos, or Tobson on Great Bernera, for an accommodating boatowner.

Anchorages: No recommended anchorage and beware submerged rocks in Kyles Vuia. There is a rough stone jetty of uncertain depth.

1. Occasional anchorage in suitable conditions in N-exposed cove on E side, SSW of Eunay Mór. Anchor in centre of bay, W of the cairn on Rubha na h-Athadh, 4m, sand.

2. Temporary anchorage in suitable weather conditions SE of Rubha Liath, the SE extremity, and W of Sgeir nan Sgarbh (dries 1.5m), in 6m.

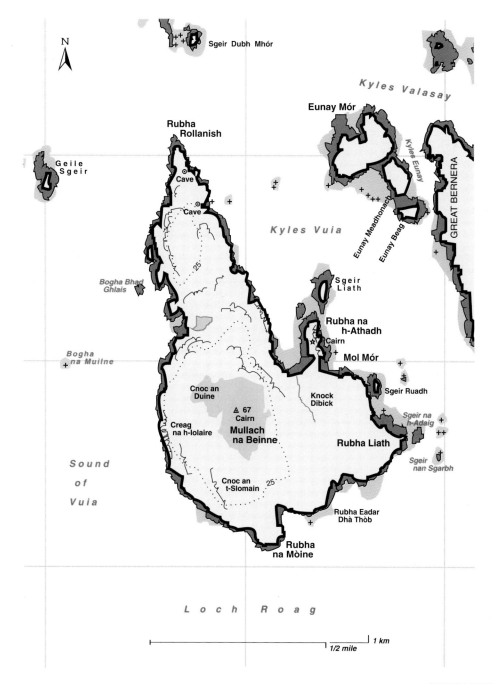

8.20 Vacsay

(G. Bhacsaidh) (ON vagr-øy – bay island) or (ON bakki-øy – island with a hillock or peat-bank). The present owner wants to change the name to 'Robert Burn's Island' although the poet had no historic association with Vacsay.

OS Maps: 1:50000 Sheet 13 1:25000 Sheet 69
Admiralty Charts: 1:200000 No.2721 1:12500 No.3381

AREA: 41ha (101 acres)
HEIGHT: 34m (112 ft)

OWNER: Previously part of the Uig (Valtos) Estate. Sold in 1983 for £9500 to a private buyer but the Uig Estate retained the grazing rights. Resold for £80,000 in 1993 to Sirdar Iqbal Singh, a retired Sikh property dealer from London, now living in Lesmahagow, Strathclyde. Mr Singh purchased the English title 'Lord of Butley Manor' in 1986.

POPULATION: 1861 – 9. No permanent habitation since then.

GEOLOGY: Lewisian gneiss with peaty soil.

HISTORY: In 1827 Vacsay became part of Linshader Farm and was partly cleared for sheep.

VACSAY in West Loch Roag lies off the beautiful white beach of Tràigh na Berie – a popular camping and caravanning spot among the sand dunes.

The island has a very irregular coastline with a confusion of islets and skerries to the north; a small cove between Sionaso and **Liacam** – a drying islet – on the rocky east coast; a larger cove, **Tòb an t-Seann Bhaile** (G. – cove of the old settlement) on the west coast; and a sizable drying island, **Trathasam**, on the south coast enclosing a shallow pool which forms a natural fish-trap. In between there are a number of irregular hillocks, the highest at 34m in the south-west.

Between Vacsay and the village of Kneep on Lewis is the conspicuous islet **Shiaram Mór** and across the loch to the north-east, beside Great Bernera, is another islet, **Grèinam**. Shiaram Mór was bought in 1983 for £11,000 by Mr Sati Gulhati, a London hotelier.

ACCESS: No regular access. Enquire at Valtos.

Anchorages:
1. Occasional anchorage in central bay on W side, 4m, sand. On approach from SW (vicinity of Shiaram Mór) beware Three Hook Rock (covered) and Bogha Thearbaso (dries 1.5m).

8.21 Pabay Mór

(ON pap-øy, G. mór – big island of the priest)

OS Maps: 1:50000 Sheet 13 1:25000 Sheets 68 and 69
Admiralty Charts: 1:200000 No.2721 1:12500 No 3381

AREA: 101ha (250 acres)
HEIGHT: 68m (223 ft)

OWNER: Bought for £19000 in 1983 by Mr Hobbs(?), reputed to be either an ornithologist or a surgeon (or both?) and resident in London. He visits Pabay Mór for a month each summer and has restored two of the old black houses. Valtos crofters retain the right to graze sheep on the island as allowed for by the Crofting Act of 1886.

POPULATION: Cleared for sheep in 1827. In 1861 there were two crews totalling fifteen fishermen and two female cooks, all from Banffshire, living in one of the caves. In 1881 nine Uig men were living in a tent on the island at the time of the census. Uninhabited since then except for occasional brief visits by fishermen and shepherds.

GEOLOGY: Lewisian gneiss with a light soil.

HISTORY: Pabay was a MacLeod island and at one time Norman, brother of the last chief, Ruaridh ('Old Rory'), lived there when 'he wald be quyeit, or yet fearit'. But MacLeod power waned and about 1800 the island was given to Sergeant Evander MacIver in lieu of a pension on his retiral from the Seaforth Regiment. The MacIver family settled on the island, but in 1827 or thereabouts they were evicted to provide unimpeded grazing for the sheep of Linshader farm. The family moved to Kneep and their descendants still live in Valtos. Both Valtos and Kneep overlook the Kyles Pabay and Pabay Mór. I was told that when the MacIvers were cleared from the island their youngest child was a little girl aged one. For the rest of her life she was known as 'Pabay-one-year-old' – 'in the Gaelic, of course'.

The Lewis coastline opposite **PABAY MOR** has superb shell-sand beaches backed by dunes. The tide runs briskly through the narrow stretch of sea, Kyles Pabay, and in bad weather the surface is broken and dangerous where the Kyle opens out into the Atlantic. But between Pabay Mór and its little brother, **Pabay Beag**, there is a wide and pleasant pool, well-sheltered from the weather, which is reputed to have been the haunt of pirates in times long past.

After the First World War some locals claim that boxes of provisions were found, proving that a German U-boat had visited the island secretly. An even more tenuous claim to fame is that the founder of the Cunard shipping line is thought to have been closely related to the MacIvers of Pabay.

A cairn marks Pabay Beag's highest point (42m) and there is another one near the summit (68m) of **Beinn Mhór** (G. – big hill) on Pabay Mór. East of Beinn Mhór, in a shallow valley beside **Cnoc an Cille** (G. – church knoll), are the ruins of a church and burial ground [NB105377]. A burn runs past the ruin and across a white sandy beach into a sheltered cove. It comes from a heart-shaped lochan, **Loch an Teampull** (G. – temple loch), between Beinn Mhór and Cnoc an Cille. There is another, slightly larger, loch to the north-west, **Loch Mhamoil** (G. – loch by the pap), with its stream discharging into Geodha Chalmoir on the steep-sided west coast.

There are many rocky caverns on Pabay and a natural stone arch in the north-east where the sea sucks and blows through a passage penetrating the hillside before it reaches an inland pool [NB104386]. This is the formation called a 'Gloup' in the Northern Isles.

North of the Pabays is the solitary rock, **Harsgeir**, and a dramatic group of islets and attendant rocky stacks guarding the entrance to Loch Roag, **Bearasay**, **Floday**, and **Old Hill** which rises 90m sheer above the sea like a giant loaf of bread.

ACCESS: No regular access but enquire at Valtos.

Anchorages:

1. Tràigh na Cille (Church beach), inlet NW of Sgeir na h-Aon Chaorach on E coast. Approach from NNE and keep slightly S of centre of the inlet, 2-3m, sand. (Church ruins are above the beach).

2. The WC Pilot states that the channel between Pabay Mór and Pabay Beag forms an excellent little harbour with depths from 0.4m to 3.2m (the large scale chart shows less depth than this), sand, where boats with local knowledge can lie safely in any weather. Use W entrance after quarter flood owing to rocks that dry. If using the narrow E entrance beware Bogha Dubh.

3. Rubha Caol, S extremity of the island. Occasional anchorage off sandy beach, 3m. Beware Three Hook Rock 2c SE of SE corner and drying rock W of Sgeir Chnapach.

4. S of Tràigh na Cille (S of Sgeir na Cille) giving Bogha Bhealt a wide berth. Anchor off cave in 5m, sand. Some swell at HW.

8.22 Little Bernera

(ON bjarnar-øy – bear island) or, possibly, (ON – Bjorn's island)

OS Maps: 1:50000 Sheet 13 1:25000 Sheet 59
Admiralty Charts: 1:200000 No.2721 1:12500 No.3381

AREA: 138ha (341 acres)
HEIGHT: 41m (134 ft)

OWNER: Comte Robin de la Lanne Mirrlees had owned the island for thirty-one years when he put it up for sale in 1993. He also owns Floday, Kealasay, and possibly, Bearasay.

POPULATION: Two inhabitants were recorded in 1807 – Neil and Donald Macdonald – (who may have had families) but they later moved to Great Bernera. However by 1831 numbers were sufficient for a school to be established by the Edinburgh Gaelic School Society and nineteen boys, twenty girls, and one adult were enrolled. But in 1832 or 1833 most of the islanders were cleared or 're-settled' at Dun Carloway on the Lewis 'mainland' (including two families called MacAuley) and the school was closed. The last record of any inhabitants was in the 1861 Census.

GEOLOGY: Lewisian gneiss with a light soil and acidic pockets.

HISTORY: Most of the small islands had connections with one or other of the early Celtic saints and in Little Bernera's case it is St Donan who is so honoured. He may have been a Pict and he is noted for his monastic centre on Eigg but the reason for his association with Little Bernera is obscure.

Following the clearance of Little Bernera for sheep-farming, and dissatisfaction with the intolerable demands of Sir James Matheson's factor, crofters on Great Bernera revolted in 1874. It was a relatively minor incident, an altercation with a sheriff officer, but it became known as the Bernera Riot and aroused public sympathy.

WILDLIFE: Cattle of the Scaliscro estate on Lewis have grazed the island for twenty-five years. A rogue bullock took charge in 1992 and for two years the cattle refused to be rounded up and ran wild.

LITTLE BERNERA lies immediately north of Great Bernera in Loch Roag on the north-west coast of Lewis. According to that intrepid 16th century traveller Dean Munro it was full of rough little craigs with fertile earth between. That description still applies today except that after a century of rough grazing the earth is probably no longer as fertile or 'manurit' as it once was. When Bernera Beag was populated and productive, apart from good pasturage for sheep and black cattle, it had a yield of 200 bolls of barley a year, which is approximately forty-two tonnes.

The ruins, no longer clearly visible, of an old fish-curing building overlook the Kyles of Little Bernera. At its west end the channel becomes very narrow at **Caolas Cumhang** (G – constricted strait) before reaching the wide, rock-fringed Camas Bosta.

Tordal is Little Bernera's highest hill (41m) but only fractionally so as there are a number of such 'little craigs', all of nearly similar height. Beneath Tordal on the north coast is the beautiful wide sweep of shell-pink sand, **Tràigh Mhór** (G. – big beach). This borders a lagoon, Kyles Kealasay, where the deep blue sea on a sunny day has a touch of South Sea magic, provided one avoids putting a foot in the water! Opposite are **Eilean Fir Crothair** (G. – isle of the shepherd) and **Kealasay**, both surrounded by low cliffs, and **Sgeir na h-Aon Chaorach** (G. – lone sheep rock). Further north and exposed to the full brunt of the Atlantic gales is **Campay**, another steep, rocky, islet with a natural stone arch at its north end and a large sea cave in the south. Màs Sgeir (G. – seagull skerry) is about a mile further north.

East of Tràigh Mhór, by a small bay among the skerries off Little Bernera's east coast is the ruin of **St Donan's chapel**.

Bearasay, the small rocky island to the north-west, was the retreat of Neil MacLeod, the great Lewis patriot, in the 16th century. He assisted in the defeat of the Fife Adventurers – the merchants who were offered Lewis by James VI and who tried to take over the herring fishing industry. James VI had a prejudice against the Gaels and wanted them to be exterminated and replaced by Lowlanders. In his words: 'As for the Highlanders, I shortly comprehend them all in two sorts of people: the one that dwelleth in our mainland that are barbarous, and yet mixed with some show of civility: the other that dwelleth in the Isles and are all utterly barbarous.'

Neil, and forty companions, stayed on Bearasay for three years and defied the attempts of the Mackenzies, who supported the King, to capture him. On one occasion he intercepted a pirate ship, the *Priam*, with a very valuable cargo including silver and jewels and delivered both it and the skipper to the Crown in the hope of obtaining a pardon. He received a pardon but it was worthless for on leaving Bearasay he was captured by a fellow clansman and handed over to the authorities. He was put on trial, found guilty of piracy, and executed in 1613. He died, according to the official report sent to the King, 'verie Christianlie'.

ACCESS: No regular access but enquire at Croir on the north coast of Great Bernera.

Anchorages:
1. Bernera Harbour (Kyles of Little Bernera) between Little and Great Bernera. Approach from E with care following sailing instructions. Anchor WNW of Sgeir a' Chaolais where possible, 4m, mud. Safe anchorage, but may be obstructed by fish cages. Alternative E of Sgeir a' Chaolais in 5-8m, sand. Good holding, no swell.

The Atlantic Outliers

4. Rona

Sula Sgeir

Flannan Isles

3. Boreray

2. Soay

1. Hirta (St Kilda)

N

Section 9

Section 9, Table 1

No.	Name	Latitude	Longitude	Table 2* No.	Table 3** No.	Area in Acres	Area in Hectares
9.1	Hirta (St Kilda)	57° 49N	08° 35W	52	12	1656	670
9.2	Soay	57° 50N	08° 38W	15	18	245	99
9.3	Boreray	57° 52N	08° 29W	27	16	190	77
9.4	Rona (North Rona)	59° 07N	05° 50W	10	62	269	109

* Table 2: The islands arranged in order of magnitude
** Table 3: The islands arranged in order of height

Introduction

In the desert wastes of the North Atlantic a rock stack or a mountain top breaks the surface. These specks of land represent the outermost regions of the British Isles and at times they are virtually inaccessible. Modern navigational aids locate them with ease but the weather can be so atrocious that landing is often impossible. Yet long ago prehistoric man arrived in his flimsy craft, settled and maintained some sort of intermittent communication with the mainland.

The St Kilda archipelago is the largest island group in this section. It has a mystique all its own and I shall never forget our pleasure when *Jandara* first made landfall there.

The group was declared a National Nature Reserve on the 4th April 1957. It was also designated as both a National Scenic Area and an Ancient Monument by the Secretary of State for Scotland and it is, furthermore, recognised as a Reserve by UNESCO and listed by the International Union for the Conservation of Nature as a World Heritage Site. It deserves all these accolades and one hopes that no visitor will ever introduce a foreign species, whether a plant or an animal such as the domestic cat. This would wreak devastation in such a fragile environment.

The most outlying outlier of all is, of course, **Rockall**, which was only officially annexed by Britain on 18th September 1955 for security reasons when the Benbecula rocket range was opened. A party from *HMS Vidal* landed by helicopter. Earlier recorded landings were in 1810 and 1921, and possibly 1887-8. In 1955 it was merely incidental that geologists were talking of the possibility of oil reserves under the Atlantic but the addition of national fishing grounds was recognised. The Union Flag was hoisted on the rock and it was decreed that Rockall should be subject to the law of Scotland and form part of the district of Harris. A navigation beacon was added in 1972. Rockall and neighbouring Hasselwood Rock (57° 36N 13° 41W) are 230 miles west of Manish Point on North Uist so this action effectively made Scotland the same size as England!

The original Gaelic name for Rockall is Sgeir Rocail [rokawl] which could be translated as the sea-rock or skerry which roars hoarsely. No one else worried too much about ownership of this nasty little obstruction until the possibility of discovering oil became more likely whereupon the Irish Republic, Iceland and Denmark all laid claim to it. So in the 1980s John Ridgeway, British adventurer and Atlantic rower, volunteered to confirm British ownership by actually living on the rock. He did so by the remarkable feat of lying for the best part of a month in a tiny shelter bolted down on a narrow ledge.

Still out west, but somewhat nearer home, the Flannan Isles can be seen on a fine day 21 miles west of Lewis (58° 17N 07° 35W). St Flannan was St Ronan's half-brother by repute (see Rona. No.9.4). This group of islets consists of three small clusters. The most westerly cluster is **Eilean a' Ghobha** (G. – isle of the blacksmith), **Roareim** and **Bròna Cleit** (G. – sad sunk rock). The smaller south-eastern cluster consists of **Soray** (G. – eastward isle), **Sgeir Toman** and **Sgeir Righinn** (G. – princess skerry). The main group has two islets, **Eilean Mór** (G. – big island) and **Eilean Tighe** (G. – house island), and some rocks scattered to the east. Eilean Tighe still has ruined houses on it.

These tiny islands are sometimes called the Seven Hunters but Dean Munro in 1549 called them the Seven Haley Isles. He said they were uninhabited but with 'infinit wyld sheipe' which 'cannot be eaten be honest men' but make good tallow. People living in Uig on Lewis made an annual pilgrimage to worship in St Flannan's Chapel.

In Martin Martin's time (1695), landing on Eilean Mór was subject to strict conventions and newcomers had to be accompanied by someone who knew the rules. For instance, it was forbidden to relieve oneself near the mooring-place, to kill a bird after evening prayers – or at any time with a stone, to eat anything in private, or to take sheep suet back home. On reaching the plateau of the island it was essential to take one's hat off and make a *deiseil* – a sunwise turn – giving thanks to God, and when twenty paces from the altar to strip off outer garments and place them on a stone. It was also important always to refer to the Flannans as 'the country', water as 'the burn' and rock as 'the hard'.

Grazing on the Flannans is of very high quality and sheep are still grazed there by the Bernera crofters. The lighthouse, which was built in 1899, is on the largest island in the group – Eilean Mór – where there are also the ruins of the corbelled 6th century St Flannan's chapel and the Bothain Chlann 'ic Phail (G. – Macphail bothies). The light is 100m above sea level and the stubby lighthouse which has been automatic since 1971 stands on high ground at the top of 60m (200 ft) cliffs. This was the lighthouse which was the scene of a remarkable unsolved mystery.

On the night of 15th December 1900 it was noted in the log of a passing steamer that the light was not working. Before receiving this information at Oban, however, the lighthouse relief tender *Hesperus* had sailed for the Flannan Isles. She had to battle through an Atlantic gale and did not arrive until Boxing Day. The crew were surprised that there was no response to their whistle and when they landed they could find no trace of the keepers. The logbook was complete up to the 13th December and notes for the log were recorded until 9am on the 15th. A meal of cold meat, pickles and potatoes was untouched on the kitchen table and, apart from one kitchen chair being knocked over, there was nothing amiss. The island was searched from end to end but nothing was found to explain the disappearance.

A report by Superintendent Muirhead of the Commissioners of Northern Lights after a detailed examination decided that the men had gone to the West landing 'and that a large body of water going up higher than where they were, and coming down upon them, had swept them away with resistless force.' But this explanation is not entirely convincing. For instance, only two sets of oilskins were missing. If the third man had to rush out in his shirtsleeves to help how did he know there was an emergency in the first place? The landings are too far away from the lighthouse to hear a cry for help. And if he was in such a hurry, why did he close the doors and the gate?

Walter Aldebert, who was a keeper of the Flannan light from 1953 to 1957, whiled away many hours trying to find a solution. The west landing is in a narrow inlet which ends in a cave. Aldebert photographed waves to show that occasionally a giant wave would thunder into the inlet causing air pressure in the cave to explode and throw tons of water across the cliffs. His conclusion was that such a wave washed one man into the sea. The second rushed back to the lighthouse for help then as the two reached the west landing a second wave carried them away. This is plausible but the records show that such explosive waves are very rare and for two to occur at the precisely critical time would be an extraordinary coincidence.

Suffice it to say that when the news from Eilean Mór was first published the press had a heyday, with sea monsters, the ghost of St Flannan, and murder by the Secret Service all put forward as plausible explanations. The mystery has exercised lively imaginations ever since but, like the Marie Celeste, it is probably a better story left unsolved.

Eight miles west of the Sound of Harris (57° 42N 07° 42W) are two islets – Haskeir Island, on which it is proposed to build a lighthouse, and Haskeir Eagach (ON – wild skerry, G. *eagach* – notched). Their bold geometric silhouettes have an almost classical quality when seen through a pale sunlit summer mist – as though Jason and the Argonauts had just passed by. Haskeir Island is studded with vertical rock formations and natural rock arches and Haskeir Eagach is a colonnade of stumpy rock stacks like a crude Greek temple.

North (59° 06N 06° 08W), in the direction of the Faeroes, the cries of the birds on **Sula Sgeir** (ON – gannet skerry) are carried for long distances by the wind. The Butt of Lewis is forty-one miles south of here and the men of Lewis still traditionally collect their supplies of *guga*, or young gannet, from these rocks every year. It is said that St Ronan's sister, Brianuil, lived with him on Rona until one day Ronan admired her beautiful legs. 'It's time to leave,' she said. She went to Sula Sgeir and died there after several years of solitude.

Rona (No.9.4) with its ancient history lies due east of Sula Sgeir and far beyond Rona are **Sule Stack** (59° 02N 04° 30W), also known as Stack Skerry, a single rock column sticking unexpectedly out of the sea to a height of 37m, and **Sule Skerry** (59° 05N 04° 24W) which is four miles further on and thirty-seven miles from Mainland Orkney. Sule Skerry (ON – lone skerry) is identified by its lighthouse. Both Sule Stack and Sule Skerry are part of Orkney district.

9.1 Hirta

(G. Hiort) Possibly, (EI hirt – dangerous, deathlike, ON -øy – island)

St Kilda

The name for the archipelago rather than the island, first appears on a Dutch map of 1666. There was no saint of that name but the derivation may be (ON sunt kelda – sweet wellwater) or that Dutch sailors assumed the popular watering hole above the village, Tobar Childa (G. tobar – well, ON kelda – well) followed the normal practice of dedication to a saint.

Dùn

[doon] (G. – castle or fort)

OS Maps: 1:50000 Sheet 18 1:25000 Sheet 1373
Admiralty Charts: 1:500000 No.2635 1:200000 No.2721 various scales No.2524 – the outliers

AREA: 670ha (1,656 acres)
HEIGHT: 430m (1,410 ft)

OWNER: National Trust for Scotland. Part-occupied by the

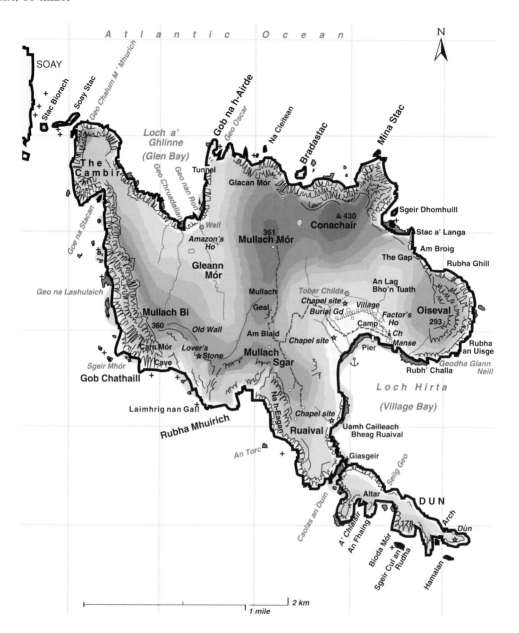

Ministry of Defense and the nature reserve is managed by Scottish Natural Heritage.

POPULATION: Continuous habitation for at least 2000 years until evacuation in 1930. 1695 – about 180. 1810 – about 200 (this may be an unreliable figure). As demand for the island's 'exports' declined (fulmar oil for lamps, feathers, tweed), some of the men had to find work on the mainland. Thirty-six islanders emigrated to Australia in 1852 with State aid. Men were also lost at sea and in accidents on the cliffs, and there was severe infant mortality due to *tetanus infantus*. 1861 – 78. 1881 – 77. 1891 – 71 (18 houses). 1911 – 80 (18 houses). 1921 – 73. 1930 – 36. 1931 – 0. 1961 – 65 (military establishment) 1971 – 65. 1981 – 46. 1991 – 0.

GEOLOGY: Hirta is almost entirely composed of two igneous rocks, a light-coloured granite or granophyre and a darker gabbro. The east part of the island is chiefly granite but interspersed with some gabbro. Some of the rock is highly magnetic. The coastline is honeycombed with caves and the sharp jagged skylines are because the Ice Age missed the St Kilda archipelago and the rocks are unworn.

HISTORY: In a recent study of Hirta on behalf of the National Trust for Scotland an ancient stone building was discovered near the top of a high cliff. The structure, possibly a place of worship or a tomb, is thought to date from the Bronze Age. Archaeologists have still to make a detailed investigation but this may show that Hirta has been inhabited for about 3500 years.

Glen Bay is the site of a pre-Viking settlement but it was not until Dean Monro visited Hirta in 1549 that the first written record appeared. He described a 'simple, poor people, scarce learnit in aney religion.'

Martin Martin, during his visit in 1697 estimated that 180 St Kildans ate about 22600 birds annually. Stac Lee alone provided about 6000 gannets a year. Rye grass and barley were cut green and stored in the 'cleitean'. Martin found the population 'happier than the generality of mankind, as being the almost only people in the world who feel the swetness of true liberty.'

One separate dwelling or cleit, south of the main 'street' is known as Lady Grange's house. She was exiled on the island for eight years to prevent her revealing her husband's Jacobite sympathies. She died in 1745, the year of the Rebellion, and is buried on Skye. (See Section 5 appendix and No.7.20).

In the early 18th century there were outbreaks of cholera and smallpox introduced by visiting ships and after 1750 the population possibly never exceeded 70. The islanders paid rent to the owners, the MacLeods of Harris and Dunvegan in Skye, who had been given the islands by a descendant of the Lord of the Isles. The rent was paid in the form of produce such as tweed, wool, feathers or oil from the sea-birds and once a year a steward called from Harris to collect the goods. At this time visitors reported a surprising level of general prosperity among the islanders although they held everything in common ownership and had no personal property. They also had no leadership

structure. A 'Parliament' would meet each day to decide what work had to be done. This was by general agreement, but there were occasions when it could take all day to reach a decision!

Apart from imported diseases the islanders were healthy except for 'eight-day sickness'. This killed eight out of every ten babies born but was considered to be God's will. In the 1890s it was discovered that the source of the disease was because the island midwife traditionally anointed the umbilicus with fulmar oil mixed with dung. The minister then had a battle persuading the islanders that God disapproved of this treatment.

The *Glen Albyn* was the first tourist ship to call at the island in 1834 and it marked the start of the loss of the islanders' independence and the end of St Kilda. They were almost completely naive and were cheated out of many of their essential possessions by the tourists. They came to rely on modern communications and a post-office was opened on the island in 1899 but this was really to satisfy tourists.

The other vital contribution to the eventual collapse of society on the island was the hell-fire and damnation of crusading Christian ministers. By far the most notorious was the Rev. John Mackay who was resident from 1865 to 1889. By the end of his evil ministry the islanders had been browbeaten into so much church attendance every day of the week that there was insufficient time for growing and gathering food.

Because the community was near starvation in 1912, a

HIRTA'S 'HIGH STREET'

wireless transmitter was installed by the Government. During the First World War this resulted in a German submarine shelling the island. The church was damaged and a store destroyed but no one was hurt and the submarine was later captured by an armed trawler. A gun was installed south-east of the present army camp to stop a repetition of this incident but it has never been fired.

After the war, conditions continued to deteriorate. Many of the active young men emigrated leaving the aged and the very young. Eventually matters became so desperate that the thirty-six remaining St Kildans were more-or-less compelled to agree to evacuation. They were persuaded to do so by Nurse Williamina Barclay who, in 1927, had been sent to assist them.

The sad event took place on the 29th of August 1930. The St Kildans were given jobs and housing near Loch Aline, planting trees for the Forestry Commission, but they never really adjusted to life on the mainland. They were industrious and intelligent but they did not appreciate the use of money, the way of life, the type of diet, and they had never seen piped water, a staircase, or for that matter, a tree.

In 1957 Hirta was resettled with an army base and missile-tracking radar station on Mullach Mór. This brought new life to the island. National Trust volunteers are restoring the village houses and those who have spent twenty-four hours on the island can join the exclusive St Kilda club. But the native St Kildans are no more although, sadly, everything that they needed to provide a viable community is now available on the island.

WILDLIFE: Due probably to the high winds there are no plants which grow above grass level, but even so there is a wealth of species. Scurvy grass, scentless mayweed, moss campion, plantago sward, and common sorrel are widespread. In the wet ground there are common cotton-grass, tormentil, lousewort, St John's wort, field gentian, bog pimpernel, sphagnum, and bog asphodel to name a few. On the hillsides there are primrose, roseroot, heath-spotted orchid, calluna, crowberry, butterwort, heath milkwort, sundew, tiny willow, deer grass and ragged robin. On Dùn can be found lesser celandine, wild angelica, sea campion, red fescue and thrift. In all, more than 130 flowering plants have been recorded and 194 varieties of lichen – including some that are very rare. There are also many tasty mushrooms.

Hirta is noted for some unique forms of wildlife: the St Kilda wren, a sub-species; the mouflon sheep recently introduced from neighbouring Soay; and a species of long-tailed fieldmouse which is twice as heavy as the mainland variety, with larger ears and a very long tail. There was also a St Kilda housemouse, *mus muralis*, but this poor little creature died out when the islanders left.

On Dùn, the St Kilda wren, puffins, and Leach's petrels nest in large numbers, and the cliffs and peaty turf of Hirta are home to eighteen breeding species of seabirds including the oldest and largest colony of fulmar in Britain.

HIRTA is the largest of the spectacular **ST KILDA** group of lonely Atlantic islands, owned by the National Trust of Scotland. This remote outpost of the British Isles is one of the dream destinations of any committed collector or explorer of islands. All the members of the group are of granite and gabbro forming dramatic jagged stacks and towering cliffs. **Conachair**, the highest peak on Hirta is 430m high (over 1400ft) but there are four other high peaks and the awesome sea cliffs are over 300m (1000ft) high.

Dean Monro in 1549 wrote that there are '. . .three grate hills, quhilk are ane pairt of Hirta, quhilk are seen affar off from the fore landis. In this fair ile is fair sheipe, falcon nests and wild fouls biggand, but the streams of the sea are stark, and are verey eivil. . .'

Village Bay in the south-east shelters the main settlement. Among the cottages and scattered up the mountain side are hundreds of small dry-stone structures with turf roofs called 'cleits' (G. – a stone beehive bothy, water-tight but cross-ventilated). These were mainly used as larders for storing the sea-birds which were the St Kildans' staple diet, but they were also used as general stores for fishing tackle, ropes, etc. Village Bay is an impressive example of a

THE ST KILDA FIELD-MOUSE AND THE ST KILDA WREN

Road to Radar Station

Tobar Childa (Well)

Calum Mòr House

Cleits

Christ Church (site) ☆Earth House

Cleits

Grave Yard

Lady Grange House

An t-Sruthan

Amhuinn Mhór

An Gearraidh

Amhuinn Riasg

Dry Burn

Factor's House

Military Base

Underground Chamber (found 1835)

St Columba's Church (site)

Landing Craft

Church

Tobar Gille Chille (Well)

Pier

Gun

Village Bay

250m
800ft

N

LAYOUT OF THE VILLAGE ON HIRTA

stone-age culture. The area is covered with dry-stone structures which are the product of centuries of effort.

In 1830 much of the original village was demolished and new black houses were built but most of the present cottages, which are gradually being restored by the National Trust, were built in the 1860s to Victorian standards and using mortar joints. The Army camp is beside the pier and near the church, manse and schoolhouse. It is unsightly, but the island environment is so overpowering that it can be largely disregarded, and the military authorities have in fact been of benefit to the island in many ways. Through the camp and among the village ruins wander primitive Soay sheep, untidily shedding their umber-coloured fleeces in the summer months. The population fluctuations of these evil-eyed, goat-like creatures are being studied with interest by scientists. The native St Kildans only kept domestic sheep on Hirta. They left the Soay sheep on their home territory of Soay (No.9.2).

There are a number of archaeological sites in Village Bay. Less than 40m north-east of **Lady Grange House** [NF101993] stone coffins were discovered in 1835. In the same year an underground chamber was found by the path north of the church. The small stone-walled grave-yard is just behind the line of houses [NF100994]. It was

too small for the number of burials so older corpses were removed in rotation to make way for new arrivals. Just north of it is the **Earth House**, a souterrain dating from the period 400BC-500AD. A number of artefacts have been found – Hebridean Iron Age pottery, two Christian crosses engraved in stone, Viking brooches and a Viking sword.

Above the village there are fox-holes in the west scree slope which are invisible from below. These were dug by the islanders in case they had to hide from pirates – the great fear of every islander.

Martin mentioned three churches and monkish cells in the 17th century which have now disappeared. One of these, Christ Church, was beside the Earth House, and St Columba's Church was west of Amhuinn Mhór (G. – big river) which is west of the village [NF099991].

At the opposite end of the island is Loch a' Ghlinne or **Glen Bay**. Here there is a ruin called the **Amazon's House** [NA087001] and complexes of small chambers similar to Iron Age settlements. The bay is enclosed by a western peninsula, **The Cambir**, and high cliffs covered with nesting seabirds. On the east side at **Gob na h-Airde** (G. – nose of the point) the sea tumbles through a large deep tunnel which penetrates the rock and frames Boreray beyond [NA088008]. High above, **Mullach Mór** (G. – big top) (361m) broods over the bay with its twin peak **Mullach Bì** (G. – pitch-black top) (360m) on the other side of **Gleann Mór** (G. – big valley). The side of Mullach Bì facing the sea is like a cataclysmic land-slip with an abrupt drop from the summit to the sea. Close to the highest point is the **Lover's Stone** [NF085990] where there is a terrifying drop on to the rocks in the surf far below.

St Kilda men were agile climbers and would scale the awesome heights with homemade ropes to collect thousands of sea-birds and their eggs. Fulmars were the most important catch as the body of each bird provides a quarter litre of oil. This oil was used for lamps and also exported. Gannets and fulmars were eaten and puffins were caught for their feathers but nothing was wasted and the entrails were used for manure. Before marriage each suitor had to prove his climbing ability by balancing on one heel right on the edge of the Lover's Stone while holding the other foot with his hands.

These cliffs are matched or even surpassed by Conachair's cliffs on the north-east coast. They are the highest cliffs in the British Isles although Foula's (No.11.6) cliffs are considered more precipitous. Conachair is the highest point of a ridge which runs past Mullach Mór and then curls southwards and descends in two steps, **Mullach Geal** (G. – bright top) and **Mullach Sgar** (G. – the dividing summit). The ridge descends further to **Ruaival**, the south-western arm of Village Bay. **Oiseval** is the opposite arm of the bay.

DUN is almost joined to Hirta at Ruaival but there is a narrow separating channel, **Caolas an Duin**, which is thickly strewn with rocks and reputed to dry during exceptionally low tides. This channel does, however, obstruct invasion by the sheep which roam freely on Hirta with the result that vegetation on Dùn is much more lush. The island is nearly a mile long and looks, with its deeply serrated backbone, like a dragon hanging on to Hirta.

Old maps show the remains of a dun or fort on the headland furthest from Hirta, Gob an Duin (G. – Dùn's beak), but there is no obvious trace of it today [NF109972].

Almost two miles beyond Dùn, the rock ridge which runs through Mullach Sgar, Ruaival and Dùn, and then disappears into the sea, resurfaces at **Levenish**, a lone guano-spattered stack.

ACCESS: Those wishing to land should obtain permission from the National Trust (which also organises summer work parties). There are a number of cruises to St Kilda but passengers rarely land and then only when weather conditions are ideal. The army service the island with a 'rat-free attested' landing craft. This sometimes arrives at night.

Anchorages:
1. Village Bay is the only safe anchorage but can be untenable in winds NE-
S. There is usually a swell. Squalls during gales can be violent. Anchor off beach midway between leading lights and pier, S and clear of the LST slipway. Holding good, firm sand. There is a concrete pier on the N side of Village Bay with steps and an iron ladder on its W side and a boat slip behind it. The pier is usually accessible but landing can be difficult due to the swell. (In 1993 most of Village Bay beach and part of the landing craft slip was reported to have been swept away in a storm).
2. Loch a' Ghlinne. (G. – glen bay). Temporary anchorage in SE gales. A valley and stream runs SE between the hills at head of bay. Landing possible beside the stream. Bay sheltered except from N, but too deep to anchor except very close to shore. Swell uncomfortable and there are strong winds off the cliffs.

9.2 Soay

[soa-ay] or *[soy]* *(ON so-øy – sheep island)*

OS Maps: 1:50000 Sheet 18 1:25000 Sheet 1373
Admiralty Charts: 1:500000 No.2635 1:200000 No.2721 various scales No.2524 – the outliers

AREA: 99ha (245 acres)
HEIGHT: 378m (1240 ft)

OWNER: Together with the rest of the St Kilda group, Soay is owned by the National Trust for Scotland and managed by Scottish Natural Heritage as a Nature Reserve.

POPULATION: Uninhabited and has probably never been permanently inhabited.

GEOLOGY: Formed by a single precipitous mountain peak rising straight from the seabed it is composed mostly of a dark breccia of gabbros and dolerites, but with some granite. It has escaped any Ice Age erosion.

HISTORY: Although the St Kildans held everything in common ownership, the one exception was sheep. These could be personally owned, although there was communal interest in their well-being. Thus the Neolithic sheep on Soay belonged to a few St Kilda families. When these families emigrated to Australia in the 1850s the laird, MacLeod of MacLeod, paid them for their sheep to help defray their expenses.

After Hirta was evacuated in 1930 the Earl of Dumfries arranged for a balanced flock of 107 sheep to be collected from Soay by some St Kildans who had made a summer visit to their old home. The sheep were transported to, and released on, Hirta (No.9.1) and these form the basis of today's sheep population which is being studied by the Soay Sheep Research Team. All the islanders' domestic sheep were removed from Hirta at the time of the evacuation.

WILDLIFE: Soay is the home of the species of horned sheep which were first brought to the British Isles about

5000BC. They are like mountain goats in appearance, wild, but unconcerned with man so long as man is unconcerned with them. Until the 1930s the sheep were entirely confined to Soay and were not to be found anywhere else. When conditions permitted the St Kildans would climb the steep slopes of Soay to the lush grazing plateau and sometimes kill a beast for fresh meat. But mutton was considered a rare and special delicacy and the main interest was the wool. Soay sheep are never shorn. The fine soft wool is merely plucked when it is being shed naturally. The St Kildans used it to make tweed.

The soaring cliffs which surround Soay afford nest space for many thousands of gannet, fulmar, storm petrel, Manx shearwater, razorbill, great skua, and Leach's petrel although larger numbers of the latter bird nest on the

Cambir on Hirta, opposite Soay Stac. Colonies of puffins inhabit the cliff tops.

Ancient **SOAY** has no dinosaurs but it has primaeval yellow-eyed sheep as compensation.

The inclined grassy plateau reaches a rounded summit, **Cnoc Glas**, (G. – grey eminence) 378m high where it falls away on the west coast in a nearly vertical black cliff, and it forms a very steep grassy incline to the east coast. The north and south have almost vertical cliffs but the cliff at the south-east end is less precipitous. The only objectional quality in this solid chunk of rock is that it overshadows the north end of Hirta at sunset.

The plateau is cut off abruptly at the Atlantic cliffs like a sliced piece of cheese at **Bearraidh na Creige Chaise**

(G. – edge of the rocky precipice). On a level patch beneath a shallow escarpment on the west coast is **Tobar Ruadh** (G. – red well) [NA060015]. No doubt this provided water for the men from Hirta, when they spent some days on Soay wool-gathering. It is however quite a distance from the bothy site, **Tigh Dugan** (G. – Dugan's house), which is on the more-sheltered south-eastern slope [NA068013]. Far below at sea-level in the Sound of Soay is a rocky projection, **Laimhrigna Sròine** (G. – nose of a landing-place), which is the only reasonable landing place on Soay. Off the end of the 'nose' stands a 15m-high rock called **Stac Dona**.

There are two more rock stacks in the Sound, the awesome **Stac Biorach** [peerich] and **Soay Stac**. Young St Kilda men were tested for their climbing ability on Stac Biorach (G. – sharply-pointed stack) which at 72m (236ft) is certainly not the highest stack in the St Kilda group but is regarded as the most difficult and dangerous to climb. It was nicknamed the 'Thumb Stack' because the only hold on the rock was no bigger than a thumb. An interesting description was written by Sir Robert Murray in 1698: '. . .after they landed, a man having room for but one of his feet, he must climb up 12 or 16 fathoms high. Then he comes to a place where having but room for his left foot and left hand, he must leap from thence to another place before him, which if hit right the rest of the ascent is easy, and with a small cord which he carries with him he hales up a rope where by all the rest come up. But if he misseth that footstep (as often times they do) he falls into the sea and the (boat's) company takes him in and he sits still until he is a little refreshed and then he tries it again, for everyone there is not able for that sport.' The first recorded outsider to climb both this stack and Stac Lee was Charles Barrington in 1883 (he also made the first ascent of the Eiger).

It is reckoned that only three days in a summer month on average are suitable for landing on Soay and there is always the danger that a rapid change in the weather may leave you marooned.

Sailing through the deep but narrow channel between Soay Stac (61m) and Hirta is possible provided, of course, the weather is agreeable.

THE NEOLITHIC SHEEP OF SOAY

ACCESS: No normal access.

Anchorages: There are no anchorages. The usual landing place at Laimhrigna Sròine near the SE corner can be used in settled weather. The Poll Adinet landing place, Laimhrig Adinet, entails mountaineering. The NTS warden from Hirta must be present during any landing.

9.3 Boreray

[**baw**-rĕ-ray *or* -rĕ] (*ON* borv-øy – *fort island or island like a castle*)

OS Maps: 1:50000 Sheet 18 1:25000 Sheet 1373
Admiralty Charts: 1:500000 No.2635 1:200000 No.2721 various scales No.2524 – the outliers

AREA: 77ha (190 acres)
HEIGHT: 384m (1,260 ft)

OWNER: The National Trust for Scotland.

POPULATION: No census records and uninhabited.

GEOLOGY: Boreray is almost entirely gabbro and there has been no Ice Age erosion.

HISTORY: Inextricably linked with Hirta and used as another food source by the St Kildans. The traces of lazybeds near the summit ridge may indicate a bygone settlement, but by the end of the 19th century the St Kildans were only visiting Boreray three or four times a year for fowling and tending the sheep.

WILDLIFE: In spite of its remote position and barren, rocky appearance there are at least 130 types of flowering plant on Boreray including some alpines which probably relish the cool climate and absence of disturbance.

The St Kildans kept some crossed black-face/cheviot sheep on Boreray which had originally been introduced to Hirta from the mainland. Although the domestic sheep on Hirta were cleared in 1930 Boreray was fairly inaccessible and the sheep were abandoned when the islanders were evacuated. They have now reverted to a wild state.

A count in 1959 showed 45,000 pairs of gannets on Boreray and its two adjoining stacks, nearly half the British population and nearly 40% of the world population. On the relatively level top of Stac Lee alone there was a solid concentration of 6000 nests in 1971.

Many other seabirds also nest on Boreray in great numbers.

BORERAY is a quite remarkable, jagged heap of black volcanic rock rearing 386m (1260ft) above the sea. It is an unforgettable sight, particularly when the cloud swirls around its summit and the gannets plunge from breathtaking heights. It is an island of superlative emotions that change with the weather. In the words of the yachtsman, R A Smith, who sailed there in *Nyanza* in 1879: 'Had it

Stac an Armin

196

Am Biran

Rubha Bhriste

Gearrgeo

An t-Sail

A t l a n t i c

Geo na Tarnanach

O c e a n

Udraclete

Mullach
an Eilean
▲ 384

Geo Shunadal

Na Roachan

S u n a d a l

Tigh Stellar

Clais na Runaich

Mullach an Tuamail

Clesgor

Clagan na Ruskochan

238

Geo an Fheachdaire

Creagan na
Rubhaig
Bana

Rubha Langa

172

Cleitean
McPhaidein

Geo Lee

Stac Lee

Geo an Araich

Creagan Fharspeig

Geo na Leachan Moire

Coinneag

Sgarbhstac

Geo Sgarbhstac

Rubha Bhrengadal

Laimhail

Gob Scapanish

1 km

1/2 mile

been a land of demons it could not have appeared more dreadful.' But he probably saw it on a wild, grey day. It lies about 3½ miles to the north-east of Hirta and it has two enormous stacks standing guard beside it, Stac an Armin, and Stac Lee. It is possible to sail between Boreray and Stac Lee – quite an experience – but the channel between Boreray and Stac an Armin is littered with rocks and should not be attempted.

Landing can be dangerous and considerable skill is required. The mountaineers, Williamson and Boyd, reported that a short distance above where they landed near **Sgarbhstac** (G. – cormorant stack) they came to a chasm in the southern crags. It is nearly two metres wide at the

narrowest point and they had to jump across with the sea surging 30m below them.

A party from the University of Durham succeeded in landing on the island in July 1980 with Army assistance. They stayed on the island for about a fortnight studying the ecology and wildlife. They were helped by the presence of an old bothy which was used by the St Kildans for shelter and which may date from the Iron Age. There may be other undiscovered archaeological remains.

In spite of its exposed situation the skewed summit of Boreray is covered in lush grass. There are still traces of lazybeds and one can only marvel at the thought of carrying loads of seaweed up these high cliffs to manure the

STAC LEE,
STAC AN ARMIN AND
BORERAY

potato beds. Understandably, by 1889, sheep had replaced the lazybed culture and the St Kildans only made occasional visits each year.

The most dangerous annual visit took place in September. The gannets, or guga (G. *guga* – a young solan goose, or a fat silly fellow), had to be killed at night when they were on their nests. Normally, about seven men would land, wearing woollen socks at this stage to avoid slipping on the slimy rock. The boat would then stand off with a crew of five and drift around all night. Gannets always post a 'sentry' and this bird had to be killed silently first. Then the sleeping birds were quietly clubbed to death or strangled with fowling rods – which sounds easy until one remembers that the gannet is a big bird, ferocious when disturbed, and the rocky ledges are narrow and treacherous in the dark. Some birds would be gutted and left stored in the cleits on Boreray, but several hundred would be loaded aboard the Hirta boat at daybreak. Despite this annual massacre nature kept an equilibrium. Birds still survive on St Kilda, it is the human beings who have gone.

In April or May the St Kildans visited Boreray to collect eggs and count the sheep. In June they returned to collect the wool. These were not Soay sheep and had to be partly sheared but this was done with a penknife. Dogs were carried up the cliff to help gather the flock. After several days, the men would cut out an area of turf. This could be seen from Hirta and was the signal to send a boat – weather, of course, permitting. In earlier times women ac-

companied the men and while the men tended the sheep the women would catch and kill puffins.

Stac an Armin (G. or ON – stack of the warrior or steward) at 196m (643ft) is the highest monolith in the British Isles and yet it was regularly climbed by the St Kildans to collect eggs and birds. Sadly, it was on Stac an Armin that the last great auk seen in Britain was killed by two St Kildans who beat it to death in July 1840. They thought it was a witch.

Stac Lee (Martin called it Stac-Ly) is certainly not in the lee of Boreray so far as the prevailing wind direction is concerned so the name probably derives from the Norse (ON *ly* – shelter) in a more general sense. A small, ancient bothy or shelter sits on top of Stac Lee, dry inside, and able to accommodate two people. When it was climbed by mountaineers in 1969 the south-east corner was considered the best landing point but best is a relative term – even on a calm day the Atlantic swell will move a boat up or down by five metres or more. Apparently the St Kildans lassoed an iron peg when landing. As the boat reached the top of the swell they would jump, find slippery hand and footholds, and start to climb.

ACCESS: No normal access.

Anchorages: There are no anchorages but there is one place at the south end, close to Sgarbhstac, a rock lying close off the SW side of Boreray, where it is possible to land when conditions are unusually calm. The NTS warden from Hirta must be present during any landing.

9.4 Rona

Probably (ON hraun-øy *– rough island) but, maybe, (G. ròn, N -øy – seal island), or named after St Ronan to whom the island chapel is dedicated.*

OS Maps: 1:50000 Sheet 8 1:25000 Sheet 39
Admiralty Charts: 1:200000 No.1954 1:25000 No.2524

AREA: 109ha (269 acres)
HEIGHT: 108m (354 ft)

OWNER: Barvas Estates Ltd.

POPULATION: 1796 – 1 family. 1841 – 3 (last inhabitant evacuated in 1844). Uninhabited since, apart from one brief interlude (see below).

GEOLOGY: Gneiss and hornblende schist with pegmatite intrusions.

HISTORY: Dean Monro comments: 'Towards the north northeist from Lewis, three score myles of sea, lyes and little ile callit Roney, laiche maine land, inhabit and manurit be simple people, scant of ony religione.'

Monro found a people which had continuously inhabited North Rona for at least 700 years. The first inhabitant

THE RONA CROSS

PLAN OF ST RONAN'S CHAPEL
AND CEMETERY

was supposed to have been St Ronan, who built a hermitage there during the 8th century, but the island may well have been occupied from earlier times. In 1680 Martin recorded the report of the Rev. Donald Morison who had visited Rona that there were five families living in their own stone and thatched houses, each with a barn, storehouse, cattle-shed and 'a porch on each side to keep off the rain or snow'. He said they were simple and contented people who took their surname 'from the colour of the sky, rainbow and clouds'. Their only interest in the outside world was in the north part of Lewis which they very occasionally visited. They had no interest in money or wealth, using barter if necessary as they had enough food and raiment for all their needs. They restricted their population to 'thirty souls', by sending their 'supernumerary' people to Lewis.

Martin reported that soon after this came tragedy. Rats from a ship invaded the island and ate all the food. Then some seamen landed and killed the only bull. Within the space of a year 'all that ancient race of people' were dead.

The disaster was discovered by a party from St Kilda (100 miles away!) who were shipwrecked on Rona after being blown there by a storm. They lived for seven months on the island while they built a boat out of driftwood which they then sailed to Stornoway.

The minister of Barvas on Lewis had the island resettled. But by 1796 there was only one family left on Rona, that of a shepherd, as the rest had apparently drowned in a fishing accident. The island was rented by a Ness tacksman for £4 sterling per annum paid to the owner, MacLeod of MacLeod, and he in turn received produce from the islanders in the form of corn, butter, cheese, wild fowl and feathers, a few sheep and sometimes a cow.

When Dr MacCulloch landed on Rona in 1815, the shepherd, Kenneth MacCagie, with his wife, three children, and old deaf mother, ran away and hid. They had 'seen no face' for seven years and had taken MacCulloch's party for 'pirates or Americans'. MacCulloch managed to persuade them that he meant no harm. There was plenty of food and six or seven acres planted with potatoes and cereals. The shepherd was indentured for eight years at an annual wage of £2 worth of clothing. He had no boat in case he deserted but he caught fish without difficulty with a rod. His house was mostly underground. The MacCagies left Rona about 1820.

About this time, with the herring industry booming, it was seriously suggested that six fishermen from Great Bernera on Lewis should be settled on Rona to form a fishing 'station' at a rent of £30 per year but there were no volunteers. So in 1829 John MacDonald, known as Iain Buidhe, took over as shepherd on Rona accompanied by his wife Cirstina and daughter Catherine. Three more children were born on the island. The family returned to Lewis about 1834 and their recorded experiences are a valuable record of life on the island.

In 1844 Rona's single inhabitant, Donald MacLeod, the 'King of Rona', was evacuated after spending a year there and in 1850 the island was offered free to the Government for use as a penal settlement. This was not accepted.

Rona lay deserted until 1884-5 when two men from Ness went there in a fit of pique after an argument with their minister. They vowed never to return to the parish. In February 1885 a relief boat called and found them both dead, one from natural causes, the other from 'exhaustion after nursing his friend.'

WILDLIFE: Harvie-Brown, a Victorian yachtsman, reported seeing whimbrel on Rona in June 1885. He was excited by the extensive bird-life and also listed the island plants – about forty-three different species in all.

Rona (including Sula Sgeir) was declared a National Nature Reserve in 1956 because of its importance as a breeding ground for guillemot, puffin, kittiwake, and fulmar. There are also large numbers of petrel, both Leach's and stormy, which breed in burrows.

Another reason for the importance of this wildlife station is that it is one of Britain's largest breeding grounds for the grey seal. About 7500 of them breed here every autumn resulting in the birth of some 2500 calves annually.

There are no rabbits.

RONA is an uninhabited island situated about ten miles east of Sula Sgeir and forty-four miles from the Butt of Lewis. It is roughly triangular in shape and covered with undulating turfy moorland but on the south-east corner there is a steep hill, **Toa Rona**, 108m high with a vertical cliff on its south side. Along the north-west coast the ocean storms have piled up an embankment of boulders over 20m (66ft) high. In spite of this protection sheets of seawater come splashing over the embankment during gales and the water has eroded deep channels in the turf which go right down to the bedrock.

During the many centuries of human habitation this remote little island was not only self-sufficient but even produced a surplus. Dean Monro said that there was an abundance of corn grown on the island and clover-grass for sheep. (The name of the hill, Toa Rona, may come from the Norse for a patch of grass.) A fine bere-meal (ground barley) was stuffed into the skins of sheep and sent with mutton and fowls to MacLeod each year as rent.

Nowadays the land supports only sheep which are sheared and tended by a party of Lewis shepherds on an annual visit.

St Ronan's Chapel is possibly the oldest unaltered Christian building in Britain [HW809323]. Certainly the Royal Commission on Ancient Monuments lists it as one of the three oldest known structures of the Celtic Church. The other two are Annait in Skye and the nunnery on Canna (No.4.4). The ruin, which is near the remains of some houses, stands in pasture sloping down between the south-western and eastern promontories. The 'village' was possibly founded by Norse settlers in the 8th century.

In the burial ground beside the chapel there once stood a stone cross with three holes through it and the much-eroded figure of a naked man carved on it, possibly as a fertility symbol. This cross was removed in the 1930s and placed in Teampull Mholuaidh at Europie on Lewis (No.8.16). It is reputed to be 6th-7th century work and may have marked St Ronan's grave.

No one is very sure who St Ronan was. There were twelve saints of that name in Donegal, and two were recorded in Scotland. There are dedications to St Ronan on both North Uist (No.7.16) and Islay (No.2.4). Whether the island was named after this particular St Ronan or the saint was named after the island is a moot point.

Sula Sgeir, eleven miles south-west of Rona, is a narrow goose-neck shaped islet which is appropriately named gannet skerry (ON *sula skeri*). It is a small rocky island almost surrounded by cliffs and with a sea-cave running right through it. Although this is now a Nature Reserve the men of Ness in Lewis have special permission to harvest the young gannets (G. *guga*) once a year in September as this is an ancient tradition. The oily flesh of guga is considered a great delicacy but it is definitely an acquired taste.

The Lewismen used to row the forty-one miles to Sula Sgeir in an open six-oared boat without a compass and yet accidents were very rare. A ring is fixed to the rocks at the only landing place, Geodha a' Phuill Bhàin, as there is no anchorage or beach. Nor is there any soil or fresh water on the islet but there are five stone bothies which the guga-hunters live in for a few days during their annual expedition.

ACCESS: No regular access but Ness (Lewis) crofters graze their sheep on the island and generally call there during July or August. It may be possible to negotiate a visit. Permission to land is required from Barvas Estates Ltd, North Lewis and from Scottish Natural Heritage, Inverness, 01463-239431.

Anchorages: Approach Rona carefully, especially from the SW.
1. There is no recognised anchorage and landing is generally difficult, but the best places, depending on wind direction and sea state, are a) Geodh' a' Stoth, b) Poll Thothatom or Poll Heallair, or c) Sgeildige (requiring a climb up a cliff).

Stroma and the Orkney Islands

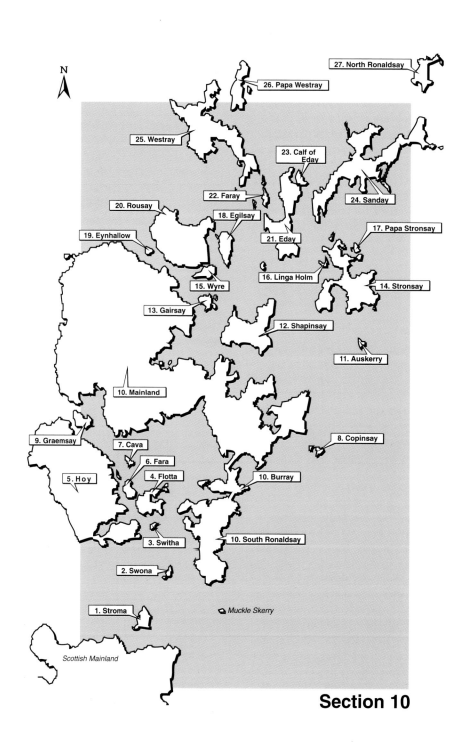

N

27. North Ronaldsay

26. Papa Westray

25. Westray

23. Calf of Eday

22. Faray

24. Sanday

20. Rousay

18. Egilsay

19. Eynhallow

21. Eday

17. Papa Stronsay

15. Wyre

16. Linga Holm

14. Stronsay

13. Gairsay

12. Shapinsay

11. Auskerry

10. Mainland

9. Graemsay

7. Cava

8. Copinsay

6. Fara

5. Hoy

4. Flotta

10. Burray

3. Switha

10. South Ronaldsay

2. Swona

1. Stroma

Muckle Skerry

Scottish Mainland

Section 10

Section 10, Table 1

No.	Name	Latitude	Longitude	Table 2* No.	Table 3** No.	Area in Acres	Area in Hectares
10.1	Stroma	58° 41N	03° 07W	62	117	927	375
10.2	Swona	58° 45N	03° 03W	117	133	227	92
10.3	Switha	58° 48N	03° 06W	161	154	101	41
10.4	Flotta	58° 50N	03° 07W	46	109	2165	876
10.5	Hoy	58° 51N	03° 18W	10	8	35380	14318
10.6	Fara	58° 51N	03° 10W	72	130	729	295
10.7	Cava	58° 53N	03° 10W	112	139	264	107
10.8	Copinsay	58° 54N	02° 41W	131	102	180	73
10.9	Graemsay	58° 56N	03° 17W	59	104	1011	409
10.10	Mainland (Orkney)	59° 00N	03° 05W	6	26	129295	52325
	South Ronaldsay	58° 47N	02° 57W			12306	4980
	Burray	58° 51N	02° 54W			2231	903
	Hunda	58° 51N	02° 59W			247	100
	Glimps Holm	58° 53N	02° 55W			136	55
	Lamb Holm	58° 53N	02° 53W			99	40	58308
10.11	Auskerry	59° 02N	02° 34W	120	163	210	85
10.12	Shapinsay	59° 02N	02° 52W	25	103	7285	2948
10.13	Gairsay	59° 05N	02° 58W	81	69	593	240
10.14	Stronsay	59° 07N	02° 36W	23	127	8093	3275
10.15	Wyre	59° 07N	02° 58W	68	146	768	311
10.16	Linga Holm	59° 08N	02° 40W	144	165	141	57
10.17	Papa Stronsay	59° 09N	02° 35W	130	164	183	74
10.18	Egilsay	59° 09N	02° 56W	54	141	1606	650
10.19	Eynhallow	59° 09N	03° 07W	129	150	185	75
10.20	Rousay	59° 10N	03° 02W	19	28	12009	4860
10.21	Eday	59° 12N	02° 46W	27	70	6783	2745
10.22	Faray	59° 13N	02° 49W	92	148	445	180
10.23	Calf of Eday	59° 14N	02° 44W	80	119	600	243
10.24	Sanday	59° 15N	02° 34W	18	99	12461	5043
10.25	Westray	59° 18N	02° 57W	20	41	11646	4713
10.26	Papa Westray	59° 21N	02° 53W	44	125	2268	918
10.27	North Ronaldsay	59° 22N	02° 25W	51	161	1705	690

* Table 2: The islands arranged in order of magnitude
** Table 3: The islands arranged in order of height

Introduction

The islands to the north of Scotland are not easily confused with those of the west. Not only is the geology very different from that of, say, the Hebrides, but the entire social structure and language is distinctive. Both areas came under Norse influence in the first millennium but whereas within a few centuries Celtic civilisation had gained control in the west, the north remained a Norse dominion until comparatively recent times. Gaelic has never been a natural language in the north. When Norn (partly Old Norse, partly Icelandic) died out it was replaced by English or Lowland Scots.

Apart from a very few outliers, the islands in this region form two archipelagoes and just as the northern isles as a group are very different from the western isles so too does each archipelago have its own distinctive characteristics. The Orkney archipelago is agriculturally rich thanks to its base of Old Red Sandstone, while the Shetland archipelago, 50-miles further north, has poorer soil and its economy therefore depends on the wealth of the sea. Hence the well-known saying that 'an Orcadian is a farmer with a boat while a Shetlander is a fisherman with a croft.' The richness of the Orkney soil has always made fishing a secondary occupation. The sea is all around, but it is primarily for transport or recreation rather than for sustenance, whereas in Shetland it is a life-giving force.

Between Duncansby Head (beside John o'Groats) on the

Scottish mainland and Brough Ness at the southern tip of South Ronaldsay is only a matter of six miles, or a mere ten kilometres. But this narrow strip of water contains the treacherous Pentland Firth in parts of which the spring tides run faster than almost anywhere else in coastal Britain. The western end of the Firth has a notorious tidal race called the Merry Men of Mey which forms on the ebb and which is so turbulent that a small vessel can be put in severe danger.

The eastern end also has its troublesome areas, such as near the Pentland Skerries in mid-firth. There are heavy breaking seas in this area which are particularly lethal when the wind is against the tide. **Muckle Skerry**, the largest of the Pentland Skerries, is a sizeable islet with a lighthouse (built in 1794) and a roadway up from the landing point in Scartan Bay. It has three tiny lochans and a table-shaped northern promontory called 'Tenniscourt'. In 1841 this islet had a population of eleven persons which by 1881 had increased to seventeen people living in four houses. After that the population declined, and in recent years it only consisted of the lighthouse keepers; that is, until 1994, when the light was automated. Now, after 200 years, the lighthouse keepers have left for good and the isle is deserted.

It would be a pity to discuss Orkney without mentioning the strange story of Henry Sinclair.

When the wealthy Order of the Knights Templar was branded heretical by the Vatican in 1307 many Knights fled to Scotland and set up their headquarters in Midlothian on the lands of the St Clair family. The St Clairs, or Sinclairs, were descended from Vikings and held powerful earldoms in Caithness and Orkney. Their connection with the Templars brought enormous additional wealth.

Henry Sinclair was born in 1345. Tall and strong, he could speak fluent Latin, Norse and Lowland Scots, and he hunted, crusaded, fathered thirteen children, and dreamed of conquest. He became a Knight Templar – a defender of the Holy Grail – and he wanted a kingdom so much that he was nicknamed 'Prince'.

Prince Henry had heard all the Norse tales of a land far west of Greenland so he persuaded two of his Venetian friends, Nicolo and Antonio Zeno, who had made vast profits from ship-building, to come to Orkney and join his venture. Nicolo died after an initial exploratory voyage to Greenland, but Antonio carried on and described events in long detailed letters to his family in Venice. These became known as the Zeno Narratives when they were eventually published in 1558.

According to these letters the adventurers fitted out a small fleet and Antonio armed it with Pietro cannons which he brought from Venice. In 1398 Prince Henry, Antonio Zeno and 300 colonists set sail for the west in twelve ships. They eventually reached Newfoundland and spent their first winter in Nova Scotia.

The Mi'Kmaq Indians tribal history tells of the arrival centuries ago of a bird with a broken wing, and a prophet called 'Kluskap' and it was about this time that the Mi'Kmaqs started fishing with European-style nets. A couple of hilltop castle ruins in Nova Scotia have been dated to this period by Canadian archaeologists and two brass canons dredged from Digby Harbour in Nova Scotia in 1990 have been identified as 14th century Pietro canons. Hardly conclusive evidence but interesting nevertheless.

The following spring (1399), the colonists sailed down the coast to look for land on which to settle. Once again there is circumstantial evidence. In Rhode Island an ancient round stone tower, called the Newport Tower, has a striking resemblance to the church tower of Egilsay (No 10.18) and rock carvings in Westford, Massachusetts, accurately depict a medieval Scottish knight in full regalia.

It is known that Prince Henry sailed back to Orkney in 1400, possibly to collect more prospective colonists or essential provisions, but according to the Narratives he was killed by the English. (Henry IV of England invaded Orkney at that time.)

No one knows what became of the settlement. The colonists may have been massacred, starved to death, or they may have merely intermarried with the Indians and slowly vanished from sight – modern genetic testing might have a story to reveal.

Some years later – in 1446 – the Sinclair family built Rosslyn Chapel on their land near Edinburgh, and it clearly features stone carvings of Indian maize and aloe cacti.

Yet all these events took place nearly a century before Christopher Columbus 'discovered' America.

10.1 Stroma

(*ON straum-øy – island in the tidal stream*)

OS Maps: 1:50000 Sheet 7 1:25000 Sheet 41
Admiralty Charts: 1:200000 Nos.1942 or 1954 1:50000 No.2162
1:26000 No.2581

AREA: 375ha (927 acres)
HEIGHT: 53m (174 ft)

OWNER: James Simpson, a Stroma man by birth and a former haulage contractor, has owned Stroma since 1960.

POPULATION: 1841 – 186 (42 houses). 1881 – 341. 1891 – 327 (66 houses). 1931 – 193. 1961 – 12. Uninhabited since 1950s except for lighthouse keepers and their families. 1971 – 8. 1981 – 5 (lighthouse keepers). 1991 – 0.

GEOLOGY: Weathered Middle Old Red Sandstone in flat layers known as Rousay flags. There is a fault line running north to south through the centre of the island – almost on the line of the road.

HISTORY: Svein Asleifsson (see Gairsay, No.10.13) had to spend a night on Stroma sheltering from a gale according to the Orkneyinga Saga. The sagas make no other mention of Stroma.

It is usually true to say that the survival of an island population in the present day depends on the availability of good education and good communication. Well, Stroma is the exception that proves the rule.

There was an active and viable population of eighty people living on the island in the early 1950s with a good primary school to serve the children. But tide-wracked Stroma lacked adequate harbour facilities. Officialdom rose to the occasion and in 1955 a new harbour was constructed at great expense. The contractors were pleased to employ the local people to carry out the work and wages were good. By the time the harbour was complete many of the islanders had made sufficient money to leave and establish themselves on the mainland. Too few were then left to maintain a viable population and within a few years the island was deserted except for the lighthouse keepers;

and they too left in 1996 when the lighthouse was automated.

WILDLIFE: Always a popular breeding ground for seals, the numbers have dramatically increased since the island became uninhabited.

STROMA is officially part of Caithness and not one of the Orkney isles. The powerful ocean tides, deflected by the British mainland, funnel into the Pentland Firth – the gap between Caithness and Orkney. Stroma obstructs their flow and turbulent seas are the result. Only a short distance west is the wide and dangerous tidal race known as the Merry Men of Mey and off Swilkie Point at Stroma's northern shore the sea can be equally violent.

The Picts are thought to have first settled in Orkney and the name of the Pentland Firth is a corruption of Pictland Firth. Stroma lies in the southern part of the Firth with the Inner Sound separating it from the mainland. The west side of the island is mainly cliffs but the east side is fairly low and flat. The ruin of **Castle Mestag** [ND340764] caps Mell Head in the south-west and in the far north, beside the lighthouse, there is a chambered cairn [ND353791].

The evidence of Stroma's recent depopulation is there to be seen. A roadway runs down the centre of the island from the lighthouse in the north to the harbour in the south connecting what were the two main settlements, **Nethertown** in the north and **Uppertown** in the south. The main island farmhouse, **Mains of Stroma**, is central. **Cairn Hill** (53m), the highest point, is in the south-east.

The church and school, and the old croft houses, stand derelict. Only the sheep find shelter in them now.

A deep rocky pit in the north-west, known as **The Gloup** (ON *glup* – hollow, ravine), is filled with sea water which feeds in through a subterranean passage under the cliffs. This is a particularly fine example of this type of feature of which there are many in the Northern Isles. Just north of the gloup are the remains of an Iron Age fort [ND350785].

ACCESS: Summer excursions from John o' Groats.

Anchorages:
1. Small harbour on S coast. Least depth of 2m at entrance. Good shelter and easy entrance at slack water.

10.2 Swona

(ON svín-øy – pig island) or, possibly, (ON – Sveinn's island). Old records call it 'Swinna'. The Norse was sometimes used perjoratively – 'a swine of an island'.

OS Maps: 1:50000 Sheet 7 1:25000 Sheet 38
Admiralty Charts: 1:50000 No.2162 1:26000 No.2581

AREA: 92ha (227 acres)
HEIGHT: 41m (134 ft)

OWNER: Alexander Annal (b.1910). His wife's family was the last to leave the island.

POPULATION: 1841 – 54 (8 houses). 1881 – 47. 1891 – 42 (7 houses). 1931 – 6. 1961 – 3. 1971 – 3. Abandoned 1974 and uninhabited since.

GEOLOGY: Weathered Middle Old Red Sandstone.

HISTORY: In spite of the difficulty of access, archaeological evidence would suggest that Swona was probably first occupied 5000 years ago.

In the 12th century this was the home of Grim, father of two of Sweyn Asleifsson's close friends.

WILDLIFE: A small herd of feral cattle still survives. The original herd, which was abandoned in 1974, consisted of a mixture of black Aberdeen Angus and brown Shorthorns. The cattle eat seaweed during the grassless winter months, shelter from the cold in derelict buildings, and the young bulls fight for dominance in the spring. Such herds of feral cattle are very rare and this herd is being studied with interest by scientists from Cambridge University. How long it will survive is uncertain.

Thousands of rabbits breed unchecked, crop the grass which the cattle need and provide an occasional meal for the seagulls.

There is such a wealth of birdlife that the RSPB would like to have Swona declared a site of scientific interest (SSI).

SWONA lies in the south approach to Scapa Flow. The Tails of the Tarf (?N – the end of the seaweed) is the most southerly point marked by the small white tower of **Swona Light**. The east side of Swona is mainly cliff with the rounded green summit of **Warbister Hill** (41m) rising close above the cliffs midway along the east coast and a cave further to the north.

The settlement on Swona was in the lowest-lying part near the north end of the island. On the east side is a little cove called the **Haven**, Swona's best attempt at a harbour and on the west side is the **Brook**, an indentation with a wide stretch of shallow, treacherous rock and reef.

Associations with the distant past include a prehistoric chambered cairn [ND384837] in the extreme south of the island, an early Christian burial ground, and Viking remains.

In the 19th century the islanders' main occupation was line-fishing for cod. This was supplemented on occasion by piloting ships through the treacherous waters of the Pentland Firth – waters which they knew so well. Crofting was a marginal existence and by 1932 only one family remained on the island. The last inhabitant in 1974 was Jim Rosie. He was unmarried and had to leave when he developed Parkinson's disease. Now the solid stone and slated buildings have fallen into disrepair and

Tidal Race

Cause **The North Head**

Bn

**The Clump
o' the Ness**

Tidal Race

The Haven

The Brook

+

Cave

Radio
Mast

Dyke End

25

Filliberry

*Selki
Skerry*

**Warbister
Hill**

40 ▲ Cave

Bn

*Chambered
Cairn*

South Clett

**The Tails of
the Tarf**

West Wini Skerry

N

Tidal Races

P e n t l a n d   F i r t h

old agricultural machinery rusts among the nettles.

Throughout history Swona has been the scene of many shipping disasters. Most of these have been on the west side of the island during the east-going tidal stream. The trouble is that the tide is deceptive and carries a boat on to the northern skerries with accelerating speed. By the time the danger is recognised it can be too late.

Martin Martin's (1695) solution should not be taken too seriously: '. . .Swinna isle, remarkable only for a part of Pentland Firth lying to the west of it, called the Wells of Swinna. They are two whirlpools in the sea, which run about with such violence, that any vessel or boat coming within their reach, go always round until they sink. These

wells are dangerous only when there is a dead calm; for if a boat be under sail with any wind, it is easy to go over them. If any boat be forced into these wells by the violence of the tide, the boat-men cast a barrel or an oar into the wells; and while it is swallowing it up, the sea continues calm, and gives the boat an opportunity to pass over.'

ACCESS: No normal means of access.

Anchorages: Swona is surrounded with very tricky tides and it is often impracticable to approach the island. There are tidal races at both N and S ends of the island and the west coast is particularly dangerous.
1. The Haven, a small cove on the NE side of the island, 2c S of North Head is the best landing place on Swona when an approach can be made.

10.3 Switha

Derivation uncertain but may be (ON sviv-øy – island that appears to be floating or swinging).

OS Maps: 1:50000 Sheet 7 1:25000 Sheet 37
Admiralty Charts: 1:50000 No.2162 1:26000 No.2581

AREA: 41ha (101 acres)
HEIGHT: 29m (95 ft)

POPULATION: No record of any habitation.

GEOLOGY: Well-weathered Old Red Sandstone of the Middle period.

WILDLIFE: There are many storm-petrel burrows in the light soil and barnacle geese winter here.

There is no written record of **SWITHA** ever having been inhabited in historic times and the Norse sagas make no mention of this little island. But Neolithic man lived here or, at least, visited the island for religious purposes, because he left two standing stones as evidence. The remarkable seamanship of these men in their flimsy craft never fails to astonish!

Sheep are grazed on Switha and probably have been for centuries. Every June, for at least a few days, the island echoes to the sound of human voices when shepherds, and occasionally members of their families, land on the island to clip the sheep.

Switha lies on the west side of the Sound of Hoxa amid tidal races beside the southern approach to Scapa Flow. Its most southerly point is called **The Ool** and between it and **The Kiln**, a point halfway along the south-east side, the cliffs reach a height of 29m. This is the highest part of the island and the ground falls away behind the cliffs except for a small hill (24m) to the north with one of the standing stones on its summit. A shallow cove in the south-west, **The Pool**, lies between the Ool and a low promontory, Point of the Pool.

ACCESS: No regular access.

Anchorages: Approach from N if possible to avoid dangerous tides at SE entrance to Cantick Sound, or time the passage carefully.
1. Temporary anchorage in the Pool, at SW end of Switha off Cantick Sound, in suitable conditions.

10.4 Flotta

(ON flott-øy – flat grassy island)

OS Maps: 1:50000 Sheet 7 1:25000 Sheets 36 and 37
Admiralty Charts: 1:200000 Nos.1942 or 1954 1:50000 No.2162
1:30000 No.35 1:26000 No.2581 1:12500 No.2568 oil terminal

AREA: 876ha (2,165 acres)
HEIGHT: 58m (190 ft)

POPULATION: 1841 – 405 (82 houses). 1881 – 425. 1891 – 423 (88 houses). 1931 – 282. 1961 – 123. 1971 – 73. (1975 – introduction of oil industry) 1981 – 300. 1991 – 126.

GEOLOGY: The whole island is Middle Old Red Sandstone but the larger south-west portion is of Rousay Beds weathered into low hills, whereas the Golta peninsula and Quoy Ness are of Eday Beds – flagstones and sandstone of building quality.

HISTORY: During the First World War Flotta became a naval base but after the war it returned to its former happy rural state. There were fields to be ploughed and lobsters to be caught in the rocky pools. Then the Second World War turned the island into an armed camp festooned with so many barrage balloons that it almost took off – the aim being to protect the southern entrance to Scapa Flow. Two new concrete piers were built with excellent access, and communication with Kirkwall and Stromness was improved. After the war the island once again slowly recovered from the shock, but, as with so many of the small islands, the population was decreasing and becoming more elderly. Improvement work was carried out, such as the laying of a water pipe in 1970 to bring fresh water from Hoy, but even so, the outlook was rather bleak.

Then Flotta, for the third time, was thrown irrevocably into the modern age because this flat little island, balanced near the edge of extinction, had the best-protected deep-water facilities in all of Orkney.

In 1974 the Occidental Group started construction of an oil terminal and linked it to the Piper and Claymore fields in the North Sea by 230km of pipeline. Many of the islanders were given employment but, inevitably, the work brought newcomers to the island and their assimilation was not always without problems. However, Flotta now has a thriving community with many young families and children, and good prospects for the foreseeable future.

The oil-terminal facilities are second only in size to those of Sullom Voe in Shetland but, unlike Shetland, practically all of the oil-related development is confined to this one small island and has relatively little impact on the Mainland community.

WILDLIFE: Large number of Arctic tern, goodly population of Arctic skua and a compact seabird colony at Stanger Head.

Scapa Flow is no longer filled with men-of-war, iron-clads, or even sleek grey frigates of the modern fleet. The only continual signs of life and industry are the gas-flares of the huge oil terminal on **FLOTTA** sparkling on the water.

The island is almost rectangular except for the gaping mouth of **Pan Hope** in the east (the site of 17th century salt pans). This wide bay cuts deep into the island with a northwards twist at Sands Taing. It then dries out in **Curries Firth**. Unfortunately all the inner part of the bay is too shallow to be of any use as an anchorage – but the waders don't mind.

In the pre-oil-terminal days the island was mostly moorland with some grazing and cultivated land and most of the farms were small. Lobster fishing was needed to augment the meagre return from farming, yet there was always an air of vitality despite the number of old people. Now more than half the total land area is covered with all the paraphernalia of industry and houses. **West Hill** (58m), Flotta's highest point, is relatively clear but the airstrip lies below it by Rotten Gutter on the west coast. North-west of the terminal the **Golta** (ON – barren, sterile) peninsula is more open, but that is all there is now to be seen of the old Flotta. The south-east corner at **Stanger Head** is covered with the derelict military installations of the Second World War, fascinating, or a suitable set for a disaster movie, depending on one's viewpoint.

Calf of Flotta is a tiny island off Roan Head in the north. It nearly rates as a drying island because the water in Calf Sound which separates it from Flotta is very shallow.

ACCESS: Frequent car ferry of Orkney Islands Shipping,

CAVA

2 kms
1 mile

S C A P A   F L O W

Wrecks of German Fleet scuttled in 1919

Ferry

Calf of Flotta

Wreck of HMS Vanguard

Calf Sound

Pier

Roan Head

Tween the Wicks

Golta

Villigar

Row Taing

FARA

Heyspan

Pan Hope

Oil Terminal

Pier

Flare Stack

Sands Taing

Curries Firth

Weddel Sound

Sutherland Pier

Quoy Ness

Pan Pier

S o u n d

Rotten Gutter

Blackawall

West Hill △58

Whome

Lee Craig

o f

Airstrip

Dam

PO

Sch

Greenslide

H o x a

Weddel

Newhouse

Castlewell

Lensty

Wharth

Overgate

Banks

Kirk Bay

Cave

House Geo

Hullderow
Hole of Row

Stanger Head

Scat Wick

Head of Banks

Innan Neb

S w i t h a   S o u n d

N

Flotta

HOY
(South Walls)

SWITHA

01856-811397, from Houton, 17km SW of Kirkwall.

Anchorages:
1. Pan Hope, large bay on E side of Flotta. Good fair weather anchorage in 4-5m N of pier and clear of underwater cable.
2. Kirk Bay, on S side. Temp anchorage but rocky and exposed in S winds.
3. West Weddel Sound, bay in NW of Flotta. Shallow and rocky but good anchorage in settled weather. Gibralter Pier on E side and Sutherland Pier on S side (0.6m at head).

10.5 Hoy

(ON há-øy – high island)

OS Maps: 1:50000 Sheet 7 1:25000 Sheets 33 and 36
Admiralty Charts: 1:200000 No.1954 1:75000 No.2249 north Hoy
1:50000 No.2162 south Hoy 1:30000 No.35 east coast

AREA: 14,318ha (35,380 acres)
HEIGHT: 479m (1,571 ft)

OWNER: Sold in 1973 by the owner, Malcolm Stewart, to The Hoy Trust. After the passing of the Crofting Reform Act many crofters purchased their own land-holdings from the Trust which also sold 3237ha to the Royal Society for the Protection of Birds (including the Old Man of Hoy). The Trust hopes to encourage resettlement on the parts of Hoy which it still owns.

POPULATION: 1841 – 1486 (294 houses). 1881 – 1380. 1891 – 1320 (271 houses). 1931 – 955. 1961 – 511. 1971 – 419. 1981 – 519. 1991 – 450.

GEOLOGY: Hoy is unique in being almost entirely composed of Upper Old Red Sandstone although there are a few small volcanic intrusive dykes in the north-west and some small areas of exposed basalt. This particular type of sandstone – massive, hard, and red or orange-coloured – is to be found nowhere else in Orkney. Its mode of weathering has resulted in the fantastic precipices of the west coast.

The sandstone lies above a basalt lava layer which is about 120m thick. This has been exposed by erosion at, for instance, the foot of the Old Man of Hoy where it forms a pedestal. The south-east of the island is of Middle Old Red Sandstone. In the extreme north there is a small area of Lower Stromness Flags – a finely-laminated Middle Old Red Sandstone which weathers to a good soil.

HISTORY: It was on South Walls, according to the sagas, that Olaf Tryggvason, King of Norway from 995 to 1000, forced Sigurd Hlodvisson the Stout, Earl of Orkney and a fearless warrior, to submit to baptism on pain of death. The Earl duly became a Christian – but in name only.

WILDLIFE: Hoy is a treasure-house of plantlife – by far the best in Orkney and including a number of rare alpines but there is also deep heather covering many of the hill-slopes. The only remaining fragment of native woodland is at Berrie Dale west of the Old Man of Hoy with willow, birch, aspen and rowan, and a few indigenous trees still growing in the clefts of Ward Hill and Cuilags – rowan, hazel – *corytus avellana*, aspen, birch – *betula pubescens*, and sallow – *salix atrocinerea*. Strangely, although it is common in the Highlands, there is no bog myrtle on Hoy.

Mountain hares are to be found in the north of Hoy and nowhere else in Orkney although the brown hare is quite common. This area is also supposed to support Orkney's only grasshoppers.

North Hoy is an RSPB Nature Reserve. Breeding species of bird to be seen – if you can survive the midges – are red grouse, golden plover, dunlin, snipe and curlew, with some hen harrier, merlin and short-eared owl. There is an important skua population – over 400 pairs of Arctic and 1500 great skuas (bonxies) were recorded in 1982 and the lochans support half the 110 pairs of red-throated divers recorded on Orkney. Stonechat, wheatear, some ring ousel and many twite are in evidence. On the cliffs there are huge numbers of fulmar, shag, kittiwake, guillemot, razorbill, puffin, black guillemot, and rock dove. There are also buzzard, peregrine and raven, and barnacle geese appear in late winter at South Walls.

May to July are the best bird-watching months.

HOY is the highest and wildest and wettest (1500mm of rain) of all the Orkney islands. The high ground rises in three rugged masses, divided by 300m deep gaps, with **Ward Hill** in the middle. Ward Hill is the highest peak in Orkney (479m). Legend has it that on the steep north side of Ward Hill, where it hangs above the Hoy Outdoor Centre, there used to be a great carbuncle which gleamed ruby red in the dark but which disappeared whenever you approached it. There has never been an explanation for this.

The outstanding view of the Hoy cliffs from the Scrabster ferry gives newcomers a very misleading impression of Orkney. As can be seen from Table III, most of the Northern Isles are low-lying. **St John's Head** on the NW coast is, at nearly 350m, one of the highest sea-cliffs in Britain with the world-famous rock pinnacle, the **Old Man of Hoy** (137m), to the south and the remarkable echoing valley of the **Kame** in the far north. In 1970, mountaineers spent two days descending St John's Head as it was almost impossible to abseil in the vicious sea-wind, and the subsequent hair-raising ascent took five days.

Many legends attach to the **Dwarfie Stane** – a huge block of red sandstone (8.5m long x 4.3m wide x 1.8m

THE OLD MAN OF HOY

high) lying within a natural amphitheatre – the Dwarfie Hamars (ON *hamars* – crags), south-east of Ward Hill [HY243004]. This is the only example in Northern Europe of a rock tomb similar to the rock-cut chamber tombs of the Mediterranean region. The tomb, which was probably cut in Neolithic or Early Bronze Age times *c.* 2000-1600BC, consists of a passage and two chambers hollowed out of the stone. Martin Martin thought there was a domestic purpose – 'at one of the ends. . . there is cut out a bed and pillow capable of two persons to lie in, at the other end there is a void space cut out resembling a bed, and above both these there is a large hole which is

supposed was a vent for smoke.' Martin said that the 'common tradition is that a giant and his wife made this their place of retreat.' Sir Walter Scott said that 'the necromantic owner may sometimes still be seen sitting by the Dwarfie Stone'. He considered the owner to be a troll, rather than a giant. Certainly the mysterious **Trowie Glen** (ON *troll* – evil monster, ogre or goblin) is beside the Dwarfie Hamars.

Even the **Dwarfie Hamars** have their legend. They are named after the dwarfs who, as everyone knows, are excellent smiths and who were responsible for forging Thor's famous hammer.

The track of roadway running through this legendary valley and past the Dwarfie Stane comes from **Moaness Pier** and the village of Hoy and ends up on the Atlantic coast at **Rackwick**, west of Rora Head. This picturesque old fishing village, stretching up the glen from a pebble beach, is Orkney's most isolated spot. The school closed in 1954 and the population has faded away although some of the cottages are reinhabited by visitors in the summer months and the famous composer, Peter Maxwell Davies, lives and composes in a converted croft in the hills above the village. Many years ago the men of Rackwick were known as fine fishermen and even finer country dancers. They cheerfully walked 6km over the ghostly hills to Hoy village, danced the night through, and then walked back home again.

Most of the north of Hoy is now sadly depopulated. The main road runs down the east coast overlooking Scapa Flow, to **Lyness** opposite the island of Fara (No.10.7). During the Second World War Lyness was home to about 30,000 men when it was the headquarters for the Scapa Flow naval base. The village has never recovered from this invasion and the Navy left behind a desolate landscape of abandoned structures.

The secluded natural harbour of **Longhope** (ON – long bay) is south of Lyness. On each ness, guarding the harbour entrance like a Pictish broch, is a **Martello Tower** [ND324935 and 338913]. These were built for protection against U.S. privateers during the Napoleonic War (1813-1815). As this was an assembly point for convoys, the Towers were each equipped with a 24-pounder canon on top, quarters for the gunners in the middle, and ammunition stores at ground level. A century later, they were armed once again for the First World War.

Melsetter House at the head of Longhope is one of Orkney's finest historic buildings [ND269893]. It was a laird's house for the Moodie family until the late 19th century when it was bought by a wealthy Englishman, J. G. M. Heddle, who enlarged it in the tradition of William Morris with furniture designed by Ford Maddox Brown and Dante Gabriel Rosetti.

The renowned **Longhope Lifeboat Station** is at Brims, in Aith Hope [ND291887]. This station has a remarkable record of daring rescues and will always be remembered for the loss of its entire crew when it went to the assistance of the Liberian cargo ship *Irene* in 1969. A force nine gale had raged for three days and the sea state was appalling. Eight men died including the coxswain and his two sons and the second coxswain and both his sons.

The south of Hoy is more green and mellow than the northern part and there is an active farming community on **South Walls**. South Walls was a tidal island until a narrow causeway – **The Ayre** – was constructed over the sandbank.

ACCESS: No bus service but car hire available. Foot and bike ferry from Stromness to Moaness, 01856-850624. Ro-ro service from Houton, Mainland to Lyness and Longhope (via Flotta), 01856-811397. Loganair service from Kirkwall (not on Sunday) to South Walls, 01856-872494.

Anchorages:
1. Mo Ness and Bay of Quoys. Temp anchorage in 3m, SE of ferry pier. The bay is mostly shoal.
2. Aith Hope, between Brims Ness and South Walls on the S coast, is not secure but can offer temp shelter in 6-9m, sand, during N winds or while waiting for a favourable tide.
3. Kirk Hope. Temp anchorage in 7m in centre of bay beyond fish farm. Exposed N and E.
4. Longhope, between S Walls and Hoy. Anchor in 4-6m E of pier on S Ness avoiding fish farm. There is 4m depth at outer end of pier but avoid obstructing ferry. Heavy squalls can occur with NW winds and use plenty of cable because of the weed. Snug anchorage in 7-10m about 2$^{1}/2$c NW of South Ness beyond submarine cables.
5. Ore Bay and Mill Bay, opposite Fara, are not recommended as the bottom is foul with old hawsers and there are fish cages.
6. Pegal Bay, in Rysa Sound. Attractive anchorage with good holding but part obstructed by fish cages and in W gales there can be violent squalls.
7. Lyrawa Bay, S of Green Head is generally too deep and exposed for comfortable anchorage but excellent holding. Head of bay is shoal.

10.6 Fara

Possibly, (ON vaer-øy – ram island). Previously called South Pharay.

OS Maps: 1:50000 Sheet 7 1:25000 Sheet 36
Admiralty Charts: 1:200000 Nos.1942 or 1954 1:50000 No.2162
1:30000 No.35 1:26000 No.2581 large scale No.2568

AREA: 295ha (729 acres)
HEIGHT: 43m (141 ft)

POPULATION: 1841 – 55 (10 houses). 1881 – 68. 1891 – 76 (15 houses). 1931 – 28. 1961 – 5. 1971 – 0. 1981 – 0. Uninhabited.

GEOLOGY: Rousay Flags of Middle Old Red Sandstone.

HISTORY: In the 19th century both Fara and Rysa Little were part of the Melsetter estate (Hoy and Walls) belonging to the Moodie family.

FARA has always had a good reputation for its rich pastures but, as with so many little islands which have a viable economic potential, it was abandoned because of poor communications. Without an adequate pier more and more of the inhabitants were attracted to secure centres of population. It became uneconomic to employ a teacher for the few remaining children and as numbers decreased further the pressure on the remainder increased. Eventually the number dropped below the critical minimum capable of manning a boat and carrying out similar communal tasks and the population collapsed. For Fara this point was reached in the 1960s yet the island lies close to the east side of Hoy and almost a stone's throw from Flotta, both populated areas. Today the ferry routes almost circumnavigate it, and neighbouring Flotta prospers. There is always hope that one day the island will be re-inhabited.

The cultivated area was mainly on the north-east side and most of the abandoned houses are in the north. The summit, **Thomson's Hill** (43m), is in the centre of the island.

There is a small pier with a windmill close behind it on the west coast south-west of Thomson's Hill. A track runs up the hill from the pier to Upper Quoy (ON *koie* – hut or shelter).

Peat Bay on the north-west coast is small and shallow with a stony beach, and **Kirka Taing** in the centre of the east coast means 'church point' – but there is little now to be seen of the chapel [ND331961].

ACCESS: No regular access. By arrangement from Lyness.

Anchorages: Most areas foul with old wire hawsers so tripping line essential.
1. SW of Peat Point in Gutter Sound. Occasional anchorage in 4-6m, sand and shingle. Peat Bay is foul but suitable for landing by dinghy.
2. SW of Thomson's Hill. Temp anchorage S of small pier. Beware rocks close inshore further S.
3. West Weddel Sound opposite Sutherland Pier on Flotta. Settled weather anchorage in 3-4m, 1¹/₂c offshore.

10.7 Cava

(ON kálf-øy – calf island)

OS Maps: 1:50000 Sheet 6 or 7 1:25000 Sheets 33 and 36
Admiralty Charts: 1:200000 Nos.1942 or 1954 1:75000 No.2249
1:30000 No.35

AREA: 107ha (264 acres)
HEIGHT: 36m (118 ft)

POPULATION: 1841 – 23 (4 houses). 1881 – 25. 1891 – 13 (3 houses). 1931 – 14. 1961 – 0. 1971 – 0. 1981 – 3. 1991 – 2.

GEOLOGY: The underlying rock forms layers of flagstones and firm sandstones known as the Eday Beds of Middle Old Red Sandstone.

HISTORY: In 1724 a notorious Orkney sailor, John Gow, became a pirate and returned to home waters. Having unsuccessfully tried to rob Clestrain House opposite Stromness, he visited Cava and kidnapped two or three girls which he took aboard his ship. A few days later they returned home. One story claims that they were laden with riches while the other declares that they were badly beaten and that one later died.

Gow went on to raid Eday (No.10.21) but he was caught, tried, and sentenced to death by hanging. In life, Gow bungled every action and in death he was equally maladroit – or unlucky. The rope broke and he had to be hanged a second time. His total career in piracy lasted only six months.

A low grassy island with a stony shoreline, **CAVA** nowadays is mainly used for grazing.

Any small island lying off a larger island was often called Calf Island by the early settlers. Cava is distinct in being a Calf Island which has in turn its own Calf Island lying to the north – **Calf of Cava**. This is really a small peninsula which is joined to the north of Cava by a stony ridge. A small octagonal lighthouse stands on it.

A modest half-knot tide runs through the channel between Cava and **Rysa Little** (ON and E. – little heap of stones), an islet which does rise a little – 17m to be precise. A small wrecked ship on this side of Cava lies to the north-west of a windmill standing near the shore. This is not exceptional as Scapa Flow is littered with wrecks.

After the German Fleet had surrendered to Admiral Beatty at the Firth of Forth on 21st November, 1918, all the ships were transferred to Scapa Flow and held under the terms of the armistice. Most of the sailors were sent home and only skeleton German crews stayed aboard while the Allies argued about division of the spoils. The armistice was due to expire on 19th June, 1919, with a return to hostilities so on the 17th June Admiral Von Reuter sent orders from his flagship *Emden* to make 'preparations for scuttling'. He was unaware that the armistice had been extended and the terms of a German surrender agreed.

On the 21st June, 1919 – a quiet clear Saturday morning with the British Fleet away on exercise – all the mighty ships, some of the most modern fighting machines in the world, sank slowly beneath the waves. The entire fleet of more than 200 vessels was fully dressed with flags and the crews were in full dress uniform.

'Where they were sunk, they will rest and rust,' said the Admiralty in disgust. But in the following years many of the ships were salvaged or stripped of their valuable metal. The wrecks that remain are now a great tourist attraction and seen by thousands of divers.

The wrecks lying nearest to Cava, taken clockwise from the north-west, are the light cruiser *Karlsruhe*, the battleship *Bayern*, the light cruiser *Kron Prince Wilhelm*, the battleship *Markgraf*, the light cruiser *Koln*, the light cruiser *Dresden* and the battleship *Konig*.

Cava Lodge, which is a conspicuous white house standing in the middle of the north part of the island, is an interesting example of a traditional old Orkney house. Only a very few examples still survive in fair condition.

Barrel of Butter to the north-east of the collection of wrecks is a small rock showing just above sea-level but marked by a beacon. Its quaint name comes from early times when the people of Orphir paid an annual rent of a barrel of butter to the local laird in return for permission to kill seals on the rock.

ACCESS: No regular access. Enquire at Lyness on Hoy or Houton on Mainland.

Anchorages: No recommended anchorages.
1. Point of the Ward, S extremity of Cava. Temp anchorage in settled weather on sandspit about 1¹/₂c S of Ward Point, 3-6m, sand and shingle. Tides are weak in this area.

10.8 Copinsay

(ON kobbunge-øy – seal-pup island) or (ON Kolbeinsøy – Kolbein's island)

OS Maps: 1:50000 Sheet 6 1:25000 Sheet 35
Admiralty Charts: 1:200000 Nos.1942 or 1954 1:75000 No.2250

AREA: 73ha (180 acres)
HEIGHT: 64m (210 ft)

OWNER: Former lighthouse-keeper's cottage bought in 1991 by Paul Craig of Burston, Staffordshire as a holiday home. In 1993 he was very upset when Scottish Hydro-electric quoted nearly £1m to connect his house to the electricity mains.

POPULATION: 1841 – 13 (1 house). 1881 – 5. 1891 – 9 (1 house). 1931 – 25. 1961 – 3 (lighthouse keepers). 1971 – 3. 1981 – 4. 1991 – 0.

GEOLOGY: Tilted and eroded Rousay flags of Middle Old Red Sandstone with a top-skin of reasonable turf.

HISTORY: According to the sagas a great sea-battle was fought north of Copinsay, off the Mainland coast of Deerness. King Karl (there is some uncertainty who King Karl was but he might be King Duncan of Scotland, father of Macbeth) fought a battle with Thorfinn the Mighty. The ships were laid side by side and Earl Thorfinn leapt off his poop into the King's ship and struck out boldly. The King had eleven ships while Thorfinn only had five but his attack was so merciless that the King fled.

WILDLIFE: Copinsay has its fair share of seals but it is best known nowadays for its bird-life. The most interesting time for bird-watching is from May to July but there is also much to be seen in the autumn. Copinsay is a Nature Reserve which has been administered by the Royal Society for the Protection of Birds since 1972 as the James Fisher Memorial Island. There are about 10,000 pairs of kittiwake, 30,000 guillemot, 1,000 razorbill, and many fulmar, eider, ringed plover, rock dove, raven and twite breeding here and even a few corncrake. No gannets have nested here since 1860. The adjacent Holms – which are accessible at low tide – also have arctic tern, puffin and black guillemot, plus a few common tern. The Horse rock-stack is covered with birds including a small colony of cormorant.

COPINSAY is a steeply-tilted green island which reaches a height of 64m right at the edge of the cliffs on its southeast side as though it had been abruptly sliced with a giant knife. From this high point the ground slopes steadily down to the west. The cliff summit is dominated by the lighthouse, a white tower standing 16m above the cliff-top and in summer the rock ledges are heavily populated with gulls, guillemots, razorbills, kittiwakes and shags.

A track runs down the hill from the lighthouse to the old farmhouse. This was still a working farm after the Second World War and although its isolation caused problems it was considered quite a good productive farm.

The **Giant Stone** is a huge boulder which according to

THE CLIFFS OF COPINSAY – GUILLEMOTS AND KITTIWAKES
SPRINKLED LIKE CONFETTI

legend was thrown at the island by a giant who lived on
the farm of Stembister in Deerness on Mainland. The
name Stembister means stone farm.

Apart from the south-eastern cliff-face the island is surrounded by reefs, holms and skerries. The farmhouse
stands on a small peninsula with a long rock saddle, Isle
Rough, connecting Copinsay to **Corn Holm** in the west.
This divides North Bay from South Bay and can be walked
across at low water. There was once a little chapel on
Corn Holm but the difficulty of access must have been a
problem for the islanders intending to worship in it.

Corn Holm is linked by drying reefs to **Ward Holm** in
the south and **Black Holm** in the west. Ward Holm has a
prehistoric cairn on it.

Horse Sound which is about half a mile wide separates
the **Horse of Copinsay**, a grass-topped rectangular stack
18m high, from North Nevi (ON *nøv* – fist), the north-east
extremity of Copinsay. As with so many small islands the
demand for grazing was so great that the islanders would
carry sheep to the top of the Horse, but it was said that it
could fatten one sheep and feed two, but that three would
starve. In the spring pigs were also hoisted to the top to
fatten on the huge 'crop' of sea-birds' eggs. The pigs'
coarse hair was used to make the strong rope needed for
fowling. 'Lee-running' was the local name for the organised collection of seabirds' eggs which was still practised
on Copinsay until the 1940s.

A hole through the Horse is called **Blaster Hole** be-

cause of the power of the water-jet which is forced
through it and 60m into the sky by easterly gales.

ACCESS: Enquire at Skaill in Deerness, East Mainland,
01856-74252.

Anchorages: No recommended anchorages but there is a landing jetty.
1. Horse Sound. Temp anchorage in 6-8m slightly E of the line of the W
coast of Copinsay (main island) and about 1¹/₂c offshore to avoid inshore
rocks.

10.9 Graemsay

(ON Gríms-øy – Grim's island)

OS Maps: 1:50000 Sheet 6 or 7 1:25000 Sheet 33
Admiralty Charts: 1:200000 No.1954 1:30000 No.35 large scale No.2568

AREA: 409ha (1,011 acres)
HEIGHT: 62m (203 ft)

OWNER: Mr A. D. Johnston of Stromness (part owner?).

POPULATION: 1841 – 214 (48 houses). 1881 – 236.
1891 – 223 (47 houses). 1931 – 114. 1961 – 51. 1971 –
39. 1981 – 22. 1991 – 27.

GEOLOGY: Mostly Lower Stromness Flags, a finely-laminated Middle Old Red Sandstone, which has eroded on the
surface to a fine soil. Two major volcanic faults on a
north-south axis roughly divide the island into three equal
sections. Apart from the outcrops of ancient granites and
schists through the Old Red Sandstone there is a larger
patch of granite-schist complex on the north coast – one
of the few such outcrops to be found in Orkney.

HISTORY: Two early Celtic sites on Graemsay are dedicated respectively to St Bride and St Columba.

There are a number of crofts on the island but only
one farm which is at Bu in Sandside. This was the original
settlement of the natural son of Earl Robert Stewart when
he was given the island by his father.

The 19th century herring industry led to an increased
interest in navigational safeguards and the construction of
the two lighthouses, Hoy High and Hoy Low – both of
which were built in 1851.

Navigational lights were introduced to the comely island
of **GRAEMSAY** in 1851 to help the fishermen and they
were surely needed. In Hoy Sound the tide can run so fast
that the surface of the sea forms high ridges with whirlpools in the troughs. The ridges slowly but constantly
move, like sand dunes during a sandstorm. These areas of
violent turbulent water are called 'roosts' (ON *rost* – maelstrom) and Hoy Sound is a good example.

Graemsay is a green refuge with fertile soil encompassed by savage reefs, wrecks and shoals. It has two low hills, **East Hill** (49m) and **West Hill** (62m), the summit. The small lighthouse, **Hoy Low**, is on the north-western extremity, Point of Oxan, and a coastal battery was built beside it in the Second World War. The big lighthouse, **Hoy High** (33m), is in the north-east on the Taing of Sandside (ON – Sandside point) next to the island's only bay, the **Bay of Sandside**, also known as **The Hap**. It is shallow and rocky and guarded by the **Skerry of Cletts** and a dangerous rock called **The Lash**.

The small fishing pier and the ferry pier are east of Hoy High lighthouse. Further south a projection called **The**

Nevi (ON *nøv* – promontory or fist) ends in the dangerous Sow Skerry.

A road runs across the island between the Bay of Sandside and a church at Kirk Geo on the south coast. Other roads feed off to the scattered dwellings and there is a small school beside West Hill. The school's future must be in some doubt as the population has been steadily dwindling for decades. (Hopefully it will survive as the closing of any island school usually spells eventual death for a community.)

The islanders own a number of boats. These are mainly used for lobster fishing but they are sometimes needed for last-minute shopping at Stromness as, although it has a Post Office, Graemsay has no shop. The islanders are good innovative farmers and fishermen. It was Patrick Honeyman of Graemsay who first introduced the Scots plough to Orkney. He even risked buying two of them at a time when only single-stilted ploughs were in general use.

ACCESS: There are two sailings by ro-ro ferry every Wednesday from Houton, Orphir, to Stromness via Graemsay, 01856-811397, allowing a 5¹⁄₂hr Graemsay visit.

Anchorages: There is no recommended anchorage and there are many hazards. Temp lying alongside the pier must be timed to avoid causing obstruction.

10.10 Mainland

(ON megenland – mainland) An alternative Norse name was 'Hrossey' – the island of horses. 16th century Latinist George Buchanan mistakenly called Mainland 'Pomona' and for a time the name was widely used but never by the islanders themselves. To Orcadians the Scottish mainland is simply 'Scotland'.

South Ronaldsay

(ON – Rognvald's island)

Burray

(ON borgr-øy – fort or broch island)

Hunda

(ON hund-øy – dog island)

OS Maps: 1:50000 Sheet 6 1:25000 Sheets 28,31,32,33,34,35,37, and 38
Admiralty Charts: 1:200000 No.1954 1:75000 Nos.2249 and 2250
1:30000 No.35 part S coast 1:25000 No.2584 part NE coast 1:12500
Kirkwall large scale No.2568 Stromness

AREA: 58,308ha (14,4079 acres)
HEIGHT: 268m (879 ft)

OWNER: Multiple ownership.

POPULATION:

	1841	1881	1891	1931	1961	1971	1981	1991
Mainland	16022	17165	16498	13352	13495	12747	14279	15123
S. Ronaldsay	2331	2557	2315	1312	980	776	886	943
Burray	532	685	681	379	262	209	299	363
Hunda	6	8	7	0	0	0	0	0
Glims Holm	0	0	0	0	0	0	0	0
Lamb Holm	?	12	8	7	0	0	0	0
	18903	20423	19508	15043	14737	13732	15464	16429

GEOLOGY: As with all the Orkney islands, Mainland is sedimentary rock of Devonian (Old Red Sandstone) age except for some small patches of granite-schist complex. One

of these is Brinkies Brae above Stromness which is the oldest place, geologically, in Orkney. The Dalradian foliated-granite rock was once an island in a great freshwater loch.

The sandstones in the west of Mainland are Upper and Lower Stromness Flags separated by a Fish Bed. These Stromness Beds are finely laminated and account for the dramatic cliff scenery in this area. The sandstones of the east are of the Rousay type although the Scapa Flow coastline, the Kirkwall area, Deerness and most of South Ronaldsay are Eday Beds, which are fine building stone. Deerness has some thick lava intrusions and the Gloup of Deerness on the east coast is a great rock hole connected to the sea by an underground fissure.

HISTORY: Mainland Orkney has so many notable relics dating from the late Stone Age that one must assume there was an advanced social structure on the island and considerable relative prosperity.

This age was followed by that of the broch-builders and the Picts (who may or may not have been the same people) but the Norsemen were not far behind them and sometime in the 9th century the Earldom of Orkney was established. A dynasty followed which is well-chronicled in the Norse Sagas and this reached its zenith in the 11th century under Earl Thorfinn the Mighty. Thereafter there was much infighting between rival descendants culminating in the death of Earl John in a drunken brawl in Thurso in 1231. He was the last of the Norse earls.

The succession passed to a son of the Earl of Angus, and various pale shadows followed him. King Haakon died in Kirkwall in 1263 and the Norse hold became ever more tenuous.

In 1379 Henry Sinclair of Roslin inherited the earldom and was formally invested by the King of Norway. He was a great sailor-adventurer and there is good circumstantial evidence that he sailed to America and established settlements there long before Columbus.

In 1468 King Christian of Norway and Denmark included Orkney and Shetland as part of Margaret, Maid of Norway's, dowry but subject to a cash redemption. The total cash failed to be paid so Scotland wasted no time in annexing the islands in 1471.

WILDLIFE: Mainland has over 600 species of flowering plant including wild lupins, daffodils and twenty-one species of wild orchid. At places near the water's edge the rare Oyster Plant, *Mertensia maritima*, can be seen but the clifftop home of the magenta-coloured Scottish Primrose, *Primula scotica*, is a secret.

Brown hares are very common on Mainland and so are rabbits. There are no frogs but there are toads. The otter is not nearly so common here as it is in Shetland, probably due to the amount of cultivation.

West of Kirkwall there are three areas of heather moorland providing one of the finest moorland bird communities in Britain. Moor breeders include hen harrier, short-eared owl, red grouse, merlin, arctic and great skua, golden plover, dunlin, snipe, curlew, reed bunting, wheatear, stonechat, sedge warbler, twite, kestrel, woodpigeon and hooded crow. Lochan breeders are the

red-throated diver, wigeon, teal, red-breasted merganser, eider and shelduck. On the lochs and wetlands are mallard, shelduck, wigeon, teal, pintail, shoveller, tufted duck, red-breasted merganser, dunlin, snipe, redshank, corncrake, sedge warbler and reed bunting. On the coasts there are kittiwake, guillemot, fulmar, razorbill and a few puffin. The Loch of Harray can sometimes hold 10,000 wintering duck and it is one of Britain's most important sites for pochard. Particular sites are: Birsay Moors and Cottascarth RSPB Reserve; Loch of Banks; The Loons RSPB Reserve; Loch of Boardhouse; Brough of Birsay; Marwick Head RSPB Reserve; Loch of Harray and Loch of Stenness; Binscarth Wood; Hobbister RSPB Reserve; and Stromness Harbour.

East of Kirkwall, Burray, and South Ronaldsay herring and lesser black-backed gulls predominate as breeders in the narrow band of moorland whereas the farmland is most noted for migrants rather than breeders and many rare ones have been recorded. Among coast breeders curlew predominate. Particular sites are: Graemeshall Loch; Deer Sound; Scapa Bay; Kirkwall Harbour; Loch of Tankerness; The Churchill Barriers; and Echnaloch Bay.

ST MAGNUS' CATHEDRAL

A narrow neck of land divides east and west **MAINLAND**. This is the strategic site of Orkney's 'capital', Kirkwall.

Kirkwall (ON *kirkjuvagr* – church bay) was established by the Norse in the 11th century but reached prominence and city-status in the 12th century thanks to its harbour and its new **Cathedral of St Magnus**. This massive edifice in early Norman style, founded in 1137 by Magnus's nephew, Rognvald III, contains the remains of both its founder and its saint built into the great piers in the central bay. The transepts, part of the choir and part of the nave with its interlacing wall-arcades are the oldest parts. It is almost surprising to find this magnificent Gothic structure in a town of less than 7000 inhabitants but, I suppose, this is a true picture of what a medieval cathedral city was really like. The small houses clustered like chickens round the mother-hen cathedral. The building was completed in the 15th century and was saved by the townsfolk from destruction during the Reformation but when Cromwell's men arrived they used it as a prison and for stabling their horses. After that only the choir continued to be used as a parish church and the neglected structure deteriorated. It was restored in 1912-1920.

Close to the cathedral is the **Bishop's Palace** which is mostly a 16th century reconstruction of the original 12th century building. It was here that King Haakon died in 1263 after his defeat by the Scots at Largs. Across the road is the **Earl's Palace** which has been called the finest structure of 16th century Scotland. This magnificent building was built with forced labour by Earl Patrick, known as 'Black Pate', a man who was so ignorant that his sentence of death was delayed for a week to allow him to 'better inform himself'.

When entering the harbour, after passing the little islet called **Thieves Holm**, it is difficult to appreciate that much of the inner part of the bay, sheltered by The Ayre and called the **Peerie Sea**, was filled in during the 1800s to allow the town to expand to the west. Originally the cathedral and the Bishop's Palace would have dominated the harbour as well as the town. The shallow Peerie Sea must have provided excellent protection for Norse longboats.

For Orkney history it is worth visiting the Orkney Library in Laing Street and **Tankerness House Museum**, a well-restored example of a merchant's house.

Kirkwall is a charming town which was made a royal burgh by James III in 1486 when he also gifted the cathedral to the citizens. The main street, which used to run close to the seafront, is Albert Street, irregular and narrow, known simply as **The Street**.

East of Kirkwall and south of Inganess Bay is **Kirkwall Airport** set in an area of fertile fields and fat cattle. The road continues to the eastern extremity of Mainland – Deerness parish – the old Norse hunting ground where the bones of red deer are still to be found in the peat bogs. Beside the road that crosses the narrow Deerness isthmus are the remains of the broch of Dingieshowe, and, to the north, the wide sands of St Peter's pool covered with wading birds. At the **Brough of Deerness**, after passing The Gloup (ON *gljúfr* – hollow or ravine) [HY592079], a growling subterranean sea-vent caused by the sea breaking through the roof of a large cave, a rough walk of about 1km brings you to the remains of an ancient monastery which was a place of pilgrimage until the 17th century [HY595088]. Male pilgrims walked barefoot round and round the holy building chanting and scattering water and sharp stones behind them.

The road running due south from Kirkwall reaches the pleasant village of St Mary's in the parish of Holm [ham]. Here there is the first of the **Churchill Barriers**.

On 14th October 1939 a German submarine slipped past the blockships in the eastern approaches to Scapa Flow and torpedoed *HMS Royal Oak*. 833 men were lost. Britain had only been at war for one month and the disaster had a serious effect on morale. Churchill later ordered barriers to be built between the eastern islands and Italian prisoners-of-war provided the labour for this task. The Italians handled the engineering with skill and supported their faith by converting two Nissen huts into the delightful little **Italian Chapel** on Lamb Holm [HY488006]. This pious work was so appreciated by the Presbyterian Orcadians that in 1960 Signor Chiocchetti, and others who had done the original work, were invited to return to Orkney and restore the chapel paintings and interior to its wartime glory.

Churchill Barrier No 2 crosses from **LAMB HOLM** to **GLIMS HOLM**, an islet which provides peat for local use, and the next Barrier reaches Burray. The old blockships can still be seen beside these causeways.

BURRAY has a great stretch of beach in its eastern bay, and the Reef linking it to **HUNDA**, which is particularly rich in birdlife, on its west coast. Burray is remembered for its colourful Jacobite laird, Sir James Stewart, who, in 1725, was involved in a murder in Kirkwall. He fled into exile and twenty years later joined the battle at Culloden. He survived the defeat and considered it safe after all these years to return home to Burray. But on arrival who should he meet but the son of his murder victim who promptly handed him over to the authorities. He died in a London prison.

Cross the 4th Barrier to **SOUTH RONALDSAY** and you are immediately greeted by an enormous windmill built for generating electricity [ND460938]. This was a trial to see if commercial electricity could be produced from Orkney's great power source – wind – but it has been a failure due to the enormous cost of maintenance. There is now talk of demolition of this obtrusive and noisy structure.

Norse grave robbers broke through the roof in the 12thC and claimed to have found 'great treasure'.

Corner piers constructed of massive monoliths.

MAGNIFICENT MAES HOWE

Corbelled roof to central chamber mainly constructed of single stone slabs over 4.5m long

Earth mound

Cell closure stones

Three cells about 1m high, each roofed with a single stone slab.

Huge stone slabs over 5m long form the roof and walls of the entrance passage.

N

Axonometric projection.

2   4   6   8 metres
10   20   30 feet

Nearby is **St Margaret's Hope** where there once was a chapel dedicated to Malcolm Canmore's Queen Margaret. It is sometimes wrongly claimed that the Hope is named after Margaret, Maid of Norway, who died in 1290. King Haakon's huge fleet of 120 ships anchored here at the start of August, 1263 – the largest fleet in history ever to enter Scapa Flow before the 20th century. There was an eclipse of the sun that day which some would claim foretold the disaster that awaited him at Largs and his subsequent death in Kirkwall.

To the west is the Hoxa peninsula with a ruined broch where, according to the *Orkneyinga Saga*, Thorfinn Skull-splitter is buried [ND425940].

Travelling southwards down the island the road passes **Ward Hill**, the summit of which is only 118m high but is a memorable viewpoint. From this distance tidal rips and treacherous seas fade into a vast expanse of untroubled ocean. But it was off this coast in 1969 that the Longhope lifeboat was lost with all on board while attempting to reach the wreck of the *Irene*.

In the south-west there is another 'Gloup' [ND472856], a chambered cairn [ND470845], and a burnt mound [ND465841]. These are all worth seeing, but they lie about a kilometre from the nearest road. **St Mary's Kirk** at Burwick is easier to reach. It contains a penitent's stone, a block of whin with two foot-shaped hollows [ND439842]. One story claims that a man called Gallus prayed to the Virgin Mary for help when his ship sank. She sent a porpoise who carried him ashore and then immortalised the poor beast by turning it into stone. Gallus built the church in gratitude.

The larger part of Mainland lies to the west of Kirkwall. The southern road from Kirkwall (A964) runs along the shores of Scapa Flow and through the **Hobbister Hill Nature Reserve** where raptors can be seen while waders frequent the shores of Waukmill Bay. The next bay, Swanbister, was renowned in the 1830s for having a monster similar to the one which is reputed to inhabit Loch Ness (see also No.11.5).

Mainland's highest peak, **Ward Hill** (268m), is north of here and the last battle on Orkney soil was fought in the valley to the east of it. That was in 1529 when William Sinclair tried to wrest the earldom from his uncle, Sir William Sinclair. He raised an army with the support of the Earl of Caithness and sailed into Scapa Flow but his cousins raised a local army which defeated him.

This is the parish of Orphir (ON *or-fjara* – 'out of' low water) and beside **Orphir Bay** is a tiny church probably built by Earl Haakon Paulsson, the murderer of St Magnus [HY335044]. He must have done penance by a pilgrimage or crusade to the Holy Land, because the design echoes that of the Holy Sepulchre in Jerusalem. Only the apse now remains (the rest was demolished in 1757 for a Presbyterian preaching box) but the church is mentioned in the sagas as a 'magnificent church' facing the 'drinking-hall'. The Vikings had very clear priorities!

The car ferry to Hoy sails from **Houton Bay** and the road then turns north up the coast of Clestrain Sound.

The northern road out of Kirkwall crosses a causeway and skirts **Wideford Hill** (225m) which is another marvellous view-point with a chambered cairn on its slopes [HY409121]. At **Rennibister** there is a good example of a souterrain or earth-house discovered in 1926 when a plough broke through the roof [HY397126]. The road continues along the south shore of Bay of Firth in which there are two small islands. The **Holm of Grimbister** is farmed, and **Damsay** (ON – pond island), which has several small pools on it, is mentioned in the sagas. It was in the days when Erlend and Sweyn were at war with Earls Rognvald and Harald. Erlend celebrated Christmas on Damsay with his men and then, dead-drunk, he returned to his ship to sleep. Although it was a full moon he and his men were taken by surprise and slaughtered. Tradition says that there was a nunnery on the island at one time and that no rats or mice are able to survive there.

This area of central Mainland is littered with prehistoric monuments but possibly the greatest concentration is around Lochs Harray and Stenness. By Tormiston Mill, a 19th century watermill, there is the green tumulus of **Maes Howe** (ON – great mound), Britain's largest chambered cairn and an example of truly breathtaking megalithic craftsmanship [HY318127]. A long, low, narrow passage leads into a large chamber with corbelled walls and smaller side chambers. The work has a flavour of Egyptian design and constructional similarity to the Treasury of Atrius in Greece although the proportions are more modest. The smaller chambers are floored and roofed with single massive stones. Maes Howe was raided by the Vikings – howebreaking was a very popular pastime – and they also indulged in graffiti in the form of runic inscriptions. One comment refers to a great treasure but does not

THE ITALIAN CHAPEL – A WARTIME WORK-OF-ART

5   10 metres

a   Cell
b   Paved Area
c   Passage
d   Hearth
e   Midden
f   Drain
(8) House number

PLAN OF
SKARA BRAE
(C. 2800BC)

N

make it clear whether it was Norse or neolithic treasure. The longest inscription has been translated as 'These runes were incised by the best runester in the west, using the axe that Gauk Thrandilsson once owned in south Iceland.' Other comments are timeless in character – 'Thorny was bedded; Helgi says so,' and 'Ingigerd is the best of them all'.

Close to Maes Howe, and possibly contemporary with it, are the **Standing Stones of Stenness** (ON *steine-nes* – promontory of the stones)[HY307125]. One of the remaining four stones is over 5m high and nearby is the, even higher, Watch Stone. Only 1½km north, on the narrow isthmus between Lochs Harray and Stenness, is the dramatic **Ring of Brodgar**, with twenty-seven of the original sixty stones still standing [HY294133]. I remember after a visit to the Ring at dawn, looking back to see it washed with pale sunlight against an ominous dark sky, surrounded by the vast expanse of grey loch and windswept grassland.

Further west, where the waters of Loch Stenness spill into the Bay of Ireland is **Unstan Cairn** [HY283117]. This is an important chambered cairn which was excavated in 1844 and produced the largest collection of Stone Age pottery found in Scotland (now housed in the Royal Museum, Queen Street, Edinburgh) as well as two

seated human skeletons.

Stromness was a prosperous port for many centuries although its role today is little more than a terminal for the ferry from Scrabster on the Scottish mainland. It has less than 2000 inhabitants but has a very long waterfront dating back to the time when it was overcrowded and busy with ships on the northern sailing routes. From 1670 to 1891 it was a base for the Hudson Bay Company, in the 18th and 19th century it was a supply base for the Davis Strait whaling fleet, and for a short time it was involved in the North American rice trade. The ships of Captain Cook were serviced here after his last ill-fated Pacific expedition as also were those of Sir John Franklin on the way to look for the North-West Passage. **Login's Well**, which provided the ships with fresh water, can still be seen, and the **Natural History Museum** has many interesting exhibits from Stromness' past.

Stromness is the home of the poet and writer, George Mackay Brown.

Some 10km north of Stromness on the west coast at the Bay of Skaill is possibly Orkney's most exciting archaeological site, **Skara Brae** [HY230187]. This astonishing prehistoric village dating from *c.* 3100BC only came to light when it was exposed by a storm in 1824. A sandstorm buried the original village in about 2450BC, thus preserving a moment of time for posterity, and 5000 years later another storm revealed it. It was conscientiously excavated in 1928 and this has given us a marvellous chance to spy on the every-day domestic life of our ancient ancestors. The tiny individual 'houses' are closely linked by passages and each contains items of primitive Stone Age fur-niture – beds, dressers, lockers, hearth, fish-larder pools, – and personal effects made of pottery, stone and whalebone. To the north of the Bay of Skaill a great Viking treasure was found in 1858 – the Skaill Hoard – enormous brooches, rings, ingots of silver, and coins. The Vikings were anything but pa-rochial – some of the coins had been minted in Baghdad!

Further north the coast road passes between **The Loons**, an area of pools and swamps and breeding wad-ers, and **Marwick Head**, whose cliffs support vast num-bers of seabirds. Both are Nature Reserves.

Marwick Head is the site of the **Kitchener Memorial** [HY227251]. Field-Marshal the Earl Kitchener of Khar-toum was invited by the Czar to visit Russia and discuss the progress of the First World War. He travelled to Thurso by night-train, crossed the Pentland Firth in a destroyer, lunched with Admiral Jellicoe on the *Iron Duke* in Scapa Flow and then boarded the cruiser *Hampshire*. It was 4th June 1916. In spite of a severe gale the *Hampshire* left by Hoy Sound and turned north. Then in very heavy seas off Marwick Head she struck a German mine and sank within fifteen minutes. There were only seven or eight survivors. Government secrecy was such that local Orcadians were forbidden to assist in the rescue attempt or speak to the press afterwards, and the eventual official report was mis-leading and obscure. Naturally, this encouraged talk of a cover-up and many wild stories circulated that Kitchener was still alive, or even that he had been deliberately executed.

The north-west corner of Mainland is Brough Head (ON *borg* – broch, or the island at the end of a tidal isth-mus) in the parish of Birsay (ON – broch island). **Brough of Birsay** is a drying or tidal island with extensive re-mains of a Viking settlement and an early medieval chapel [HY240285]. The chapel is built on the remains of an earlier, 6th or 7th century, chapel. The settlement may have been part of a well-garrisoned fortress. This island well repays a visit but avoid being trapped by the incoming tide covering the causeway.

Overlooking Brough of Birsay is **Earl Stewart's Pal-ace** [HY248279]. The palace was rebuilt in 1574 but this is the site where the earls of Orkney had their palace be-fore moving to Kirkwall in the 12th century. The present ruin shows little of the original splendour.

The north coast road passes Loch of Swannay, (thought by some to be the best trout-fishing loch on Mainland), and skirts Eynhallow Sound in the parish of

THE RING OF BRODGAR

Evie (ON – swirling tide). Here, like a sentinel on wind-swept Aiker Ness, stands **Gurness Broch** [HY382268]. This is the best-preserved broch in Orkney but there is a great complex of ruins surrounding it which are also fas-cinating to explore.

About 6km south-west of Gurness Broch by an undu-lating minor road is Orkney's last surviving example of a **Click Mill** [HY325228]. These were old horizontal watermills, once common in Scandinavia and still to be found in North Pakistan. South of here is the parish of Harray (ON – hunting territory), the only land-locked par-ish in Orkney.

ACCESS: P&O Ferries from Scrabster to Stromness daily except most Sundays, 01856-850655. Also twice-weekly, Aberdeen to Stromness (and then on to Shetland), 01224-572615. By air: BA Express daily (except Sundays) to Kirkwall from Aberdeen, Birmingham, Edinburgh, Glas-gow, London, Manchester, Sumburgh, and Wick: BA also (week-days only) from Belfast, Inverness, and Stornoway, 0345-222111. Kirkwall airport, 01856-872494. Limited bus service on Mainland.

Anchorages: Considerable care and experience is needed due to the many er-ratic tidal conditions. Eynhallow Sound is particularly hazardous.

1. Stromness Harbour. Enter by buoyed channel using leading lights. Secure anchorage beyond piers in Hamna Voe as directed by harbour master. Lim-ited area, congested, but good holding. Keep clear of ferry terminal.

2. Bay of Ireland. Anchorage 4c NE of Bu Point in 5-6m, sand. Exposed to S.

3. Bay of Houton. Enter E side of Holm of Houton (Howton) and keep nearer Holm side of mid-channel, depth 3m. Anchor in centre of bay, 4-5m, clean sand. Good shelter, good holding, but restricted space.

4. Swanbister Bay. Occasional anchorage in offshore winds, NE of pier in 5-8m, sand and mud.

5. Waulkmill Bay, E of Ve Ness dries out 3c from head. Not recommended.

6. Scapa Bay (about 2km S of Kirkwall). Approach on leading line. Leave buoyed wreck of HMS Royal Oak (sunk by German sub in Oct 1939) to starboard and Scapa Skerry buoy to port on approach. Anchor mid-bay off the stone pier, or lie alongside pier-head (3m), or small yachts can anchor

N of pier. Good anchorage, except in S'lies which bring a swell. Untenable in SW gales.

7. Bay of Ayre (village of St Mary's on N shore with two piers). Anchor in settled weather off village in 2-6m, holding slightly doubtful, or lie alongside E of pier-head.

8. Echnaloch Bay on NW side of Burray. Sandy beach at head with small pier on NE side. Temp anchorage in S'lies.

9. Hunda Sound. Excellent in any weather. Best mid-sound, in 7-11m, sand over clay, very good holding. Head and sides are shoal.

10. St Margaret's Hope (bay on S side of Water Sound). Approach with care on leading line. Fairway only 2.7m depth. Anchor in centre in 6m. 100m-long pier on W side has 2.7m at end. Head and shores are foul.

11. Widewall Bay. Bottom sandy and shelves gradually. Give Herston Head a 2c berth. Useful when awaiting slack water for passage S.

12. Sand Wick is shallow and exposed.

13. Bur Wick (SW tip of S Ronaldsay) is fringed with reefs but has a sandy beach at its head. Temp anchorage off beach in 5-7m in quiet weather.

14. Wind Wick, between Hesta and Halcro Heads. Temp anchorage in light W'lies, 5-10m.

15. Holm Sound. Temp anchorage well off the sandy beach which heads the bay on the NE side of Burray, in 6-7m, sand, good holding but if wind is between NE and SE leave at once.

16. E Weddel Sound, SW Holm Sound. Excellent anchorage in centre of Bay, E of blockship, E of barrier, 2-4m, sand. Best anchorage in this area.

17. Kirk Sound. Temp anchorage in Mainland bay N of E end of Lamb Holm, close inshore, 3-6m, sand and rock. Exposed SE. (Visit Italian Chapel, Lamb Holm.)

18. Deer Sound. Take care when entering and give shores a reasonable offing. Good shelter, good holding and very few squalls. Anchor off the stone pier on NW side of the Sound, below Hall of Tankerness, or off Mirkady Point, mid-channel in 4-5m. Small craft could use shallow St Peter's Bay in about 2m.

19. Inganess Bay (Shapinsay Sound). Shelter from W and S and good holding in 6-8m, sand and shells. There are reefs and shallows off both entrance points.

20. Bay of Meil, W of Head of Holland. Good anchorage in centre of S part of bay, 6-8m, sand. Exposed N.

21. Bay of Carness. Fringed with reefs but good anchorage in centre.

22. Bay of Kirkwall. Approach on leading line and anchor between Hatston Boat Slip and the CG lookout near W side of bay. SW side of bay is shoal. Exposed to N winds but these do not raise a heavy sea. Good holding. Harbourmaster's permission required to berth alongside the quays.

23. Bay of Firth, shallow and many hazards. But with care and local knowledge offers good anchorage.

24. Bay of Isbister. Anchor 3¹/₂c ENE of Wald Taing in 8-10m, mud.

25. Wood Wick (Eynhallow Sound) dries out 3c from head. Temp anchorage in suitable conditions 1¹/₂c S of Scara Taing, 6-8m.

26. Aiker Ness (Eynhallow Sound). In bay SE of Aiker Ness, SE of Aikerness House, 1c offshore in 5-6m, mud. Beware extensive shoal in centre and S of bay.

27. Sands of Evie (Eynhallow Sound). Rocky bottom, poor holding and not recommended.

28. Bay of Skaill. Centre of west coast of Mainland. Temp anchorage (to visit Skara Brae). Exposed to W. Approach with caution.

10.11 Auskerry

(ON *østr sker* – east skerry)

OS Maps: 1:50000 Sheet 5 1:25000 Sheet 32
Admiralty Charts: 1:200000 Nos.1942 and 1954 1:75000 No.2250

AREA: 85ha (210 acres)
HEIGHT: 18m (59 ft)

OWNER: The proprietor of Housebay on Stronsay (No.10.14). He grazes his sheep on the island.

POPULATION: 1881 – 8. 1891 – 7 (2 houses). 1931 – 4 (lighthouse keepers). 1961 – 3. 1971 – 0. 1981 – 0. Now uninhabited.

GEOLOGY: Middle Old Red sandstone in the form of weathered Rousay Flags.

HISTORY: This small island has now been uninhabited for many decades (even the lighthouse was made automatic in the 1960s) but it has an ancient history with standing stones making an abrupt statement on the wind-blown landscape, a burnt mound, and the ruins of a medieval chapel [HY677160]. This is just the type of lonely outpost sought by the early Celtic Christians in their search for peace and communion with God, and any lonely Christian today could forget the passage of time. There are only the sheep for company, and the solitude is accentuated by the crashing of the surf and the screaming of the wind and seagulls.

WILDLIFE: Seabirds and seals a-plenty. A large colony of storm petrel, and a breeding site for puffin, arctic tern, and black guillemot.

AUSKERRY is a flattish grassy islet with a rocky shoreline and a conspicuous white lighthouse at **Baa Taing** (ON – tongue or promontory at the sea-rock). To sailors it could be easily confused with Muckle Skerry in the Pentland Firth which is very similar in appearance except that Muckle Skerry has two light towers.

Auskerry is about three miles south of Stronsay (No.10.14) and is separated from it by Auskerry Sound – a turbulent reef-rimmed stretch of sea. The food and mail at one time were delivered by a local fishing boat from Whitehall village on Stronsay but in the last years of occupation the lighthouse keepers provisions came from Kirkwall.

The inlet called **Hunters Geo** (ON *gja* – gully, creek) beneath the lighthouse on Baa Taing dates from the time when this was a favourite spot for seal-hunters. It is still a favourite spot for the grey seal, *halichoerus grypus*, with its Roman nose, sad eyes (and halitosis) – known throughout the islands as the 'selkie'. In the late autumn many congregate on the skerries to pup and sing together.

Although the grey seal was one of the rarer species

numbers have been rising dramatically while the battle between fishermen and conservationists continues over the
question of culling. It is now much more common in Orkney than the so-called common seal.

ACCESS: No regular access. Enquire in Kirkwall or at
Whitehall Village, Stronsay, to make arrangements with a
local fishing boat.

*Anchorages: No anchorage. Many hazards and strong tides in Auskerry
Sound.*

10.12 Shapinsay

Possibly, (ON hjalpandis-øy – helpful island) – because of a good harbour?

OS Maps: 1:50000 Sheet 6 1:25000 Sheets 29, 30, and 32
Admiralty Charts: 1:200000 Nos.1942 or 1954 1:75000 Nos.2249 or
2250 1:25000 No.2584

AREA: 2,948ha (7,285 acres)
HEIGHT: 64m (210 ft)

OWNER: Multiple ownership. The Balfour family owned

the entire island until the early 20th century when they sold the freehold to their tenant farmers.

POPULATION: 1798 – 730 (and about eighty boats). 1841 – 935 (199 houses). 1881 – 974. 1891 – 903 (179 houses). 1931 – 584. 1961 – 421. 1971 – 346. 1981 – 345. 1991 – 322.

GEOLOGY: This is a fertile island due to the breakdown of the Rousay Beds sandstone which covers all of it except the south-east corner. Here is extruded basaltic lava and Eday Beds of Middle Old Red sandstone which is a much

better building stone than the Rousay Beds variety.

HISTORY: In 1263 King Haakon assembled his large fleet of galleys in Elwick before sailing south to Largs but the island itself was never mentioned in the sagas.

Always agriculturally fertile and reasonably prosperous, Shapinsay also enjoyed the kelp boom in the 18th century. The island produced over 3000 tons of burned kelp every year which brought in about £20,000 of income for the inhabitants.

WILDLIFE: In 1805 the minister on Shapinsay first noted

that the Orkney vole was a unique sub-species of the European vole, *microtus arvalis*. This little creature is something of a puzzle as it is found nowhere else in the British Isles. It has Spanish characteristics but is unlikely to have come from an Armada wreck because, unlike rats, voles hate sailing and avoid ships like the plague.

The best time for birdwatching on Shapinsay is in the winter. Oystercatcher, lapwing and curlew nest on the farmland, and there are a few skua, gulls and terns in the south-east moorland. Inland is generally disappointing. In winter there are shelduck on The Ouse, an inlet on the north coast, and whooper swan on the Mill Dam which is an RSPB Nature Reserve. Breeding waders such as redshank and snipe can be seen in spring and also various duck species. Balfour Castle woodland has many breeding birds and a variety of migrant species although the trees are generally small and stunted by the wind.

Intensively cultivated and close to Kirkwall, **SHAPINSAY** is a suburban sort of island. It is relatively low-lying with centrally-situated **Ward Hill** (64m) its highest point flanked by two hummocks. The east coast has modest cave-riddled cliffs between **The Fit O'Shapinsay** in the south-east and **Ness of Ork** (C. *orc* – boar) in the north-east. There is another minor escarpment flanking the north-west peninsula called **The Galt** (ON – boar) or Galt Ness. The rest of the coastline has little in the way of distinctive features with the exception of **Helliar Holm** (ON – holy island), a green tidal island with a beacon on it protecting the entrance to Elwick.

Elwick (ON – holy bay) is another of the long line of famous anchorages used by King Haakon's fleet in 1263. As a harbour it was described by Rev. Cruttwell's Gazateer in 1798 as 'excellent for its extent as almost any one in this country. On the west side of it is a fine beach, with abundance of excellent fresh water'. The west side now has a ferry pier and a village with shops and a post office. Cruttwell, incidentally, made an interesting claim: 'In this harbour it is high water at three quarters of an hour after nine o'clock, when the moon is new and full.'

Beside Elwick is the Victorian extravaganza of **Balfour Castle** [HY475164] with the only patch of woodland on Shapinsay. The building was completed in Scottish Baronial style in 1848.

The family of Balfour of Trenabie on Westray (No 10.25) has a long association with Shapinsay. In the 18th century John Balfour made a fortune in India and then married the widow of a certain Colonel Mackennan. The Colonel had lent money to the Rajah of Tanjore and a number of other British expatriates were also caught in the same trap. The Rajah failed, or refused, to repay the loans so the lenders appealed for help from the British Government. They eventually received compensation, but only after John Balfour, by then (1790) MP for Orkney

COLONEL BALFOUR'S CASTLE

and Shetland, actively promoted their claim. Of course his wife, being Colonel Mackennan's widow, gained a substantial benefit from the settlement which contributed handsomely to John Balfour's fortune. Balfour bought estates on Shapinsay and several neighbouring islands and started building Balfour Castle.

But it fell to his son, Colonel Balfour, to complete most of the present structure with David Bryce as his architect. Colonel Balfour had raised a troop of volunteers and promoted himself to the status of colonel. The kelp industry had collapsed so he set about reforming the island's agriculture – squaring the fields into 10-acre units separated by open drains. He also built the attractive little village of **Balfour** populated with imported craftsmen such as joiners and weavers and the watermill which can be seen one kilometre north of the castle. A natural marsh beside it was dammed in the 1880s to provide the water. This is the **Mill Dam**. Balfour's improvements were generally of great benefit to the island but he himself is remembered as a petty tyrant. This is perhaps unfortunate as it was an age when many other landlords were clearing their islands for sheep.

Soon after the Second World War an expatriate officer of the Polish Lancers who had escaped the Katyn massacre, Tadeus Zawadski, bought Balfour Castle and the Balfour estate on Shapinsay. Like Balfour, he farmed it successfully, and he was a popular laird and resident of the island. He died in 1979.

Quholm in the north-east of Shapinsay [HY521218] was the family home of the parents of the American author, William Washington Irving. He was famous in his time and has been called the 'father of American literature' but is now often only remembered for his story of Rip Van Winkle. His father emigrated to the States in 1783 and set up shop as a hardware merchant in New York and his son was christened in honour of the first President.

ACCESS: Orkney Isles Shipping Co. ferry from Kirkwall, several sailings every day, 01856-872044. Balfour Castle Tour and cruise round Hellier Holm, Tourist Office, 01856-872856.

Anchorages: There are turbulent tides in The String off Helliar Holm.

1. Elwick. Anchor anywhere suitable in the bay, but note that shores are fringed by a shallow bank. Bottom sand. Pier on W side at village. Avoid obstructing ferry. Good shelter.

2. Veantrow Bay. Exposed to N and uncomfortable. Best on E side, 6-9m, sand and coral.

3. Helliar Holm. Temp anchorage E of Helliar Holm and clear of prohibited area, sand.

10.13 Gairsay

(ON Gáreksøy – Gárekr's island). Gárekr is a man's name.

OS Maps: 1:50000 Sheet 6 1:25000 Sheet 29
Admiralty Charts: 1:200000 Nos.1942 or 1954 1:75000 Nos.2249 or 2250 1:25000 No.2584

AREA: 240ha (593 acres)
HEIGHT: 102m (335 ft)

OWNER: Bought in 1971 by Val and David McGill of Cornwall who are resident on the island and farm it.

POPULATION: 1841 – 71 (15 houses). 1881 – 33. 1891 – 33 (5 houses). 1931 – 5. 1961 – 0. 1971 – 7. 1981 – 8. 1991 – 3.

GEOLOGY: Fertile soil over Rousay type Middle Old Red sandstone.

HISTORY: Gairsay will always be remembered as the home of the boisterous Sweyn Asleifsson, one of the last of the great Vikings. (His story would make a great opera but there is only space here for a 'potted' version.)

In the 12th century, Sweyn's father, Olaf Rolfsson of Gairsay, had supported Earl Paul of Orkney in a sea-battle off Deerness against Olvir Rosta in which Olvir was defeated. Seeking revenge Olvir set fire to Olaf's home and Olaf and five of his men were burnt to death. Sweyn was fishing in the Pentland Firth at the time but when the young man returned and saw the carnage he crossed to Orphir on Mainland to tell Earl Paul what had happened.

It was the night of the Yule feast. A big surly man called Sweyn Breastrope, the Earl's favourite and foremost fighter, was belligerent with drink. After the Earl had gone to bed there was a quarrel and in the ensuing fight Sweyn Asleifsson killed him. Fearing Earl Paul's anger Sweyn ran for cover and appealed to Bishop William of Egilsay for help and advice. The Bishop was sympathetic and suggested that he lie low for a while. He sent him to stay with friends on the island of Tiree (No 3.10).

The following spring Sweyn visited Earl Maddad in Atholl and there learned that Earl Paul had declared him an outlaw. Maddad was married to Margaret, the beautiful but scheming sister of Earl Paul. She reckoned that both her son Harald, and her nephew Erlend, had a justifiable claim to the Orkney Earldom. Sweyn promised to support Harald's claim and in return he was paid compensation for the death of his father and given a merchant-ship with a crew of thirty men. Sweyn promptly sailed to Orkney, kidnapped Earl Paul (see Rousay No.10.20), and delivered him unharmed to Atholl. The Earl was never seen again and Margaret is reputed to have had her brother blinded and murdered.

Sweyn sailed back to Orkney and went openly to the assembled Parliament at Kirkwall. In a meeting with Bishop William, Kol, and Kol's son Rognvald – the good-natured earl-presumptive – he explained what had happened. His explanation was accepted and after the meeting Parliament acknowledged Rognvald's authority as Earl of Orkney.

Sweyn inherited his father's lands including Gairsay and persuaded Earl Rognvald to lend him two ships. He then sailed to Scotland and landed at Helmsdale. He failed to capture Olvir Rosta, which was his intention, so he plundered and burned Rosta's homestead. Turning south, Sweyn then spent two years fighting and pillaging in the Irish Sea and followed this by marrying Ingrid, the rich widow of the chieftain of the Isle of Man.

Back in Orkney, after a further successful cruise, the volatile Sweyn fell out with Earl Rognvald, and after a nominal revolt, slipped away to Edinburgh and the court of David I, King of Scots. There he persuaded David to intercede on his behalf with Earl Rognvald. Rognvald duly forgave him and Sweyn returned to Gairsay.

Earl Rognvald meanwhile went on a crusade to the Holy Land and was absent for over two years leaving Harald in charge. Earl Maddad of Atholl had died and Harald was furious to discover that his widowed mother Margaret was having a child by Gunni, a brother of Sweyn Asleifsson. Harald outlawed Gunni but this enraged Sweyn. However Margaret by this time had already tired of Gunni and fallen instead for a handsome young Shetlander who carried her off to Mousa (No.11.2).

When Rognvald returned home he found Harald absent in Norway raising a force, possibly to usurp him. Sweyn and Erlend were jointly running his earldom. He sent Sweyn and Erlend north to defend Shetland against Harald and they captured three of Harald's ships. Taking advantage of Sweyn's absence in the north Harald approached Rognvald and asked for reconciliation. He explained that Rognvald had put him in charge during his absence but that Sweyn had turned against him. The easy-going Rognvald accepted this so he and Harald joined forces with a fleet of ships and lay in wait for Sweyn. As Rognvald and Harald had fourteen ships while Sweyn and Erlend had only seven Sweyn did not try to gain access to Mainland Orkney for supplies and assistance but chose instead to wait. Winter approached and Rognvald's fleet sheltered in Scapa Bay. It was a cold, dark, night with storm-force winds, poor visibility and gusts of sleet. Suddenly out of the spray Sweyn's ships appeared and his men leapt aboard the anchored ships. Rognvald was ashore and Harald escaped, but nearly everyone else was caught off-guard and slaughtered.

Strangely, in spite of all this bloodshed, Rognvald the peacemaker eventually arranged a reconciliation between Harald and Sweyn who, thereafter, became close friends.

Sweyn returned to his buccaneering exploits which included a raid on Port St Mary in the Scillies but a few years later, in 1158, Rognvald, the good-hearted warrior-poet, died in a skirmish in Caithness and Earl Harald succeeded him.

Sweyn continued to live on Gairsay. He farmed in the summer, drank away the winter in his drinking hall with his eighty men-at-arms, and went a-viking every spring and autumn. In one exploit, about 1171, with a fleet of five ships off Dublin he captured two English ships with a cargo of wine and cloth. They let the sailors go, stitched the brightly-coloured cloth to their sails for show, and drank so much that they could not remember how they sailed home to Orkney. They called it their Cloth Cruise.

Eventually Sweyn decided to have one last cruise before

retirement. He sailed south again to Dublin which was then held by the English. Fearless as ever, he stormed the city, captured it and held it to ransom. But the next day on his way to collect the ransom he was ambushed and killed.

One translation of the saga says: '. . .it is the judgement of men that he has been the biggest man in every way in the lands of the west, both in days present and days past, among men who were not of higher rank than he.'

WILDLIFE: Arctic and great skuas breed on the heather-covered moorland and arctic terns, sandwich terns and cormorants frequent the surrounding skerries.

Although **GAIRSAY** is much the same size as Wyre, its neighbour to the north, it has a distinctive summit (102m) with a cairn on top whereas Wyre is low-lying. The south-east corner of Gairsay, which is over 20m high and is called **Hen of Gairsay**, is only attached to the rest of the island by a narrow neck of land. It shelters a small cove on its west side which is the island's only anchorage. The sea south of Gairsay has many deceptive rock patches and skerries, and there are three tiny islets – **Holm of Boray**, **Grass Holm**, and **Holm of Rendall**. North of Hen of Gairsay is a more substantial islet – **Sweyn Holm** (ON – Sveinn's or servant islet) – is probably named after Sweyn Asliefsson.

Near the end of the 17th century Gairsay was bought by Sir William Craigie, a wealthy merchant who had been a tacksman of the Earl. There was an existing house on a prominent site opposite the shores of Rendall and he developed this into the imposing small mansion of **Langskaill**. Langskaill or Skaill is a name given to a Viking drinking-hall although in Norway it usually refers to a farmhouse or store. This particular Langskaill is sited on top of the remains of Sweyn's drinking-hall.

The front of the mansion courtyard has a curtain wall with a walkway along the parapet and there is an arched doorway with an armorial shield above it. A bowling green used to be between the house and the sea with access to a solid stone pier. After Craigie's death the house was deserted and eventually part of the decaying building was used as a farm steading. New owners renovated and occupied the building but after the Second World War it was once more abandoned and neglected for a period until it was again renovated by the present owners.

Gairsay provides good pasturage for sheep under a tenancy agreement but this may not help the economics of running an island farm.

ACCESS: No regular access but arrangements may be made at Tingwall.

Anchorages:
1. Millburn Bay, on S coast beside Hen of Gairsay. A submerged ridge (1.5m) joins W side of Millburn Bay to Holm of Boray. Shores are shoal.

Anchor in centre, 6m, mud.
2. Langskaill, by The Taing. Stone pier for owner's use.

10.14 Stronsay

Possibly, (ON strjóns-øy – good fishing and farming island) – the inference being 'profitable property'.

OS Maps: 1:50000 Sheet 5 1:25000 Sheets 27 and 30
Admiralty Charts: 1:200000 Nos.1942 or 1954 1:75000 No.2250
1:25000 No.2622 Papa Sound

AREA: 3,275ha (8,093 acres)
HEIGHT: 44m (144 ft)

OWNER: Multiple ownership.

POPULATION: 1798 – 887. 1841 – 1234 (250 houses). 1881 – 1274. 1891 – 1275 (269 houses). 1931 – 953. 1961 – 497. 1971 – 436. 1981 – 462. 1991 – 382.

GEOLOGY: Most of the island is the Rousay type of Middle Old Red sandstone weathered into good soil and low hills but the south-west side of the Bay of Holland and a patch at Links Ness in the north-west is of the Eday variety of sandstone.

HISTORY: From the early 17th century to 1914 Stronsay was a fishing centre of constant importance. It was first exploited by the Dutch and built up to such an extent that by 1900 it had become the capital of the herring industry. This then declined but was revived for a time in the 1920s and 1930s. At one stage Whitehall had fifteen fish-curing stations (and forty pubs!) operating during the season, with a constant traffic of ships delivering the catch and exporting the cured and salted herring, mainly to Baltic markets. About 1960 there was an attempt to revive the industry with the formation of a co-operative to process white fish for export to the USA, but the great days are over.

WILDLIFE: In common with most of the Orkney islands this is a treeless landscape but the rich pastures have many wildflowers in spring and summer and examples of the rare blue-flowered oysterplant can be found near the shoreline at Lea Shun and on the shingle on the south side of St Catherine's Bay. A large area of naturalised Patagonian Ragwort (from south Chile) grows beside the path to The Pow, while Frog Orchids and Adder's Tongue can be found west of the beautiful Sand of Rothiesholm.

There is an enormous winter population of wildfowl including whooper swan and Greenland white-fronted geese, plus dabbling and diving duck and visiting shore-birds.

This is an excellent place for spotting rare migrant birds. American golden plover, tawny pipit, pied wheatear, Radde's, marsh and sub-alpine warblers, rustic bunting, Arctic redpoll and scarlet rosefinch have all been recorded.

The lochs and wetlands are breeding haunts for redshank, snipe, shoveller and pintail and there are still a few corncrake and corn bunting nests and the occasional quail. Fairly large seabird colonies occupy the area be-tween Odness and Lamb Head on the east coast.

Recommended bird-watching sites are: the Rothiesholm Peninsula, where there are breeding skua, gull, tern and various wildfowl and waders on the moorland, and also red-throated diver and twite. This is one of the best moorland sites in the Northern Isles. The cliffs are tenanted by shag, guillemot, razorbill, fulmar and black guillemot.

Mill Bay and Meikle Water, which are good for observing migrant passerines, sea-duck, divers, and waders. White-fronted and greylag geese frequent the area in the winter together with whooper swan, many duck and waders.

STRONSAY is a low-lying island of rich green pastures and wide beaches. **Burgh Hill** (44m) in the south-east is the highest of several rounded hills scattered across the island, all of similar height. Many typical maritime heath plants grow on its slopes.

Whitehall is the main settlement and ferry port. Its name comes from a house built in the 1670s by Patrick Fea, a retired privateer. For over two centuries, up to the outbreak of the Second World War, this was the most active herring port in the northern Orkney isles and the large two-storeyed houses are a reminder of days of prosperous fishing, large families, and many lodgers. Today, Whitehall is a modest little place, with a fish factory, post-office, and hotel, and a few fishing boats in the harbour. At one time there was a fleet of 300 boats in Papa Sound, fifteen fish-curing stations, and 1500 'fishwives'. Occasional whaling occurred when there was the opportunity. A school of fifty whales was driven into Mill Bay in 1834 and slaughtered, yielding £100 worth of whale oil.

The road from Whitehall joins a road which runs north and south down the spine of the island, with a separate branch across the neck of land between St Catherine's Bay and Bay of Holland to the **Rothiesholm** [**Row**sum] peninsula.

The airstrip is in the far north beyond John's Hill near the tidal wetland of **Oyce of Huip**, and across Huip Sound is **Holm of Huip** with a cairn on it and many Atlantic grey seals. To the north-west is rocky Links Ness and the islet of **Little Linga** (ON – heather isle).

Wardhill with its village and school is in the geometric centre of the island and immediately west of **Mill Bay**. There is a long beach round Mill Bay with a rock seat in the middle called the **Mermaid's Chair** [HY655262]. Scota Bess, one of Orkney's storm witches, would sit here casting evil spells until finally the fisherfolk could stand no more of it. They beat her to death and buried her body but in the morning the corpse was found lying on the ground beside the grave. This happened several times so, in desperation, the islanders flung the body into **Meikle Water** (S. – little water), the loch south of Wardhill and it was never seen again. But it is said that any girl who sits in the Mermaid's Chair will be able to foretell the future.

Stronsay has long been a place of progressive farming and relatively large landholdings although there has been a natural change of character of the farming through the years. The kelp industry also played its part in the 18th

century and circular, stone-lined kilns for burning the kelp can be seen dotted about the shores. James Fea of Whitehall started the industry in 1722 but the islanders feared the vengeance of *Nuckelavee*, a sea monster who hated smoke. Even forty years later they blamed the kelp industry for bad harvests and poor fishing and brought a case against James Fea which they won. However, the next generation had a different attitude and the smoke from Stronsay's kelp kilns could be seen for miles.

The waters of Stronsay's **Well of Kildinguie** [HY654273] have long held the reputation for curing everything except the black death provided they are mixed with dulse from the adjoining seashore. However, close examination of the water may persuade one that the sickness is better than the cure.

Balanced on top of each of three rock stacks in Odin Bay, **The Malme**, **Tam's Castle**, and **Burgh Head**, are the precarious ruins of anchorite cells. Here too is **Vat of Kirbister**, a dramatic 'gloup', boasting the finest natural rock arch in Orkney [HY686239].

The southern cliffs of Stronsay, on each side of the **Bay of Holland** (there has long been a strong Dutch presence in this area), are rich in birdlife. It was from here that the islanders would collect the seabirds and eggs which were once an essential part of their normal diet. The Norse considered the area important because the adjoining Bay of Houseby indicates a farm which was an administrative and tax-collecting centre (ON *husabyr* – royal administrative farm). This also appears to have been a favoured area in prehistoric times as there are a number of tumuli, and on **Lamb Head**, the southern extremity, there are cairns and a small broch with a stone construction beside it which may be a Pictish or Norse pier [HY690214]. Here too is Hell's Mouth, a narrow, rocky, chasm in which breaking seas make a frightening sound.

ACCESS: Orkney Islands Shipping run a daily ro-ro ferry service from Kirkwall and adjacent islands to Whitehall on Stronsay, 01856-872044. Scheduled flights by British Airways from Kirkwall, Sanday and Westray, 01856-872494 and 0345-222111. Tourist information 01856-872856.

Anchorages:
1. Whitehall Harbour. Good anchorage but many reefs and shoals. Use N entrance and anchor where space and depth available S of Papa Stronsay. There is water both sides of both piers but avoid obstructing ferry. Alternatively anchor about 1c W of red can buoy in Jack's Hole.
2. Linga Holm (St Catherine's Bay). Occasional anchorage E of SE extremity in 6-10m. In E winds temp anchorage off W side of Linga Holm in 9-10m. Tidal streams negligible.
3. Bay of Holland. Good anchorage in suitable weather on W side of bay in 6-8m, sand. Exposed S.
4. Mill Bay. Fringed by shoals and bottom foul, not recommended, but anchor S of Grice Ness in emergency.

10.15 Wyre *or* Weir

(ON vigr *– spear head or javelin) – derived from shape of island? There is a Norwegian island with a similar name and shape – and another off Iceland.*

OS Maps: 1:50000 Sheet 5 or 6 1:25000 Sheet 29
Admiralty Charts: 1:200000 Nos.1942 or 1954 1:75000 No.2249

AREA: 311ha (768 acres)
HEIGHT: 32m (105 ft)

POPULATION: 1841 – 96 (20 houses). 1881 – 80. 1891 – 67 (14 houses). 1931 – 44. 1961 – 47. 1971 – 36. 1981 – 27. 1991 – 28.

GEOLOGY: Middle Old Red sandstone of the same variety as neighbouring Rousay which weathers to a good fertile soil.

HISTORY: Wyre is noted for what is possibly the earliest stone castle to have survived in Scotland. This was built by Kolbein Hruga, remembered affectionately as 'Cubbie Roo', a mid-12th century chief and descendant of Earl Paul I. He was born in Sunnfjord, Norway, and was established by Thorfinn the Mighty as a *gøding*, or best man.

Cubbie Roo's son was Bjarni (1188-1223). He became Bishop of the See of Orkney in about 1190 and he probably prevailed upon his father to build the delightful little romanesque chapel on Wyre. Bjarni was also a poet who composed a lay about the legend of the Jomsvikings which is the only contribution to Norse literature to have come from the Scottish islands.

Cubbie Roo's castle is where Snaekoll Gunnason and fellow rebels sought refuge after killing Earl John, the last of the Viking earls, in 1232.

WILDLIFE: A large number of divers and sea-duck winter in the shelter of the adjoining sounds.

The flat little island of **WYRE** with its famous castle ruin is mentioned in the Norse Sagas. The *Orkneyinga Saga* speaks of 'Kolbein Hruga – the most haughty of men. . . He had a good stone castle built there that was a safe stronghold.' And *King Haakon's Saga*, eight years later, refers to the last Norse earl, Earl John, being slain in a Thurso cellar and how his murderers took refuge in Wyre castle. They were besieged, but as the castle was easily defended a truce was arranged.

Cubbie Roo's castle ruin is in the centre of the island just north of the only hillock (32m) [HY442263]. The castle is a stone keep about 7½m square surrounded by a deep stone-faced ditch. The stonework is of high standard and there is evidence of at least one upper floor. A water tank is cut into the stone floor at ground level. The en-

Detail of the Chancel Arch from a drawing by T S Muir

PLAN OF THE 12TH
CENTURY CHAPEL
ON WYRE

Plan

| 5 metres
| 15 feet

Cubbie Roo's Chapel on Wyre (12th Century)

trance was from the east with a door at upper level so that a ladder could be lowered for visitors. There are other ruins just visible around the castle but their purpose is uncertain.

North-east of the castle is the home farm, **The Bu of Wyre** [HY443264]. The farm buildings may have been built on top of Cubbie Roo's original farmhouse where Bishop Bjarni spent his boyhood.

Close to the castle ruin and farm buildings is a rectangular roofless chapel standing in a burial ground [HY443263]. The chapel dates from the late 12th century and was dedicated to either St Mary or St Peter. It has been partially restored and is of Romanesque design showing the influence of architectural ideas introduced to Orkney by Kol and Rognvald. The Vikings travelled widely and absorbed a remarkable amount of culture when they were not engaged in piracy.

In the centuries after the demise of 'haughty' Kolbein Hruga island folklore ascribed to him the character of a lumbering, well-meaning giant who could step from island to island. It was said that he tried to build bridges and causeways between the islands but the stones kept breaking his kishie (a straw basket normally used for carrying peat) which is why there are now so many rocks and skerries.

The renowned Orcadian poet, Edwin Muir, who was a contemporary and friend of the Orcadian painter, Stanley Cursiter, was born on Wyre in the late 1880s. 'I'm an Orkneyman, a good Scandinavian,' he said. In his autobiography he recalls his happy childhood on the island.

ACCESS: Daily vehicle ferry from Tingwall by Orkney Islands Shipping 01856-751360 or 01856-872044.

Anchorages: Negotiate Wyre Sound with great care.
1. Wyre Sound. Reasonable anchorage and shelter E of the pier and close inshore out of the tide.

10.16 Linga Holm

(ON lyng-øy, OE holm – heather island islet). Locally, sometimes called Midgarth Holm after the adjoining farm on Stronsay.

OS Maps: 1:50000 Sheet 5 1:25000 Sheet 30
Admiralty Charts: 1:200000 Nos.1942 or 1954 1:75000 No.2250

AREA: 57ha (141 acres)
HEIGHT: 10m (33 ft)

OWNER: The proprietor of Midgarth, Stronsay.

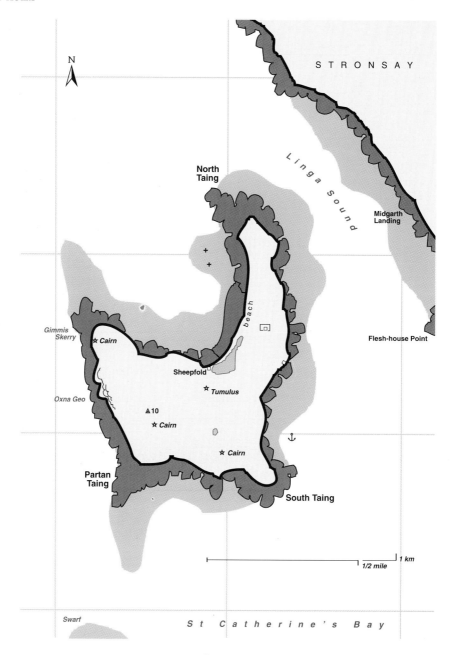

N

STRONSAY

Linga Sound

North
Taing

Midgarth
Landing

beach

Gimmis
Skerry
★ Cairn

Flesh-house Point

Sheepfold

★ Tumulus

Oxna Geo

△10
★ Cairn

★ Cairn

Partan
Taing

South Taing

1 km
1/2 mile

Swarf

St Catherine's Bay

POPULATION: 1841 – 6 (1 house) 1891 – 0. 1931 – 0. Uninhabited.

GEOLOGY: Middle Old Red sandstone of the Rousay variety.

WILDLIFE: Grey seals breed here in October and November and common seals are regular visitors. This is a reserve for the rare breed of North Ronaldsay (No 10.27) sheep.

Greenland white-fronted geese find this a favourite spot in winter.

Stretching open its arms to try to block the north-west winds which blow at intervals into St Catherine's Bay, **LINGA HOLM** is rather unsuccessful as this small island is only 10m high at its highest point. It has had a long association with Mid Garth on Stronsay which is only separated from it by narrow Linga Sound. The Sound can look deceptively peaceful but can suddenly become turbulent with very little warning.

The eastern arm which stretches in a narrow tongue up the side of Linga Sound to North Taing has a building on it which has been in use as a boathouse. West of it is an extensive shallow pond beside a beach. The rest of the island is mainly open grassland rising gradually to its highest level in the south-west where there are the walls of a ruined house. Sometimes Shetland ponies can be seen grazing here. Prehistoric cairns in this area are evidence of the presence of early man but the most noteworthy archaeological item is the excellently preserved Pictish House.

Partan Taing (G. – edible crab, ON *taing* – point) is a reef on the south-west side which runs out towards the **Swarf** (ON *svarf* – grit), a dangerous skerry in the middle of the entrance to St Catherine's Bay.

ACCESS: No regular access. Enquire at Stronsay Hotel or Post Office, Whitehall, Stronsay.

Anchorages: Avoid passage through Linga Sound if possible and beware Swarf south of Linga Holm.

1. St Catherine's Bay. Occasional anchorage E or NE of South Taing (SE extremity) in 6m. In light E winds temp anchorage off W side of Linga Holm in 9-10m. Tidal streams negligible.

10.17 Papa Stronsay

(ON – priest's island of Stronsay). The Norse called it Little Papey (ON papøy hin litli).

OS Maps: 1:50000 Sheet 5 1:25000 Sheets 27 and 30
Admiralty Charts: 1:200000 Nos.1942 or 1954 1:75000 No.2250
1:25000 No.2622

AREA: 74ha (183 acres)
HEIGHT: 13m (43 ft)

OWNER: Bought in 1988 for £115,000 by Charles Smith from Battersea, London. He has been the sole resident and farmed Papa Stronsay since then but he put it up for sale in 1994.

POPULATION: 1841 – 28 (5 houses). 1881 – 23. 1891 – 27 (4 houses). 1931 – 18. 1961 – 4. 1971 – 3. 1981 – 0. 1991 – 0.

GEOLOGY: Middle Old Red sandstone of the Rousay Flags variety.

HISTORY: Following the occupation of the island by pre-historic man, Papa Stronsay became a hermitage for Culdee monks.

In the early years of the 11th century fair-haired Earl Rognvald, gallant but unprincipled, arrived from Norway to take his share of the Orkney earldom granted to him by King Magnus of Norway. This Rognvald should not to be confused with the later Earl Rognvald of St Magnus cathedral fame. The incumbent Earl Thorfinn of Orkney accepted the position and agreed that two-thirds of the rev-enue should go to Rognvald but asked, in return, for Rognvald's support and friendship. Rognvald agreed.

For several years Thorfinn and Rognvald enjoyed themselves rampaging up and down the west coast of Scotland, fighting and laying waste parts of the Hebrides, Ireland, Galloway and the north-west of England.

Then Kalf Arnison, a relative-in-law of Thorfinn who had fallen out with King Magnus, asked for refuge and hospitality in Orkney for himself and his men. Thorfinn agreed but Rognvald would not and a quarrel ensued. The two Earls prepared for battle and their fleets eventually met in combat off the west coast of Hoy. Only when Kalf's six ships joined the fray was the issue decided and the defeated Rognvald fled to Norway. But later, in mid-winter, Rognvald returned in a single ship and caught Thorfinn unprepared in a house in Orphir and set fire to it. Thorfinn escaped by leaping through the flames carrying his wife Ingibjorg and disappeared into the night. In a tiny skiff he then rowed across the Pentland Firth to safety.

Rognvald went to Papa Stronsay to obtain malt barley which was grown on the island, probably by the Culdee monks, as he planned to brew ale for Christmas and hold a victory celebration, but while he and his men huddled by the fire in bitter December weather Thorfinn suddenly encircled them in flames. It was now Rognvald's turn to leap through the flames like Thorfinn, but he was carrying a lap-dog instead of a wife. He hid among the rocks and seaweed on the shore but the dog yapped and he was caught and slain by Thorkel Fosterer, one of Thorfinn's men.

And so Papa Stronsay played an important part in the history of Orkney for this episode led to a long period of peace and prosperity under the magnanimous rule of Thorfinn the Mighty.

WILDLIFE: Whooper swans winter on Mill Loch. The owner banned duck shooting on the island and there are now many birds including breeding arctic terns and visitors such as snow bunting.

For many centuries **PAPA STRONSAY** was known for its fertility and its luxuriant crops of grain. And from the early 17th century until 1914 it also prospered from the fishing industry as, in spite of limited acreage, it had no less than five fish-curing stations. These worked in co-operation with the fifteen stations at Whitehall, just across the harbour on Stronsay and much of the produce went for sale to the Baltic ports. In the 1950s the farm was producing excellent crops of oats, and root crops such as turnips and potatoes.

Papa Stronsay is low and flat, only reaching 13m above sea-level but it has an ample water supply from Mill Loch which covers about 5% of the surface area. Most of the buildings are in the south of the island overlooking Whitehall Harbour and close to a mound (8m high) known as

Earls Knoll [HY668292]. There are two noteworthy cairns and a burnt mound in the centre of the island beside Mill Loch. Several derelict crofts dot the landscape and two medieval chapel sites can still be seen. Reminders of Papa Stronsay's popularity in the heady days of the herring boom are everywhere. A stone quay and a number of old piers are south of the house but the curer's huts have long since been dismantled.

The owner was a London vintner by trade who was keen to take up farming. He arrived in Orkney almost by chance and bought the island on impulse in 1988. For the first year he regretted the move but then became certain that he could live nowhere else. The farm is mainly stocked with sheep and the laird's house is rambling and comfortable with gas lighting to avoid the noise of an electric generator at night. As so often happens, however, euphoria wears off and city lights beckon.

A thin tongue of land curls out to the west and then southwards to **Point of the Graand** (ON *graand* – spit or sandbar). The whole area is very shallow and tidal and encloses the **Bight of Stackaback**. The light beacon at **The Ness** in the north-east is a white tower which is automatic and only 8m high.

It is well-known in Orkney that when there is a spring tide on a Midsummer Night the grey seal or 'selkie' strips off his skin and becomes human and dances for sheer joy. A Papa Stronsay woman once fell in love with a selkie. The proof? Her children had thick horny skin on their hands and feet and always smelled of fish.

ACCESS: No regular access. For private arrangements enquire at Stronsay Hotel or Whitehall post-office.

Anchorages:
1. Whitehall Harbour. Good anchorage but many reefs and shoals. Use NW entrance and anchor where space and depth available S of Papa Stronsay.

10.18 Egilsay

(G. eaglais or EI ecclais, ON -øy – church island) or, possibly, (ON – Egil's island). In 1529 described as 'insularum ecclesia'. The possible Celtic derivation, very unusual in Orkney, is supported by the drying island at the north extremity being called Kili Holm which could be (G. cille – chapel or cell islet).

OS Maps: 1:50000 Sheet 5 or 6 1:25000 Sheets 26 and 29
Admiralty Charts: 1:200000 Nos.1942 or 1954 1:75000 Nos.2249 or 2250

AREA: 650ha (1,606 acres)
HEIGHT: 35m (115 ft)

POPULATION: 1795 – 210. 1841 – 190 (35 houses). 1881 – 165. 1891 – 147 (33 houses). 1931 – 85. 1961 – 54 (15 houses). 1971 – 39. 1981 – 24. 1991 – 46.

GEOLOGY: Middle Old Red sandstone similar to that on Rousay.

HISTORY: Erlend's son, Magnus, reluctantly accompanied King Magnus of Norway when he plundered Wales in 1098 but he refused to fight, although to prove he was no coward he stood on the poop-deck singing psalms during the battle. Needless to say this was not a popular gesture and soon after the battle was won young Magnus had to make a quick exit. He took refuge for a number of years at the court of Edgar, King of Scots (the son of Malcolm Canmore) avoiding all contact with King Magnus. The Norwegian King was by then known as Magnus Barelegs presumably because he chose to wear a kilt. In 1103 Magnus Barelegs was killed in Ireland so young Magnus returned to Orkney in 1106 and claimed his earldom and half the Orkney revenues. The other half belonged to Earl Haakon, his cousin.

FAMOUS EGILSAY LANDMARK – THE 12TH CENTURY CHURCH OF ST MAGNUS

In spite of his piety Magnus was a fairly unpredictable character but nevertheless he had the popular support of many Orcadians. He married a girl called Ingigerd but never consummated the marriage. Apparently cold water helped him to maintain a state of chastity. After some years he lost interest in marital life and travelled south to stay at the court of King Henry I of England. Henry was married to King Edgar of Scotland's sister.

Haakon took advantage of Magnus' absence to assert his complete authority in Orkney when suddenly Magnus reappeared with five warships. Haakon rushed to arms but the Althing, or Parliament, counselled peace and arranged a parley on the island of Egilsay during Easter week, 1117. Both parties were to take no more than two ships and equal numbers of men. Magnus landed first, but then saw Haakon approaching with eight ships and many men.

Magnus refused to let his men defend him and spent the night praying in a small chapel while Haakon camped on the shore. With Magnus was a Celt called Holdbodi who recorded what then happened.

In the morning Magnus came out of the chapel, met Haakon on the shore and offered, for the sake of peace, to go into exile – to Rome or the Holy Land – but Haakon dismissed the idea.

Magnus then said he would accept imprisonment, but this too was rejected. He next offered to be maimed or blinded and to this Haakon agreed, but Haakon's men objected as they did not wish Orkney to continue to be divided between two earls. They said they would prefer to kill either cousin outright – no matter which. Haakon is then reported to have said: 'I like my Earldom better than death, so kill him.' But no one was keen to strike the fatal blow in such a cold-blooded fashion.

Magnus said nothing, knelt, prayed, and then commanded Lifolf, (who was Haakon's cook), to use his axe to hew a great wound in his head. This Lifolf did, and also struck a second time.

ROUSAY

Point of
Pitten

Point of
Ridden

Marlow

★ *Cairn*

Kili Holm

*Bay
of Ham*

Sound of Longstaing

Roe
Ness

Smithy Sound

1 km

1/2 mile

Varaquoy

Eri Clett

Broad Geo

Grory

Sound

Weyland

Howie Sound

**Holm of
Scockness**

Mae Ness

Point of Crook

Howe

Maeness

Point of
Steedie

Grugar

North
Toft

★ *St Magnus Church*

Mae Banks

⚓

Skaill

✦ Sch

Pier

North Culdigo

⊚ *Monument*

*Manse
Loch*

Ossin

Whistlebare

PO

Warsett

Kirbist

R o u s a y   S o u n d

Cott

Howan

*Bay of
Skaill*

Ferry

The Hubbet

▲ 35

Vady

Whitelett

*Bay of
Vady*

Orchin

Onziebust

*Chambered
Cairn* ★

*Loch of the
Graand*

Sheep Skerry

N
↑

The
Graand

**Point of
the Graand**

W Y R E

Holdbodi's account has since been supported by the discovery in 1919 of what is almost certainly Magnus' skeleton entombed in St Magnus' cathedral in Kirkwall. The skull has been pierced with an axe and the upper jaw severed.

WILDLIFE: Breeding ducks, waders and black-headed gulls frequent the many small lochs. In winter the coastline supports about 1,000 waders including many purple sandpiper and turnstone and large numbers of divers and sea-duck occupy the sounds round the island.

EGILSAY is a spear-head shaped island with a low central ridge rising to 35m. Conspicuous on the ridge is the great round tower of **St Magnus' Church** [HY466304]. From the distance it could, unromantically, be a factory chimney or grain silo but closer inspection reveals the beautiful masonry of this well-preserved 12th century tower. The style is unique in Orkney and follows an Irish ecclesiastical style of the 11th century. Even on mainland Scotland there are only a limited number of examples. The tower was reduced in height in the 19th century to improve its stability but it is still nearly 15m high. Originally, it was probably about 20m high and included several storeys. Its internal diameter at ground level is about 3m and the walls are over 1m thick.

The church nave, originally covered with Orcadian stone slabs, is now roofless but the church was in use until well into the 19th century. The walls are almost complete but they are dotted with 'put-log' holes, possibly for scaffolding, and there used to be a second storey above the chancel, roofed with a barrel vault.

This is not the church where St Magnus kept vigil before his death although it is dedicated to him and quite probably stands on the site of the earlier chapel. The place where the saint was murdered is not far away and marked by a stone pillar.

There is a good little road running from the pier at **Skaill** (ON *skáli* – hall), on the west side of Egilsay, up to the schoolhouse near St Magnus' Church. Here a road runs along the spine of the island serving the dozen or so small farms. Apart from a chambered cairn [HY474278] near the southernmost tip, **Point of the Graand** (ON – spit or sandbank), there are few other known prehistoric relics.

At the north of Rousay Sound which separates Egilsay from Rousay there is a small island like a stepping stone, **Holm of Scockness** (ON – islet of the crooked headland). **Kili Holm**, the islet to the north of Egilsay, is tidal. Both are used as rough grazing for sheep.

ACCESS: Vehicle ferry service several times daily, if required, from Tingwall by Orkney Islands Shipping, 01856-751360 or 01856-872044.

Anchorages:
1. Skaill. Anchor in Rousay Sound off the Skaill pier, 3-6m, sand. Avoid obstructing ferry. Subject to swell in S'lies.

10.19 Eynhallow

(ON øyin helga – holy island)

OS Maps: 1:50000 Sheet 6 1:25000 Sheet 28
Admiralty Charts: 1:200000 Nos.1942 or 1954 1:75000 No.2249

AREA: 75ha (185 acres)
HEIGHT: 30m (98 ft)

OWNER: Bought in 1980 for £60,000 by Orkney Islands Council.

POPULATION: 1841 – 26 (4 houses). 1891 – 0. 1931 – 0. 1981 – 0. Uninhabited.

GEOLOGY: Middle Old Red sandstone of the Rousay variety.

HISTORY: This was probably the site of one of the earliest monastic settlements in Orkney and may only have been preceded by Christ Church on the Brough of Birsay. Although it was established after Earl Thorfinn's period of rule at the height of Norse dominance, it almost certainly had Celtic antecedents.

WILDLIFE: It used to be claimed that rats and mice could not live on this enchanted isle but, at least, encouraged by the lack of human habitation there are large numbers of seals. Even these may be Merfolk or Fin Folk because their enchanted summer home is called Hildaland and some think Hildaland is really Eynhallow.

On a more practical note this is a sea-bird sanctuary run as a Nature Reserve by Orkney Islands Council. Thirty-three species nest regularly on the island, including the fulmar (the 'malliemak'), whilst many others come as visitors. The fulmar is now quite common but was unknown in Orkney before 1900.

With the exception of the exposed west side, **EYNHALLOW** is surrounded by reefs, shoals and dangerous tides. One can only marvel at the seamanship and grit (or foolhardiness) of the early Christians who founded a monastic settlement here. The island has a compact shape with the highest ground (30m) being just north-west of the centre. The ruins of the small medieval church on what may be a Benedictine monastery site can be seen facing across Eynhallow Sound to the parish of Evie on Mainland [HY359288]. Evie means 'swirl' and the Reef of Burgar opposite the church creates the dangerous Burgar Rost, a vicious tidal rip that has to be treated with great respect. On the other side of the island is the even more turbulent Cutlar Rost.

The recent history of the ruined church is of interest because it was only rediscovered about a century ago. In the middle of the 18th century the owner cleared the island by evacuating the four families. This was said to be because they were suffering from a virulent disease and it is possible that typhoid was the problem from a contaminated well. After they had gone the thatched roofs were stripped off the dwellings to make them uninhabitable. It was only then that it was realised that one of the houses was in fact an early church which had been converted into a house. It is now believed that the conversion took place in the 16th century.

The church itself is thought to be early 12th century but beside it are a number of other roofless apartments. Whether or not these are anything to do with a monastery is debatable. Even the existence of a monastery itself is by no means certain although the references in the sagas together with the name of the island would make this a high probability.

Eynhallow is not often visited, and understandably so, as it is difficult to reach. It is an island rich in tradition and mystery and in the past was known as the enchanted island. It has, for instance, been known to vanish as one approaches it. The only way to avoid this navigational disaster (so they say) is for the helmsman to keep his eyes resolutely fixed on the island while clasping a metal object.

ACCESS: No regular access. Try the Eviedale Centre at Evie, 0185 675 270/254, or make enquiries in Tingwall.

Anchorages: Local knowledge is essential. The tidal stream (Burgar Rost) S of island is very strong, unpredictable, and conditions can change suddenly. Tidal stream on NE side is dangerous. There is no recommended anchorage.

10.20 Rousay

(ON Hrólfs-øy – Hrolf's island)

OS Maps: 1:50000 Sheet 6 1:25000 Sheets 26, 28, and 29
Admiralty Charts: 1:200000 Nos.1942 or 1954 1:75000 No.2249

AREA: 4,860ha (12,009 acres)
HEIGHT: 250m (820 ft)

OWNER: Multiple ownership.

POPULATION: 1841 – 982 (225 houses). 1881 – 873.
1891 – 774 (187 houses). 1931 – 468. 1961 – 237.
1971 – 181. 1981 – 213. 1991 – 217.

GEOLOGY: The Middle Old Red sandstone of which
Rousay is almost entirely composed has been adopted as a
standard for its particular type – it yields greyish-coloured
flagstones. These underlie the peat-covered uplands.

HISTORY: In the on-going struggle for control of Orkney,
Earl Rognvald had landed and mustered his forces on
Westray (No.10.25) and Earl Paul, known as Paul the Silent, who was effectively in control, had established his defences on Mainland. Battle seemed imminent until
Rognvald asked Bishop William to mediate. The Bishop
agreed, and a fortnight's truce was declared.

Paul decided that a few days' holiday would do him
good so he sailed over to Rousay to stay with his friend
Sigurd of Westness and early in the morning he, and a
group of his men, went down to the shore to hunt otters.

The wild card in this idyllic scenario, however, was
young Sweyn of Gairsay (No.10.13) – Sweyn Asliefsson –
who had been rather unjustly outlawed a year before by
Earl Paul. Sweyn had stayed on the Scottish mainland
with Earl Maddad of Atholl and his wife, Margaret, whose
son Harald also had claims to the Orkney title. He promised to support Harald's claim and Margaret's uncle provided him with a merchant ship and a crew of thirty men.

When Paul failed to return to the house for his morning ale, Sigurd sent out a search party which found the
bodies of Paul's men and six strangers. There had obviously been a fight but no trace of Paul could be found. It
was only discovered later that Sweyn had sailed his new
ship through Scapa Flow, up the Atlantic coast of Mainland, and into Eynhallow Sound – waters which he knew
well from his life on Gairsay. There he had surprised and
kidnapped Paul and slain his followers.

Paul was taken to Atholl and given a friendly reception
although held as a prisoner but later, when Sweyn had returned to Orkney, the ruthless Margaret had him blinded
and then murdered.

WILDLIFE: There is a lot of angelica to be seen on Rousay
– the plant which the Norsemen are said to have introduced. It looks something like hogweed.

The brown hare is fairly common but the enormous
population of rabbits is most in evidence. There are more
families of otters on these coasts than elsewhere in Orkney.

Bird-watching on Rousay is good at any time but probably best from May to July. Inland, there are many breeding species such as the red-throated diver, hen harrier,
merlin, curlew, golden plover, short-eared owl and five gull
species. The common sandpiper can be seen here although
it is generally uncommon in Orkney.

The best sites are: Brings Heath and Quendale in the
north-west where there are some 4000 pairs of Arctic
tern, 100 pairs of Arctic skua and some great skua. Many
fulmar, kittiwake, guillemot and razorbill are to be found
on the cliffs.

Trumland RSPB Reserve in the south-east; here the
red-throated diver, hen harrier, and golden plover breed,
while merlin, Arctic and great skua, and short-eared owl
can be seen.

Great northern diver, eider, long-tailed duck, velvet
scoter and red-breasted merganser winter in Eynhallow
Sound.

ROUSAY is a hilly island and the sandstone strata have
given the hills a terraced appearance. From the summit of
Blotchnie Fiold (250m) in the south-east it is possible to
see Foula (No.11.6) on a clear day nearly 100km distant
on the Atlantic horizon.

This is possibly the most interesting of all the Orkney
islands and one of the best of the Northern Isles for anyone interested in prehistory. It has the added advantage
that some of the best sites are quite near the ferry pier on
the south coast. West of the pier are three remarkable
burial cairns: **Taversoe Tuick** [HY426276] has two storeys and separate entrance passages, **Blackhammer**
[HY414276] has seven divisions in the chamber (in 1936
two skeletons were found in it), and **Knowe of Yarso**
[HY405280], a stalled cairn with four compartments.
When this latter cairn, which is about 3km from the pier,
was excavated in 1934 a large collection of mixed bones
were discovered including the remains of twenty-one humans, several sheep, thirty deer, and a dog.

The pier and village settlement were built in the 1870s
by General Traill Burroughs who is sometimes given the
dubious distinction of being Orkney's most-detested 19th
century landowner. His home, **Trumland House,** was designed in a truly-Victorian Scottish Baronial style by David
Bryce in 1873 [HY428278]. The General made his money
in India and married the heiress to the Traills of Rousay.
She took an interest in the landscaping around the house
– which has resulted in a pleasant patch of woodland –
and chose a knoll for a viewpoint and on which to place a
seat. This led to the discovery that the knoll was a 5000-
year-old burial cairn with an adjacent earth-house
(Taversoe Tuick).

The Traill family home was at **Westness** [HY383289], a couple of kilometres beyond Knowe of Yarso. It was burnt down when John Traill, a Jacobite supporter, was hiding in the Gentleman's Cave on Westray (No.10.25) but was rebuilt later in the 18th century.

Excavations were started in 1978 on a number of Viking buildings beyond Westness. According to the *Orkneyinga Saga* this was the home of Sigurd where Earl Paul was kidnapped while hunting otters although there is some dubiety because not far away, at **Skaill** (ON *skáli* –

hall), a farmer in 1963 started digging a hole to bury a cow and broke into a Norse grave. A young woman was buried in it with three magnificent silver brooches dating from about the 9th and 10th century. There is an old church at Skaill which may be pre-Reformation [HY374302].

Without doubt, the most significant archaeological site on Rousay is **Midhowe** [HY372306] which is just beyond Skaill and opposite Eynhallow (No.10.19). Here there is an enormous chambered cairn which predates Maes howe on Mainland. The Midhowe chamber is 23m long and over 2m wide with 12 burial stalls arranged along each side. Unstan type pottery was found here and the remains of twenty-five individuals. There were also the remains of cattle, deer, sheep and even an Orkney vole. The original chamber height would have been about 2½m. Midhowe was excavated in the 1930s having been discovered, and the work paid for, by W. G. Grant who had bought Trumland House and much of the south-west of the island. It was Grant's forebears who founded the Highland Park whisky distillery at Kirkwall.

Near the tomb is an Iron Age broch [HY370307] which is over 9m in diameter and with walls over 4m high and clustered by it are the remains of later buildings like a small village. During excavation many domestic implements were revealed, some of which were of Roman origin.

Rousay is littered with the relics of prehistory. There are two more brochs in the immediate vicinity of Westness, at least fifteen brochs on the shores of Eynhallow Sound, and any number of cairns and burnt mounds.

After the road turns northwards it crosses Quendale where the old mansion of **Tofts** stands – said to be the oldest two-storeyed domestic house in Orkney. The site is south of Brae of Moan [HY373326]. There is interesting cliff scenery all along this coastline due to the regular rock strata, with caves, geos, and a natural rock arch.

The place names by Saviskaill Bay on the north coast confirm associations with the Norse period, **Wasbister** (ON – west farm), Langskaill (ON – longhouse drinking-hall) and a number of 'quoy' suffixes (ON *koie* – shelter or enclosure), often applied to hillcrofts.

The north-east corner of the island forms a protuberance ending at Faraclett Head. Here, on the farm of Bigland, there is a fine example of a Stone Age village of the Skara brae type called **Rinyo** [HY438321]. This has been dated to about 3700BC from pottery shards discovered at foundation level and this, in turn, has assisted the dating of Skara Brae. It also shows that these dwellings were contemporary with the chambered cairns.

On Faraclett farm nearby there is an enormous standing stone called **Yetnes-steen** (ON *jötna-steinn* – the giant's stone) [HY447327]. To prove there is no discrimination, at Swandale to the west, some rock-outcrops are called the **Gyro-stones** (ON *gyger* – a female giant).

There are a number of lochs on Rousay all rich in birdlife, such as **Loch of Wasbister** in the north-west, and in the desolate centre of the island where there is marvellous hill-walking, **Muckle Water** (big), **Peerie Water** (little) and **Loomachun** (ON – lochan of the red-throated diver or loon).

Although Rousay supported about 1000 people at the start of the 19th century it has always been restricted by its lack of agricultural land. Only the coastal strip can be profitably worked.

ACCESS: Vehicle-ferry service by Orkney Islands Shipping Company from Tingwall, 01856-872044 or 01856-751360, several times daily. Rousay History Tour, 01856-821234. Tourist Office, 01856-872856.

Anchorages:
1. Bay of Ham, N of Rousay Sound, good shelter from N and W. Anchor in 3½-6m. (Access to the Stone Age village of Rinyo).
2. Saviskaill Bay. Not recommended. Rocky bottom and exposed.
3. Wyre Sound. Anchor E of Rousay ferry pier. Close inshore out of the tide gives reasonable shelter from all directions. (Access to Taversoe Tuick, etc.)

10.21 Eday

(ON eid-øy – isthmus island). Eday has a narrow waist.

OS Maps: 1:50000 Sheet 5 1:25000 Sheets 24, 27 and 30
Admiralty Charts: 1:200000 Nos.1942 or 1954 1:75000 No.2250

AREA: 2,745ha (6,783 acres)
HEIGHT: 101m (331 ft)

OWNER: Multiple ownership since 1925. Previously owned by the Hebden family. Most small farms are owner-occupied.

POPULATION: 1841 – 944 (193 houses). 1881 – 730. 1891 – 647 (138 houses). 1931 – 430. 1961 – 198. 1971 – 179. 1981 – 154. 1991 – 166.

GEOLOGY: Most of Eday is of an eponymous type of Middle Old Red sandstone which is an excellent and attractive building stone. The fine yellow sandstone used in St Magnus Cathedral was quarried here. This is a true sandstone which is stratified in distinct slabs that are easily fashioned into blocks. It over-lies the Rousay type of sandstone except in a small patch at Backaland where Rousay Beds reach the surface.

The ridge of hills running down the spine of Eday is covered with peat. Only the narrow coastal strip is suitable for cultivation. The islands of Sanday (No.10.24) and North Ronaldsay (No.10.27) obtained most of their fuel requirements from Eday and the peat was also exported to a number of whisky distilleries throughout Scotland.

HISTORY: Near the start of the 17th century the youthful John Stewart, second son of the Earl of Orkney, was accused of poisoning his brother Patrick. It was claimed that he had colluded with a witch called Alysoun Balfour. Alysoun was tortured but John was acquitted and in 1628 was created Earl of Carrick. In 1632 he was granted the island of Eday and immediately set about building a home in the pleasant Bay of Carrick overlooking Calf Sound. The date 1633 is still to be seen inscribed over the courtyard gateway at Carrick House.

The notoriously inept pirate, John Gow, after raiding Cava (No.10.7) in 1724 tried to raid Carrick House on Eday. He sailed into Calf Sound but was unaware that the fast tides always set onto the Eday shore. His ship *Revenge* got into difficulties and ran aground. He spent some time in full view of the House struggling for control and by the time he came ashore his old schoolmate James Fea, the owner of Carrick House, was waiting for him. He was arrested and handed over to the authorities. His ship's bell is still in Carrick House.

WILDLIFE: This is the only Orkney island on which bog myrtle, *myrica gale*, can be found. The hills are used for rough grazing for sheep and are regularly burned to encourage the growth of young heather.

A number of otters, fairly uncommon in Orkney, frequent these coasts, particularly in the south-west between West Side and War Ness. There are lots of rabbits but no hares.

Eday has some special treats for birdwatchers, particularly from May to July. On Mill Loch there are several pairs of red-throated divers, probably representing the densest concentration of these fine birds in Britain, and a few pairs of whimbrel nest on the moors which is a rare sight on Orkney. The moors also harbour arctic and great skua, curlew, snipe and golden plover. Fulmar and herring gull breed on Red Head in the extreme north and black guillemot can be seen on the shore. There are many migrants in the woodland at Carrick House particularly in spring and autumn.

EDAY can be dark and bleak with hills clothed in a deep layer of peat moorland. Only the southern part is cultivated and although there are many farms they are mostly very small and owner-occupied. This is a long island with a low narrow waist where the airstrip is sited beside the shallow Loch of Doomy.

The north extremity is called **Red Ness** and the islet beside it in the Sound of Faray is **Red Holm**. These names are explicit – the red rock colour is distinctive, and because Red Ness is so much higher (70m) than its surroundings it is a useful landmark clearly indicating the entrance to Calf Sound. **Carrick House** [HY567385] was built in 1633 by the Earl of Carrick, younger son of the unpopular Earl Robert Stewart. Carrick Farm and the village of Calfsound look north across the narrow tide-rippled sound to Calf of Eday (No.10.23). The Bay of Carrick is sheltered by the western ridge of Noup Hill (ON *gnupr* – headland crag), Muckle Hill of Linkertaing, and Vinquoy Hill. The remains of chambered cairns in these hills can be seen but the best example, although little remains, is at **Huntersquoy** (ON *koie* – shelter or enclosure) [HY563377]. This, like Taversoe Tuick on Rousay (No.10.20), has two storeys with separate entrances. **The Stone of Setter** stands proudly between Huntersquoy and Mill Loch, where red-throated divers can be seen among the reeds [HY564372].

A road runs southwards for the entire length of the island, from Calfsound to the standing stone at Southside. There are more chambered cairns and other evidence of early man, particularly among the moorland hills – Fersness, Whitemaw, Flaughton, Leeniesdale, and **Ward Hill** (101m), the highest on the island. Although the ferry route leads through Calf Sound in the north the ferry pier is at **Backaland** in the south-east.

The thick layers of peat on Eday were its salvation in the 18th and 19th century as it provided much-needed fuel for the other islands and prosperity also came from its quarries which supplied Kirkwall with slate. But increasing imports of coal destroyed the peat trade in the 1860s and the island has not yet fully recovered its self-esteem.

South-west of Warness, across the Fall of Warness where North Sea gales stir up fierce tidal rips, are **Muckle Green Holm** and **Little Green Holm**. They are occupied by a small cormorant colony and a number of nesting shags while Otter Pool on Muckle Green Holm still shelters a family of otters.

ACCESS: Orkney Islands Shipping ro-ro ferry daily from Kirkwall or neighbouring islands, 01856-872044. BA Express flights from Kirkwall, Weds. only, 01856-872494. Tourist information, 01857-622248.

Anchorages:
1. Bay of Carrick, Calf Sound. Follow the white sectored light identifying the fairways in the Sound. Bay of Carrick is SE of Calf Sound Light-tower. Good shelter. Anchor below Carrick House off the stone jetty close inshore out of the tide in 5m, sand. Avoid lobster boat moorings.
2. Fersness Bay. Shelter from all S'lies. Anchor off S shore in 3½-7m, sand and weed. Good holding.
3. Bay of Backaland, an indentation on the E coast ½M N of Veness. Temp anchorage in suitable conditions, bottom stony, or possibly lie alongside pier but keeping a constant watch.
4. Bay of London, small inlet at centre of E coast. Occasional anchorage at entrance to bay.
5. Mill Bay, small inlet on the E coast ¾M SSW of Greenybrae. Occasional anchorage at entrance to bay.

10.22 Faray

(ON vaer-øy – ram island). Previously called North Pharay.

OS Maps: 1:50000 Sheet 5 1:25000 Sheet 26 or 27
Admiralty Charts: 1:200000 No.1942 or 1954 1:75000 No.2249 or 2250

AREA: 180ha (445 acres)
HEIGHT: 32m (105 ft)

POPULATION: 1841 – 67 (14 houses). 1871- 83. 1881 – 72. 1891 – 58 (8 houses). 1931 – 40. 1961 – 0. 1971 – 0. 1981 – 0. 1991 – 0. Only occasional habitation.

GEOLOGY: Middle Old Red sandstone of the Rousay type with the exception of a small area of Eday type sandstone on the south-east coast.

HISTORY: A lone chambered cairn near Lavey Sound is the only apparent historic artefact on the island.

WILDLIFE: The islet due west of Faray, Rusk Holm, is a favourite spot for grey seals which can often be seen lying on the wet rocks like well-cooked giant chipolatas.

FARAY is part of a ridge which almost connects Fers Ness on Eday to Weather Ness on Westray. There is a wider gap to the south through which the Kirkwall Ferry sails into the Sound of Faray and a narrower gap at the north forming Weatherness Sound. In the middle, Faray is separated from Holm of Faray by Lavey Sound which dries out at low water but through which it is possible to sail after half-tide.

Faray rises to a height of 32m near the centre of the island.

A road still runs up the central axis serving the scattered empty houses. It was reported that during the General Election of 1992 three voters on Faray were unable to deliver their votes because the rudder of their boat was broken. Democracy was saved by the use of a pet homing skua which carried their voting papers to Mainland.

One of the crofts on the ridge is called 'Holland' – a name which is quite common throughout Orkney. Although the Dutch were well-known to the Orcadians the name is, in most cases, actually derived from (ON *há-land* – high land).

In the late 1930s there were eight families living on the island. They had crofts and supplemented their income by a spot of lobster-fishing. Then the Second World War intruded and a new world opened up. Comparisons were drawn and the simple but strenuous island life seemed less than perfect. By 1947 the last hard-working family had

Red Head

The   North   Sound

2 kms
1 mile

East Lesses

East Toe

Grey Head
The Knees

The Auks

N

Grotties Geo
Head of Pernealy

△ 50

The Graand

Bight of
the Graand

Quern Geos

Old Saltworks

The Bow

Starling Ayre
Lashy Taing
Grassy
Geos

Bay of
Carrick

Goreys
Saddle

Lashy
Skerries

Stalled Cairn,
Chambered Tombs
& Iron Age House

25

Natural Arch

Furrowend

EDAY

The Castles

Ferry

Calf of Eday

left and the island was deserted except for occasional summer occupation.

The only notable prehistoric relic is the chambered cairn beside Lavey Sound but there is also a cairn on the neighbouring island skerry of Rusk Holm which lies to the west of Faray.

ACCESS: No regular access. Try T. Rendall, Westray, 018577-216; or Eday Tourist Information, 018572-248.

Anchorages: There are no recommended anchorages but temp anchorage may be found using the chart. In S'lies anchor in Fersness Bay, Eday and in N'lies anchor by Weatherness, Westray to await suitable conditions for an approach to Faray. Avoid shoal area SW of Faray, and Lavey Sound which dries.

10.23 Calf of Eday

See Eday (No.10.21). 'Calf' refers to a satellite of a larger island.

OS Maps: 1:50000 Sheet 5 1:25000 Sheets 24 and 27
Admiralty Charts: 1:200000 No.1942 or 1954 1:75000 No.2250

AREA: 243ha (600 acres)
HEIGHT: 50m (164 ft)

POPULATION: 1841 – 0. 1891 – 0. 1931 – 0. 1981 – 0. 1991 – 0. Uninhabited.

GEOLOGY: The island is composed of Middle Old Red sandstone, mostly of the Eday variety but there is a thin intersection of Rousay flags on the north-south axis.

HISTORY: In the 18th and 19th century most of Orkney's salt came from the salt pans on this small island.

WILDLIFE: On Grey Head and the eastern cliffs there are large colonies of guillemot, razorbill and kittiwake, with black guillemot around the shores and moorland-nesting black-backed gulls on the heather top. A large cormorant colony thrives on the south side of the island.

Narrow Calf Sound between Eday and **CALF OF EDAY** is scenically attractive. The approach by sea from the north lies between the imposing **Red Head** of Eday and **Grey Head** of the Calf. The stone colours are subtle and dramatic.

The savage spring tide runs through the sound at six knots at both flood and ebb and in gales is whipped up into a turbulent race but at slack water in fine weather the sea becomes idyllic.

Among the group of chambered cairns on the heather slopes opposite Calfsound village, one is of particular interest as it has been built above an even earlier stone structure – whether a tiny dwelling or a tomb it is hard to say [HY579386].

The old saltworks [HY575390] are within a stone's throw of the chambered cairns.

ACCESS: No regular access. Try Eday Tourist Information, 018572-248; or T. Rendall, Westray, 018577-216.

Anchorages:
1. Bay of Carrick, Calf Sound. Follow the white sectored light identifying the fairways in the Sound. Bay of Carrick is SE of Calf Sound Light-tower on Eday. Good shelter. Anchor below Carrick House off the stone jetty close inshore out of the tide in 5m, sand. Avoid lobster boat moorings. Cross the sound at slack water for dinghy landing. (Both tidal streams set towards the Eday shore).

10.24 Sanday

(ON sand-øy – sand island)

OS Maps: 1:50000 Sheet 5 1:25000 Sheets 25 and 27
Admiralty Charts: 1:200000 Nos.1942 or 1954 1:75000 No.2250

AREA: 5,043ha (12,461 acres)
HEIGHT: 65m (213 ft)

OWNER: Multiple ownership. Most of the farms are owner-occupied.

POPULATION: 1798 – 1772. 1841 – 1892 (372 houses). 1881 – 2082. 1891 – 1929 (402 houses). 1931 – 1160. 1961 – 670. 1981 – 531. 1991 – 533.

GEOLOGY: Well-weathered Middle Old Red Sandstone with a greyish colour. This is mostly of the Rousay type which accounts for the good soil but the south-western extremity is of the firmer Eday type of sandstone. A fault crosses the island from Ness of Brough to Tresness.

WILDLIFE: The Site of Scientific Interest (SSI) at North Loch includes Early March and Frog Orchids. Seaweed is plentiful around the coasts and *Laminaria digitata*, *Laminaria Cloustonii* and wracks such as *Fucus nodosus* and *Fucus serratus* are collected by the farmers for alginate processing.

Sanday has prolific birdlife. There are colonies of Arctic tern, large numbers of ringed plover, and some corncrake and corn bunting. Many waders settle on the shoreline in winter including grey and golden plovers, bar-tailed godwit, dunlin, and turnstone. Probably the spring and autumn migrants are the greatest interest.

Lady Parish in the south-west has many migrants and breeding wildfowl such as teal, widgeon, shoveller, tufted duck, red-breasted merganser, eider and some breeding waders. At Gump of Spurness there are Arctic skua and short-eared owl.

Eric Linklater thought that, from the air, **SANDAY** looked like a fossilised, gigantic bat but we can be sure that the Norsemen never saw it from this angle. There are three peninsulas projecting from a common central base. The island is low-lying, the highest point being **The Wart** (65m) and the peninsulas divide the long coastline into a large number of fairly shallow and exposed bays with beautiful wide white sandy beaches. These are usually deserted except for multitudes of wading birds. From a comparison with old maps it is possible that the sandbanks are slowly being extended by the sea and that the island is growing.

At sea level, in dark misty weather, this large sprawling island is virtually invisible. Consequently, before the days of radar, there was a constant supply of shipwrecks to keep the inhabitants warm. There is no peat on the island so wooden ships were very welcome and it is even said that prayers in church asked for the Lord's assistance in this respect.

The light, sandy soil is very fertile. It is tied in at the coasts by the roots of marram grass although thousands of rabbits do their best to disturb this delicate balance. A golf course spreads across the dunes of the Plain of Fidge at Newark. Kelp was the major industry in the 18th century with one quarter of Orkney's total production coming from Sanday. When the kelp boom died it was of little concern as during the 19th century the farms here were the most prosperous in Orkney. It is still productive but nowadays the farming is possibly more relaxed and supplemented by lobster fishing and seaweed-gathering for alginate.

Although there are a few small lochs, the sandy soil is not good at retaining moisture, and as the rainfall is sometimes low, water shortage can be a problem.

For many centuries agriculture took precedence over the preservation of ancient monuments on Sanday so there are few visible ruins although almost every ness has the faint trace of a broch. **Els Ness**, which at one time would have been a separate island but is now connected by an ayre, is on the south coast overlooking Sanday Sound. It has escaped the plough and is spattered with cairns like convex craters on the surface of the moon. Here there is a very interesting chambered cairn (central chamber and six cells) at **Quoyness** (ON – hut or shelter headland) which is the largest such cairn yet excavated in Orkney (key available at Lady post-office). Bones found in it were radiocarbon dated to about 2900BC [HY676378].

Stone Age burial mounds were treated with fear by the old crofters. This was because every mound had a resident hogboon. The hogboon was bad-tempered and untrustworthy and could cause a lot of trouble. At Hellihowe on Sanday one hogboon created so much trouble that the desperate farmer sold the croft and moved out. But as he carried his possessions into his new crofthouse the hogboon stuck its head out of a kirn and said: 'We're gettan a fine day tae flit on, guidman.'

Maybe the most interesting relic yet found is that of a Viking ship-burial north-east of **Scar** (ON – cleft) on the north-central peninsula of Burness [HY678458]. This was discovered in 1991 when about half the boat (6.5m long) had already been washed away by the sea. But the remaining – lengthwise – half contained a compartment with the skeletal remains of a man, a woman and a child. Beside the man was a sword, a quiver of arrows and some bone gaming pieces. Beside the woman were two spindle whorls, a pair of shears, and some iron objects which might be parts of a wooden box. There was also a decorated whalebone plaque, a sickle, a brooch and some other remains possibly of textiles.

Scar itself is the site of the **Saville Stone**, a 20-ton block of Scandinavian gneiss – an obvious glacial erratic. It is said that this was thrown by a furious witch on Eday at a man on Sanday with whom her daughter had eloped. She missed, and the couple lived happily ever after.

Not far from Scar, on the shores of Otterswick, is the attractive little 19th century fishing village of Ortie – straight from a picture postcard.

At the eastern extremity of Sanday, the lighthouse stands above Tobacco Rock on the tidal island of **Start Point**.

ACCESS: Orkney Islands Shipping ro-ro ferry service daily, 01856-872044. BA Express scheduled flights from

Kirkwall and Stronsay, 01856-872494 or 0345-222111.

Anchorages:
1. Kettletoft Bay, on S coast. Possible to lie alongside ferry pier on W side of bay, 3.5m depth at head, or anchor in bay in 4m. Approach bay using leading line. Very exposed. SE and S'lies bring in a swell.
2. Otterswick, on N coast. Large shallow bay. Care needed on entering and give shores a wide berth. Good shelter but quite uncomfortable in N and E winds. Anchor to suit wind direction.
3. North Bay, on W coast, S of Holms of Ire. Enter from NW. Anchor in 3-5m. Exposed to W'lies.

10.25 Westray

(ON vestr-øy – western island)

OS Maps: 1:50000 Sheet 5 1:25000 Sheets 23, 24, and 26
Admiralty Charts: 1:200000 No.1942 or 1954 1:75000 No.2249
1:37500 No.2622 NW coast

AREA: 4,713ha (11,646 acres)
HEIGHT: 169m (554 ft)

OWNER: Multiple ownership. Most of the larger farms are owner-occupied. Westray has a policy of giving local Orcadians first refusal when farms are for sale.

POPULATION: 1841 – 1791 (387 houses). 1881 – 2200. 1891 – 2108 (433 houses). 1911 – 1668. 1931 – 1269. 1961 – 872. 1971 – 735. 1981 – 741. 1991 – 704.

GEOLOGY: Westray is entirely composed of Middle Old Red sandstone of the Rousay Beds variety. The harder bedrock has a bluish colour, but most of the rock is a greystone flag which used to be used for building and slating. There is only a limited quantity of poor-grade peat and most of the island is fertile soil.

HISTORY: Earl Rognvald landed on Westray in 1136 on his second expedition to Orkney and gained the submission of the two local chieftains, Kugi of Rapness and Helgi of Hofn (Hofn was the old name for Pierowall).

During the Reformation, in the mid-16th century, the last Catholic Bishop of Orkney, Adam Bothwell, followed the example of many of his brethren at the time and bestowed part of the Church lands, the island of Westray, on his sister Margaret and her husband. Margaret was married to Gilbert Balfour, scion of an ancient Fife family and one who, as Master of the Household to Mary Queen of Scots, had been involved in the murder of Mary's husband, Darnley, in 1567. (He had previously been implicated in the murder of Cardinal Beaton in 1546.) Gilbert, who was also Sheriff of Orkney and Captain of Kirkwall Castle, immediately set about building a magnificent castle in his new domain. It is possible that the ground-work was already there in the form of an unfinished castle

started by Bishop Thomas Tulloch a century earlier. However, in due course Noltland Castle was completed and after Mary had married the Earl of Bothwell she instructed Gilbert to make it ready for the reception of herself and her new husband. At the same time she created him Duke of Orkney.

Mary was deposed before her visit could take place but Bothwell fled north to Orkney hoping for refuge. Gilbert, though, refused to let him stay and as he also failed to find shelter in Shetland, he had to sail on to Bergen where he was arrested and given a life sentence in a Danish prison.

Gilbert Balfour meanwhile joined an uprising in favour of the exiled Queen but it was defeated and he was found guilty of treason. He fled to Sweden but could not resist being involved in a plot against the Swedish King for which he was arrested and executed.

In spite of all Gilbert's unfortunate conspiracies and Lord Robert Stewart's occupation of Noltland Castle for a time, the Balfour family held on to Westray and their ownership of the island continued for many generations. This might be attributed to the fact that Bishop Bothwell after his deposition as a Catholic Bishop suddenly chose to become a staunch Protestant.

WILDLIFE: Common plant species are bird's foot trefoil, lady's smock, bog orchis, grass of parnassus, butterwort, eyebright and scabious. In the spring there are primroses everywhere including examples of the rare *primula scotica*.

Mice, and the Orkney vole, are common but otters are only occasionally to be seen. The first rats only appeared on the island during the Second World War after an enemy grain ship ran onto the rocks.

The seabird colonies on the west coast are probably the main interest for birdwatchers. The cliffs between Noup Head RSPB Reserve and Inga Ness are packed with birds including some 60,000 guillemot, 3,000 razorbill, and 30,000 pairs of kittiwake, as well as shag, puffin, black guillemot and occasional continental migrants. On the inland heath near the cliffs there are about 2,000 pairs of arctic tern, fifty pairs of arctic skua, and eider, oystercatcher, ringed plover and four species of gull. On the lochs and wetland areas there are breeding wildfowl and waders many of which over-winter here. A few corncrake can be heard. In winter, purple sandpiper and turnstone can be seen on the rocky foreshore, with sanderling in the sandy bays. The most interesting time is possibly mid-May to mid-July.

Other sites of interest are Stanger Head in the southeast for puffin, Aikerness Peninsula in the north near the airstrip for black guillemot, and Loch of Burness near Pierowall which is the northernmost habitat of the little grebe. Here also are mute swan, teal, shoveller, tufted duck, moorhen, coot, snipe and redshank.

Although the hills and sea-cliffs of **WESTRAY** are not as

high as others in the Orkneys, they are very impressive and beautiful. In fact there is such a diversity of scenery that this is often called the 'Queen of the North Isles'. The inhabitants are also noted for their own distinctive brand of 'bloody-Mary' humour.

In the south-west are three cairn-pimpled hills, Knucker Hill, Gallo Hill and Fitty Hill which is the highest point on the island at 169m. Cliffs separate them from the sea and run northwards to **Noup Head** (ON *gnupr* – craggy headland) which projects into the Atlantic and

towers above the swell – when it can be seen through the clouds of wheeling seabirds. North again is Bay of Noup and Rack Wick culminating at **Bow Head**, the northern extremity of a dangerous but dramatic coastline. Near Bow Head are **The Querns of Aikerness** which is a huge cauldron surrounded by rock pillars and arches.

South of the airstrip at Aikerness and overlooking the tidal race in Papa Sound is **Bay of Skaill** (ON *skáli* – hall). On the south side of the bay the Hole o' Rowe penetrates the headland. Climbers can descend the cliff face for a good view of the huge waves bursting and foaming up through the hole while the spent water cascades back into the bay.

The cliffs in this region and on the west coast in particular are riddled with caves. One of the most famous of these is **Gentlemen's Cave** on the south side of Noup Head [HY398486]. The Westray islanders are said to have been the only Orcadians who supported the Jacobite cause and after the defeat at Culloden in 1746 a number of the local lairds are thought to have hidden in this cave throughout the winter to avoid Hanoverian vengeance. Among them was one of the Balfours of Trenabie whose descendant John Balfour became landowner of a large part of Shapinsay (No.10.12) in the 18th century. For many years after the uprising supporters would meet in the cave to drink the health of the 'King over the Water'. For the inexperienced it is a fairly risky climb down to the cave.

The principal village is **Pierowall** tucked in to the sheltered Bay of Pierowall. Viking graves dating back to 800 have been found here, and there are the remains of two ancient churches, **Lady Kirk** and **Cross Kirk**, both of the Norse period.

On the slope of a hill west of the village is mysterious **Noltland Castle** [HY429487]. Mysterious, because it is unclear why such a mammoth structure was ever built by Gilbert Balfour. It stands alone like a man-of-war, a great stone fort with walls 2m thick pierced with tiers of gun-loops. It could have withstood a massive siege – but who would want to attack it? Gilbert Balfour, of course, had the character of a robber-baron so possibly he and his brother-in-law, the Bishop-about-to-be-deposed, had dreams of starting up their own mini-kingdom in Orkney using the combined fortresses of Noltland and Kirkwall.

Inside the forbidding bulk of the castle is a large and elegant staircase installed later by Earl Patrick Stewart, son of Queen Mary's bastard brother, Robert Stewart. It is graceful but quite out-of-keeping with the original design. More to the point is the inscription over the arched doorway – 'When I see the blood I will pass over you in the night.'

On a lighter note, the length of festivity following a wedding in the Northern Isles is renowned. The longest party on record was held at Noltland Castle. It continued from Martinmas to Candlemas without a break – three months!

Another Skara Brae-type Stone Age village has been excavated on the shore near the golf course at Links of Noltland.

A road runs the length of Westray from the airstrip in the north to **Point of Huro**, the southern extremity, where the tiny islet of **Wart Holm** lies near Rull Rost, a frenetic tidal rip in the middle of the Westray Firth.

ACCESS: Orkney Islands Shipping ferry on weekdays from Kirkwall and nearby islands, 01856-872044. Wide Berth Ferries in summer, 01856-741351. BA Express scheduled flights from Kirkwall and Papa Westray, 01856-872494 or 0345-222111.

Anchorages:
1. Bay of Swartmill, Papa Sound. Temp anchorage in offshore winds but holding unreliable.
2. Bay of Cleat. As above.
3. Bay of Brough. As above.
4. Pierowall Harbour. Excellent anchorage in 2m, clear of the pier, but restricted space.
5. Pierowall Road, Papa Sound. Good anchorage where depth suitable. Good holding, bottom chiefly sand and weed, weak tidal streams and no swell.
6. Bay of Skaill. Shallow and not recommended.
7. Bay of Tuquoy on S coast. Temp anchorage in settled weather, sand, 3-6m. Exposed, but negligible tidal stream.
8. Rapness Sound, SE side of Westray (Weather Ness). Useful temp anchorage in N'lies. Exposed S and heavy swell in bad weather. Good holding.
9. Rack Wick too deep and Skel Wick has rocky bottom. Neither is suitable.

SEABIRDS GALORE AT THE NOUP

10.26 Papa Westray

(ON papøy meiri – big Papay or priest's island).

OS Maps: 1:50000 Sheet 5 1:25000 Sheet 23
Admiralty Charts: 1:200000 No.1942 or 1954 1:75000 No.2249 or 2250 1:37500 No.2622

AREA: 918ha (2,268 acres)
HEIGHT: 48m (157 ft)

OWNER: Belonged to the Traill family for three centuries but now in multiple ownership.

POPULATION: 1841 – 340 (69 houses). 1881 – 345. 1891 – 337 (76 houses). 1931 – 237. 1961 – 139. 1971 – 106. 1981 – 94. 1991 – 85.

GEOLOGY: The geology of Papa Westray is similar to that of Westray – Middle Old Red sandstone of Rousay Beds with a fertile soil.

HISTORY: According to the *Orkneyinga Saga*, after Earl Rognvald Brusasson was murdered by his uncle in 1046 he was buried on Papay, but the location of his grave is a mystery. It is thought by some to be in the vicinity of Munkerhoose because an ornate cross with a gilt finish was found there in the St Boniface churchyard.

In 1567 Gilbert Balfour, Master of the Queen's Household, Captain of Kirkwall Castle and Sheriff of Orkney, and Margaret, his wife, were granted both Papa Westray and Westray by Margaret's brother, Adam Bothwell, Bishop of Orkney. The Westrays belonged to the Catholic church but with the Reformation came a rapid disposal of church lands. Gilbert (together with his two brothers) had been implicated in the murder of Cardinal Beaton in 1546 and also the later murder of Darnley, Mary Queen of Scots' husband.

WILDLIFE: The dwarf shrub-heath in the north of the island is rich in herbs and specialised plants which will only grow on old red sandstone. Among them is the Scottish primrose, *primula scotica*, which has a purple flower with a yellow eye.

The low cliffs on the east coast were possibly the last breeding site of the great auk before its extinction. Early in the 19th century a pair nested here, but the female died or was killed and the male bird was shot in 1813.

Some rare migrants have been recorded on Papa Westray particularly during easterlies in spring and autumn.

The best sites are: North Hill RSPB Reserve. This is the largest ternery in Europe with about 100,000 Arctic tern and some common and sandwich tern. There are also arctic skua (constantly nagging the terns), eider, four gull species, several wader species, and colonies of guillemot, kittiwake, razorbill, puffin and some black guillemot. Sooty shearwater and long-tailed skua can be seen at sea.

Holm of Papa: here there is, possibly, the largest breeding colony of black guillemot in Britain – some 130 pairs at the last count. There are also gulls, terns and some storm petrel.

Loch of St Tredwell: this was a former breeding site of the red-necked phalarope and many varieties of wildfowl and waders breed here.

Mid-May to July, and August to mid-October, are the best birdwatching times.

The attractive 'priest' island of **PAPA WESTRAY** has a long association with early Christianity. In fact it is claimed that this was the fountainhead of Christianity in Orkney.

But it has a much longer association with early man. The **Knap of Howar** on the west coast is a settlement that has been dated to about 3700BC [HY483518]. Two solidly-built stone houses, which are thought to be the oldest preserved domestic dwellings in northern Europe, stand side by side, facing the turbulent 'Röst' of Papa Sound. They are near the airstrip and the **House of Holland** (ON *há-land* – high land), former home of the Traills of Holland, past owners of the entire island [HY488515].

The flight across Papa Sound from Westray is the shortest scheduled air-flight in the world according to the *Guinness Book of Records*. It normally takes two minutes but was once accomplished in fifty-eight seconds; the distance between the two airstrips is less than the length of Heathrow's longest runway.

North of the airfield is Munkerhoose religious site where the early Christian anchorites probably set up camp. A small pre-Reformation **Church of St Boniface** is built on the site of a much earlier building [HY488527]. Boniface was known as the 'German Apostle' for as a missionary bishop he converted much of Germany to Christianity. Several stone Celtic crosses from the graveyard can now be seen in the Tankerness Museum at Kirkwall and the Royal Scottish Museum at Edinburgh. A Viking grave remains on the site with a carved hog-backed gravestone of red sandstone. Nearby, a roundhouse (*c.* 900BC) has recently been excavated where the cliffs are being eroded by the sea.

Papa Westray's fertile soil supports a number of active smallholdings, although some are now owned by absentee Westray farmers. The islanders are fighting to maintain their community in spite of a dwindling population. The shop closed in the 1980s and the resident doctor left but they formed a co-operative to run a community shop and hostel.

The north of the island is devoted to the RSPB's famous **North Hill Nature Reserve**, a wonderland for birdwatchers. **North Hill** is the island's highest point at 48m. Beneath the low cliffs of the northern tip, Mull

Head, there is a notoriously dangerous tidal race called 'The Bore'. During gales even the sea bottom 40m below the surface is savagely scoured by the cross-currents, and erosion is almost continuous.

The large expanse of the Loch of St Tredwell, with many wildfowl nesting on its shallow shores, is at the opposite end of the island. On a small peninsula on its east bank is a tiny ruined chapel, the **Chapel of St Tredwell** [HY496509]. Triduana or Tredwell was a devout 8th century Celtic girl who is said to have lived alone on this little peninsula. Nechtan, King of the Picts, told her that he

was aroused to passion by her beautiful eyes and attempted to rape her but his ardour was quickly dampened when she plucked out her eyes and handed them to him. It is said that this proves that spiritual attributes are more important to a true Christian than physical ones. The blind girl was later rewarded by being made abbess of a nunnery at Restalrig in Midlothian and in due course she was canonised.

The chapel, which is dedicated to her, became by the 12th century a place of pilgrimage for anyone with eye troubles. There used to be a spring beside it at which pilgrims would bathe their eyes. Bishop John of Caithness claimed to have regained his sight here in 1201 after being blinded by Earl Harald.

The east coast has two large bays, North and South Wick, which are separated by an islet, **Holm of Papa**. Even this tiny piece of Orkney has its remnants of prehistory for there are several cairns and the largest is a chambered cairn, 35m long by 16m wide [HY509518]. The walls are as thick as those of Midhowe (See Rousay No.10.20). There is a narrow central chamber with compartments at each end and small cells opening off it – ten single and two double cells. On the walls are unusual 'eyebrow' decorations. The cairn was first opened in 1849 but no human remains were found in it. However, it is contemporary with the houses at Knap of Howar – older than Maes howe on Mainland – and may have been the place where these people buried their dead.

ACCESS: Orkney Islands Shipping vehicle-ferry from Kirkwall and surrounding islands, weekdays, 01856-872044. BA Express scheduled flights from Kirkwall, Westray and Eday, 01856-872494 or 0345-222111. The island boat (T. Rendall), 01857-677216. Accommodation enquiries, 01857-644267.

Anchorages:

1. Bay of Moclett, between Head of Moclett and Vest Ness, the S extremity. Excellent anchorage, sand. Avoid submarine cable and ferry approach. Good holding but exposed S.

2. South Wick, on E coast, W of Holm of Papa. Very shallow, sandy bay, 2m and less in depth. Anchor off pier on E side or off Holm of Papa ESE of the pier.

3. North Wick. Occasional anchorage, sand and stones, 4-5m. Best approach at LW to avoid reefs. Beware rock and shoal in NW area.

10.27 North Ronaldsay

The name is of uncertain derivation. The Norse name was Rinansøy (?Ringa's isle) so it is almost certainly not derived from (ON Ragnvalds-øy – Ronald's island).

OS Maps: 1:50000 Sheet 5 1:25000 Sheet 22
Admiralty Charts: 1:200000 No.1942 or 1954 1:75000 No.2250

AREA: 690ha (1,705 acres)
HEIGHT: 20m (66 ft)

OWNER: Multiple ownership. Bought by James Traill, an Edinburgh lawyer, for £2,222 in 1727 and held by the Traill family until quite recently when some of the tenants purchased their properties and became owner-occupiers.

POPULATION: 1841 – 481 (92 houses). 1881 – 547. 1891 – 501 (86 houses). 1931 – 298. 1961 – 161. 1971 – 134. 1981 – 121. 1991 – 92.

GEOLOGY: Old Red Sandstone of Rousay Flags mainly greyish or bluish in colour. The south and east coasts have wide sandy beaches, north and west is more rocky. There is no peat and a shortage of fuel has always been a problem.

HISTORY: In spite of its remote location the island has been continuously occupied since prehistoric times.

King Harfagar of Norway had a son called Halfdan Highlegs who fought a sea battle against Earl Einar (Torf Einar – the first man to cut peat for fuel) in North Ronaldsay Firth. Halfdan lost the battle and swam ashore but Einar followed and slew him.

Rinansøy (North Ronaldsay) is mentioned on a number of other occasions in the Norse sagas.

In November 1983 North Ronaldsay was connected to the national grid and received electricity for the first time.

WILDLIFE: The range of habitat and lack of human interference encourages a wide selection of wildlife – everything from breeding seals to a wealth of botanical varieties.

Apart from the usual Orkney plant-life there are rare examples of the Arctic sandwort, *arenaria norvegica*, and skull-cap, *scutellaria galericubata*.

The island is noted for its primitive sheep which exist on a diet of seaweed except when lambing. They are small, goat-like in shape, and variously coloured, and they produce very fine wool and delicious dark mutton. They are descendants of the original Orkney sheep, well adapted to the environment and producing their best mutton in mid-winter just when it is most needed. The flock is maintained at around 4000 head with each family having an agreed allocation according to an elected committee – The Sheep Court. Because of their diet of seaweed an oil-spill could have disastrous consequences so a small flock is now kept in England as a safeguard.

This remote island also has wonderful birdlife – in many ways equal to Fair Isle (No.11.1) and a bird observatory was therefore established here in 1987. There are records of fifty-one breeding species of which thirty-four are regular and there is a colony of about fifty pairs of cormorant on Seal Skerry. Mute swan, shelduck, teal, gadwall, pintail, mallard, eider, shoveller, coot, moorhen, water rail, oystercatcher, ringed plover, lapwing, snipe, curlew, redshank, common and herring gulls, rock dove, sandwich tern, skylark, meadow and rock pipits, pied wagtail, wren, blackbird, hooded crow, starling, house sparrow, reed bunting, twite, raven, and the rare corncrake are all in evidence.

Hedgehogs were thoughtlessly introduced in 1972 (although fortunately there are still no rats) with a consequent loss of many ground nests but a scheme to remove them was introduced. Many migrant birds can be seen including continental passerine migrants. Rarities which have been recorded are the olive-backed pipit, Spanish sparrow, Pallas's rosefinch, snowy owl and the pine bunting. At sea, Sabine's gull, long-tailed skua, Leach's petrel and sooty shearwater may be seen.

Apart from birds, Seal Skerry – Orkney's most northern rock – supports large colonies of both grey and common seals during the breeding season.

NORTH RONALDSAY has many similarities with Papa Westray (No.10.26), in size, population, and land use but its situation is even more remote. It is low-lying – nowhere is the ground higher than 20m above sea-level – extensively cultivated and studded with cottages. The inhabitants make up a closely-knit and competent community, well-able to cope with their isolated situation. The County Library apparently has a full-time job keeping them supplied with books, while even the average Orcadian has quite a struggle understanding the local dialect. This contains many similarities to the traditional Norn dialect which was at one time the language of Orkney.

Because of its unique, primitive, seaweed-eating sheep the entire island is surrounded by the **Sheep Dyke**, a wall about 2m high. This great construction which was completed in the mid-19th century ensures that the sheep stay on the seashore because, although they survive well on seaweed, they would eat the local agricultural produce for choice. It is only when they are lambing that they are allowed to vary their diet.

Normally the dyke is maintained by the islanders as a matter of course, but in 1993 the worst storms in fifty years knocked down more than 3km of the 20km of wall allowing the scruffy little sheep to wander all over the farmland. The island community was much too small to undertake such a massive repair by itself so the Royal Navy came to the rescue and helped to rebuild the wall and save the crops.

In the past, communal farms or groups of smallholdings in Orkney were defined by boundary walls which have, in general, long since disappeared. But this is not so on North Ronaldsay where many farming traditions can still be identified and two old boundary dykes, **Matches Dyke** and **Muckle Gersty** stretch right across the island in the form of raised mounds, dividing the island into three roughly equal portions.

Another old tradition is the use of 'plantiecruives,' miniature walled gardens outside the sheep dyke by the seashore. These are used as cold frames to bring on the young kale plants, wind-proof and relatively frost-free.

North Ronaldsay was first occupied in the remote past and the first settlers have left much evidence of their activities. There is a standing stone near **Loch Gretchen** which is about 4m high and pierced by a hole [HY752529]. Two hundred years ago the islanders still danced round this stone on the night of the New Year but the meaning of the ritual has been forgotten.

The remains of a settlement at **Kirbist** [HY758523] may be another Skara Brae (see No.10.10) and there is also an unusual ruin near Hooking Loch which could be a primitive house.

At **Strom Ness**, the southern tip of the island,

Burrian Broch has walls 4$\frac{1}{2}$m thick and four concentric ramparts on the side facing the land [HY762514]. Objects inscribed with Pictish symbols have been found in it and there are the remains of a settlement alongside. Unfortunately this site is now in some danger of being washed away by the sea.

A hazardous patch of rocks called **Reef Dyke** lies off Bride's Ness in the south-west. Many ships have been wrecked here including, the wreck of an armed merchant ship of the Swedish East India Company, the *Svecia*, which went down in 1740 with two-thirds of its crew and a valuable cargo of silks and spices. It was investigated by marine archaeologists in 1975.

ACCESS: One return service weekly by Orkney Islands Shipping, 01856-872044. BA Express scheduled flights from Kirkwall, Eday and Sanday, 01856-872494 or 01345-222111.

Anchorages:
1. Linklet Bay, S of Dennis Head. Occasional anchorage in 7m-9m, sand. Best off jetty at N of bay. Exposed to E.
2. South Bay between Twingess and Strom Ness. Temp anchorage in middle of bay, 7m, sand. Exposed S to W and liable to swell. Sufficient depth to lie alongside pier but also subject to swell.

THE SEAWEED-EATING SHEEP OF NORTH RONALDSAY

Fair Isle and the Shetland Islands

N

Out Skerry

29. Unst

28. Balta

27. Linga

26. Uyea

24. Fetlar

23. Yell

25. Hascosay

21. Brother Isle

20. Bigga

22. Lamba

19. Samphrey

18. Out Skerries

16. West Linga

17. Linga

15. Whalsay

13. Vementry

Ve Skerries

12. Papa Little

14. Papa Stour

11. Mainland

10. Vaila

7. Noss

9. Hildasay

4. Oxna

5. Papa

8. Bressay

6. Foula

3. South Havra

2. Mousa

1. Fair Isle

Section 11

Section 11, Table 1

No.	Name	Latitude	Longitude	Table 2* No.	Table 3** No.	Area in Acres		Area in Hectares
11.1	Fair Isle	59° 32N	01° 38W	49	30	1898		768
11.2	Mousa	60° 00N	01° 10W	91	113	445		180
11.3	South Havra	60° 02N	01° 21W	141	132	146		59
11.4	Oxna	60° 07N	01° 22W	135	136	168		68
11.5	Papa	60° 07N	01° 21W	142	147	146		59
11.6	Foula	60° 08N	02° 04W	37	13	3126		1265
11.7	Noss	60° 09N	01° 01W	65	39	847		343
11.8	Bressay	60° 09N	01° 05W	26	29	6931		2805
11.9	Hildasay	60° 09N	01° 21W	111	149	267		108
11.10	Vaila	60° 12N	01° 36W	66	75	808		327
11.11	Mainland	60° 15N	01° 20W	2	9	239388	96879	
	Muckle Roe	60° 22N	01° 25W			4381	1773	
	West Burra	60° 05N	01° 20W			1836	743	
	East Burra	60° 04N	01° 19W			1273	515	
	Trondra	60° 07N	01° 17W			680	275	
	Uyea	60° 37N	01° 25W			111	45	100230
11.12	Papa Little	60° 20N	01° 23W	83	84	558		226
11.13	Vementry	60° 20N	01° 28W	63	79	914		370
11.14	Papa Stour	60° 20N	01° 42W	47	82	2046		828
11.15	Whalsay	60° 21N	00° 58W	31	58	4868		1970
11.16	West Linga	60° 22N	01° 02W	104	118	309		125
11.17	Linga (Olna Firth)	60° 22N	01° 22W	133	95	173		70
11.18	Housay (Out Skerries)	60° 25N	00° 46W	84	116	403	163	
	Bruray	60° 25N	00° 45W			136	55	218
11.19	Samphrey	60° 28N	01° 09W	138	153	163		66
11.20	Bigga	60° 30N	01° 11W	126	145	193		78
11.21	Brother Isle	60° 31N	01° 13W	165	159	99		40
11.22	Lamba	60° 31N	01° 17W	160	143	106		43
11.23	Yell	60° 35N	01° 05W	9	34	52412		21211
11.24	Fetlar	60° 36N	00° 52W	22	44	10077		4078
11.25	Hascosay	60° 37N	00° 59W	73	152	680		275
11.26	Uyea	60° 40N	00° 54W	86	120	507		205
11.27	Linga (Bluemull Sd)	60° 40N	00° 59W	159	158	111		45
11.28	Balta	60° 45N	00° 47W	124	128	198		80
11.29	Unst	60° 46N	00° 52W	12	23	29820		12068

* Table 2: The islands arranged in order of magnitude
** Table 3: The islands arranged in order of height

Introduction

It is extremely rare to find a map of the British Isles in which the Shetland archipelago is shown in its true position. Almost invariably it is squeezed into a small inset. The result is that nearly everyone on mainland Britain fails to appreciate that Shetland, as the northern outpost of the British Isles, is closer to Bergen than to Aberdeen – and that Muckle Flugga is further from the Scottish/English border than Lands End.

Shetland was to the Norsemen what Gibraltar was to the British – a key naval base conveniently situated where world sea-routes converged. When the North Atlantic is seen from the correct viewpoint it is clear why the Vikings used Shetland as their first landfall, whether to raid Ireland, trade with the Isle of Man, or cross the Atlantic to Greenland.

Although they had no magnetic compasses these remarkable navigators could not only use a crude sextant and gnomonic (sun/shadow) compass by day, and follow the stars at night, but they also knew how to read the ocean swell – a method still known to the Polynesians –

and follow natural indicators such as the drift of seaweed and the flight of seabirds.

Take the story of 'Raven' Flokki and his two beautiful daughters. There was said to be a Land of Ice and Volcanoes beyond the Faeroes and Flokki wanted to find it and make it his home. So he set sail from Norway but when he had reached Shetland one of his daughters, Geirhild, died and he buried her beside the loch which still bears her name, Loch of Girlsta. Flokki then sailed on to the Faeroes where his second daughter met and married an islander and would travel no further. Flokki was determined to continue although no one could tell him how to reach the land of Ice – only that they thought it was in the direction of the setting sun. So Flokki captured three ravens and sailed west. After a few days he released the first raven and saw it fly back the way he had come. The next day he released the second raven, but it flew ever higher and was lost to sight. The following day he released his last raven which flew high, but then set course to the north-west. He followed it and reached his chosen land, and that is how Flokki became the first Ice-lander.

In the Icelandic sagas, which were put in writing in the 13th century, Shetland is consistently called *Hjaltland* and that is still the Icelandic name. This has led to all sorts of scholarly assumptions regarding the derivation of the Norse name although in the Faeroe Islands and West Norway it was known as *Hetland*. In 1221 one of Henry III's clerks at Westminster called Shetland *Heclandensis* and the pope's clerk in 1226 called it *Ihatlandensis*. But in 1289 the Norwegian king in a letter to the English king called it plain *Shetland* although in 1299 in Shetland itself it was written as *Hiatlandi*.

The pre-Norse name for Shetland was *Inse Catt* according to early Irish documents, i.e. the islands of the Catt tribe, whose totem was a cat. This was the same tribe that gave its name to Caithness – Catt Cape. The equivalent name for Orkney was *Inse Orc* – islands of the tribe of Orc, whose totem was an *orc* or boar.

The Icelandic, and assumed early Norse, name of *Hjaltland* has been variously interpreted by the experts as

Viking settlement c. 870AD

GREENLAND

Arctic Circle

4 " ....then south of Iceland from where you meet birds and whales."

3 " ....and south of the Faeroes of which only half the height emerges above the horizon..."

2 "You steer north of Shetland which is only just visible..."

1 "From Hernum in Norway you sail due west towards Greenland..."

Extracts of text from the Viking 'Hauksbok'

The Viking route to Greenland and beyond...

meaning 'high land', 'land shaped like the hilt of a sword', or 'Hjalti's land' (whoever Hjalti may have been). I am sure these are all carefully considered and learned interpretations but the Norwegian historian, A W Brøgger, has suggested that the Norsemen were merely talking of the land of Catt, or Cattland. As they would have pronounced Catt as 'chat', i.e. chatland, – this seems to me to be an absolutely brilliant piece of common sense.

In spite of its northern situation Shetland's winter climate is only marginally colder than that of mainland Britain thanks to the North Atlantic Drift. This is an extension of the Gulf Stream. Summers are certainly cooler but the very long hours of daylight tend to compensate. In fact in midsummer the Simmer Dim (the summer gloaming) is an unforgettable experience. Wind speeds can be high, and sometimes very high, but rainfall is not excessive and less than that of many areas of the British mainland.

Shetland's geology is very different from that of Orkney,

although there are some large areas of Orkney's ubiquitous Old Red Sandstone. Generally, though, the rocks are Precambrian and of the Dalradian group giving an undulating rather than a slab-shaped profile. These rocks do not decompose into fertile soil. Consequently, there are large areas of blanket peat and few rock outcrops. The coastlines have been eroded to form high cliffs and whereas Orkney's cliffs are mainly limited to its Atlantic coast – Shetlands intrude everywhere.

Shetland, like the south of England, and the Outer Hebrides to a lesser degree, is sinking and at a rate sufficient to make a marked difference in the last few centuries. A mere century ago one could walk from Muckle Roe to Mainland at low water.

The geology and poor soil combine to create a landscape which is more primitively picturesque than that of Orkney but in spite of the poverty of much of the soil there is a feeling of affluence which is not entirely due to the oil industry. Perhaps it can be attributed to the rich character and open generosity of the Shetland islanders themselves.

11.1 Fair Isle

Referred to in the sagas as (ON frioar-øy – *fair isle) but a derivation from (ON* feoer-øy – *far off isle) seems more plausible.*

OS Maps: 1:50000 Sheet 4 1:25000 Sheet 22
Admiralty Charts: 1:200000 No.1942 or 1119 1:25000 No.2622

AREA: 768ha (1,898 acres)
HEIGHT: 217m (712 ft)

OWNER: Acquired by the National Trust for Scotland (NTS) in 1954 from Mr George Waterston with the help of Lord Bruntisfield.

POPULATION: In 1701 the population was decimated by smallpox but it recovered and in 1790 was 220. 1841 – 232 (35 houses). 1861 – 380. 134 emigrated to Nova Scotia in 1862. 1881 – 214. 1891 – 223 (34 houses). 1931 – 108. 1955 – about 50. There was talk of evacuation but the NTS improved amenities and encouraged repopulation. 1961 – 64. 1971 – 65. 1981 – 69. 1991 – 67.

GEOLOGY: Red sandstone cliffs and natural sandstone arches and stacks surround the island. The highest cliffs are in the north but Sheep Rock in the south-east has some of the finest arches. There is copper ore on Fair Isle at Copper Geo.

HISTORY: In the Norse saga of *Burnt Njal*, Kari the viking came from Iceland and landed on Fair Isle. He spent the winter there, staying with his good friend David the White. And in the *Orkneyinga Saga* Earl Rognvald sent Uni to Fair Isle in preparation for his invasion of Orkney. When the time was due, Uni soaked a warning beacon with water so that it could not be lit and the Earl was able to pass Fair Isle and land on Westray (No.10.25) unopposed.

In 1588 the 38-gun *El Gran Grifon*, a Spanish fleet auxiliary flagship was wrecked at Fair Isle. After the Armada's defeat she had withstood an attack in the English Channel by Sir Francis Drake's *Revenge* but managed to escape northwards. Then on a night in late summer there was a severe squall and she ran onto the rocks in Sivars Geo, on the south-east side of Fair Isle. About 200 men survived the catastrophe and struggled ashore. They had already been without food for days and were weak and starving. The islanders supplied what little food they had but found it difficult to support such a large number of extra mouths. As the rations were small the men set about raiding the winter stocks, killing poultry and slaughtering the few precious cattle and sheep until, in desperation, the islanders managed to round them up and ship them off to Shetland. There they were well-fed and well-treated until they were repatriated. In 1984 a Spanish delegation dressed as conquistadors dedicated an iron cross in the island's kirkyard to those who had died.

This was just one wreck out of many. A survey has shown that, up to the advent of radar, there was a major shipwreck on the rocks of Fair Isle every four to five years on average.

In 1630 Fair Isle became part of the Shetland estates of Sinclair of Quendale and it was held by his family until 1750. They obtained rent from twenty-four households in four townships and a 'Hamburg Merchant's' booth by the south harbour.

For several centuries the Dutch had turned herring fishing into a very profitable industry. Their fishing boats or 'busses' crowded the waters of Orkney and Shetland protected by naval men-of-war and the catches were exported to Europe, the Mediterranean, and even South America. The French cast covetous eyes on this wealth and in a famous sea-battle in 1702 their navy attacked

FAIR ISLE POST OFFICE, SHIRVA. A POST OFFICE WAS OPENED AT SOUTH HARBOUR IN 1877. IT MOVED HERE IN 1948.

Dutch men-of-war off Fair Isle with some success.

In 1770 Fair Isle was purchased by Stewart of Brough in Sanday, Orkney, and in 1866 was sold to J. Bruce of Sumburgh.

WILDLIFE: About 240 different species of flowering plant have been recorded, including juniper, which is rarely found elsewhere in Shetland. White campion and reed grass are widespread with swathes of blue spring squill and thrift. There are also examples of the rarer orchids. Heather and cranberry are common, and dwarf willow

and alpine bistort can be found in the hilly moorland.

Like Hirta (No.9.1), Fair Isle has its own distinctive sub-species – the Fair Isle wren (*troglodytes troglodytes fridarienis*) and the Fair Isle fieldmouse (*apodemus sylvaticus fridarienis*). The rabbits are so multi-coloured that some could be wearing Fair Isle jerseys, but they have not yet achieved the status of a separate sub-species.

The Bird Observatory was founded in 1948 by George Waterston, a well-known ornithologist, who bought the island because of its exceptionally interesting birdlife. Over 345 species of bird have been recorded, which is more than anywhere else in Britain, and well over 220,000 birds of about eighty different species have been ringed such as puffin, pipit, wheatear, brambling, fieldfare, redwing, crossbill, siskin and sometimes, Lapland bunting, barred warbler and pied woodpecker.

There are large colonies of seabirds including great and arctic skua. Other breeding species are eider, oystercatcher, ringed plover, lapwing, and snipe. Curlew, whimbrel and dunlin occasionally breed here and breeding passerines include raven, wren, starling, house sparrow, twite, wheatear, white and pied wagtail, skylark, and rock and meadow pipit.

The best all-round months for birdwatching are April, late June to early September, and late October. The best time to spot rare migrants is between mid-September and late October when the wind is from the east.

FAIR ISLE lies twenty-four miles south-west of Shetland's Sumburgh Head which is roughly half-way between the two northern archipelagoes. It has a distinctive outline with high red sandstone cliffs in the north sloping down to a low, bare southern coastline. **Ward Hill** (217m) in the north-west is the highest part of the island. The Hill Dyke and the ancient Feelie Dyke separate the northern hill-grazing land from the southern fields.

The majority of the inhabitants live in the south where there is a limited amount of ground suitable for cultivation. Here, the scattered settlement of **Stonybreck** (ON *brekke* – hillside) includes a post-office, general store, school, museum, Church of Scotland kirk, and Methodist chapel (each used on alternate Sundays).

The airstrip is centrally situated and to the east of it is the **Bird Observatory and Hostel**. East again, **Bu Ness** (ON – home headland) is only joined to the island by a very narrow isthmus dividing two relatively sheltered bays, North and South Haven. **North Haven** is the port for the passenger ferry, *The Good Shepherd*. Rough roads continue north from the airstrip and the Bird Observatory (roads south of the airstrip are macadamed). One road leads to the radio mast by Ward Hill, and the other serves the lighthouse on **The Nizz** (ON *nes* – the headland). Both the island lighthouses were built by Stevenson in 1892. In this area, known as **Skroo** (ON – stack of oats built to withstand winter gales), the cliffs have been savagely bent by primaeval forces and perforated with caves and natural arches by the sea. But this is in keeping with the whole north of the island which is generally wild and barren. In summer the Ward Hill area becomes a test of nerve as the great skua, or 'bonxies', dive-bomb all intruders.

Once again long sea crossings obviously did not deter early man for there are a number of tumuli which date back to about 3500BC (Houlalie is the largest) and an Iron Age fort is at Landberg near the Observatory [HZ226722].

The population decline was halted thanks to the timely intervention of the ornithologist George Waterston who gained international recognition for the island by publicising its varied birdlife. He had visited it regularly since 1935 but while a prisoner-of-war in Germany he dreamed of purchasing the island and setting up a bird observatory. After the war he realised his dream and in due course he also enabled the National Trust for Scotland to continue the good work. The Trust improved the mail-boat pier, good communications being the essential ingredient for a viable island community, and also improved much of the property. The Bird Observatory and Hostel was rebuilt in 1969 with accommodation for twenty-four visitors.

The one-teacher school which was built in 1880 is still going strong. At the age of twelve pupils go to a boarding school in Lerwick for their secondary education. In 1980 a new school hall was built by the community, with help from the authorities and the NTS. Although it is used by the school during the day it becomes a popular community hall in the evenings.

Apart from those directly involved with the Nature Reserve or in community service, the main occupation is crofting, supplemented by some fishing, and the knitting of traditional jerseys. The distinctive, brightly-coloured and non-repetitive geometric patterns of Fair Isle knitwear are sometimes said to have been introduced by the shipwrecked Spanish sailors from *El Gran Grifon* but it is almost certain that they were an insular development from traditional Nordic designs.

Although this rocky island would seem to be a climber's paradise, with the semi-detached headland of **Sheep Rock** south of Bu Ness considered a prime test of climbing ability, the stone is reported to be of poor quality and unreliable. However as the top of Sheep Rock provided four hectares of valuable pasture the islanders used to climb it with chains and then used ropes to raise and lower the sheep.

A few examples of the traditional Shetland boat – the 'yoal' – can still be found at Fair Isle. She is a lightweight craft with a raked stem and stern, clinker-built, and very similar to the Danish Gokstad ship of 1000 years ago. The islanders used their yoals to trade with passing ships but the construction of the lighthouses stopped this practice as ships then gave the island a wide berth.

The Thief's Hole in the cliff face of **Malcolm's Head**, behind Fogli Stack, was the traditional smugglers' or press-gang hideout. Another feature of interest is an 80m subterranean passage, the **Kirn of Scroo**, at the North Light which ends in a 'gloup' or borehole.

ACCESS: Regular passenger boat service from Grutness (Sumburgh), Shetland to North Haven; bi-weekly in summer, fortnightly in winter, weather permitting, 01595-760222. Regular flights by Loganair from Tingwall,

01595-840246. Permission to stay at Bird Observatory hostel (ornithologists get priority) from Warden, 01595-760258. There are NTS work parties in the summer to restore buildings, 0131-226 5922.

Anchorages:

1. North Haven, Bu Ness. Small secure harbour (built 1992) but limited space for lying alongside. Anchorage possible but occasional swell and very restricted space. Follow leading marks for entry. Mail-boat pier was built 1958 and slipway 1981.

2. South Harbour, a small bay at the S end between Meo Ness and Head of Tind. Recognised anchorage and landing place but full of dangers and probably best avoided.

3. South Haven, Bu Ness. Temp anchorage in N'lies but poor holding due to rocky bottom. Anchor in 4m. Careful entry required.

11.2 Mousa

[moo-së] (ON mós-øy – moor or mossy island)

OS Maps: 1:50000 Sheet 4 1:25000 Sheet 20
Admiralty Charts: 1:200000 No.1119 1:75000 No.3283

AREA: 180ha (445 acres)
HEIGHT: 55m (180 ft)

POPULATION: 1774 – 11 families. 1841 – 12. 1861 – 0 and uninhabited since.

GEOLOGY: The old quarry on Mousa was the source of many of the flagstones used for the streets of Lerwick.

Copper ore is to be found at Sand Lodge on Mainland, just opposite Mousa.

HISTORY: Mousa, and its famous broch, are best remembered for their part in the sagas.

According to the Icelandic *Egil's Saga* about 900AD a young man in Norway, Bjorn, fell in love with a girl called Thora Jewel-hand. They eloped from her family home and he took her to his mother's house on the Sogne fjord where she stayed throughout the winter, virtue intact. In the spring Bjorn's father gave him a trading-ship and suggested that he make for Dublin where business was good. His parents wanted Thora to remain with them until his return but the couple would not be separated and Thora sailed with him. A violent storm blew up and they were in grave danger but they managed with difficulty to run the ship aground on Mousa. The young lovers married and made the ancient broch into their honeymoon home for the winter. Meanwhile the crew set about repairing the ship.

The following spring news came that Thora's family had persuaded King Harald of Norway to outlaw Bjorn. As his ship was now ready for sea Bjorn and Thora sought refuge in Iceland. It was another stormy voyage but they were given a very friendly welcome on arrival. Not long after, Thora produced a daughter called Asgerd and they all lived happily ever after.

In the Norse *Orkneyinga Saga* the story is told of

THE BROCH
OF MOUSA

Map labels:

The Tara · Caves · Cave · Round Geo · Catti Geo · North Croo Geo · 41 The Hamars · South Croo Geo · NORTH ISLE · East Ham · Tidal Pond · Caves · Holes of Burro · Blow Geo · Piltock Geo · Jetty · Hamlee Taing · Footpath · Burnt Mound · Cave · Under Lee · West Ham · Natural Arch · Hesti Taing · Private Ferry · Mid Field · 55 · Perie Bard · Scarfi Stack · Ca. · 25 · SOUTH ISLE · East Pool · Jetty · Bard Sound · Homestead · Mousa Sound · Burgi Ayre · Knowe (ruin) · Muckle Bard · Broch of Mousa · Burnt Mounds · West Pool · Pond · Piltock Geo · Natural Arch · The Haa · Well · The Swarf · Cave · 35 · Green Head · Masti Geo · Hoga · Caves · Broch (ruin) · The Cellar · MAINLAND (Shetland)

2 km · 1 mile

Margaret, wife of Earl Maddad of Atholl, daughter of Earl Haakon and mother of Earl Harald. After the death of her husband, the mature but beautiful Margaret, wasted no time in moving in with Gunni, brother of the buccaneering Sweyn Asleifsson of Gairsay (see No.10.13). She soon became pregnant but Margaret was mercurial, oversexed, and not really made for motherhood. She gave birth to the child in 1153 but, growing tired of Gunni, she turned her attention to a handsome young man from Shetland, Earl Erland Ungi son of Harald the Fair-spoken. She was of course only too delighted to be carried off to Shetland by Erland and taken to the broch on Mousa. There the couple established their love nest and, although the broch does not look particularly cosy by present-day standards, no doubt love overcame all discomforts. At least the chosen spot was private and defensible, which was important as it

was not long before Margaret's twenty-year-old son, Earl Harald Maddadson, besieged it. He was enraged by his mother's behaviour but her hide-out proved 'an unhandy place to get at'. So, in the end, after a long siege he agreed to forgive her provided she married Erland. This she did and after the ceremony Harald sailed them over to Norway for a legitimate honeymoon.

WILDLIFE: The most noticeable life-forms are sheep, seals, and sea-birds. The seals, both common and grey, particularly favour East and West Ham.

Botanically the island has an interesting mixture of moorland and salt-water plants.

Breeding species of birds include great and arctic skuas, eider, storm petrel, fulmar, many arctic tern and black guillemot. A colony of storm petrel and a few rock doves nest in the broch's drystone walls and migrant waders frequent the lochans.

Two men fishing in a small boat off **MOUSA** in September 1779 were surprised when a strange ship approached from the south and asked for help. They climbed aboard only to discover that it was a French warship wanting to be piloted into Lerwick harbour. They immediately lied to the French saying that two powerful British warships were waiting in Lerwick. They were able to describe the ships because they had seen them sailing south some months before. This persuaded the French not to attack Lerwick but they refused to release the two fishermen. Months later the French man-of-war – still with its two prisoners aboard – was captured by a British ship, and strangely enough it turned out to be one of the actual British ships which the men had lied about! So nearly a year after their abortive fishing trip the two well-travelled fishermen returned home.

To the Vikings an island was a piece of land which a boat could circumnavigate but the term 'circumnavigation' included transporting a boat across dry land. It was for this reason that the Mull of Kintyre was judged to be an island. Similarly little Mousa counted as two islands, **North Isle** and **South Isle**, because it has a narrow waist or isthmus which a boat could be carried across.

North Isle is the smaller part and rises to a height of 41m. It is divided from South Isle by two bays, **West Ham** (ON *ham* – harbour) and East Ham. South Isle's highest point is **Mid Field** at 55m and there is a further small hill in the south which rises to 35m. The south-east is indented to form what are almost two drying islands with saltwater pools separating them, **Muckle Bard** and **Perie Bard** (ON – big and subordinate sandbar or reef). A lighthouse stands on Perie Bard.

There are two tiny lochans on Mousa, one on each 'island', with ancient tumuli beside the southern loch. The remains of old farm-buildings are on an attractive site above this loch and nearer the east coast is a ruined water mill. There is also an old two-storeyed building known as **The Haa** [HU458236]. On the east coast itself the wreck of the first *St Sunniva* can be seen. She ran aground in 1930 in thick fog.

On the western shore, the world's finest, best-preserved, and most complete broch can be clearly seen from Mainland across the Mousa Sound. The **Broch of Mousa**, dating from the Iron Age, has lost its upper courses but is still some 13m tall. It is a very fine example of the craft of the ancient builders. Unlike many other brochs there is no sign of a surrounding settlement – the broch of Mousa appears to stand alone. The external diameter at ground level is about 15m with the walls gracefully curved inwards so that the upper diameter is about 12m. The circular internal courtyard is approximately 6m in diameter and contains a wheelhouse which was probably added in the 2nd or 3rd century. The stairs between the double walls lead upwards through six galleries.

Many brochs have been built in tandem facing each other over a stretch of water, and this broch is no exception as on a headland projecting into Mousa Sound there are the remains of its sister Broch of Burraland. The real purpose of these structures, built before the Roman invasion of British waters, is still a mystery.

Mousa's broch is built of small stones of a local schistose slate meticulously laid dry to give a smooth exterior. The workmanship is quite remarkable when one remembers that timber was an exceptionally scarce commodity and the curved walls were probably built without templates and to a line depending on the eye of the stonemason. This skill and accuracy has resulted in a building, possibly 1000 years old at the time of the Vikings and now 1000 years older still, appearing today as though the builders had just laid the last stone and gone home for the night.

ACCESS: Boat by private arrangement in summer from Leebotten pier, (Mr Tom Jamieson – 01950-431367). 15 min. crossing time. No dogs allowed.

Anchorages: Near the broch the bottom is rock and unsuitable for anchoring. 1. West Ham, Mousa Sound – a bay 1/2M N of the broch. There is a cottage and boat slip. Anchor in 4m, sand. Sheltered from NW through N to E. Fresh S'lies cause a swell.

11.3 South Havra

(ON hafr-øy – ewe island). Less probable alternatives are (ON havari-øy – shipwreck island) or (ON – Halvor's island). Formerly written as Halvera and Hevera.

OS Maps: 1:50000 Sheet 4 1:25000 Sheet 20
Admiralty Charts: 1:75000 No.3283 1:25000 No.3294

AREA: 59ha (146 acres)
HEIGHT: 42m (138 ft)

POPULATION: 1841 – 37. 1881 – 35. 1891 – 24 (4 houses). Uninhabited since 1923.

GEOLOGY: Soil with no peat deposits over an area of epidotic syenite, undifferentiated schist and gneiss.

HISTORY: South Havra was the home of the Foud (Magistrate) of all Shetland, Olaf Sinclair, in the 16th century. He was also laird of the great odal estate of Brew.

South Shetland occasionally suffered raids by men from Lewis (No.8.16). There was one such raid which ended in a pitched battle at Sumburgh in which sixty men died. It is said that Olaf Sinclair only escaped death by diving off the high cliffs at Sumburgh Head.

SOUTH HAVRA could easily be called the island of shipwrecks as it lies directly across the southern approach to the comparatively sheltered waters of Clift Sound and the Burras. The east side is steep-to but elsewhere there are reefs and skerries galore particularly in the channel between South Havra and Little Havra and also stretching north from Little Havra to the west of Croo Taing. The cliffs and broken shoreline of both islands are made up of a tumble of interesting rock formations perforated with caves and arches.

Eight families were living on the island until May 1923 when they all decided to leave. Up to that time it seems to have been a viable small community with a full-time schoolteacher and eight pupils. The ground was fertile and productive and, although there was no peat for fuel, this could be found at Deepdale on the Mainland shore. However, the operation was not easy as the peat had to be brought down the hillside on a sledge, controlled by ropes to stop it falling over the cliff and into the sea. It then had to be manhandled across the slippery rocks and into a heaving boat. It must have been difficulties such as these which persuaded the islanders to abandon their homes.

The island's summit is 42m high and on top of it stands the conspicuous ruin of a **windmill** which itself is nearly 8m high. This was, strangely, the only corn-grinding windmill in Shetland, a land of wind-whipped islands with a long association with the Dutch. This windmill was built by the islanders in the middle of the 19th century to grind their corn as there was no stream to operate a water mill. The ruin is worth visiting and the island is an exciting place to explore.

The two larger coves on the south coast are optimistically called the Harbour and West Ham (ON *ham* – harbour). Both bays are exposed and partly filled with drying rocks.

The Havra rock formations are repeated on the adja-

Oxna

cent Mainland with a tiny rocky islet, **Holm of Maywick**, in the centre of the separating channel.

ACCESS: No regular access. Make enquiries at Scalloway.

Anchorages:
1. In the S inlet on the E coast. (There are two narrow inlets close together but the N inlet is foul with rocks). Anchor in middle of pool in 2m with warps ashore.

11.4 Oxna

(ON yxn-øy – ox island)

OS Maps: 1:50000 Sheet 4 1:25000 Sheet 19
Admiralty Charts: 1:75000 No.3283 1:25000 No.3294

AREA: 68ha (168 acres)
HEIGHT: 38m (125 ft)

POPULATION: 1841 – 19 (2 houses). 1871 – 29. 1881 – 30. 1891 – 31 (5 houses). 1901 – 36. 1931 – 0. Uninhabited since.

GEOLOGY: Much of the rock is epidotic syenite which is like a dark granite.

HISTORY: At the end of the 19th century a young Oxna boy was playing with his friends near a skarf's (cormorant's) nest. The surrounding turf had been scalped away by the islanders to improve the soil in the arable areas and consequently the ground was bare. Something glinted in the sunlight and with some difficulty the boy prised the object from the roots and took it proudly home. A visiting schoolteacher from Burra was shown the find and he informed the museum authorities in Edinburgh. I hope the bright-eyed lad or his family were paid 'treasure trove'. They deserved it because he had unearthed an exquisite example of Norse jewellery – a solid gold armlet about 7cm (3 inches) in diameter, plaited from four heavy gold wires.

OXNA has a compact shape, uneven surface and a number of small lochans. Its summit to the south of the centre is 38m high. Extending for a considerable distance to the north is a broken line of islets and skerries. Joined to Oxna by a drying reef are the **Hoggs of Oxna** with a narrow channel, Bulta Sound, separating them from the next group called the **Cheynies**. Bulta Sound is navigable, but only 100m wide.

The Cheynies are a group of three drying islets forming a single unit and to their south-east is a further little islet called **Spoose Holm**.

When Oxna was inhabited the main settlement was beside the narrow inlet called **Sandy Voe**, facing the island of Papa (No.11.5). It seems that the First World War was the beginning of the end for Oxna. With the menfolk away it was virtually impossible for the women and children to maintain a viable community in such a demanding environment. Difficulties of transport and communication, fishing and subsistence crofting, hard enough at the best of times, must have become insurmountable. And even when the war was over many of the islanders never returned – mere statistics among the losses on the Somme or at sea.

ACCESS: No regular access. Enquire at Hamnavoe.

Anchorages:
1. Anchor NNE or SSE of Spoose Holm, 6-9m, sand over rock. Area partly obstructed by fish cages. Beware reef close S of Spoose Holm. Reasonably sheltered except from the N.

11.5 Papa

(ON pap-øy – priest or hermit island)

OS maps: 1:50000 Sheet 4 1:25000 Sheet 19
Admiralty Charts: 1:75000 No.3283 1:25000 No.3294

AREA: 59ha (146 acres)
HEIGHT: 32m (105 ft)

POPULATION: 1841 – 21. 1881 – 14. 1891 – 23 (2 houses). 1931 – 0. Uninhabited since.

GEOLOGY: Much of the bedrock is epidotic syenite which is similar to a coarse granite.

WILDLIFE: The island is said to be infested with rats but if so, they are well-concealed.

All Shetland's holy islands are clustered in the south-west of the archipelago and it has been suggested that by the time the early Irish Christians had sailed in their coracles all the way to Shetland they were only too content to settle down where they had landed and go no further.

Why the first missionary chose **PAPA** and not Oxna or Langa (an islet to the north) will never be known but maybe Oxna was already inhabited and the poor chap was just too tired to sail over to Langa. Certainly Papa has a lot to commend it. It has some pools of fresh water, enough land to cultivate for food, and reasonable proximity to Mainland.

Before the island was vacated in the 1920s it supported three or four crofts.

There is a deep and narrow channel separating Papa from Oxna and the coast of Papa is indented with a series of small inlets. Off the north-east headland is the **Hogg of Papa** – to balance the Hoggs of Oxna at the opposite side of the group – and the west side of the island has a tidal channel joining it to a fair-sized islet called **West Head of Papa**. This tidal islet alone is actually larger than the aforementioned **Langa** (ON – long island) and yet Langa supported one croft and a population of nine souls in 1841 and thirteen in 1881 although it was deserted by the 1890s. Papa has a goodly stock of peat and the Trondra (Mainland) islanders have the right to cut it as they have none of their own.

Even smaller islets lie to the east of Papa in the centre of the shipping route into the port of Scalloway – **Green Holm** with **Merry Holm** and a scattered group of skerries beside it. To the north is **Burwick Holm** by the Ness of Burwick.

In May 1903 the crew of *Adelong* fishing near Papa reported that a sea-monster, known locally as a 'sifan', had ruined ten of their nets.

A similar report from the other side of Shetland was given in a sworn account by six men crewing the *Bertie* in

Middle Channel

Papa Skerry

West Head
of Papa

21

Croo
Bight

North Voe

Hogg of Papa

Sheepfold

25

Well

Settlement
(ruins)

Well

32

Sheepfold

East Head
of Papa

Tangi Voe

OXNA

South Voe

Robie's
Point

South Channel

N

1 km
1/2 mile

Atla Holm

Bullia Skerry

Atla Ness

Hamna Voe

MAINLAND
(West Burra)

June 1882. They had been fishing south-east of Fetlar for two days. Their holds were full of fish and they were hauling in their lines to return home when they saw a sifan heading for their boat. It was 150 feet long with a huge head covered with barnacles, a square mouth with bright green whiskers – 'probably of seaweed' – and it had humps and a long neck. They fired at it at close range and threw ballast stones at it but that only infuriated it and it followed the boat for three hours.

ACCESS: No regular access. Enquire at Hamnavoe or Scalloway.

Anchorages: A tripping line is advised.
1. North Voe. Temp anchorage in 6m in centre of gut.
2. West Head of Papa. Temp anchorage in 5m in bay between Papa and West Head of Papa. Beware rocks on Papa shore and keep nearer the West Head of Papa shore. Head of bay is shoal.
3. NNE of Spoose Holm. (See Oxna, No.11.4). Safest anchorage except in N'lies but a considerable dinghy distance from Papa.
4. Temp anchorage in South Voe in centre of gut, 6m.

11.6 Foula

[**foo**-lë] (ON fugl-øy – bird or fowl island). Sometimes called Uttrie – the outer isle.

OS Maps: 1:50000 Sheet 4 1:25000 Sheet 18
Admiralty Charts: 1:75000 No.3283 1:75000 No.3281 NE part only

AREA: 1,265ha (3,126 acres)
HEIGHT: 418m (1,371 ft)

OWNER: South Foula has been owned by the family of P R H S Holbourn of Pendre, Brecon, Wales since 1900.

POPULATION: In the early 18th century the 'Mortal Pox', or smallpox, almost depopulated the island but it was replenished from Mainland. 1841 – 215 (38 houses). 1881 – 267 (and 7 fishing boats or 'sixareens'). 1891 – 239 (47 houses). 1901 – 222. 1931 – 118. 1951 – 70. 1961 – 54. 1971 – 33. 1981 – 39 (15 occupied houses). 1991 – 40.

GEOLOGY: The west and centre is sedimentary (Old Red Sandstone) and the land terminates abruptly with high sandstone cliffs of variegated colours. The north-east side is metamorphic, consisting mainly of schists and gneiss. Foula has some of Shetland's best arable land.

HISTORY: In 1490 Foula became the possession of Alv Knutsson. Previously it had belonged to the Norwegian family of Ciske. When the last Queen of Foula, Katherine Asmunder, died in the late 17th century Norse udal law was still recognised by the islanders who were unaware of the advent of Scots law in the rest of Shetland.

About this time, according to island tradition, a ship's surgeon named Scott visited the island and gained the trust of the islanders. He persuaded them to hand over their old Norse title-deeds on the pretext that they needed to be registered in Edinburgh. They never saw them again and the family of Scotts of Melby, owners of Vaila (No.11.10) and various estates on Shetland Mainland, thereby acquired possession of the island. This was merely another reputed case of the theft of land by 'carpetbaggers' from the south which had become widespread throughout the Northern Isles during the previous two centuries. As a result crofters lost their udal rights under which they were freemen land-owners. Instead they became tenants and virtual bondsmen subject to the whims of their landlords. Luckily, as fishermen, the islanders were more rent-productive than those depending solely on crofting and this saved them from clearance for sheep-farming. But their insecurity continued until 1882, when they gained some protection under the Crofting Acts.

Until 1800 Norn was still the normal tongue of this isolated community although it was no longer spoken anywhere else in Britain. Even in 1894, Jacobsen, the Faroese linguist, was surprised at the similarities with Faroese.

Foula still uses the old Julian calendar which the rest of Britain discarded in 1753 and Christmas on the island is therefore still celebrated on the 6th of January. And New Year's Day, or 'Nuerday', is on 13th January. According to the islanders this is neither old-fashioned nor heathen, but just downright independent.

WILDLIFE: Foula is yet another island with its own variety of sheep although they are not as distinctive as the Soay (No.9.2) sheep of the St Kilda group or even the seaweed-eating sheep of North Ronaldsay (No.10.27). They are known as Shetland 'hardback' sheep and, in common with all primitive sheep, they have exceptionally hairy fleeces. They were possibly introduced by the Vikings. Recently the sheep have been found to have a carniverous streak – they bite the heads off young Arctic tern and skua nestlings. Red deer on Rum (No.4.3) have a similar habit. The RSPB has suggested that the sheep should be given mineral feeding blocks as they are probably trying to compensate for a mineral deficiency in the vegetation. On the other hand the sheep may have just discovered a new gastronomic treat.

Foula, like Fair Isle (No.11.1), has its own sub-species of field mouse, *Apodemus sylvaticus thuloe* – a charming little creature with big feet.

The Viking name of Foula is still apt for this is an internationally recognised seabird station with over 125,000 breeding birds (twelve species) including the rare Leach's petrel. It is the most prolific breeding site in the North Atlantic for that ponderous pirate, the great skua or 'bonxie'. In the 19th century bonxies bred nowhere else in Britain except Foula and Unst (No.11.29) but, thanks to the attention of egg-collectors, only about fifteen pairs were left by the late 19th century and only *three* pairs by 1920. However, with protection, it has made a remarkable recovery and there are about 3000 breeding pairs on Foula's cliffs and boulder fields. The great skua – large, dark brown and heavily built – will attack even a gannet or black-backed gull forcing it to vomit up its catch. During the nesting season it will fearlessly attack men or dogs yet, strangely, the smaller arctic skua, or 'scootie-allan', shows no fear of it.

Parts of the sheer northern cliffs provide no foothold for nesting birds but elsewhere the narrow ledges are packed with noisy activity. The south-east of the island, which is almost bare of peat, has high densities of nesting oystercatcher, ringed plover, arctic skua and arctic tern. Unfortunately, there are now greatly reduced numbers of puffin (or 'Tammy Norie'). This may be due to a reduction in sand-eels caused by over-fishing or it may be a result of the increased numbers of bonxies. After all, a bonxie will even take an occasional lamb so puffins are an easy meal.

FOULA is the most isolated inhabited island in the British Isles and the most westerly of the Shetland group, lying fourteen miles out in the Atlantic. Bad weather can cut off the island for up to six weeks at a time so the difficulty for a visitor is not merely the matter of getting there, but the twin problem of getting there *and* getting back. Be sure to carry ample provisions in case of an enforced stay and if you are visiting in your own boat remember to keep a very close watch on the weather as there is no adequate harbour.

The land rises from east to west with low, broken cliffs and some small coves on the east coast, but a west coast of precipitous cliffs rising to a height of 150-365m. There are five distinct peaks all leaning to the north; the **Sneug**, which is the highest at 418m, just west of centre; the **Hamnafield** or Hamnafjeld (344m) at the centre; the **Noup** (248m)(ON – precipitous crag) on the south-west coast; the **Kame** (376m) on the west coast; and **Soberlie Hill** (221m) on the north-west coast. The Noup is separated from the other peaks by a glacial valley called the **Daal** (ON *dal* – valley).

At one time the menfolk of Foula were almost entirely engaged in fishing but nowadays crofting has had to take precedence. All the crofts are on the east side with about

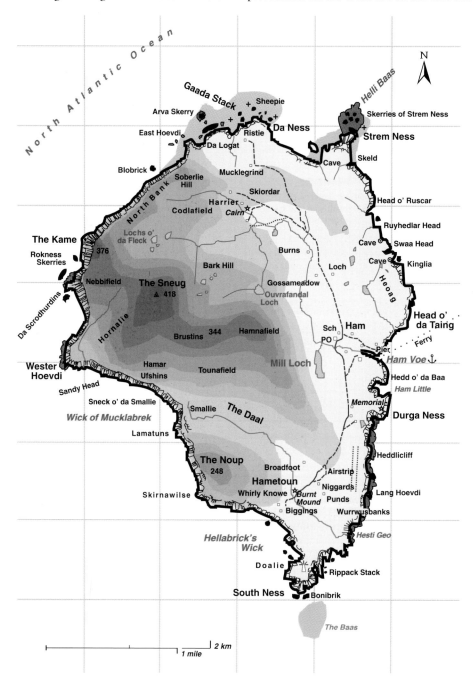

half the population settled in **Hametoun** (S. – home town) in the south-east and the remainder living at **Ham** near Ham Voe (ON – harbour inlet). Here there is a post-office, a school (rebuilt at considerable expense), a church and a chapel. The 'smiddy' sells items made by the island-ers like colley lamps, ram's head knives, sheepskin rugs and items made from copper salvaged from the *Oceanic,* sister ship to the *Titanic.* She was wrecked off Foula in 1914.

Ham Voe is the best that Foula can provide in the way of harbour facilities. The island's only 'beach' is at the head of the narrow little voe and the fishing boats have to be drawn well up to clear the big waves which tumble in, particularly when the wind is in the east. Even the mailboat/ferry (an old RNLI lifeboat of 11m overall length) which served until 1989 was power hoisted onto a concrete pad above the pier whenever it was not in use. A monthly mailboat service began in 1879 when the local minister wrote to Queen Victoria and received a reply from Disraeli. But 'monthly' was an optimistic term as there was no harbour and passengers and goods had to be landed on the rocks. It was not until 1914, after thirty years of petitioning, that a tiny concrete pier was built us-ing local labour and shingle from the back of Smell Geo. It included a step for a gun because of the advent of the First World War. The officials chose to site the pier along-side the only skerry in the Voe so consequently one side of the pier is inaccessible. Many years later a power-driven crane and winch was fitted to allow the mailboat to be lifted out instead of being manhandled. The winter service from Walls is entirely dependent on the weather but there have been many problems since 1990 as a new ferry was built which was found to be unable to cope with the se-vere conditions.

The strong sense of community in this gaunt and beautiful outpost is very evident. For about a century the population was slowly disintegrating and in 1965 Eric Linklater claimed that this 'old folks' home remote in the pitiless Atlantic will not survive much longer as a human habitation'. Yet today the population has stabilised, shows signs of increasing, and new houses and a school for the next generation have been built. There is no doubt that this is the result of better communications; access to an airstrip, a telephone, and a radio transmitter. But a differ-ent attitude by mainlanders is also helping to save the last few populated islands from complete desolation. Local au-thorities have at last realised that island schools may be uneconomic but that they are an essential element in maintaining a population, and that this also applies to im-proved harbours and services.

Foula has many physical similarities to Hirta, St Kilda (No.9.1). Both these Atlantic islands have high moun-tains, skyscraping cliffs and little land suitable for cultiva-tion. In both cases an essential source of food was seabirds and eggs collected from the terrifying cliffs. But there the similarity ends because the St Kildans were basically croft-ers who had virtually no concept of private property. All decision-making had to be communal following the tenet that the community is more important than the indi-vidual.

On Foula on the other hand the islanders were fisher-men rather than crofters and like all sailors they were in-tensely independent and self-assured. They believed in pri-vate enterprise and standing on their own feet. The com-munity was important, but only as a collection of indi-viduals. Even the houses on Foula stand apart whereas on St Kilda they cling together.

Is there a lesson to be learned? The St Kildans have gone, but Foula is still a thriving community.

Foula's stacks are not as high as those of Hirta but they are just as interesting. For instance, near **Hellibaas** (ON – flagstone rocks on which the sea breaks in bad weather) on the north coast there is a high square-topped stack with a natural arch at its base which looks like a ru-ined castle. But Foula's cliffs are unequalled in dramatic impact even if they just fail by 2m to match the height of the awesome St Kildan cliffs. There is a narrow chimney on top of **Hamnafjeld** (ON – harbour mountain) which is so deep it is said to go straight down to Hell; and at the head of the Daal in the **Wick of Mucklabrek** is the Sneck of the Smallie, another secret chimney which plunges down between the sea cliffs in a narrow slit until only the sky is visible 60m above.

Relics of the quaint Norn language still linger in the dialect on Foula, noticeable in place names such as Hedd o' da Baa (head of the underwater rock) and Wester Hoevdi (western height). Linklater recalled how when the menfolk had finished fishing they would dance the Foula Reel to the tune of *The Shaalds of Foula* (shaald – shoal) – 'Up wi' da lines and link it awa, awa, ta da shaalds o Foula.'

One of these famous, but dangerous, shoals – **Hoevdi Grund** (ON – high ground) – which were once rich in cod, haddock, mackerel, halibut, saithe and ling, lies only three miles east of South Ness.

ACCESS: By mail boat/ passenger ferry, May to Sept. weather permitting, from Walls, twice weekly, or Scalloway alternate Thurs., 01595-753232, or 01426-986763 for in-formation. Advance booking essential. Loganair charter flights, weather permitting, 01595-840246.

Anchorages: There is no adequate harbour. Local boats are hauled out and even the mailboat/ferry is lifted out by crane each trip.
1. Ham Voe. Very restricted. Beware rocks on N and S sides of Ham Voe and on E side of pier. Approach with care on a WNW course to just off the SW corner of the pier. The stone pier is 27m long with steps half-way along its NW side and a depth of 1.8m at its head. Anchor in corner of Voe with warp to hold stern off. Best to leave promptly if bad weather likely.

11.7 Noss

(ON nos – nose, or high rocky promontory) or (ON nes – headland)

OS Maps: 1:50000 Sheet 4 1:25000 Sheet 17
Admiralty Charts: 1:75000 No.3283 1:17500 No.3291 excludes E coast

AREA: 343ha (847 acres)
HEIGHT: 181m (594 ft)

OWNER: Noss is part of the Garth Estate. The laird is Mr John Hamilton Scott of Garth.

POPULATION: 1841 – 24 (3 houses). After 1871 partly cleared by Walker, the owner's factor. 1881 – 3. 1891 – 3 (1 house). 1931 – 4. Only summer habitation since. 1961 – 0. 1971 – 3. 1981 – 0. 1991 – 0.

GEOLOGY: Old Red Sandstone cliffs stratified and eroded in horizontal slabs which provide perfect shelves for nesting birds with occasional traces of volcanic vents.

HISTORY: A small chapel existed in front of the old homestead at Gungstie (now the SNH visitor centre) in 1633, built by 'shipwrakt' persons. The walls were still standing in 1774 and the burial ground beside the Sound was used until the middle of the 19th century. There is good reason to believe that the chapel site was originally Celtic and pre-Norse but, unfortunately, the burial ground is now being eroded by the sea. In 1969 the tenant found an underground passage beside the house.

The homestead was built some 400 years ago and for a time was the only inhabited house on Noss. In the early 19th century the farm was reputed to produce the best butter and milk in Shetland. The tenant farmer at the time was the father of Dr James Copland who published the *Dictionary of Medicine* in 1832.

In 1869 the Marquis of Londonderry leased the island and turned it over to pasture for his prize breed of Shetland stallions. These were used in his Durham coal mine as a substitute for child labour. The mares were kept on Bressay to allow controlled breeding.

Since 1900 Noss has been used for sheepfarming providing pasturage for about 420 Shetland ewes.

WILDLIFE: The island, which has been a National Nature Reserve since 1955, is managed by Scottish Natural Heritage. Explanatory leaflets are available at the visitors' centre. Visitors are required to keep to the cliff-top path and no camping is permitted.

There are 150 species of flowering plants here including the semi-parasitic Lousewort or 'Sookie Flooer', but Noss is best known for its seabirds, more than 160,000 of them. The first gannet colony only became established on Noss in 1911. Now there are over 5,000 pairs nesting on the headland with over 10,000 pairs of kittiwake and 65,000 pairs of guillemot. Twenty pairs of arctic skua and 300 pairs of great skua (bonxie) nest inland. There are also many fulmar, eider (dunter), great black-backed gull, razorbill, puffin, shag and black guillemot (tystie).

The best bird-watching period is mid-May to July.

The isle of **NOSS** is a veritable metropolis of seabirds and the cacophony of sound from their cries is so loud that it can sometimes be heard far to seaward when even the island itself is out of sight. The cliffs of Noss are made up of narrow horizontal beds of sandstone which the sea has carved into thousands of attractive ledges. These are ideal sites for seabirds' dream-houses and competition is intense in Bird City.

The **Noup of Noss**, towering 180m above the waves, is the highest point on Noss and the 'city centre'. Every precipitous dormitory suburb has a suitable name which rolls off the tongue delightfully: the Cletters, Whiggie Geo, Point of Heogatoug, and the Rump to the north; and southwards – Rumble Wick, Geordie's Holes, Feadda Ness and Holm of Noss. The best viewpoint is from the sea.

Holm of Noss, also known as Cradle Holm, is a stack standing 48m high and considered now to be almost impossible to climb. It is separated by a 20m gap from the cave-riddled cliffs of Feadda Ness. This used to provide a handy anchorage for small boats until a rockfall blocked it. In the 17th century a crofter was wagered a cow that he could not reach the top of the Holm and he won the wager, reputedly by climbing a ship's mast for part of the way. While on the top he fixed stakes in the turf and constructed a replaceable rope railway which could support a box cradle large enough to carry a man and a sheep. Unfortunately, after completing the work he slipped and fell to his death. It was of little consolation to him that his engineering was faultless and that his famous 'Cradle of Noss' was used every summer for over 200 years to graze sheep on the top of the Holm. It was dismantled in 1864 by Mr Walker, the laird's factor, who considered it unsafe. He had a safety wall built along the cliff-head.

Noss Sound is shallow, rocky and narrow (less than 200m) and wind and tide can funnel through, making it decidedly unpleasant at times. It has been the scene of many shipwrecks. An old track along the south shore ends at **Setter** where there are still the ruins of a settlement. In Norse times there were five settlements along this south coast according to the records. The visitors' path continues from here and circumnavigates the island.

The old house at Gungstie was restored as staff accommodation in 1986 and includes a visitor information room. The Pony Pund – the stables building built by the Marquis of Londonderry in 1870 – was converted at the same time and contains an interpretive display.

The name of **Papil Geo** (G. – priest's inlet) on the north coast below the **North Croo** might be a reminder that an early Christian hermit once lived on Noss – possibly in the caves which open on to the Geo, or it may be related to the chapel site at Hametoun.

From the landing place at Gungstie the ground climbs towards the west, gently at first and then quite steeply. The 'Hill Dyke' crosses the island's neck and during the lambing season this separates the lambs from the nesting bonxies. The ground cover is mostly coarse grass but the grazing was once fine grass pasture for the Marquis of Londonderry's ponies. In the nesting season when climbing up the slopes to the cliff-head the bonxies dive-bomb with determination. This is rarely dangerous but is certainly intimidating. On the cliff-top path expect also to have your senses assaulted. The sight of prolific birdlife is unbelievable, the noise is deafening, and the smell overpowering.

ACCESS: Lerwick to Bressay (See No.11.8). Bus, taxi or on foot (5km) to Noss Sound. For crossing Noss Sound by inflatable from Bressay (mid-May to mid-August) hail the Scottish Natural Heritage warden at Gungstie on Noss. Scottish Natural Heritage, 01595-693345. There are also summer boat trips round Bressay and Noss (2½hrs) but no landings – details from Lerwick Tourist Office, 01595-693434.

Anchorages: Caution necessary if passing through Noss Sound. It is shallow, rocky, and has a strong tidal current.

1. Nesti Voe, at S end of Noss Sound. Occasional anchorage. Enter mid-channel and anchor in the middle, sand. Exposed S.

2. Voe of the Mels, W of Nesti Voe. Occasional anchorage. Approach E of mid-channel and anchor near head of voe in 4m, sand. Exposed S.

3. Noup of Noss, steep-to. There are mooring rings on the rocks below the Noup for use in quiet weather to watch the birds.

11.8 Bressay

In 1490 called (ON Brús-øy – Brusi's island) from a proper name, but in 1263 was possibly referred to as (ON breid-øy – broad island).

OS Maps: 1:50000 Sheet 4 1:25000 Sheets 17 and 19
Admiralty Charts: 1:75000 No.3283 1:17500 No.3291

AREA: 2,805ha (6,931 acres)
HEIGHT: 226m (741 ft)

OWNER: Mr John Hamilton Scott of Garth who farms Maryfield Farm is the principal landowner. He inherited the Bressay estate from his uncle, Mr Norman Ogilvie Mouat Cameron of Garth.

POPULATION: 1841 – 904 (167 houses). 1881 – 847. 1891 – 799 (166 houses). 1931 – 448. 1961 – 269. 1971 – 248. 1981 – 335. 1991 – 352.

GEOLOGY: Almost entirely composed of Middle and Upper Old Red Sandstone with a few volcanic outcrops and some thin bands of tuff between the flagstones on the east coast. Much of Shetland is roofed with 'slates' – thin flagstone slabs – from Bressay, and building stone was quarried at Aith.

HISTORY: A selection of prehistoric remains are scattered across Bressay but the best known early historical artefact is probably the Bressay Stone which was found near Culbinsbrough churchyard and which can be seen in the Scottish National Museum of Antiquities in Edinburgh. It is a Pictish cross-slab with an ogam inscription which includes two Gaelic words and one Norse word which could indicate that the early inhabitants were co-operating peacefully. It is exquisitely carved with a Celtic cross, representations of priests, a horseman, some animals and, possibly, Jonah and two whales.

In the 11th century Harald Hardrada's ships lay in Bressay Sound (ON *Breideyjarsund*) before sailing south to a Viking defeat by Harold Godwinsson at Stamford Bridge. In the 13th century King Haakon's fleet also sheltered in the Sound before meeting a similar fate at Largs.

From the 15th to the mid-17th century most of Bressay was owned by Sigurd Jonsson, a Norwegian nobleman. John Neven the Younger of Unst became owner of the estate in 1660 and then it passed to the Hendersons,

who were also of Norwegian origin. Most of the remainder of the island belonged to the Bolts of Cruister, Magnus Bolt being 'Foude' of Bressay in 1612. The Bolts lived in the Haa of Cruister but the building was abandoned – it is now a ruin – when the Mouats of Garth acquired the Bolts' estate in the early-19th century.

In 1640 ten Spanish men-of-war sailed into the Sound and attacked four Dutchmen, two of which were sunk. Later, an English fleet of ninety-four ships commanded by Admiral George Monk anchored here for several days in 1653 while searching for Van Tromp and the Dutch fleet.

In the early 18th century French privateers sailed through and 'pillaged like gentlemen' and a French fleet in a fishing war with the Dutch burnt 150 busses anchored in the Sound. The area was a favourite fishing ground for the Dutch and in 1774, for instance, over 400 busses – mostly Dutch – anchored in the Sound. It was said that Amsterdam was built 'oot o' da back o' Bressa'.

During the Peninsular War, naval press-gangs raided the area and removed numerous young Shetlanders, magnificent seamen whom the islands could ill-afford to lose, for service with Nelson's fleet.

1871 was 'da year 'at Walker made da uproar'. The laird at that time was Miss Mouat and her factor, Walker, cleared many of the crofts for sheep. He built Maryfield House for himself and named it after his wife. The site, opposite Lerwick, was previously a croft called Troubletoon.

The German High Seas Fleet visited the Sound in the early years of the 20th century and Bressay boasted gun emplacements in both World Wars.

WILDLIFE: Many migrant birds reach the crofts in the west of the island. Waders and whooper swans can be seen at the Loch of Grimsetter on the east coast. Further south, bonxies nest near Sand Vatn, seabirds nest on the cliffs and a colony of arctic skua nests near Bard Head.

Lerwick and **BRESSAY** are symbiotic. Lerwick could not exist if it were not for the protection which the island gives to its excellent harbour; Bressay owes much of its livelihood to close proximity to Lerwick.

The merits of an anchorage in Bressay Sound were known by the Vikings but it was the Dutch fishermen in the 15th century who turned it into a port. The Dutch busses – two-masted craft of over 80 tons – and their accompanying men-of-war which would now be called 'fishery protection vessels' would crowd into the Sound in vast numbers. At times it was said one could cross from Mainland to Bressay by stepping from boat to boat. For the Dutch this was a great government-protected industry with more than 2000 busses exporting their catch of Scottish herring to countries throughout the western world. James VI (James I of England) tried to introduce a licensing system to control them but it was ignored. Later Charles I enlisted the help of the Navy and after an ex-

Easter Rova Head · Holm of Beosetter · Outer Score · Inner Score · Score Head · Score Minni · Bars Geo Cave · Baa Berg · Scarfi Taing · White Hill · Ness of Beosetter · Holm of Gunnista · Sweyn Ness · Elvis Voe · Score Hill 66 · Blue Geo · Hill of Beosetter · B.Mound · Gunnista · Aith Ness · Minni of Aith · Aith Voe · Bay of Heogan · Heogan · Lochs of Beosetter · Hill of Gunnista · Hog's Kailyard · Loder Head · Rules Ness · Hill of Cruester · Standing Stone · Loch of Aith · Bruntland · Voe of Cullingsburgh · Bay of Cuppa · Holm of Cruester · Burnt Mound · Gardie Ho · 1 · Hill of Setter · St Mary's Church · Broch · B.Mound · Geo of Vatsvie · Maryfield · Cruetoun · Setter · Ander Hill · Noss Sound · Ferry · Leira Ness · Hoversta · Clodisdale · Loch of Setter · Everby · Brough · B.Mound · Ferry · Broch (ruin) · NOSS · (Lerwick) · Sch · PO · Uphouse · Loch of Brough · Sildries · Ullins Water · MAINLAND · B Mound · Midgarth · Virdick · ruin · Bressay Sound · Brei Wick · Voe of Learaness · Will Houll · B Mound · Pettifirth · Loch of Grimsetter · Muckle Hell · Bight of Ham · Grindiscol · Wart · West Hill 150 · Millburn Geo · Natural Arch Huster Roo · Taing of Ham · Ham · Souterrain · White Gate · Hope Wick · Cro of Ham · Grey Head · Loch of Seligeo · Seli Geo · Ward of Bressay ▲226 · Grut Wick · Green Head · Stoura Clett · Whinna Skerry · Hevdi · Kirkabister · Mana Berg · Lourie's Stane · Mossy Hill · Kirkabister Ness · Daal · The Black Hill · Sand Vatn · Gore's Kirn · Round Point · Ovluss · Burn of Veng · Hamar · 165 Mills of the Ord · Waterfalls · Hole of Bugars · The Ord · Flada Cap · Maatruf · Geos of the Veng · Bard · Cave of the Bard · Giant's Leg · Mid Dublin · Bard Head

2 km
1 mile

change of fire the Dutch agreed to pay an annual fee and obey the rules. One such rule was that fishing could not begin before the Feast of St John the Baptist (Johnsmas – 24th June). By mid-June the Sound would fill with boats preparing for the start and the Shetlanders meanwhile would make what profit they could from the event by setting up booths and bars on the shore.

By 1798 a few Shetland boats had succeeded in joining the bonanza. According to the Rev. Cruttwell: 'The inhabitants of Bressay fit out about twenty-six large fishing boats.'

It is a sad historical fact that the social structure in the Scottish islands denied most of the inhabitants the chance to own an ocean-going fishing boat with the result that the vast wealth of the northern seas was largely exploited by foreigners. It is only in very recent times that Scottish fishermen have had the opportunity to participate.

The south and east coasts are high, barren and precipitous whereas the north and west coasts are lower with rocky foreshores and productive crofts. **Ward of Bressay** – 'Da Wart' – is a pyramid-shaped hill in the centre of the southern part of the island. It is the highest point on the island at 226m but its interesting silhouette is not appreciated by the inhabitants of Lerwick as on sunny winter mornings it casts a shadow across the town.

On the south coast above the cliffs there is another hill called **The Ord** which reaches a height of 165m. East of here is the bleak expanse of **Sand Vatn** and the most southerly point of Bressay, **Bard Head**. The sandstone cliffs which stretch round this point and up the west coast are composed of interesting rock formations. Beside the aptly-named **Giant's Leg** is the Cave of the Bard, better known as **Orkneyman's Cave** [HU514360]. No one is certain now who the Orkneyman was: he might have been a Jacobite, or a fugitive from the naval press-gangs, or the name might come from an earlier age. The cave is only accessible by boat but is well worth the trouble. The entrance is a symmetrical archway which is wide enough for several boats to enter abreast and the water within is clear and deep with extraordinarily beautiful variegated colours on the roof and walls. The cave then narrows but opens up again into a spacious hall with stalactites. It is possible to go in by dinghy for a considerable distance.

Bressay has had its brochs but only traces of these remain. In Culbingsbrough Voe (ON Kolbeinsborg) in the north-east, called Cullingsburgh by the Ordnance Survey, there is one on a small promontory [HU521423]. Beside it is the ruined wall of a chapel, **St Mary's Church**, which is claimed to have been the only cruciform church in Shetland and which may date back to the Norse era. In the burial ground is a stone commemorating a Dutch captain, Claes Bruyn, who was master of a merchantman *Amboina*. In 1636 after a foray with Portuguese ships off Mozambique, he took on a cargo of Persian silk at Surat in India, was delayed by violent gales off the Cape of Good Hope, lost twenty-nine of his crew from disease, and then at last, months later, reached Bressay Sound. He dropped anchor thankfully and promptly dropped dead.

St Mary's is overlooked by **Ander Hill** which has a derelict lookout tower on top of it built by the Admiralty before the First World War. Ander Hill has a similar profile when viewed from every point of the compass.

Gunnista was also the site of an early church dedicated to St Ola or Olaf and the parish church until 1722. It was demolished by the laird, William Henderson of Gardie, despite the minister's protests, to use the materials for a new church to be built nearer Gardie House. **Aith Voe**, between Gunnista and twisted Aith Ness, is a fair anchorage with its entrance guarded by two islets, **Holm of Beosetter** and **Holm of Gunnista**.

A third early church existed at **Kirkabister** in the south-west dedicated to St John, but it has long since disappeared. **Bressay Lighthouse** is close by, at Kirkabister Ness, marking the southern entrance to Bressay Sound. It was built in 1858 and is now automatic.

The ferry docks by **Maryfield**, the main house for Maryfield Farm (452ha). To the north is the charming little mansion, **Gardie House**, the laird's house, which was built in 1724 but had its facade remodelled about 1900.

ACCESS: By car ferry from Lerwick, 5 minutes, hourly service, 01595-692024. Tourist Office, 01595 693434.

Anchorages:
1. Lerwick Harbour, (on Mainland). Berth in Small Boat Harbour or Albert docks subject to HM's agreement or temp anchorage S of Small Boat Hr. Busy port and long stay not recommended.
2. Bard Head. Mooring rings for use while visiting the Cave of the Bard (Orkneyman's cave) by dinghy in settled conditions.
3. Aith Voe, N coast. Enter E of Holm of Gunnista. Anchor in 4-7m. Perfect shelter in all weathers, but anchorage part obstructed by fish cages.

11.9 Hildasay

Possibly, (ON hildis-øy – battle island). Hild was the battle goddess of Norse mythology. The Vikings liked to settle a quarrel by single combat on an uninhabited island in order to avoid interference by spectators. The island name is sometimes spelt Hildesay. Alternatively, (ON Hildirs-øy – Hildir's island) Hildir is a man's name.

OS Maps: 1:50000 Sheet 4 1:25000 Sheets 16 and 19
Admiralty Charts: 1:75000 No.3283 1:17500 No.3294

AREA: 108ha (267 acres)
HEIGHT: 32m (105 ft)

POPULATION: 1881 – 7. 1891 – 30 (5 houses). 1901 – 0. Uninhabited since.

GEOLOGY: The high-quality 'granite' on Hildasay – actually an epidotic syenite – was quarried for many years and was even said to have been exported to Australia but with the advent of concrete the quarry became uneconomic and closed down.

HISTORY: Hildasay was bought by an American with Shetland family connections in 1897.

HILDASAY is an oval island, shaped like a yeti's footprint. It reaches a height of 32m near its north end. There are rocky escarpments on the west and north coasts and the south coast has three 'toes' formed by two narrow inlets, Cusa Voe and Tangi Voe (ON – seaweed inlet). A large loch, **West Loch**, with a lone islet covers a considerable part of the west side of the island. A tiny balancing lochan is on the east side.

Hildasay has a satellite island – the yeti's big toe, – called **Linga** (ON – heather island). It is close to the south-east coast and it was a separate croft in the 19th century.

To the north-west, but separated by a deep navigable channel, is a long reef of skerries and holms including **North Score Holm**, **Easter Score Holm** and **Sanda Little**. It culminates in **Sanda Stour** (ON – big sand island) at its south end. This little islet is 19m high and the sea has carved its rocks into a natural arch.

The ruins of Hildasay's small settlement, which reached its maximum size of five houses towards the end of the 19th century, is on the hillside in the north. At that

time the island was going through a relatively prosperous stage. Apart from three or four crofts there was a curing-station for herring and a granite quarry. The quarry had a small railway-track to carry the cut stone down to the landing-place – the only such railway-track in Shetland. The owner allowed islanders from Burra and Trondra to cut peat on the island as they had none on their own islands. The peat on Hildasay was of particularly good quality and the peat-cutting visits were always a good excuse for a social occasion.

Unfortunately, the good times came to an end. The quarry closed down when the sale of its stone became uneconomic and almost simultaneously the curing-station

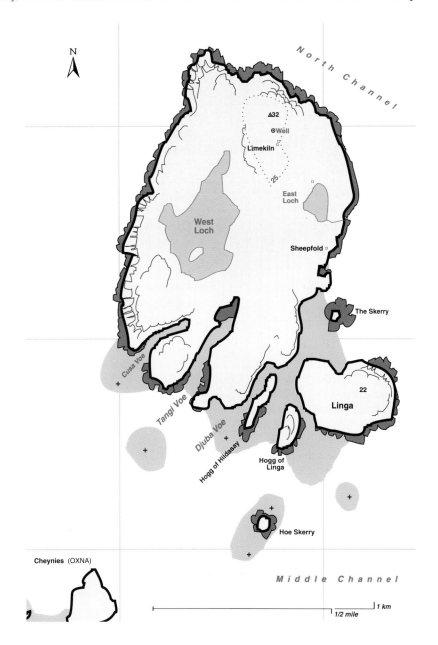

was closed because of the decline in the herring industry. Only sheep remained. The island was abandoned about 1900.

ACCESS: No regular access. Enquire at Scalloway or Hamna Voe.

Anchorages: There is no recommended anchorage and temp anchorage by The Skerry (N of Linga) is risky owing to the proximity of fish cages but there is an old pier for a landing place.

11.10 Vaila

Probably, (ON val-øy – falcon island), but could also be horse island, battlefield island, or round island.

OS Maps: 1:50000 Sheets 3 and 4 1:25000 Sheet 16
Admiralty Charts: 1:75000 Nos.3283 or 3281 1:25000 No.3295

AREA: 327ha (808 acres)
HEIGHT: 95m (312 ft)

OWNER: Dorota Rychlik and Richard Rowland, of London. Purchased in 1993 from Mr Henry Anderton. The new owners are restoring Vaila Hall and expect to take up full-time residence.

POPULATION: 1841 – 29 (4 houses). 1881 – 9. 1891 – 19 (2 houses). 1901 – 30. 1931 – 5. 1961 – 9. 1971 – 5. 1981 – 0. 1991 – 1.

GEOLOGY: Fine, dark-grey sandstone typical of the Walls region. It was deposited about 400 million years ago but has since been folded and metamorphosed and subsequently glaciated. The south-east corner has an intrusion of complex Sandsting granite seen in the red cliffs by the Gaada Stacks.

HISTORY: A Neolithic house site has been discovered and there are Bronze Age burnt mounds in the fertile north-west of the island.

In 1490 the estates of the Norwegian family of Ciske were divided and Vaila and Foula (No.11.6) became the possession of Alv Knutsson. Gorvel Fadersdatter 'of Geskie' succeeded to the title in 1537 and she leased Vaila, and Walls, to Robert Cheyne of Ury (later to become Commissioner of Zetland) in 1576 with permission to build a fortress for safety from 'Heland men, perattis and utheris invasionis'. There was some confusion concerning national ownership of all the Northern Isles at this time as they had been mortgaged to Scotland for Princess Margaret of Norway's dowry in 1468 and Scotland had later foreclosed on the unpaid debt and annexed them. Consequently, Andrew Hawich of Scatsa contested Cheyne's claim to Vaila but Cheyne was able to produce proof of title from the Scottish king. Two years later

(1582) Gorvel transferred all her estates to the King of Denmark but he too confirmed Cheyne's right to lease the property for 66 'good dollars' a year.

The Scandinavian claim became more and more tenuous and by 1661 the Danes were complaining that the rent was seldom received.

In 1698 the Cheyne's sold Vaila to James Mitchell, a Scalloway merchant and he built a house on the island which now forms part of the south wing of Vaila Hall. In 1736 the island was inherited by James Scott of Melby and it was the Scott family who leased it to that notable Shetlander, Arthur Anderson.

Arthur Anderson was born in Shetland in 1792. He was a beach-boy (fish-drier) who acquired some education and volunteered to join the Navy. He became a midshipman and, in due course, a Captain's clerk. He then left the Navy and obtained employment with a London shipowner, Willcox, who eventually offered him a partnership. This gave him time to travel during which he intervened successfully in a civil war in Portugal and founded a Liberal newspaper in Shetland. In 1837 he and Willcox started the Peninsular Steam Company which, three years later, became the Peninsular and Oriental (P & O), running regular mail services to India and China with a strict discipline that almost matched the Royal Navy.

Meanwhile Anderson continued to take a great interest in Shetland's welfare. He presented Queen Victoria with a fine knitted Shetland shawl which made these shawls instantly popular in fashion-conscious London society and created a new cottage industry. Also in 1837 he leased Vaila and established the Shetland Fishery Company – breaking the existing feudal system by which all catches, and most of the boats, belonged to the laird. And in the following year he started a regular steamship mail-service to Shetland which still exists today in the form of the P & O ferries serving the Northern Isles.

This untiring and benevolent man was Member of Parliament for Orkney and Shetland for several years – establishing a Liberal tradition which has remained part of the philosophy of the islands. But his outlook was far from insular: for instance, he suggested the cutting of a Suez canal long before de Lessops. He was philanthropic, founding the Widows' Homes in Lerwick for widows of seamen and fishermen, never priggish, and always retained a great sense of humour.

Arthur Anderson, who died aged seventy-seven, may have had only a passing connection with the island of Vaila but the island gains much by association with one of the truly great Shetlanders.

In 1893 Herbert Anderton, a rich Yorkshire mill-owner on a wool-buying business trip to Shetland, fell in love with Vaila and bought it. He immediately carried out a massive building programme with similarities to the Bullough developments on Rum (No.4.3). Anderton used

MAINLAND
(West Shetland)

Pier

Holm of Breibister

Linga

Vaila Voe

Vaila Sound

Wester Sound

Vaila Holm

Cloudin
(farmhouse)

Baa of Linga

Quoy Hill

Boathouse
Pier

Ham

Galta
Skerry

Pier

Vaila Hall
★ Burnt Mound   ★ Burnt Mound

Mucklaberry
Castle
(tower)

Cave

Burn of Ham

25

MAINLAND

Easter Sound

Natural Arch

Reitta
Ness

Maamy's Hole

Cairn ★

Natural Arch

Ram's
Head

Nouns Geo

Cairn ★

Cairn
★

East Ward

△ 95

Cave

West Ward
81

75

Mid Ward

75

Caves
56

Humla
Stack

Caves

Green Head

Vine Geo

Coukie Geo

Cave

*Muckle
Bight*

Rock Arch

Strom
Ness

Gaada Stacks

N

1 km
1/2 mile

Vaila Hall as a summer residence and accommodated large house parties. His brother, Francis Swithin, a Royal Acadamician, assisted with other developments on the island and his brother-in-law and fellow mill-owner, Colonel Foster, bought nearby Burrastow House.

During the slump Mr Anderton's fortune largely disappeared as he tried to maintain full employment for his mill-workers. He retired to the island in 1933 and lived there in virtual isolation until he died in 1937. Colonel and Mrs Foster then inherited Vaila but they had both died by 1953 and their daughter was confined to the deteriorating building with multiple sclerosis. Meanwhile, the farm also fell into disrepair so that when, on Miss Foster's

death in 1969, Herbert Anderton's great-nephew inherited the island, it was almost too late for him to take remedial measures to stop further serious deterioration of the property. To assist in the cost of maintenance he ran banquets in the Hall, and opened a hostel for bird watchers and sea anglers. He sold Vaila to the present owners in 1993 but has retained possession of Burrastow House (built 1759) on Mainland which he runs as a hotel with a first-class restaurant, 01595-71307.

WILDLIFE: Over 100 different species of wild flower have been recorded on Vaila.

The peat and heather moorland and cliff fringe provide

nesting sites for many seabirds. The sea eagle nested here in the 19th century.

Green fertile ground on the north of **VAILA** slopes upwards to moorland in the south. Here there are two cairn-topped rounded hills, West Ward (81m) and **East Ward**, (95m) the island summit. The moor has some scattered pools and lochans and on the south-east coast it falls abruptly to the sea in red granite cliffs which rear up again in arches and rocky stacks like Dracula's teeth where they are split by narrow geos.

On the west coast the cliffs are of more modest height but they also have a natural arch and the explosive **Maamy's Hole** where the waves are forced under pressure through a fissure into a 'gloup' [HU221464].

Vaila is separated from Mainland by Wester Sound and Easter Sound which form entrances to **Vaila Sound** with its good natural harbour of Walls. This used to be a port of call for ships from Aberdeen and Leith, and for the Shetland deep-sea fishing fleet, and is still the terminus for the Foula passenger ferry (No.11.6). The islet of **Linga** (ON – heather isle) which lies in the middle of Vaila Sound had a population of nine in 1841. This increased to thirteen in 1881 and there were still two inhabitants in 1931.

Derelict cottages by Vaila's west beach were probably built in the early 17th century. Near them, on the narrow peninsula running parallel with Wester Sound, is **Mucklaberry Castle** [HU221468], an ancient two-storey watch tower of unknown origin but which may have been of use to smugglers watching for excisemen. The tower was restored by Herbert Anderton with added crenellations and an angle turret.

West Pier is sheltered by **Vaila Holm** at this north-west corner. It is the landing-point for the boat from Burrastow House on Mainland which crosses the narrows of Wester Sound, passing the **Holms of Breibister** and **Burrastow**.

There is another pier at **Ham** (ON – harbour) in the north-east – the **East Pier**. The boat-house with studio above was possibly the first reconstruction project undertaken by Anderton. Both he and his wife were keen artists and his brother was a member of the Royal Academy. Anderton's work had often taken him abroad and among the many artefacts he brought back was a Buddha from Japan. With true Victorian abandon he constructed a small Buddhist temple beside the studio. (This is quite unique for Shetland but not for Scottish islands in general. Both Eilean Righ (No.2.8) and Holy Island (No.1.3) also have Buddhist connections.) Unfortunately, the temple and studio later fell into serious disrepair but the gardens at Ham, which Herbert Anderton created, still shelter his tomb.

The fertile ground in the north supported a productive farm and **Cloudin Farmhouse** was built in 1894. When Lord Londonderry's famous stud of Shetland ponies on Bressay (No.11.8) was sold Anderton bought foundation stock and built up a large herd. He also had sheep, Clydesdale horses and a small herd of dairy cows.

Work started on **Vaila Hall**, which is the largest house of its kind in Shetland, in 1895. The south wing incorporates James Mitchell's laird's house as well as the original entrance doorway with the Mitchell coat-of-arms above it inscribed with the date 1696. The north wing of the hall was reconstructed from various outbuildings with a central courtyard which became the hall itself. Some of the stone and skilled labour for the work was imported from England and many of the ornaments and contents came from further afield. The stone griffons flanking the entrance steps, for instance, are thought to have come from Germany.

As befitted an island laird, a brass canon made in Yorkshire was ceremoniously fired from the terrace whenever the Andertons arrived on Vaila.

ACCESS: Crossing from Burrastow pier, by prior arrangement, 01595-809363 or -809213.

Anchorages:
1. Ham (East Pier). Reasonable shelter in all winds. Anchor off pier but avoid old moorings.
2. Burrastow pier. Anchor off pier and fairly near fish cages. Sheltered W-N.

11.11 Mainland
(ON megenland – mainland)
Muckle Roe
(S. and ON – big red island)
West and East Burra
(E. and ON – west and east broch island)
Trondra

Probably, (ON – boar island) but may be from the man's name (ON – Prondr's isle) or, improbably, the Norse tribe's name (ON – Praendir island) from which Trondheim in Norway derives.

OS Maps: 1:50000 Sheets 1, 3 and 4 1:25000 Sheets 3, 6, and 8 to 21 inclusive
Admiralty Charts: 1:500000 No.219 1:200000 Nos.1119 and 1233 1:75000 Nos.3281, 3282 and 3283 1:30000 No.3298 Yell Sound 1:17500 No.3291 approaches to Lerwick various scales: No.3294 Clift Sound, Scalloway, Sand and Hos Wick, Seli, Sandsound and Weisdale Voes: No.3295 Vaila Sound, Gruting, Dales and Ronas Voes, Bay of Quendale, Swarbacks Minn, Olna and Ura Firths 1:12500 No.3297 Sullom Voe

AREA: 100,230ha (247,668 acres)

HEIGHT: 450m (1,476 ft)

OWNERS: Multiple ownership.

POPULATION:

	1841	1881	1891	1931	1961	1971	1981	1991
Mainland	20572	20821	19741	15172	13282	12944	22184	17562
E. & W. Burra	586	642	695	767	653	565	838	889
Muckle Roe	214	230	213	154	103	94	101	115
Trondra	244	133	154	91	20	17	92	117
	21616	21826	20803	16184	14058	13620	23215	18683

GEOLOGY: Mainland is formed from a ridge of very old rocks made up of granite, schist, and gneiss. The southern leg or promontory is mainly of dark blue and grey slates and mica-schists but with a band of Old Red Sandstone on the east coast. North of here the ridge of stratified metamorphic rocks continues in more crystalline forms of schist and gneiss interrupted by long bands of limestone as far north as Laxfirth. West Mainland is generally of Old Red Sandstone but North Mainland is a very complex structure with granites and diorites predominating and basaltic lavas and tuffs on the west side.

On top of the ancient core of igneous and metamorphic rocks great beds of sediment (Old Red Sandstone) were laid down in geologically-recent times. There were occasional volcanic intrusions with the lava forming layers of igneous rock.

INSIDE AN IRON AGE WHEEL-HOUSE AT JARLSHOF

During the last Ice Age the Scandinavian ice sheet spread across Shetland and scoured the surface, removing much of the 'new' Old Red Sandstone from the central spine and smoothing the topography into rounded hills, wide valleys and many small lochs. The ice brought debris with it. There is a two-ton boulder of laurvikite in the roadside wall of Dalsetter croft in Boddam (near Sumburgh) which was deposited there by the ice. It has come from just south of Oslo.

HISTORY: There are none of the Orkney-style chambered cairns on Shetland which could lead one to suppose that these islands were inhabited by a different prehistoric race or, at least, a people with its own distinctive social and religious code.

Christianity filtered north into Shetland slightly later than to Orkney which is understandable and the islands played a lesser part in Norse history. This is possibly due to their geographical position as a staging post on the route to the Faeroes, Iceland, Greenland, western Scotland, and Ireland. In general terms, however, the history of Shetland in the Norse period was similar to that outlined for Mainland Orkney (No.10.10).

In 1468 King Christian of Norway and Denmark mortgaged both Shetland and Orkney to the Scottish Crown as part of Margaret of Norway's marriage dowry. As the cash redemption was not forthcoming Scotland foreclosed and annexed the islands in 1471.

Apart from a few churchmen there were virtually no Scots living in Shetland at that time but the next one hundred years saw a considerable influx of land-hungry Scots. It was in this period also that the Lowland Scots dialect started to mingle with the native tongue. The Sinclair family was there before 1469 and by 1600 Sinclair was the commonest surname among the one-third of the population which used Scottish surnames. The native Shetlanders still used patronymics.

In 1564 Mary, Queen of Scots, granted the feu of Orkney and Shetland in perpetuity to her half-brother, Lord Robert Stewart. By 1568 Lord Robert had forced the Bishop to resign, gained the right to all crown, church and earldom property together with the right to claim revenue from every islander, and had made himself the chief magistrate. No Norse earl had ever held such power.

By 1571, Lord Robert had installed his half-brother, Laurence Bruce, as foud (chief magistrate) and Bruce used and abused this position to confiscate land on every excuse. He soon lost his position as chief magistrate but, nevertheless, by 1638 the Bruce family held one-eighth of all the lands of Shetland.

In 1581 Lord Robert was made Earl of Orkney and in 1591 his son, Earl Patrick Stewart, succeeded him. He built the castle at Scalloway, and the house at 'Jarlshof' and as chief magistrate he nominally supported the Norse legal forms, but would confiscate land readily. However, his main interest was in reducing the land holdings of the entrenched landowners such as the Bruce family of Muness and this made him many powerful enemies. He was imprisoned in 1609 and executed in Edinburgh in 1615 by James VI. Norse law was superseded by Scots law; udal was replaced by feudal. The landowning families had now gained enormous power and fought among themselves to divide the spoils.

WILDLIFE: There are very few trees to be found, but the largest plantation in Shetland is at Kergord, north of Weisdale. Many interesting alpine plants grow on Ronas Hill including dwarf specimens of willow, *Salix herbacea*.

Shrubs generally are heather and juniper as much of the landscape consists of upland peat bog, grass, and moorland, with many small lochs, but about 680 flowering plants and ferns, and nearly 1000 varieties of fungi, have been recorded. The Alpine Mouse-Ear Chickweed, *Cerastium Arcticum Edmondstonii*, can be found nowhere else in the world but the Shetland Isles and there are also a number of unique microspecies of Hieracium, or Hawkweed. White water lilies, *Nymphaea alba*, flourish in some of the lochans.

Native domestic mammal species are the small, hardy, Shetland ponies (about 1m high) and the distinctive black and brown Shetland sheep which are thought to be identical to Siberian wild sheep. Arctic hares, introduced for sport about 200 years ago, are common.

There is good fishing in many of the lochs but in Loch Spiggie the fish are reported to be 'dour'.

Mainland Shetland is of ornithological interest throughout the year with the great asset of nineteen hours of summer daylight. East and south-east winds bring in migrants with May, September and October being best for unusual sightings. The red-necked phalarope and the Slavonian grebe are scarce and the black-throated diver can probably not be found.

Sites: Sumburgh and Fitful Head for breeding seabirds. About 2500 moulting eider offshore in autumn and long-tailed skua occasionally seen. Pool of Virkie, north of Sumburgh has intertidal sand and mud flats for wintering and migrant shore-birds.

Quendale Bay, sand-dunes and machair. Wintering divers and sea-duck with Loch of Hillwell to the north an important breeding site for wildfowl. Corncrake sometimes heard here.

Loch of Spiggie RSPB Reserve is the most important winter wildfowl site in Shetland. Shelduck, teal, oyster-catcher and curlew nest here. Great and arctic skuas, kittiwake and arctic tern are often present, and whooper swan, sometimes, in autumn. Greylag geese, wigeon, tufted duck, pochard, goldeneye and long-tailed duck in spring.

At Boddam Voe, on east coast opposite Loch of Spiggie there are wintering divers, grebe, sea-duck, gulls and waders. Great skua and raven are attracted by the nearby slaughter-house.

Scalloway and Lerwick Harbours, gulls and black guillemot. Migrant passerines in town gardens. Loch of Clickhimin on west side of Lerwick is a wintering wildfowl site.

Lochs of Asta and Tingwall, pochard, tufted duck, and possibly the only mute swans in Shetland.

Weisdale, Sandsound, and Tresta Voes for goldeneye, sea-duck, grebes and wintering divers.

Kergord woodland, north of Weisdale, gives cover for nesting birds, rook, tree sparrow, goldcrest, and migrant species.

Sandness, west extremity of Mainland, wintering wildfowl and sea-birds.

Lunna Ness, red-throated diver on the lochans, migrants in the sycamore trees.

Sullom Voe, wintering great northern diver, slavonian grebe, eider, long-tailed duck and velvet scoter. Also ravens, waders and gulls.

Esha Ness, guillemot and kittiwake colonies in the Old Red Sandstone cliffs. Nearby breeding terns, whimbrel and skuas.

MAINLAND, the principal island of the Shetland group, lies at about the same latitude as the south of Greenland. It has a landscape of hills which are mostly smooth, low and covered with rough grass, heather and upland peat bog. The highest point is the massive barren crest of **Ronas Hill** at 450m (1467ft). This is also the highest point in all Shetland.

The long leg of land stretching from **Sumburgh** in the south to Lerwick in the north is undulating peat moorland with a border of neat meadows. The great tilted wedge of Sumburgh Head is set between Grutness Voe and West Voe of Sumburgh with busy **Sumburgh Airport** straddling the connecting isthmus.

Grutness Pier on the east is the departure point for *The Good Shepherd* on its trips to Fair Isle (No 11.1) and on the west, facing **Horse Island** and Scat Ness with its substantial ruined Iron Age Fort **Ness of Burgi**, are the world-famous ruins of Jarlshof.

Jarlshof [HU397096] was given its fanciful Viking name by Sir Walter Scott in his novel *The Pirate* but it is rather misleading because the site covers at least five dis-

SCALLOWAY CASTLE

tinct archaeological periods over a span of some 3000 years. The ruins are complex and fascinating. There are Bronze Age huts and farm buildings, earth-houses from the Iron Age with a broch and wheel-houses (1st-8th century), a variety of Norse long-house remains (9th-14th century), the foundations of a medieval farmhouse (14th-16th century), and the walls of the house belonging to Earls Robert and Patrick Stewart (16th century). The wheel-houses are particularly interesting as they seem to be family homes with recesses arranged like wheelspokes around a central hearth.

BODDAM CROFT MUSEUM. THE SMOKESTACK OF THATCH AND TIMBER IS CALLED A 'TEØFI'.

The land stretches west to the awesome heights of **Fitful Head** (ON – *hvitfugla* – white birds). It encloses the wide sandy sweep of Bay of Quendale, scene of the 1993 *Braer* tanker disaster. South of the bay are two islets, **Lady's Holm** and **Little Holm**.

East of the main road by Gallow Hill and south of the village of **Boddam** is the **Croft House Museum** which portrays croft life in the 19th century beside a working horizontal water-mill of original Norse design [HU399147].

Although the main road continues north to Channer Wick, a more interesting secondary route branches west at Boddam by the eutrophic **Loch of Spiggie** (Sc *spigg* – stickleback), rich in water-plants, fish and wildfowl. Beyond, the bleak Bay of Scousburgh shelters behind the island of **Colsay** with its prehistoric cairn.

St Ninians Isle is Shetland's answer to Mont St Michel but most of the remains of the early-Christian monastic settlement have now disappeared. Only the lower courses of a 12th century chapel [HU367209] can be seen amid the bare sheep-grazed downs where a sandy isthmus crosses to the island. But in 1958 excavation revealed the remains of an earlier (pre-Norse) church, and a hoard of 8th century Celtic silver was found under a stone slab in a box made of Norwegian larch. This may have been hidden by the monks before a Viking raid. South of the chapel is a Holy Well – a spring of crystal-clear water.

North of St Ninians Isle the tiny islet of **Griskerry** lies close to the Ness of Ireland with a road running up the Ness to Maywick.

Back on the east coast after rejoining the main road a number of scattered settlements surround Sandwick and the pier at **Leebotten** where the boat leaves for Mousa (No.11.2) on pre-arranged visits.

Hollanders Knowe is where a secondary road cuts off to the west through the hills to Scalloway while the main road continues to Lerwick. This was once a Dutch trading post.

Scalloway [skalaway or -awa] (ON *skallivaagr* – voe of the booths) is on the west coast and only 8km from Lerwick. It was the capital of Shetland until Lerwick claimed that title about two centuries ago but it is still an impor-

tant little village port and a centre for the fish-processing industry. The pier was built in the 1830s for the export of salt cod to Spain and it was extended in 1896. The most prominent feature is **Earl Patrick's Castle**, built with forced labour in 1600 to a medieval design which was already out-of-date. It was abandoned only fifteen years later when its owner was executed. A resident told me that the lime mortar was mixed with 'the hair of maidens'.

In 1942 Prince Olaf, later, King of Norway, visited Scalloway in recognition of the many Norwegians who were carrying out clandestine wartime operations. Fascinating information on these operations (and the 'Shetland Bus') can be found in **Scalloway Museum** on the waterfront.

Mainland is now connected by bridges with the long, narrow islands of **TRONDRA**, **WEST BURRA** and **EAST BURRA**. The busy fishing port of **Hamna Voe** is on West Burra.

The main road to Lerwick passes Sandy Loch Reservoir and as it enters the town, the Loch of Clickhimin is on the left – unfortunately now surrounded by new housing. In it, but connected to the shore by a causeway, is possibly Lerwick's most memorable feature [HU464408], the massive structure of **Clickhimin Broch** [klich-imin]. The broch is 20m in diameter, has walls 5$\frac{1}{2}$m thick and 4$\frac{1}{2}$m high, and the entire structure stands on a great stone platform with a gateway leading into an enclosure. The site is thought to have been occupied from the 6th century BC up to possibly the 7th century AD and to have been in turn a dun, a broch and, latterly, a wheelhouse. There are a number of inexplicable features and the ruin is so tidy that one must wonder whether the Victorian lady who carried out the excavation was occasionally overcome by idealism. (Such questions however should not be allowed to spoil your appreciation.)

LERWICK (ON *leir vik* – mud creek) is a cosmopolitan town built round a lively waterfront and harbour. Nowadays visiting Dutch sailors have been largely replaced by Russians but the close association with Scandinavia continues. Although Norsemen probably founded the town and appreciated the safe anchorage in Bressay Sound, it was the Dutch who developed it in the early 17th century by using Lerwick as a base for their fishing activities. The Shetlanders were glad to sell their wares to the visiting sailors and consequently a shanty town of booths, shacks, bars and brothels grew up leading to 'great abominatioun and wickednes'. In 1640 ten Spanish warships sailed into Bressay Sound and sunk two of the four Dutch men-of-war who were there to protect the fishing 'busses'. In 1653 Cromwell, instead of knocking Lerwick about, tried to impose an English claim to the fishing grounds by sending Admiral George Monk with ninety-four ships to search for Van Tromp. He landed an army of troops to build what is now **Fort Charlotte**, possibly Lerwick's first permanent building. But twenty years later the Dutch returned, set fire to it and carried on fishing. Then the French took an interest and in 1702 their privateers attacked the Dutch and sailed around the Shetlands which they 'pillaged like gentlemen.' They burned 150 busses off Lerwick.

Strangely, neither Shetland, nor for that matter, Scotland, seem to have had much to say in these Continental battles over the local fishing grounds. In 1798 the Rev. Cruttwell reported that: 'The herring fishery is carried on almost wholly by foreigners, 200 busses from Holland, 50 from Denmark, 40 from Prussia, 20 from Dunkirk and about the same from the Netherlands.'

Flagstoned **Commercial Street**, Lerwick's main street, meanders behind the waterfront buildings, attractively irregular and criss-crossed with narrow alleys and dark wynds. **Fort Charlotte** at its north-west end was first repaired after the Dutch attack and then it was thoroughly renovated and a barrack block added in 1781. It is, today, the only Cromwellian military structure which survives intact in Scotland.

The district of Hillhead, a chaotic composition of old stone gables and slated roofs, is above Commercial Street. It contains the **Town Hall**, 1882 Scottish baronial with fine stained glass windows and a Victorian interpretation of a Viking drinking hall. Nearby is the interesting and comprehensive **Shetland Museum**. Both of these are certainly worth visiting. The Fort is rather uninspiring but provides commanding views from its ramparts and the town itself has fascinating corners to explore. A replica Viking longship makes trips around the bay (information at the Tourist Office) and in many ways this is Lerwick's best viewpoint.

A winter visit to Lerwick should be timed for the last Tuesday of January when the nostalgic Viking fire festival of Up-Helly-aa is celebrated with great gusto by the locals. There are 'guisers', lighted torches, songs, revelry and a burning longship.

North of Lerwick Harbour the town fades away into rough land round the Bight of Vatsland. A small group of rocks called the **Holms of Vatsland** lie in the bay. The road runs to the head of Dales Voe and then turns north to the scattered community of Veensgarth and **Tingwall**

Airfield where a route strikes off to Weisdale and the west Mainland. Near the **Tingwall Agricultural Museum** a secondary road runs south to Scalloway and passes Loch of Tingwall. This is an interesting diversion as the Viking parliament and law court, the Althing, used to meet here in the valley. The actual site is thought to be **Law Ting Holm** [HU418434], a small promontory at the north end of the loch which was an island in Norse times. There is a standing stone at the foot of the loch and on **Gallow Hill**, to the west, a mother and daughter were burned as witches in the early 18th century.

North of Tingwall the road runs alongside the **Loch of Girlsta** named after a Norse maiden, Geirhilda, who is said to be buried on the island in the loch. The districts of North and South Nesting, a remote area of low hills skirted by the loop of a secondary road, lie to the east. Off their indented coastline are the **North** and **South Isles of Gletness** with **Green Holm** far to the south, **Hoo Stack**, **Eswick Holm**, **Cunning Holm**, **Holm of Skellister**, **Hog Island** and **Green Isle**. A line of skerries called the **Stepping Stones** runs far out to sea punctuated by **Muckla Billan** and **Muckle Fladdicap**.

Near the head of Dury Voe (South Voe) at **Laxo** (ON *lax* – salmon) is the pier of the car ferry to Whalsay (No.11.15). A secondary road skirts the Voe and becomes unclassified as it turns north. Halfway up the Ness is **Lunna Kirk** which was built in 1753 [HU486691].

West Lunna Voe is remembered as the anchorage for the 'Shetland Bus', small fishing boats which courageously dodged the Germans to assist the Norwegian resistance during the Second World War. This was a lifeline for supplies, rescuing refugees and transferring agents, but in the end, fuel shortages in Norway so reduced the local fishing fleet that the Shetland boats became more and more conspicuous. German patrols also became more efficient with the result that many brave men and their ships were lost. **Lunna House** (1660), now a summer hotel, was the headquarters for the operation. For cover, most of the trips had to be undertaken in the long, dark, sub-Arctic nights of winter when the weather was at its worst. Lt-Com David Howarth (in *The Shetland Bus*) recalled five days of November storm with winds of over 100mph. 'At Lunna the salt water snatched from the wave crests in Vidlin Voe streamed over the isthmus and over the house to a height of a hundred and fifty feet. From the upper windows the spray looked as solid as streamers of grey silk. . . .'.

Just beyond Lunna, at Grut Wick, the Ninian oil pipeline to Sullom Voe makes its first landfall after 103 miles on the seabed. **Lunna Holm** marks the extreme end of Lunna Ness.

The main road divides again at **Voe**. One branch leads north up Dales Voe to **Booth of Toft** where the car ferry leaves for Yell (No.11.23). The other takes a north-westerly direction along the shore of the Olna Firth, scene of the last whaling station in Shetland, and up to the uninspiring village of **Brae** (ON *breio eio* – broad neck) on Busta Voe. Here, a road turns off for the oil terminal at **Sullom Voe**. These sheltered waters supported an active flying-boat base during the Second World War and they are now the setting for giant tankers visiting Europe's largest oil terminal. Part of the area is reclaimed land where excavated material was dumped in Orka Voe. The Ninian and Brent pipelines – both of nearly one metre diameter – discharge their oil here.

Beyond Brae, a road crossing a bridge to the south-west links the round, hilly island of **MUCKLE ROE** with Mainland. Almost completely encircled with high cliffs of red granite there are some crofts in the south-east but the rest of the island is of broken high moorland – wild walking country.

At **Mavis Grind** (ON *maev eids grind* – gate of the narrow isthmus) Mainland almost splits into two islands [HU34-0684]. To the right of the road are the head waters of Sullom Voe, to the left is a small sea-loch and the waters of St Magnus Bay. **Egilsay**, a group of drying islets, lies offshore, and further north, **Isle of Gunnister** and **Isle of Nibon** with **Oe Stack** and a rock arch. This is the district of Northmavine, an area of scenic beauty. After about 8km the road divides with the left fork heading for **Hillswick** (ON *hildiswik* – battle bay) on the shores of the Ura Firth. The Ness of Hillswick is a peninsula with many multi-coloured rock formations. Off its west coast is **Isle of Westerhouse**, **Isle of Niddister** and **The Drongs** – spiky stacks and grotesque shapes carved by the sea out of the old red sandstone with one huge perpendicular column over 30m high. Hillswick was developed in the 18th century as a haaf fishing station by Thomas Gifford of Busta. A haaf (ON *haf* – sea) is a deep-sea fishing ground in the Northern Isles. Gifford provided all the equipment and the fishermen provided all the fish – a somewhat inequitable arrangement, but normal practice at that time.

A secondary road continues westward into the forbidding landscape of **Esha Ness** eventually reaching Stenness (ON – stone headland) where there was also a small haaf fishing-station partly sheltered by **Isle of Stenness** which has a natural arch on it. In 1933 Joan Grigsby camped on the isle and wrote a successful book about the experience called *An Island Rooin*. Nearby stack-shaped **Dore Holm** (ON – doorway islet) has a flying buttress on its north-west side making a natural arch 21m high and the islet is completely perforated by a cavernous passage which looks like a giant doorway. The Esha Ness area has many prehistoric relics and interesting walks. Moorland lochans sprinkle the ground above the western cliffs which are broken into fantastic shapes, weathered and tilted and a home for many seabirds. There are arches, caves and subterranean passages and the precipitous view north from the lighthouse track to **Grind of**

the Navir (ON – gateway of the giants) is particularly dramatic.

The north side of Esha Ness is indented by **Hamna Voe** (ON – harbour bay), an anchorage and one-time whaling station with a narrow rocky entrance which is difficult to identify from the sea. Luckily three islets lie to the north, **Muckle Ossa**, **Little Ossa** and **Fladda**, and Muckle Ossa has a hole right through it. A line of sight through the hole leads directly to the voe entrance.

A certain John Williamson who was born here in 1740 became known as Johnny Notions. He was a blacksmith, clock repairer, weaver, joiner and bonesetter at different times in his life but he became renowned for protecting people from smallpox when the disease was rife and the medical profession could only advocate leeches. He is said to have collected vesicles from victims of the disease, dried them by a peat fire and buried them for several years. These were then inoculated under his patients' skin and the wound was dressed with a cabbage leaf.

An unclassified road near Hillswick leads to the head-waters of lovely **Ronas Voe**. Beside the voe is a knowe called **Hollanders' Grave** where Dutch seamen were buried in 1674 [HU299804]. They were on a crippled Dutch East-Indiaman, the *Wapen van Rotterdam*, which sheltered here during the war with the English. She was discovered by the frigate *Newcastle* and taken after a fight.

Another Dutch East-Indiaman, the *Wapen van Alkmaar* carrying ivory from Ceylon foundered in a Shetland storm in 1689. (These ships took the long route past Shetland in order to avoid the English Channel.) In the early 1930s a fishing boat dredged up two tusks thirty miles north-east of Shetland which were sent to Aberdeen University for identification. The University claimed they had come from a Shetland mammoth and this myth was not dispelled until they were radio-carbon dated in 1993.

Across Ronas Voe is Shetland's highest hill, **Ronas Hill** (450m), with a chambered cairn at the summit. An invigorating hill-walk to the top is rewarded by a striking panoramic view stretching from the Atlantic, with the little islets of **The Cleiver** and **Gruna Stacks** beyond the entrance to the cutlass-shaped Ronas Voe, Foula (No.11.6) on the horizon, Sullom Voe to the south-east, Yell Sound to the east with the **Holms of Burravoe**, and **Muckle** and **Little Holm**. Beyond the northern tip of Mainland lies **Gruney**, **Outer Stack**, **Scordar**, **Turla**, **Fladda**, and assorted skerries collectively known as **Ramna Stacks** – a group designated as a 'Special Protection Area' on account of its prolific birdlife. The district of North Roe lying at the foot of Ronas Hill and west of the road is a huge expanse of trackless wilderness peppered with lochs and bog pools.

Heading north the road skirts Colla Firth and passes the **Loch of Housetter**. Beside the road are two standing stones [HU361855] and chambered cairns. The road ends at Isbister by Sand Voe. Mainland tapers away at **Point of**

Fethaland, 4km to the north, while to the north-west is the drying island of **Uyea** [oe-yë]. Climbers consider the cliffs and stacks in this region offer a worthwhile challenge but, whether climbing or not, it is a place of extraordinary beauty.

Taking the left fork where the road divides at Veensgarth and passing west of the Tingwall Airstrip the road climbs **Wormadale Hill** with its magnificent view down **Whiteness Voe**. There is a workshop here (called Hjaltasteyn) making, and selling, handmade jewellery from Shetland's own gemstones. **Loch of Strom** has the ruin of a medieval castle on a crannog-like islet [HU396475]. This may have been a residence of the Sinclairs before the castle at Scalloway was completed.

Weisdale Voe has a strange claim to fame. It was the birthplace in 1786 of John Clunie Ross who was recognised by Queen Victoria as 'King' of the Cocos Islands. Far down the voe, off the shores of Strom Ness are the islands of **Flotta** (ON – flat island) and **Hoy** (ON – high island).

The road crosses the hills and runs along the shore of Tresta Voe and **The Firth** to **Bixter**. Here a secondary road meanders northwards for 16km eventually meeting the main north road at Voe on the Olna Firth. At the head of Bixter Voe another minor road runs south to Sand where there are the arched remains of **St Mary's Chapel** which is said to have been built by the crew of a wrecked Spanish Armada galleon but is actually of Norse origin [HU346472]. At the entrance to the voe are two tiny islets, **Fore Holm** and **Kirk Holm** with the latter, surprisingly, having the remains of an ancient settlement on it. This road continues through Easter Skeld to the south coast at Culswick where, 2kms away beside a cave, are some remnants of the **Broch of Culswick** [HU254448]. The islet of **Giltarump** lies to the south and **Muckle Flaes** is near the broch. A hermit is reputed to have lived at one time on the storm-lashed **Burgi Stack**.

OLD LODBERRIES SOUTH OF LERWICK HARBOUR

A more interesting archaeological site, well sign-posted, is to the north at **Stanydale** – a large heel-shaped cairn on the open moors. It dates from about 1600BC and is thought to have been a neolithic temple or meeting place of religious significance. The nearest known similar structure is in Malta. The walls are nearly 4m thick and they enclose an oval chamber with stalls. The floor has post holes in which are traces of spruce. Live spruce was almost certainly only introduced to Scotland in the 16th century so driftwood is the most likely explanation. There are many settlement remains round about indicating that this windswept moorland once supported a sizeable community.

An abandoned village at **West Houland** is reminiscent of the cleared settlements in the Western Isles – thankfully a rather uncommon sight in this part of the world.

Near here an unclassified road runs north to West Burra Firth where the ferry sails to Papa Stour (No.11.14). **Galta Stack** is in the middle of the firth and at the entrance are **The Heag** and **Isle of West Burrafirth**.

Walls (ON – voes) is a little township with a snug harbour which once knew a certain prosperity providing barrels of salted fish for export to Aberdeen and Leith. The Foula ferry (No 11.6) sails from here. The mapmakers thought the Shetlanders' pronunciation, which sounded like Wa's, was a Scottish form of 'walls' so they anglicised the name accordingly. It actually comes from the Norse *vágar*, or *voes*, the 'v' being pronounced as a 'w'.

Unclassified roads from Walls service a fairly large area of crofts but to the north the landscape is wild and barren. The road ends at Melby which looks past the **Holm of Melby** in the Sound of Papa to Papa Stour (No.11.14) and the North Atlantic.

ACCESS: P&O overnight ro-ro service Aberdeen/Lerwick, about five times weekly, 01224-572615. Also ro-ro service Stromness (Orkney)/Lerwick, about twice weekly, 01856-850655.

British Airways, 0345-222111, and Business Air, 0500-340146, have frequent flights to Sumburgh Airport from Aberdeen, Edinburgh, Glasgow, Inverness, etc. Sumburgh Airport, 01950-460654.

Shetland Tourist Organisation publish an Inter-Shetland Transport Timetable – Scottish Tourist Office, Market Cross, Lerwick ZE1 0LU. 01595-693434. Inter-island transport information, 01426-986763.

Anchorages:
1. Grutness Voe, 1½M N of Sumburgh Head. Well-sheltered except that NE'lies and E'lies bring a swell. Beware shallows in S half of entrance. Noisy due to airport (but convenient for Jarlshof visit). Concrete pier has depth of

2.7m alongside but avoid obstructing it. Anchor off pier in 6m. A small boat marina is in Pool of Virkie, behind breakwater.

2. Voe Bay. Reasonable shelter in NE'lies. Head and N shore are shoal and also avoid S headland. Anchor off SW shore in 6m, sand.

3. Leven Wick. Good shelter from S and W. Anchor ³/₄c off beach in 6m, sand.

4. Hos Wick. Good shelter from N and W. Anchor at NW corner but beware rocky patches. Head is shoal. Alternative anchorage in bight N of Broonies Taing. (Sea-cave with blowhole to explore on Ness of Cumliewick.)

5. Sand Wick. Anchoring prohibited due to submarine cables.

6. Wick of Sandsayre, (N Mousa Sound). Rocky ridge extending 1c from SE side affords some shelter for temp anchorage. There is a small stone pier on S side.

7. Aith Voe is shallow, narrow and partially obstructed with rocks. Temp anchorage when conditions allow.

8. Gulber Wick. Holding good but exposed SE. Anchor near head.

9. Voe of Sound. Foul ground and submarine cables restrict anchorage. Best avoided.

10. Lerwick Small Boat Harbour. Temp anchorage to S. Berthing alongside breakwater not recommended. For a berth in Small Boat Harbour contact HM (Office opposite Victoria Pier). (Easy access to town centre.)

11. Lerwick Harbour. For berth in Albert docks contact HM.

12. Dales Voe. Reasonable shelter except from NE. Beware entrance dangers and keep mid-channel. Anchor just beyond promontory on SE side in 6m, mud.

13. Lax Firth. Good shelter. Keep W of mid-channel. Anchor at head beyond the ayre on E shore in 5-6m.

14. Wadbister Voe. Excellent shelter in SW winds. Beware centre rock at entrance.

15. Cat Firth. Excellent shelter but holding may be unreliable. Anchor N of Little Holm in 6m between the burns and W of mid-channel. Beware two wrecks which cover.

16. Vassa Voe. Excellent shelter but little room. Enter close to SE shore.

17. South Voe of Gletness. Temp anchorage in fair weather off W side of South Isle of Gletness in 4m, sand.

18. North Voe of Gletness. Exposed N and E. Approach with care. Anchor near head of voe in 4m, sand. Bilge keelers can dry out in pool beyond the reef.

19. Dock of Ling Ness (South Nesting Bay). Temp anchorage (longer stay for bilge keelers). Numerous rocks to be avoided.

20. Dury Voe, Bight of Bellister S of Green Isle. Narrow access E and W of Green Isle but many rocks and bottom probably foul.

21. Grunna Voe, S side of head of Dury Voe. Excellent anchorage in 5-10m, black mud, good holding. Approach keeping towards N shore of Dury Voe and turn into Grunna Voe when fully open. Keep 1c off both shores.

22. Vidlin Voe. Sheltered anchorage in pool off pier in 4m, mud. If insufficient room anchor S of Vidlin Ness clear of fish cages in 6-10m, mud but in NE and E gales a swell sets in to this area. Careful attention to charts needed.

23. Boatsroom Voe, at head of Hamna Voe, W side of Lunna Ness. Excellent anchorage in SW corner but partly obstructed by fish cages. On approach keep over 1c off Lunna Ness and to W side or centre when in

Boatsroom Voe.

24. West Lunna Voe (Shetland Bus anchorage). Excellent anchorage about ¹/₂c offshore below the tower, 10-12m, but mostly obstructed by fish cages. There are several rocks to avoid. Follow sailing instructions carefully for approach.

25. Swining Voe. Good anchorage but most parts too deep for small craft, mud and shingle.

26. Dales Voe, beyond Colla Firth. Excellent holding and free of swell but subject to violent gusts in W'lies. Keep ³/₄c off when passing Scarvar Ayre and anchor in 5-15m, mud.

27. Firths Voe. Temp anchorage in summer weather. Both sides clear beyond ¹/₂c and head dries 2c.

28. Garths Voe, off Sullom Voe. Tug and boat harbour for oil terminal.

29. Sullom Voe. Excellent anchorage anywhere above the Ness of Haggrister in depth to suit. For approach through Yell Sound to Sullom Voe it is essential to contact Harbour Control (Ch.16) and follow sailing instructions.

30. Gluss Voe. Good sheltered anchorage in pool at head of voe in 4-12m, sand. W end of pool dries. Easy approach up centre of voe.

31. Bay of Ollaberry. Occasional anchorage with good shelter from W. Anchor at head of bay in 5m.

32. Quey Firth. Temp anchorage only.

33. Colla Firth. Good shelter from W. Best anchorage off pier in Voe of the Brig or anywhere on W shore. On approach keep 1c off shores. Pier is 32m long with 4m at its head.

34. Burra Voe (North Roe). Drying rocks at middle of entrance. Keep less than ¹/₂c from Burgo Taing when entering. Good anchorage centrally off N shore in 4-6m, sand. Temp anchorage in SW opposite the houses.

35. Easter Wick of Fethaland. Temp anchorage in good weather.

36. Sand Voe on N coast. 60° 36.2N 10° 20.0W. Good sheltered anchorage close to W side of inner part of Sand Voe in 4-5m but difficult to get out in NW'lies. Good anchorage in outer voe in depths over 7m when winds are offshore but exposed to NW.

37. Ronas Voe, NW Mainland. Subject to violent squalls. Secure anchorage at head of voe in 4-10m but winds fitful. Enter mid-channel till S of Burries Ness then tend towards the NE shore, then mid-channel above the narrows. Dramatic scenery. (Access to climb Ronas Hill.)

38. Hamna Voe. Tricky entrance only 65m wide needs careful attention to sailing instructions. Reasonably sheltered anchorage in E of the voe or temp anchorage off the beaches on SE side.

39. Brae Wick and Sand Wick. Coast foul but with local knowledge temp anchorage possible.

40. Hillswick, Ura Firth. Excellent shelter in 4-10m, sand, but holding unreliable.

CLICKHIMIN FORT, BLOCKHOUSE AND BROCH

41. Ura Firth, N of Hillswick. Good shelter in 4-10m, sand, but holding unreliable.

42. Hamar Voe, Ura Firth. Excellent shelter and holding good. The head of the pool at the head of the voe is shoal but has no hidden dangers. Anchor where depth suitable.

43. Mangaster Voe. Good anchorage near the head in 4-6m but north of the moorings. Partly obstructed by fish cages.

44. Roe Sound. Approach with care and avoid in W'lies. Good anchorage just W of islet, Crog Holm, but exposed W.

45. Busta Voe, Swarbacks Minn. Fair anchorage off Brae in 6m but bottom mainly seaweed. Use slip by church for landing. Approach mid-channel W of Linga.

46. Olna Firth, Swarbacks Minn. Excellent shelter. Anchor in 4-8m above the narrows. Centre of firth clear for approach. Stone pier at Voe has 1.8m at head.

47. Gon Firth. Well-sheltered anchorage in bight at SE corner.

48. Sound of Houbansetter. Good shelter. Anchor at any suitable depth.

49. Aith Voe. Well-sheltered. Anchor anywhere to suit and if strong N'lies tuck into entrance to East Burra Firth.

50. Uyea Sound, S side of Swarbacks Minn. Good shelter in bay on N side but fish cages and many weedy patches. Approach with care. Landing possible at pier in tiny harbour on S side and passage through to Cribba Sound best tackled at near HW.

51. Vementry Sound. Many sheltered anchorages but the entrance to the sound is not well-defined and there are many dangers. Interesting area to explore but not for the faint-hearted.

52. West Burra Firth, St Magnus Bay. Occasional anchorage subject to a heavy swell. Anchor about 2c beyond narrows towards W shore in 9-12m sand. Approach needs great care. New pier for ferry to Papa Stour built 1992.

53. Voe of Snarraness, St Magnus Bay. 60° 17.7N 01° 34.7W. Clear of dangers beyond 1/2c offshore. Excellent holding, and more sheltered than West Burra Firth. Anchor in 9-14m in pool centre (fish cages) or in shallow bay on E side.

54. Lera Voe, Vaila Sound. Approach through Easter Sound. Anchor N of pier on S side of voe. Several hazards.

55. Vaila Voe. Excellent anchorage N of Salt Ness in 4-5m, mud. Better anchorage than Lera Voe. Beware Baa of Linga NW of Galta Skerry beacon, otherwise approach is relatively simple.

56. Gruting Voe. Well-sheltered anchorages in any of the voes leading off Gruting Voe: Browland Voe, Scutta Voe, or Seli Voe. Olas Voe is shallow. Keep midchannel but at entrances to Browland Voe and Scutta Voe keep N of mid-channel. Anchor anywhere suitable for depth and wind, mud generally.

57. Skelda Voe, The Deeps, (W of Hildasay). 60° 11N 01° 26W. Secure anchorage in pool at NE head in 5.5m but can be subject to some swell in S'lies. Several dangers on approach.

58. Rea Wick, Seli Voe and Sand Voe. Best visited at LW. Temp anchorages in quiet offshore winds.

59. Sandsound Voe. Pier at Omunsgarth suitable for boats at all times. Anchor in bight N of Omunsgarth or wherever suitable in The Firth, Bixter Voe, Effirth Voe or Tresta Voe. Beware Billy Baa off Fora Ness on first approach and there are several reefs and shoals to be avoided at Salt Ness and the upper reaches.

60. Weisdale Voe. Good anchorage N of narrows at Hellister Ness sheltered except for S'lies. Head of voe is shoal. In S'lies use Bay of Haggersta.

61. Stromness Voe and Whiteness Voe. Best visited at LW. Temp anchorages in quiet offshore winds.

62. Scalloway harbour. Well-sheltered. Anchor off the town on a line between Blacks Ness and Gallow Hill, 6-10m, soft mud. Below the castle there is a quay with depths exceeding 3m alongside. In W'lies better shelter E of the castle but landing difficult. Approach to Scalloway is fairly tortuous.

63. West Burra Firth, S of Scalloway entrance. Good shelter and holding. Approach mid-firth and anchor in centre N of bridge in 10-12m, sand.

64. Hamna Voe, NW extremity of West Burra. Good shelter and fairly easy approach but busy fishing port, restricted room, and bottom foul with moorings. There is a 75m long jetty at the head of the voe with 3.4m depth alongside its head.

65. West Voe leading to South Voe. Small marina behind breakwater at Bridge End between West and East Burra.

66. Clift Sound. Good shelter except from strong S'lies in entrances to Voe of North House, and N parts of Stream Sound and West Voe of Quarff (submarine cables in Clift Sound cross the S part of W Voe of Quarff to Stream Sound).

67. May Wick. Temp anchorage off pleasant sandy beach.

68. Bigton Wick, St Ninians Isle. Good shelter except from N. Anchor on W side as near the isthmus as possible, sand. (Visit St Ninian's Isle.)

69. St Ninians Bay. Good shelter except from S. Anchor on W side as near the isthmus as possible, sand. (Visit St Ninian's Isle.)

70. Bay of Scousburgh. Temp anchorage in quiet conditions.

71. Bay of Quendale not safe except as temp anchorage in very settled weather.

11.12   Papa Little

(ON pap-øy litla – little island of the priest) Shetlanders call it Papa Litla.

OS Maps: 1:50000 Sheet 3 1:25000 Sheets 11 and 14
Admiralty Charts: 1:75000 Nos.3281 and 3282 1:25000 No.3295

AREA: 226ha (558 acres)
HEIGHT: 82m (269 ft)

POPULATION: 1841 – 11 (1 house). Uninhabited since.

GEOLOGY: Papa Little lies at the junction of two faults: the Walls Boundary Fault (which may be an extension of the Great Glen Fault), and a lesser fault running westwards to Sandness Hill. Most of the island is Old Red Sandstone but the west is peat-covered metamorphic schists and phyllite.

HISTORY: Although this was obviously recognised by the Norsemen as a 'papar' island it is not known whether it was associated with any specific religious figure. It was, more likely, merely the home of an anonymous religious recluse, a holy man, or hermit. It was inhabited, possibly for centuries, by a population of fisherfolk, but abandoned or cleared in the mid-19th century. The islanders of Papa

Stour (No.11.14) have a traditional right to cut peat on Papa Little and this became essential in the 1870s when their own stocks ran out.

The south-west side of **PAPA LITTLE** is steep with low cliffs surrounding the projection of Moo Ness (ON – ness like a heap of stones). These dwindle to Green Banks in the south. There are several small hills with the highest being **North Ward** (82m), and South Ward (also 82m) topped with a cairn.

The large deep bay on the west coast is defined by two projecting entrance points. The southerly of these is called **Point of Hamna-ayre** (E. and ON – point of the shingle-spit of the harbour) where boats were once drawn up on the shingle beach when the island was inhabited. There are vivid patches of sea pinks in the grass round the shore – a plant known locally as 'banksflooer.'

Papa Little no doubt served its early inhabitants well with its bare but pleasant slopes, generous stock of peat for fuel, relatively sheltered position, and two little lochans, one in the north and one in the south, to provide fresh water.

The advantage of having peat on one's doorstep cannot be overestimated. To collect it from the mainland, or another island required an enormous amount of toil and trouble and even an element of danger. After the peat blocks had been cut and dried they were loaded into each individual's 'kishie' – a large basket slung on the back – to bring them to the shore, or to a steep-sided rock which a boat could approach. There they were stacked up in preparation for the loading which often had to be carried out fairly promptly because of weather and tide. If the boat lay off a beach the people would wade out to it while the skipper or one of the crew stowed the peats neatly. As the boatload increased the boat had to be moved further out into deeper water making access more difficult.

If the boat could come alongside a rocky shore distance was less but the work was just as back-breaking and unpleasant. Controlling the boat in a swell, or if the weather was poor while the peats were being emptied into it and stowed, required skilful seamanship. And carrying a full kishie over slippery seaweed-covered rocks could be difficult and dangerous.

After the heavily-laden boat had arrived at its destination the whole procedure began all over again but in reverse, and even when the peats were finally delivered to each croft door the work was not over, for they still had to be stacked expertly to keep each precious particle dry and safe from winter storms. It is little wonder that some said there was more heat generated by the peat-gatherers than by the peat itself.

ACCESS: No regular access. The best bet would be to ask the fish-farm operator or a friendly boat-owner at Aith.

Anchorages:
1. Bight of Warwick, Sound of Houbansetter. Anchor off E shore of Papa Little in the bight S of the drying sandspit in 7-10m. Good holding and well-sheltered except, possibly, from N-NE.

11.13 Vementry

(ON Vémundr-øy – Vémundr's island) Vémundr is a man's name.

OS Maps: 1:50000 Sheet 3 1:25000 Sheets 11 and 14
Admiralty Charts: 1:75000 No.3281 1:25000 No.3295

AREA: 370ha (914 ft)
HEIGHT: 90m (295 ft)

POPULATION: 1841 – 2 (1 house). No permanent habitation since.

GEOLOGY: Although the area is predominantly of undifferentiated schist and gneiss Vementry has a large intru-

MAA LOCH, VEMENTRY

sive sheet of coarse granite on the north-west side composed mainly of pink orthoclase, felspar, and quartz, but with very little mica. Across the Cribba Sound near Clousta there are volcanic rocks and Old Red Sandstone.

HISTORY: Swarbacks Minn was an important naval anchorage during the First World War and Vementry was fortified with two 6-inch guns to protect it.

VEMENTRY, in the parish of Aithsting, is probably as good an example as any of a typical small Shetland island with its bare and broken landscape of lochs and voes, rock-girt shoreline, windy heath, the cries of seabirds, and a scattering of relics from man's ancient past.

Swarbacks Head (ON and E. – headland of the black-backed gull) in the north, guards the entrance to the large irregular area of sheltered water called Swarbacks Minn. Above its rocky bluff and skerry there are two old gun emplacements from the 1914-18 war [HU290619]. **Northra Voe** (ON – northern creek), the small inlet beside Swarbacks Head has a chambered cairn on its west side beside a small burn [HU290612].

There are several small hills on Vementry. The highest, **Muckle Ward** (90m), has a magnificent, circular (8m diam.), stone-faced cairn on its summit [HU295609]. It stands on a heel-shaped platform made of big stone blocks with an 11m wide facade. A passage with some of its lintels still in position leads to a trefoil-shaped chamber. This type of tomb is to be found only in Shetland and has its chambers laid out like the heel of a shoe. These cairns are usually built in a prominent position, such as at the top of a hill, but the size varies and may depend on the importance of the interred individuals. This tomb on Muckle Ward is a large one and one of the best-preserved in Shetland – probably because its situation is not readily accessible. It is also unusual because it has no entrance and was presumably closed after the last burial.

The west coast is divided by shallow, rocky, Suthra Voe (ON – southern creek) which penetrates into the heart of the island. Two islets almost obstruct the entrance, **The Heag**, and **Gruna** (ON – green island) while **Linga** to the south spreads half-way across the sound. Only a shallow, narrow channel separates Vementry from Mainland as a neck of land projecting out of Mainland divides Cribba Sound from Uyea Sound. Vementry House stands, white-walled, at the root of this peninsula with its snug little harbour beside it.

St Magnus Bay

Swarbacks Minn

Swarbacks Skerry

Swarbacks Head

59

Crooie Geo

John's Head

Corbie Geo

Geo of the Ward

Northra Voe

Swaba Stacks

Chambered Cairn ★

Whal Geo

Muckle Ward ★ 90 *Chambered Cairn*

Turr Geo

Lamba Wick

North Voe

Holms of Uyea Sound

61

25

Heill Head

25

Loch of Reva

Egga Field

Cow Head

Uyea Sound

The Heag

Suthra Voe

Maa Loch

★ *Homestead*

Gruna

Miilder Ness 56

Vementry

Shaabers Head

Seggi Bight

Cribba Sound

Linga

25

57

MAINLAND

Trea Wick

Sonso Ness

Green Point

Whaal Voe

Green Holm

North Voe of Clousta

The Brigs

Brindister Voe

MAINLAND (Aithsting)

Voe of Clousta

N

Vementry

1 km
1/2 mile

ACCESS: No regular access but a boat-owner in Vementry harbour (Mainland) may take you across the 200m-wide sound.

Anchorages: Vementry Sound has a number of suitable anchorages but passage is difficult with many rocks and dangerous reefs. Proceed with great care using large-scale chart and sailing instructions.
1. Uyea Sound. Reasonable shelter. Anchor in bay on N side in 4-8m, good holding when not in weed, but restricted by fish cages. Narrow passage through to Cribba Sound has minimum depth of 1m.
2. Cribba Sound. Good shelter in NW half. Fish cages.

11.14 Papa Stour

(ON papøy stóra – big island of the priests)

OS Maps: 1:50000 Sheet 3 1:25000 Sheet 13
Admiralty Charts: 1:75000 No.3281

AREA: 828ha (2,046 acres)
HEIGHT: 87m (285 ft)

OWNER: Multiple ownership.

POPULATION: 1841 – 382 (66 houses). 1871 – 351. 1881 – 254. 1891 – 244 (44 houses). 1931 – 100. 1961 – 55. 1971 – 24. 1981 – 29. 1991 – 33.

GEOLOGY: Formed from volcanic lava and ash and then sculpted by the sea resulting in some of the finest sea caves in Britain. These, however, are only accessible in fine weather. There are also many interesting skerries, stacks and voes.

HISTORY: Papa Stour, with its fertile soil, is thought to have been first settled about 3000BC. When the Norsemen came they presumably found monks or hermits in residence but they settled here themselves nevertheless. A fascinating piece of archaeological detective work by Dr

Barbara Crawford of St Andrews in the early 1980s has revealed what is almost certainly the 13th century residence of Duke Haakon, later King of Norway, who had a farm on the island beside Housa Voe.

In the early 16th century merchants from Hamburg and Bremen considered the island of sufficient importance to build a summer trading booth to buy fish and fish oil from the islanders and exchange various commodities. But the haaf (ON deep-sea) fishing decreased and herring fishing had taken its place by the mid-19th century. A herring station was constructed at Hamna Voe and curers and gutters came from far afield, even from Ireland. Fuel was so scarce and the fishermen so busy that the islanders started burning the turf and even today large areas lie scalped and bare. By the 1870s the situation was so bad that people started to leave.

In 1970 the school closed because there were no more young children. In fact the total population by then was only sixteen fairly elderly people. Although the Sound of Papa is relatively narrow, tides rage through it and the island can be isolated for days at a time. But after an advertisement was placed in *Exchange and Mart* mentioning that crofts would be granted free together with five sheep each, young people started to flood in from all over Britain. It was a refuge from the rat-race – a place for 'human values' and flower-power. Shetlanders started calling it the 'Hippy Isle'. Most of the incomers gave up quickly when they discovered the rigours of island existence but a few remained and they gave the island new life. The population rose to about thirty. By 1992, however, numbers were once again falling and a new search was on for anyone – even 'barefoot hippies' – said an islander.

WILDLIFE: This is a fertile island and it is said that fishermen can locate the island in a summer haar by the pungent smell of the wild flowers – 'Fir da scent o flooers in Papa leds wis aa da wye'.

Papa Stour and Foula (No.11.6) were the last refuges of the primitive and goat-like Shetland sheep. These were classified as an endangered species, but a flock is now kept on Mainland.

The stacks and inlets support many sea-birds and there are quite large colonies of cormorant and Manx shearwater. It is interesting to learn that although the fulmar is relatively widespread now, in 1890 an ornithologist visiting Papa Stour noted with delight that he had seen one.

Common seals breed on the skerries.

Each volcanic island being formed today off the coast of Iceland will become a **PAPA STOUR** tomorrow. Already their soft ash is being eaten away by the sea from its hard volcanic base leaving tunnels and arches and weird, grotesque, tortuous shapes. On the surface, where the sea cannot wash them away, seeds dropped by the seabirds take root and the ash is converted into fertile soil, rich in essential nutrients.

Papa Stour is one of the most fertile of the Shetland Islands, its only failing being a total lack of fuel in the form of peat. It has exciting volcanic forms and a precipitous coastline, indented and eroded, above a tumble of detached rocks, stacks and skerries – a wonderland for climbers and potholers. In the north-west there is an immense cliff with a natural tunnel, the **Hole of Bordie**,

VOLCANIC SEA-CAVES BY BREI HOLM, PAPA STOUR

penetrating it for nearly 1km (½M)! **Virda Field**, the highest hill (87m), sits above it. Beyond the narrow cleft of Akers Geo are the **Fogla** (ON *fugl* – bird) and **Lyra** (ON *lyrie* – Manx shearwater) **Skerries**. They also have subterranean passages through which the tide surges. Here too a great column of rock, the **Stack of Snalda**, reaches skywards, and far out to sea the **Ve Skerries** (ON – suffering skerries), a favourite seal-hunting ground in days gone by, lie low and menacing among the Atlantic waves.

Probably Britain's finest sea cave, **Kirstan's** (or Christie's) **Hole**, is on the south-west side of the island [HU152606]. It is at the head of a narrow creek and confined between vertical rock faces about 30m high. A columnar stack stands like a sentry beside the 27m-wide natural arch forming the cave entrance. Within there is an enclosed space with glistening walls standing open to the sky. The cave then continues for about another 70m, ending at a beach.

John Tudor, a Victorian traveller, raved about the caves of Papa Stour. His favourite was **Francie's Hole** nearer Hamna Voe. This is smaller than Christie's Hole, but in his view more beautiful. The entrance is perfectly arched and inside you are 'in fairyland, so exquisite is the colouring of the roof and sides, and so pellucid is the water'. Caves branch off on one side and at the back is a small pink beach above which 'are alcoves or recesses like stalls in a church'.

Hamna Voe (ON – haven or harbour creek) is an almost land-locked lagoon. Red cliffs on the east side by the entrance conceal the modest island airstrip and the school. There is a natural rock arch in these cliffs with the remnants of two chambered cairns above it. The church is above a small beached cove known as **Kirk Sand** and there are more cairns and burnt mounds nearby. The odds are that the church, which looks across the Sound of Papa to Melby on Mainland, was built on the most sacred pagan site. **Forewick Holm** lies offshore.

All the habitation is in the east mainly around **Housa**

Voe (ON – voe of the houses). Although more exposed than Hamna Voe, Housa Voe has a pier for the small ferryboat from West Burra Firth on Mainland. Off the headland between Kirk Sand and Housa Voe there are many interesting rock formations and a small islet, **Brei Holm**, joined to the ness by a drying reef. Until the 18th century this tiny patch of land supported a leper colony although it is now thought that many of the so-called lepers actually only suffered from vitamin deficiency.

Near Brei Holm is an isolated stack with the vestige of a stone house to be seen on its narrow top. This is the **Maiden Stack**, or Frau Stack. In the early 14th century Lord Thorvald Thoresson is said to have built this for his daughter to live in to ensure that she would not be in the company of men. But it was all to no avail for when he released her she was found to be pregnant.

The group of houses which cluster behind the Post Office at Housa Voe is known as **Biggings** (ON *byggja* – buildings) and is probably the island's earliest settlement. At the start of the 19th century the Hon. Edwin Lindsay was sent here in disgrace by his family for refusing to fight a duel. They had him declared insane and he was kept under guard on the island for twenty-six years. It was a Quaker preacher, Catherine Watson, who arranged his escape and he was then able to claim his inheritance. There is a spring at the south of the island called Lindsay's Well where he was allowed to bathe.

Papa Stour's mood changes with the weather and at times it has either a magical or a sinister quality. This is particularly noticeable on the north coast when a haar creeps in and blankets the wicks and geos. But even Housa Voe is not immune. The islanders tell of a strange ship that sailed into the voe on a sunny day long ago. The crew were seen to be preparing to attack the village so the local witch, Minna Baaba, immediately created a storm which blew the ship far out to sea.

ACCESS: Boat from West Burrafirth, Monday, Wednesday, Friday and Saturday, 30 minutes, 01595-873227. Weather permitting and prior booking essential. Loganair flights on request, Tues. only, 01595-840246.

Anchorages: Passage in the Sound of Papa requires great care as there are strong tides and many off-shore dangers. There are severe overfalls off the NW coast.

1. Hamna Voe. Shelter from all weather but entry impossible in strong S'lies. At the narrows there is only 2m depth at LWS, and 20m width. Follow instructions for entry, which requires care. Anchor N or S in 4-6m.

2. Housa Voe. Reasonable shelter in 4-6m, sand. Good holding. There is a pier. Enter from N 1c off and parallel to NW shore to avoid Housa Baa.

3. West Voe. Not recommended.

4. Culla Voe. Shelter from all weather. Approach mid-channel to avoid sunken rocks at entrance. Anchor near head of voe.

11.15 Whalsay

(ON hvals-øy – whale island)

OS Maps: 1:50000 Sheet 2 1:25000 Sheet 12
Admiralty Charts: 1:75000 No.3282

AREA: 1,970ha (4,868 acres)
HEIGHT: 119m (390 ft)

OWNER: Multiple ownership.

POPULATION: 1841 – 628 (112 houses). 1881 – 870. 1891 – 927 (167 houses). 1931 – 900. 1961 – 764. 1971 – 870. 1981 – 1026. 1991 – 1041.

GEOLOGY: The bedrock is almost entirely of gneiss with granite veins. There are good stocks of peat which the Out Skerries islanders are entitled to cut.

HISTORY: The Bruces of Muness in Unst gained possession of Whalsay from its crofter-owners and brought in a period of harsh rule. In the 19th century the punishment for any small misdemeanour was exile from the island.

Naval press-gangs valued the sailing ability of Whalsay men and would sometimes remove them from their sixerns when they were out fishing. The families were not informed.

The recent history of Whalsay is the 'boom and bust' history of fishing for this is an island of fishermen. In 1832 many lost their lives when there was a great storm at sea but fishing continued and 1834 was the peak year for herring catches. Second-hand 'half-deckers' were bought on the Scottish mainland to replace the native 'sixerns' and improve the Whalsay fleet. But this optimism was followed in 1839 by a slump in the herring market followed in 1840 by another violent storm in which many men were drowned. Bankruptcy and poverty were rife.

By the late 19th century, however, the industry had recovered and bigger boats were introduced. For a time all was well, and then steam drifters created new problems as the Whalsay men lacked capital to compete.

BENIE HOOSE – A NEOLITHIC RETREAT

Between the two World Wars Whalsay fishermen survived by catching what herring they could in the summer and supplementing this with inshore haddock fishing in the winter, but after the Second World War conditions improved when Government grants and loans assisted the purchase of superior dual-purpose vessels.

This 'mini-boom' continued until 1965 when 200 Norwegian ships appeared fitted with power tackle and sonar and swept the seas of fish. The Shetlanders tried to follow the Norwegian example and for a few years there were huge catches but by 1977 the stocks had disappeared and herring-fishing was banned. Since 1983 there has been limited intermittent fishing, complicated by the requirements of the European Community.

WILDLIFE: The Shetland record brown trout – 9lb 4oz – was caught in Whalsay's Loch of Huxter.

Small colonies of kittiwake and puffin nest at the south

end of the island and whimbrel, arctic tern and arctic skua nest on the moors and by the lochans. A few red-throated diver, known as 'rain geese' in Shetland, may also be seen. This is an important staging-post for migrant birds; unusual species such as the red-rumped swallow, hoopoe, and Pallas' warbler have been recorded.

WHALSAY is the 'Bonny Isle'. Pleasant green pastures could easily support livestock but few do, for the islanders are fishers not farmers and the economy revolves round fish. Offshore there are rocks, reefs and skerries with fascinating names like the **Hogo Baas** and **Rumble Holm** which give shelter to lobsters, prawns, and a surprising number of white fish. Efficient foreign fleets which vacuum the seas and create deserts cannot operate in such an area; it takes a local to know all the sandbanks and crevices. As a result and in spite of the complications of deep-sea fishing there is an expanding and relatively prosperous population, a fish-processing plant, and a desire by every young man to get to sea in his own boat. Why waste time milking cows when there are fish in the sea? Lerwick can supply all the milk required.

Ward of Clett, a well-defined hill in the south of the island is the highest point at 119m. It rises south-west of the **Loch of Huxter** (ON – prehistoric-mound farm) with its Iron Age holm fort [HU559620]. This is thought to be one of the earliest versions of a broch – the idea from which the later versions evolved. Unfortunately, many of the stones were removed to build cabbage enclosures or 'plantiecruives', but sufficient remains to be of interest.

Generally, the island has an attractive rolling landscape of low hills and small lochs, with activity mainly centred around the small port at **Symbister** in the south. The airstrip is at the other end, at **Skaw** (ON – point) in the north. There are two islets off Skaw Taing, **Outer** and **Inner Holm of Skaw**, with a ruined chapel on Inner Holm.

The lighthouse on **Symbister Ness** in the south-west is

BREMEN BÖD – A 17TH CENTURY HANSEATIC TRADING-POST

close to the busy, little harbour which is in the most southerly of two small voes. **Bremen Böd**, near the Symbister pier, has an old wooden windlass beside it. This is a Hanseatic store set up by German merchants in the 17th century to trade brandy, tobacco, linen, muslin, fruit, and salt for haddock, fish oil, cod and other fishy delicacies. It is the only complete surviving example in Scotland of such a building. It was rescued from dereliction and is now used as a visitors' interpretive centre.

Symbister House is an extravagant solid-granite Georgian mansion sited east of the harbour which has served as a Junior High School since 1940 [HU543622]. It was built in 1823 by the head of the distinguished Shetland family of Bruce at great cost (£30,000), not because he needed a second home – he already had a fine house on Mainland – but for the rather petty reason that he did not wish to leave the money for his heirs to enjoy. The grounds, incidentally, are reputed to be haunted by an old sailor who was murdered by the gardener for winning a game of cards.

Between Symbister and Loch of Huxter is the ruined cottage where the poet Christopher Grieve (Hugh MacDiarmid) lived from 1933 to 1942. The place name is **Sudheim** (ON – south home) but the Ordnance Survey had anglicised this to **Sodom**! – much to MacDiarmid's amusement.

A shallow bay on the south coast, Sand Wick, has Bronze Age burnt mounds beside it. Several skerries and an islet, **Holm of Sandwick**, obstruct entrance to the bay.

Half-way up the north-west coast the village of **Brough** (ON – stronghold) is beside Kirk Ness with a narrow isthmus leading to a church [HU555655] and at Suther Ness there is another lighthouse. Directly across on the other side of the island is **Isbister** (ON – east farm), a settlement of houses clustered beside a loch and looking south-east over two strings of islets. Nearby are the delightfully named **Nista** (ON – northmost isle), **Mooa** (ON – narrow isle), and **Isbister Holm** with **Nacka Skerry** to the north, and further out are **East Linga** and the **Grif**, **Swarta**, **Longa**, and **Rumble Skerries** (ON – beside the deep sea, black, long and round-rocks skerries respectively). The Grif Skerry was a haaf fishing station where the boats could be beached in bad weather while the men sheltered in primitive huts.

Some of these names can be very confusing. For instance, the Admiralty Chart attaches names to the rocks south of Whalsay which are incorrect according to the Whalsay fishermen. They say that a sailor should read **Muckla Fladdacap** as Muckle Fladdacap, **Muckla Billan** as Peerie Fladdacap, **Litla Billan** as Haerie, and **Haerie** as Ooter Vooder!

Midway between Loch Isbister and Loch of Huxter is pewter-coloured **Nuckro Water** (ON nøkk – water monster). This is the home of a vicious water demon, known in Shetland as the 'njuggle', which usually appears in the form of a beautiful, friendly, horse. But once seated on its back the human victim is carried into the water and drowned. The njuggle can also appear in other forms and it is most dangerous after sunset. Another njuggle lives in Njugals Water near Tingwall on Mainland.

Between Isbister and Skaw the **Yoxie Biggins** may date from about 3000BC. This is a heel-shaped structure somewhat like Staneydale on Mainland. It was first assumed to have religious significance but now it is thought more likely to have been a Neolithic farmhouse. Another ruin

from the same period, **Bunzie** (or **Benie**) **Hoose**, is adjacent and it has a clover-leaf layout [HU587652].

ACCESS: Frequent car ferry service from Laxo (Mainland), 30 minutes, 01806-566259. Loganair charter flights from Tingwall, 01595-840246. Local information, 01806-566483.

Anchorages:
1. Symbister Harbour. Sheltered but busy fishing-boat harbour on W coast. No anchorage in N or S owing to underwater cables. Tie alongside S breakwater/jetty, 102m-long, provided those already berthed are agreeable.

West Linga

WEST LINGA SEEN FROM SODOM (HUGH MACDIARMID'S COTTAGE) ON WHALSAY

11.16 West Linga

(E. and ON – west heather-island)

OS Maps: 1:50000 Sheet 2 1:25000 Sheet 12
Admiralty Charts: 1:75000 No.3282

AREA: 125ha (309 acres)
HEIGHT: 52m (171 ft)

POPULATION: Uninhabited.

GEOLOGY: Coarse micaceous and hornblendic gneiss with granite veins. There is a raised beach above Croo Wick (ON – sheep-pen bay) at the south extremity.

HISTORY: Liv Schei in her fascinating book, *The Shetland Story*, notes that on the 7th August 1485 at Korskirken in Bergen a meeting was held to discuss an illegal purchase of various lands in Shetland. The most important piece of land listed was ten merks on 'Liungøuo i Hwalsøyo.'

WEST LINGA is a long narrow island covered in rough heath with its highest point (52m) almost in the exact geometrical centre. There is a further minor hill in the southern part with a cairn on it and two small lochans in the northern half. It is somewhat surprising that an island of this size with a supply of drinkable, if brackish, water has so little sign of human habitation but this is probably due to the lack of an anchorage. There is not even a suitable place to beach a boat easily for any length of time. However, in spite of such difficulties the island seems to have been inhabited intermittently until, possibly, the end of the 18th century.

It is said that while the Bruce family were 'acquiring' Whalsay the udaller of West Linga went out fishing. While he was absent his young son got his head stuck in a large jar and his mother was frantic with worry. The Bruce representative happened to land on the island during this incident and the mother appealed to him for help. He re-fused until the mother signed over the land whereupon he calmly broke the pot. This story may have grown with the telling but it no doubt had some basis in fact.

The **Calf of Linga** is a drying islet off the Skate (ON – a rock or sand shelf) at the southern extremity. At the opposite extreme in the north there is another islet called **Wether Holm**. This is separated from West Linga by a narrow 3m-deep channel.

West Linga divides the sea area between Whalsay and Mainland into two Sounds, Linga and Lunning. Both have fierce tides but Lunning Sound is broken up with many islets and skerries which create swirls and eddies understood only by the Whalsay fishermen. The islets are **Hunder Holm** according to the Ordnance Survey but known locally as 'Unerim' (ON – Arnorr's holm), **Bruse Holm** or 'Brusim' (ON – Brusi's holm), **Ketill Holm** or 'Kettlim' (ON – Ketill's holm), **Score Holm** or 'Skurim' (ON – Skori's holm) and **Little Linga**.

The poet and author, Hugh MacDiarmid, who lived in a Whalsay cottage which overlooked West Linga, claimed in *The Uncanny Scot* to have spent three days on the island. He said that he asked a boatman to leave him there and not to look for him for three days and that he had with him only a good stock of matches, some thick black tobacco, and two books. He slept in a cave in the rocks and caught four sillocks with a bent pin on a string. It transpired later that the story was entirely imaginary – although he had spent part of a day on the island with the man who grazed his sheep there.

ACCESS: No regular access but a friendly boat-owner ot fisherman at Symbister on Whalsay may assist.

Anchorages: No recommended anchorages.

11.17 Linga

(ON lyng-øy – heather island)

OS Maps: 1:50000 Sheet 3 1:25000 Sheet 11
Admiralty Charts: 1:75000 Nos.3281 or 3282 1:25000 No.3295

AREA: 70ha (173 acres)
HEIGHT: 69m (226 ft)

POPULATION: Uninhabited and no census records.

GEOLOGY: Gneiss, schists and some quartzite and pelite.

A circumnavigation of **LINGA** reveals all. From every

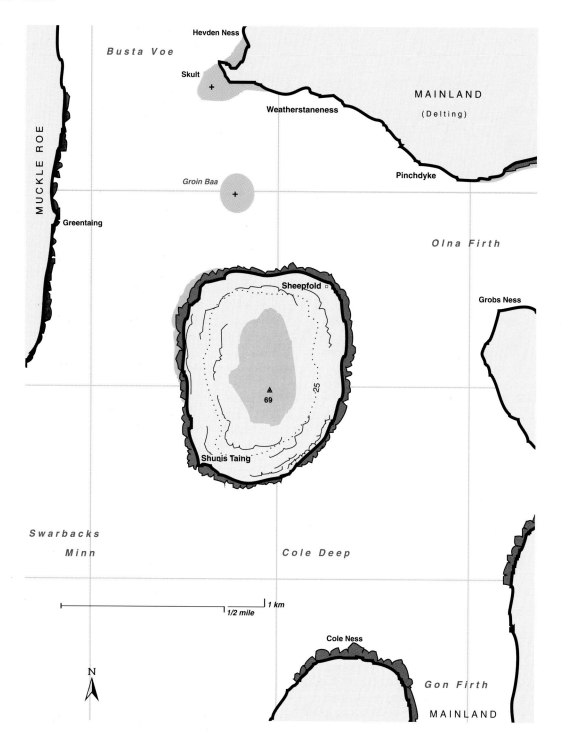

viewpoint its rounded surface of rough grass and heather resembles a well-cooked pudding in a rock-encrusted pie-dish. There are no coves or caves or crags, no hidden se-crets, no ancient ruins. To its credit the view from the top of the dumpling (69m) is striking and worth the effort of achieving a landing. To be fair, Linga is not unwelcoming to visitors – merely indifferent.

ACCESS: No regular access. There is an adjacent fish farm and one of the service boats may be persuaded to put you ashore.

Anchorages: No recommended anchorages. Beware Groin Baa in the north channel.
1. Possible temporary anchorage, if conditions are suitable, off NE side in 12-15m but use tripping line.

11.18 Housay
or West Isle

(ON hús-øy – house island)

Bruray *or* East Isle

(ON brúar-øy- island forming a bridge) - together with

Grunay

(ON – green island) these are known as the Out Skerries (ON út-skeri – outer skerries) or just 'The Skerries', (ON austrskeri – eastern skerries).

OS Maps: 1:50000 Sheet 2 1:25000 Sheet 10
Admiralty Charts: 1:75000 No.3282

AREA: 218ha (539 acres)
HEIGHT: 53m (174 ft)

OWNER: Housay, Bruray and the nearby stacks and skerries are owned by Cussons Estate. They were bought by A. S. Cussons (of Imperial Leather fame) in 1967. The only exception to this is Laurence Anderson who owns his own property of 'Sunnyside' beside Da Stripe.

Grunay has changed hands many times in the last decade. The last owner of whom I have record was Torquil Johnson-Ferguson of Dumfriesshire but he put it up for sale in 1993.

POPULATION:

	1841	1881	1891	1931	1961	1971	1981	1991
Housay		71	86	68	71	63	48	58
Bruray		59	54	34	34	35	31	27
Sub-total		130	140	108	105	98	79	85
Grunay		25	25	6	0	0	0	0
Total	122	155	165	114	105	98	79	85

GEOLOGY: The Mio Ness peninsula (joined to Housay by The Steig which is a collapsed cave) is granite. Apart from a strip of fragmented limestone which stretches from the southern coast of Housay through the centre of Housay and Bruray the rest of the islands are of gneiss. Grunay has granite bedrock.

HISTORY: The extent of settlement by early man still awaits scientific investigation. Norse habitation is much more clearly recorded by the hundreds of Norse place-names. These could never have arisen from a few transitory visits and point to continuous settlement over a long period of time.

But the really history of the Skerries is the history of the sea that surrounds them because through the centuries many ships have foundered on these treacherous rocks and the people of the Skerries have had to live with, and understand, the sea in all its moods. One of the earliest recorded wrecks was a Spanish Armada horse-carrier which was said to have sunk in the narrow channel called The Rett.

With the outbreak of the second Anglo-Dutch war in 1664 Dutch East-Indiamen, being merchant ships, avoided the English Channel and preferred to take the longer route ('Achter Om') round the north of Scotland. Although, following the accession of a Scottish King to the English throne in 1603, Scotland and England had a shared monarchy, both countries still had independent Parliaments and the Scots were not at war with the Dutch. On the night of the 11th December 1664 the *Kennermerland*, bound for the Cape of Good Hope ran hard on to Stoura Stack and broke up in the South Mouth. The foremast fell ashore and three men in the rigging survived. The rest were swept out to sea and drowned. The only body washed ashore, a drummer-boy, is buried near the old fish factory. The Earl of Morton, who owned the islands at that time, recovered about 120,000 guilders by promptly setting up a primitive salvage operation but King Charles II stepped in and claimed ownership. There was a court case in Edinburgh which the King won and the Earl lost both the guilders and his Orkney and Shetland estates. The islanders also got nothing, but at least enough barrels of spirits had been washed ashore to keep them inebriated for weeks and it is still said that a chest of gold was hidden on the seashore. It is also said that the first hens on Out Skerries came from this wreck.

The *De Liefde*, one of a convoy of ships laden with gold and silver coins to pay for exotic goods in Java, ran into Mio Ness on 8th November 1711 and was lost with all hands except for the look-out in the crow's-nest who was thrown onto the grassy top of the cliff. He reported that there were millions of guilders and several chests of gold coins on board. Most of the money may still be somewhere on the seabed. Occasional coins turn up unexpectedly and an official dive in 1967 recovered a chestfull of silver coins and some gold ducats. Diving to these wrecks without official permission is forbidden and strictly enforced.

More recently, in 1906, the wreck of the *North Wind* with a cargo of wood allowed the islanders to lay wooden floors in every house – a great luxury.

But shipwrecks only brought occasional and limited

THE SKERRIES SHORELINE – A GRAVEYARD FOR SHIPS

prosperity. Fishing is the historic means of livelihood and in the 19th century Out Skerries provided a valuable haaf fishing station and intermittently throughout the 20th century it has been a centre for the industry.

WILDLIFE: Very well-placed to receive continental migrants when the wind is in the east so, apart from islanders' relatives, divers and island-hoppers, the majority of visitors are bird-watchers. The islands support small breeding colonies of gulls, terns, eider and black guillemot but, otherwise, there is only limited birdlife on the cliffs which are not high enough to provide attractive nesting sites.

HOUSAY and **BRURAY** are linked by a concrete bridge built in 1957, replacing the first bridge built in 1899 and a subsequent 'improvement', and they are nowadays the only inhabited islands in the Out Skerries group. Although this cluster of little islands and skerries, exposed and isolated, reach tentatively into the vast inhospitable wastes of the North Sea they are considered to be one of the happiest and most flourishing parts of Shetland. On approach by sea the cliffs, which are not particularly high, still look forbidding and impregnable. But on a close approach a gap appears and once through the narrow 'mouth' a different picture presents itself. In between the three main is-

lands of the archipelago, Housay, Bruray and Grunay is a landlocked haven and a pier, completed in 1986, where the ferry docks. Neat, trim and colourful cottages scattered around deep-green miniature fiords create a Nordic flavour. Behind, are low grassy hills which are used for grazing. There is a little cultivation on a belt of relatively fertile soil but generally the people of the Out Skerries are like those of Whalsay – fisherfolk, not farmers.

The Skerries is a world in miniature with about 1500 tiny geographical features each of which is specifically named by the islanders. Housay has a long precipitous leg stretching south-westwards and ending at **Mio Ness** (ON – narrow headland). It humps up like a bent knuckle to a height of 48m near its south extremity. The island itself has a hill on each side of **West Voe**, a deep inlet on the west coast and a modest settlement with a Post Office and a cemetery in the middle. At the northern extremity is **Wether Holm**.

North Hill is covered with mounds of stones like 2m-long upturned boats. These are said to be prehistoric graves. There is other evidence of early man – lengths of walls built of Cyclopean masonry, 'skeos' round West Voe (a 'skeo' is the Shetland equivalent of a St Kildan 'cleit', or stone larder), and a mysterious stone rectangle of large boulders called **Battle Pund**. This has some similarity to

Hjaltadans on Fetlar (No.11.24). There are varying explanations for both it and its name.

Across the bridge, on Bruray there are more houses, a school overlooking the harbour, and the airstrip beyond. North of the airstrip is the highest point on the archipelago at 53m where a much-needed fresh-water collection system was installed in 1957. Even so, water sometimes has to be brought over by tanker from Mainland.

As ever in such small communities, the school is a vital requirement for stability and the islanders insisted that their children should be fully educated on the island. Consequently a new school was built in 1965. It has two teachers and provides both primary and secondary education – including a course in computer graphics! It is the smallest secondary school in Britain. The old school was converted into a church and a new Community Hall was built in 1981.

There is about a mile of surfaced road which can be quite busy as, since the introduction of the ro-ro ferry, there are about twenty cars. Every family owns a boat, and a fish-processing factory was built here in the productive early 1970s but fish is no longer such a prolific commodity and the factory is idle.

The small island of **Grunay** on the east side of the harbour is separated from the others by South Mouth and Northeast Mouth. The entrance to South Mouth is guarded by both **Stoura Stack** – cause of the *Kennermerland* (or *Carmelan*) disaster – and **Old Man's Stack**, while **Lamba Stack** stands by Northeast Mouth. East of Grunay is **Bound Skerry** with a lighthouse which is now automatic. It was twice bombed by the Germans in the Second World War as they thought it was a munition factory! The lighthouse was built in 1857 for £21,000 and the keepers were housed on Grunay. Robert Louis Stevenson's signature is in the visitor's book.

On its route to Out Skerries the ferry passes a group of islets and skerries stretching south from Mio Ness – **Benelip**, consisting of linked islets – **North and South Benelip** and **Easter Skerries** – is the largest, while the ferry is named after **Filla** which lies immediately to the south.

ACCESS: Ro-ro ferry on prior booking from Vidlin, two hours, several sailings, Fri., Sat., Sun., or Lerwick on Tues., and Thurs., 01806-566226. Loganair charter flights from Tingwall, 01595-840246.

Anchorages:
1. Between Housay and Bruray. Anchor in 6m towards the bridge, abreast the school, if space can be found among the moorings. Use tripping line. Reasonable shelter but some swell possible.
2. Between Bruray and Grunay. Anchor in 4m off Bruray shore about 1c NE of perch. Use tripping line. Reasonable shelter but NE'lies bring an uncomfortable swell.
3. North Mouth, pool N of bridge (Stringa Voe). Sheltered but not recom-

mended as room very restricted.
4. West Voe on W side of Housay. Mouth obstructed by the Hogg, a rocky islet 2c long. The narrow difficult entrance is at S end of the Hogg where a bar restricts least depth to only 0.6m. Inside the depth increases and there is excellent shelter but the entrance at HW is tricky.

11.19 Samphrey

(ON Sandfridar-øy – Sandfridr's island) Sandfridr is a woman's name.

OS Maps: 1:50000 Sheet 2 or 3 1:25000 Sheet 9
Admiralty Charts: 1:75000 No.3282 1:30000 Nos.3292 or 3298

AREA: 66ha (163 acres)
HEIGHT: 29m (95 ft)

POPULATION: 1841 – 36 (6 houses). 1881 – 0. Uninhabited since then.

GEOLOGY: Coarsely-crystalline gneiss with occasional granite veins.

HISTORY: In late 1832 a terrible storm blew up unexpectedly and caught six Samphrey men out fishing on the haaf. Their sixern was blown through mountainous seas until it eventually ended up on a Norwegian beach. It suffered only minor damage and the men were given accommodation and treated very hospitably by the Norwegians. In the spring they returned home, none the worse for their holiday abroad, to a great welcome from their families who had believed they were dead.

WILDLIFE: The grazing is reasonably good for sheep but wildflowers are scarce, not only because of the grazing but also, because the island is so flat, it catches the worst of the salt-spray.

A number of sea birds breed here and both Samphrey and neighbouring Fish Holm are managed by the RSPB as a bird sanctuary.

SAMPHREY defensively straddles the southern entrance to Yell Sound. The tides can run fast past its shores. It is low-lying, shaped something like the jaw-bone of an ass, and the highest ground in the centre of the island is only 29m above sea-level.

Unlike so many Shetland islands, Samphrey is relatively clear of rocks in the surrounding sea and it is possible to sail fairly close to the coastline, except for the shallow **Bunglan** promontory on the west side. A large pool or lochan on this headland is only cut off from the sea by narrow margins of land on two sides.

Many of the remnants of human occupation have already disappeared but there is a wee kirkyard. It is reputed to have very few men buried in it as according to tradition: 'Samphrey men are always taken by the sea.' Such certainty could only have arisen in a community dedicated to fishing and the sea which, in the end, may have taken too many, for slowly during the 19th century the number of fishermen and their families dwindled until the island was entirely depopulated. Samphrey is now merely habitation for seabirds and sheep.

South of Samphrey there is an island, **Linga** (ON – heather island) which only just fails to meet my target of forty hectares. It is higher than Samphrey but otherwise I have found nothing of particular note. South of it is yet another, **Wether Holm** (ON – islet of the castrated ram), and to the north is **Fish Holm**.

A rock outcrop, The **Rumble**, north-east of Samphrey

is marked by a beacon. Orfasay (ON *orfyrisøy* – tidal island), is across the sound and linked to the south coast of Yell (No.11.23).

ACCESS: No regular access. Make local enquiries at Mossbank, or Boath of Toft, Mainland.

Anchorages:

1. Temp anchorage in suitable weather in the bight N of Bunglan, the W promontory. Approach with care and anchor in 5m. Use tripping line. Beware submarine cable which is on a line between the W extremities of the two headlands.

11.20 Bigga

(ON bygd-øy – island of the building)

OS Maps: 1:50000 Sheet 2 or 3 1:25000 Sheet 9
Admiralty Charts: 1:75000 No.3282 1:30000 No.3298

AREA: 78ha (193 acres)
HEIGHT: 34m (112 ft)

POPULATION: 1841, 1881 and 1891 – no separate census records. 1931 – 1. Since uninhabited.

GEOLOGY: Moine bedrock of coarsely-crystalline gneiss and quartzite.

WILDLIFE: Storm petrel and puffin occasionally breed here. Uynarey to the north is a nature reserve managed by the RSPB.

BIGGA is now a 'sheep isle' but it appears to have been intermittently inhabited until the 1930s. It is long and narrow with a head and torso. The neck is between two bays, **Easter** and **Wester Hevda Wick** (ON – east and west bays of seaweed or manure). The torso rises to a central height of 34m and there is a small hill at the north extremity or head with a prehistoric cairn on its eastern slope.

In the south of the island there is a house which is used as a shepherd's bothy. The local newspapers reported the story of two sailors from Yell (No.11.23) who were given home leave during the Second World War. They were home-sick and desperate to rejoin their families in time for Yule. The weather was very wild and the ferry from Mainland refused to sail so they borrowed a small open boat from a friend and set off. The snow-covered hills of Yell could just be seen through the spume over the wind-whipped open Sound and the tide was in full racing flood but they were accomplished sailors and knew the waters well. However, they could make no headway as the storm increased in strength and it was many hours later

before they managed to struggle ashore on Bigga. They sheltered in the bothy but it was so cold that they spent the night playing the fiddle and dancing Shetland reels to keep warm. The next day they were given assistance by a passing drifter and arrived on Yell just in time to join their family celebrations.

There is a reef at the north end of Bigga which crosses the narrow sound separating Bigga from Uynarey. **Uynarey** (ON – venerated island) is slightly higher than Bigga with steeper sides.

ACCESS: No regular access. The assistance of a local boat-owner is required. The Yell ferryman may advise.

Anchorages: Strong tides and a number of rocks make this area hazardous.
1. Temp anchorage when conditions suitable in Wester Hevda Wick. Beware rock with less than 1.8m over it ¹/₂c off NW extremity.

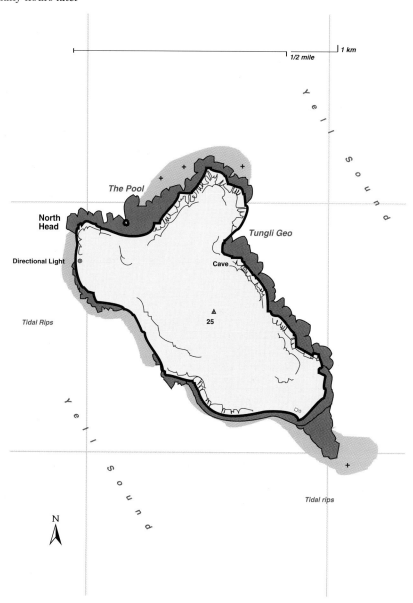

Brother Isle

11.21 Brother Isle

(ON breidare-øy – broad beach island). The alternative, (ON brodur-øy – brother island), is improbable.

OS Maps: 1:50000 Sheets 1, 2 or 3 1:25000 Sheet 7
Admiralty Charts: 1:75000 No.3282 1:30000 No.3298

AREA: 40ha (99 acres)
HEIGHT: 25m (82 ft)

POPULATION: Uninhabited and no census records.

GEOLOGY: Undifferentiated Moine gneiss and quartzite.

WILDLIFE: Occasional site for breeding storm petrel.

BROTHER ISLE does not extend a welcome to visitors. If an anchorite or hermit monk ever did live on it, he must certainly have enjoyed solitude for Brother Isle like a pirate ship repels boarders on all sides. The shallow depression on the north side, known as **The Pool**, is full of hidden rocks and there is an evil drying rock called Stoura Baa lurking a short distance away. The southern tip has a long reef of rocks extending to the south-east amid vicious tidal rips. There are also tidal rips off the east and west coasts.

When gales are blowing against the tides in Yell Sound the surface of the sea is whipped into a demonic frenzy. It

THE 'BONXIE', OR GREAT SKUA, LORD OF THE SKIES

is then that the South Yell folk refer to the tides familiarly as 'bitin' grices' – or, in other words, swine.

The island itself, (with an area of just under one hundred acres it is the smallest in my over-forty-hectares classification), is unremarkable. There is a central hillock of 25m height and a dent on the east side called **Tungli Geo** (ON – gloomy inlet). Nearby is a substantial cave which could, I suppose, have provided some shelter for a hermit.

To the west of Brother Isle the ugly head of **Tinga Skerry**, rears 5m above the dark waters of Yell Sound and, like an iceberg, conceals most of its body beneath the surface.

ACCESS: No regular access.

Anchorages: No recommended anchorages.

11.22 Lamba

(ON – lamb island)

OS Maps: 1:50000 Sheets 1, 2 or 3 1:25000 Sheet 6
Admiralty Charts: 1:75000 Nos.3281 or 3282 1:30000 No.3298

AREA: 43ha (106 acres)
HEIGHT: 35m (115 ft)

POPULATION: Uninhabited.

GEOLOGY: Intrusive igneous rocks – mainly granite and syenite.

WILDLIFE: A family of otters is to be seen quite often in the cleft on the north-east side beside the eponymous Otter Had.

Storm petrel and puffin usually take up residence in the nesting season.

LAMBA's main claim to distinction is the tall (27m) light tower at its southern extremity, **South Head**. This helps to define the entrance to busy Sullom Voe oil terminal.

There are caves in the steep bluff beside the light tower and a cleft called **Hesti Geo** (ON – horse inlet). On the east coast a wider indentation called the **Wick of Lamba** (ON – Lamba Bay) is at least partly sheltered from the tidal currents in this area. These are clearly seen in the turbulence which builds up off both South Head and North Point. There is another small bay on the north-west side but it is full of rocks and dries out at low water.

Lamba is surrounded by low escarpments which means that access can be something of a scramble but once above the shore the ground rises more gradually to a height of about 35m at the centre.

An interesting wreck of a Norwegian steamer – the *SS Robert Lee* – lies near Lamba in a depth of only 10 metres but divers should be very wary of the strong currents.

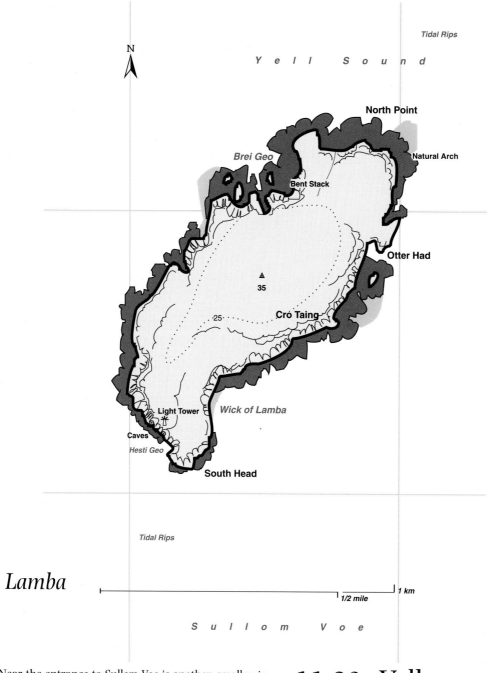

N

Tidal Rips

Y e l l   S o u n d

North Point

Brei Geo

Natural Arch

Bent Stack

Otter Had

△
35

25

Cró Taing

Light Tower

Wick of Lamba

Caves

Hesti Geo

South Head

Tidal Rips

Lamba

1 km

1/2 mile

S u l l o m   V o e

Near the entrance to Sullom Voe is another, smaller, island with a light beacon. This is **Little Roe** which in 1841 was inhabited by eleven people sharing a single house.

ACCESS: No regular access.

Anchorages: No recommended anchorages.
1. Temp anchorage in suitable weather conditions in Wick of Lamba, 7-10m.

11.23 Yell

(ON gjall – barren) but some think the name may be Pictish. The early Norse name was 'Jala' or 'Jela' which might mean white island (i.e. sandy beaches).

OS Maps: 1:50000 Sheets 1 and 2, or 1 and 3 1:25000 Sheets 2, 3, 4, 7, and 9
Admiralty Charts: 1:75000 No.3282 1:30000 Nos.3292 and 3298 1:12500 No.3293 Basta Voe

AREA: 21,211ha (52,412 acres)
HEIGHT: 205m (672 ft)

OWNER: Multiple ownership.

POPULATION: 1841 – 2611 (550 houses). 1881 – 2529. 1891 – 2511 (525 houses). 1931 – 1883. 1961 – 1155. 1971 – 1143. 1981 – 1168. 1991 – 1075.

GEOLOGY: Precambrian rocks under a thick blanket of peat. Most of the island is of garnetiferous mica plagioclose gneiss but the north-eastern coast and the south-east corner have an underlay of striped granulitic oligoclase gneiss and some bands of calc-silicate rock. The central highland is thick lenticular quartzite and the western cliffs are muscovite biotite gneiss with some silvery mica schists.

HISTORY: Early prehistoric remains are scattered around the coasts of Yell with hardly any to be found inland and there are a number of Iron Age structures such as the important broch at Ness of Burraness, overlooking Fetlar. About twelve broch sites have been identified and at least fifteen sites of ancient chapels.

Yell moorland was possibly of less interest to the past landowners because it was never formed into really large estates and has always had multiple ownership. The largest landowners in the 19th century were Mouat in the north, Leask in the west and MacQueen in the Burravoe district.

WILDLIFE: The moors and heaths of Yell provide a habitat for most of Shetland's eight species of orchid with the heath spotted orchid by far the most common.

The coasts are otter territory and the lochans are well-stocked with brown trout. The west coast in particular is favoured by grey seals but a bearded seal which must have strayed from the Arctic drift ice was recorded here in 1977.

At the Lumbister RSPB Reserve in the north-west near Whale Firth there are typical breeding species for the Shetlands – red-throated diver, red-breasted merganser, golden plover, eider, merlin, curlew, snipe, lapwing, arctic and great skuas, dunlin, great black-backed gull, raven, twite and wheatear. Oystercatcher, black guillemot, puffin and ringed plover breed on the coast.

Generally speaking, the waters of Yell Sound offer an important wintering area for divers, eider, and long-tailed duck.

The ferry to **YELL** docks at Ulsta. As you cross the Sound, what appears to be a reef at the southern extremity of the island turns out to be the lonely remains of a broch built precariously on a skerry. Yell itself has a gloomy appearance – low-lying hills blanketed in peat bog – yet for many this is the real Shetland. The peat of course has its merits as the Rev. Cruttwell pointed out in the 18th century: 'The inhabitants have plenty of fuel, catch immense quantities

of small fish and live comfortably.' On the other hand, Buchanan in the 16th century claimed that Yell was 'so uncouth a place that no creature can live therein, except such as are born there'. By the 1960s Yell's danger of serious depopulation became a matter of grave concern. Some said that part of the problem was the islanders' 'social egalitarianism,' which denied anyone the opportunity to be a leader or entrepreneur. This is unlikely but airing the matter seems to have helped because the numbers now appear to have stabilised. Yell is quite a large island – half the size of Arran – but it has such a bleak landscape that human settlement, and attitudes, tend to cling to the edges.

Two roads run north from **Ulsta**, the main road on the west coast and a secondary, more scenic and interesting, road following the south and east coasts.

This secondary road skirts Hamna Voe (ON – harbour voe) and runs into **Burravoe** (ON – broch voe) in the extreme south-east. The white crow-stepped **Old Haa of Burravoe**, built in 1637, is the oldest surviving building on the island [HU522796]. It is used as a local museum and craft centre. Burravoe has a tiny well-protected harbour which discourages visitors by its welter of skerries surrounding the islet, **Green Holm**, at its entrance.

The east coast has pleasant hamlets and crofts and touches of cultivation to relieve the dark peat mosses on the slopes of Yell's highest hill, **Ward of Otterswick** (205m). Beyond the cliffs the expanse of steel-blue sea is broken by Fetlar (No.11.24) and when the weather is favourable Out Skerries (No.11.18) can be seen on the horizon.

In 1924 a German 3-masted barque, *Bohus*, ran aground and broke up here with the loss of two of its crew. The figurehead lay for many years on the shore until it eventually rotted and disintegrated but not before a fibreglass reproduction had been made and set up on the shore as a monument. This is known as the '**White Wife of Queyon**' [HU529853].

The only settlement of note on the main road up the west coast is **West Sandwick**, a pretty spot with houses clustered round the sandy beaches of Southladie Voe [HU440887]. The remains of a broch on a drying islet on the coast look across to the **Holm of West Sandwick** which has a rock arch through which the sea breaks. A challenging walk along these west coast cliffs past the prehistoric settlement at **Birrier** [HU438913] beside **Sweinna Stack**, and **Ern Stack** (which was the last recorded nesting-place of the sea-eagle in Shetland) leads to Stuis of Graveland at the entrance to **Whale Firth**.

Yell is almost bisected where the west and east coast roads rejoin at **Mid Yell**, the island's main settlement. It is here that the narrow twisted Whale Firth nearly meets the sheltered anchorage of **Mid Yell Voe**, a suitable venue for many sailing regattas. The dramatic ruin of haunted

Windhouse at the head of Whale Firth is on a site which has been occupied since Neolithic times.

The ruined herring curing station half way up Whale Firth at **Grimister** closed shortly after the Second World War – and apart from a few crofts the firth is deserted. The Germans claimed that their U-boats often sheltered here during the First World War and one could hardly imagine a better hiding-place! The whole west coast area beyond Whale Firth to North Neaps at the remote northern extremity of Yell is an untouched wilderness of peaty heath and mire with many small lochans rippled by the continual wind. Yet this desolate expanse containing the **Lumbister RSPB Reserve** has some of the most interesting scenery and hill-walks on the island. The coast is wildly indented with green hollows, great rock arches, caves and tumbled cliffs.

The main road continues beyond Mid Yell – with its islet of **Kay Holm** hidden by a headland – round the length of Basta Voe, and ends at **Gutcher** which is the ferry terminal for Fetlar (No.11.24) and Unst (No.11.29). But before jumping aboard at this point remember that the best of Yell lies north where a secondary road continues up the shores of attractive Bluemull Sound through the rural village of **Cullivoe**.

As the road passes the priests' loch on Papil Ness, and turns along the north coast at **Brough**, the roofless **Kirk of Ness** [HP532049] can be seen by the west shore of Kirk Loch. This medieval parish church was dedicated to St Olaf but has been deserted since 1750. There is no historical proof but legend claims that it is from here that Leif the Lucky set off on his expedition to America. The rough wilderness is, incomprehensibly, covered with the remains of ancient settlements which have never yet been adequately investigated. To the west on the cliff top is the broch which has given the area its name [HP540051]. There is a delightful walk along these cliffs and the views are stunning but it is important to keep clear of the edge which is brittle and crumbles easily.

Skeletons have been found in the sands of the **Wick of Brekken** which may once have had a settlement like Jarlshof.

The road ends at **Gloup Voe** (ON – ravine creek) although there is a track continuing round the head of the voe to West-a-Firth on the far side. The **Fishermen's Memorial** [HP507044] here on the hillside above the voe commemorates yet another devastating island disaster. The entire male community in this remote northern haven (ten sixerns with fifty-eight fishermen on board) was lost at sea in a savage storm on the 20th July 1881.

A track leading north from Gloup connects with the Coastguard Lookout Station which is set on the cliffs between two wicks. To the west is **Gloup Holm** with jagged **Eagle Stack**, **Whilkie Stack** and **The Clapper**. To the east, Muckle Flugga lighthouse is on the horizon – convincing proof that this is the end of the road.

ACCESS: Ro-ro ferry from Toft, Mainland to Ulsta, Yell – twenty mins., approx. half-hourly. Ro-ro ferry from Belmont, Unst to Gutcher, Yell – ten mins., approx. half-hourly. Ro-ro ferry from Odsta, Fetlar to Gutcher, Yell – twenty mins., approx. eight times daily. 01957-722259.

Anchorages:
1. Hamna Voe on S coast. Exposed SE-S. Anchor W of Ness of Galtagarth in 8-10m, good holding. Head is shoal. Approach on central course and beware Burga Skerry 3c S of Green Holm.
2. Burra Voe at SE extremity of Yell. Approach from S and enter with great care. There are many rocks and at the entrance there is a bar with 2.4m over. Anchor anywhere inside in 4-6m. Good shelter but bottom foul with old moorings.
3. Wick of Gossabrough on E coast. Small stone pier on S side. Easy access but beware Wick Skerry at entrance. Exposed N to E. Anchor off beach in

SW bay. Holding unreliable.
4. Otters Wick has many rocks and careful use of chart required. Exposed E to SE.
5. Mid Yell Voe, mid E coast, good secure anchorage. Head dries for 1/2M. Approach on mid-channel course and anchor anywhere in wide part of voe in 3-10m, mud and sand. Gusty in N winds.
6. Basta Voe. Good shelter. Both sides clear to 3/4c from shore. Shingle bank off point on NE shore. Anchor beyond the shingle bank in 5-11m, clay, good holding mostly.
7. Wick of Gutcher, small bay in Bluemull Sound with vehicle ferry terminal. Berthing reserved exclusively for ferry.
8. Culli Voe, in Bluemull Sound, is shallow but concrete pier at entrance to voe projects 42m from shore and has 3.5m depth at head. Fair anchorage as far into the voe as depth permits or temp anchorage south of pier in 5m, holding good, sand and shells. There is tidal turbulence between Culivoe Ness and Grimsetter Point.
9. Wick of Brekken (Breakon) on N coast. Temp anchorage in S or E winds, holding poor (Lunda Wick on Unst is better).
10. Gloup Voe, not recommended. Mostly too deep, heavy sea rolls in with N-NW winds, and voe dries out halfway to head.
11. Whale Firth on W coast. Quiet, secluded anchorage. Beware sunken rock 2c NE of Nev of Stuis at entrance and rocks off S shore at Grimister. Otherwise clear of dangers.
12. Southladie Voe, close E of Ness of West Sandwick. Good anchorage except in S'lies. Keep to W side at narrow passage off Urabug ayre where there is only 2m depth. Anchor in the pool beyond, 3m, soft mud.

11.24 Fetlar

(ON – fat/prosperous land). Intriguing alternative derivation suggested by Liv Schei (ON fetill – a strap or tie) with (ON -ar) as the plural form. See below.

OS Maps: 1:50000 Sheet 1 or 2 1:25000 Sheet 5
Admiralty Charts: 1:75000 No.3282 1:30000 No.3292 west part

AREA: 4,078ha (10,077 acres)
HEIGHT: 158m (518 ft)

OWNER: Most of the island was inherited by Mrs Borland, Edinburgh, on the death of her aunt, Lady Nicolson (c. 1980). Fetlar has been owned by Nicolsons since the early 1800s but the recent owners were not direct descendents of Sir Arthur Nicolson.

POPULATION: 1841 – 761 (137 houses). 1881 – 431. 1891 – 363 (70 houses). 1931 – 217. 1961 – 127. 1971 – 88. 1981 – 102. 1991 – 90.

GEOLOGY: There is gneiss in the west including Lambhoga. East of a fault line there are magnificent serpentine outcrops which are only equalled by those of Cornwall and which account for the interesting cliff formations. There is also mettagabro and phyllite. The sand in the Wick of Houbie is magnetic and at Moo Wick at the

YELL
Burra
Ness
Sound
Gruney
Urie Lingay
Ferries
The Fludir
Hamars
Ness
Daaey
Tressa
Ness
Il Holm
Scuta
The Flaeshins
Basta Voe
Pier
Oddsta
Gors
Geo
Funzie Girt
Cairns
△158
East Neap
Busta
Hill
Stack of Birrier
The Clett
Swarta Skerry
Ness of
Snabrough
Sna Broch
(ruin)
Vord
Hill
Kirn of Gula
Outer Brough
Settlement
Hascosay Sound
Pier
Ness of
Brough
Brough Lodge
& Folly
Hamara Field
Stackaberg
Cairn ★
★Fiddler's Crus
Loch
of
Winyadepla
Hesta
Ness
Strandburgh
Ness
HASCOSAY
Sand of Sand
★Haltadans
Caves
Wick of
Gruting
Grut
Ness
Yogli
Geo
Whale Geo
Corbie
Head
Ponsil
North Dale
Airstrip
Skutes
Water
Caves
Swart
Houll
Kegga
Head
of Hosta
South Sound
Gallow
Hill
PO
Southdale
Sch
Waters
of Cruss
Caves
Strand
Bunwell
Everland
Gruna W
Heilinabretta
Baa-neap
Natural Arch
Cluster
Papil
Water
Tresta
Broch
(ruin) ★
Feal
Leagarth Ho
Ripple
Stone
HOUBIE
Pier
Aith
Still
The Heog
Ch.Cairn
Muckle
Wirawil
Funzie
The Tind
Nat Arch
Head of Bresdale
Nat Arch
Wick of
Houbie
Broch (ruin)
Wick
of Aith
Aith Ness
Caves
Loch
of Funzie
Woodenbreck
Houlls Geo
Nousta Ness
Funzie Bay
YELL
Lamb Hoga
Colgrave Sound
Silda Wick
Wick of Tresta
Gerdiesberg
CG
Furra Stacks
Muckle Birriers Geo
Hawks Geo
Helliers Ness
Rett Geo
Cave
Cave
Moo
Wick
Head of
Lambhoga
Likilk
Cave
The Snap
Butsa
Funzie Ness
Rams Ness
The Snap
Funzie Ness

N

5 kms
3 miles

tip of Lambhoga there is a residual deposit of kaolin. At Hesta Ness in the north-east the serpentine has been altered to antigorite and steatite. Here too there are bands of pure talc which was mined at one time.

HISTORY: The story of Fetlar goes back a long way. Yet Fetlar, in spite of its great contrast to its neighbour, the rather desolate Yell, has never achieved a distinctive place in Shetland history, probably due to its lack of a safe harbour. The first Norse settlers are thought to have landed here, and swashbuckling King Harald the Fair-haired landed on Fetlar during his pursuit of 'vikings' in the 9th century but he swiftly moved on to a secure anchorage at Unst.

The first large-scale clearances in Shetland started here on the Lamb Hoga peninsula in 1822 when the landowner, Sir Arthur Nicolson, evicted the crofters to make room for sheep. By 1858 he had emptied the whole of the north and west part of the island and cleared nearly 30 townships. He built himself the three-storey tower folly at Grutin using stone from the crofters' houses.

A serious drop in population during the 1980s led to the local community council advertising for settlers in *Country Life* and *Scottish Field*. The biggest drawback for young families today is that children aged eleven and over

have to travel to Yell for schooling but in other respects this is an idyllic island.

Like so many Shetland islands, Fetlar has a history of shipwrecks. An incomplete list illustrates this:

1601 – a Danish vessel. 1699 – a packet, wrecked at Hamars Ness. 1710 – a vessel from Emden. 1737 – *Wendela*, Danish. 1765 – a vessel at Whale Geo. 1773 – *James*. 1794 – a vessel at Aith. 1799 – *Good Intent*. 1811 – *Stadt Memel*. 1847 – *Clarenden*. 1848 – *Neptune*. 1870 – *Johan Caesar*, Hamburg. 1882 – *Lizzie*. 1897 – *Flosta*. 1897 – *Anna*. 1900 – *Hedevig*, Norway. 1962 – *Maia*, Russian trawler.

WILDLIFE: More than 200 different species of wildflower have been recorded on this verdant isle. Rarer species include frog orchid and northern gentian, but the rarest are members of the sedge family. In the sheltered area at Leagarth House there used to be a number of quite exotic trees.

There are many grey and common seals around the coasts and otters can often be seen, particularly between Brough Lodge and Urie.

The lochs, some with restricted access, offer fly fishing for brown trout.

Fetlar is an outstanding bird sanctuary, especially for

breeding waders of which there is the highest density in Britain. All visitors should please first contact the RSPB warden, 01957-83246. Lapwing, oystercatcher and ringed plover breed on the crofts, and golden plover, dunlin, curlew, and many whimbrel nest on the moorland. Snipe, redshank and red-necked phalarope breed on the lochans and wetlands. There are also breeding seabirds. Manx shearwater, storm petrel, shag, kittiwake, guillemot and puffin are to be seen on the cliffs, particularly on the Lamb Hoga peninsula which has Britain's largest colony of storm petrels. There are common tern and about 4500 pairs of arctic tern.

Fetlar is probably most renowned for the snowy owls which were found nesting at Stakkaberg in 1967. This is the extreme southern limit of their breeding range. Unfortunately the old male, having driven off all competitors, died of old age in 1975 leaving several morose females without a mate. Consequently, there are now no resident snowy owls although they still occasionally make an appearance.

Other breeders on the island are red-throated diver, eider, raven and twite and recorded migrants include two-barred crossbill and greenish warbler. In the autumn there are many fieldfare and redwing.

Let your imagination take over for a moment and think of **FETLAR** in the dark ages of prehistory – a fair and fertile land populated by mesolithic farmers.

Now let us suppose that two tribes live on the island and because the grass is always greener next door they engage in intermittent feuding and fighting. The wars go on for years until at last someone decides to call a truce. There is a meeting at which, after argument, they agree to a division of land, and so that there can be no further dispute whatsoever, they join forces and build a big wall right across the centre of the island. With their territories now clearly defined they live happily ever after.

This idyllic state continues until the 7th or 8th century AD and then the unexpected happens. Land-hungry Norwegian settlers, following in the wake of the first marauding Vikings, come to Shetland. Their first landfall is Fetlar which is about as near to Norway as you can get and here they see a land of milk and honey. History does not record the viewpoint of the original islanders but we can be sure the land was acquired while they were slaughtered, enslaved or merely absorbed.

The Norsemen would be surprised to find Fetlar divided by a huge wall and, as they lacked a scientific definition for an island, they thought of it as two islands. This is much the same as their view that a mountain barrier divided Lewis and Harris into two separate islands or a narrow isthmus turned the Mull of Kintyre into an island. At this point an element of fact creeps into our reconstruction because early Norse records always spoke of Fetlar as

Est Isle and Wast Isle. Fetlar, as a name for the whole island, is first found in a document dated 1558 although an earlier document in 1490 talks of Foetilør. As 'fetill' means a strap or a tie in Norse one might guess that they thought of Fetlar as two islands tied together.

Meanwhile, the ancient wall itself took on an aura of mystery. 'Who had built it?' the settlers wondered. And as time passed their descendants attributed its creation to the Finns, magical figures in Norse folklore, who might have been Laplanders, or giants, or trolls, or all three rolled together. It was said that the Finns built the wall in a single night in exchange for a farmer's best cow.

Today, the one-metre wide wall, or what little is left of it, is still called **Funzie Girt** [fin-ee girt] which means the Finns' dyke and it cuts round the west side of Vord Hill but disappears near Whilsa Pund. It then reappears south of Skutes Water, crosses the Vallahamars and ends by the Stack of Billaclett where there is a cave in which the trolls lived. It divides Fetlar into two almost equal sections.

There are other mysteries too in this mid-island region. Between Vord Hill and Skutes Water, are the **Fiddler's Crus** [HU618927]. These are three mysterious stone circles set in a triangular pattern and almost touching each other. Each circle is about 13½ metres in diameter. Nearby, about 200 metres north of Skutes Water, there is another strange monument called **Haltadans** (or Hjaltadans) which means 'limping dance' [HU622924]. This is an outer circle of thirty-eight serpentine stones, about 11½ metres diameter, with an internal, low and concentric earth bank. Two stones lie at the centre. Both these structures seem to be related but archaeologists have no satisfactory explanation of their purpose. The local explanation is that a fiddler and his wife were dancing in the moonlight one night with trolls and all were enjoying it so much that they failed to notice the dawn. Everyone was instantly petrified by the light of the rising sun. The stone circles are the dancing trolls and the two prostrate central stones are the fiddler and his wife. This is a typical Norse legend with trolls as creatures of the night coupled with a Christian flavour of retribution for ungodly pleasures.

Fetlar is Shetland's most fertile island and it is still known as the Garden of Shetland although it is not quite as well-tended as it once was. It is quite hilly with **Vord Hill** (ON – watch hill) at 158m being the highest point. Two Neolithic heel-shaped cairns on the hill are possibly 5000 years old. The shelter in the southern cairn was built during the First World War [HU622936].

It is a pity that such an attractive island has no secure anchorages although it is usually possible to find shelter provided there is no sudden change of wind. The survival of any island's population today depends on reliable communications and on-site education. In Fetlar's case the former criterion was satisfied in 1974 when a vehicle ferry service to a pier at Oddsta was inaugurated but the island still lacks the facilities for secondary education which Out Skerries (No.11.18) already has.

Fetlar's single road runs west to east across the island. To the south there is the great **Lamb Hoga** (ON – sheep pasture) peninsula with its steep gneiss cliffs. Shetland ponies sometimes graze here on the open moorland. The lairds of **Brough Lodge** [HU580926], the Nicolsons, crossed the native stock with Norwegian to achieve an improved breed. Beneath the stretch of **Papil Water** (ON – priests' water) is the magnificent sweep of beach at **Tresta**, well-sheltered from the prevailing wind.

The adjoining cove at **Houbie** (ON *hopr* – light), with the airstrip to the north of it, also has a pleasant, but much smaller, beach. Prominent **Leagarth House**, by the small pier, was built by Sir William Watson Cheyne in 1900. He was a Houbie lad who became a famous surgeon after assisting Joseph Lister in his development of antiseptic surgery in 1867. Sir William died in 1932. The **Fetlar Interpretive Centre**, almost opposite Leagarth House should not be missed. It is a treasure trove of island history.

The road continues through pleasant green valleys to the east coast settlement, and old haaf station, of **Funzie** [fin-ee], a picturesque collection of cottages, many of which are unfortunately deserted. As the name suggests it was here that the very first Vikings are said to have settled. The land in summer is swathed in wildflowers and on almost every rocky headland there is a lichen-covered ruined broch. The cliffs here are not as high as elsewhere but their rugged serpentine rock faces are full of colour. **Funzie Bay** was the site of a haaf fishing station in the 19th century.

Under Baa-naap is a rocky point called **Heilinabretta** where the Danish ship, *Wendela*, ran aground and sank in 1737 [HU675911]. She was carrying a large quantity of unspecified silver currency, most of which was immediately salvaged by the islanders. A diving team in the 1970s investigated the wreck and collected a number of silver coins in the area. Unauthorised diving is forbidden.

Broken cairns top Vord Hill and, below, the landscape is dotted with ancient mounds. The view from here is magnificent. The whole island can be seen stretching from The Snap, a headland beneath the Coastguard Lookout-point in the south-east, to **Hamars Ness** near the ferry pier in the north-west; and from **Rams Ness** in the south to **Strandburgh Ness** in the east. The latter has a tiny islet, **Outer Brough**, beside it with the remains of a broch and ancient settlement. Great natural arches in the Wick of Gruting (ON – stony area) flank **Kirn of Gula**, a blowhole, where fishermen took refuge in the 18th century when the press gangs called [HU645931]. Beneath the cliffs of East Neap are rock stacks including the remarkable shape of **The Clett** [HU641944] off Busta Pund with, believe it or not, a hermitage perched on it! The sea between Fetlar and Bluemull Sound is sprinkled with low-

lying islets including **Daaey**, **Urie Lingey** and **Sund Gruney** (ON – south green island).

ACCESS: Ro-ro ferry about eight times daily from Gutcher (Yell), 01957-722259.

Anchorages:
1. Vehicle-ferry terminal at Oddsta, Hamars Ness, in NW is reserved for ferry only.
2. Brough Lodge, W coast. Convenient temp anchorage in E winds. Anchor off the slip and below the tower, N of Ness of Brough, in 4-6m.
3. Wick of Tresta. Good shelter if wind W or N, but swell comes in with W gales. Open to SE. Head shoals. Anchor in 6-8m, sand, good holding. Approach on central course and beware rock 2c E of Head of Lamb Hoga. Magnetic anomalies.
4. Wick of Gruting. Good shelter in S winds. Open N. Keep 1c off all shores. Anchor centre-bay E or W of Ness of Gruting in 10m, sand, good holding.
5. Hamars Ness. Temp anchorage and some shelter in S'lies. Anchor ENE of extremity of Hamars Ness distant 2¹/₂c in 11m. Beware extensive foul area in the bay.

11.25 Hascosay

[ha-skoa-say] (ON haf-skogen-øy – sea-wood or driftwood island) or, possibly, (ON housecarl's or retainer's island)

OS Maps: 1:50000 Sheet 1 or 2 1:25000 Sheet 4
Admiralty Charts: 1:75000 No.3282 1:30000 No.3292

AREA: 275ha (680 acres)
HEIGHT: 30m (98 ft)

OWNER: Part of the Nicolson of Fetlar estate inherited in the 1980s by Mrs Borland of Edinburgh, a niece of Lady Nicolson.

POPULATION: 1841 – 42 (6 houses). 1851 – 13. 1861 – 0. Uninhabited since.

GEOLOGY: The bedrock is a coarse micaceous gneiss.

HISTORY: A branch of the Edmondston family once owned the island and a James Edmondston is named as laird of Hascosay in 1645.

Hascosay was home to a small but thriving community until it was bought by Sir Arthur Nicolson, the laird who cleared much of Fetlar for sheep in the mid-19th century. His house on Fetlar, Brough Lodge, overlooked Hascosay and this may have been why the islanders decided to leave before they were forcibly evicted. On the other hand, the trouble may merely have been lack of a good supply of fresh water and nothing to do with Sir Arthur.

WILDLIFE: Hascosay, like Eynhallow (No.10.19) in Orkney, is reputed to have soil of a magic quality which keeps mice away. Other islands even used the soil as a mouse-deterrent but its efficacy has not been recorded.

Basta Ness

YELL

Taingar

Gruna Taing

Djuba Wick

Virdi Taing

Natural Arch

Punds Geo

·25·

Oxna Geo

Cave

Skulia Geo

Hascosay Sound

The Bow of Hascosay

·25·

△ 30

Housa Wick

Ramna Geo

Greybearded Man

Point of the Gunnald

28

The Rett   Ba Taing

Colgrave Sound

South Sound

Baa of Hascosay

Ness of Vatsetter

YELL

1 km
1/2 mile

The BBC cameraman, Hugh Miles, visited Hascosay with the renowned Shetland ornithologist, Bobby Tulloch, in 1979, to make a BBC 'Wildtrack' programme on otters. Hascosay is noted for its otters but on this occasion they failed to appear and the film was eventually shot on Fetlar and (Basta Voe) Yell. Nevertheless, Tulloch's books include many of his beautiful photographs of the Hascosay otters.

HASCOSAY has an undulating surface, the highest point being 30m above the south-west bluff. The island is criss-crossed with burns or rivulets fed by several small pools, none of which is large enough to merit the title of lochan and none of which provides a supply of good drinking wa-

ter. Even when the pools are filled with rainwater they quickly turn brackish with the salt-spray and there is only one rather inadequate well. **Housa Wick** (ON – house bay) is an attractive rocky inlet which cuts deep into the island in the south-west. On a shallow isthmus behind it are the walls of the Edmondston's old hall which they vacated before 1800. There is also the site of a chapel but it is not known to whom it was dedicated.

A smaller bay on the north side is used for fish farming. It is called **Djuba Wick** (ON – deep bay) but with a depth of less than 10m according to the Admiralty Chart the derivation of the name is open to conjecture.

The broken cliffs in the south fall away to **The Rett**

(ON – the straight) and **Ba Taing** (ON – point of the underwater rock). On the opposite headland of Housa Wick there are more cliffs and an offshore stack called **Greybearded Man**. Continuing up the west coast there is **Skulia Geo** (ON – hiding-hole inlet) with a submerged rock concealed in the middle of the geo and a fair-sized cave to explore on its shore. Nearby the rocks form a natural arch. There are a number of fine caverns on Hascosay.

ACCESS: No regular access, but a boat owner at Sellafirth may be cooperative.

Anchorages: No recommended anchorages.

1. The Bow of Hascosay, Hascosay Sound. Temp anchorage at N end of Bow in 5-10m.

2. Housa Wick. Temp anchorage in centre of Wick, 8-10m. The head is foul. Beware Baa of Hascosay 3½c SSE of Ba Taing.

11.26 Uyea

[yoo-ay] Possibly, just, (ON øy-øy – island island) but might be (ON ve-øy – home island or island of the sacred place)

OS Maps: 1:50000 Sheet 1 1:25000 Sheet 4
Admiralty Charts: 1:75000 No.3282 1:30000 No.3292

AREA: 205ha (507 acres)
HEIGHT: 50m (164 ft)

OWNER: Sold by Jim Smith, a local farmer, in 1990 for about £100,000 including the livestock (320 sheep) and the islet of Wedder Holm. The new owner is Peter Hunter of Uyeasound on Unst, a crofter and salmon farmer.

POPULATION: 1841 – 23 (3 HOUSES). 1881 – 5. 1891 – 8 (1 HOUSE). 1931 – 12. 1961 – 0. 1971 – 0. 1981 – 0. 1991 – 0.

Uyea

GEOLOGY: Hornblende-schists in the west, mica-schists in the east.

HISTORY: Uyea Hall was the five-bedroom home of Basil Neven-Spence who was the Member of Parliament for Orkney and Shetland from 1935 until he was defeated in 1950 by Jo Grimond. Sir Basil is buried in the chapel cemetery.

WILDLIFE: Although mice are plentiful on Unst, there are none on Uyea. Maybe some of Hascosay's magic soil is responsible (see No.11.25).

Otters can be seen by the shores, and many seals.

UYEA is only two-thirds the size of Vaila (No.11.10) but is similar in respect that it is dominated by a single large house originally built by the owner. On Uyea **The Hall** stands amid a group of structures on the central ridge near the middle of the island and is therefore fairly conspicuous. The highest point on the ridge is 50m.

Farm roads or tracks lead from a bay on the north-coast with a rough jetty on the foreshore to the main house.

There are a number of antiquities which mirror those just across the sound on Unst. Part of the old chapel beside **Brei Wick** (ON – broad bay) dates from the 12th century [HU608985], while **Tur Ness**, just north of Brei Wick, is the site of an ancient settlement. At the northern end of the island there is a chambered cairn representing even earlier times.

Quite close to **Hawks Ness**, the southern extremity, is an islet called **Wedder Holm** (ON – ram islet) and further away to the east is the small island of **Haaf Gruney** (ON *hafgroenøy* – green island in the fishing grounds). This island is now classified as a national nature reserve on account of its colony of breeding storm petrel. The remains of a disused chromate mine are on it and its green pastures have for long been used for grazing.

In the early 18th century two young girls from Uyea rowed themselves over to Haaf Gruney to milk the cows. On their return a storm blew up and increased in fury. For several days they could do nothing but bail and hang on until they were at last cast ashore on the island of Karmøy off the south-west coast of Norway. The superstitious islanders at first took fright but when one of the girls made the sign of the Cross they helped them. In any case there was a severe shortage of women on Karmøy at the time so, needless to say, before long the girls were happily married and their descendants still live there today.

ACCESS: No regular access but a boat owner in Uyeasound might be helpful.

Anchorages:

1. Skuda Sound, bay W of Scarfa Taing. Anchor off the jetty in 5-6m, mud and sand. Reasonable shelter and holding. Beware Cliva Skerries, W of the bay.

2. Bay on S side between Winna Ness and Hawks Ness. Temp anchorage in

suitable conditions. Approach and anchor centrally towards the head in 5-6m.

3. Brei Wick. Avoid. Shallow and foul.

11.27 Linga

(ON lyng-øy – heather island)

OS Maps: 1:50000 Sheet 1 1:25000 Sheet 4
Admiralty Charts: 1:75000 No.3282 1:30000 No.3292

AREA: 45ha (111 acres)
HEIGHT: 26m (85 ft)

OWNER: The island was bought in the 1980s by a Mr Renwick who started building a psuedo-Norman castle at North Booth, but was refused planning permission. He abandoned the project (concrete blocks can still be seen) and sold out to Charles Henderson of Yell. He, in turn, sold Linga to an American lady but kept the crofting rights and uses the land for grazing sheep.

POPULATION: No census records and uninhabited.

GEOLOGY: A bedrock of coarse mica-schist and gneiss.

WILDLIFE: In spite of its name, very little heather is to be found on Linga. Many seabirds breed here, particularly guillemot, and there are resident otters. Seals breed in the season.

Linga is a long narrow island lying roughly parallel to the coast of Yell, and separated from it by Linga Sound. This is a fairly secluded corner of Shetland – if anywhere in this part of the world can truly be called secluded. Yell holds out two tentative arms, Head of Gutcher and Burra Ness (with a ruined broch on it) to shelter the waters of Linga Sound. There is often little in the way of activity in or near the Sound except for the ferry plying its path between Gutcher on Yell and Oddsta on Fetlar.

The long low ridge of Linga reaches a maximum height of 26m near its southern end. It has few known antiquities but there is the site of an old chapel [HU559986] which would indicate that it might have had a number of inhabitants at some time. The source of an adequate supply of fresh water is a puzzle although it may have been brought over by boat from neighbouring Yell. The island is now used for grazing sheep.

There is said to be a green ring on the island (although its position is elusive!) called the **Bear's Bait**. An ancient Norse tale says that Jan Tait of Fetlar killed one of the King of Norway's men after an argument and the King had him brought to Norway to answer for the crime. After the King had spoken to Jan he was so impressed by his courage and candour that he promised to grant him his freedom provided he captured a giant bear that was causing trouble in the district. Jan put out a barrel of drugged butter for the bear to eat and had no trouble capturing it

Linga

YELL

and taking it to the King. The King kept his promise and granted him his freedom but he was surprised that Jan had not killed the bear. He ordered him to do so and then to leave Norway forthwith. Jan, however, was proud of his capture and wanted to show it to his friends so he brought the bear back to Shetland and kept it tethered on Linga. The ring marks the spot where the poor old bear walked round and round its stake for the rest of its days.

ACCESS: No regular access but it may be possible to obtain advice or assistance at Gutcher on Yell.

Anchorages: No recommended anchorages.
1. Linga Sound. Temp anchorage in suitable conditions off the mid-point of the W coast in 3-6m. Approach with caution and use tripping line.

11.28 Balta

Perhaps (ON Balti-øy – Balti's island) from the man's name.

OS Maps: 1:50000 Sheet 1 1:25000 Sheet 2
Admiralty Charts: 1:75000 No.3282 1:12500 No.3293

AREA: 80ha (198 acres)
HEIGHT: 44m (144 ft)

POPULATION: No census records and uninhabited now.

GEOLOGY: Hornblende-schist interspersed with gabbro.

HISTORY: The remains of a broch at South Sail at the top of the northern cliffs may once have had a 'brother' broch across the Sound on Swinna Ness – they often came in pairs – but there is no record of it. It does suggest, however, that Balta was inhabited at that time.

WILDLIFE: The eastern cliffs provide residential sites for nesting seabirds. A glaucus gull nested for several years on nearby Huney during the 1980s.

BALTA is a long narrow island like Linga (No.11.27) but with a more complex shape. It has three hills spaced along its length, the central one at **Muckle Head** (S. – big head) being the highest (44m). The southern hill is 38m high.

The east coast, facing the stormy North Sea, consists of steep cliffs broken by fissures and rocky coves and with

tumbled half-submerged rock-falls close to the foot where they have not slipped away down the steep submarine slopes. There is a shallower patch, **Salta Skerry**, where the cliffs fade out at the southern extremity of the island, over which the white lighthouse stands guard. Heavy seas break over this area when the wind is in the south-east. The whole of this east coast is slowly being eroded by the sea which pounds against it relentlessly.

The rock strata tips the whole island up towards the east while the west side is low-lying with patches of sandy beach. With some limited shelter from the winds, and a consequent reduction in the salt-spray, the grass is green and makes excellent pasture for sheep.

Apart from the broch ruin at **South Sail** [HP660089]

N

The Rett

Swinna Ness

North Channel

Ruined Broch

South Sail

Beacon

Natural Arch

B a l t a

S o u n d

House

Muckle Head

⚓

▲ 44

Swarta Skerry

UNST

25

South Head

38

S o u t h

The Yel

The Givv

C h a n n e l

Salta Skerry

Huney

1 km

1/2 mile

another site of archaeological interest is that of an ancient chapel dedicated to the popular Norse saint, St Sunniva.

Balta Sound was a busy and popular harbour in the early 1900s and the island must have seen a lot of activity as hundreds of brown-sailed luggers of the Scottish fishing fleet bustled in and out to off-load their herring catches.

In 1917 a Royal Navy submarine, *E49*, struck a mine and sank in Balta Sound. The wreck, which lies at a depth of thirty-five metres, is classed as a 'war grave' and permission to dive must be obtained from the Ministry of Defence.

On the west side of South Channel is the small uninhabited island of **Huney** which has a flat grassy top about 19m high. There is a narrow channel called the Yei between Huney and the coast of Unst which is full of rocks and sandbanks but which the local fishermen negotiate with ease.

ACCESS: No regular access but a boat owner at Baltasound may be persuaded to help.

Anchorages: Approach mid-channel by S Channel when entering Balta Sound. The N Channel is tricky and requires great care.
1. Mid E-side of Balta. Good anchorage and well sheltered except for S-SW in which case move to the Unst side. Best spot with Buness House, Unst, in line with Skeo Taing but may be obstructed by fish cages. Anchor as near Balta as depth permits, sand.

11.29 Unst

[unst – not, oonst] Derivation obscure and may be of Pictish origin, but possibly (ON ørn-vist – home of the eagle or erne).

OS Maps: 1:50000 Sheet 1 1:25000 Sheets 1, 2 and 4
Admiralty Charts: 1:75000 No.3282 1:30000 No.3292 southern part only 1:12500 No.3293 Balta Sound only

AREA: 12,068ha (29,820 acres)
HEIGHT: 284m (932 ft)

OWNER: Multiple ownership. The Sandison family are the largest landowners but the families of Saxby (who wrote *Birds of Shetland*) and Edmondston (*A Flora of Shetland*), also have sizable landholdings.

POPULATION: 1798 – 1688 (300 houses) approx. 1831 – 2730. 1841 – 2808 (517 houses). 1881 – 2173. 1891 – 2269 (470 houses). 1931 – 1326. 1961 – 1148. 1971 – 1124. 1981 – 1206. 1991 – 1055.

GEOLOGY: Unst has a complex but fascinating geology. The western side, defined by Loch of Cliff and the Loch of Watlee by Valla Field is coarse-grained gneiss, sometimes studded with tiny garnets, under peat moorland which is

very similar to that of adjacent Yell. The eastern side is composed of metagabbro and serpentine interspersed with schists. The serpentine has veins of iron chromate, and black and green jasper. A complex dislocation zone divides these two zones.

Limestone can be found in the south and talc at Haroldswick in the north-east. Unst has the only surviving talc mine in Britain.

HISTORY: Harolds Wick is named after King Harald Haarfagr (Fair-hair) who anchored here in 875 after first visiting Fetlar (No.11.24). Norway was being harassed by viking, or pirate, raids from Shetland and Orkney so the king visited the islands and annexed them in the name of Norway. The pirates were, in any case, probably descendants of Scandinavian settlers.

WILDLIFE: This was the home of Thomas Edmonston who published *A Flora of Shetland* in 1845 when he was still in his teens. He discovered the Norwegian Sandwort here in the Keen of Hamar which is found nowhere else in Britain but North Ronaldsay (No.10.27) and Rum (No.4.3), and protected by law since 1981, and the Shetland Mouse-ear Chickweed which is unique to Unst. Edmondston was killed accidentally by a musket during an Amazon expedition when he was still a young man.

The Keen of Hamar is now a National Nature Reserve and the Warden's permission is needed to enter, 01463-239431. It is a remarkable site of broken serpentine scree. A number of other unusual and rare plants such as the fragrant and frog orchids can also be found here and occasionally elsewhere on Unst.

Small groups of Shetland ponies, whose numbers are in decline elsewhere, can still be seen on Unst. There are no bats, weasels, frogs, toads, hedgehogs or adders but there are plenty of rabbits. Rats were first recorded in 1903, and otters are common.

Hermaness National Nature Reserve is one of the few breeding sites of a rare moth and the cliffs of this, Britain's most northerly peninsula, hold one of our largest seabird colonies. 10,000 pairs of fulmar, the same of gannet, 5,000 pairs of kittiwake, 16,000 pairs of guillemot, 2,000 pairs of razorbill, and some 25,000 pairs of puffin have been recorded. There are a small number of Arctic skua and, this being with Foula the last stronghold of the bonxie (great skua) when it was nearing extinction, now boasts at least 800 pairs.

It is also at Hermaness that the famous black-browed albatross has returned each spring since the early 1970s. A vagrant from the South Seas and trapped in the northern hemisphere it keeps hoping to find a mate. It occasionally winks at a passing gannet but is always violently rebuffed.

Many seabirds visit Bluemull Sound, particularly in winter and early spring, when eider and tysties (black guillemot) breed here.

Britain's most northerly inhabited island, **UNST** is one of the most interesting in the Shetland group. It has its share of dreich peat moorland, particularly in the west but the cliff scenery is spectacular.

The ferry from Yell (No.11.23) docks at the chunks of serpentine which make up Belmont pier. The shell of **Belmont House**, a Lowland-style mansion built in 1777, can be seen across the fields [HP565010]. The main road branches off to Uyeasound, past standing stones, and on

to **Muness Castle** [HP629011]. This desolate ruin in a desolate landscape could have been devised by Edgar Allen Poe for the Fall of the House of Usher. It was built in 1598 by Lawrence Bruce of Cultmalindie in Perthshire, an evil man and a relative of the notorious tyrant Earl Patrick. Bruce also built the castle at Scalloway on Main-land (No.11.11). Muness is a handsome ruin, a high stone rectangle with circular towers and similarity of detail to the Earl's Palace in Kirkwall (No.10.10) built in the same period. Above the entrance is inscribed (the Shetland phonetics are unmistakable):

> 'List ze to knaw yis bulding quha began Laurence the Bruce he was that worthy man quha ernestly his airis and ofspring prayis to help and not to hurt this vark aluayis – the zeir of God 1598'

In spite of this urgent plea, the work at Muness Castle was soon destroyed, for the castle burnt down in the 17th century. The history of the disaster is confused. One story in Norn verse claims it was a certain Hakki of Dikkeram, possibly in response to the abduction of a girl called Helga and the murder of her father by one of the Bruce family. Another story claims the castle was sacked and torched by French privateers.

Beside Mu Ness (ON – maiden headland) is the islet of **Hunts Holm** and to the north a Norse settlement has been excavated at **Sandwick**.

A branch to the west off the main spinal road leads to a track which passes **Bordastubble**, Shetland's largest standing stone [HP579034], and arrives at **Lunda Wick**. Here there is the ruin of the 12th century **Lund Church**, last used for worship in 1785 [HP566041]. In the cemetery are the 16th century graves of two Bremen merchants, probably representatives of the Hanseatic trade. (See Whalsay, No.11.15.) Lund Church – or St Olaf's Chapel – is built on **Blue Mull**, the headland which gives its name to Bluemull Sound. The mull is best admired from the sea, where it has a distinct blue colour when seen from the distance. On the opposite side of Lunda Wick at **Underhoull** are grass-covered earthworks surrounding the ruin of a broch [HP575044]. A 9th century Viking longhouse, excavated in the 1960s, was built on an earlier Iron Age site. Further north, where the road crosses a burn, there is a restored Norse-type horizontal click mill.

Islets are scattered about North Sound, north of Lunda Wick, called **Lang Holm**, **Round Holm**, **The Vere**, and **Brough Holm**. As expected this latter islet has the remains of yet another broch on it. Further north up this dramatic coastline are two more groups, **North Holms**, and **South Holms** which has a subterranean passage.

The main road continues over a relatively featureless landscape with the ridge of **Valla Field** (ON – hill of mythological battle) to the west reflected in the brown waters of **Loch of Watlee**. The wishing well of **Helia Brune** [HP594046] is beside the loch and there are a few scattered chambered cairns. It is interesting, by the way, to note a resemblance between the map of Unst and Robert Louis Stevenson's map of Treasure Island. RLS visited Unst after his Uncle David had built Muckle Flugga lighthouse. Not long after the visit he began writing *Treasure Island*.

Baltasound is Unst's 'capital' with two hotels and an airstrip. The Swedish Church was built in 1910 and used by Scandinavian fishermen until the 1950s. The Sound used to be the centre of the northern herring industry and in its heyday had a seasonal population of 10,000, but its main use as a port today is for the export of talc. It is also a collection point for the oil industry – hence the busy little airfield.

To reach the large scattered settlement of **Haroldswick** the road skirts **Crussa Field** and **Muckle Heog**, hills which have clusters of ancient cairns on them. One is called Harald's Grave and is supposed to be the burial site for King Harald the Fair-haired. Haroldswick has the most northern post-office in Britain and is always happy to frank your letters accordingly.

Nor Wick, a bay with a glorious sweep of beach and weathered rocks, is an old haaf fishing station site. In 1700 a sea-eagle stole a baby girl, Mary Anderson, from the croft on the hill above the wick and carried her off to its eyrie on the cliffs of Fetlar. This was seen by a Fetlar islander and a young boy, Robert Nicolson, was lowered down to the nest by rope. He rescued the baby and she was returned unharmed to Unst and, according to the story which is sworn to be true, when Mary grew up, Robert married her and the happy couple settled in Yell and raised a family.

At **Wick of Skaw**, Britain's most northerly dwelling, a croft farmhouse, nestles among marsh marigolds in a small valley by the beach. One of the outhouses is made from an old upturned boat [HP658164], normal island practice where nothing is wasted.

A visit to the summit of **Saxa Vord** (ON – Saxa's lookout), Unst's highest point at 284m is no 'big deal' as there

TERN WATCHERS AT NOR WICK

is a road climbing the one thousand feet or so to the top. The view is breathtaking. The furthest outpost of the British Isles, **Out Stack**, or 'Oosta', is only 3km further north. Lady Franklin landed on this bare rock in 1849 and prayed for her husband when he failed to return from his North West Passage expedition. Out Stack may be in the lead but **Muckle Flugga** with its lighthouse, built by David Stevenson in 1858 for £32,000 and surrounded by wheeling seabirds, is close behind. (It was automated in 1995.) Beneath one's feet are some of Shetland's most spectacular cliff-scenery and the deep, beautiful, but ominous, cleft of **Burra Firth**. At the entrance to Burra Firth there is a 100m-long natural tunnel through the rock at **Hol Hellier** through which a dinghy can sail on a calm day. Looking back, to the south, the firth almost meets the long and narrow Loch of Cliff, which in turn leads to a distant valley stretching the length of Unst, splitting the island longitudinally. Across the Burra Firth, the **Herma Ness** peninsula is a wild area almost uncontaminated by man. It is a Nature Reserve run by Scottish Natural Heritage.

The Ministry of Defence has installations on and around Saxa Vord. In 1962 an unofficial all-British wind speed record of 177mph was recorded here as the anemometer blew away.

Saxa was a giant who lived on Saxa Vord and Herma was another giant who lived on Hermaness Hill and they were always quarrelling; or so the story goes. One day, Herma, using a ship's mast as a fishing rod, caught a whale for supper and asked Saxa to boil it for him in his kettle. (Saxa's Kettle is a huge rock-cup in Nor Wick in which the tide boils and gurgles.) Saxa agreed provided he could keep most for himself but Herma objected to this. The giants started throwing stones at each other and one of the stones which Herma threw can be seen on the west side of Saxa Vord and a stone which Saxa threw is a skerry on the west shore of Burra Firth called **Saxa's Baa**.

I suppose it is fitting that the end of the world should be a land of giants, for there is nothing beyond here but the icy wastes of the Arctic.

ACCESS: Frequent ro-ro ferry service from Gutcher, Yell, 10 minutes, 01957-722259. Frequent BA Express (Loganair) flights from Tingwall, Sumburgh, Edinburgh, and Wick, 01595-840246 or 0345-222111.

Anchorages:
1. Uyea Sound. Fairly good shelter except from SW'lies. There is a pier on NW side at head of sound. Anchor NE side in suitable depth, mud and sand. If caught by SW'lies try Skuda Sound. See Uyea (No.11.26).
2. Sand Wick, Ham of Muness. Exposed NW-N-E. Temp anchorage towards head of bay in 3-6m. Head shoals to shingle beach. Approach needs care.
3. Balta Sound, only safe all-weather anchorage on Unst. Anchor where
suitable but best off N shore between Buness House and Sandison Wharf, 4-8m, mud. Good holding. Avoid stony shoal patches and skerries as charted.
4. Harolds Wick. Exposed SE-E. Temp anchorage near E side of head but hard bottom and holding poor. Approach mid-channel.
5. Nor Wick, on NE coast. Unsafe in E'lies. Temp anchorage near centre of head, 8-10m, good holding in stiff grey sand.
6. Wick of Skaw. Dangerous due to tidal roost. Best to avoid this area by at least 1M.
7. Burra Firth. Exposed N. Sides high and steep-to but wide sandy beach 2¹/2M up firth at head. Easy access. Temp anchorage off beach, holding good.
8. Muckle Flugga. No anchorage and landing only possible in fine weather at steps cut in rock.
9. Lunda Wick, just E of Blue Mull. Sheltered S and E, otherwise exposed. Anchor in SE towards head, sand and mud, holding good. Approach with care S of mid-channel.
10. Wick of Belmont, off Bluemull Sound. Vehicle ferry terminal at head with berthing reserved exclusively for ferry. Rocky bottom.

The East Coast

1. Isle of May

Inchcolm

Bass Rock

Inchkeith

Section 12

Section 12, Table 1

No.	Name	Latitude	Longitude	Table 2* No.	Table 3** No.	Area in Acres	Area in Hectares
12.1	Isle of May	56° 11N	02° 33W	157	121	111	45
12.A	Bass Rock	56° 05N	02° 38W			19	8

* Table 2: The islands arranged in order of magnitude
** Table 3: The islands arranged in order of height

Introduction

It is remarkable that over the entire length of the east coast of mainland Scotland, from John o'Groats – or more accurately, Duncansby Head – to the border north of Berwick-upon-Tweed, there is only one island which comes within the terms of classification for this book by having an area of forty hectares or more. And even this single example – the Isle of May – only just meets the conditions as it is a mere forty-five hectares (111 acres) in area.

There is no islet really worth mentioning north of the Tay except, possibly, the **Halliman Skerries** off Branderburgh and Lossiemouth – a mere line of seaweed-covered rocks, a few broken shards of land at the extreme head of the Cromarty Firth and **Keith Inch** which is actually part of the docks at Peterhead.

In the Firth of Tay itself there is only quaintly-named **Mugdrum Island** (G. – hog-back island) while out in the open sea beyond the Firth is the lonely and infamous **Bell Rock**. During the 1980s, radio broadcasts had to drop Bell Rock readings from the inshore shipping forecasts when a fire gutted the interior of the lighthouse. The Bell Rock, incidentally, is also known as **Inchcape** (G. – island stumbling-block) which is understandable as this tiny rock chip with some skerries around it is only just large enough to support a lighthouse and seems to be there for no logical reason. It was certainly the cause of many shipping tragedies before the lighthouse marked its position.

We have to look to the Firth of Forth to find every other islet on the east coast. The Isle of May has been mentioned. The Bass Rock, although below the classified size, is of such historic interest that it has been included as an appendix to this section. But the remaining little islands also have fascinating histories.

To the west of the Bass Rock is the rugged island of **Fidra** with a broken reef, called the Briggs of Fidra, spanning between it and the shore. On the Briggs are the remains of a Cistercian Hermitage which belonged to a Nunnery founded at North Berwick in the 12th century. At the time of the Dissolution of the Monasteries in Scotland (1561) the North Berwick and Fidra sisterhood consisted of eleven nuns, each drawing an annual income of £20. Although this was a very comfortable income, and they came of good families, not one of them could sign her name. It is possible to anchor on the east, west or south sides of Fidra although there is often an uncomfort-

able swell. On the east side there is a landing jetty for the lighthouse. The south anchorage is tricky because of the rocks and submarine cables.

Two smaller islets lie between Fidra and the Bass Rock – **Craigleith** and **Lamb**. The Lamb has a Dog guarding each side of it (they are skerries) while Craigleith's claim to fame is that it was used as a rabbit warren.

Further up the Forth, standing conspicuously four-square in the middle of the seaway opposite the Port of Leith is **Inchkeith**. It is about half the size of the Isle of May but slightly higher and also has a lighthouse on the summit. It is now unkempt but it once supported a viable small farm with good pasturage and there are several springs providing drinking water. The geology, apart from a few beds of sandstone, is chiefly sheets of igneous rock separated by thin strata of sedimentary deposits – shale with many fossils, coal, and limestone.

The plant-life is varied and I can vouch for the virility of the birdlife. During the nesting season the gulls strafe visitors relentlessly.

Sometime between 679 and 704 St Adomnan, abbot of Iona, founded a 'school of the prophets' on the island and it was here that he met St Serf who had just arrived in Scotland from Rome. In 1010 Malcolm II rewarded Robert de Keth of the Catti (Chattan) clan from Caithness (Cattiness) for his assistance in repelling the Danes and gave him large estates which included Inchkeith and Dalkeith. This is the probable derivation of the name of the island although there are other possibilities. In 1497 the sufferers from a contagious disease called 'grandgore' were shipped from Edinburgh to a Hospital on Inchkeith. The crew of a plague-stricken ship was also quarantined here in 1580; more plague-victims were sent over in 1609; and in 1799 many Russian sailors who had died of an infectious disease were buried on the island.

In 1547 after the battle of Pinkie Cleugh, the victorious English general – the Duke of Somerset – landed marines on Inchkeith and ordered them to fortify the island. A large square fort with corner towers was accordingly built on the summit (site of the present lighthouse). Italian mercenaries held the fort for the English until 1549 when D'Essé, a French general, led a joint Scottish and French force in a brilliant manoeuvre which recaptured the island. The Queen Regent, Mary of Guise, landed on

Inchkeith the following day to see the 'three and four hundred of her dead foes still unburied'. As the date of capture was June 29th – the day of *Fête Dieu* in France – she renamed the island *L'ile de Dieu*. D'Essé demolished the fort and built a larger and stronger one on the same site with an outer surrounding wall and a moat crossed by a drawbridge. Mary Queen of Scots inspected the French garrison of this fort in 1564 and the commemorative stone from the original gateway with the inscription 'M.R. 1564' can still be seen where it has been built into a wall beside the lighthouse.

After Mary's deposition the Castle of Inchkeith was ordered to be 'raisit' but ended up instead being used as a prison. However, it was refortified during the Cromwellian Wars and, even when the ubiquitous Dr Johnson visited Inchkeith with Boswell in 1773, Boswell noted that the fort was strongly built. It was not until 1808 that it was at last 'raisit' to make room for the lighthouse.

In 1878, after twenty years of deep thought, the Admiralty realised that Inchkeith had a commanding position in the Forth and decided to fortify it once again. They installed elaborate batteries at the three corners of the island designed by the Royal Engineers as three separate fortresses. Each battery is partly underground and these magnificent fortifications can still be explored today. In fact Inchkeith is an island so rich in history that it is surprising that it has not received more detailed archaeological study, particularly before all its valuable artefacts disappear. It also has, incidentally, Scotland's *lowest average rainfall* (21.75ins). Dr Johnson said: 'I'd have this island: I'd build a house. . . A rich man of an hospitable turn here, would have many visitors from Edinburgh.' Inchkeith was purchased from the Lighthouse Commissioners when the lighthouse was made automatic, by Mr Tom Farmer, a well-known Edinburgh businessman, but he has not yet followed Dr Johnson's advice.

Inchmickery (G. *innis na bhicaire* – isle of the vicar) is an insignificant islet lying between **Cramond Island** (which is a drying island, accessible at low water) and Inchcolm. It probably had some past connection with the abbey on Inchcolm. The story goes that James IV, who had an enquiring mind, wanted to discover the 'Original Language' of the human race. So he sent two newly-born infants with a dumb nurse to live on uninhabited Inchmickery. After a year or two he and his courtiers seriously agreed that the children 'spak extremely guid Ebrew'.

The remnants of various Second World War fortifications make Inchmickery today an interesting piece of abstract sculpture.

Inchcolm (G. – island of St Columba) was named in the 12th century in memory of Columba's visit to it in about 567. Its old name was Aemonia or Emona. It is best known for the monastery which dominates its skyline and

INCHCOLM ABBEY

which was founded in 1123 by Alexander I. A century earlier when a Danish force under King Sueno entered the Firth of Forth and pillaged Fife with the support of an English force sent by Sueno's brother King Canute, Macbeth drove them off. In return for 'a great summe of gold' Macbeth agreed that the defeated invaders could bury their dead on St Colme's holy island (Shakespeare put the price at 'ten thousand dollars').

Naturally, as a well-endowed monastery, Inchcolm was fair game for plunder and an English ship first raided it in 1335 carrying off all the treasures including a famous image of St Columba. A storm almost wrecked the ship on Inchkeith so the sailors vowed to return the image if they survived. In due course they landed at Kinghorn, sent the image back to Inchcolm, and then sailed for home with the rest of the booty, a clear conscience, and a fair wind. There was another English raid in 1384 and this time the raiders tried to burn down the monastery, but St Columba sent a change of wind which put the fire out.

In 1547, after the battle of Pinkie Cleugh, the Monastery was fortified, and there were occasions when it was, like the Castles of Inchkeith and Inchgarvie, also used as a state prison. Euphemia, mother of Alexander, Lord of the Isles, was imprisoned here, as was Patrick Graham, Archbishop of St Andrews. But there were dark secrets too as revealed in the 1880s when a human skeleton, standing upright, was found built into one of the walls.

The various buildings on Inchcolm are too extensive to discuss in detail here but they form a most interesting group and some parts of the monastery are remarkably well-preserved. The site is maintained by the Government and has a resident custodian. During the summer there are occasional boat excursions from South Queensferry and for yachtsmen the best anchorage is in the north bight.

The island beneath the Forth (rail) Bridge – **Inchgarvie** (G. – rough island) – also has a long and interesting history but as the bridge has destroyed its insularity it is not a subject for this book. Like Inchkeith it had its castle fortification which was considered an important stronghold and was also used as a state prison on occasions, and even a hospital for the quarantine of infectious diseases. It was demolished by Cromwell but rebuilt in 1779 for protection against John Paul Jones. In the end stone from the castle was used to help build the bridge caissons in 1883.

For the defence of the bridge a gun emplacement was maintained on Inchgarvie during the Second World War.

12.1 Isle of May

(ON maa-øy – gull island) In 13th century recorded as 'Maeyar' leading to a comparison with (G. machair – level land) because of the island's plateau-like structure but this is not convincing.

OS Maps: 1:50000 Sheet 59 1:25000 Sheet 364
Admiralty Charts: 1:75000 Nos.175 or 190 1:25000 No.734

AREA: 45ha (111 acres)
HEIGHT: 50m (164 ft)

OWNER: The Commissioners of Northern Lights. Scottish Natural Heritage (SNH) manage it as a National Nature Reserve.

POPULATION: 1881 – 22. 1891 – 27. 1931 – 10. 1961 – 7. 1971 – 10. 1981 – 6. 1991 – 0.

GEOLOGY: The rock is mainly hard fine-grained basalt of a dark-grey colour with tinges of green and greenstone. There are fewer sea-caves than there are on the Bass Rock as the rock here is harder.

HISTORY: The island became a celebrated place of pilgrimage after St Adrian, first Bishop of St Andrews, was discovered and murdered when attempting to shelter here from the Danes in about the year 870. He was buried on the island but half his stone coffin is supposed to have miraculously floated over to Anstruther and ended up in Anstruther Wester churchyard. Six thousand Fife Christians are said to have been slaughtered in this attack, including another saint – Monance.

David I (1124-53) gifted the May to the Benedictine Monastery of Reading in Berkshire on the promise that nine priests would say mass for his soul and that of his successors in perpetuity. He built a chapel on the island dedicated to St Adrian for the new Priory.

The May was sold by the abbot of Reading privately to William Wishart, archbishop of St Andrews *c.* 1270. This may have been encouraged by Alexander III who disliked the idea of the May being under English control, and certainly the brethren in Reading tried to rescind the deal when they learned of it.

When Edward I installed John Balliol on the throne of his 'vassal kingdom' of Scotland in 1292, the very first

Parliament was asked to return the May to the Benedictines of Reading. Bishop Fraser of St Andrews however appealed to the Pope for a ruling and this delayed any settlement. The Battle of Bannockburn in 1314 eventually resolved the matter, although the Scottish monks had meanwhile deserted the island and established themselves in more comfort at Pittenweem. For the next two centuries the monks continued to till the island but live elsewhere while the English demolished the island Priory during many incursions. Later, however, a small Hermitage was built among the ruins.

In 1549 the Provost of St Andrews took a feu on the island which was described then as waste land providing no income, due to the rabbit warrens having been destroyed by the English. It was agreed that a chaplain should stay in the Hermitage and continue to conduct services in the chapel 'out of reverence to the relics and tombs of the saints buried in the island; and for the reception of pilgrims. . .' Two years later a feu charter was conferred on the Balfours of Montquhanny and in 1558 it passed to the family of Forret of Fyngask. Then sometime before 1636 the island was bought by the Cunynghames of Barnes and it was agreed that together with James Maxwell of Innerwick they could levy an 'impost' on ships for erecting and maintaining a Light on the Isle of May. Parliament ratified this in 1641 and again in 1645 for the 'true and thankful service done to his hieness . . . Be his Majesty's Lovitt Johne Cunnynghame of Barnes In bigging and erecting upoun the yle of Maij belonging to him Lyand in the mouth of the firth Of ane Lighthous. . .'

In 1672 the Earl of Kellie is recorded as the owner but he sold it to the Scotts of Scotstarvet. The Marquis of Tichfield, 4th Duke of Portland, inherited it from the Scotts by marriage in 1795 and the Duchess eventually sold it to the Northern Lighthouse Commissioners for the sum of £60,000 in 1815.

WILDLIFE: A number of interesting plant communities are to be found and over sixty varieties of seaweed have been recorded here. Samples were taken in 1994 to try to

THE LIGHTHOUSE – A FINE TOWN HALL

reconstruct the vegetational history of the island, as well as that of the medieval fish industry.

Renowned for its birdlife, in early summer this is a great nesting place for many seabirds but, unlike the Bass Rock, there are no gannets. April/May and August/October are the best periods for birdwatching. Breeders: Large numbers of shag, kittiwake, guillemot, razorbill, puffin, and also, fulmar, herring gulls and lesser black-backed gulls, eider, oystercatcher and a few common and arctic terns, wheatear and rock pipit.

Over 240 bird species have been recorded and in au-
tumn there are often enormous numbers of relatively common birds. Species seen include wryneck, bluethroat, icterine, barred and yellow-browed warblers, great grey and red-backed shrikes, red-breasted flycatcher, Lapland and ortolan buntings, and scarlet rosefinch. Rarities recorded include the red-footed falcon, spoonbill, Pallas's sandgrouse, Daurian redstart, Siberian thrush, pied wheatear, Pallas's-, paddyfield-, melodious-, olivaceous-, and subalpine warblers, red-throated pipit, yellow-breasted and rustic buntings, and pine grosbeak. At sea: divers, shearwaters, sea-duck, petrels and skuas.

The verdant islet May,
Whose fitful lights amid surrounding gloom,
. . .from danger warns the home-bound mariner.
                                    Fergusson, 1772

The **ISLE OF MAY** is well known for three diverse reasons, its archaeological interest, its historic lighthouse, and its birdlife. The island itself is a long narrow slab of hard basalt with a grassy and reasonably fertile surface partly surrounded by cliffs. The highest point at 50m is near the centre with the lighthouse on it.

Most of the antiquities are at the southern end not far from **Kirkhaven** where there is a jetty and crane built for the lighthouse keepers. The main ruin is of a rectangular building nearly 10m long with two Norman-style window openings in the west wall [NT658990]. The building is on a north-south access and has had several alterations such as the addition of a defensive tower. The north part of the structure, defined by a partition wall, may have been a chapel but about 1600 a small smithy and forge were constructed inside the ruins of the church which had probably been abandoned years before. Although this building was joined to St Ethernan's Priory (*c.* 1140), the Priory itself was demolished in a succession of English invasions. However, during archaeological excavations in 1992, a monastic church was uncovered. The cloister garth and numerous graves were investigated in 1995 and excavation under the 13th century Benedictine church has revealed signs of an earlier building. Large quantities of pottery included a 13th or 14th century decorated jug which probably came from Scarborough and shards of Iron Age and Beaker vessels.

David I was the son of the saintly Queen Margaret and he was determined to substitute the Roman faith for the Culdee faith of St Columba and the other early Christians. He spent money lavishly on abbeys, cathedrals, and churches, gave generous donations to Augustinians, Cistercians, and Benedictines and was profligate in his distribution of Crown lands to the Church. His friendship with the Benedictines of the House of Reading on the Thames came about through his marriage to Henry I of England's sister. His endowment made the Priory of May one of the kingdom's wealthiest establishments.

There are records that shortly after David had founded the Priory Sweyn Asliefsson (See Gairsay, No.10.13), the likable buccaneering Orcadian, plundered it and then sailed up the Firth of Forth to Edinburgh to be received by King David with great honour. It seems that he proudly told David of his exploits and was severely reprimanded so he promptly sailed back down the Forth, restored all the plunder to the monastery, and then sent his greetings to David whereupon he was restored to his position of honour.

A creek at the south-west corner of the island is known as the **Pilgrims' Haven**. It has two outlying rock stacks

A CHAPEL IN THE CLIFFS NEAR ST ADRIAN'S PRIORY

(one of these isolated pinnacles is 24m high and supposed to look like a bishop's mitre but I found that to be somewhat imaginative) and a shingle beach in the cove on which a small boat can rest. In the 14th and 15th century a steady stream of pilgrims landed here and flocked up the slope to pay their respects at St Adrian's shrine. On the way they would stop to drink brackish water from the **Pilgrim's Well** [NT659989] which was reputed to cure many ailments and bring about remarkable miracles. One of these pilgrims was Mary of Gueldres, *en route* from the Netherlands in 1449 to marry James II. Another was James IV who made the pilgrimage on a number of occasions – 1490, 1503, 1505 and 1513. James V may also have visited the May in 1540.

In the 17th century there was a small village just south of the Priory and there is a tradition that the inhabitants lived by ship-wrecking and smuggling. Contraband was kept in the cave near the **South Ness** which the excisemen were told was inhabited by a colony of kelpies. The May caves were also used by Fife fishermen to avoid the press-gangs and one well-concealed cave is still called 'Press Cave'. At the time of writing archaeologists are proposing to investigate the village remains.

In a hollow near the cliff-edge is a solitary tombstone for a John Wishart who died in 1730. This was probably the site of the village cemetery.

West of the lighthouse keepers cottages and outbuildings there is a deep gorge which has been dammed to provide a water supply. Prior to this there was no satisfactory source of fresh water as, although there are several wells, they are either brackish or dry out at intervals. The lighthouse is now automatic but on an earlier visit to the island a keeper proudly showed us his walled garden, well-protected to keep out the rabbits and full of superb vegetables.

The lighthouse is a handsome structure which would make a fine town hall but is quite out-of-keeping with the landscape. It was started in 1816 and contains a square light-tower with mock battlements and a spacious two-storey building with accommodation for the superintendent keeper.

The track running past the lighthouse and on to **Altarstones Landing** in the north-west is called

Holyman's Road because it was the path customarily taken by the Prior.

In the centre of the island and not far from the modern lighthouse is a platform-like structure which is all that remains of the original lighthouse or **Beacon** [NT657994]. When Alexander Cunningham had it built in 1635 it was the first and only lighthouse in Scotland – a mere platform 12m high with a burning beacon on it. When Cunningham's son, John, together with James Maxwell, obtained permission to charge ships an impost for the light, they improved the design by raising the beacon platform to 18m and constructing the tower like a Border keep. This was in 1656. The impost was four Scots shillings a ton for foreign ships and two shillings for home vessels collected by Customs officers on the Fife coast and bringing in about £280 sterling per year. The light came from burning a ton of coal each night in a grate or chauffer at the top of the tower. In gales, up to three tons of coal were consumed.

The architect for the beacon tower was drowned when his boat capsized while on a supervision visit. Several old ladies of Pittenweem were blamed for the tragedy and burned as witches.

The lighthouse was rather unsatisfactory, particularly as in a gale very little light could be seen on the dangerous windward side. In January 1791 the light was out for two nights during a severe storm. It was found that the lighthouse keeper, his wife, and five children, had been asphyxiated by the fumes although a baby survived. There were many shipwrecks and complaints but nothing was done until two Royal Navy frigates, *Pallas* and *Nymph*, were wrecked on the rocks near Dunbar in 1810. The pilots said they thought a limekiln at Broxmouth was the May light, and that the May light was the Bell Rock. At last the Government acted. The Commissioners of Northern Lights bought the island in 1815 and started construction of the present lighthouse – using the latest design of oil lamps and reflectors.

Maiden Hair Rock, near the Pilgrims' Haven, is supposed to be named in honour of St Thenaw. King Loth of Lothian was reputed to have been gifted his kingdom by King Arthur of the Round Table. The legend claims that in the year 516, Princess Thenaw, Loth's young unmarried daughter, was found to be pregnant. The king was furious and ordered her to be cast headlong from Traprain Law (then known as Dunpender) as punishment for fornication. After praying for forgiveness the girl was thrown from the height, but she landed on soft ground and suffered no injury. King Loth was convinced that only a witch could have had such a remarkable escape and decreed that she be put to death by drowning. So she was rowed out from Aberlady and cast into the water near the Isle of May. She managed to clutch on to the seaweed on Maiden Hair Rock for a time but after crying for help from God she was swept away by the tide far up the Forth. She was at last washed ashore beside the Monastery at Culross and it was here, lying on the beach, that she gave birth to her son, Kentigern, later known as St Mungo, patron saint of Glasgow. Soon after, mother and son were discovered by a monk and St Serf, Abbot of Culross, looked after them.

ACCESS: Boat trips from Anstruther in summer, 01333-31 013.

Anchorages: Use plenty of chain as holding is poor.
1. Altarstanes Landing, W side. Subject to surge and exposed to all W'lies. Occasional anchorage in 5m, opposite the steps. Moored dinghies subject to damage except in flat calm. Hoist inflatables clear of sea.
2. Kirkhaven, E of S Ness. Long, narrow gut entered from SE with jetty at head. Pleasant in calm weather but subject to surge in S-SW winds and dangerously exposed to E'lies and breaking seas. Depth only 1.2m but with space for small yacht to tie to rings. Very narrow, but mid-channel approach under power is straightforward.
3. East Tarbet or Tarbet Hole. Subject to swell and exposed to E. Awkward landing on rocks. Occasional anchorage in 4m.

12-Appendix Bass Rock

Derivation uncertain. Possibly named after a man named Bass mentioned in the Book of Lecain (Chronicles of Picts and Scots) who may have owned the rock, or, maybe (G. bathais – brow or forehead). In Old Norse 'Baa' is a sunken rock on which the sea breaks in bad weather – maybe this is an inaccurate application meaning 'a dangerous rock'.

OS Maps: 1:50000 Sheet 66 1:25000 Sheet 396
Admiralty Charts: 1:75000 No.175 1:50000 No.734

AREA: 7½ha (19 acres)
HEIGHT: 107m (350 ft)

OWNER: Sir Hew Hamilton-Dalrymple.

POPULATION: Uninhabited.

GEOLOGY: A volcanic plug of phonolite rock.

HISTORY: Most of the rock belonged to the Bishopric of St Andrews when Malcolm Canmore is said to have granted the remaining part of it to the Lauder family in 1056. The Lauders became known as the Lauders of the Bass and they held it until the mid-17th century. In 1706 it became the property of Sir Hew Dalrymple and it is still in the ownership of his family.

St Baldred, an Irish missionary may have been the first inhabitant. He died in 606.

In 1338, the siege of Dunbar Castle by the English was broken because the Bass Rock was able to provide Black Agnes, Countess of March and Dunbar, with provisions.

The date when the fortress was built, probably by the Lauders, is not on record. It is first mentioned in 1405

1/2 km

1/4 mile

Firth of Forth

The Middens

Stone Dyke

West Cove

The Pulpit

△ 111

Path

Well

St Baldred's Chapel (ruin)

Castle (ruin)

Crane Bastion

West Landing

East Cove

East Landing

N

when Prince James, the twelve-year old son of Robert III, later to become James I, was sent here for safety by his father until a vessel could be found to take him to France, as the king's brother, the Duke of Albany, had designs on the throne. Albany tipped off the English who intercepted James' ship, and imprisoned the prince in the Round Tower at Windsor for nineteen years. When James was eventually ransomed for £400,000 he, understandably, decided to get his own back and imprisoned the son of the Duke of Albany in the fortress on the Bass Rock.

In 1542 the crude little chapel which had been built about 1491 was consecrated and dedicated to St Baldred.

When Cromwell stormed north and defeated the Presbyterians at Dunbar (they had offered allegiance to Charles II), there was an attempt to send the Church Records over to the Bass Rock for safe keeping. But the

Rock surrendered to Cromwell's forces in 1651, the Records were removed to London, and it is thought they were lost in the fire at the House of Commons in 1834.

When Charles II was restored as monarch in 1660 he set about destroying the Church of Scotland, but the Covenanters fought back with secret 'conventicles'. Many Presbyterians were arrested and in 1671, the Bass Rock was bought (for £4000) and used as a prison for the recalcitrant Covenanters. It was not until 1688 that many of these men were released when James VII was relieved of the Crown and William of Orange proclaimed king. Much of Scotland however remained faithful to James until the Battle of Killiecrankie after which the only remaining Jacobite stronghold was the Bass Rock. It held out for nearly two years under its Governor, Sir Charles Maitland, but was eventually starved into submission in 1690.

THE BASS ROCK FROM THE RAMPARTS OF TANTALLON CASTLE.
THE ISLE OF MAY LIES ON THE HORIZON.

It was now the turn of four Jacobites to be held prisoner. But not for long, because while the new Governor, Fletcher of Saltoun, was away they captured the garrison and with only a gunner and sixteen friends from Lothian to help them they held the Bass Rock from 1691 until 1694. Even then they only surrendered because they were granted an amnesty.

In 1701, the fortress was dismantled and the island was sold to Sir Hew Dalrymple, whose family still own it. Its main use at this time was for grazing sheep and collecting gannets to eat.

In 1902 the lighthouse was constructed and the island was once again temporarily inhabited.

WILDLIFE: Forty-eight species of wildflower have been recorded here. This includes the tree mallow, *lavatera arborea*, a tall biennial with attractive rose-coloured flowers. Apart from some examples on Ailsa Craig (No.1.1) it was until relatively recently found nowhere else in Scotland although it is reputed to have grown also on Inchmickery and Inchgarvie at one time. However, a few began to be seen in North Berwick gardens and now it is a widespread and popular garden plant. Another unusual plant is the Pheasant's-eye Daffodil, *narcissus poeticus* which comes from central Europe. Examples can also be found of the native Sea Beet, *beta vulgaris maritima*.

Birdlife is prolific. There are common inland species such as blackbird, hedge sparrow and rock pipit while seabirds are packed onto every steep rock ledge. The island is most famous for its huge gannet colony of over 7500 pairs and the bird is even named after the island, *sula bassana*. There are also large numbers of kittiwake, razorbill, shag, fulmar, herring gull, guillemot and puffin.

The **BASS ROCK** can be thought of as the Ailsa Craig (No.1.1) of the East Coast but it is very much smaller.

There was a fortress on it for centuries and most of the materials were brought over from the mainland. Considering the difficulty of landing in even comparatively quiet conditions, one can only marvel at the dogged determination of the builders.

There is a huge cave which cuts right through the base of the Bass Rock from east to west. The sea – and the seals – slip through, and it can be explored by dinghy in calm weather. Its least height is about 10m, length 170m, and there is a patch in the middle where there is a small gravel beach.

Sailing around the rock is an unforgettable experience. The view of the cave may be beautiful and fascinating but it is the assault on all the senses which is beyond belief. The eyes are dazzled by clouds of wheeling and diving birds set against rock formations draped in guano and deep shadows of caverns and overhanging ledges. The ears are deafened by the high-pitched cries of the seabirds as a descant to the surging bass tones of the sea growling in the rock clefts – what a subject for Mahler! And the nose really suffers. The smell is overpowering.

The rock itself appears from the mainland to slope gradually down to the sea but this slope is in fact divided into three rough terraces. The lowest terrace with the landing place has the remains of the fortress on it which was purchased by the Government in 1671 as a state prison. On the second terrace are the ruins of **St Baldred's Chapel**, probably built on the site of his original anchorite cell. The highest terrace has what was once a walled garden and a well – although this is no more than a catchment for surface water. There is a cairn at the summit (111m).

ACCESS: There are boat trips from North Berwick in the summer months. The owner's permission is required for landing.

Anchorages: No anchorages.
1. Landing jetty on S side, below lighthouse. Unless flat calm (very rare) advisable to lie off and approach in dinghy. Even then, landing can be difficult due to the swell.

Table 2

Islands arranged by order of magnitude

NO.	NAME	TABLE I NO.	AREA IN HECTARES	NO.	NAME	TABLE I NO.	AREA IN HECTARES
1	Lewis/Harris	8-16	220020	36	Canna	4-4	1314
2	Mainland (Shetland)	11-11	100230	37	Foula	11-6	1265
3	Mull	3-3	87794	38	Kerrera	3-2	1214
4	South Uist	7-16	72827	39	Great Cumbrae	1-6	1168
5	Islay	2-4	61956	40	Scarp	8-15	1045
6	Mainland (Orkney)	10-10	58308	41	Soay	5-1	1036
7	Arran	1-4	43201	42	Berneray	8-1	1010
8	Jura	2-5	36692	43	Rona	5-9	930
9	Yell	11-23	21211	44	Papa Westray	10-26	918
10	Hoy	10-5	14318	45	Iona	3-1	877
11	Bute	1-8	12217	46	Flotta	10-4	876
12	Unst	11-29	12068	47	Papa Stour	11-14	828
13	Rum	4-3	10463	48	Pabbay	8-5	820
14	Tiree	3-10	7834	49	Fair Isle	11-1	768
15	Coll	3-13	7685	50	Eriskay	7-13	703
16	Barra	7-6	6835	51	North Ronaldsay	10-27	690
17	Raasay	5-7	6405	52	Hirta (St Kilda)	9-1	670
18	Sanday	10-24	5043	53	Scalpay	8-8	653
19	Rousay	10-20	4860	54	Egilsay	10-18	650
20	Westray	10-25	4713	55	Mingulay	7-2	640
21	Colonsay	2-6	4617	56	Ronay	7-18	563
22	Fetlar	11-24	4078	57	Muck	4-1	559
23	Stronsay	10-14	3275	58	Shuna	2-10	451
24	Eigg	4-2	3049	59	Graemsay	10-9	409
25	Shapinsay	10-12	2948	60	Sandray	7-4	385
26	Bressay	11-8	2805	61	Wiay	7-17	375
27	Eday	10-21	2745	62	Island of Stroma	10-1	375
28	Scalpay	5-3	2483	63	Vementry	11-13	370
29	Ulva	3-7	2415	64	Ceann Ear (Monach Isles)	7-20	357
30	Lismore	3-9	2351	65	Noss	11-7	343
31	Whalsay	11-15	1970	66	Vaila	11-10	327
32	Luing	2-13	1543	67	Little Cumbrae Island	1-5	313
33	Taransay	8-11	1475	68	Wyre	10-15	311
34	Scarba	2-9	1474	69	Tanera Mór	6-7	310
35	Gigha Island	2-3	1395	70	Handa	6-9	309

NO.	NAME	TABLE I NO.	AREA IN HECTARES	NO.	NAME	TABLE I NO.	AREA IN HECTARES
71	Isle of Ewe	6-2	309	119	Eilean Righ	2-8	86
72	Fara	10-6	295	120	Auskerry	10-11	85
73	Hascosay	11-25	275	121	Vuia Mór	8-19	84
74	Seaforth Island	8-14	273	122	Fuiay	7-8	84
75	Eilean Mór (Crowlin I.)	5-6	270	123	Lunga	3-8	81
76	Inchmarnock	1-7	266	124	Balta	11-28	80
77	Lunga	2-11	254	125	Muldoanich	7-5	78
78	Holy Island	1-3	253	126	Bigga	11-20	78
79	Pabbay	7-3	250	127	Boreray	9-3	77
80	Calf of Eday	10-23	243	128	Eilean Kearstay	8-18	77
81	Gairsay	10-13	240	129	Eynhallow	10-19	75
82	Fuday	7-11	232	130	Papa Stronsay	10-17	74
83	Papa Little	11-12	226	131	Copinsay	10-8	73
84	Housay (Out Skerries)	11-18	218	132	Hermetray	7-21	72
85	Carna	3-14	213	133	Linga (Olna Firth)	11-17	70
86	Uyea	11-26	205	134	Gunna	3-11	69
87	Berneray	7-1	204	135	Oxna	11-4	68
88	Boreray	8-2	198	136	Tanera Beg	6-8	66
89	Gruinard Island	6-3	196	137	Cara	2-2	66
90	Ensay	8-4	186	138	Samphrey	11-19	66
91	Mousa	11-2	180	139	Eilean Dubh Mór	2-14	65
92	Faray	10-22	180	140	Isay	5-8	60
93	Killegray	8-3	176	141	South Havra	11-3	59
94	Isle Martin	6-4	157	142	Papa	11-5	59
95	Shuna Island	3-12	155	143	Floddaymore	7-19	58
96	Sanda Island	1-2	151	144	Linga Holm	10-16	57
97	Wiay	5-5	148	145	Eileach an Naoimh	2-12	56
98	Garbh Eilean (Shiant I.)	8-10	143	146	Inch Kenneth	3-4	55
99	Hellisay	7-9	142	147	Horse Island	6-6	53
100	Garbh Eileach	2-15	142	148	Tahay	7-22	53
101	Eilean nan Ron	6-10	138	149	Longay	5-4	50
102	Little Bernera	8-22	138	150	Eileanan Iasgaich	7-14	50
103	Longa	6-1	126	151	Eilean Macaskin	2-7	50
104	West Linga	11-16	125	152	Scotasay	8-9	49
105	Eilean Iubhard	8-13	125	153	Stockinish Island	8-7	49
106	Mealista Island	8-17	124	154	Texa	2-1	48
107	Pabay	5-2	122	155	Shillay	8-6	47
108	Priest Island	6-5	122	156	Soay Mór	8-12	45
109	Eorsa	3-6	122	157	Isle of May	12-1	45
110	Rona (North)	9-4	109	158	Stuley	7-15	45
111	Hildasay	11-9	108	159	Linga (Bluemull Sound)	11-27	45
112	Cava	10-7	107	160	Lamba	11-22	43
113	Pabay Mór	8-21	101	161	Switha	10-3	41
114	Ailsa Craig	1-1	99	162	Fiaray	7-12	41
115	Soay	9-2	99	163	Vacsay	8-20	41
116	Gighay	7-10	96	164	Flodday (E Barra)	7-7	40
117	Swona	10-2	92	165	Brother Isle	11-21	40
118	Little Colonsay	3-5	88				

Table 3

The islands arranged in order of height

NO.	NAME	TABLE I NO.	AREA IN METRES		NO.	NAME	TABLE I NO.	AREA IN METRES
1	Mull	3-3	966		36	Berneray (Bishop's Isles)	7-1	193
2	Arran	1-4	874		37	Kerrera	3-2	189
3	Rum	4-3	812		38	Eriskay	7-13	185
4	Lewis/Harris	8-16	799		39	Noss	11-7	181
5	Jura	2-5	785		40	Pabbay (Bishop's Isles)	7-3	171
6	Uists/Benbecula	7-16	620		41	Westray	10-25	169
7	Islay	2-4	491		42	Carna	3-14	169
8	Hoy	10-5	479		43	Shiant Islands	8-10	160
9	Mainland (Shetland)	11-11	450		44	Fetlar	11-24	158
10	Scarba	2-9	449		45	Muldoanich	7-5	153
11	Raasay	5-7	443		46	Colonsay/Oronsay	2-6	143
12	Hirta	9-1	430		47	Tiree	3-10	141
13	Foula	11-6	418		48	Soay	5-1	141
14	Eigg	4-2	393		49	Muck	4-1	137
15	Scalpay	5-3	392		50	Great Cumbrae	1-6	127
16	Boreray	9-3	384		51	Lismore	3-9	127
17	Barra/Vatersay	7-6	383		52	Rona	5-9	125
18	Soay	9-2	378		53	Handa	6-9	123
19	Ailsa Craig	1-1	338		54	Little Cumbrae Island	1-5	123
20	Holy Island	1-3	314		55	Sanda Island	1-2	123
21	Ulva/Gometra	3-7	313		56	Tanera Mór	6-7	122
22	Scarp	8-15	308		57	Isle Martin	6-4	120
23	Unst	11-29	284		58	Whalsay	11-15	119
24	Bute	1-8	278		59	Ronay	7-18	115
25	Mingulay	7-2	273		60	Crowlin Islands	5-6	114
26	Mainland (Orkney)	10-10	268		61	Garbh Eileach	2-15	110
27	Taransay	8-11	267		62	Rona (North)	9-4	108
28	Rousay	10-20	250		63	Fuiay	7-8	107
29	Bressay	11-8	226		64	Gruinard Island	6-3	106
30	Fair Isle	11-1	217		65	Scalpay	8-8	104
31	Seaforth Island	8-14	217		66	Coll	3-13	104
32	Canna/Sanday	4-4	210		67	Lunga	3-8	103
33	Sandray	7-4	207		68	Wiay	7-17	102
34	Yell	11-23	205		69	Gairsay	10-13	102
35	Pabbay (Sound of Harris)	8-5	196		70	Eday	10-21	101

Bibliography

The relevant section(s) are in square brackets after each entry. [G] = general.

Admiralty Hydrographer. *North Coast of Scotland Pilot.* [G]
——————*West Coast of Scotland Pilot.* [G]
Allen, J. Romilly, *The Early Christian Monuments of Scotland.* 1903. [G]
Anderson, A. O., and M. O., *Adomnan's Life of Columba.* 1961. [G]
Anderson, Joseph (ed), *The Orkneyinga Saga.* 1873. [10,11]
Anderson, R. S. G. *The Antiquities of Gigha.* 1978. [2]
Arbman, H. *The Vikings.* 1961. [G]
Atkinson, Robert, *Island Going.* 1949. [G]
——————*Shillay and the Seals.* 1980. [7,8]
Bailey, Patrick, *Orkney.* 1971. [10]
Barclay, R. S., *The Population of Orkney 1755-1961.* 1965. [10]
Barry, G., *History of the Orkney Islands.* 1805. [10]
Blake, George, *The Firth of Clyde.* [1]
Booth, C. Gordon, *A Guide to Islay and Jura.* 1984. [2]
Boswell, James, *The Journal of a Tour to the Hebrides. 1785.* [G]
Botanical Society of the British Isles. *Proceedings.* [G]
Bray, Elizabeth, *The Discovery of the Hebrides. Voyagers to the Western Isles 1745-1883.* 1986. [G]
Brøgger, A. W., *A History of the Norse Settlements in Scotland.* 1929. [G]
Brown, G. M., *An Orkney Tapestry.* 1969. [10]
Brown, P. Hume, *Early Travellers in Scotland.* 1891. [G]
Budge, Donald, *Jura, an Island of Argyll.* 1960. [2]
Butler, David, *Isle of Noss.* 1990. [11]
Buxton, Ben, *Mingulay. An Island and Its People.* 1995. [7]
Campbell, A. J., *Fifteen Centuries of the Church in Orkney.* 1938. [10]
Campbell, J. F., *Popular Tales of the West Highlands.* 1860-2. [G]
Campbell, John Lorne, *Canna: the Story of a Hebridean Island.* 1984. [4]
Carmichael, Alasdair, *Kintyre.* [G]
Carmichael, Ian, *Lismore in Alba.* 1947. [3]
Childe, V. Gordon, *Prehistory of Scotland.* 1935. [G]

——————*Skara Brae: A Pictish Village in Orkney.* 1931. [10]
Clouston, J. Storer, *A History of Orkney.* 1932. [10]
Clouston, J. Storer, *The Orkney Parishes.* 1927. [10]
Cluness, A. T., *The Shetland Isles.* 1951. [11]
Clyde Cruising Club Publications Ltd. Sailing Directions (1992 amendments).
Clyde Area. 1985. [1]
Kintyre to Ardnamurchan. 1981. [2,3]
Ardnamurchan to Cape Wrath. 1984. [4,5,6]
Outer Hebrides. 1988. [7,8]
Shetland. 1978. [11]
Orkney, North and North-East Coasts. 1990. [10]
Cooper, Derek, *Hebridian Connection.* 1977. [G]
——————*Skye.* [5]
——————*The Road to Mingulay.* 1985. [7,8]
Council for Scottish Archaeology,
Discovery and Excavation in Scotland. [G]
Scottish Archaeological News. [G]
Cruttwell, Clement, *The New Universal Gazeteer.* 1798. [G]
Craig, David, *On the Crofters' Trail.* 1990. [G]
Craig, G. Y., *Geology of Scotland.* 1991. [G]
Cursiter, J. W., *List of Books relating to Orkney and Shetland.* 1894. [10,11]
Darling, Dr Frank Fraser, *Island Farm.* 1944. [6]
——————*Island Years.* 1942. [3,6,9]
——————*A Naturalist on Rona.* [9]
——————*West Highland Survey.* [G]
Darling, F. Fraser and Boyd, J. Morton, *The Highlands and Islands.* 1969. [G]
Dasent, G. W., *The Orkneyingers' Saga.* 1894. [10]
Delaney, Frank, *The Celts.* 1989. [G]
Dey, Joan, *Out Skerries.* 1991. [11]
Dickson, John, *Emeralds Chased in Gold.* 1899. [12]
Donaldson, M. E. M. *Further Wanderings - Mainly in Argyll.* 1926. [G]
Drever, W. P., *Udal Law in the Orkneys and Zetland.* 1914. [10,11]
Drummond, Maldwin, *West Highland Shores.* 1990. [G]
Edmonston, T., *Glossary of Shetland and Orkney Dialect.* 1866. [10,11]

Fabian, D. J. *et al. The Islands of Scotland including Skye*. [G]

Faux, Ronald, *The West*. 1982. [G]

Feacham, R., *A Guide to Prehistoric Scotland*. [1963] [G]

Fenton, Alexander, *The Northern Isles: Orkney and Shetland*. 1978. [10,11]

Fenton, Alexander and Palsson, Hermann, *The Northern and Western Isles in the Viking World*. [G]

Forth Yacht Clubs' Association Pilot Handbook. *Berwick-on-Tweed to Peterhead*. 1974. [12]

Garms, Harry, *The Natural History of Europe*. 1967. [G]

Gear, Sheila, *Foula. Island West of the Sun*. 1983. [11]

Gordon, Seton, *Highways and Byways in the West High lands*. 1935. [G]

Gorrie, D., *Summers and Winters in the Orkneys*. 1868. [10]

Graham, Henry Grey, *The Social Life of Scotland in the Eighteenth Century*. 1899. [G]

Grant, I. F., *The Lordship of the Isles*. 1982. [G]

Grant, James Shaw, *Discovering Lewis and Harris*. 1987. [8]

Gregory, D., *History of the Western Highlands and Islands*. 1881. [G]

Grieve, Symington, *The Book of Colonsay and Oronsay*. 1923. [2]

Grigsby, Joan, *An Island Rooin*. 1933. [11]

Grimble, Ian, *Highland Man*. 1980. [G]

——————*Scottish Islands*. 1985. [G]

Groome, F. Hindes, *Ordnance Gazetteer*. 1900. [G]

Gunn, J., *The Orkney Book*. 1909. [10]

Harker, Alfred, *The West Highlands and the Hebrides*. 1941. [G]

Heddle, J. G. F. M. and Mainland, T., *Orkney and Shetland*. 1920. [10,11]

Henderson, Isabel, *The Picts*. 1967. [G]

Hewison, James King, *Bute in the Olden Time*. 1893. [1]

Higgins, L. R., *A Tangle of Islands*. 1971. [G]

Hogg, Garry, *The Far Flung Isles*. 1961. [G]

Hossack, B. H., *Kirkwall in the Orkneys*. 1900. [10]

Howarth, David, *The Shetland Bus*. 1953. [11]

Jakobsen, Jakob, *Old Shetland Dialect and Place-Names of Shetland*. [11]

——————*Etymological Dictionary of the Norn Language in Shetland*. [11]

Jamieson, Peter, *Letters on Shetland*. 1949. [11]

Johnson, Samuel, *Journey to the Western Isles of Scotland*. 1775. [G]

Knox, John, *Tour of the Highlands of Scotland and the Hebride Isles in 1787*. 1787. [G]

Lacaille, A., *The Stone Age in Scotland*. 1954. [G]

Lamont, W. D., *The Early History of Islay*. 1966. [2]

Lawrence, Martin, *Clyde to Colonsay*. 1989. [1,2]

——————*Crinan to Canna*. 1987. [2,3,4]

——————*Castlebay to Cape Wrath*. 1990. [5,6,7,8]

Lawson, Bill, *The Teampull on the Isle of Pabbay*. 1994. [8]

Linklater, Eric, revis. J. R. Nicolson. *Orkney and Shetland*. 1990. [10,11]

Linklater, Eric, *The Ultimate Viking*. 1955. [G]

Loder, J de V., *Colonsay and Oronsay in the Isles of Argyll*. 1935. [2]

MacCaig, Norman, *Collected Poems*. 1988. [G]

MacCormack, John, *Island of Mull*. 1923. [3]

MacCulloch, J., *The Highlands and Western Isles of Scotland*. 1824. [G]

Macdonald, Donald, *Lewis. A History of the Island*. 1978. [8]

MacDonald, James, *General view of the agriculture of the Hebrides or Western Isles of Scotland: with observations on the means of their improvement, together with a separate account of the principal islands*. 1811. [G]

McEwen, John, *Who Owns Scotland*. 1981. [G]

Mackenzie, Compton,; Campbell, J. L.; Borgström, Carl, *The Book of Barra*. 1936. [7]

McKerral, Andrew, *Kintyre in the Seventeenth Century*. 1948. [1,2]

MacKillop, Donald, *Sea-Names of Berneray*. 1990. [7,8]

Mackintosh, W. R., *Around the Orkney Peat Fires*. 1914. [10]

McLellan, Robert, *The Isle of Arran*. 1970. [1]

Macnab, P. A., *Mull & Iona*. 1982. [3]

McNeill, F. Marion, *Iona*. 1959. [3]

Madders, Michael, and Welstead, Julia, *Where to Watch Birds in Scotland*. [G]

Marshall, David, *The Story of Inchkeith*. [12]

Martin, Martin, *A Description of the Western Isles of Scotland*. 1703. [G]

——————*A Late Voyage to St Kilda*. 1698. [8,9]

Marwick, H., *Ancient Monuments of Orkney. Official Guide*. 1952. [10]

——————*Orkney*. 1951. [10]

——————*Orkney Farm Names*. 1952. [10]

——————edit. Nicolaisen, W. F. H., *The Place-Names of Birsay*. 1970. [10]

——————*The Place-Names of Rousay*. 1947. [10]

Mercer, John, *Hebridean Islands: Colonsay, Gigha, Jura*. 1982. [2]

Millman, Lawrence, *Last Places*. 1992. [7]

Mitchison, Rosalind, *A History of Scotland*. 1982. [G]

Mooney, J., *Eynhallow. The Holy Isle of the Orkneys*. 1923. [10]

Morton, Tom, *Hell's Golfer - a good walk spoiled*. 1995. [7,8,10,11]

Muir, Edwin, *Autobiography*. [10]

Munro, Dean Sir Donald, *Description of the Western Isles of Scotland*. 1549. [G]

Munro, Neil, *Children of the Tempest*. [7]

——————*The Clyde River and Firth*. [1]

New Statistical Account of Scotland. 1845. [G]

Murray, Frances, *Summer in the Hebrides*. 1887. [G]

Murray, W. H., *The Islands of Western Scotland*. 1973. [G]

——————*The West Highlands of Scotland*. 1988. [G]

Newton, Norman S., *Colonsay and Oronsay*. 1990. [2]

——————*Islay*. 1988. [2]

Nicolaisen, W. F. H., *Scottish Place-Names*. 1976. [G]

Nicolson, A., *History of Skye*. 1930. [5]

Nicolson, James R., *Traditional Life in Shetland*. 1990. [11]

O'Dell, A. C. and Watson, Kenneth, *The Highlands and Islands of Scotland*. 1962. [G]

O'Dell, Andrew, *Historical Geography of the Shetland Isles*. [11]

Orkney Antiquarian Society.
Proceedings. [10]

Pennant, T., *A Tour in Scotland, and Voyage to the Hebrides*. 1776. [G]

Perrot, David, *Guide to the Western Isles*. 1986. [G]

Philip, Kathleen, *The Story of Gigha*. 1979. [2]

Rendall, R., *Orkney Shore*. 1960. [10]

Robson, Michael, *Rona, the Distant Island*. 1991. [9]

Royal Commission on the Ancient and Historical Monuments of Scotland.
Argyll. 1971-92. [1,2,3]
Orkney. 1946. [10]
Outer Hebrides, Skye and Small Isles. 1928. [4,5,6,7,8]

Sawyer, P. H., *The Age of the Vikings*. 1962. [G]

Schei, Liv Kjørsvik and Moberg, Gunnie, *The Orkney Story*. 1985. [10]
——————*The Shetland Story*. 1988. [11]

Scott, M. A., *Island Saga. The Story of North Ronaldsay*. 1968. [10]

Scottish Mountaineering Club. District Guide Books,
Islands of Scotland
Munro's Tables

Shaw, Frances J., *The Northern and Western Islands of Scotland: their Economy and Society in the Seventeenth Century*. 1980. [G]

Shaw, Margaret Fay, *From the Alleghenies to the Hebrides*. 1993. [G]

Sharpe, Richard, *Raasay: a Study in Island History*. 1982. [5]

Sheddon, Hugh, *The Story of Lorn*. [3]

Simpson, W. Douglas, *The Ancient Stones of Scotland*. 1965. [G]
——————*The Celtic Church in Scotland*. 1935. [G]

Simpson, Sir James Y., *Inchcolm*. [12]

Sinclair, Andrew, *The Sword and the Grail*. 1993. [10]

Sissons, J. B., *The Evolution of Scotland's Scenery*. 1967. [G]

Skene, W. F., *Celtic Scotland*. 1876. [G]

Smout, T. C., *A History of the Scottish People*. 1985. [G]

Smith, G. Gregory, (ed.) *The Book of Islay: Documents Illustrating the History of the Island*. 1895. [2]

Society of Antiquaries of Scotland.
Proceedings. [G]

Steel, Tom, *The Life and Death of St. Kilda*. 1975. [9]

Steven, Campbell, *The Island Hills*. 1955. [G]

Storrie, Margaret C., *Islay: Biography of an Island*. 1981. [2]

Teignmouth, Lord, *Sketches of the Coasts and Islands of Scotland*. 1836. [G]

Tennent, Norman, *The Islands of Scotland*. [G]

The Statistical Account of Scotland. 1791-99. 1800. [G]

The Third Statistical Account of Scotland. 1961. [G]

Thompson, Francis, *Harris and Lewis, Outer Hebrides*. 1968. [8]
——————*Northern Scotland & the Islands*. [G]
——————*The Uists and Barra*. 1976. [7]

Tranter, Nigel, *Argyll & Bute*. 1977. [1,2,3]

Tulloch, Bobby, *Bobby Tulloch's Shetland*. 1993. [11]

Tulloch, Vie, *The Isle of Gigha*. 1988. [2]

Wainwright, F. T. (ed.) *The Northern Isles*. 1962. [G]
——————*The Problem of the Picts*. 1955. [G]

Walker, John, edit. McKay, Margaret M., *The Rev Dr John Walker's Report on the Hebrides of 1764 and 1771*. 1980. [G]

Watson, W. J., *The History of the Celtic Place-Names of Scotland*. 1926. [G]

West, R. G., *Pleistocene Geology and Biology*. 1968. [G]

Westwood, Jennifer, *Albion. A Guide to Legendary Britain*. 1985. [G]

Whitehouse, G. K., *The Wild Goats of Britain and Ireland*. 1972. [G]

Whittow, J. B., *Geology and Scenery in Scotland*. 1979. [G]

Williams, Ronald, *The Lords of the Isles: the Clan Donald and the Early Kingdom of the Scots*. 1984. [G]

Williamson, Kenneth and Boyd, J. Morton, *Mosaic of Islands*. 1963. [G]
——————*St. Kilda Summer*. 1960. [9]

Wilson, Neil, *Scotch and Water: an Illustrated Guide to the Hebridean Malt Whisky Distilleries*. 1985. [G]

Youngson, Peter, *The Long Road: a Driver's Guide to Jura*. 1987. [G]

Index of Islands

The section and island reference number is given for each entry. Int = Introduction. Ap = Appendix

Eilean na Creig Duibhe   5-Int
Eilean na Daoine Beaga   8-16
Eilean na Gearrabreac   8- 8
Eilean na h-Acairseid   4-Int
Eilean na h-Aon Chaorach   3- 1
Eilean na h-Uamha   3- 7
Eilean nam Bairneach   4-Int
Eilean nam Ban   2- 6, 3-3
Eilean nam Beathach   2-Ap
Eilean nam Feannag   8-19
Eilean nam Freumha   2-Ap
Eilean nam Meann   3- 9
Eilean nam Muc   3- 3
Eilean nam Mult   7-Int
Eilean nan Cabar   4-Int
Eilean nan Caorach   2- 1, 3- 9
Eilean nan Coinean   2-Int, 2-5, 2-7
Eilean nan Each   4- 1
Eilean nan Eildean   3-14
Eilean nan Gabhar   2- 5, 3-14,
   4-Int
Eilean nan Gamhna   3- 2, 3- 9
Eilean nan Gearr   7-19
Eilean nan Imireachean   7-14
Eilean nan Leac   2-Int
Eilean nan Naomh   5- 6
Eilean nan Ron   2- 6
EILEAN NAN RON   6-10
Eilean nan Uan   6-Int
Eilean na Praise   8- 8
Eilean na Rainic   6-Int
Eilean na Saille   6- 7
Eilean na Sgaite   8- 8
Eilean Olmsa   2- 6
Eilean Orasaig   3- 2
Eilean Port a' Choit   6-Int
Eilean Quidnish   8-16
Eilean Ramsay (See Lismore)   3- 9
Eilean Raonuill   4-Int
Eilean Ràrsaidh   5-Int
Eilean Reamhar   5-Ap
Eilean Reilean   3- 7
Eilean Riabhach   6-Int
EILEAN RIGH   2- 8
Eilean Rosaidh   8-16
Eilean Ruaridh   5-Ap
Eilean Rubha an Ridire   3- 3
Eilean Seamraig   5- 9
Eilean Scarista   8-18
Eilean Sgorach   5-Ap
Eilean Sheumais   7- 8
Eilean Sìorruidh   7-20
Eileans, The   1- 6
Eilean Thinngarstaigh   8-16
Eilean Thòraidh   8-16
Eilean Tigh (See Raasay)   5- 7
Eilean Tighe   9-Int
Eilean Tioram   5-Int
Eilean Tornal   2-Ap
Eilean Troddday   5-Ap
Eilean Trosdam   8-18

ENSAY   8- 4
EORSA   3- 6
Erisgeir   3- 5
Eriska   3-Int
ERISKAY   7-13
Ern Stack   11-23
Erraid (See Mull)   3- 3
Eswick Holm   11-11
Eunay Mór   8-19
EWE, ISLE OF   6- 2
EYNHALLOW   10-19
Faihore   7-16
FAIR ISLE   11- 1
Fairy Isles   2-Int
FARA   10- 6
FARAY   10-22
Ferramas   7-16
FETLAR   11-24
Fidra   12-Int
Finsbay Island   8-16
FIARAY   7-12
Filla   11-18
Fiola an Droma (See Lunga)   2-11
Fiola Meadhonach (See Lunga)   2-11
Fish Holm   11-19
Fladda   2-11, 3-8, 11-11
Fladda-chùain   5-Ap
Fladday   8-15
Flannan Isles   9-Int
Floday   8-19, 8-21
Flodday   7- 4, 7-16
FLODDAY   7- 7
Floddaybeg   7-19
FLODDAYMORE   7-19
FLOTTA   10- 4
Flotta   11-11
Fogla Skerry   11-14
Fore Holm   11-11
Forewick Holm   11-14
FOULA   11- 6
Frank Lockwood's Island   3- 3
Fraoch Eilean   2-13, 5-7, 6- 1
Fraochlan   6-Int
Frau Stack   11-14
Fuam an Tolla   8- 8
FUDAY   7-11
FUIAY   7- 8
Gaeilavore Island   5-Ap
Gairbh Eilean   5- 8
GAIRSAY   10-13
Galta Stack   11-11
Gamhnach Mhór   3- 3
Garay Island   5- 8
GARBH EILEACH   2-15
Garbh Eilean   3- 5, 3-7, 3-14, 5-9,
   8-19
GARBH EILEAN (Shiant Islands)
   8-10
Garbh Eilean Mór   7-16, 7-18
Garbh Lingay   7- 8
Garbh Rèisa   2- 7

Garbh-Sgeir   4-Int
Gasay   7-Int, 7-14, 7-16
Gasker   8-15
Gearran Island   5-Ap
Geasgill Beag   3- 4
Geasgill Mór   3- 4
Geirum Beag   7- 2
Geirum Mór   7- 2
Gigalum   2- 3
GIGHA   2- 3
GIGHAY   7-10
Gilsay   8- 3
Giltarump   11-11
Glas Eilean   1-Int, 2-5, 2-6, 2-13, 4-Int,
   5-Int, 6- 1
Glas Eileanan   3- 3, 7-Int
Glas-eilean Mór   7-15, 7-16
Glas-eilean na Creige   7-Int
Glas Leac   6-Int
Glas-leac Beag   6- 5
Glas-leac Mór   6- 8
Glims Holm (See Mainland-Orkney)
   10-11
Gloraig a' Chaimbeulaich   8- 8
Gloup Holm   11-23
Glunimore Island   1- 2
Gometra (See Ulva)   3- 7
Gousam   8-19
Gousman   8- 3
GRAEMSAY   10- 9
Grass Holm   10-13
Greanamul   7-Int, 7-3, 7-11
Greanamul Deas   7-Int
Greanen   7-21
Great Bernera (See Lewis)   8-16
GREAT CUMBRAE   1- 6
Great Stack   6- 9
Green Holm   11- 5
Green Holm   11-11, 11-23
Green Island   6-Int
Green Isle   11-11
Grèinam   8-18
Greineim   8-17, 8-20
Greinem   8- 8
Grif Skerry   11-15
Grimsay (See South Uist)   7-16
Griskerry   11-11
Groatay   7-21
Groay   8- 3
GRUINARD ISLAND   6- 3
Gruna   11-13
Gruna Stack   11-11
Gruney   11-11
Guillamon Island   5- 3
Guirasdeal   2-11
Gumersam Bheag   8- 3
Gumersam Mhór   8- 3
GUNNA   3-11
Haaf Gruney   11-26
Haerie   11-15
Halliman Skerries   12-Int

JANDARA